ABC OF RUGBY LEAGUE

The Code's First Real Encyclopaedia

MALCOLM ANDREWS

an
ABC
BOOK

TO LACHLAN

A 2010 Kangaroo?

Published by ABC Enterprises for the
AUSTRALIAN BROADCASTING CORPORATION
GPO Box 9994 Sydney NSW 2001

Copyright © Malcolm Andrews, 1992

First published 1992

National Library of Australia
Cataloguing-in-Publication entry
Andrews, Malcolm, 1944–
    The ABC of rugby league: the code's first real encyclopaedia.

    ISBN 0 7333 0176 2.

    1. Rugby League football - Australia - Encyclopedias. 2. Rugby
    League football players - Australia - Biography -
    Encyclopedias. I. Title.

796.3330994

Designed by Howard Binns-McDonald
Cover Photography by Andrew Varley, courtesy RUGBY LEAGUE WEEK
Set in 9 point Cheltenham by Midland Typesetters, Maryborough, Victoria
Printed and bound in Australia by Australian Print Group, Maryborough, Victoria
7.5–2495

ABOUT THE AUTHOR

Malcolm Andrews is a respected Australian journalist. In his 27-year career he has worked for such media organisations as *The Australian*, the *Daily Telegraph* (Sydney), the *Daily Express* (London), Sydney radio station 2UW and the Nine Network's current affairs program, *Today*.

In the early 1970s he spent five years in Munich working for the US State Department at Radio Free Europe, which broadcast news behind the Iron Curtain.

Over the years, Andrews has also ghosted many newspaper columns for such international sporting names as Johnny Raper and Les Johns (Rugby League) and Joe Mercer (English Soccer).

He is now a freelance based in Brisbane, writing extensively on a wide variety of subjects for a whole spectrum of publications including *The Australian Magazine, Ita, Women's Weekly, Woman's Day, Australasian Post, Penthouse, Turf Monthly*, and several News Limited capital city newspapers. He is also correspondent for the respected British Rugby League publications, *League Express* and *Open Rugby*, and he has a weekly column on football history and trivia in *Big League*, the official NSW Rugby League program.

Andrews has written twelve books. They include light-hearted looks at Australian life compiled in tandem with Bill Mitchell, cartoonist for *The Australian—Great Aussie Stuff-Ups, Great Aussie Trivia, Great Aussie Sports Heroes* and sequels to the latter two. Others include *Encyclopaedia of Australian Sports, Encyclopaedia of Australian Cricket, Rugby League— the Greatest Game of All, Rugby League Heroes* and *101 Australian Sporting Heroes*.

THE ABC OF RUGBY LEAGUE

Horrie Miller was one of the longest serving secretaries on the NSW Rugby League. The Eastern Suburbs winger was appointed to the post in a 'palace coup' in 1909, one year after the game began in Australia, and was secretary, on and off until March 1946. In the 1920s, Miller coined the phrase 'The Greatest Game of All' to describe Rugby League. Australian Rules fanatics may scoff, and first-generation Soccer supporters may shake their heads, but to millions of Rugby League people, that is exactly what it is—the greatest game of all.

It is the major winter sport in both New South Wales and Queensland and is making inroads in other states. In 1990, some 23 566 Western Australians turned out at the WACA Ground to watch a Premiership clash between Canberra and Manly-Warringah. It was a record for the famous Perth ground. Only the lack of a major arena of suitable size in Sydney has prevented Rugby League from breaking all Australian sporting records.

During the football season, the major daily newspapers devote one third of their sporting pages to the game. Private firms sell team posters, bubble-gum cards, T-shirts etc. Major companies sponsor teams and competitions— and the ratings for big games on television are higher than those of blockbuster movies and other much-vaunted programs. Yet, despite this incredible interest in the game, Rugby League has rarely spawned comprehensive books on the sport, its history and the names which made it famous. With *The ABC of Rugby League*, I have tried to rectify this.

The book covers every aspect of the sport in Australia. The history is detailed. All international tours and matches are covered. The fortunes of every club in the NSWRL Premiership are examined, and there are pen-portraits of hundreds of the great players, coaches and administrators. Famous names from overseas are included—those with sufficient impact on the game in Australia as separate entries, those who never played club football here under their respective country's entry. Minor and extinct competitions, such as the famous Maher Cup, are not forgotten either.

The book would have been impossible without the help of dozens of League lovers including Harry Edgar (publisher of the respected British magazine, *Open Rugby*), Mike Rylance (editor of the British weekly, *League Express*), Ian Heads (former managing editor of *Rugby League Week*) and George Crawford (Rugby League historian and for many years chief League writer for the Sydney *Daily Telegraph*). David Middleton, the *Rugby League Week* journalist with an encyclopaedic knowledge of the Greatest Game of All, pored over the manuscript to eliminate the work of the inevitable gremlins.

All statistics were accurate at January 1, 1992.

A

ABORIGINAL AND ISLANDER FOOTBALLERS

Aborigines and Islanders have a proud record in Australian Rugby League. Arthur Beetson had few equals as a player and he had a distinguished coaching career, too. Another, Eric Simms, was such a prolific scorer of field goals that the authorities changed the rules to curb his points harvest.

The first Aborigine to wear the green and gold was Queensland winger Lionel Morgan, who played two Tests against France and a World Cup match in 1960. In 1990, Mal Meninga, a Solomon Islander who has often been represented as being Aboriginal, skippered the Kangaroos.

In 1987, as a highlight of National Aborigines Week, a hypothetical team of the finest Aboriginal and Islander players was chosen. Beetson, named as coach, reckoned it could have beaten any Test side in the world. It was: Dale Shearer (Manly-Warringah), David Liddiard (Penrith), Tony Currie (Canterbury-Bankstown), Mal Meninga (Canberra), John Ferguson (Canberra), Steve Ella (Parramatta), Scott Gale (Balmain), Jeff Hardy (Illawarra), Ron Gibbs (Manly-Warringah), Sam Backo (Canberra), Mal Cochrane (Manly-Warringah), Paul Roberts (South Sydney). Reserves: Ricky Walford (St George) and Craig Salvatori (Eastern Suburbs).

Australia's Aboriginal and Islander Internationals

Player	Tests	World Series Matches	Others	Total
Lionel Morgan (1960)	2	—	—	2
Arthur Beetson (1966–77)	14	14	1	29
Ron Saddler (1967–68)*	—	—	—	—
Eric Simms (1968–70)	—	8	—	8
John Sattler (1969–71)	4	—	—	4
George Ambrum (1972)	2	—	—	2
Larry Corowa (1978–79)	2	—	—	2
Mal Meninga (1982–91)	34	—	1	35
Steve Ella (1983–85)	4	—	1	5
John Ferguson (1985)	3	—	—	3
Dale Shearer (1986–90)	16	—	1	17
Sam Backo (1988–89)	6	—	1	7
Tony Currie (1988–89)	7	—	—	7
Cliff Lyons (1990–91)	7	—	—	7
Craig Salvatori (1991)	2	—	—	2

* toured with 1967–68 Kangaroos

ABORIGINAL TOURING SIDES

In 1973 an Australian Aboriginal side made a tour of New Zealand. The lightning visit was an experimental venture. The Aborigines, led by Penrith's Ron Mason, played nine games in 10 days against minor sides, winning seven.

1973
Aborigines in New Zealand

Played 9, Won 7, Lost 2, Points for 251, Points against 172.

Match Results

Opponents	For	Against
Te Atatu A	17	13
Te Atatu B	45	3
Otahuhu A	22	30
Otahuhu B	19	17
Rotorua Central	47	17
Mangakino	43	19
Wellington Petone	26	24
Marist	26	13
Canterbury XIII	6	36

In 1990 a second Aboriginal side went overseas—this time to Tonga for the Pacific Cup. The 20-man side comprised 17 from the Under-21 ranks and three older players from the Sydney competition to provide experience and depth. The three were Ron Gibbs (Gold Coast), Ricky Walford (St George) and Graham Lyons (South Sydney). A fourth, Cliff Lyons (Manly-Warringah), would also have played but for being chosen in the Kangaroo side to tour Britain and France. The Aborigines finished fourth after being beaten by Western Samoa in the semi-finals and by Tonga in the play-off for third place.

DON 'BANDY' ADAMS

Five Tests for Australia (1956). Also played in 13 minor games on one Kangaroo tour (1956–57).

Two former Kangaroos had a hand in the path to success of Don 'Bandy' Adams, a dairy farmer from Maitland in the NSW Hunter Valley—1911–12 tourist Robert 'Botsy' Williams and 1948–49 captain Col Maxwell.

Williams spotted his potential early and it was Maxwell, Adams' first senior coach, who switched him from five-eighth, where he played all his schoolboy football, to the wing, where he was to make his mark as an international. Adams was a sensation with the fans once he made his first appearance for New South Wales, as a 21–year-old, in 1955. He looked ungainly with his bandy legs—but his speed and swerve left many an opponent grasping for thin air.

Adams played Test football for only one year but was a huge success. He made his international debut in the First Test, at the Sydney Cricket Ground, against the 1956 New Zealand Kiwis, going over for two tries. In the Third Test he performed even better, snaring a hat-trick of tries. The flying flankman was selected in the 1956–57 Kangaroo squad. But his reputation had preceded him to Britain and he was closely spotted in most matches. He scored four tries against Liverpool City in the opening match, but was later plagued by injury, finishing the tour with one Test against both Britain and France and a tally of 15 tries.

Back home he was never able to make it to the top again, with wingers of the calibre of Brian Carlson and Peter Dimond keeping him out of the NSW and Australian sides.

ADIDAS GOLDEN BOOT see *Golden Boot Award*

FRED AH KUOI

Twenty-four Tests for New Zealand (1978–85). Also played four matches in two World Championships (1975 and 1977).

When 22–year-old Fred Ah Kuoi led New Zealand in the Third Test against the touring 1979 British Lions, he became the youngest player ever to lead the Kiwis. It was a fitting tribute to the fine, attacking five-eighth from Auckland. Five years later, Ah Kuoi led the Kiwis against the next British side to tour down-under, and his side became the first ever to win a series 3–0. His combination with centre James Leuluai was sensational—more than the tourists could contain.

Ah Kuoi was one of the first New Zealanders to pursue an overseas club career while still approaching his peak international form. In 1981 he joined the great New Zealand captain Mark Graham at North Sydney. It was not a successful stay in the Sydney Premiership competition and at the end of his three-year contract he could not regularly make the first-grade side. However he went to England and gained a new lease of life with his old team-mate Leuluai at Hull. The highlight of his stay was a Challenge Cup Final appearance at Wembley in 1985. He played outside the Australian halfback genius Peter Sterling, with Leuluai and fellow Kiwis Dane O'Hara and Gary Kemble also in the Hull lineup. Unfortunately, Wigan triumphed over them, 28–24, in one of the great finals of Rugby League history.

Ah Kuoi's Test career saw him on two tours of Britain and France (1980 and 1985). He played centre in the side which scored a shock 19–12 victory over Australia at Brisbane's Lang Park in 1983—the first success on Australian soil in 20 years.

GREG ALEXANDER

Six Tests for Australia (1989–90). Also played 26 minor matches on two Kangaroo tours (1986 and 1990) and one New Zealand tour (1989).

Greg Alexander was one of the most talked-about schoolboy footballers in the history of the televised Commonwealth Bank Cup. He had moved from St Dominic's in Penrith to Fairfield Patrician Brothers in 1982. For two seasons halfback Alexander was the inspiration behind the side which won the prestige competition. He was Player-of-the-Series in 1983.

The following season he played just two reserve-grade matches for Penrith before being called into the senior side. He was a permanent first-grader from then on. His phenomenal play soon paid dividends. In 1985 he won the Dally M Award as the Player-of-the-Year. During that season he played his first representative game (for City Seconds) and in the Premiership competition scored 196 points (14 tries, 69 goals and 2 field goals)— a record for Penrith. Twelve months later he notched 183 points. By 1990 he had set a new club record for the total number of points scored by a player during his career, 594. In the following two seasons he extended that record to 883.

Alexander was a last-minute selection in the 1986 Kangaroo side, after winger Eric Grothe failed a fitness test. With other fine halfbacks, Peter Sterling, Des Hasler and Allan Langer in good form Alexander had to wait until the 1989 tour of New Zealand to play his first Test match.

In 1990, Penrith coach Phil Gould switched the versatile Alexander to fullback and, until an injury forced him out of the City side, he was in superb form in his new position. In the latter stages of the season Gould switched him back to half for Penrith's surge to its first grand final.

However this new-found versatility was of great use on the Kangaroo tour of Britain and France later that year. Alexander was chosen as a utility back—but found himself playing most of his games as understudy to fullback Gary Belcher. A sensational French leg helped Alexander become the tour top-scorer with 156 points (14 tries and 50 goals). Alexander scored 46 points (five tries and 13 goals from as many attempts) in the Kangaroos' 78–6 thrashing of France B at Lyon—a world record tally for an individual in an international game. When he came on as a replacement, 18 minutes into the First Test, at Avignon, he set about the task of posting a new individual record for Franco-Australian Tests with 26 points (from three tries and seven goals). This beat the previous best of 20 by Ken Irvine in 1964 and Michael O'Connor in 1986.

Alexander was a vital cog in the Penrith side which, in 1990, made the grand final for the first time in the club's history. He scored a try and kicked a goal, but it was not enough. Canberra, the reigning Premiers won 18–14. 'Brandy' had his revenge a year later when he captained the Panthers to their first Premiership—in the 25th year of the club—with a 19–12 success over the Canberra Raiders. He was later chosen to tour Papua New Guinea with the Australian side but was forced out through injury.

TREVOR ALLAN

Trevor Allan was one of the first post-World War II Rugby Union stars to cash in on his ability and turn professional.

He was lured over to the Rugby League code in 1950, with an offer of £5000 by the English club Leigh. At that stage he was one of Australia's most brilliant and popular Union players, with a record of 15 Test appearances in just three years, including five on the 1947–48 Wallaby tour of Great Britain and France. He was captain in 10 of those Tests, and he was top-scorer on the Wallaby tour with 66 points.

Allan proved to be a great hit at Leigh and played for Other Nationalities in their international match against Wales in his first season in Britain. Recurring injuries, possibly the legacy of his fearsome tackling, forced him to quit England in 1954.

Back home he tried to make the big time again as captain-coach of

North Sydney but was only a shadow of his former self, with injuries restricting him to just 11 games in three seasons before he hung up his boots for the last time in 1960 to return to Rugby Union as a radio and television commentator for the ABC.

AMCO CUP see *Midweek Cup*

AMCO SHIELD see *Commonwealth Bank Cup*

AMERICAN ALLSTARS

Efforts to establish Rugby League in North America resulted in a tour of Australasia in 1953 by a group of gridiron players under manager-player Mike Dimitro. They were coached by Balmain stalwart Norm 'Latchem' Robinson. Their outfits were nothing if not colourful—royal blue jumpers with red and white stars on the shoulders and royal blue shorts with red and white stripes down the sides.

But the tour was a failure. The Americans won just six of the 26 matches played and would have lost a lot more but for the late inclusion of several Australian players to bolster their ranks. One of the Americans, winger Al E Kirkland, returned to Australia to play for Parramatta during the 1956 season.

American Allstars in Australia

Played 18, Won 3, Lost 13, Drew 2, Points for 406, Points against 560

Tour match results

Opponents	Venue (Attendance)	For	Against
Monaro & Southern Division	Canberra (4827)	34	25
Sydney	Sydney (65 453)	25	52
New South Wales	Sydney (32 554)	41	62
Combined NSW Country	Wollongong (11 787)	9	35
Western Division	Dubbo (4717)	21	24
Newcastle	Newcastle (14 160)	19	10
Northern Division & North Coast	Coffs Harbour (5400)	18	26
Queensland	Brisbane (24 397)	36	39
North Queensland	Cairns (6042)	17	17
Central West Queensland	Longreach (1635)	21	26
Central Queensland	Rockhampton (5332)	26	33
Brisbane	Brisbane (7000)	26	39
Toowoomba	Toowoomba (5778)	15	29
Ipswich	Ipswich (3155)	16	15
Wide Bay	Maryborough (6166)	33	33
Riverina	Gundagai (2560)	14	30
New South Wales	Sydney (19 686)	18	27

American Allstars in New Zealand

Played 8, Won 3, Lost 5, Points for 157, Points against 211

Tour Match Results

Opponents	Venue	For	Against
Auckland	Auckland	28	54
Taranaki	New Plymouth	21	18
Wellington	Wellington	17	18
West Coast	Greymouth	10	27
Canterbury	Christchurch	8	39
Northland	Whangarei	25	6
Maoris	Auckland	26	40
South Auckland	Hamilton	22	19

AMPOL CUP see *Extinct Competitions*

CHRIS ANDERSON ────────────────────────

Eight Tests for Australia (1978–80). Also played three matches in one World Championship (1975), one minor international (1982) and 23 minor games on two Kangaroo tours (1978 & 1982) and one New Zealand tour (1980).

Chris Anderson was a no-frills footballer, but he achieved results many of his flashier counterparts could only dream about. Two Kangaroo tours, two English Challenge Cup winners' medals (including one as captain-coach), an English Championship success and a Sydney Premiership are some of the honours which came his way.

English fans were the first to see Anderson at his very best. While still a raw winger with Canterbury-Bankstown, Anderson went to Britain in the 1974–75 off-season in an effort to gain experience. He was an immediate sensation. In 19 games for the Widnes club he scored 18 tries. Widnes officials were so impressed that they outlayed $2000 (no small figure in those days) to fly him back to England for the Wembley Cup Final. Widnes' 5–0 success over Warrington earned Anderson the first of his coveted Cup-winners medals.

Less than a month later, Anderson found himself in the line-up for Australia's World Championship match against New Zealand. He was also used as a substitute in later home games against France and England. Anderson missed a place in the next Championship (1977), but good late season form won him a spot in the 1978 Kangaroo side. On that tour he played in all five Tests. He also made appearances in the next two international series, against the touring 1979 British Lions and while on tour of New Zealand the following year. A severe bout of glandular fever in 1981 seemed to herald the end of Anderson's big match career, but he bounced back to make the 1982 Kangaroo squad. Although he did not play in any of the Tests he did appear in an international against Wales.

Anderson finished his career with Canterbury in 1984, after playing a then-record 232 first-grade games and scoring a record 117 tries. This, and his 19 touch-downs in the 1983, season remain a Bulldog record. Anderson was also a member of the side which took out the Premiership in 1980.

Back in England, Anderson turned the game upside down. He took over as captain-coach of the lowly-rated Halifax side, and with the injection of some young Australian players, including Martin Bella, Michael Hagan and Paul Langmack, steered it to the 1986 English Championship. The following year he achieved the ultimate. Despite carrying painful rib injuries, Anderson inspired Halifax to a 19–18 Challenge Cup Final victory over St Helens before 91 267 people at Wembley. Graham Eadie, the Australian Test fullback who Anderson had persuaded to come out of retirement, scored the match-winning try and won the Lance Todd Trophy as Man-of-the-Match.

Anderson then quit as a player, but had Halifax back at Wembley the following year only to see his side humbled by a great Wigan combination,

38–10. He returned home and, in 1990, took over as coach of his beloved Canterbury.

Everyone wrote off the Bulldogs at the beginning of 1991 when there was a mass exodus of experienced players, including internationals David Gillespie, Paul Langmack and Andrew Farrar. But Anderson surprised everyone by steering his side to a playoff for the fifth semi-final spot.

ANNANDALE

Annandale was one of the early clubs of the Sydney Premiership competition. It played only 11 seasons between 1910 and 1920—and with little success. It won only 23 of its 151 first-grade games. Four times it collected the wooden spoon for running last. In one of those years, 1918, it played its way into the record books as the first club which failed to notch a competition point all season. This has since been equalled by South Sydney in 1946 and Eastern Suburbs in 1966. Annandale's best season was 1911 when it finished fifth of the eight teams.

VIC ARMBRUSTER

Eight Tests for Australia (1924–30). Also played 16 minor games on one Kangaroo tour (1929–30).

Vic Armbruster was one of the stars of the 1929–30 Kangaroos

Tall. Tough. Talented. Vic Armbruster was all of these and more. He was the complete Rugby League forward, equally at home at lock or in the second-row. For almost a decade he was a dominant force in Australian representative football.

Armbruster, who hailed from the NSW north coast, first played for his State in 1922. It wasn't a happy debut as Queensland beat the Blues 25–9 to notch its first-ever success after 22 successive losses since the first interstate clash in 1908. Armbruster later moved north to Toowoomba and then on to Brisbane, where he played for Grammars and Valleys. It was while in the northern State that he forced his way into the Test side for the first time, against the 1924 British Lions touring side.

His Test debut was also a match of disappointment for Armbruster. On one occasion he dived and missed a loose ball lying over the British line. A try would have given Australia a narrow win (Britain eventually succeeded 5–3). During the match, Armbruster was injured and spent considerable time off the field. After the game he was rushed to hospital suffering from concussion.

His second international appearance was more to his liking, as he was on the winning side and scored a fine try after a cross-kick from centre Tommy Gorman. Armbruster appeared in two other series against Britain (the latter during the 1929–30 Kangaroo tour). He continued in the Queensland side until 1931, quitting after his 26th appearance.

KEN ARTHURSON

Ken Arthurson was a top-class halfback in the early 1950s. Some said he was as good, if not better than, the then-Test representative Keith Holman. However a bad injury in 1953—Arthurson's skull was fractured in a trial match at Parkes, in the NSW central-west—put paid to any international hopes this brilliant attacking player may have had. Arthurson, however, soon made his name in other spheres of Rugby League—as a coach and an administrator.

His best performance as a coach was in 1957 when he guided his old club, Manly-Warringah, to the grand final. He took over as secretary of Manly and in the next 21 years helped the Sea-Eagles through their best years, in which they at last managed the elusive Sydney Premiership. Then, in 1983, after the sudden retirement of Kevin Humphreys and with Rugby League at the centre of a media controversy, Arthurson took over the top job in the country—that of Chairman of the Australian Rugby League.

He was at the helm for one of the most exciting eras of the game— a period which saw the Sydney competition expand to Newcastle, Brisbane and the Gold Coast and the opening of the multi-million dollar Sydney Football Stadium, which was the venue for the 100th Anglo-Australian Test during Australia's Bicentennial year, 1988.

OPAI ASHER

One Test for New Zealand (1910). Also played in two internationals for Australasia (1910) which for many years were regarded as Tests.

Winger Albert 'Opai' Asher was one of New Zealand's first great players.

Asher (Maori name, Wharepapa) was nicknamed 'The India-Rubber Man' for his ability to swerve away from and slip out of tackles. He was a member of the NZ Maori sides which visited Australia in 1908 and 1909. And he represented New Zealand against the touring 1910 British Lions and on the tour of Australia in 1913 (although there were no Tests played against the Australians).

In 1910 Asher was one of two New Zealanders who played for Australasia against the British Lions in Sydney matches at the R A S Showground and Wentworth Park. In the second match Asher was involved in a spectacular clash with British winger Billy Batten. The Englishman had a habit of hurdling opponents. In the Sydney match Batten leaped into the air. But Asher was ready for him and jumped, too. His head came into contact with Batten's knee and a nasty gash needing 10 stitches was opened, forcing him off the field for some time.

THE ASHES

Just when the press and the public began to describe Rugby League Test clashes between Australia and Great Britain as being for 'The Ashes' is not certain. The term however, borrowed from cricket's most famous prize, has stuck. Since 1928, the two nations have actually played for the Ashes Cup, a splendid gold trophy—although it has gone missing in suspicious circumstances on a couple of occasions.

The longest period one side has held The Ashes is 30 years (Great Britain). The run stretching over 10 series, was broken when Australia pulled off an upset win at home in the 1950s clashes. The 100th Test between the two countries was played at the Sydney Football Stadium in 1988.

Results of the Anglo-Australian Series

Series	Venue	Result	Tests to Australia	Tests to Britain	Drawn
1908–09	Britain	Great Britain	—	2	1
1910	Australia	Great Britain	—	2	—
1911–12	Britain	Australasia	2	—	1
1914	Australia	Great Britain	1	2	—
1920	Australia	Australia	2	1	—
1921–22	Britain	Great Britain	1	2	—
1924	Australia	Great Britain	1	2	—
1928	Australia	Great Britain	1	2	—
1929–30	Britain	Great Britain	1	2	1
1932	Australia	Great Britain	1	2	—
1933	Britain	Great Britain	—	3	—
1936	Australia	Great Britain	1	2	—
1937	Britain	Great Britain	1	2	—
1946	Australia	Great Britain	—	2	1
1948	Britain	Great Britain	—	3	—
1950	Australia	Australia	2	1	—
1952	Britain	Great Britain	1	2	—
1954	Australia	Australia	2	1	—
1956	Britain	Great Britain	1	2	—
1958	Australia	Great Britain	1	2	—
1959	Britain	Great Britain	1	2	—
1962	Australia	Great Britain	1	2	—
1963	Britain	Australia	2	1	—
1966	Australia	Australia	2	1	—
1967	Britain	Australia	2	1	—
1970	Australia	Great Britain	1	2	—
1973	Britain	Australia	2	1	—
1974	Australia	Australia	2	1	—

Continued

Results of the Anglo-Australian Series *continued*

Series	Venue	Result	Tests to Australia	Tests to Britain	Drawn
1978	Britain	Australia	2	1	—
1979	Australia	Australia	3	—	—
1982	Britain	Australia	3	—	—
1984	Australia	Australia	3	—	—
1986	Britain	Australia	3	—	—
1988	Australia	Australia	2	1	—
1990	Britain	Australia	2	1	—

Anglo-Australian Test Records

Largest Test crowd in Australia: 70 204 at the Sydney Cricket Ground for First Test, June 6, 1932

Largest Test crowd in Britain: 52 569 at Wembley Stadium, London, for First Test, October 27, 1990

Smallest Test crowd in Australia: 15 944 at Sydney Football Stadium for Third Test, July 9, 1988

Smallest test crowd in Britain: 2000 at Park Oval, Park Royal, London, for First Test, December 12, 1908

Top pointscorer: Graeme Langlands (Australia), 104 (6 tries, 43 goals)

Top British pointscorer: Jim Sullivan, 62 (31 goals)

Top tryscorer: Ken Irvine (Australia), 12

Top British tryscorer: Billy Boston, 9

Most points in a series: Mick Cronin (Australia), 54 (2 tries, 24 goals), in 1979

Most points in a Test: Michael O'Connor (Australia), 22 (3 tries, 5 goals), First Test, Old Trafford, Manchester, 1986

Most points by a Test side: 50 by Australia, Second Test, Swinton, 1963
Most points by Great Britain: 40, in Third Test, Sydney Cricket Ground, 1958

Biggest winning margin: 38 points, by Australia (50–12), Second Test, Swinton, 1963

Biggest winning margin by Great Britain: 23 points (40–17), Third Test, Sydney Cricket Ground, 1958

Leading Scorers in Anglo-Australian Tests
(Figures to the end of the 1990 Series)

Player (Country)	Tries	Goals	Field goals*	Points
Graeme Langlands (Aust)	6	43	—	104
Mal Meninga (Aust)	4	32	—	86
Mick Cronin (Aust)	2	35	—	76
Michael O'Connor (Aust)	5	23	—	66
Jim Sullivan (GB)	—	31	—	62
Noel Pidding (Aust)	3	26	—	61
Neil Fox (GB)	3	26	—	61
Roger Millward (GB)	5	14	—	43
Ken Irvine (Aust)	12	3	—	42
Keith Barnes (Aust)	—	19	—	38
Dave Brown (Aust)	3	13	—	35
Gordon Clifford (Aust)	—	17	—	34
Eric Weissel (Aust)	1	15	—	33
Lewis Jones (GB)	—	15	—	30
Garry Schofield (GB)	7	—	2	30
Dally Messenger (Aust)	3	10	—	29
Ernest Ward (GB)	2	11	—	28
Brian Carlson (Aust)	8	2	—	28
Reg Gasnier (Aust)	9	—	—	27
Billy Boston (GB)	9	—	—	27

* *Field goals scored when worth two points are included in tally of goals. Also note some tries worth three points, others four*

ANGLO-AUSTRALIAN TESTS
1908–09

First Test
At Park Oval, Park Royal, London, Saturday, 12 December 1908
Crowd: 2000
AUSTRALIA 22 (Devereux 3, Butler tries, Messenger 5 goals) drew with GREAT BRITAIN 22 (Batten 2, Thomas, Brooks, Tyson, Robinson tries, Brooks 2 goals)
Australia: M Bolewski, W Heidke, S Deane, H Messenger (c), J Devereux, A Halloway, A Butler, P Walsh, E Courtney, J Abercrombie, A Burdon, S Pearce, L O'Malley
Great Britain: H Gifford, W Batten, B Jenkins (c), G Dickenson, C Tyson, E Brooks, J Thomas, A Robinson, A Smith, W Longworth, W Jukes, J Higson, A Mann
Referee: JH Smith (Great Britain)

Second Test
At St James' Park, Newcastle-upon-Tyne, Saturday, 23 January 1909
Crowd: 22 000
GREAT BRITAIN 15 (Thomas, Lomas, Tyson tries, Lomas 3 goals) d AUSTRALIA 5 (Messenger try and goal)
Australia: M Bolewski, D Frawley, H Messenger (c), A Rosenfeld, A Morton, A Conlon, A Butler, P Walsh, E Courtney, T McCabe, J Abercrombie, S Pearce, L O'Malley
Great Britain: H Gifford, G Tyson, J Lomas (c), B Jenkins, W Batten, E Brooks, J Thomas, J Silcock, A Robinson, A Smith, W Longworth, W Jukes, W Higson
Referee: WJ McCutcheon (Great Britain)

Third Test
At Villa Park, Birmingham, Wednesday, 10 February 1909
Crowd: 9000
GREAT BRITAIN 6 (Thomas, Tyson tries) d AUSTRALIA 5 (Frawley try, Devereux goal)
Australia: C Hedley, D Frawley, W Heidke, J Devereux, M Bolewski, S Deane, A Anlezark, P Walsh, E Courtney, R Graves, A Burdon (c), S Pearce, L O'Malley
Great Britain: F Young, W Batten, B Jenkins, J Lomas (c), G Tyson, J Brooks, J Thomas, F Boylen, A Mann, W Longworth, A Smith, R Padbury, W Jukes
Referee: JH Smith (Great Britain)

1910

There has always been a great deal of confusion about which games played in 1910 were, in fact, Test matches. Great Britain played five internationals while on tour. The first was against Australia, the next against the Kangaroos, the third against Combined New South Wales and Queensland and the last two against Australasian sides which included two New Zealanders, winger Albert 'Opai' Asher and fullback Riki Papakura. For years, Australia recognised the clashes with Australia and Australasia as Test matches. At the same time, Britain claimed the games with Australia and one of the Combined XIIIs were the Tests. No doubt, the fact that if Australia had its way the series would have been drawn and if Britain was right the tourists would have won had something to do with their respective attitudes.

Even as late as 1960, one respected British reference book, *Sport International*, took the Australian point of view—and the Australian case is strengthened by the fact that Queenslander Bill Heidke was captain of the Combined XIII in Brisbane and not the regular Test captain, New South Welshman Dally Messenger. As well, seven of the thirteen were Queenslanders—a huge percentage considering most Test sides at that time had only one or two players from north of the border. Eventually, however, the Australians fell into line with Britain, enabling the 100th Test to be played at the Sydney Football Stadium in 1988.

First Test
At RAS Showground, Sydney, Saturday, 18 June 1910
Crowd: 42 000
GREAT BRITAIN 27 (Jukes 3, Leytham 2, Thomas, Batten tries, Lomas, Thomas, Leytham goals) d AUSTRALIA 20 (Hickey, Messenger, Woodhead, Barnett tries, Messenger 4 goals)
Australia: C Russell, C Woodhead, J Hickey, H Messenger (c), A Broomham, W Farnsworth, C McKivat, R Craig, C Sullivan, E Courtney, W Spence, J Barnett, W Noble
Great Britain: J Sharrock, J Leytham, J Lomas (c), B Jenkins, W Batten, J Thomas, T Newbould, A Avery, E Curzon, R Ramsdale, W Jukes, F Webster, W Ward
Referee: T McMahon (Australia)

Second Test
At Brisbane Exhibition Ground, Saturday, 2 July 1910
Crowd: 18 000
GREAT BRITAIN 22 (Leytham 4, Thomas, Kershaw tries, Lomas 2 goals) d AUSTRALIA 17 (Barnett, Messenger, McKivat, Craig, Nicholson tries, Hickey goal)
Australia: D McGregor, C Woodhead, J Hickey, W Heidke (c), H Messenger, W Farnsworth, C McKivat, H Nicholson, J Barnett, R Tubman, E Buckley, R Craig, H Brackenreg
Great Britain: J Sharrock, W Batten, J Lomas (c), J Riley, J Leytham, J Thomas, F Smith, R Ramsdale, W Winstanley, W Jukes, F Webster, H Kershaw, G Ruddick.
Referee: J Fihelly (Australia)

11

International
At RAS Showground, Sydney, Saturday, 9 July 1910
Crowd: 50 000
AUSTRALASIA 13 (V Farnsworth, Courtney, McKivat tries, Messenger 2 goals) drew with GREAT BRITAIN 13 (Leytham, Avery, Winstanley tries, Lomas, Thomas goals)
Australasia: R Papakura, A Asher, H Messenger (c), V Farnsworth, A Broomham, W Farnsworth, C McKivat, H Brackenreg, R Craig, W Cann, C Sullivan, S Pearce, E Courtney
Great Britain: J Sharrock, W Batten, J Lomas (c), B Jenkins, J Leytham, J Thomas, F Newbould, H Kershaw, A Avery, W Jukes, W Winstanley, R Ramsdale, F Webster
Referee: T McMahon (Australia)

International
At Wentworth Park, Sydney, Wednesday, 13 July 1910
Crowd: 50 000
AUSTRALASIA 32 (McKivat 2, Broomham, Messenger, Brackenreg, Spence tries, Messenger 5, Brackenreg 2 goals) d GREAT BRITAIN 15 (Riley 2, Winstanley tries, Thomas 3 goals)
Australasia: R Papakura, A Asher, H Messenger (c), V Farnsworth, A Broomham, W Farnsworth, C McKivat, W Noble, W Spence, H Brackenreg, C Sullivan, S Pearce, E Courtney
Great Britain: J Sharrock, W Batten, J Riley, B Jenkins (c), J Leytham, J Thomas, F Smith, E Curzon, F Shugars, G Ruddick, F Webster, W Winstanley, W Jukes
Referee: T McMahon (Australia)

1911-12

First Test
At St James' Park, Newcastle-upon-Tyne, Wednesday, 8 November 1911
Crowd: 5317
AUSTRALASIA 19 (Farnsworth 2, Cann, Francis, Hallett tries, Francis, Cann goals) d GREAT BRITAIN 10 (Davies 2 tries, Thomas 2 goals)
Australasia: C Fraser, A Broomham, H Hallett, H Gilbert, C Russell, V Farnsworth, C McKivat (c), W Cann, P McCue, A Francis, R Craig, R Williams, E Courtney
Great Britain: J Sharrock, W Davies, B Jenkins, H Wagstaff, J Miller, J Thomas (c), F Smith, B Gronow, A Avery, F Harrison, O Burgham, L Clampitt, W Winstanley
Referee: B Ennion (Great Britain)

Second Test
At Tynecastle Park, Edinburgh, Saturday, 16 December 1911
Crowd: 8000
AUSTRALASIA 11 (Frawley, McKivat, Russell tries, Francis goal) drew with GREAT BRITAIN 11 (Wagstaff 2, Lomas tries, Wood goal)
Australasia: H Hallett, C Russell, V Farnsworth, H Gilbert, D Frawley, W Farnsworth, C McKivat (c), W Cann, R Craig, A Francis, E Courtney, W Noble, P McCue
Great Britain: A Wood, H Jenkinson, J Lomas (c), H Wagstaff, W Batten, J Davies, F Smith, B Gronow, D Clark, R Ramsdale, W Winstanley, T Woods, F Harrison
Referee: F Renton (Great Britain)

Third Test
At Villa Park, Birmingham, Monday, 1 January 1912
Crowd: 4000
AUSTRALASIA 33 (Berecry 2, McKivat 2, Frawley 2, McCue 2, V Farnsworth tries, Frawley 2, Gilbert goals) d GREAT BRITAIN 8 (Lomas, Clarke tries, Wood goal)
Australasia: H Hallett, D Frawley, V Farnsworth, H Gilbert, T Berecry, W Farnsworth, C McKivat (c), W Noble, R Craig, W Cann, P McCue, R Williams, C Sullivan
Great Britain: A Wood, W Batten, J Lomas (c), B Jenkins, A Jenkinson, W Davies, F Smith, A Avery, F Harrison, T Woods, D Clark, W Winstanley, R Ramsdale
Referee: R Robinson (Great Britain)

1914

First Test
At RAS Showground, Sydney, Saturday, 27 June 1914
Crowd: 40 000
GREAT BRITAIN 23 (Moorhouse 2, Clark, Holland, Robinson tries, Longstaff 2, Robinson 2 goals) d AUSTRALIA 5 (Norman try, Bolewski goal)
Australia: H Hallett, M Bolewski, S Deane (c), W Kelly, H Horder, R Norman, A Halloway, J Watkins, P McCue, C Sullivan, F Burge, S Pearce, E Courtney
Great Britain: W Jarman, J Robinson, B Jenkins, H Wagstaff (c), S Moorhouse, W Hall, F Smith, D Clark, F Longstaff, J Chilcott, R Ramsdale, A Coldrick, D Holland
Referee: T McMahon (Australia)

Second Test
At Sydney Cricket Ground, Monday, 29 June 1914
Crowd: 38 000
AUSTRALIA 12 (Fraser, Burge tries, Messenger 3 goals) d GREAT BRITAIN 7 (Coldrick try, Rogers 2 goals)
Australia: H Hallett, D Frawley, S Deane (c), W Messenger, R Tideyman, C Fraser, A Halloway, W Cann, C Sullivan, R Craig, F Burge, S Pearce, E Courtney
Great Britain: G Thomas, F Williams, H Wagstaff (c), W Hall, J Robinson, JH Rogers, F Smith, J Chilcott, D Clark, D Holland, A Coldrick, R Ramsdale, W Jarman
Referee: T McMahon (Australia)

Third Test
At Sydney Cricket Ground, Saturday, 4 July 1914
Crowd: 34 420
GREAT BRITAIN 14 (Davies, Johnson tries, Wood 4 goals) d AUSTRALIA 6 (Messenger, Deane tries)
Australia: H Hallett, R Tidyman, W Messenger, S Deane (c), D Frawley, C Fraser, A Halloway, W Cann, R Craig, E Courtney, C Sullivan, S Pearce, F Burge
Great Britain: A Wood, F Williams, H Wagstaff (c), W Hall, W Davies, S Prosser, J Smith, A Johnson, A Coldrick, D Holland, D Clark, R Ramsdale, J Chilcott
Referee: T McMahon (Australia)

1921–22 Kangaroos (*l* to *r*) Back Row—J Craig, W Richards, P Laing, S Pearce, R Vest *Third Row*—W Lindsay, H Peters, W Schultz, A Gray, JC Ives, C Blinkhorn, H Caples, R Townsend, R Latta, N Potter, H Sunderland *Second Row*—DF Thompson, R Norman, F Burge, WA Cann, L Cubitt (captain), SG Ball, C Fraser, E McGrath, G Carstairs *Front Row*—J White, ES Brown, A Johnston, WN Broadfoot, H Horder, JC Watkins, CW Prentice, F Ryan, E Gill

1920

First Test
At Brisbane Exhibition Ground, Wednesday, 23 June 1920
Crowd: 32 000
AUSTRALIA 8 (Fraser, Burge tries, Horder goal) d GREAT BRITAIN 4 (Gronow 2 goals)
Australia: H Fewin, R Vest, V Farnsworth, N Broadfoot, H Horder, C Fraser, A Johnston (c), F Burge, B Gray, W Richards, W Schultz, S Pearce, N Potter
Great Britain: G Thomas, W Stone, D Hurcombe, H Wagstaff (c), J Bacon, J Parkin, JH Rogers, B Gronow, A Milnes, A Johnson, H Hilton, D Clark, F Gallagher
Referee: L Kearney (Australia)

Second Test
At Sydney Cricket Ground, Saturday, 3 July 1920
Crowd: 40 000
AUSTRALIA 21 (Potter, Farnsworth, Horder, Vest, Gilbert tries, Fraser, Horder, Burge goals) d GREAT BRITAIN 8 (Johnson, Gallagher tries, Gronow goal)
Australia: C Fraser, R Vest, V Farnsworth, H Gilbert (c), H Horder, A Johnston, D Thompson, W Richards, B Gray, N Potter, W Schultz, S Pearce, F Burge
Great Britain: G Thomas, J Bacon, H Wagstaff (c), D Hurcombe, W Stone, R Lloyd, JH Rogers, A Johnson, A Milnes, B Gronow, D Clark, H Hilton, F Gallagher
Referee: T McMahon (Australia)

Third Test

At RAS Showground, Sydney, Saturday, 10 July 1920
Crowd: 32 000
GREAT BRITAIN 23 (Hilton 2, Stone 2, Bacon tries, Rogers 3, Stockwell goals) d AUSTRALIA 13 (Gray,
Thompson, Burge tries, Burge 2 goals)
Australia: C Fraser, R Vest, V Farnsworth, H Gilbert (c), H Horder, A Johnston, D Thompson, W Richards,
B Gray, F Burge, W Schultz, S Pearce, N Potter. Replacement: J Robinson (for Horder)
Great Britain: G Thomas (c), J Rogers, W Stone, J Bacon, S Stockwell, E Jones, J Parkin, W Cunliffe,
J Cartwright, G Skelhorne, F Gallagher, D Clark, H Hilton
Referee: T McMahon (Australia)

1921–22

First Test

At Headingley, Leeds, Saturday, 1 October 1921
Crowd: 31 700
GREAT BRITAIN 6 (Stone, Stockwell tries) d AUSTRALIA 5 (Blinkhorn try, Craig goal)
Australia: C Fraser (c), H Horder, R Vest, J Craig, C Blinkhorn, A Johnston, D Thompson, J Watkins,
F Ryan, B Gray, C Prentice, S Pearce, F Burge
Great Britain: G Thomas, W Stone, H Wagstaff (c), J Bacon, S Stockwell, J Parkin, J Rogers, J Price,
J Morgan, J Beames, W Cunliffe, J Cartwright, G Skelhorne
Referee: F Renton (Great Britain)

Second Test

At The Boulevard, Hull, Saturday, 5 November 1921
Crowd: 21 504
AUSTRALIA 16 (Blinkhorn 2, Vest, Horder tries, Thompson 2 goals) d GREAT BRITAIN 2 (Rogers goal)
Australia: C Fraser (c), H Horder, R Vest, G Carstairs, C Blinkhorn, H Caples, D Thompson, F Burge,
R Latta, J Watkins, C Prentice, S Pearce, W Schultz
Great Britain: G Thomas, W Stone, W Batten, J Bacon, S Stockwell, J Parkin (c), JH Rogers, J Cartwright,
W Cunliffe, G Skelhorne, D Morgan, J Beames, J Price
Referee: R Robinson (Great Britain)

Third Test

At Weaste Ground, Salford, Saturday, 14 January 1922
Crowd: 22 000
GREAT BRITAIN 6 (Hilton, Gallagher tries) d AUSTRALIA 0
Australia: C Fraser (c), C Blinkhorn, R Vest, G Carstairs, H Horder, H Caples, D Thompson, F Burge,
W Richards, R Latta, F Ryan, W Schultz, C Prentice
Great Britain: G Thomas, D Hurcombe, J Bacon, H Wagstaff (c), J Owen, J Greenall, JH Rogers, W Cunliffe,
J Cartwright, G Skelhorne, R Taylor, H Hilton, F Gallagher
Referee: R Jones (Great Britain)

1924

First Test

At Sydney Cricket Ground, Monday, 23 June 1924
Crowd: 50 005
GREAT BRITAIN 22 (Parkin 2, Price, Rix tries, Sullivan 5 goals) d AUSTRALIA 3 (Aynsley try)
Australia: E Frauenfelder, C Blinkhorn, H Horder, T Gorman, C Aynsley, A Blair, J Craig (c), R Latta,
J Bennett, A O'Connor, A Oxford, H Watt, N Potter
Great Britain: J Sullivan, S Rix, T Howley, J Ring, C Carr, D Hurcombe, J Parkin (c), F Gallagher, J Darwell,
J Price, W Burgess, J Bennett, W Cunliffe
Referee: T McMahon (Australia)

Second Test

At Sydney Cricket Ground, Saturday, 28 June 1924
Crowd: 33 842
GREAT BRITAIN 5 (Parkin try, Sullivan goal) d AUSTRALIA 3 (Aynsley try)
Australia: E Frauenfelder, H Horder, J Craig (c), T Gorman, C Aynsley, J Hunt, D Thompson, R Latta,
V Armbruster, A O'Connor, J Bennett, H Watt, N Potter. Replacement: C Ives (for O'Connor)
Great Britain: J Sullivan, S Rix, C Carr, T Howley, F Evans, F Gallagher, J Parkin (c), W Burgess, W Cunliffe,
A Brough, J Bennett, J Darwell, J Thompson
Referee: T McMahon (Australia)

Third Test

At Brisbane Exhibition Ground, Saturday, 12 July 1924
Crowd: 39 000
AUSTRALIA 21 (Paton, Armbruster, Oxford tries, Aynsley 2, Thompson 2, Craig, Oxford goals) d GREAT
BRITAIN 11 (Evans 2, Parkin tries, Sullivan goal)
Australia: E Frauenfelder, C Aynsley, J Craig (c), T Gorman, W Paten, J Hunt, D Thompson, A O'Connor,
V Armbruster, R Latta, J Bennett, H Watt, N Potter. Replacement: A Oxford (for O'Connor)
Great Britain: J Sullivan, S Rix, T Howley, J Bacon, F Evans, J Parkin (c), D Hurcombe, F Gallagher,
J Darwell, J Price, W Cunliffe, J Bennett, W Burgess
Referee: J Roche (Australia)

1928

First Test
At Brisbane Exhibition Ground, Saturday, 23 June 1928
Crowd: 39 300
GREAT BRITAIN 15 (Fairclough, Horton, Ellaby tries, Sullivan 3 goals) d AUSTRALIA 12 (Armbruster, Aynsley tries, Craig, Freestone, Aynsley goals)
Australia: J Craig, C Aynsley, T Gorman (c), N Hardy, J Freestone, F Laws, A Edwards, V Armbruster, D Dempsey, G Treweek, C York, A Justice, H Steinohrt
Great Britain: J Sullivan (c), T Askin, J Oliver, J Brough, A Ellaby, L Fairclough, W Rees, W Horton, R Sloman, A Fildes, H Bowman, N Bentham, W Burgess
Referee: C Broadfoot (Australia)

Second Test
At Sydney Cricket Ground, Saturday, 14 July 1928
Crowd: 44 548
GREAT BRITAIN 8 (Parkin, Ellaby tries, Sullivan goal) d AUSTRALIA 0
Australia: N Hardy, H Byrne, T Gorman (c), J Craig, P Maher, E Weissel, J Busch, V Armbruster, D Dempsey, G Treweek, H Steinohrt, A Justice, C York
Great Britain: J Sullivan, T Askin, J Brough, J Oliver, A Ellaby, W Rees, J Parkin (c), W Burgess, N Bentham, J Thompson, R Sloman, W Horton, A Fildes
Referee: L Deane (Australia)

Third Test
At Sydney Cricket Ground, Saturday, 21 July 1928
Crowd: 37 000
AUSTRALIA 21 (Wearing 2, Pearce tries, Wearing 3, Craig 3 goals) d GREAT BRITAIN 14 (Fairclough 2 tries, Sullivan 4 goals)
Australia: N Hardy, B Wearing, T Gorman (c), J Craig, C Pearce, E Weissel, J Busch, J Kingston, V Armbruster, D Dempsey, G Treweek, A Justice, H Steinohrt
Great Britain: J Sullivan (c), A Ellaby, T Askin, J Oliver, T Gwynne, L Fairclough, W Rees, W Horton, A Fildes, R Sloman, W Burgess, H Bowman, N Bentham
Referee: L Deane (Australia)

1929-30

First Test
At Craven Park, Hull, Saturday, 5 October 1929
Crowd: 20 000
AUSTRALIA 31 (Shankland 2, Treweek, Prigg, Bishop, Spencer, Weissel tries, Weissel 5 goals) d GREAT BRITAIN 8 (Middleton, Feetham tries, Thompson goal)
Australia: F McMillan, W Spencer, C Fifield, T Gorman (c), W Shankland, E Weissel, J Busch, W Prigg, G Treweek, V Armbruster, W Brogan, G Bishop, M Madsen
Great Britain: J Rees, T Gwynne, R Kinnear, W Dingsdale, A Frodsham, L Fairclough (c), W Rees, N Bentham, J Thompson, H Bowman, A Middleton, W Horton, J Feetham
Referee: R Robinson (Great Britain)

Second Test
At Headingley, Leeds, Saturday, 9 November 1929
Crowd: 31 402
GREAT BRITAIN 9 (Atkinson try, Sullivan 3 goals) d AUSTRALIA 3 (Shankland try)
Australia: F McMillan, W Spencer, T Gorman (c), C Fifield, W Shankland, E Weissel, J Busch, W Prigg, D Dempsey, G Treweek, M Madsen, G Bishop, H Steinohrt
Great Britain: J Sullivan, A Ellaby, A Atkinson, W Dingsdale, S Smith, W Rees, J Parkin (c), W Burgess, N Bentham, D Jenkins, A Fildes, M Hodgson, F Butters
Referee: R Robinson (Great Britain)

Third Test
At Station Road, Swinton, Saturday, 4 January 1930
Crowd: 33 809
AUSTRALIA 0 drew with GREAT BRITAIN 0
Australia: F McMillan, W Spencer, T Gorman (c), C Fifield, W Shankland, E Weissel, J Busch, J Kingston, V Armbruster, G Treweek, W Brogan, A Justice, H Steinohrt
Great Britain: J Sullivan, A Ellaby, A Atkinson, H Halsall, S Smith, J Oster, J Parkin (c), W Burgess, N Bentham, A Thomas, F Butters, M Hodgson, A Fildes
Referee: R Robinson (Great Britain)

Fourth Test
At Athletic Grounds, Rochdale, Wednesday, 15 January 1930
Crowd: 16 743
GREAT BRITAIN 3 (Smith try) d AUSTRALIA 0
Australia: F McMillan, W Shankland, C Fifield, T Gorman (c), W Spencer, F Laws, J Busch, J Kingston, G Treweek, V Armbruster, W Brogan, A Justice, H Steinohrt
Great Britain: J Sullivan (c), S Smith, T Blinkhorn, S Brogden, A Atkinson, B Evans, W Rees, W Williams, N Bentham, A Thomas, A Fildes, H Crowther, H Young
Referee: R Robinson (Great Britain)

1929-30 Kangaroos

A Justice, C Fifield, F Laws, L Sellars, A Ridley, P Madsen, W Brogan, G Bishop, A Henderson, W Prigg, DV O'Dempsey, G Treweeke, LV Armbruster, AS Hennessey (Coach-Trainer), J Kingston, H Steinohrt, W Shankland, W Spencer, H Finch, J Upton, P Maher (Vice-Captain), J Lorne Dargan (Joint Manager), Harry Sunderland (Joint Manager), T Gorman (Captain), F McMillan, E Root, AEG Edwards, E Weissel, J Busch, J Holmes, H Kadwell

1932

First Test
At Sydney Cricket Ground, Monday, 6 June 1932
Crowd: 70 204 (World Test Record)
GREAT BRITAIN 8 (Ellaby, Atkinson tries, Sullivan goal) d AUSTRALIA 6 (Weissel 3 goals)
Australia: F McMillan, J Wilson, F Laws, E Weissel, C Pearce, E Norman, H Gee, W Prigg, S Pearce, D Dempsey, M Madsen, J Little, H Steinohrt (c)
Great Britain: J Sullivan (c), A Ellaby, A Atkinson, S Brogden, S Smith, E Pollard, B Evans, J Thompson, L White, N Silcock, W Horton, M Hodgson, J Feetham
Referee: W Neill (Australia)

Second Test
At Brisbane Cricket Ground, Saturday, 18 June 1932
Crowd: 26 574
AUSTRALIA 15 (Gee 2, Wilson tries, Weissel 2, Pearce goals) d GREAT BRITAIN 6 (Smith, Pollard tries)
Australia: F McMillan, C Pearce, E Norman, J Wilson, E Weissel, H Gee, F O'Connor, S Pearce, L Heidke, M Madsen, D Dempsey, H Steinohrt (c)
Great Britain: J Sullivan (c), A Ellaby, A Atkinson, S Brogden, S Smith, E Pollard. L Adams, J Thompson, L White, N Silcock, W Horton, M Hodgson, J Feetham
Referee: J Simpson (Australia)

Third Test
At Sydney Cricket Ground, Saturday, 16 July 1932
Crowd: 50 053
GREAT BRITAIN 18 (Smith 3, Brogden tries, Sullivan 3 goals) d AUSTRALIA 13 (O'Connor try, Weissel 5 goals)
Australia: F McMillan, J Wilson, C Pearce, F Laws, F Neumann, E Weissel, H Gee, W Christie, F O'Connor, S Pearce, M Madsen, L Heidke (c)
Great Britain: J Sullivan (c), A Ellaby, A Atkinson, S Brogden, S Smith, A Risman, B Evans, J Thompson, W Williams, M Hodgson, A Fildes, L White, W Horton
Referee: L Deane (Australia)

1933-34

First Test
At Belle Vue Zoological Gardens, Manchester, Saturday, 7 October 1933
Crowd: 33 000
GREAT BRITAIN 4 (Sullivan 2 goals) d AUSTRALIA 0
Australia: F McMillan (c), A Ridley, C Pearce, D Brown, J Why, V Hey, V Thicknesse, W Prigg, F O'Connor, S Pearce, M Madsen, D Dempsey, R Stehr
Great Britain: J Sullivan (c), A Ellaby, A Risman, S Brogden, S Smith, W Davies, B Evans, J Miller, L White, N Silcock, M Hodgson, W Horton, J Feetham
Referee: F Peel (Great Britain)

Second Test
At Headingley, Leeds, Saturday, 11 November 1933
Crowd: 29 688
GREAT BRITAIN 7 (Woods try, Sullivan 2 goals) d AUSTRALIA 5 (Brown try & goal)
Australia: W Smith, F Gardner, C Pearce, D Brown, A Ridley, V Hey, V Thicknesse, W Prigg, J Doyle, J Gibbs, F O'Connor, A Folwell, M Madsen (c)
Great Britain: J Sullivan (c), B Hudson, A Risman, W Dingsdale, J Woods, S Brogden, B Evans, N Silcock, L White, J Miller, W Horton, M Hodgson, J Feetham
Referee: F Peel (Great Britain)

Third Test
At Station Road, Swinton, Saturday, 16 December 1933
Crowd: 10 990
GREAT BRITAIN 19 (Hudson, Feetham, Smith tries, Sullivan 5 goals) d AUSTRALIA 16 (Hey, Prigg tries, Brown 5 goals)
Australia: F McMillan (c), C Pearce, D Brown, F Laws, J Why, V Hey, L Mead, W Prigg, S Pearce, J Gibbs, R Stehr, A Folwell, M Madsen
Great Britain: J Sullivan (c), B Hudson, A Atkinson, A Risman, S Smith, E Jenkins, W Watkins, J Miller, T Armitt, N Silcock, W Horton, M Hodgson, J Feetham
Referee: F Peel (Great Britain)

1936

First Test
At Sydney Cricket Ground, Monday, 29 June 1936
Crowd: 63 920
AUSTRALIA 24 (Brown 2, Ridley, Pearce tries, Brown 4, Beaton 2 goals) d GREAT BRITAIN 8 (Beverley, Edwards tries, Hodgson goal)
Australia: J Beaton, A Ridley, V Hey, D Brown (c), A Crippin, E Norman, V Thicknesse, W Prigg, S Pearce, L Heidke, F Curran, P Fairall, R Stehr
Great Britain: W Belshaw, A Edwards, A Atkinson (c), S Brogden, J Morley, E Jenkins, T McCue, H Beverley, H Woods, M Hodgson, J Miller, H Field, N Silcock
Referee: L Deane (Australia)

Second Test
At Brisbane Exhibition Ground, Saturday, 4 July 1936
Crowd: 29 486
GREAT BRITAIN 12 (Edwards 2, Risman 2, Hodgson goals) d AUSTRALIA 7 (Crippin try, Beaton, Brown goals)
Australia: J Beaton, A Ridley, V Hey, D Brown (c), A Crippin, E Norman, V Thicknesse, W Prigg, L Heidke, S Pearce, F Curran, P Fairall, R Stehr
Great Britain: J Brough (c), A Edwards, A Risman, W Belshaw, S Brogden, E Jenkins, W Watkins, H Beverley, H Woods, J Arkwright, M Hodgson, T Armitt, N Silcock
Referee: F Moynihan (Australia)

Third Test
At Sydney Cricket Ground, Saturday, 18 July 1936
Crowd: 53 546
GREAT BRITAIN 12 (Hudson, Brogden tries, Hodgson 3 goals) d AUSTRALIA 7 (Hey try, Brown 2 goals)
Australia: J Beaton, A Ridley, D Brown (c), E Norman, A Crippin, V Hey, F Gilbert, W Prigg, S Pearce, L Heidke, F Curran, M Madsen, R Stehr
Great Britain: W Belshaw, A Edwards, A Risman (c), S Brogden, B Hudson, E Jenkins, W Watkins, H Beverley, M Hodgson, J Arkwright, H Woods, T Armitt, N Silcock
Referee: L Deane (Australia)

1937–38

First Test
At Headingley, Leeds, Saturday, 16 October 1937
Crowd: 31 949
GREAT BRITAIN 5 (Jenkins try, Hodgson goal) d AUSTRALIA 4 (Beaton 2 goals)
Australia: L Ward, J Reardon, J Beaton, R McKinnon, B Williams, E Norman, P Williams, W Prigg (c), E Lewis, J Gibbs, F Curran, H Pierce, R Stehr
Great Britain: W Belshaw, A Cunliffe, A Croston, A Risman (c), J Morley, E Jenkins, T McCue, H Beverley, M Hodgson, J Arkwright, H Woods, T Armitt, N Silcock
Referee: A E Harding (Great Britain)

Second Test
At Station Road, Swinton, Saturday, 13 November 1937
Crowd: 31 724
GREAT BRITAIN 13 (Edwards 2, Hudson tries, Risman 2 goals) d AUSTRALIA 3 (Dawson try)
Australia: L Ward, B Williams, J Beaton, E Norman, L Dawson, J Reardon, P Williams, W Prigg (c), H Narvo, E Lewis, L Heidke, H Pierce, J Gibbs
Great Britain: W Belshaw, A Edwards, A Risman (c), S Brogden, B Hudson, E Jenkins, W Watkins, H Beverley, J Arkwright, K Jubb, N Silcock, T Armitt, H Higgins
Referee: A E Harding (Great Britain)

Third Test
At Fartown, Huddersfield, Saturday, 18 December 1937
Crowd: 9403
AUSTRALIA 13 (Norval, Reardon, Narvo tries, Beaton 2 goals) d GREAT BRITAIN 3 (Hudson try)
Australia: L Ward, L Dawson, R McKinnon, J Beaton, A Norval, J Reardon, F Gilbert, W Prigg (c), E Lewis, H Narvo, L Heidke, H, Pierce, F Curran
Great Britain: W Belshaw, B Hudson, S Brogden, A Risman (c), A Edwards, E Jenkins, W Watkins, H Beverley, K Jubb, J Arkwright, D Prosser, T Armitt, H Higgins
Referee: A E Harding (Great Britain)

1946

First Test

At Sydney Cricket Ground, Monday, 17 June 1946
Crowd: 64 526
AUSTRALIA 8 (Cooper, Bailey tries, Jorgenson goal) drew with GREAT BRITAIN 8 (Horne, Whitcombe tries, Risman goal)
Australia: D Parkinson, L Cooper, J Jorgenson (c), R Bailey, E Newham, P Devery, J Grice, N Mulligan, A Clues, R Kay, F Farrell, G Watt, R Westaway
Great Britain: A Risman (c), E Batten, E (Ernest) Ward, J Kitching, A Johnson, W Horne, T McCue, I Owens, D Phillips, L White, K Gee, J Egan, F Whitcombe
Referee: T McMahon (Australia)

Second Test

At Brisbane Exhibition Ground, Saturday, 6 July 1946
Crowd: 40 500*
GREAT BRITAIN 14 (Bassett 3, Johnson tries, Ernest Ward goal) d AUSTRALIA 5 (Cooper try, Jorgenson goal)
Australia: D Parkinson, L Cooper, R Bailey (c), J Jorgenson, E Newham, P Devery, J Grice, J Hutchinson, A Clues, R Kay, F Farrell, G Watt, R Westaway
Great Britain: E (Ernest) Ward, A Bassett, A Risman (c), E (Ted) Ward, A Johnson, W Horne, T McCue, I Owens, D Phillips, L White, F Whitcombe, J Egan, K Gee
Referee: S W Chambers (Australia)
(* an estimated 10 000 other fans scaled fences to get into the ground after the police shut the gates)

Third Test

At Sydney Cricket Ground, Saturday, 20 July 1946
Crowd: 35 294
GREAT BRITAIN 20 (Bassett 2, Curran, Owens tries, Risman 3, Ted Ward goals) d AUSTRALIA 7 (Kennedy try, Jorgenson 2 goals)
Australia: D Parkinson, L Cooper, J Jorgenson (c), T Eather, N White, P Devery, C Kennedy, N Mulligan, A Clues, R Kay, F Farrell, G Watt, J Armstrong
Great Britain: E (Ernest) Ward, A Bassett, A Risman (c), E (Ted) Ward, E Batten, W Horne, T McCue, I Owens, D Phillips, L White, G Curran, J Egan, K Gee
Referee: T McMahon (Australia)

1948-49

First Test

At Headingley, Leeds, Saturday, 9 October 1948
Crowd: 36 394
GREAT BRITAIN 23 (Pimblett 2, McCormick 2, Foster 2, Valentine tries, Ward goal) d AUSTRALIA 21 (McMahon 2, Graves, Froome, Hall tries, Graves 3 goals)
Australia: C Churchill, J Graves, D McRitchie, J Hawke, P McMahon, W O'Connell (c), K Froome, N Mulligan, J Rayner, D Hall, A Gibbs, K Schubert, J Holland
Great Britain: J Ledgard, J Lawrenson, E Ward (c), A Pimblett, S McCormick, W Horne, G Helme, D Valentine, T Foster, R Nicholson, G Curran, J Egan, K Gee
Referee: A S Dobson (Great Britain)

Second Test

At Station Road, Swinton, Saturday, 6 November 1948
Crowd: 43 500
GREAT BRITAIN 16 (Lawrenson 2, Pimblett 2 tries, Ward 2 goals) d AUSTRALIA 7 (Horrigan try, Graves 2 goals)
Australia: C Churchill, P McMahon, C Maxwell (c), J Horrigan, J Graves, W O'Connell, W Thompson, W Tyquin, N Mulligan, J Rayner, N Hand, K Schubert, A Gibbs
Great Britain: M Ryan, J Lawrenson, E Ward (c), A Pimblett, S,McCormick, R Williams, G Helme, D Valentine, T Foster, R Nicholson, G Curran, J Egan, K Gee
Referee: G S Phillips (Great Britain)

Third Test

At Odsal Stadium, Bradford, Saturday, 29 January 1949
(Postponed from 18 December 1948, because of fog)
Crowd: 36 294
GREAT BRITAIN 23 (Curran 2, Ward, McCormick, Williams tries, Ward 4 goals) d AUSTRALIA 9 (Hall, Lulham, de Belin tries)
Australia: C Churchill, R Lulham, D McRitchie, J Hawke, P McMahon, W O'Connell, K Froome, W Tyquin (c), N Mulligan, F de Belin, D Hall, K Schubert, A Gibbs
Great Britain: M Ryan, J Lawrenson, A Pimblett, E Ward (c), S McCormick, R Williams, G Helme, D Valentine, J Featherstone, W Hudson, K Gee, J Egan, G Curran
Referee: G S Phillips (Great Britain)

1950

First Test
At Sydney Cricket Ground, Monday, 12 June 1950
Crowd: 47 215
GREAT BRITAIN 6 (Hilton 2 tries) d AUSTRALIA 4 (Pidding 2 goals)
Australia: C Churchill (c), N Pidding, D McRitchie, K Middleton, J Troy, F Stanmore, K Holman, L Cowie, F de Belin, A Thompson, J Holland, K Schubert, D Hall
Great Britain: M Ryan, G Ratcliffe, E Ward (c), E Ashcroft, J Hilton, R Williams, T Bradshaw, H Street, R Ryan, F Higgins, K Gee, J Egan, E Gwyther
Referee: G Bishop (Australia)

Second Test
At Brisbane Cricket Ground, Saturday, 1 July 1950
Crowd: 35 000
AUSTRALIA 15 (Graves, Cowie, Holman tries, Graves, Churchill, Holland goals) d GREAT BRITAIN 3 (Danby try)
Australia: C Churchill (c), D Flannery, N Andrews, K Middleton, J Graves, F Stanmore, K Holman, L Cowie, F de Belin, H Crocker, J Holland, K Schubert, A Thompson
Great Britain: J Ledgard, G Ratcliffe, E Ward (c), E Ashcroft, T Danby, R Williams, T Bradshaw, H Street, H Murphy, F Higgins, K Gee, J Egan, E Gwyther
Referee: F Ballard (Australia)

Third Test
At Sydney Cricket Ground, Saturday, 22 July 1950
Crowd: 47 178
AUSTRALIA 5 (Roberts try, Churchill goal) d GREAT BRITAIN 2 (Ward goal)
Australia: C Churchill (c), R Roberts, K Middleton, D McRitchie, J Troy, F Stanmore, K Holman, L Cowie, H Crocker, B Purcell, J Holland, K Schubert, D Hall
Great Britain: J Ledgard, T Danby, E Ward (c), E Ashcroft, J Hilton, J Cunliffe, T Bradshaw, H Street, D Phillips, F Higgins, E Gwyther, J Egan, K Gee
Referee: T McMahon (Australia)

1952

First Test
At Headingley, Leeds, Saturday, 4 October 1952
Crowd: 34 305
GREAT BRITAIN 19 (Castle, Ryder, Daniels tries, Horne 5 goals) d AUSTRALIA 6 (Pidding 3 goals)
Australia: C Churchill (c), N Pidding, N Hazzard, H Wells, B Carlson, G Hawick, K Holman, H Crocker, A Paul, F Ashton, B Davies, K Schubert, D Hall
Great Britain: J Evans, A Daniels, R Ryder, E Ward, F Castle, W Horne (c), E Toohey, K Traill, R Ryan, C Pawsey, J Featherstone, A Ackerley, A Prescott
Referee: G S Phillips (Great Britain)

Second Test
At Station Road, Swinton, Saturday, 9 November 1952
Crowd: 30 509
GREAT BRITAIN 21 (Castle 2, Greenall 2, Ward tries, Ward 2, Horne goals) d AUSTRALIA 5 (Geelan try, Carlson goal)
Australia: C Churchill (c), D Flannery, N Hazzard, C Geelan, B Carlson, F Stanmore, C Donohoe, A Collinson, T Tyrrell, B Davies, C Gill, K Schubert, D Hall
Great Britain: J Evans, A Daniels, E Ward, D Greenall, F Castle, W Horne (c), E Toohey, K Traill, D Valentine, C Pawsey, J Featherstone, T McKinney, A Prescott
Referee: J W Jackson (Great Britain)

Third Test
At Odsal Stadium, Bradford, Saturday, 13 December 1952
Crowd: 30 509
AUSTRALIA 27 (Ryan 2, Pidding, Holman, Davies tries, Pidding 6 goals) d GREAT BRITAIN 7 (Horne try, Evans 2 goals)
Australia: C Churchill (c), N Pidding, N Hazzard, C Geelan, T Ryan, F Stanmore, K Holman, A Collinson, F Ashton, B Davies, D Hall, K Kearney, R Bull
Great Britain: J Evans, D Bevan, D Greenall, E Ward, F Castle, W Horne (c), E Toohey, K Traill, D Valentine, C Pawsey, J Featherstone, T McKinney, A Prescott
Referee: A S Dobson (Great Britain)

1954

First Test
At Sydney Cricket Ground, Saturday, 12 June 1954
Crowd: 65 885
AUSTRALIA 37 (McCaffery 2, Provan, O'Shea, Hall, Pidding, Carlson tries, Pidding 8 goals) d GREAT BRITAIN 12 (Silcock, Jackson tries, Jones 3 goals)

Continued

1954 First Test *continued*

Australia: C Churchill (c), N Pidding, K McCaffery, A Watson, B Carlson, R Banks, K Holman, H Crocker, N Provan, K O'Shea, R Bull, K Kearney, D Hall
Great Britain: J Cunliffe, L Jones, E Ashcroft (c), P Jackson, F Castle, R Price, G Helme, K Traill, D Valentine, N Silcock, A Prescott, T McKinney, J Wilkinson
Referee: D Lawler (Australia)

Second Test

At Brisbane Cricket Ground, Saturday, 9 November 1954
Crowd: 46 355
GREAT BRITAIN 38 (Boston 2, Pawsey, Williams, Jackson, Helme tries, Jones 10 goals) d AUSTRALIA 21 (Carlson 2, Provan, Hall, Holman tries, Pidding 3 goals)
Australia: C Churchill (c), N Pidding, N Hazzard, A Watson, B Carlson, R Sullivan, K Holman, H Crocker, N Provan, K O'Shea, D Hall, K Kearney, R Bull
Great Britain: L Jones, W Boston, P Jackson, E Ashcroft, T O'Grady, R Williams (c), G Helme, D Valentine, N Silcock, C Pawsey, J Bowden, T McKinney, A Prescott
Referee: D Lawler (Australia)

Third Test

At Sydney Cricket Ground, Saturday, 17 July 1954
Crowd: 67 577
AUSTRALIA 20 (Watson, Wells, Pidding, Diversi tries, Pidding 4 goals) d GREAT BRITAIN 16 (Williams 2, Ashcroft, Valentine tries, Jones 2 goals)
Australia: C Churchill (c), B Carlson, H Wells, A Watson, N Pidding, R Banks, K Holman, P Diversi, N Provan, K O'Shea, B Davies, K Kearney, D Hall
Great Britain: L Jones, W Boston, P Jackson, E Ashcroft, T O'Grady, R Williams (c), G Helme, D Valentine, N Silcock, C Pawsey, A Prescott, T McKinney, J Bowden
Referee: D Lawler (Australia)

1956

First Test

At Central Park, Wigan, Saturday, 17 November 1956
Crowd: 22 473
GREAT BRITAIN 21 (Boston 2, Grundy, Davies, Sullivan tries, Mortimer 3 goals) d AUSTRALIA 10 (Moir, Poole tries, Holman 2 goals)
Australia: C Churchill, I Moir, R Poole, A Watson, D Adams, R Banks, K Holman, K O'Shea, W Marsh, T Tyquin, R Bull, K Kearney (c), B Davies
Great Britain: F Mortimer, W Boston, P Jackson, A Davies, M Sullivan, R Price, J Stevenson, E Dawson, G Robinson, J Grundy, B Shaw, T Harris, A Prescott (c)
Referee: N T Railton (Great Britain)

Second Test

At Odsal Stadium, Bradford, Saturday, 1 December 1956
Crowd: 23 334
AUSTRALIA 22 (Holman, Banks, Davies, Bull tries, Clifford 5 goals) d GREAT BRITAIN 9 (Stevenson try, Mortimer 3 goals)
Australia: G Clifford, D Flannery, A Watson, R Poole, D McGovern, R Banks, K Holman, I Doyle, D Furner, K O'Shea, R Bull, K Kearney (c), B Davies
Great Britain: F Mortimer, W Boston, P Jackson, A Davies, M Sullivan, R Price, J Stevenson, D Turner, G Robinson, J Grundy, B Shaw, T Harris, A Prescott (c)
Referee: M Coates (Great Britain)

Third Test

At Station Road, Swinton, Saturday, 15 December 1956
Crowd: 13 515
GREAT BRITAIN 19 (Little, Turner, Gunney, Sullivan, Boston tries, Davies 2 goals) d AUSTRALIA 0
Australia: G Clifford, D Flannery, R Poole, A Watson, D McGovern, R Banks, K Holman, I Doyle, K O'Shea, T Tyquin, R Bull, K Kearney (c), B Orrock
Great Britain: G Moses, W Boston, P Jackson, A Davies, M Sullivan, R Price, J Stevenson, D Turner, G Gunney, J Grundy, S Little, T Harris, A Prescott (c)
Referee: R Gelder (Great Britain)

1958

First Test

At Sydney Cricket Ground, Saturday, 14 June 1958
Crowd: 68 777
AUSTRALIA 25 (O'Shea, Mossop, Carlson, Kite, Provan tries, Clifford 5 goals) d GREAT BRITAIN 8 (Southward, Bolton tries, Southward goal)
Australia: G Clifford, R Kite, H Wells, B Carlson, I Moir, A Brown, K Holman, K O'Shea, N Provan, R Mossop, B Davies (c), K Kearney, W Marsh
Great Britain: E Fraser, I Southward, P Jackson, A Davies, M Sullivan, D Bolton, A Murphy, J Whiteley, M Martyn, B Edgar, A Terry, T Harris, A Prescott (c)
Referee: D Lawler (Australia)

Second Test
At Brisbane Exhibition Ground, Saturday, 5 July 1958
Crowd: 33 563
GREAT BRITAIN 25 (Southward 2, Challinor, Sullivan, Murphy tries, Fraser 5 goals) d AUSTRALIA 18 (Marsh, Holman, Carlson, Dimond tries, Clifford 3 goals)
Australia: G Clifford, P Dimond, B Carlson, G Hawick, R Kite, A Brown, K Holman, K O'Shea, N Provan, R Mossop, B Davies (c), K Kearney, W Marsh
Great Britain: E Fraser, I Southward, E Ashton, J Challinor, M Sullivan, D Bolton, A Murphy, V Karalius, R Huddart, J Whiteley, A Prescott (c), T Harris, B McTigue
Referee: D Lawler (Australia)

Third Test
At Sydney Cricket Ground, Saturday, 19 July 1958
Crowd: 68 720
GREAT BRITAIN 40 (Sullivan 3, Southward, Terry, Murphy, Davies, Whiteley tries, Fraser 8 goals) d AUSTRALIA 17 (Provan, Holman, Hawick tries, Clifford 4 goals)
Australia: G Clifford, I Moir, H Wells, B Carlson, P Dimond, G Hawick, K Holman, K O'Shea, N Provan, R Mossop, B Davies (c), K Kearney, W Marsh
Great Britain: E Fraser, I Southward, E Ashton, A Davies, M Sullivan, P Jackson (c), A Murphy, V Karalius, D Huddart, J Whiteley, B McTigue, T Harris, A Terry
Referee: J Casey (Australia)

1959

First Test
At Station Road, Swinton, Saturday, 17 October 1959
Crowd: 34 964
AUSTRALIA 22 (Gasnier 3, Wells tries, Barnes 5 goals) d GREAT BRITAIN 14 (Turner, Boston tries, Fraser 4 goals)
Australia: K Barnes (c), J Riley, H Wells, R Gasnier, E Lumsden, B Clay, B Muir, B Hambly, R Mossop, G Parcell, D Beattie, I Walsh, W Wilson
Great Britain: E Fraser, W Boston, A Davies, E Ashton (c), M Sullivan, D Bolton, A Murphy, D Turner, R Huddart, M Martyn, A Terry, T Harris, B McTigue
Referee: R Gelder (Great Britain)

Second Test
At Headingley, Leeds, Saturday, 21 November 1959
Crowd: 30 301
GREAT BRITAIN 11 (Robinson, Fox, Whiteley tries, Fox goal) d AUSTRALIA 10 (Carlson 2 tries, Carlson, Barnes goals)
Australia: K Barnes (c), E Lumsden, H Wells, R Gasnier, B Carlson, B Clay, B Muir, B Hambly, R Mossop, E Rasmussen, W Wilson, I Walsh, G Parcell
Great Britain: F Dyson, I Southward, E Ashton, N Fox, M Sullivan, D Bolton, J Stevenson (c), J Whiteley, B McTigue, D Vines, A Terry, T Harris, D Robinson
Referee: R Gelder (Great Britain)

Third Test
At Central Park, Wigan, Saturday, 12 December 1959
Crowd: 26 089
GREAT BRITAIN 18 (Fox, Southward tries, Fox 6 goals) d AUSTRALIA 12 (Raper, Carlson tries, Barnes 3 goals)
Australia: K Barnes (c), E Lumsden, H Wells, R Gasnier, B Carlson, B Clay, B Muir, J Raper, R Mossop, B Hambly, D Beattie, I Walsh, W Wilson
Great Britain: G Round, I Southward, E Ashton, N Fox, M Sullivan, D Bolton, J Stevenson (c), J Whiteley, B McTigue, D Robinson, A Terry, T Harris, J Wilkinson
Referee: E Clay (Great Britain)

1962

First Test
At Sydney Cricket Ground, Saturday, 9 June 1962
Crowd: 70 174
GREAT BRITAIN 31 (Sullivan 2, Ashton 2, Turner, Huddart, Boston tries, Fox 5 goals) d AUSTRALIA 12 (Irvine, Gasnier tries, Parish 3 goals)
Australia: D Parish, M Cleary, R Gasnier (c), R Hagan, K Irvine, A Summons, B Muir, J Raper, R Lynch, E Rasmussen, D Beattie, I Walsh, G Parcell
Great Britain: G Round, M Sullivan, N Fox, E Ashton (c), W Boston, D Bolton, A Murphy, D Turner, R Huddart, B Edgar, B McTigue, W Sayer, N Herbert
Referee: D Lawler (Australia)

Second Test

At Lang Park, Brisbane, Saturday, 30 June 1962
Crowd: 34 766
GREAT BRITAIN 17 (Boston 2, Murphy tries, Fox 3, Ashton goals) d AUSTRALIA 10 (Irvine, Summons tries, Barnes 2 goals)
Australia: K Barnes (c), E Lumsden, R Gasnier, A Gil, K Irvine, R Banks, A Summons, G Smith, M Veivers, W Owen, D Beattie, I Walsh, W Carson
Great Britain: G Round, M Sullivan, E Ashton (c), N Fox, W Boston, H Poynton, A Murphy, L Gilfedder, R Huddart, B Edgar, B McTigue, W Sayer, N Herbert
Referee: J Casey (Australia)

Third Test

At Sydney Cricket Ground, Saturday, 14 July 1962
Crowd: 42 104
AUSTRALIA 18 (Irvine 2, Summons, Drake tries, Irvine 3 goals) d GREAT BRITAIN 17 (Fox, Murphy, Ashton tries, Fox 4 goals)
Australia: F Drake, K Irvine, P Dimond, A Gil, E Lumsden, J Lisle, A Summons (c), J Raper, M Veivers, E Rasmussen, D Beattie, I Walsh, W Carson
Great Britain: G Round, M Sullivan, E Ashton (c), N Fox, W Boston, H Poynton, A Murphy, D Turner, R Huddart, B Edgar, B McTigue, W Sayer, N Herbert
Referee: D Lawler (Australia)

1963

First Test

At Wembley Stadium, London, Wednesday, 16 October 1963
Crowd: 13 946
AUSTRALIA 28 (Gasnier 3, Langlands, Irvine, Thornett tries, Langlands 5 goals) d GREAT BRITAIN 2 (Fox goal)
Australia: K Thornett, K Irvine, R Gasnier, G Langlands, P Dimond, E Harrison, B Muir, J Raper, R Thornett, B Hambly, N Kelly, I Walsh (c), P Gallagher
Great Britain: K Gowers, W Burgess, E Ashton (c), N Fox, N Field, D Bolton, A Murphy, V Karalius, K Bowman, J Measures, J Tembey, W Sayer, B Tyson
Referee: D Davies (Great Britain)

Second Test

At Station Road, Swinton, Saturday, 9 November 1963
Crowd: 30 843
AUSTRALIA 50 (Irvine 3, Dimond 2, Langlands 2, Gasnier 2, Harrison, Kelly, R Thornett tries, Langlands 7 goals) d GREAT BRITAIN 12 (Measures, Stopford tries, Fox 3 goals)
Australia: K Thornett, K Irvine, R Gasnier, G Langlands, P Dimond, E Harrison, B Muir, J Raper, R Thornett, K Day, N Kelly, I Walsh (c), P Quinn
Great Britain: K Gowers, M Sullivan, E Ashton (c), N Fox, J Stopford, F Myler, A Murphy, V Karalius, R Morgan, J Measures, C Watson, L McIntyre, W Robinson
Referee: D Davies (Great Britain)

Third Test

At Headingley, Leeds, Saturday, 30 November 1963
Crowd: 20 497
GREAT BRITAIN 16 (Smith, Stopford, Ward tries, Fox 2 goals) d AUSTRALIA 5 (Irvine try, Langlands goal)
Australia: K Thornett, K Irvine, R Gasnier, G Langlands, P Dimond, E Harrison, B Muir, J Raper, R Thornett, B Hambly, P Quinn, I Walsh (c), N Kelly
Great Britain: K Gowers, G Smith, K Holden, A Buckley, J Stopford, D Bolton, T Smales (c), D Fox, K Roberts, R Huddart, F Collier, J Ward, C Watson
Referee: E Clay (Great Britain)

1966

First Test

At Sydney Cricket Ground, Saturday, 25 June 1966
Crowd: 57 962
GREAT BRITAIN 17 (Burgess, Hardisty, Watson tries, Keegan 3 goals, Bishop field goal) d AUSTRALIA 13 (Banks try, Barnes 3 goals)
Australia: K Barnes, K Irvine, G Langlands, J McDonald, J King, G Banks, W Smith, J Raper, A Crema, W Bradstreet, R Crowe, I Walsh (c), L Weier
Great Britain: A Keegan, W Burgess, I Brooke, A Buckley, J Stopford, A.Hardisty, T Bishop, D Robinson, W Bryant, J Mantle, B Edgar (c), P Flanagan, C Watson
Referee: J Bradley (Australia)

Second Test

At Lang Park, Brisbane, Saturday, 16 July 1966
Crowd: 45 057
AUSTRALIA 6 (Barnes 3 goals) d GREAT BRITAIN 4 (Keegan 2 goals)

▶

Australia: K Barnes, K Irvine, G Langlands, J Greaves, J King, J Gleeson, W Smith, R Lynch, R Thornett, M Veivers, N Kelly, I Walsh (c), J Wittenberg
Great Britain: A Keegan, G Wriglesworth, F Myler, I Brooke, W Burgess, A Hardisty, T Bishop, W Ramsey, W Bryant, J Mantle, C Watson, P Flanagan, B Edgar (c)
Referee: C Pearce (Australia)

Third Test
At Sydney Cricket Ground, Saturday, 23 July 1966
Crowd: 63 503
AUSTRALIA 19 (Irvine 3, King, Lynch tries, Johns 2 goals) d GREAT BRITAIN 14 (Hardisty try and penalty try, Gowers 4 goals)
Australia: L Johns, K Irvine, P Dimond, J Greaves, J King, J Gleeson, W Smith, R Lynch, A Beetson, M Veivers, N Kelly, I Walsh (c), J Wittenberg. Replacement: R Thornett (for Beetson)
Great Britain: K Gowers, W Burgess, I Brooke, A Buckley, G Wriglesworth, A Hardisty, T Bishop, D Robinson, W Ramsay, J Mantle, B Edgar (c), P Flanagan, C Watson. Replacement: W Bryant (for Mantle)
Referee: C Pearce (Australia)

1967

First Test
At Headingley, Leeds, Saturday, 21 October 1967
Crowd: 22 293
GREAT BRITAIN 16 (Young, Millward tries, Millward 3, Holliday goals, Bishop field goal) d AUSTRALIA 11 (Langlands try, 4 goals)
Australia: L Johns, J McDonald, G Langlands, R Gasnier (c), J King, J Gleeson, W Smith, J Raper, E Rasmussen, R Lynch, P Gallagher, N Kelly, D Manteit
Great Britain: A Keegan, C Young, I Brooke, M Price, W Burgess, R Millward, T Bishop, D Robinson, R Irving, J Mantle, C Watson, P Flanagan, W Holliday (c)
Referee: F Lindop (Great Britain)

Second Test
At White City Stadium, London, Friday, 3 November 1967
Crowd: 17 445
AUSTRALIA 17 (Langlands, King, Coote tries, Langlands 4 goals) d GREAT BRITAIN 11 (Bishop try, Fox 3 goals, Bishop field goal)
Australia: L Johns, J Greaves, G Langlands, J McDonald, J King, A Branson, J Gleeson, R Coote, E Rasmussen, R Lynch, P Gallagher (c), N Gallagher, N Kelly
Great Britain: A Keegan, C Young, I Brooke, N Fox, W Francis, R Millward, T Bishop, F Foster, R Irving, J Mantle, C Watson, P Flanagan, W Holliday (c)
Referee: F Lindop (Great Britain)

Third Test
At Station Road, Swinton, Saturday, 9 December 1967
Crowd: 13 515
AUSTRALIA 11 (Coote, Branson, King tries, Langlands goal) d GREAT BRITAIN 3 (Price try)
Australia: L Johns, J King, J Greaves, G Langlands, J McDonald, J Gleeson, W Smith, J Raper (c), R Coote, E Rasmussen, D Manteit, N Kelly, P Gallagher
Great Britain: A Keegan, C Young, I Brooke, M Price, G Jordan, R Millward, T Bishop, D Robinson, R Valentine, R Irving, C Watson, P Flanagan, W Holliday (c). Replacements: A Burwell (for Young) and C Renilson (for Watson)
Referee: F Lindop (Great Britain)

1970

First Test
At Lang Park, Brisbane, Saturday, 6 June 1970
Crowd: 42 807
AUSTRALIA 37 (Morgan 2, King 2, McDonald tries, Langlands 9 goals, Hawthorne 2 field goals) d GREAT BRITAIN 15 (Flanagan, Watson, Laughton tries, Price 3 goals)
Australia: G Langlands (c), J King, J McDonald, J Brass, J Cootes, P Hawthorne, W Smith, R Coote, A Beetson, R Lynch, J Wittenberg, E Walters, J Morgan. Replacement: C Weiss (for Lynch)
Great Britain: T Price, C Sullivan, F Myler (c), M Shoebottom, J Atkinson, A Hardisty, K Hepworth, M Reilly, D Laughton, D Robinson, C Watson, P Flanagan, D Chisnall. Replacement: R Irving (for Robinson)
Referee: D Lancashire (Australia)

Second Test
At Sydney Cricket Ground, Saturday, 20 June 1970
Crowd: 60 962
GREAT BRITAIN 28 (Millward 2, Atkinson, Fisher tries, Millward 6 goals & field goal, Hynes field goal) d AUSTRALIA 7 (King try, McDonald goal, Hawthorne field goal)
Australia: R Laird, J King, J Brass, J McDonald, J Cootes, P Hawthorne, W Smith, C Weiss, R Coote, A Beetson, J Wittenberg, B Fitzsimmons, J Sattler (c)
Great Britain: D Edwards, A Smith, S Hynes, F Myler (c), J Atkinson, R Millward, K Hepworth, M Reilly, D Laughton, J Thompson, C Watson, A Fisher, D Hartley. Replacement: M Shoebottom (for Edwards)
Referee: D Lancashire (Australia)

23

Third Test
At Sydney Cricket Ground, Saturday, 4 July 1970
Crowd: 61 258
GREAT BRITAIN 21 (Atkinson 2, Hynes, Millward, Hartley tries, Millward 3 goals) d AUSTRALIA 17 (McCarthy try, McKean 7 goals)
Australia: A McKean, J McDonald, R Fulton, J Brass, J King, P Hawthorne (c), R Grant, R Coote, R Costello, R McCarthy, J Morgan, E Walters, A Beetson
Great Britain: M Shoebottom, A Smith, F Myler (c), S Hynes, J Atkinson, R Millward, K Hepworth, M Reilly, D Laughton, J Thompson, C Watson, A Fisher, D Hartley
Referee: D Lancashire (Australia)

1973

First Test
At Wembly Stadium, London, Saturday, 3 November 1973
Crowd: 9875
GREAT BRITAIN 21 (Lowe 2, Clarke, Lockwood tries, Clawson 4 goals, Nash field goal) d AUSTRALIA 12 (Fulton, Branighan tries, Langlands 3 goals)
Australia: G Langlands (c), R Branighan, R Fulton, G Starling, E Goodwin, T Pickup, T Raudonikis, P Sait, K Maddison, R McCarthy, A Beetson, E Walters, R O'Reilly
Great Britain: P Charlton, C Sullivan (c), S Hynes, C Hesketh, J Atkinson, D Topliss, S Nash, R Batten, G Nicholls, P Lowe, B Lockwood, C Clarke, T Clawson
Referee: W Thompson (Great Britain)

Second Test
At Headingley, Leeds, Saturday, 24 November 1973
Crowd: 16 674
AUSTRALIA 14 (McCarthy try, Eadie 5 goals, Fulton field goal) d GREAT BRITAIN 6 (Clawson 3 goals)
Australia: G Eadie, L Williamson, G Starling, R Branighan, D Waite, R Fulton, T Raudonikis, P Sait, G Stevens, R McCarthy (c), A Beetson, E Walters, R O'Reilly. Replacement: K Maddison (for McCarthy)
Great Britain: P Charlton, C Sullivan (c), S Hynes, C Hesketh, J Atkinson, D Topliss, S Nash, R Batten, J Mantle, P Lowe, B Lockwood, C Clarke, T Clawson. Replacements: D Eckersley (for Topliss) and C Dixon (for Mantle)
Referee: W Thompson (Great Britain)

Third Test
At Wilderspool Stadium, Warrington, Saturday, 1 December 1973
Crowd: 10 019
AUSTRALIA 15 (Maddison 2, Fulton, Starling, Walters tries) d GREAT BRITAIN 5 (Millward try & goal)
Australia: G Eadie, L Williamson, G Starling, R Branighan, D Waite, R Fulton, T Raudonikis, P Sait, G Stevens, K Maddison, A Beetson, E Walters, R O'Reilly. Replacement: T Pickup (for Eadie)
Great Britain: P Charlton, A Smith, S Hynes, C Hesketh, C Sullivan (c), D Eckersley, R Millward, D Laughton, P Lowe, C Nicholls, M Harrison, C Clarke, T Clawson. Replacements: D Watkins (for Millward) and C Dixon (for Clawson)
Referee: W Thompson (Great Britain)

1974

First Test
At Lang Park, Brisbane, Saturday, 15 June 1974
Crowd: 30 280
AUSTRALIA 12 (Orr try, Langlands 4 goals Fulton field goal) d GREAT BRITAIN 6 (Clawson 2, Watkins goals)
Australia: G Langlands (c), D Waite, R Fulton, M Cronin, W Orr, G Richardson, T Raudonikis, R Coote, P Sait, R Higgs, A Beetson, E Walters, R O'Reilly
Great Britain: P Charlton, D Redfearn, D Watkins, C Hesketh (c), J Bevan, R Millward, S Nash, G Nicholls, C Dixon, J Thompson, J Mills, J Bridges, T Clawson. Replacements: J Gray (for Nicholls) and D Eckersley (for Bridges)
Referee: D Lancashire (Australia)

Second Test
At Sydney Cricket Ground, Saturday, 6 July 1974
Crowd: 48 006
GREAT BRITAIN 16 (Chisnall, Dixon, Gill tries, Gray 3 goals & field goal) d AUSTRALIA 11 (Fulton, Lang, Coote tries, Cronin goal)
Australia: G Eadie, D Waite, R Fulton, M Cronin, W Orr, G Richardson, T Raudonikis, R Coote, P Sait, G Stevens, A Beetson (c), J Lang, R O'Reilly. Replacements: R Branighan (for Eadie) and R McCarthy (for O'Reilly)
Great Britain: P Charlton, L Dyl, D Eckersley, C Hesketh (c), R Millward, K Gill, S Nash, G Nicholls, C Dixon, E Chisnall, J Thompson, J Gray, J Mills. Replacement: S Norton (for Gray)
Referee: K Page (Australia)

Third Test
At Sydney Cricket Ground, Saturday, 20 July 1974
Crowd: 55 505
AUSTRALIA 22 (Williamson, Langlands, McCarthy, Coote tries, Langlands 5 goals) d GREAT BRITAIN 18 (Dyl, Richards tries, Gray 6 goals)
Australia: G Langlands (c), L Williamson, R Fulton, M Cronin, R Branighan, T Pickup, T Raudonikis, R Coote, G Stevens, R McCarthy, A Beetson, R Turner, J O'Neill
Great Britain: P Charlton, M Richards, L Dyl, C Hesketh (c), J Bevan, K Gill, S Nash, G Nicholls, C Dixon, E Chisnall, J Thompson, J Gray, T Clawson. Replacements: R Millward (for Gill) and P Rose (for Dixon)
Referee: K Page (Australia)

1978

First Test
At Central Park, Wigan, Saturday, 21 October 1978
Crowd: 17 644
AUSTRALIA 15 (Boustead, Fulton tries, Cronin 4 goals, Fulton field goal) d GREAT BRITAIN 9 (Bevan try, Fairbairn 3 goals)
Australia: G Eadie, K Boustead, S Rogers, M Cronin, C Anderson, R Fulton (c), T Raudonikis, R Price, R Reddy, G Gerard, C Young, M Krilich, G Olling
Great Britain: G Fairbairn, S Wright, E Hughes, E Cunningham, J Bevan, R Millward (c), S Nash, S Norton, L Casey, G Nicholls, P Rose, D Ward, J Thompson. Replacements: J Holmes (for Cunningham) and P Hogan (for Casey)
Referee: R Campbell (Great Britain)

Second Test
At Odsal Stadium, Bradford, Sunday, 5 November 1978
Crowd: 26 761
GREAT BRITAIN 18 (Wright 2 tries, Fairbairn 6 goals) d AUSTRALIA 14 (Price, Rogers tries, Rogers 4 goals)
Australia: G Eadie, K Boustead, S Rogers, M Cronin, C Anderson, R Fulton (c), T Raudonikis, R Price, R Reddy, G Gerard, C Young, M Krilich, G Olling. Replacements: A Thompson (for Cronin) and L Boyd (for Gerard)
Great Britain: G Fairbairn, S Wright, J Joyner, L Dyl, J Atkinson, R Millward (c), S Nash, S Norton, P Lowe, G Nicholls, B Lockwood, A Fisher, J Mills. Replacements: J Holmes (for Millward) and P Rose (for Norton)
Referee: M Naughton (Great Britain)

Third Test
At Headingley, Leeds, Saturday, 18 November 1978
Crowd: 30 604
AUSTRALIA 23 (Raudonikis, Peponis, Gerard, Boyd tries, Cronin 5 goals, Fulton field goal) d GREAT BRITAIN 6 (Bevan, Millward tries)
Australia: G Eadie, K Boustead, S Rogers, M Cronin, C Anderson, R Fulton (c), T Raudonikis, R Price, L Boyd, G Gerard, R Morris, G Peponis, C Young. Replacements: A Thompson (for Rogers) and I Thomson (for Boyd)
Great Britain: G Fairbairn, S Wright, J Joyner, J Bevan, J Atkinson, R Millward (c), S Nash, S Norton, P Lowe, G Nicholls, V Farrar, A Fisher, J Mills. Replacements: J Holmes (for Atkinson) and P Rose (for Fisher)
Referee: M Naughton (Great Britain)

1979

First Test
At Lang Park, Brisbane, Saturday, 16 June 1979
Crowd: 23 051
AUSTRALIA 35 (Price 2, Boustead 2, Corowa tries, Cronin 10 goals) d GREAT BRITAIN 0
Australia: G Eadie, L Corowa, S Rogers, M Cronin, K Boustead, A Thompson, T Raudonikis, R Price, L Boyd, R Reddy, C Young, G Peponis (c), R Morris
Great Britain: J Woods, D Barends, J Joyner, E Hughes, R Mathias, J Holmes, G Stephens, S Norton, G Nicholls, D Laughton (c), J Mills, D Ward, T Skerrett. Replacements: P Hogan (for Mills) and S Evans (for Joyner)
Referee: E Ward (Australia)

Second Test
At Sydney Cricket Ground, Saturday, 30 June 1979
Crowd: 26 857
AUSTRALIA 24 (Cronin 2, Rogers, Reddy tries, Cronin 6 goals) d GREAT BRITAIN 16 (Joyner, Hughes tries, Woods 5 goals)
Australia: G Eadie, L Corowa, S Rogers, M Cronin, K Boustead, A Thompson, T Raudonikis, R Price, L Boyd, R Reddy, C Young, G Peponis (c), R Morris
Great Britain: G Fairbairn, D Barends, J Joyner, J Woods, E Hughes, J Holmes, G Stephens, M Adams, L Casey, J Grayshon, G Nicholls (c), D Ward, T Skerrett. Replacements: S Evans (for Holmes) and D Watkinson (for Skerrett)
Referee: G Hartley (Australia)

Third Test
At Sydney Cricket Ground, Saturday, 14 July 1979
Crowd: 16 844
AUSTRALIA 28 (Reddy, Price, Eadie, Boyd tries, Cronin 8 goals) d GREAT BRITAIN 2 (Fairbairn goal)
Australia: G Eadie, C Anderson, S Rogers, M Cronin, T Fahey, A Thompson, T Raudonikis, R Price,
L Boyd, R Reddy, R Morris, G Peponis (c), C Young
Great Britain: G Fairbairn, E Hughes, J Joyner, J Woods, S Evans, D Topliss, A Redfearn, S Norton,
P Hogan, J Grayshon, L Casey, D Ward, G Nicholls (c). Replacements: J Holmes (for Topliss) and M
Adams (for Casey)
Referee: E Ward (Australia)

1982

First Test
At Boothferry Park, Hull, Saturday, 30 October 1982
Crowd: 26 771
AUSTRALIA 40 (Grothe, Meninga, Boustead, Kenny, Boyd, Pearce, Reddy, Price tries, Meninga 8 goals)
d GREAT BRITAIN 4 (Crooks 2 goals)
Australia: G Brentnall, E Grothe, M Meninga, S Rogers, K Boustead, B Kenny, P Sterling, R Price, W Pearce,
R Reddy, L Boyd, M Krilich (c), C Young
Great Britain: G Fairbairn, D Drummond, E Hughes, L Dyl, S Evans, J Woods, S Nash (c). S Norton,
L Crooks, L Gorley, T Skerrett, D Ward, J Grayshon. Replacement: D Heron (for Crooks)
Referee: J Rascagnares (France)

Second Test
At Central Park, Wigan, Saturday, 20 November 1982
Crowd: 23 126
AUSTRALIA 27 (Price, Sterling, Grothe, Meninga, Rogers tries, Meninga 6 goals) d GREAT BRITAIN 6 (Mumby
3 goals)
Australia: G Brentnall, K Boustead, M Meninga, S Rogers, E Grothe, B Kenny, P Sterling, R Price, R Reddy,
W Pearce, L Boyd, M Krilich (c), C Young. Replacements: W Lewis (for Grothe) and R Brown (for Reddy)
Great Britain: K Mumby, D Drummond, M Smith, D Stephenson, H Gill, J Holmes, K Kelly, D Heron,
C Burton, B Eccles, T Skerrett, J Dalgreen, J Grayshon (c). Replacements: J Woods (for Holmes) and
A Rathbone (for Burton)
Referee: J Rascagnares (France)

Third Test
At Headingley, Leeds, Sunday, 28 November 1982
Crowd: 17 328
AUSTRALIA 32 (Boustead, Ribot, Rogers, Kenny, Krilich, Pearce tries, Meninga 7 goals) d GREAT BRITAIN
8 (Evans try, Crooks 2 goals & field goal)
Australia: G Brentnall, K Boustead, M Meninga, S Rogers, J Ribot, B Kenny, P Sterling, W Pearce, R Reddy,
P McCabe, R Morris, M Krilich (c), L Boyd. Replacements: W Lewis (for Ribot) and R Brown (for Boyd)
Great Britain: G Fairbairn, D Drummond, D Stephenson, M Smith, S Evans, D Topliss (c), A Gregory,
M Crane, L Crooks, P Smith, P Rose, B Noble, M O'Neill. Replacement: N Courtney (for O'Neill)
Referee: J Rascagnares (France)

1984

First Test
At Sydney Cricket Ground, Saturday, 9 June 1984
Crowd: 30 190
AUSTRALIA 25 (Lewis, Price, Boustead, Murray tries, Conlon 4 goals, Lewis field goal) d GREAT BRITAIN
8 (Schofield try, Burke 2 goals)
Australia: G Jack, R Conlon, G Miles, B Kenny, K Boustead, W Lewis (c), M Murray, R Price, W Pearce,
B Niebling, G Dowling, G Conescu, D Brown. Replacements: C Close (for Kenny) and C Young (for Brown)
Great Britain: M Burke, D Drummond, G Schofield, K Mumby, E Hanley, D Foy, N Holding, M Adams,
M Worrall, C Burton, L Crooks, B Noble (c), A Goodway. Replacements: J Lydon (for Holding) and
D Hobbs (for Crooks)
Referee: R Shrimpton (New Zealand)

Second Test
At Lang Park, Brisbane, Tuesday, 26 June 1984
Crowd: 26 534
AUSTRALIA 18 (Grothe, Pearce, Meninga tries, Meninga 3 goals) d GREAT BRITAIN 6 (Schofield try, Burke
goal)
Australia: G Jack, E Grothe, M Meninga, G Miles, K Boustead, W Lewis (c), M Murray, W Pearce, P Vautin,
B Niebling, D Brown, G Conescu, G Dowling. Replacements: S Mortimer (for Murray) and W Fullerton
Smith (for Brown)
Great Britain: M Burke, D Drummond, G Schofield, K Mumby, E Hanley, A Myler, N Holding, M Worrall,
A Goodway, C Burton, K Rayne, N Noble (c), L Crooks. Replacements: A Gregory (for Burke) and
M Adams (for Crooks)
Referee: R Shrimpton (New Zealand)

Third Test
At Sydney Cricket Ground, Saturday, 7 July 1984
Crowd: 18 756
AUSTRALIA 20 (Grothe, Conescu, Jack tries, Meninga 4 goals) d GREAT BRITAIN 7 (Hanley try, Burke goal, Holding field goal)
Australia: G Jack, E Grothe, G Miles, M Meninga, K Boustead, W Lewis (c), S Mortimer, R Price, W Pearce, W Fullerton Smith, G Dowling, G Conescu, B Niebling. Replacements: B Kenny (for Miles) and D Brown (for Fullerton Smith)
Great Britain: M Burke, D Drummond, G Schofield, K Mumby, E Hanley, A Myler, N Holding, M Adams, A Goodway, C Burton, B Case, B Noble (c), D Hobbs
Referee: A Drake (New Zealand)

1986

First Test
At Old Trafford, Manchester, Saturday, 25 October 1986
Crowd: 50 583
AUSTRALIA 38 (O'Connor 3, Miles 3, Jack tries, O'Connor 5 goals) d GREAT BRITAIN 16 (Schofield, Marchant, Lydon tries, Crooks, Gill goals)
Australia: G Jack, M O'Connor, B Kenny, G Miles, L Kiss, W Lewis (c), P Sterling, R Lindner, B Niebling, N Cleal, P Dunn, R Simmons, G Dowling. Replacements: M Meninga (for Kiss) and T Lamb (for Lindner)
Great Britain: J Lydon, T Marchant, G Schofield, E Hanley, H Gill, A Myler, D Fox, A Goodway, I Potter, L Crooks, J Fieldhouse, D Watkinson (c), K Ward
Referee: J Rascagnares (France)

Second Test
At Elland Road, Leeds, Saturday, 8 November 1986
Crowd: 30 808
AUSTRALIA 34 (Jack 2, Kenny, O'Connor, Lewis, Lindner tries, O'Connor 5 goals) d GREAT BRITAIN 4 (Schofield try)
Australia: G Jack, M O'Connor, B Kenny, G Miles, D Shearer, W Lewis (c), P Sterling, R Lindner, B Niebling, N Cleal, P Dunn, R Simmons, G Dowling. Replacements: T Lamb (for Sterling) and M Meninga (for Niebling)
Great Britain: J Lydon, B Ledger, G Schofield, T Marchant, H Gill, A Myler, D Fox, A Goodway, I Potter, L Crooks, J Fieldhouse, D Watkinson (c), K Ward. Replacements: S Edwards (for Myler) and A Platt (for Watkinson)
Referee: J Rascagnares (France)

Third Test
At Central Park, Wigan, Saturday, 22 November 1986
Crowd: 20 169
AUSTRALIA 24 (Miles, Lewis, Lindner tries, Shearer penalty try, O'Connor 4 goals) d GREAT BRITAIN 15 (Schofield 2 tries, Lydon 2, Gill goals, Schofield field goal)
Australia: G Jack, M O'Connor, B Kenny, G Miles, D Shearer, W Lewis (c), P Sterling, R Lindner, B Niebling, M Meninga, P Dunn, R Simmons, G Dowling. Replacements: T Lamb (for Meninga) and L Davidson (for Dunn)
Great Britain: J Lydon, H Gill, G Schofield, D Stephenson, J Basnett, A Myler, A Gregory, H Pinner, A Goodway, C Burton, L Crooks, D Watkinson (c), K Ward. Replacement: I Potter (for Burton)
Referee: J Rascagnares (France)

1988

First Test
(100th Test between Australia and Great Britain)
At Sydney Football Stadium, Saturday, 11 June 1988
Crowd: 24 480
AUSTRALIA 17 (Jackson 2, Backo tries, O'Connor 2 goals, Lewis field goal) d GREAT BRITAIN 6 (Hanley try, Loughlin goal)
Australia: G Jack, A Ettingshausen, M O'Connor, P Jackson, A Currie, W Lewis (c), P Sterling, B Lindner, P Vautin, W Fullerton Smith, S Backo, G Conescu, P Daley. Replacements: G Belcher (for Sterling) and S Folkes (for Vautin)
Great Britain: P Loughlin, P Ford, G Schofield, D Stephenson, M Offiah, D Hulme, A Gregory, E Hanley (c), A Platt, M Gregory, P Dixon, K Beardmore, K Ward. Replacements: H Gill (for Loughlin) and R Powell (for M Gregory)
Referee: F Desplas (France)

Second Test
At Lang Park, Brisbane, Tuesday, 28 June 1988
Crowd: 27 130
AUSTRALIA 34 (O'Connor, Ettingshausen, Jackson, Backo, Pearce, Lewis tries, O'Connor 5 goals) d GREAT BRITAIN 14 (Ford, Offiah tries, Loughlin 3 goals)
Australia: G Jack, A Currie, P Jackson, M O'Connor, A Ettingshausen, W Lewis (c), P Sterling, W Pearce, P Vautin, W Fullerton Smith, S Backo, G Conescu, P Daley. Replacements: G Belcher (for Ettingshausen) and R Lindner (for Conescu)

Continued

1988 Second Test *continued*
Great Britain: P Loughlin, H Gill, P Ford, E Hanley (c), M Offiah, D Hulme, A Gregory, M Gregory, A Platt, P Dixon, R Powell, K Beardmore, K Ward. Replacements: D Wright (for Ford) and P Hulme (for Platt)
Referee: F Desplas (France)

Third Test
At Sydney Football Stadium, Saturday, 9 July 1988
Crowd: 15 944
GREAT BRITAIN 26 (Gill 2, Offiah, Ford, M Gregory tries, Loughlin 3 goals) d AUSTRALIA 12 (Lewis, Backo tries, O'Connor 2 goals)
Australia: G Jack, A Ettingshausen, M O'Connor, P Jackson, A Currie, W Lewis (c), P Sterling, W Pearce, P Vautin, W Fullerton Smith, S Backo, G Conescu, M Bella. Replacements: G Belcher (for Sterling) and R Lindner (for Fullerton Smith)
Great Britain: P Ford, M Offiah, P Loughlin, D Stephenson, H Gill, D Hulme, A Gregory, E Hanley (c), M Gregory, R Powell, H Waddell, P Hulme, K Ward. Replacement: B Case (for Waddell)
Referee: F Desplas (France)

1990

First Test
At Wembley Stadium, London, Saturday, 27 October 1990
Crowd: 52 569 (British record)
GREAT BRITAIN 19 (Eastwood 2, Offiah tries, Eastwood 3 goals, Schofield field goal) d AUSTRALIA 12 (Meninga, McGaw tries, Meninga 2 goals)
Australia: G Belcher, M Hancock, M Meninga (c), M McGaw, A Ettingshausen, R Stuart, A Langer, R Lindner, P Sironen, J Cartwright, S Roach, K Walters, M Bella. Replacements: G Lazarus (for Bella), D Hasler (for Cartwright), G Alexander (for Langer) and D Shearer (for Hancock)
Great Britain: S Hampson, M Offiah, D Powell, C Gibson, P Eastwood, G Schofield, A Gregory, E Hanley (c), D Betts, R Powell, P Dixon, L Jackson, K Harrison. Replacements: K Ward (for R Powell) and K Fairbank (for Harrison)
Referee: A Sablayrolles (France)

Second Test
At Old Trafford, Manchester, Saturday, 10 November 1990
Crowd: 46 615
AUSTRALIA 14 (Shearer, Lyons, Meninga tries, Meninga goal) d GREAT BRITAIN 10 (Dixon, Loughlin tries, Eastwood goal)
Australia: G Belcher, A Ettingshausen, M Meninga (c), L Daley, D Shearer, C Lyons, R Stuart, B Mackay, R Lindner, P Sironen, S Roach, B Elias, G Lazarus
Great Britain: S Hampson, M Offiah, D Powell, C Gibson, P Eastwood, G Schofield, A Gregory, E Hanley (c), P Dixon, D Betts, A Platt, L Jackson, K Harrison. Replacements: P Loughlin (for Offiah) and K Ward (for Harrison)
Referee: A Sablayrolles (France)

Third Test
At Elland Road, Leeds, Saturday, 24 November 1990
Crowd: 32 500
AUSTRALIA 14 (Ettingshausen, Meninga, Elias tries, Meninga goal) d GREAT BRITAIN 0
Australia: G Belcher, A Ettingshausen, M Meninga (c), L Daley, D Shearer, C Lyons, R Stuart, B Mackay, R Lindner, P Sironen, S Roach, B Elias, G Lazarus. Replacements: D Gillespie (for Lazarus), G Alexander (for Shearer), D Hasler (for Mackay) and M Sargent (for Lazarus)
Great Britain: S Hampson, M Offiah, C Gibson, D Powell, P Eastwood, G Schofield, A Gregory, E Hanley (c), D Betts, P Dixon, A Platt, L Jackson, K Harrison. Replacements: J Davies (for Gibson), M Gregory (for Dixon) and R Powell (for Harrison)
Referee: A Sablayrolles (France)

ASHES TROPHY

It's all very confusing—but as well as fighting for The Ashes in Tests against Great Britain, there is a second Ashes Trophy for Franco-Australian Tests. The trophy was donated in 1951 by the City Tattersalls Club in Sydney. It was not until the 1956–57 series in France that Australia managed to win it for the first time, but since then, with rare exceptions, Australia has dominated the clashes. Indeed, in the last two series played in France (1986 and 1990), Australia's four victories netted 190 points to France's 16 (an average of 47–4). By 1991, Australia had won 28 Tests to France's 12, with two drawn.

Results of the Franco-Australian Test Series

Series	Venue	Result	Tests to Australia	Tests to France	Tests Drawn
1938* _____	France _____	Australia	2	—	—
1949* _____	France _____	Australia	2	—	—
1951 _____	Australia _____	France	1	2	—
1952–53 _____	France _____	France	1	2	—
1955 _____	Australia _____	France	1	2	—
1956–57 _____	France _____	Australia	3	—	—
1959–60 _____	France _____	Australia	3	—	—
1960 _____	Australia _____	Drawn	1	1	1
1963–64 _____	France _____	Australia	2	1	—
1964 _____	Australia _____	Australia	3	—	—
1967 _____	France _____	France	—	2	1
1973 _____	France _____	Australia	2	—	—
1978 _____	France _____	France	—	2	—
1981 _____	Australia _____	Australia	2	—	—
1982 _____	France _____	Australia	2	—	—
1986 _____	France _____	Australia	2	—	—
1990 _____	Australia _____	Australia	1	—	—
1990 _____	France _____	Australia	2	—	—

* Not for Ashes Trophy

(For results, teams and scorers for every Test, see entry for France)

FERRIS ASHTON

Eight Tests for Australia (1952–53). Also played 21 minor games on one Kangaroo tour (1952–53) and one New Zealand tour (1953).

Ferris Ashton was a tough second-row forward for the Eastern Suburbs side in the Sydney competition during the early 1950s.

He made his Test debut against the touring New Zealand Kiwis in 1952 and in the next year and a half appeared in eight Tests (three each against Britain and New Zealand and two against France). In the same period he made two overseas tours with Australian representative sides—to the Northern Hemisphere with the 1952–53 Kangaroos and across the Tasman for the 1953 series against New Zealand.

After he retired as a footballer, Ashton spent several years as a television commentator with Channel 7.

ATTENDANCES

Australian Rugby League matches over the years have consistently outdrawn similar games overseas, but in recent years the trend has changed. Where British crowds once were often counted in merely hundreds, the influx of so many Australasian stars has helped pack the grounds of the more successful clubs. And when the Kangaroos tour, the British officials have been forced to turn to Soccer grounds, such as Manchester United's home, Old Trafford, to accommodate the crowds.

Significantly, the lack of an adequate arena in Australia has prevented it claiming the world record attendance. Until recent changes in seating, each year almost 100 000 spectators would turn up at Wembley Stadium in London to watch the Challenge Cup Final. And in 1954 a mammoth 102 569 poured into Odsal Stadium, Bradford, for the Cup Final replay, after Warrington and Halifax had drawn at Wembley.

The Australian crowd record will not be beaten in the foreseeable future. In 1965 some 78 056 fans went through the turnstiles at the Sydney Cricket

Ground to see the Premiership grand final between St George and South Sydney. Many thousands more scaled the walls after the house-full signs were raised and the gates shut and were not counted in the official crowd figure. Today, grand finals, which are held at the adjacent Sydney Football Stadium, are all-ticket affairs catering for a capacity crowd of just under 42 000.

Record Australian Attendances
(All at the Sydney Cricket Ground)

All matches: 78 056 for grand final, St George v South Sydney, September 18, 1965
Test matches: 70 204 for First Test, Australia v Great Britain, June 6, 1932
Interstate matches: 56 487 for NSW v Queensland, July 2, 1927

Record Club Home Ground Attendances
Balmain (Leichhardt Oval): 22 750 v Penrith, August 12, 1989
Brisbane (Lang Park): 33 245 v Parramatta, August 20, 1989
Canberra (Bruce Stadium): 24 460 v St George, August 25, 1991
Canterbury-Bankstown (Belmore Sports Ground): 26 120 v St George, May 20, 1979
Cronulla-Sutherland (Caltex Field): 19 753 v St George, July 29, 1979
Eastern Suburbs (Sydney Football Stadium): 20 685 v South Sydney, March 11, 1988
Gold Coast (Seagulls Stadium): 13 423 v Brisbane, May 8, 1988
Illawarra (Wollongong Showground): 15 296 v St George, April 29, 1990
Manly-Warringah (Brookvale Oval): 27 655 v Parramatta, August 31, 1986
Newcastle (Newcastle International Sports Centre): 32 217, v Balmain, August 26, 1990
North Sydney (North Sydney Oval): 22 037 v Manly-Warringah, August 4, 1991
Parramatta (Parramatta Stadium): 27 243 v South Sydney, August 17, 1986
Penrith (Penrith Park): 21 956 v Manly-Warringah, August 14, 1988
St George (Kogarah Oval): 23 582 v South Sydney, May 4, 1975
South Sydney (Sydney Football Stadium): 24 275 v Parramatta, June 24, 1989
Western Suburbs (Campbelltown Sports Ground): 17 286 v St George, August 2, 1991

AUCKLAND

Auckland has always been the stronghold of Rugby League in New Zealand. And naturally enough, for an area which has in most years provided the bulk of the country's Test players, it has proved to be a real stumbling block for touring international sides. In the 1960s and 1970s Auckland beat touring teams in most games. But today, with so many of the top players turning out for Australian or British clubs, the representative sides are not as strong. However they still manage upsets, such as the 26–24 win over the 1989 Australian side which was striving to go through its New Zealand tour unbeaten.

The New Zealand champions joined the Australian midweek televised Cup competition (the Amco Cup) for its second season, in 1975. Auckland reached the semi-finals where it was beaten by the eventual Cup winners, Eastern Suburbs. However, after that brief tilt at glory, Auckland disappointed. It was easily beaten by a virtual second-grade Canterbury-Bankstown side in 1979 and twelve months later was thrashed by a Western Suburbs outfit which included only four regular first-graders. Eventually the promoters were forced to leave it out of the competition.

Interest in Australian football remained however. In 1991, a consortium of Auckland businessmen made overtures to the NSW Rugby League in an effort to be included in the Premiership competition when next it was enlarged. The consortium had plans for a giant stadium and sponsorship for air-travel. By joining the big guns in Australia the consortium believed the exodus of their stars could be halted.

Results of Matches between Auckland and Touring Sides from Australia

Year	Opponents	Result	For	Against
1912	New South Wales	Won	10	3
1913	New South Wales	Lost	2	27
1922	New South Wales	Lost	25	40
1925	Queensland	Drawn	18	18
1935	Australia	Lost	6	16
1949	Australia	Lost	18	36
1953	Australia	Lost	4	26
1961	Australia	Won	13	8
1965	NSW Country	Won	18	5
1965	Australia	Lost	2	18
1966	NSW Country	Won	23	2
1969	Australia	Won	15	14
1970	NSW Country	Won	20	12
1971	Australia	Won	15	14
1972	Queensland	Lost	17	18
1975	Australia	Lost	6	17
1976	Sydney	Won	17	7
1977	Australia	Won	19	15
1980	Australia	Lost	7	21
1985	Australia	Lost	10	50
1989	Australia	Won	26	24

AUCKLAND TOUR OF GREAT BRITAIN

In 1987 Auckland made a trail-blazing tour of Great Britain. Although the side included a number of Test players, poor promotion resulted in generally disappointing crowds.

Record in Great Britain

Played 6, Won 3, Lost 3, Points for 117, Points against 137

Match Results

Opponents	Venue (Attendance)	For	Against
Leeds	Leeds (6639)	29	25
Warrington	Warrington (3750)	22	16
St Helens	St Helens (5901)	26	52
Hull	Hull (1921)	24	26
Wigan	Wigan (10 743)	10	6
Chairman's XIII	Leeds (2698)	6	12

CEC AYNSLEY

Four Tests for Australia (1924–28)

New Zealand critics were so enthralled by the play of Queenslander Cec Aynsley when the Maroons toured the Shaky Isles in 1925 that they dubbed him 'The Gloaming of Rugby League'. Rare praise, indeed! For Gloaming was one of the fastest, most dominant racehorses New Zealand (or, indeed, Australasia) has ever known.

Aynsley, an elusive winger who played for Brisbane Western Suburbs, was the undoubted star of the 11–match tour. He scored 34 tries, including four in one match against the full New Zealand Test side. He finished the tour with a personal tally of 124 points. Aynsley, a brilliant goalkicker, would have racked up a phenomenal tally but for the fact that another great kicker, Jimmy Craig, took most of the attempts at goal on the tour. The Queensland winger played only four Tests (against Great Britain, in 1924 and 1928) but had the enviable record of scoring in each international.

B

SAM BACKO

Six Tests for Australia (1988–89). Also played for Australia in Bicentennial international against the Rest-of-the-World (1988), for Rest-of-the-World against Great Britain (1988) and for Australia in three minor matches on one tour of New Zealand (1989).

In eight decades of Rugby League Tests between Australia and Great Britain only three players have managed to score a try in each of the three Tests of a single series. One is the great Australian winger Ken Irvine who did it twice (1962 and 1963). Another is the champion centre Mal Meninga (1990). The third, surprisingly, is a player who packed down in the front row—not normally known for its scoring opportunities—Sam Backo. In the first three Tests of his career (against the touring 1988 Great Britain side) the Canberra prop Backo scored a try. He lost his perfect record for Australia against the Rest-of-the-World later that year, but went close to scoring before setting up a try for centre Mark McGaw.

It was a big season for the tough, straight-running forward. Backo was one of the stars of Queensland's 3–0 whitewash of New South Wales in the State-of-Origin series, scoring two tries in one match and one in another, as well as taking out two of the three Man-of-the-Match awards.

On the club scene, Backo was one of the stars of the Canberra push to the 1987 grand final. But at the end of the 1988 season, after 97 first-grade games with the Raiders, he elected to return to his native Queensland, joining the Brisbane Broncos. There he continued in good form and was once again one of the stars of Queensland's second straight 3–0 defeat of the New South Welshmen, and Australia's 3–0 defeat of New Zealand in the Trans-Tasman Test clashes. Unfortunately, his decision to return to Queensland meant that he missed out on the glory of Canberra's first ever Premiership victory. After being plagued by recurring knee injuries, which forced him out of the Test side in 1990, Backo bowed to medical opinion and announced a premature retirement from the Broncos at the end of that season. However, in 1991, he made a limited return to football with Logan City in the Brisbane competition.

SG BALL

SG (George) Ball was one of the most famous Australian Rugby League officials. He was one of the five men responsible for the formation of the famous South Sydney club. Ball served as its treasurer at the outset, in 1908, and became secretary two years later, holding this job for more than half-a-century.

He was, from the early days, a delegate to the NSW Rugby League and for many years headed its management committee. In 1913 he managed the NSW side which visited New Zealand—one of the first to go to the Shaky Isles.

In memory of the great administrator, in 1965, the NSW Rugby League instituted the SG Ball Cup for players under 15 years of age. In 1978, the conditions were changed to include boys under 16.

Winners of the SG Ball Cup

1965	South Sydney	1978	Canterbury-Bankstown
1966	Parramatta	1979	South Sydney
1967	Parramatta	1980	South Sydney
1968	Parramatta	1981	Penrith
1969	South Sydney	1982	Balmain
1970	St George	1983	Parramatta
1971	Western Suburbs	1984	St George
1972	Canterbury-Bankstown	1985	Parramatta
1973	Parramatta	1986	South Sydney
1974	South Sydney	1987	Parramatta
1975	South Sydney	1988	Parramatta
1976	South Sydney	1989	Illawarra
1977	Penrith	1990	Newcastle
		1991	Parramatta

BALMAIN

Balmain is one of the original clubs of the Sydney Premiership competition. It was formed on 23 January 1908, just fourteen days after the first club, Glebe, came into being.

Although the Watersiders, as the Balmain players were then known, were runners-up to South Sydney in the second season of the Premiership, it was to be eight years before they tasted any real success. And what a success it was! The club won the 1915 competition in all three grades, the first time this feat had been achieved. The three sides repeated the performance the following year and, in 1917, the first-grade combination made it three in a row. Balmain also took out the City Cup that year.

These were the days of Jimmy Craig, possibly the most versatile Rugby League champion Australia has produced. He could play in any position in the backline and once even turned out as a hooker. Then there was one of the greatest club scrum-base partnerships of all time—at halfback ex-Eastern Suburbs star Arthur 'Pony' Halloway and outside him another fine utility player Charles 'Chook' Fraser. Halloway was the Watersiders' skipper from 1916 until retirement. Balmain had yet another fine allrounder in second-row forward Bob Craig. He had been a member of Australia's Rugby Union team which won the gold medal at the 1908 London Olympic Games.

Balmain was the premier side again in 1919, 1920 and 1924, but had to wait another fifteen years for its next win, in 1939. Then the Tigers struck a purple patch. During a nine-year period they were Premiers four times and runners-up twice. Some of the greats to play for Balmain in this halcyon period were Harry Bath and Pat Devery, who both left before the peaks of their careers to play in Britain. In 50 matches for Balmain, Devery scored 32 tries and kicked 60 goals. Other fine players during this era included Sid Goodwin, Bobby Lulham and George Watt. Lulham still holds the club try-scoring record, with 28 in the 1947 season.

The only other first-grade Premiership title won by the men from Leichhardt Oval came in 1969. And it was a real shock. The Tigers were little fancied against a great South Sydney combination which had won the Premiership the previous two years (and, as history would have it, the next two as well). A clever display of tough football saw Balmain win 11–2. Much of the credit for the Tigers' showing that season must go to English Test five-eighth David Bolton, who completely outshone the rest of the halves in the Sydney competition. Ironically, one of Balmain's favourite sons, Keith Barnes, just missed out on that success. The man dubbed 'Golden Boot' had retired at the end of the previous season after playing in 194 first-grade games and scoring 1539 points in 14 seasons with the Tigers. He later served as Balmain's chief executive and managed the 1990 Kangaroo side which toured Britain and France.

Balmain went close in 1988. Forced into a midweek play-off with Penrith for the fifth and final semi-final spot, the Tigers then turned in a series of do-or-die performances. They beat, in turn, Penrith (28–8), Manly-Warringah (19–6), Canberra (14–6) and Cronulla-Sutherland (9–2) to reach the grand final. But the sudden-death run had taken its toll and Balmain was no match for Canterbury-Bankstown in the season's finale, going down 24–12. The 1988 side was star-studded. Great Britain captain Ellery Hanley proved to be a real inspiration in his eight games after the end of the Lions' Australasian tour. And then there were Australian internationals Garry Jack, Wayne Pearce, Steve Roach, Paul Sironen, Ross Conlon, Russel Gartner and Ben Elias as well as New Zealand Test halfback Gary Freeman.

Balmain were back in the grand final twelve months later. After they led Canberra 12–2 at half-time the Premiership looked likely to head to Leichhardt. But the Raiders fought back and a try by winger John Ferguson ninety seconds from the final hooter equalled the score. At 14–all the two sides played an extra ten minutes each way and a Canberra try and field goal snatched the game away from Balmain. One of the stars for Balmain that year was English centre Andy Currier, who scored 146 points in just 16 games and a few months later was to win a British Test spot against the touring New Zealand Kiwis.

One of Balmain's all-time favourites, lock-forward Wayne Pearce, decided to call it a day after the 1990 season and 192 first-grade games (2 short of Keith Barnes' club record). Tiger fans were hoping for a fairytale finish to 'Junior' Pearce's illustrious career. Sadly, it was not to be. Balmain scraped into the semi-finals after beating Newcastle in a playoff for fifth spot, but then were eliminated by Manly-Warringah, going down 16–0 in the minor qualifying semi-final.

Balmain

Founded: 1908
Entered Sydney Premiership competition: 1908
Home ground: Leichhardt Oval (Record Premiership crowd—22 750)
Colours: Gold and Black
Nickname: The Tigers (formerly The Watersiders)
Honours:
Sydney Premiership—Winners, 1915 (unbeaten), 1916, 1917, 1919, 1920, 1924, 1939, 1944, 1946, 1947, 1969; Runners-up, 1909, 1936, 1945, 1948, 1956, 1964, 1966, 1988, 1989
    Midweek Cup—1976, 1985, 1987
    Flowers' Memorial Trophy (Club Championship)—1941, 1943, 1944, 1947, 1950
    Pre-Season Competition—1967, 1976
    City Cup—1917
    Reserve-grade Premiership—1915, 1916, 1928, 1930, 1933, 1941, 1944, 1946, 1950, 1957, 1958, 1965, 1967, 1982, 1984
    Third-grade Premiership—1915, 1916, 1919, 1926, 1934, 1948, 1950, 1954, 1956, 1960, 1968
    Under-23 Premiership—1973
    President's Cup—1912, 1914, 1926, 1929, 1930, 1932, 1939, 1940, 1952, 1954, 1959, 1966, 1967, 1973
    Flegg Memorial Trophy—1973, 1982
    SG Ball Cup—1982
Most first-grade games: 194 (Keith Barnes)
Most points in a career: 1 539 (Keith Barnes)
Most tries in a career: 119 (Arthur Patton)
Most points in a season: 207 (Len Killeen, 1969)
Most tries in a season: 28 (Bobby Lulham, 1947)
Rothmans Medal: Wayne Pearce (1985)
NSW Player-of-the-Year: Bobby Lulham (1947)
Rugby League Week Player-of-the-Year: Ben Elias (1988)
Sun Herald Best-and-Fairest: Bill Marsh (1955), Laurie Fagan (1962), Peter Provan (1966)

BOB BANKS

Thirteen Tests for Australia (1953–62). Also played two matches in one World Cup (1954) and 16 minor games on one Kangaroo tour (1956–57) and one tour of New Zealand (1953).

Bob Banks had a chequered Rugby League career. The Toowoomba star was in and out of the Australian Test lineup during the 1950s and 1960s. A great tactical five-eighth with a punishing cover defence, he first appeared on the representative scene for Queensland in 1952. He made his Test debut, on a tour of New Zealand, a year later. He was to go on to play a total of 13 Test matches (six against Great Britain, four versus France and three against New Zealand).

Banks reached his peak on the 1956–57 Kangaroo tour of Britain and France when he appeared in all six Tests. He played only two internationals after that tour. The first was after a break of three years (against the 1960 touring Frenchmen) and the last after a further two years had elapsed (against the great 1962 British Lions side). He was a fine captain, skippering Queensland in 1959 and 1960. He also led Northern Queensland to victory in the State competition a few months before his 1963 retirement from the game.

KEITH BARNES

Fourteen Tests for Australia (1959–66). Also played three matches in two World Cups (1957 and 1960) and 16 minor games on one Kangaroo tour (1959–60).

Keith Barnes was one of the most prolific goalkickers Australia has known. Such was his prowess that he was affectionately known as 'Golden Boot'. Barnes kicked more than 700 goals in Sydney Premiership football during a 14-year span from 1955 to 1968, an average of around four a match. His biggest tally was 11 in one game and he kicked 10 on a number of occasions, including once for Australia (against France, in Brisbane, in 1960). His 52 points (26 goals) tops the list for Tests against France. And he is the seventh highest scorer for Australia in all Tests and World Series games with 118 (59 goals).

Keith Barnes

Welsh-born Barnes began his football career in Wollongong as a halfback and in 1954 represented NSW Country in its annual clash with the Sydney lineup. Next year he joined Balmain and soon established himself as one of the greatest fullbacks of all time. While with the Tigers, he represented Australia 14 times in Test matches (six against Great Britain, two against New Zealand and six against France). He toured Great Britain, France and Italy as captain of the 1959–60 Kangaroos (scoring 202 points in his 22 appearances). Barnes captained Australia in 14 of his 17 Test and World Cup matches.

Barnes had two great disappointments during his football career. He missed out on a spot in the triumphant 1963–64 Kangaroos lineup (a side which he had been expected to captain) and he never managed to play in a Sydney Premiership-winning team. Balmain made the grand final three times when Barnes was playing but each time was beaten. Barnes retired in 1968 after his 194th first-grade game for the Tigers. Ironically, it was to be just 12 months later that Balmain broke through for its first Premiership in 22 years.

The champion fullback later became chief executive of the Balmain club and was manager of the 1990 Kangaroo side, the first former captain to achieve this honour.

AH BASKERVILLE

Albert Henry Baskerville played an important role in getting Rugby League on a firm footing in his native New Zealand—and in Australia and Britain, too. In 1907, Baskerville organised (with champion All Black winger George Smith) the first international League tour, taking his New Zealand 'All Golds' side to Australia and Britain.

The All Golds played three matches against New South Wales in Sydney and the £200 profit enabled the fledgling code to get on its feet in Australia. In England the tourists played three Tests and an international against an England XIII. They won the series two matches to one and failed by only two points in the other international. They played 10 more games in Australia, including matches in Brisbane and Newcastle, on the way home. A three-Test series went to the All Golds 2–1. Baskerville did not, however, live to see his efforts bear fruit. He died from pneumonia in Brisbane on May 20, 1908—just 11 days after he had scored a try in the first Australia–New Zealand Test (won by the All Golds 11–10). His body was taken back to New Zealand for burial.

There is confusion about how the New Zealand pioneer spelled his surname. Most authorities spell it Baskerville, but on his grave it is spelled Baskiville.

The 1935 Australian side visit the grave in New Zealand of AH Baskerville, the man who brought the first international side to Australia in 1907

HARRY BATH

Harry Bath was possibly the finest Australian footballer never to have represented his country. He missed his chances when he left Australia to play in England in 1947. When he returned, 10 years later, it seemed the selectors had decided to punish him for deserting the ship and despite grand performances for the St George club, he was not to wear the green and gold. However, he did go close to playing a Test. After representing Queensland in 1945, the tough second-rower joined Balmain and was one of the stars for New South Wales in the two 1946 matches against his old State. But then, in the NSW-Great Britain match a week before the First Test, he badly injured his leg (and his Test selection prospects).

In England he played briefly for Barrow before transferring to Warrington where he showed his class not just as a forward but as a goal-kicker, too. In 1952–53 he topped the English goalkicking lists with 173. And it was his boot which made the difference when Warrington won the famous 1954 Challenge Cup final replay before a world record crowd of 102 569 at Odsal Stadium in Bradford.

Harry Bath scores a try for Warrington in a 1950 English Challenge Cup semi-final against Leeds

During his second season back in Australia, Bath kicked a Sydney club record 108 goals. This tally has since been topped, but only by footballers playing in an expanded competition with more games. Bath remains the only player to have topped the table in both Australia and England. His 225 points in 1958 were followed by another double-century (205) the following season. It was then that Bath hung up his boots. Regretably, in his last match, the 1959 grand final, he was sent off (with Manly-Warringah's Rex Mossop) for fighting.

In 1961 Bath began another successful career—that of coach. He steered Balmain to grand finals in 1964 and 1966, only to see his sides go down to the mighty St George juggernaut. In 1968 he took over as Australia's coach. Under his guidance the national side won two World Cups (1968 and 1970). Then, in 1977, Bath took a group of inexperienced St George players through to the Sydney grand final where, in a torrid replay, 'Bath's Babes' shocked by thrashing Parramatta to win the title. They missed out on the Premiership the following year (finishing a disappointing eighth) but the Bath magic worked again in 1979 and he steered the Dragons to an exciting win over Canterbury-Bankstown in the grand final.

BOB BAX

Bob Bax was one of Queensland's most successful coaches. During the 18 years in which he coached Brisbane A-grade sides, only once did his team miss out on the semi-finals. They made the grand final fourteen times and nine times they won the Premiership. Bax also had an impressive record as coach of the Brisbane representative sides, although he did fail when Queensland coach in 1971, 1972 and 1973, against star-studded New South Wales teams.

Bax played one season in the Brisbane competition (1947) during which he was a Bulimba Cup representative, before moving into the coaching sphere in the country. He was lured back to Brisbane in 1955. In the next five years he took Brothers into five grand finals and won two. In 1960, he moved to Norths and turned that side into Brisbane's best. From 1960 to 1964, Norths won five straight Premierships. In the next six years, Bax took them into four more grand finals, and won another two Premierships.

Bax retired as Norths' coach in 1970 but returned seven years later. It was a disappointing return. In the first season he helped steer Norths to the semis but the 1978 team slumped to finish last. Bax decided to call it a day. However, as Norths' president he played a major role in the 1980 Premiership success.

JACK BEATON

Eight Tests for Australia (1936–38). Also played 22 minor games on one Kangaroo tour (1937–38).

Jack Beaton showed more than a glimpse of his potential while still at school. He was regarded as one of the finest Rugby Union players produced by the famous St Joseph's College in Sydney's GPS competition. In 1932 he created a GPS record by scoring 114 points (15 tries and 32 goals) in just seven matches for Joeys.

Beaton, a goal kicking three-quarter, immediately proved himself when he joined Eastern Suburbs Rugby League side in 1934, playing his first representative game (Rest of NSW v NSW Kangaroos) at the start of that first season. He also made the State side later in the year, notching two tries in his first interstate game against Queensland.

He made his Test debut two years later, against the touring British Lions. The highlight of his international career was the 1937–38 Kangaroo tour.

Jack Beaton

He played in all five Tests (including the first two ever played against France) and topped the tour scoring with 127 points (six tries and 53 goals) from 27 matches. On the club scene, Beaton was a member of Easts' Premiership winning sides in 1935, 1936 and 1937.

DUD BEATTIE

Twelve Tests for Australia (1959–62). Also played three matches in one World Cup (1960), one game for the Rest-of-the-World against Great Britain (1960), one minor international for Australia (1960) and 23 minor games on one Kangaroo tour (1959–60), one New Zealand tour (1961) and one World Cup visit (1960).

There have been few forwards with courage equal to that of Queenslander Dud Beattie. A good example of Beattie's toughness was his last Test appearance—the third encounter with Great Britain in 1962. The big man dislocated his shoulder, but for a long while he refused to leave the field (there were no substitutes in those days). Eventually, realising he must quit, Beattie provoked British tough guy Derek 'Rocky' Turner into a fight. Referee Darcy Lawler sent off both men. Australia were therefore not disadvantaged and went on to snatch an 18–17 win.

Beattie, from Ipswich, first made the Queensland side in 1958 as a 22–year-old. The following year he made his Test debut against New Zealand and his play was such that he was an automatic selection for the 1959–60 Kangaroo tour of Britain and France. He was at his best in the 1960 World Cup in Britain and was one of five Australians chosen in the Rest-of-the-World side which played the British after the home side won the Cup. Beattie played all possible matches on that tour, including an international against France at Toulouse. He also missed only two games on the 1961 tour of New Zealand.

After he retired Beattie eventually returned to the international sphere as an Australian Test selector.

ARTHUR BEETSON

Fourteen Tests for Australia (1966–74). Also played 14 matches in two World Cups (1968 and 1972) and two World Championships (1975 and 1977), one minor international (1975) and 10 minor games on one Kangaroo tour (1973).

Many critics rate Arthur Beetson as Australia's finest front-row forward of the post-World War II era. But, for a time, it looked as if a gigantic appetite would bite off his promising career. A change of clubs and the prospect of overseas tours helped provide the necessary incentive for him to trim his weight and force his way back to the top.

Beetson started as a centre in the Queensland country town of Roma but switched to the forwards as a raw 21–year-old with the Redcliffe side in Brisbane. In 1966, he was lured to Sydney and made his mark so quickly that his Test debut was the same year, against the touring Englishmen. He failed to make the Test sides the following season but was recalled for the 1968 World Cup, played in Australia. After that, Beetson went to England for an off-season stint with Hull Kingston Rovers. His Sydney club, Balmain, insisted that Hull KR insure him for $25 000 against permanent injury. Beetson broke a leg at Hull but Balmain did not collect as the injury did not end his career.

Arthur Beetson

Beetson's football got a real boost when he joined Eastern Suburbs in 1971. He thrived under the coaching of Don Furner and Jack Gibson and was among the first to be chosen to wear the green and gold for Australia. He capped it all in 1975 by leading the victorious Australian World Championship side to Britain and France for the second half of the international contest. However, at the start of the next series, in 1977, Beetson was the centre of a major controversy. The selectors originally omitted him from the national squad to go to New Zealand for the first game. The Australian Rugby League refused to accept any team without Beetson, so the selectors reluctantly included him. Beetson was understandably upset when he heard what had happened and withdrew. He was, however, chosen as his country's captain for the remaining Championship matches, from which Australia emerged unbeaten.

When Jack Gibson left Easts before the start of the 1977 season, Beetson became captain-coach of the Roosters. He had mixed success. In 1977 he steered Easts to a Pre-Season Trophy success, third spot in the Premiership competition and to the final of the midweek Amco Cup. Next year Easts won the Amco Cup but narrowly missed out on the Premiership semifinals. Beetson switched to Parramatta for the 1979 and 1980 seasons before returning to his old Brisbane club, Redcliffe in 1981. As captain-coach he steered Redcliffe to the grand final of the Brisbane competition. He later returned to Sydney with moderate success as Easts' non-playing coach.

Beetson always had the interests of Queensland at heart. When State-of-Origin football was introduced in 1980 it was Beetson's captaincy which inspired the Maroons to a shock 20–10 win in the first match. He then continued his success as coach of the Queenslanders, but his one chance at coaching Australia (in 1983) was soured when New Zealand scored an upset 19–12 victory in the second encounter at Brisbane's Lang Park. After a few years out of the limelight he was all smiles on his return to big-time coaching, when his beloved Queenslanders thrashed New South Wales in a 1989 white-wash of the Blues—coached, ironically by Beetson's old mentor and mate, Jack Gibson. However, Gibbo had his revenge when New South Wales won a year later.

Beetson also spent a couple of seasons as an expert commentator for the ABC's telecasts of the Saturday Premiership matches before returning to the coaching scene in 1992 as mentor of the Cronulla Sharks.

GARY BELCHER

Fifteen Tests for Australia (1988–91). Also played 21 minor games on two Kangaroo tours (1986 and 1990), one New Zealand tour (1989) and one Papua New Guinea tour (1991).

Gary Belcher was one of the finest footballers in Australia for some time before he managed to make it into the Test arena, but as fullback he had to play second-fiddle to the elusive Garry Jack.

Belcher had attracted the attention of southern scouts during 1985 when he was a member of the Brisbane Souths Premiership-winning side. And the following year he switched to the Canberra club. The move paid off handsomely as he was able to make the Queensland State-of-Origin side—a selection which many keen critics reckoned should have been made at least 12 months earlier. At the end of that year Belcher was selected as Jack's understudy for the Kangaroo squad which toured Britain and France. Although he didn't play in any of the five Tests, Belcher gave promise of things to come.

He eventually made his Test debut in the 100th Anglo-Australian clash, in 1988, coming on as a replacement at the Sydney Football Stadium. That season Belcher topped the pointscoring in the Sydney Premiership with 218 (10 tries and 89 goals)—a record for the Canberra club. The following season, 1989, he took advantage of weeks of inactivity by an injured Jack, to establish himself as Australia's top fullback, playing in all three Tests on the tour of New Zealand. It was a great year for Belcher, who played a major role in the Raiders drive to their first Premiership. His form entitled him to the spot of the Best Fullback in the World in the ratings published by the British magazine *Open Rugby*. He retained that rating in the 1990 listings.

There were more Tests during 1990—and yet another Premiership to Belcher and the Raiders. On his second Kangaroo tour that year, he was in superb form. It was only Belcher's brilliance that kept his in-form understudy, Greg Alexander, out of the starting lineups for the Tests.

Belcher struggled for much of the 1991 season with an injury which eventually cost him his Test spot for the series against New Zealand. But he bounced back to form in the Raiders push to their third straight grand final to regain his Australian jumper for the tour of Papua New Guinea.

DEAN BELL

Twenty-five Tests for New Zealand (1983-90). Also played for New Zealand in 1988 World Cup final and for Oceania against Europe (1984), and seven games for Maoris on one British tour (1983).

Three-quarter Dean Bell was one of the cornerstones of a Kiwi resurgence as a world power in the 1980s—and he was a fine club footballer on both sides of the globe.

Bell, one of a well-known Auckland Rugby League family, first caught the eye of knowledgeable League men in 1982, when he spent a season in British football with Carlisle. The following year he made his Test debut, in the home-and-away series against Australia, and was back in Britain with the touring Maori side. As his Test career began to blossom, Bell first spent time with Leeds in England (where he played a big part in the 1984 success in the John Player Trophy). Then, with fellow Kiwis Hugh McGahan and Olsen Filipaina, he was lured by coach Arthur Beetson to Eastern Suburbs in the Sydney Premiership. He had two good seasons (1985 and 1986) before another great coach, Kiwi Test mentor Graham Lowe, persuaded him to return to England to link up with the Wigan juggernaut.

At Wigan, Bell earned Cup and Championship-winners medals, and he reached the pinnacle of success by captaining his country in the 1988 World Cup final against Australia. At 27, he was still a worthy Kiwi Test player in 1989 in the matches against Britain and France. All told, Bell played 26 Test and World Cup games (nine against Australia, 10 versus Britain, four against France and three against Papua New Guinea).

MARTIN BELLA

Eight Tests for Australia (1988-91). Also played in 26 minor games on two Kangaroo tours (1986 and 1990), one New Zealand tour (1989) and one Papua New Guinea tour (1991).

The world seemed his oyster when North Sydney prop Martin Bella was chosen in the 1986 Kangaroo squad for the tour of Britain and France. But time and time again, just when it seemed he had cemented a Test place, an indifferent game saw him on the outer. On that first Kangaroo tour, Bella showed glimpses of top form in his 10 appearances. His Test debut was delayed until the 100th clash between Australia and Britain at the Sydney Football Stadium in 1988, but an ordinary game saw others get the nod for the remaining two Tests.

The big prop was one of the real stars of the State-of-Origin clashes the following year, but on the tour of New Zealand he found himself playing second fiddle to Steve Roach, who had not played in the interstate clashes. Bella, by this time with Manly-Warringah, was also angry when, despite more great State-of-Origin form, he did not make the Test side against France in 1990. However, the late withdrawal of Canberra prop Sam Backo saw Bella drafted into the Test XIII for that match and the subsequent international against New Zealand, at Wellington. At the end of the season he was one of the first chosen for the 1990 Kangaroo tour. Unfortunately, on tour, Bella lost his Test spot to the in-form Glenn Lazarus.

But Bella was not to be denied. With some strong games in the 1991 State-of-Origin series, he found himself back in the green and gold for the home series against New Zealand and the end-of-season tour of Papua New Guinea.

JIM BENNETT

Three Tests for Australia (1924)

Jim Bennett played in only one Test series—but his brief appearance in the international arena doesn't do justice to the ability of this fine front-row forward. He was one of the toughest and most talented ever to pull on a football jumper.

He first stood out as a teenager in 1916, when he gained selection in a Brisbane side to play Maryborough. A couple of seasons in the Queensland country honed his raw ability. In 1920, when he returned to Brisbane, he was ready for greater things. During 1921 he played in the Queensland side which downed the touring New Zealand combination and he was unlucky not to have been chosen for the end-of-season Kangaroo tour of Britain. Bennett, by then playing in Toowoomba, eventually made the Test side when Britain toured Australia in 1924, appearing in all three clashes. He also played a major role in the defeat of Britain by the Toowoomba representative team—the tourists only other losses were to Australia and the two State sides.

On the club scene, Bennett was a member of the brilliant Western Suburbs combinations which went through the 1920 and 1922 Brisbane Premiership seasons unbeaten.

WAYNE BENNETT

Played in two minor games for Australia on one New Zealand tour (1971).

Wayne Bennett made the headlines only once as a player—when he was chosen to tour New Zealand with the 1971 Australian side. However as a coach he carved a niche as one of the best in Australian Rugby League.

Bennett, a strong 20-year-old winger from Toowoomba, made the Australian side after performing well in the interstate clashes with New South Wales. He did not play in the lone Test but turned out in the two minor matches (against New Zealand B and Auckland).

As a coach, Bennett experienced frustrating years in the early 1980s with Brisbane Brothers before moving to Souths which he took to the Brisbane grand final in 1984 and the Brisbane Premiership 12 months later. In 1985, Bennett took time out to coach the Queensland State-of-Origin side (which went down to the New South Welshmen) before joining Don Furner as co-coach at Canberra. The pair lifted the Raiders to the 1987 grand final.

Bennett switched to the Brisbane Broncos in 1988 for their first season in the Sydney Premiership. The same year he was back at the helm of Queensland, which gave him sweet revenge with a 3–0 win over New South Wales. His spell at the Broncos met with early disappointment. The first year Brisbane missed the semi-finals by just two points, and in 1989, the Broncos lost the play-off for the final semi-final spot to Cronulla-Sutherland.

In 1990, the Broncos finally made the play-offs in second place, vindicating Bennett, who had made several controversial decisions during the year, including the sacking of Wally Lewis as the Brisbane captain. In the semis, the Broncos were shocked 26–16 by Penrith, beat Manly-Warringah 12–4, but then were thrashed by the eventual Premiers, Canberra 32–4, in the preliminary final. 'To be beaten by a team like Canberra is no disgrace,' was the laconic Bennett's sizing up of the season.

TOM BERECRY

One Test for Australia (1912). Also played 12 minor games on one Kangaroo tour (1911–12).

North Sydney winger Tom Berecry played only one Test for Australia—a statistic which hardly does justice to his immense talent. His lone Test was at Birmingham, in the Third Test on the triumphant 1911–12 Kangaroo tour. Berecry missed much of the tour through injury, but in his 13 appearances he set the turf alight with 16 tries. They included four in a 56–4 romp against Runcorn on Christmas Day and two in the Test, won by Australia 33–8. Writing in *The Referee* newspaper at the end of the tour, English journalist Fred Marsh rated Berecry as the best winger in the team—better even than the great Dan Frawley, one of the all-time greats of the game—for not only was Berecry an elusive runner but he excelled with a rock-like defence.

BRIAN BEVAN

Sixteen international appearances for Other Nationalities in the European Championship (1949–55).

Few footballers have looked less athletic than Brian Bevan. He was thin and balding, and would run onto the field with heavy strapping on his spindly legs. But Bevan's looks were deceiving. Football has never known a try-scoring machine like him. In 18 seasons in British Rugby League, the expatriate Australian scored more tries than any other player in history. He notched a phenomenal 796 in club games and another 38 in representative and so-called friendly matches—some 300 more than his nearest rival, Welshman Billy Boston.

The great forward Harry Bath, who played hundreds of games with Bevan for the English club Warrington, said of the winger: 'Brian never had any

Brian Bevan

counterpart in Australia in my time. Maybe Dally Messenger had the same magical effect on crowds in the early days of Rugby League, but no player ever provided sustained thrills for so many fans over such a long period as Bevan. He always gave me the impression he had radar built into the toes of his football boots and that this steered him around everyone between him and the tryline.'

Bevan had made little impact on Rugby League before he joined Warrington in 1945, from the Sydney club Eastern Suburbs. Warrington recognised the talent of the Australian sailor who had arrived in Britain on the HMAS *Australia*. He had tremendous acceleration and a prodigious sidestep (reputedly perfected as a boy by sidestepping around fans as they left the Sydney Cricket Ground). He also had a penchant for multiple try-scoring feats. Twice, in Britain, he went over for seven in one match. Four times he scored six, seven times he notched five, and on 22 occasions he finished a match with four tries. Trebles were common as far as Bevan was concerned, with a career total of 69.

One major record which did elude Bevan was that of scoring the most tries in a single season. In 1952–53 he scored 72 for Warrington, eight short of the tally set by fellow-Australian Albert Rosenfeld. Bevan had three other seasons when he topped 60—1950–51 (68), 1953–54 (67) and 1954–55 (63). Bevan was in Warrington sides which won two Challenge Cups (1950 and 1954) and three Championships (1948, 1954 and 1955).

GEORGE BISHOP

Two Tests for Australia (1929). Also played 13 minor games on one Kangaroo tour (1929–30).

George Bishop was a fine hooker who toured Great Britain with the unlucky 1929–30 Kangaroos (playing in 15 matches, including two of the four Tests in that series against Great Britain). The Balmain star was also chosen to make a second tour four years later, but was ruled medically unfit because of a leg ulcer.

George Bishop is probably best remembered as one of Australia's top referees of the late 1940s and early 1950s. He controlled one Test in the 1950 Anglo-Australian series and all three of the New Zealand v Australia internationals in 1952. He was in charge of three Sydney Premiership grand finals (1948, 1949 and 1952).

Bishop was also, for a time, a Sydney, New South Wales and Australian selector. The combination of Test player, referee and selector is believed to be unique in Rugby League.

TOMMY BISHOP

Twelve Tests for Great Britain (1966–1969). Also played three matches in one World Cup (1968) and 10 minor matches on one tour of Australasia (1966).

Tommy Bishop was a star on both sides of the world. A tiny but brilliant halfback, he was the inspiration of some great British international sides in the latter half of the 1960s. He was a sensation on the 1966 tour of Australia and New Zealand and starred again when next 'Down Under', this time with the 1968 World Cup side. He was to captain his country before settling in Australia to take over as captain-coach of the fledgling Cronulla-Sutherland side.

Bishop lured ex-St Helens clubmate Cliff Watson to Cronulla and the pair helped lift the Sharks from among the also-rans to the Sydney Premiership grand final in 1973. When a ceiling on payments to players in the Sydney competition was introduced, Bishop moved north to cash in on his talents. It is perhaps significant to note that after he left Cronulla, the club dropped from number two in the competition to third last. After a successful stint in Brisbane, Bishop returned to New South Wales. At first no Sydney club was interested in using him, so he went to Wollongong where he coached the Illawarra combination (then under the auspices of the Country Rugby League) to victory in the 1978 Caltex Country Championship. Illawarra also performed well in the midweek Amco Cup, under Bishop's guidance.

North Sydney signed Bishop for three years at the start of the 1979 season. The Bears' hopes quickly faded and, after a year of bickering among club officials and only two wins by the first-grade side, Bishop quit. In 1980, Bishop was recalled to Cronulla for another try at the Premiership. Again it was to no avail.

TIGER BLACK

Tiger Black was one of Australia's most famous radio commentators. He started with 2UW in 1946 and, after stints with 2UE and 2GB, finally joined 2KY for which he called all major games, in Australia and overseas, for more than a quarter of a century. Black had played football before turning to radio, but injury cut short his Rugby League career. He was a hooker in the St George side which won the reserve grade Premiership in 1938. For many years Black was also involved in the administration of the St George club.

ANTOINE BLAIN

One Test for France (1938). Also played two internationals (1939).

Antoine Blain was a fine player. He was a member of the Second Test side which played the touring Australians in 1938. The following year he starred in the French lineup which became the first from that country to win the International (European) Championship from England and Wales.

However it was as an administrator that Blain is best remembered—and not only for his work in France. Blain was the secretary of the French Rugby League from 1951 to 1964 and managed all the French sides which made tours of Australia during that time (in 1951, 1955, 1960 and 1964). He was also at the helm of the 1957 World Cup squad for the series in Sydney and Brisbane.

CEC BLINKHORN

Four Tests for Australia (1921–24). Also played 26 minor matches on one Kangaroo tour (1921–22).

Cec Blinkhorn is remembered as half of the greatest club and international wing combination Rugby League has known. The other was Harold Horder. They wrought havoc among opposing sides while with North Sydney and South Sydney and in the Australian Test team. Blinkhorn's play was characterised by a great right-handed fend which left would-be tacklers sprawling.

He made only one tour of Britain with the Kangaroos, but the visit, in 1921–22, was never to be forgotten. The manager of the side, SG Ball, said later: 'To see Blinkhorn and Horder made all my years in Rugby League worthwhile. I doubt whether the world has ever seen better displays of the wing three-quarter's craft'. While on tour, Blinkhorn scored 39 tries—a tally not likely to be topped. Nine of Blinkhorn's tries were scored in Australia's record 92–7 win over Bramley.

On returning home, Blinkhorn's form was just as devastating. In 1922, he scored 20 tries to set a North Sydney record. Blinkhorn was a vital cog in the North Sydney squads which won that club's only two Sydney Premierships, in 1921 and 1922. Blinkhorn never really had a chance to cash in on his talents. English clubs Halifax, Huddersfield and St Helens, each offered a then-record signing-on fee of £1500, but he could not accept because of an international transfer ban.

Blinkhorn's famous fend did not just send lightweight backs sprawling—big, burly forwards were also treated with disdain. After a match at Halifax,

Blinkhorn was dressed and ready to leave when he found his path blocked by a huge local opponent. 'Take off coat, laad,' the forward demanded. Blinkhorn reckoned he was in for a fight. But it was not to be—the local only wanted to feel the muscles of his right arm. 'If anyone had told me a fend from a skinny arm like that would have put me on my backside, I would have called him a liar,' the Halifax forward said in disbelief.

WARREN BOLAND

Warren Boland is one of the few players of the modern era to have captained a Sydney first-grade side while playing on the wing. Coaches usually like their skippers calling the shots closer to the ruck.

Boland was captain of Western Suburbs during the dark days of the early 1980s when richer clubs plundered the Magpies best players. He was one of the few stars to stick with Wests. However in 1983 when the NSW Rugby League decided to kick the Magpies out of the competition (they were subsequently re-instated) he hung up his boots and moved to Brisbane. He then carved out a new career in football, calling the shots nationally for the ABC on its Saturday afternoon telecasts.

MICK BOLEWSKI

Four Tests for Australia (1908–09). Also played in 30 minor games on one Kangaroo tour (1908–09).

When versatile back Mick Bolewski was named as one of four Queenslanders in the first Kangaroo side, southern critics complained. They suggested his selection was political. Bolewski, from Bundaberg, had the last laugh. Not only did he play in all three Tests on tour, but his dependable play caught the eye of local officials who lured him back to England to play club football for Leigh. One major sporting newspaper even wrote a poem about him, the last verse reading:

'Bolewski of the Kangaroos,
However hot the fray,
Lasts out, untired,
Like one inspired,
The very longest day.
Fatigue he never seems to know,
He'd like to, it is plain,
Come up to scratch, after a match,
And play it o'er again.'

Bolewski played fullback in the first two Tests of the series against England and winger in the last. He played in the centre in the First Test against the visiting 1909 Kiwis before joining Leigh.

KERRY BOUSTEAD

Twenty-five Tests for Australia (1978–84). Also played one minor international (1982), for Oceania against Europe (1984) and in 18 minor games for Australia on two Kangaroo tours (1978 and 1982).

Kerry Boustead burst onto the international scene in 1978. A young, fresh-faced winger from Innisfail in the north of Queensland, he was one of few members of the State side to impress in the annual interstate series (in the days immediately before the introduction of State-of-Origin football). His reward was selection in the three Tests against New Zealand and a spot in the Kangaroo squad which toured Britain and France later in the year. When he ran out onto the Sydney Cricket Ground for the First Test against the Kiwis he was only 18 years and 310 days old—the youngest player ever to appear in an Australian Test team.

Boustead moved to Sydney to join the Eastern Suburbs club after the 1978 Kangaroo tour. Some critics doubted his ability to survive the rough, tough Sydney Premiership tussles, but not only did he survive, he established himself as a real superstar. His brilliance ensured that he was always one of the first chosen to wear the green and gold. Easts tried him at fullback as well as on the wing, and he confounded the pundits with superb displays. A feature of his play was copy-book, ankle-high tackling. In 1983, soon after returning from his second Kangaroo tour, Boustead followed his coach at Easts, Bob Fulton, to Manly-Warringah and helped the Sea Eagles to a midweek KB Cup success and the Minor Premiership.

Boustead's Test career came to an end the following year after 25 Tests (11 versus Great Britain, eight against New Zealand, five against France and one versus Papua-New Guinea) in which he scored 15 tries. After a serious injury in 1986 it looked like Boustead's club career was also over. However he returned to the game in Britain with Hull Kingston Rovers before returning to play out his career with North Sydney, hanging up his boots at the end of the 1990 season.

LES BOYD

Seventeen Tests for Australia (1978–82). Also played 20 minor games on two Kangaroo tours (1978 & 1982) and one New Zealand tour (1980).

Fiery forward Les Boyd earned a place in Rugby League annals for the wrong reasons—two mammoth suspensions for foul play.

On 7 June 1983, in the State-of-Origin match against Queensland, Boyd hit opposition forward Darryl Brohman with an elbow, badly smashing the Queenslander's jaw. Boyd was cited after the match and suspended for 12 months. Then, after only his fourth match following the ban he was again cited—for gouging an opponent's eye. This time he was suspended for 15 months.

Boyd was also the centre of a major court case in which he sued the NSW Rugby League for denial of natural justice over an earlier and shorter suspension. He won the case, but a second hearing confirmed the suspension.

However, Boyd deserves recognition for more than his clashes with the judiciary. He was one of the toughest and most inspiring forwards to play in the 1970s and 1980s. The boy from southern NSW was one of the stars of the 1972 schoolboys' tour of Britain. He was lured to Western Suburbs where he showed great form under the coaching of Roy Masters, the man who had been in charge of the schoolboys' side. Boyd went on the Kangaroo tour of Britain and France in 1978 and made his Test debut in England. He was one of the best of the Australian Test side which thrashed the touring British Lions the following year.

Les Boyd

At the end of that season, Boyd was one of three Western Suburbs Test men who accepted lucrative contracts to sign with Manly-Warringah. While with Manly he played in the series against New Zealand (1980 and 1982) and France (1981) before making a second Kangaroo tour in 1982. The five Tests on that tour were his last.

After his 15–month suspension ended, Boyd quit Australian football to play in England with Warrington, for which he was a great inspiration. In 1986 he captained Warrington to a 38–10 success over Halifax (skippered by fellow-Australian Chris Anderson) in the Premiership final. In the process, Boyd won the Harry Sunderland Trophy as Man-of-the-Match.

Two years later Boyd returned to Australia to play out his career in his home town of Cootamundra. In his first season he helped inspire Cootamundra from last place to take out the local Premiership. In 1990 at the age of 33, he was still playing well enough to lead Riverina into the final of the NSW Country Championships and Cootamundra to another Premiership.

RAY BRANIGHAN

Eight Tests for Australia (1971–74). Also played eight matches in two World Cups (1970 and 1972) and one World Championship (1975), one minor international (1970) and 12 minor matches on one Kangaroo tour (1973), one New Zealand tour (1971) and one World Cup tour (1970).

Ray Branighan was a member of the fine South Sydney combination which ruled the roost as the 1970s dawned and provided the nucleus of the Australian international lineups. He was given his chance as a 22–year-old, when he was one of seven Souths players chosen in the 18–man squad for the 1970 World Cup in England. He played in all seven games on the tour (four Cup clashes and three minor games). Branighan continued to star on the international scene until the 1975 World Championships. During the intervening period he appeared in four Test series, playing five Tests against Britain, two against France and one against New Zealand. A versatile utility back, Branighan played at fullback, wing and centre for Australia.

On the club scene, after two Sydney Premiership successes with the Rabbitohs (1970 and 1971), he switched to Manly-Warringah where he bagged two more Premierships (1972 and 1973). He scored a try in each of his first three grand final appearances.

JOHN BRASS

Three Tests for Australia (1970). Also played three matches in one World Championship (1975).

Before John Brass turned professional in 1968, he was one of Australia's finest Rugby Union players. In just two years he had appeared in 12 Union internationals and made two Wallaby tours to Britain.

His impact on League was no less exciting. His form slumped a little after he played all three Tests against the touring 1970 British Lions, but in 1975, he came back with a vengeance. He was one of the spearheads of the Australian attack in the side which won the World Championship that year, captaining his country in their match against the Kiwis in New Zealand.

On the club scene, Brass played a major role in Eastern Suburbs successes in the Sydney Premiership during the mid-1970s. He starred in both the 1974 and 1975 grand finals, scoring two tries and a goal in the 38–0 win over St George in 1975.

GREG BRENTNALL

Thirteen Tests for Australia (1980–82). Also played 13 minor games on one Kangaroo tour (1982) and one New Zealand tour (1980).

An emergency switch in club positions late in 1980 helped secure Greg Brentnall a permanent spot in the Australian Test side. Brentnall had appeared in the centre since first playing for Canterbury-Bankstown's first-grade side in 1977. It was in that position that he made his Test debut, as a virtual stand-in for Steve Rogers, on the 1980 tour of New Zealand. When Canterbury's regular fullback, Stan Cutler, was injured as that season was drawing to a close, the Bulldogs' selectors turned to Brentnall, a former Australian Rules footballer, as his replacement. He was an instant master in his new position and played a major role in Canterbury-Bankstown's Premiership success.

The following season, Brentnall established himself as Australia's number-one fullback, playing both Tests against the touring Frenchmen. He was at his brilliant best in 1982, starring in Australia's clean-sweep of the Test series against New Zealand, Papua-New Guinea, Britain and France. His performances for Canterbury-Bankstown won him the Rothmans Medal as the best-and-fairest player in the Sydney Premiership competition. After one more season he called it a day and moved back to his native Riverina where he worked at promoting the game in which he excelled.

BRISBANE

For years Brisbane fans wondered how a local side would stand up against the top teams in the Sydney competition. When a Combined Brisbane side beat Eastern Suburbs 12–11 in the final of the 1984 midweek National Panasonic Cup, there was a groundswell of support for a team to join the Sydney Premiership. After several false starts, in 1987 a Brisbane group decided to accept an invitation from the NSW Rugby League to take part.

The Broncos, as the Brisbane players were dubbed, had a fairytale start to their first season (1988), thrashing the reigning Premiers, Manly-

Warringah, 44–10 in their very first match, at Brisbane's Lang Park. Indeed, the Broncos went on to win their first six matches. For that first season, Brisbane included in its ranks six Queensland internationals—Wally Lewis (the Australian Test captain), Gene Miles, Colin Scott, Greg Dowling, Greg Conescu and Bryan Niebling. The team was under the guidance of Queensland State-of-Origin coach Wayne Bennett, who the previous season had guided Canberra to its first-ever grand final. Unfortunately, the winning streak did not continue. A loss to Balmain in the last match of the season saw the Broncos just miss the semi-finals.

For 1989, more stars joined up, including Test men Sam Backo and Peter Jackson (from Canberra) and Tony Currie (from Canterbury-Bankstown) and State-of-Origin representative Scott Tronc (from Western Suburbs). The Broncos form was so good that six of them made the Queensland State-of-Origin side and another two the New South Wales lineup. Young stars Michael Hancock and Kerrod Walters joined Lewis, Currie, Jackson, Miles and Backo in the Australian side chosen to tour New Zealand. (Miles withdrew from the team because of injury).

An eighth, halfback Allan Langer, would also certainly have been in the touring side but for breaking his leg in the second interstate clash. Langer had been the real discovery of the previous year, taking over from Peter Sterling as Australia's scrum-half and winning the Man-of-the-Match award in both the Test against Papua-New Guinea and the World Cup final against New Zealand. Walters was the centre of controversy at the start of the season, when coach Bennett preferred him as hooker to the incumbent Test rake Greg Conescu, who found himself in reserve grade.

As in the first two years, the 1989 season finished with disappointment for the Broncos, who went down 38–14 to Cronulla-Sutherland in the play-off for the fifth and final semi-final position.

The 1990 season opened sensationally. Bennett dropped a bombshell by sacking Australian skipper Wally Lewis from his spot as Broncos captain. Gene Miles took over. Not only that—Lewis was also moved to lock to make way for Kevin Walters (Kerrod's twin brother) who had been playing with Canberra.

Bennett was thoroughly vindicated. Kevin Walters went on to make the Kangaroo squad at the end of the year (as did his brother Kerrod) and Miles won the Dally M award for Captain-of-the-Year. Most important, the Broncos finally made the play-offs, finishing the preliminary rounds in second place. In the semis, the Broncos were shocked 26–16 by Penrith, beat Manly-Warringah 12–4, but then were thrashed by the eventual Premiers, Canberra 32–4, in the preliminary final. Bennett noted: 'To be beaten by a team like Canberra is no disgrace'.

The Broncos saw six of their team in the triumphant Kangaroo squad— the Walters brothers, Langer, Hancock and centres Dale Shearer and Chris Johns. Two young discoveries of 1990, fullback Paul Hauff and winger Willie Carne, must have been unlucky not to have also toured. Carne, 20, had scored 15 tries in his 20 first-grade games to equal Wally Lewis' club record. Lewis could not come to terms with the Broncos at the end of 1990 and left to join the Gold Coast.

Hauff and Carne got their chance the following season. Hauff was chosen in the First Test squad to take on the touring New Zealand side. But, when the Kiwis scored a shock win over Australia, Hauff was one of the scape-goats dropped for the remaining two encounters. Carne was among the new blood brought in after the First Test debacle. And he was one of the first chosen for the end-of-season tour of Papua New Guinea, nabbing a hat-trick of tries in each Test.

Other Broncos to play Tests that season were Langer, Shearer and Johns. And hard-working second-rower Andrew Gee was a late selection for the Papua New Guinea tour. Their success was not mirrored in the Premiership, with Brisbane missing the semi-finals by one point.

Brisbane

Founded: 1987
Entered Sydney Premiership competition: 1988
Home ground: Lang Park (Record club crowd—33 245)
Colours: Maroon, white and yellow
Nickname: The Broncos
Honours:
    Sydney Premiership—Nil
    Panasonic Cup—1989
    Pre-Season Competition—1991
    Reserve grade—1990
Most points in a career: 363 by Terry Matterson
Most tries in a career: 35 by Michael Hancock
Most points in a season: 152 by Terry Matterson, in 1988
Most tries in a season: 15 by Wally Lewis, in 1988; 15 by Willie Carne, in 1990; 15 by Steve Renouf, in 1991

BRISBANE PREMIERSHIP

Brisbane clubs have been playing Rugby League since the early days of the code in Australia, but their early competitions included teams from outside the Queensland capital.

The Brisbane Premiership was the brainchild of officials in the 1920s. After a dispute concerning the way the game was run in the State, the Brisbane clubs eventually won the right to conduct an autonomous competition. In 1922, the first all-Brisbane Premiership took place with six teams—Brothers, Carlton, Coorparoo, University, Fortitude Valley and Western Suburbs. Wests won that year, going through the season unbeaten. Grammars joined in next season and Wynnum Rugby Union team swapped codes in 1931.

Two years later, Brisbane introduced a district competition. Carlton became Southern Suburbs, Coorparoo and Wynnum amalgamated to become Eastern Suburbs and Grammars changed to Northern Suburbs. Other changes since then include: University went back to Rugby Union in 1934; Wynnum-Manly entered the competition in 1951, South Coast joined the following year but dropped out in 1955; and Redcliffe was admitted in 1960 and Ipswich in 1986.

The competition suffered an upheaval when the Brisbane Broncos joined the Sydney Premiership in 1988, when Logan City became the latest local club to get the chance to fight for the Brisbane Premiership. During this period Valleys tried a unsuccessful merger with the Seagulls club on the Gold Coast. Although the side, which called itself Seagulls-Diehards, won the Brisbane Premiership in 1988, the marriage of convenience was annulled the following season and Valleys resumed their old name.

Brisbane's Premier Clubs

1909	Valleys	1937	Valleys	1965	Redcliffe
1910	Ipswich	1938	Norths	1966	Norths
1911	Valleys	1939	Brothers	1967	Brothers
1912	Natives	1940	Norths	1968	Brothers
1913	West End	1941	Valleys	1969	Norths
1914	Valleys	1942	Brothers	1970	Valleys
1915	Valleys	1943	Brothers	1971	Valleys
1916	Wests	1944	Valleys	1972	Easts
1917	Valleys	1945	Souths	1973	Valleys
1918	Valleys	1946	Valleys	1974	Valleys
1919	Valleys	1947	Easts	1975	Wests
1920	Wests*	1948	Wests	1976	Wests
1921	Carltons	1949	Souths	1977	Easts
1922	Wests*	1950	Easts	1978	Easts
1923	Coorparoo	1951	Souths	1979	Valleys
1924	Valleys	1952	Wests	1980	Norths
1925	Carltons	1953	Souths	1981	Souths
1926	Brothers	1954	Wests	1982	Wynnum-Manly
1927	Grammars	1955	Valleys*	1983	Easts
1928	University	1956	Brothers	1984	Wynnum-Manly
1929	University	1957	Valleys	1985	Souths
1930	Carltons	1958	Brothers	1986	Wynnum-Manly
1931	Valleys	1959	Norths	1987	Brothers
1932	Wests	1960	Norths	1988	Seagulls-Diehards
1933	Valleys	1961	Norths	1989	Valleys
1934	Norths	1962	Norths	1990	Valleys
1935	Brothers	1963	Norths	1991	Easts
1936	Wests	1964	Norths		

* unbeaten

DAVE BROWN

Nine Tests for Australia (1933–36). Also played 31 minor games on one Kangaroo tour (1933–34) and one New Zealand tour (1935).

So great was Dave Brown's pointscoring prowess that he virtually rewrote Rugby League's record books. Such was his ability that today many football historians describe him as the Bradman of Rugby League. Three of his records still stand more than half-a-century after he retired—the 285 points (19 tries and 114 goals) scored on the 1933–34 Kangaroo tour of Britain; the 38 tries scored (in just 14 games for Eastern Suburbs) in the 1935 Sydney Premiership season; and the 45 points scored in one game, against Canterbury-Bankstown, that same season.

For more than 30 years Brown also held the record for the most points scored in an Australian club season. During the sensational 1935 season he notched 244. This figure was subsequently passed by South Sydney fullback Eric Simms and Parramatta centre Mick Cronin. However by that time, the Sydney competition had been expanded and Simms and Cronin had fifty per cent more games than Brown's 14 in which to amass their tallies. Brown scored 385 points in all matches that year (including Test and representative games). Once again, only Cronin has scored more in a calendar year.

The great footballer began his first-grade career with Easts in 1930 while he was still a schoolboy at Waverley College. The following season he made the New South Wales team for the first time. From then on there was no looking back. He became the pointscoring phenomenon on the Kangaroo tour when the team manager Wally Webb persuaded him to slow down his approach to the ball. It was the best advice ever given to the great player. In 1935, Brown (at the age of 23 years and nine months) became the youngest captain of an Australian side in Tests against Great Britain (the last three of his nine internationals).

After the 1936 season, when he starred in Easts' Sydney Premiership success, Brown was lost to Australia. He accepted a £1000 signing-on fee, £3 a week and £6 a match to play with Warrington in England. He was again a great success, although missing out on the two greatest prizes—success in the Challenge Cup or the English Championship. The closest he came was as a member of the Championship runners-up, when Warrington went down 13–11 to Salford in 1937.

Two images of Dave Brown

Dave Brown was easily recognised by his bald pate. When he was 18 an illness caused him to lose all his hair. He tried wearing a hair-piece, but a team-mate threw it overboard on the sea voyage to England with the 1933–34 Kangaroos. From then on his trade-mark was brown leather headgear.

EDWIN 'NIGGER' BROWN

Played four minor games for Australia on one Kangaroo tour (1921–22).

'Nigger' Brown, a robust centre from Toowoomba, did not play for Australia in Tests. He would surely have done so but for nagging injuries on the 1921–22 Kangaroo tour of Britain when he played in just four matches. However, he was still hailed by local critics as Australia's best inside back. Such was his form in that handful of matches that Wigan tried to sign him. The Lancashire club offered a £1000 signing-on fee and £7 a match, a huge sum in those days, but its efforts were thwarted by a transfer ban between Australia and Britain.

Brown represented Queensland for many seasons during the 1920s, forming a great centre partnership with Australian captain Tommy Gorman.

Edwin Brown's nickname would, for obvious reasons, never be countenanced today. The name had nothing to do with the colour of Brown's skin. It came about because of his snappy dressing and penchant for wearing deep brown shoes. This colour was known in the shoe shops as -'nigger brown'.

BILL BUCKLEY

Bill Buckley was one of the most famous Australian administrators. He was at the helm of the code throughout the 1960s when Australian Rugby League prospered to an unprecedented extent.

Buckley began his love affair with League as a schoolboy in the southern NSW town of Queanbeyan. He played first-grade football in Sydney with Newtown but that career ended abruptly in 1931, when he broke a leg. Buckley then became a Newtown selector for 10 years and a delegate to the NSW Rugby League. When Harry 'Jersey' Flegg died in 1960, Buckley took over as president of both the NSW and Australian Rugby Leagues— positions he held until his own death in 1973.

BOBBY BUGDEN

Two Test appearances for Australia (1960). Also played five minor games on one Kangaroo tour (1959–60).

Halfback Bobby Bugden is one of only three Australian footballers to score a hat-trick of tries in his Test debut. The other two were Jim Devereux in the first-ever Test in 1908 and Brad Mackay, who played for the same club as Bugden, St George, in 1990.

Bugden was perhaps unlucky to have been playing at the same time as two of the greatest of Australian halfbacks, Keith Holman and Barry Muir. That pair kept Bugden's Test appearances to just two—both against the touring 1960 Frenchmen. The St George half had already worn the green and gold, in minor matches with the 1959–60 Kangaroos, but an injury meant that he played only five games on the tour. When Muir was injured before the Second Test against France, at the Brisbane Exhibition Ground in 1960, Bugden was called into the Test side. It was a sensational match with Australia running up a then-record Test score of 56 points. Bugden scored three of the side's 12 tries, one of them in extra time after the half-time siren had sounded.

In his only other Test, the third 1960 encounter at the Sydney Cricket Ground, Bugden scored the only Australian try. He engineered the move from within his own 22, running 20 metres before off-loading to winger Lionel Morgan. He then backed up Morgan, who, when tackled near the line, slipped the ball to Bugden to score.

On the club scene, Bugden was a vital cog in the St George juggernaut, forming a formidable combination with five-eighth Brian Clay and playing in the Dragons' six Premiership-winning sides from 1956 to 1961. He then switched to Parramatta, helping the Eels to the semi-finals for the first time, in 1962. Parramatta, with Bugden playing a major role, reached the playoffs again in the next three years. It is significant that after Bugden quit Sydney football at the end of the 1965 season, Parramatta's form slumped and the Eels slipped back to become again one of the Premiership also-rans.

VIC BULGIN

Played 23 minor games for Australia on one Kangaroo tour (1948–49) and one New Zealand tour (1949)

Vic Bulgin is the only man ever to have represented Australia at both Rugby League and golf. He was a fine fullback, but had the misfortune to be playing at the same time as the immortal Clive Churchill. Bulgin toured Britain and France with the 1948–49 Kangaroos and New Zealand in 1949 as Churchill's understudy. The 20–year-old was a surprise selection for the Kangaroo tour. He had not played for New South Wales and his only representative appearance had been in a Possibles versus Probables match several months before. However his good form for Eastern Suburbs had made the selectors sit up and take notice.

As a golfer, Bulgin toured South Africa (1959) and Canada (1967) with Australian teams. His best effort was as runner-up to the great Kel Nagle in the 1959 Australian Open.

BULIMBA CUP

The Bulimba Cup was contested annually by representative teams from Brisbane, Ipswich and Toowoomba. It began in 1925, with a match between the latter two. The triangular series developed into one of the major trials for Queensland and Australian selection. However, in the 1960s and early 1970s, public interest in the Cup dwindled—so much so that it was scrapped in 1972. The final tally of Bulimba Cup successes was Brisbane 19, Toowoomba 16 and Ipswich 11.

Winners of the Bulimba Cup

1925	Toowoomba		1949	Brisbane
1926	Ipswich		1950	Brisbane
1927	Toowoomba		1951	Toowoomba
1928	Toowoomba		1952	Toowoomba
1929	Ipswich		1953	Toowoomba
1930	Brisbane		1954	Toowoomba
1931	Brisbane		1955	Toowoomba
1932	Brisbane		1956	Toowoomba
1933	Ipswich		1957	Ipswich
1934	Ipswich		1958	Ipswich
1935	Ipswich		1959	Toowoomba
1936	Toowoomba		1960	Toowoomba
1937	Ipswich		1961	Brisbane
1938	Ipswich		1962	Brisbane
1939	Ipswich		1963	Brisbane
1940	Brisbane		1964	Brisbane
1941	Brisbane		1965	Toowoomba
1942	No competition		1966	Ipswich
1943	No competition		1967	Brisbane
1944	Toowoomba		1968	Brisbane
1945	Toowoomba		1969	Brisbane
1946	Brisbane		1970	Toowoomba
1947	Brisbane		1971	Brisbane
1948	Brisbane		1972	Brisbane

ROY BULL

Twenty-two Test matches for Australia (1949-57). Also played three matches in one World Cup (1954) and 36 minor games on two Kangaroo tours (1952-53 and 1956-57) and two New Zealand tours (1949 and 1953).

Prop forward Roy Bull was well named. An expert scrummager and a great performer in tight play, he was as strong as the proverbial mallee bull. What he lacked in pace he made up for in strength and football know-how.

Bull, a Manly-Warringah junior, was the club's first international, touring New Zealand in 1949 when a raw 19–year-old and just two years after making his first-grade debut. From the time of his first Test, at Carlaw Park, Auckland, in October 1949, until his last, at Lyon in France, in January 1957, he was always one of the first picked in Australian sides. Indeed, from 1952 on, he was only once out of the Australian Test lineup, missing the Third Test against the 1954 British Lions because of a broken hand.

Bull's best season was undoubtedly that year. His performances for Manly in the Sydney Premiership competition and grand displays in the Tests against Britain and the World Cup in France earned him the honour of NSW Player-of-the-Year. All told, Bull made five overseas trips with Australian teams. As well as the visit to France for the inaugural World Cup he twice toured Britain and France with the Kangaroos and crossed the Tasman twice.

On the club scene, he played a then-record 177 first-grade games for Manly before retiring in 1959. He was later to serve as president of the Manly club.

ALEC BURDON

Two Tests for Australia (1908-09). Also played 24 minor games on one Kangaroo tour (1908-09).

This red-haired front-row forward holds an important place in the history of Rugby League. It was a shoulder injury to Burdon in a 1907 Rugby Union match and his subsequent loss of earnings and huge medical bills which sparked the split to form the professional code in Australia.

Alec Burdon

Burdon was a Rugby Union international with four appearances against New Zealand (in 1903 and 1905) and Britain (1904) to his credit. However the Union authorities flatly refused his request for compensation. He joined others upset about the issue at meetings above the sports store in Sydney owned by the famous cricketer Victor Trumper. Together they helped draft a constitution to form the NSW Rugby League.

Burdon toured Great Britain with the 1908–09 Pioneers (the first Kangaroos), playing in 26 games including the Test matches at London and Birmingham. In the latter he captained the Australians, only to see his side go down narrowly 6–5. After his playing days were over Burdon continued in the game as an administrator and selector of NSW State sides and Test teams.

FRANK BURGE

Thirteen Tests for Australia (1914–22). Also played 24 minor games on one Kangaroo tour (1921–22) and one New Zealand tour (1919).

Few would disagree with the notion that Frank Burge was one of the greatest forwards in the history of Rugby League. He was also one of football's finest coaches.

He was the best of four fine footballing brothers. Albert 'Son' Burge played two Rugby Union Tests (against New Zealand in 1907 and against Wales the following year), Peter Burge played three Rugby Union Tests in 1907 and toured Great Britain with the 1911–12 Rugby League Kangaroos, while Laidley Burge represented New South Wales in the 13-a-side code.

Frank 'Chunky' Burge was a boy wonder. He was a first-grade Rugby Union player at the age of 14—the youngest to play senior football in either Rugby code. After switching to Rugby League he pressed for selection with the 1911–12 Kangaroos but missed out because the selectors thought that, at 16, he was too young to mix it with the tough British forwards. However he did manage to visit New Zealand with the New South Wales side the following season.

Burge eventually did tour Britain, with the 1921–22 Kangaroos. And what a tour it was for the brilliant Burge! He wound up with 33 tries, scored in 23 matches. This was a record for a forward which still stands today. With the trend to shorter tours, it could be on the record books forever. In one match, against a Lancashire League XIII at Everton, Burge scored five tries—a feat unheard of for a forward. So great was the publicity surrounding his performance that the Everton soccer club, one of England's top sides, made Burge a huge offer of £3000 pounds to join its ranks and learn the round-ball game. He turned it down, noting some years later: 'In those days £3000 was a lot more money than it is today. But I returned to Australia and have no regrets about that.'

Chunky was also a magnificent goalkicker. One of his best performances was on the 1919 tour of New Zealand, when Australia beat Auckland 93–5. Burge booted 13 goals.

Burge played his early football with Glebe. It was while with the Dirty Reds, as the side was known, that he notched another great performance, scoring eight tries in a 1920 match against University. In 138 games for Glebe, Burge scored 137 tries. In 1927, he was lured to St George to serve

Frank Burge

as the club's captain-coach. His fee for the season was the biggest ever paid to a player in the Sydney competition. The money was well spent. Burge took St George from the bottom of the table to the 1927 Premiership final, where a fine South Sydney combination had to produce its best form of the season to win. Burge remained as coach for another three seasons and each time St George made the semi-finals.

The great coach took over at Canterbury in 1936, just two years after the club had entered the Sydney competition. The season before the Berries, as they were then known, had won just two of their 16 matches. Yet Burge steered them into the semi-finals, with only four defeats, in his first year at the helm. And two years later they won their first Premiership.

EDDIE BURNS

Eddie Burns was one of Rugby League's finest front-row forwards. Only World War II and later a diabolical selection decision robbed him of the chance to play for his country.

Burns turned out with Canterbury-Bankstown when it joined the Sydney Premiership competition in 1935 and was still with the club when he retired in 1951. During those 17 seasons, he played a then-record 232 games for the Berries, as they were then affectionately known. With hooker Roy Kirkaldy and fellow-prop Henry 'Tarzan' Porter, Burns became part of probably the greatest Australian club front-row combination of all time.

Critics still wonder at Burns' omission from the 1948–49 Kangaroo side which toured Britain and France. He played superbly for New South Wales in the Brisbane game against Queensland, but the national selectors overlooked him. After he retired as a player, Burns turned his hand to coaching and in 1963 and 1964 schooled the NSW side. Only once was it beaten, 3–2 by New Zealand in a tough, low-scoring match.

JOE 'CHIMPY' BUSCH

Six Tests for Australia (1928–30). Also played 15 minor games on one Kangaroo tour (1929–30).

'Chimpy' Busch's name is part of Rugby League legend, largely because of a vital touchdown which was disallowed in the Third Test of the 1929–30 Kangaroo tour of Britain. The incident resulted in the match being drawn 0–0. For the first and only time a fourth Test was played to decide the series. The referee admitted that Busch had scored a fair try but he could not over-rule his linesman who claimed Busch had stepped into touch before grounding the ball.

However Busch's reputation did not need to rely on controversy. He was a tall, fast halfback noted for great service from the base of the scrum. He was originally a centre, discovered by an Eastern Suburbs talent scout while playing barefoot in a match on the NSW north coast. Busch came to Sydney and within four months found himself in the Test team. Unfortunately for Australia, he played only six Tests before accepting a lucrative offer from the Leeds club to continue his top-class footballing days in Britain.

JOCK BUTTERFIELD

Twenty-eight Tests for New Zealand (1954–63). Also played seven games for New Zealand in three World Cups (1954, 1957 and 1960), one match for the Rest-of-the-World (1957) and 64 minor games for New Zealand on three tours of Australia (1956, 1959 and 1963) and two tours of Great Britain and France (1955–56 and 1961).

One of the finest hookers from anywhere in the world, Jock Butterfield went within an ace of becoming the only player in the history of the game to wear his country's colours 100 times. When he quit the international scene in 1963 he had played for the Kiwis in 99 games, including 35 Test and World Cup games. He was also a member of the Rest-of-the-World team which played Australia during the 1957 World Cup, a game given Test match status by the New Zealand authorities.

Butterfield made his debut against the touring 1954 British Lions and, a few months later made his first trip overseas, to France, for the inaugural World Cup. Including World Cups, he was to tour with the Kiwis a record eight times before he finally left the Test scene after the 1963 swing through Australia.

The following season he and fellow Kiwi international Trevor Kilkelly were signed by Manly-Warringah to play in the Sydney Premiership competition. However by that time, Butterfield's best days were over. He played just 10 games and at the end of the season made way for young local hooker Fred Jones, who was to go on to play a then-record 243 first grade games for the Sea Eagles.

C

CANBERRA

Of all the clubs to join the Sydney Premiership race in the modern era, Canberra made it to the top in the quickest time. The Raiders joined the competition in 1982. In 1987, they reached their first grand final and just two years later Canberra won the first of two straight Premierships. Yet, when the club's inclusion was first mooted there was stiff opposition to the move. The NSW Rugby League wanted to increase the size of the competition to 14 with Canberra and Illawarra, but the existing clubs were worried about Canberra because of its distance from Sydney.

However Canberra had the financial support of one of the most successful licenced clubs in Australia, the Queanbeyan Leagues Club. It had a fine ground in Seiffert Oval, near the Leagues Club (it has since moved to Bruce Stadium in the national capital). As its trump card—it was willing to pay all travelling expenses for the Sydney clubs for the first couple of seasons. And so, Canberra joined the Sydney Premiership. It chose as coach Don Furner, a man with proven ability (an ability which was later to take him to the post of Test and Kangaroo coach).

At first, the Raiders had trouble attracting name players, but finally, in 1987, everything started to click. Furner had as his co-coach Wayne Bennett, the mentor of Queensland's State-of-Origin team. Canberra shocked everyone by reaching the grand final, where it went down to a star-studded Manly-Warringah combination 18–8, before 50 201 fans in the last League match at the Sydney Cricket Ground. That year, the Raiders had the services of some of the best Queensland representatives including centres Mal Meninga and Peter Jackson and fullback Gary Belcher as well as the tough forward Sam Backo, who 12 months later was to reach Test standard.

Canberra reached the semi-finals again in 1988 under new coach Tim Sheens. Then, in 1989, the Canberra players really came of age. They slumped mid-season when they were without Test representatives involved across the Tasman in the series between Australia and New Zealand—Belcher, Meninga and Bradley Clyde (Australia) and Brent Todd (New Zealand). However they stormed home to scrape into the semis. From there it was a case of sudden-death every week. In turn, they beat Cronulla-Sutherland 31–10, Penrith 27–18, and Minor Premiers South Sydney 32–16 to reach the grand final.

In the Premiership-deciding game, everything looked lost when Balmain led 12–2 at half-time and 14–8 with 90 seconds to play. But five-eighth Chris O'Sullivan put up a bomb, centre Laurie Daley hand-balled to ageless winger John Ferguson who went over. Meninga's conversion tied the game and put it into extra time. In the 10 minutes extra each way, O'Sullivan first snapped a field goal and then replacement forward Steve Jackson put the result beyond doubt with a bullocking run to score. Canberra had won 19–14. Man-of-the-Match (and winner of the Clive Churchill Medal) was young lock forward Clyde.

Canberra showed the Premiership win was no fluke with back-to-back titles, beating Penrith 18–14 in the 1990 grand final. This time Canberra's former Rugby Union international Ricky Stuart won the Clive Churchill Medal. Five Raiders—Meninga, Belcher, Daley, Stuart and prop Glenn Lazarus—made the Kangaroo side to tour Britain and France. A sixth, Clyde, would have also been in the side but for a crippling injury suffered late in the season.

In between the two Premierships, Canberra travelled to Britain for what was billed as the World Club Championship. The match, at Old Trafford, Manchester, pitted the Raiders against English Champions Widnes. Canberra looked likely to race away to an easy win after leading 12–0 just 11 minutes after the kick-off. However a gallant display by Widnes, led by former Kiwi international Kurt Sorensen, and the loss of skipper Meninga saw Canberra wilt and finally go down 30–18.

The Rugby League world was rocked when, in 1991, it was revealed that the Canberra club was close to bankruptcy. Some bad management decisions had seen the Raiders plunge to almost $6 million into the red. No sooner had senior executives resigned, than the club was hit with a second blow. It was revealed that Canberra had exceeded the salary cap of $1.5 million imposed by the NSWRL both in 1990 and 1991. Other clubs were livid. A 'Save the Raiders' Fund was set up to try to halt an expected exodus of senior players forced to take a pay cut. But when captain Mal Meninga and coach Tim Sheens agreed to stay on for 1992, several other internationals signed up as well. There was, however, not enough money to go around. And internationals Brent Todd and Glenn Lazarus were forced to move to other clubs.

In the meantime, Canberra staged a remarkable late-season surge. Written off as Premiership contenders during the internal strife, the Raiders won seven straight matches to reach the grand final for the third consecutive year (running in 16 tries in the three final-five play-off matches). But, plagued by injuries, they could not stave off a second-half fight-back by Penrith who took out the season's finale 19–12.

Canberra

Founded: 1981
Joined Sydney Premiership competition: 1982
Home ground: Bruce Stadium (Record crowd—24 460)
Colours: Lime green, white, blue and gold
Nickname: The Raiders
Honours:
   Sydney Premiership—Winners, 1989, 1990; Runners-up, 1987

▶

Channel 10 Challenge Cup—1990
Jersey Flegg Cup—1989
Most points in a career: 527 by Ron Giteau
Most tries in a career: 60 by Chris O'Sullivan
Most points in a season: 218 by Gary Belcher, in 1988
Most tries in a season: 20 by John Ferguson, in 1988

WA CANN

Eight Tests for Australia (1908-14). Also played in one 1910 international which for many years was regarded as a Test and eight minor matches for Australia on one Kangaroo tour (1908-09).

Bill Cann was one of the pioneers of Rugby League in Australia. He served on the first South Sydney committee and was one of the club's delegates to the early meetings of the NSW Rugby League. It was a drastic step for Cann to throw his support behind the fledgling code, for he was a star Rugby Union player and had been promised a trip to England with the first Wallaby side. Cann, in fact, had two trips to England (with the Kangaroos in 1908–09 and 1911–12) and another two to New Zealand (with New South Wales sides, in 1912 and 1913).

He relished the transition to League from the amateur code, where the constant kicking curbed his natural game. The 1911–12 tour co-manager Johnny Quinlan wrote of Cann: 'WA Cann is, in my opinion, one of the greatest all-round forwards to play Rugby. The way he combines with his backs simply nonplussed the opposition. It was he who introduced the typical Australian style of fast forward play in which the backs and forwards combine so effectively and spectacularly. It is no reflection on his successors to say the original model remains the greatest gem'.

On the club scene, Cann was a major cog in the South Sydney machine which took out the first two Sydney Premierships. All told, he played 74 first-grade games for the Rabbitohs—a significantly large number in those early days of the sport. After retiring as a player, Cann became a leading Rugby League administrator and visited Britain again as co-manager of the 1921–22 Kangaroos.

CANTERBURY-BANKSTOWN

The NSW Rugby League surprised everyone when, in 1934, it agreed to allow Canterbury-Bankstown to join the Sydney Premiership race. At that time, there were eight sides playing in the competition and Canterbury's introduction meant there would be a bye each week. Canterbury's playing strength was also suspect. There was also the fact that the side had neither a ground nor training facilities.

It was later revealed that League chiefs had been swayed by an emotional speech by the then-Mayor of Canterbury, Ald SE Parry, who promised, among other things, that his council would establish a playing field and erect a grandstand on Belmore Oval. This was done, and so to this day Belmore Oval (since renamed Belmore Sports Ground) has remained the home of the Canterbury side. The critics did, however, see some of their worst fears realised in that first season, 1935. Canterbury won only two of its 16 games. It suffered some humiliating losses, including a 91–6 drubbing by St George and an 87–7 thrashing by Eastern Suburbs.

The change after one season was incredible. The great Frank Burge was appointed coach for 1936 and steered Canterbury to only four losses during the year. The babes of the competition reached the semi-finals. Two years later they won their first Premiership. In doing so, they ended the run of the classic Eastern Suburbs line-up, which had been unbeaten in the previous two seasons.

Most of the credit for Canterbury's success must go to its fine front-row trio, said to have been the best of any club, anywhere in the world, at any time. The props were Henry 'Tarzan' Porter and Eddie Burns. The rake, Roy Kirkaldy, was dubbed by journalists of that era 'The Prince of Hookers'. For about a decade these three provided the backbone of the Canterbury pack. All told, they packed down together in 138 first-grade games, a record which is unlikely to be beaten. All three played more than 150 club games, with Burns playing 235. The trio was also a major force in Canterbury's second Premiership success in 1942, when forward power proved to be the decisive factor in an 11–9 grand final victory over St George.

In 1967, Canterbury destroyed a Rugby League legend on its way to the grand final. In the preliminary final, Canterbury beat St George, who for 11 straight seasons had been virtually unbeatable in Australian club football. Ironically, it was a former St George star, front-rower Kevin Ryan, who led Canterbury when the Berries (as they were then known) beat the Dragons 12–11. Unfortunately, South Sydney accounted for Canterbury 12–10 in the grand final.

In the 1980s, Canterbury was one of the dominant sides in the Sydney competition. The Bulldogs, as the club had been renamed, won in 1980 (beating Eastern Suburbs 18–4), 1984 (downing Parramatta 6–4), 1985 (defeating St George 7–5) and 1988 (beating Balmain 24–12 in the first grand final at the Sydney Football Stadium). Canterbury also went down 4–2 to Parramatta in 1986, the lowest scoring (and only tryless) grand final in history. Three of the finest modern coaches were at the helm for these successes—Ted Glossop (1980), Warren Ryan (1984 and 1985) and Phil Gould (1988).

One of the most remarkable instances of families involved in Rugby League occurred in the 1980 grand final. Canterbury was spearheaded by two sets of brothers, the Mortimers and the Hughes. Chris and Peter Mortimer played in the centres, while brother Steve was halfback. Garry Hughes was five-eighth, Mark Hughes lock and Graeme Hughes second-row. Steve and Chris Mortimer both played for Australia—Steve in eight Tests between 1981 and 1984 and Chris in one Test in 1986. Steve eventually wrestled the record for the greatest number of first grade games from Burns. When Steve Mortimer retired because of a recurring injury he had played 267 games.

Other Canterbury international stars of that era included fullback Greg Brentnall, three-quarters Chris Anderson, Ross Conlon, Tony Currie and Andrew Farrar, five-eighth Terry Lamb, and forwards George Peponis, Paul Dunn, David Gillespie, Paul Langmack, Steve Folkes and Peter Tunks. Hooker Peponis captained Australia in Tests, while Lamb has the record of being the only player in history to play in every match on a Kangaroo tour (1986).

Anderson's 117 tries are a club record. He went on to make a name for himself as player-coach of the English club Halifax, which he took to Championship and Challenge Cup successes, before returning to ultimately take over the reins of Canterbury, in 1990. It was not a truly happy return of the prodigal son. Canterbury could manage only seventh spot on the competition table that year, and at the end of the season there was a mass exodus of stars. Farrar, Langmack, Gillespie and representative hooker Joe Thomas went to join former coach Ryan at Western Suburbs, Dunn moved to Penrith, and classy utility back Jason Alchin switched to St George.

But the Bulldogs, under Anderson, surprised everyone by finishing in equal fifth spot in 1991, going down gallantly in the play-off for the last semi-final berth to Western Suburbs.

Canterbury-Bankstown

Founded: 1935
Entered Sydney Premiership competition: 1935
Home ground: Belmore Sports Ground (Record crowd—26 120)
Colours: Blue and white
Nickname: The Bulldogs (formerly The Berries)
Honours:
  Sydney Premiership—Winners, 1938, 1942, 1980, 1984, 1985, 1988
  Runners-up, 1940, 1947, 1967, 1974, 1979, 1986
    Flowers' Memorial Pennant (Club Championship)—1938, 1939
    Pre-Season Trophy—1962, 1970
    State Championship—1939
    Reserve-grade Premiership—1939, 1971, 1972, 1980
    Third-grade Premiership—1971
    Presidents' Cup—1976, 1991
    Flegg Memorial Trophy—1963, 1971, 1976
    S G Ball Cup—1972, 1978
Most first-grade games: 267 by Steve Mortimer
Most points in a career: 1,096 by Steve Gearin
Most tries in a career: 117 by Chris Anderson
Most points in a season: 244 by Steve Gearin, in 1979
Most tries in a season: 19 by Chris Anderson, in 1983
Rothmans Medal winners: Greg Brentnall (1982), Terry Lamb (1984), Ewan McGrady (1991)
Dally M Trophy winner: Mick Potter (1984)
NSW Player-of-the-Year: Les Johns (1967)
Rugby League Week Player-of-the-Year: Ewan McGrady (1991)
Sun-Herald Best-and-Fairest Player: Barry Stenhouse (1953), Les Johns
  (1969), Garry Dowling (1974 and 1975)

BRIAN CARLSON

Seventeen Tests for Australia (1952–61). Also played six matches in two World Cups (1957 and 1960), one game versus the Rest-of-the-World (1957), one minor international (1960) and 42 minor games for Australia on two Kangaroo tours (1952–53 and 1959–60) and two New Zealand tours (1953 and 1961).

Brian Carlson was one of the finest utility backs to wear Australia's colours. He was equally at home at fullback, on the wing or in the centres. Carlson was also an accomplished goalkicker. Only a handful of Australians have scored more than the 90 points notched by Carlson in Test and World Cup football. The burly star may have had an even finer record but for the fact that his weight often soared during the summer. His early-season form suffered as a consequence.

However he was a regular representative in top football for more than a decade. His first tour of Britain and France, in 1952–53, was as a winger and he played his first three Tests on that visit. He bowed out of the

Brian Carlson

Test scene by captaining the 1961 Australian side to New Zealand as a utility back. Three years later he was still playing top-class football when he capped a good season by kicking five goals for Newcastle against the touring Frenchmen.

During his international career Carlson played 10 Tests against Britain, four versus New Zealand and three against France as well as six World Cup matches. One of the highlights came in the 1957 World Cup in Australia. Chosen as a winger, he switched to fullback after the regular custodian, Keith Barnes, was injured in the first game. Carlson's play in the remaining matches was a decisive factor in Australia's first Cup success.

He may have been one of the Cup heroes, but as far as his club was concerned, he was persona non grata. Carlson was captain-coach of the Blackall side in the Queensland country when he gained selection in the World Cup squad. The Blackall officials asked him to pull out of the squad and concentrate on club football. When he refused, the club dismissed him. Unconcerned, Carlson went ahead to become the top scorer in the Cup series with two tries and 15 goals. North Sydney was only too pleased to snap up his services once the World Series was over.

MARK CARROLL

One Test for Australia (1990). Also played in six minor games for Australia on one Kangaroo tour (1990).

Mark Carroll was one of the fine Penrith youngsters of the late 1980s, who slipped through the Panther net and went elsewhere. Carroll had been the captain of the Penrith side which won the Jersey Flegg Memorial Trophy in 1986 and finished the season in the Panthers' Under-23 side which made the playoffs. However after playing just three first-grade games (in 1989) he switched to South Sydney, where, shrugging off dreadful form by his Rabbitoh team-mates, he made a meteoric rise into the Australian Test team as a replacement in the 1990 World Cup qualifying match against France, even though he hadn't played State-of-Origin football. At the end of the season Carroll was chosen to tour Britain and France with the 1990 Kangaroos but unfortunately a bad injury restricted his appearances on tour to just six.

WILLIE CARNE

Four Tests for Australia (1991). Also played three minor matches on one Papua New Guinea tour (1991).

Queensland winger Willie Carne rocketed to stardom in his first year in senior football—1990. In the space of a few weeks he went from a reserve grade player with the Brisbane Broncos into the Queensland State-of-Origin side.

He had always shown promise in his home town of Roma, from where he represented South-west Queensland in 1988. The following year he was one of the stars of the Broncos Colts side which won the Sunshine Coast Premiership. Carne was called into the Broncos firsts for the match against Newcastle in round six of the Premiership, in April 1990. There was no looking back as the big winger (95kg or 15 st) went on a try-scoring splurge which was to net him a club record-equalling 15 touch-downs for the season.

After just five matches he was selected in the Queensland State-of-Origin side for the final match of the series. His form was such that he went close to being chosen for the Kangaroo side which toured Britain and France at the end of the season.

But Test football was not far away. After Australia was surprisingly beaten in the first Test by the 1991 Kiwis, Carne got his chance. The 22-year-old scored in both of the final two encounters, won decisively by Australia. He was one of the first chosen for Australia's end-of-season tour of Papua New Guinea. He scored three tries in each of the two Tests on tour—becoming the first Australian in history to snare a hat-trick in successive Tests.

GEORGE CARSTAIRS

Two Tests for Australia (1921–22). Also played in 15 minor games for Australia on one Kangaroo tour (1921–22).

George Carstairs had a meteoric rise in Rugby League. Before the start of the 1921 season the 19–year-old had played only junior matches, but, by the end of the year, he was in the Australian Test side, on the Kangaroo tour of Britain.

Carstairs also has a special niche in football history. The fine centre was the first player to score a try for St George. The Saints played their first match in the Sydney Premiership on April 23, 1921—fittingly St George's Day. They went down to Glebe by just one point, 4–3, with Carstairs the lone scorer.

At the end of the season Carstairs made the Kangaroo side, thus beginning a tradition which has seen at least one St George player chosen in each successive Kangaroo squad. Inexplicably, Carstairs did not get a run until the 11th match of the tour, in which Australia downed Wakefield Trinity 29–3. However his form was such that he made his Test debut in the second international clash, at Hull, in which Australia emerged triumphant. In the third and deciding Test, at Salford, Carstairs was called upon to play a major role. Fullback and captain Chook Fraser was carried off with a suspected broken leg, and Carstairs was switched back from the centre to fill the custodian's spot. He tackled grimly, but to no avail, as Britain scored a 6–0 victory.

Carstairs made a second overseas trip at the end of 1922, when New South Wales made a successful sortie across the Tasman to New Zealand. On the tour he was one of the NSW internationals who joined with New Zealand Kangaroo team-mate Bert Laing, for a special exhibition game against a combined side of players from Auckland and non-Kangaroo tourists.

JOHN CARTWRIGHT

Four Tests for Australia (1990–91) Also played eight minor games for Australia on one Kangaroo tour (1990).

John Cartwright was one of a group of fine young players blooded in the Penrith side in the mid-to-late 1980s. The youngsters laid the foundation for Penrith's charge to the elite of the Sydney Premiership competition, culminating in its 1990 grand final appearance and 1991 Premiership success.

A tough second-rower, who stood 1.88m (6ft 2in) high and weighed 108kg (17 stone), Cartwright was the son of a former Penrith club secretary. He was spotted playing for St Mary's junior club and was given a chance with a couple of first-grade games for the Panthers in 1985. There was no looking back. By 1989, this clever player, with ball-skills almost unmatched among his fellow forwards, was one of the best in the business and played in all three State-of-Origin matches that year. An injury in early 1990 proved but a minor setback, and Cartwright was firing so well at the end of the season, especially in the grand final, that he was one of the first chosen for the Kangaroo squad to tour Britain and France. His early form was good and won him a spot in the First Test lineup. However he did not live up to this promise and spent the rest of the tour playing the minor games with the second XIII—the so-called 'Emus'.

Cartwright came on as an interchange player in each of the three Tests against the touring 1991 New Zealand Kiwis. Towards the end of the season he was carrying a bad injury and it seemed he would miss out on the euphoria of Penrith's second straight grand final. But, early in the game, he was rushed onto the field from the reserves bench and, ignoring the injury pain, played a major role in what was to be the Panthers first Premiership win. He was chosen for the Australian side for the subsequent tour of Papua New Guinea—but succumbed to the injury and pulled out.

CATALAN

The Perpignan club, XIII Catalan, is one of the most famous of all French sides. The club boasted possibly the greatest of all French players, Puig Aubert, and over the years provided stiff competition for touring international teams. Indeed, it scored an historic victory over the great 1963–64 Kangaroos. In 1988, XIII Catalan made a lightning trip to Australia, losing both matches.

Record in Australia

Played 2, Lost 2, Points for 10, points against 24

1988 Tour of Australia

Opponents	Venue	For	Against
Newcastle XIII	Newcastle	10	13
NSW Country	Wyong	0	11

CHALLENGE CUP

In 1978, Sydney television station Channel 10 staged a one-off knockout competition for the seven sides which missed out on the Premiership semi-finals as well as the first semi-finalist eliminated in the playoffs. North Sydney beat South Sydney 23–14 in the final.

A competition of the same name—but at the start of the season instead of the finish—was instituted by the Ten Network in 1990. All 16 Premiership sides took part in the knock-out series televised midweek under floodlights. All matches until the semi-finals were double-headers in country areas, with crowds of more than 11 000 watching the matches in Parkes, Albury and Bathurst. Canberra, the reigning Premiers, won the first of the pre-season Challenge Cups, beating Penrith 12–2 in the 1990 final. The competition was held again in 1991, but renamed the Lotto Challenge, with the winner, Brisbane, taking away $250 000 in prizemoney.

After financial difficulties, the Ten Network lost the rights to televise the competition in 1992. Channel 9, which previously had only the State-of-Origin matches in its portfolio, took over the telecasts of all NSWRL competitions including the yet-again renamed Toohey's Challenge. Matches were held even further afield, with the semi-finals being played in the New Zealand cities of Auckland and Wellington, which were expected to join the NSWRL Premiership in 1994.

LES CHANTICLEERS

Les Chanticleers is the name given to touring French Rugby League teams. The nickname is not as common in use as the Kangaroos, Kiwis, Kumuls or Lions but probably this is because France makes only an occasional tour. The French derive their name from the badge of the Federation Francaise de Jeu a Treize (the French Rugby League), a crowing cock on a football. The bird is known as 'Le Coq Gaulois' or 'Le Chanticleer'.

The French made their first overseas visit in 1934—a short tour of neighbouring England, but their first tour of Australia and New Zealand was not until 1951. It was an experiment to see if France rated inclusion in the regular program of full-scale international visits. At first it seemed a disaster. The tourists showed indifferent form and the Australian Rugby League chiefs threatened to send them packing. However they improved—so much so that they beat Australia in the Test series. The tourists triumphed again in 1955 but failed to match Australia on four subsequent tours.

FRANCE TO AUSTRALIA, NEW ZEALAND AND PAPUA NEW GUINEA

1951

Famous sporting journalist Tom Goodman dubbed the Frenchmen who made their country's first tour of Australasia in 1951 'The Unforgettables'.

They certainly were. The touring side is remembered as the most exciting of any side to visit Australia and New Zealand in the eight decades of tours down-under. The French surprised by beating Australia in the Test series. Stars included fullback Puig Aubert, who kicked 18 Test goals from 18 attempts (and 96 on the whole Australian section of the tour) and the brilliant second-row combination of Elie Brousse and Edouard Ponsinet.

Record in Australia

Played 21, Won 15, Lost 3, Drawn 3, Points for 582, Points against 357

Test Match Results

France	26	Australia	15	(Sydney, 60 160)
France	11	Australia	23	(Brisbane, 35 000)
France	35	Australia	14	(Sydney, 67 009)

Other Matches

Opponents	Venue (Attendance)	For	Against
Monaro	Canberra (5000)	37	12
Newcastle	Newcastle (21 480)	12	8
Western Division	Forbes (5950)	26	24
Sydney	Sydney (44 522)	19	19
Riverina	Albury (4129)	10	20
Northern Division	Armidale (6000)	29	12
Queensland	Brisbane (25 847)	22	22
Central Queensland	Rockhampton (4598)	38	14
North Queensland	Townsville (11 000)	50	17
Wide Bay/Burnett	Bundaberg (4500)	44	19
Brisbane	Brisbane (10 750)	17	16
Toowoomba	Toowoomba (10 939)	20	17
NSW North Coast	Lismore (8710)	33	9
New South Wales	Sydney (45 579)	14	14
Southern Division	Wollongong (11 334)	24	13
NSW XIII	Sydney (29 304)	11	29
Australian XIII	Melbourne (4460)	34	17
Western Australia	Perth (14 500)	70	23

Record in New Zealand

Played 7, Won 6, Lost 1, Points for 124, Points against 62

Test Match Result

France	15	New Zealand	16	(Auckland, 19 229)

Other Matches

Opponents	Venue (Attendance)	For	Against
West Coast	Greymouth (3667)	5	2
Canterbury	Christchurch (6990)	13	7
Wellington	Wellington (8602)	26	13
Auckland	Auckland (20 414)	15	10
South Auckland	Hamilton (7480)	27	7
Taranaki	New Plymouth (6473)	23	7

Team members: Puig Aubert (c), O Lespes, G Gomes, J Merquey, V Cantoni, J Dop, L Mazon, M Martin, A Berand, E Brousse, E Ponsinet, G Calixte, R Duffort, R Contrastin, M Andre, R Caillon, R Perez, M Lopez, F Montrucolis, P Bartoletti, A Audobert, G Genoud, F Rinaldi, J Crespo, G Delaye, M Bellan, C Galaup, C Teisseire.

1955

The 1955 French tourists began their visit to Australia showing only average form. They were thrashed by Sydney, downed by some of the lesser country sides and soundly beaten in the First Test. But the Frenchmen, led by brilliant centre Jacques Merquey, came good when it really counted. They won the high-scoring Second Test by just one point and then took out the decider at the Sydney Cricket Ground.

Record in Australia

Played 25, Won 15, Lost 10, Points for 615, Points against 462

Test Match Results

France	8	Australia	20	(Sydney, 67 748)
France	29	Australia	28	(Brisbane, 45 745)
France	8	Australia	5	(Sydney, 62 458)

Other Matches

Opponents	Venue (Attendance)	For	Against
Western Australia	Perth (5000)	31	6
South Australia	Adelaide (1074)	48	10
Victoria	Melbourne (2311)	44	2
Monaro	Canberra (4000)	3	11
Sydney	Sydney (39 445)	0	35
Riverina	Narranderra (9000)	27	29
New South Wales	Sydney (50 488)	24	29
Southern Division	Wollongong (6500)	7	16
Brisbane	Brisbane (30 000)	21	11
Toowoomba	Toowoomba (7305)	6	35
Queensland	Brisbane (14 871)	23	17
Central Queensland	Rockhampton (7500)	40	24
West Queensland	Barcaldine (2250)	29	14
Far North Queensland	Cairns (5943)	66	21
North Queensland	Townsville (7525)	42	26
Wide Bay	Gympie (5391)	46	17
Ipswich	Ipswich (4242)	19	10
Northern Division	Casino (4500)	17	18
Newcastle	Newcastle (20 824)	15	17
Sydney Colts	Sydney (13 282)	28	26
New South Wales	Sydney (30 769)	23	27
Western Division	Parkes (8306)	11	8

Record in New Zealand

Played 8, Won 4, Lost 4, Points for 150, Points against 129

Test Match Results

France	19	New Zealand	9	(Auckland)
France	6	New Zealand	11	(Auckland)

Other Matches

Opponents	Venue	For	Against
West Coast	Greymouth	13	7
Canterbury	Christchurch	12	24
Wellington	Wellington	19	14
Taranaki	New Plymouth	46	19
Maoris	Huntly	20	28
Auckland	Auckland	15	17

Team members: J Merquey (c), G Benausse, R Contrastin, F Cantoni, M Voron, A Savonne, A Ducasse, C Teisseire, R Rey, V Larroude, F Levy, A Jiminez, A Delpoux, J Dop, S Menichelli, C Duple, R Guilhem, F Montrucolis, A Save, J Pambrun, G Berthomieu, J Jammes, J Fabre, J Vanel, A Audobert, R Moulis, A Carrere.

1960

France scored just one try in the three Tests against Australia in 1960—but it was enough to help draw the series. The First Test was shared 8–all (each side kicked four goals). The Second was a cakewalk for Australia 56–6 (the Frenchmen's points coming from three goals), but the tourists surprised with a 7–5 victory in the deciding match. Each team scored a try but an extra goal by five-eighth Claude Mantoulan gave France the edge. The French had no such luck in New Zealand, losing both Tests.

Record in Australia

Played 22, Won 12, Lost 8, Drawn 2, Points for 422, Points against 390

Test Match Results

France	8	Australia	8	(Sydney, 49 868)
France	6	Australia	56	(Brisbane, 32 644)
France	7	Australia	5	(Sydney, 29 127)

Other Matches

Opponents	Venue (Attendance)	For	Against
Northern Territoty	Darwin (1400)	42	14
Western Australia	Perth (4538)	29	8
Monaro	Canberra (3000)	25	17
Newcastle	Newcastle (15 096)	14	10
NSW North Coast	Kempsey (6500)	23	28
Riverina	Wagga Wagga (11 000)	25	14
Sydney	Sydney (41 808)	17	23
Southern Division	Wollongong (9038)	10	35
New South Wales	Sydney (32 488)	7	25
Western Division	Dubbo (5466)	7	14
Brisbane	Brisbane (17 425)	12	15
Queensland	Brisbane (22 533)	18	30
Wide Bay/Burnett	Maryborough (3982)	33	10
Central Queensland	Rockhampton (4000)	13	8
Far North Queensland	Cairns (4329)	26	15
North Queensland	Townsville (4547)	22	5
Ipswich	Ipswich (2704)	33	19
Toowoomba	Toowoomba (9818)	21	21
Northern Division	Armidale (6200)	24	10

Record in New Zealand

Played 9, Won 6, Lost 3, Points for 180, Points against 83

Test Match Results

France	2	New Zealand	9	(Auckland, 17 914)
France	3	New Zealand	9	(Auckland, 14 007)

Other Matches

Opponents	Venue (Attendance)	For	Against
Waikato	Huntly (3071)	32	2
Taranaki	Hawera (1234)	30	21
Wellington	Wellington (1701)	41	3
Canterbury	Christchurch (7529)	15	8
West Coast	Greymouth (4500)	29	5
Maoris	Rotorua (5044)	23	12
Auckland	Auckland (11 431)	5	14

Individual Records in Australia

	Matches	Tests	Tries	Goals	Points
P Lacaze	11	–	–	49	98
A Lacaze	10	–	1	22	47
R Gruppi	11	2	12	–	36
C Mantoulan	12	3	4	7	26
J Verges	7	–	8	–	24
J Dubon	9	2	5	1	17
A Marty	8	1	3	4	17
A Foussat	11	2	5	–	15
F Rossi	10	1	5	–	15
R Moulinas	6	–	2	4	14
J Giraud	7	1	4	–	12
G Benausse	8	1	4	–	12
A Casas	11	1	4	–	12
A Perducat	10	–	4	–	12
L Poletti	9	1	3	1	11
J Darricau	8	–	3	–	9
J Majoral	11	–	2	–	6
A Jiminez (c)	12	3	2	–	6
M Bescos	12	3	2	–	6
A Boldini	9	1	2	–	6
Y Mezard	8	–	2	–	6
R Benausse	4	–	1	–	3
J Barthe	9	3	1	–	3
G Fages	8	2	1	–	3
A Vadon	9	2	1	–	3
R Eramouspe	12	3	1	–	3
A Quaglio	10	2	–	–	–
B Fabre	7	3	–	–	–

1964

The abject failure of the 1964 French tourists dealt an death blow to future tours. It was to be 17 years before the Frenchmen returned. The tourists were outclassed even by moderate country sides and players had to sell autographed photos to prevent the tour from becoming a complete financial disaster. To attract even a moderate crowd to the Third Test the authorities had to stage a game bwteen NSW Colts and Other Nationalities as a curtain-raiser.

Record in Australia

Played 25, Won 9, Lost 16, Points for 402, Points against 516

Test Match Results

France	6	Australia	20	(Sydney, 20 270)
France	2	Australia	27	(Brisbane, 20 076)
France	9	Australia	35	(Sydney, 16 731)

Other Matches

Opponents	Venue (Attendance)	For	Against
Northern Territory	Darwin (2340)	36	19
North West Queensland	Mt Isa (2465)	23	14
North Queensland	Townsville (6623)	21	35
Central Queensland	Rockhampton (4100)	2	22
Sydney	Sydney (39 929)	2	49
Southern Division	Wollongong (7936)	0	11
Western Division	Orange (2200)	11	17
Newcastle	Newcastle (14 926)	14	16
NSW North Coast	Wauchope (4391)	19	21
Monaro	Queanbeyan (3000)	38	16
New South Wales	Sydney (13 507)	8	36
Riverina	Griffith (4361)	16	21
Brisbane	Brisbane (12 841)	17	23
Queensland	Brisbane (12 885)	22	28
Ipswich	Ipswich (3636)	20	15
Gold Coast	Tweed Heads (3000)	16	0
Toowoomba	Toowoomba (4750)	28	15
Wide Bay/Burnett	Bundaberg (4612)	29	11
NSW Group 10	Lithgow (1800)	17	7
Northern Division	Armidale (4300)	13	17
NSW Colts	Sydney (2545)	15	39
Western Australia	Perth (2313)	20	2

Record in New Zealand

Played 10, Won 6, Lost 4, Points for 157, Points against 117

Test Match Results

France	16	New Zealand	24	(Auckland, 10 148)
France	8	New Zealand	18	(Christchurch, 4935)
France	2	New Zealand	10	(Auckland, 7279)

Other Matches

Opponents	Venue (Attendance)	For	Against
Maoris	Whangarei (1564)	3	7
Wellington	Wellington (1301)	18	12
West Coast	Greymouth (1970)	9	6
Taranaki	New Plymouth (1200)	22	4
Auckland	Auckland (3764)	13	10
Waikato	Huntly (2737)	23	16
Bay of Plenty	Rotorua (596)	41	10

Individual Records in Australia

	Matches	Tests	Tries	Goals	Points
F Bertrand	12	–	5	42	99
C Mantoulan	20	4	8	36	96
M Boule	25	6	26	–	78
R Garnung	24	3	3	34	77

Continued

Individual Records in Australia *continued*

	Matches	Tests	Tries	Goals	Points
A Bourreil	23	3	9	–	27
J Villeneuve	21	5	3	7	21
P Plo	10	3	7	–	21
A Carrere	21	2	6	–	18
G Savonne	23	5	6	–	18
J Etcheberry	15	–	5	–	15
L Verge	20	5	5	–	15
H Chamorin	25	6	5	–	15
M Bardes	9	2	2	2	10
J Lapoterie	14	3	3	–	9
JP Lecompte	18	5	3	–	9
H Castel	13	1	1	2	7
S Estiau	21	2	2	–	6
B Fabre	2	–	1	–	3
E Duseigneur	22	3	1	–	3
P Azalbert	9	1	1	–	3

Did not score:

R Eramouspe	12	1
H Larrue	9	–
C Sabathie	15	2
J Pano (c)	10	4
F Mas	16	5
J Graciet	20	1
L Faletti	10	1

1981

The Frenchmen had their worst-ever tour down-under in 1981. They lost all Tests in Australia and New Zealand and only managed a draw against the fledgling Papua New Guinea side. They scored a mere 164 points in 15 games—a dismal average of 11 points per match.

Record in Australia

Played 6, Won 1, Lost 5, Points for 40, Points against 141

Test match results

France	3	Australia	43	(Sydney, 16 277)
France	2	Australia	17	(Brisbane, 14 000)

Other Matches

Opponents	Venue (Attendance)	For	Against
Newcastle	Newcastle (13 000)	0	29
Illawarra	Wollongong (2216)	7	26
North Queensland	Townsville (3200)	25	15
Wide Bay	Nambour (6000)	3	11

Record in New Zealand

Played 7, Won 4, Lost 3, Points for 89, Points against 93

Test Match Results

France	3	New Zealand	26	(Auckland, 12 500)
France	2	New Zealand	25	(Auckland, 13 000)

Other Matches

Opponents	Venue (Attendance)	For	Against
South Island	Christchurch (5000)	16	12
Central Districts	Wellington (2500)	22	0
Maoris	Huntly (3200)	14	5
Northern Districts	Whangarei (3000)	22	5
Auckland	Auckland (8000)	10	20

Record in Papua New Guinea

Played 2, Won 1, Drawn 1, Points for 35, Points against 27

Test Match Results

France _____ 13   Papua New Guinea _____ 13   (Port Moresby, 14 000)

Other Matches

Opponents	Venue (Attendance)	For	Against
Highlands Zone _____	Mount Hagen (12 000)	22	14

Individual Records in Australia

	Tries	Goals	Points
J Imbert _____	1	17	37
A Perez _____	–	12	24
Y Greseque _____	6	–	18
J Roosebrouck (c) _____	3	–	9
J Gine _____	2	–	6
H Ratier _____	2	–	6
H Guiraud _____	2	–	6
B Imbert _____	2	–	6
G Laforgue _____	2	–	6
G Delauney _____	1	–	3
P Fourquet _____	1	–	3
M Naudo _____	1	–	3
M Pillon _____	1	–	3
S Rodriguez _____	1	–	3
G Alard _____	1	–	3
JJ Vila _____	1	–	3
JL Bezard _____	1	–	3
M Ambert _____	1	–	3
B Gonzales _____	1	–	3
J Giradet _____	1	–	3
J Malacamp _____	1	–	3

Did not score: H Daniel, C Macalli, M Chantal, M Caravaca, D Castanon, D Hermet and C Zaldvendo.

1990

France staged a short tour of Australia in 1990, mainly so that Australia's home match in the World Cup could be staged. The authorities, worried about the Chanticleers drawing power, scheduled all matches away from the two major centres, Sydney and Brisbane. The lone Test was played in freezing conditions at Parkes in the central-west of New South Wales. Australia won easily—but the score should have been even higher, with the Australian kickers booting only one goal from eight attempts.

Record in Australia

Played 6, Won 3, Lost 3, Points for 92, Points against 119

Test Match Result

France _____ 2   Australia _____ 34   (Parkes, 12 384)

Other Matches

Opponents	Venue (Attendance)	For	Against
Western Australia _____	Perth (5625)	16	8
Queensland Country _____	Cairns (5000)	16	9
Queensland Residents _____	Rockhampton (4500)	16	22
NSW North Coast _____	Wauchope (5000)	10	26
Western Division _____	Bathurst (1500)	32	20

Individual Records

	Matches	Tests	Tries	Goals	Points
G Dumas _____	5	1	2	8	24
C Pons _____	6	1	4	–	16
J Moliner _____	4	–	3	–	12
P Chamorin _____	4	–	2	–	8
D Divet _____	5	1	2	–	8
M Tisseyre _____	2	–	–	4	8

Continued

Individual Records *continued*

	Matches	Tests	Tries	Goals	Points
P Entat	6	1	1	–	4
G Delaunay	5	1	1	–	4
D Fraisse	2	–	1	–	4
JP Marquet	2	–	1	–	4
T Valero	6	1	1	–	4
H Ratier (c)	5	1	–	–	–
P Aillieres	3	–	–	–	–
T Buttignol	4	1	–	–	–
D Cabestany	5	1	–	–	–
E Castel	4	1	–	–	–
A Alesina	3	–	–	–	–
P Fages	1	–	–	–	–
P Gestas	3	–	–	–	–
C Piredda	2	–	–	–	–
JL Rabot	6	1	–	–	–
J Ruiz	5	1	–	–	–
JB Saumitou	5	1	–	–	–
P Sokolow	2	–	–	–	–
F Lope	4	1	–	–	–

1991

France had a disastrous tour of New Zealand and Papua New Guinea in 1991. The tourists were thoroughly outplayed, winning only three of the nine matches. It was only in the last couple of matches that they showed any semblance of competitive form. Their World Cup victory over Papua New Guinea sparked off a riot amongst spectators.

Record in New Zealand

Played 5, Won 1, Lost 4, Points for 40, Points against 180.

Test Match Results

France	6	New Zealand	60	(Auckland, 7000)
France	10	New Zealand	32	(Christchurch, 2000)

Other Matches

Opponents	Venue	For	Against
Kiwi Colts	Rotorua	8	28
President's XIII	Palmerston North	2	54
West Coast	Greymouth	14	6

Record in Papua New Guinea

Played 4, Won 2, Lost 2, Points for 82, Points against 85.

Test Match Results

France	20	Papua New Guinea	18	(Goroka, 11 485)

Other Matches

Opponents	Venue	For	Against
Southern Zone	Port Moresby	22	24
Island Zone	Rabaul	24	28
Northern Zone	Lae	16	15

Team members: G Dumas (c), C Auroy, C Pons, C Sirvent, JM Garcia, P Campana, P Chamorin, D Bienes, D Despin, A Alesina, P Fages, R Palisses, P Entat, F Romano, T Bernabe, G Boyais, B Plante, D Cabestany, JB Samitou, D Verdes, Y Storer, M Tisseyre, G Delpeche, T Valero, T Butignol, P Torreilles, R Viscay.

FRANCE TO ENGLAND
1982

France made a mini-tour of England in 1982 to help prepare the players for their matches against the Australian Kangaroos a few months later.

It was a low key affair. The three British clubs fielded a number of youngsters and referees gave the Frenchmen a hiding in the penalty counts.

Record in England

Played 3, Won 2, Lost 1, Points for 35, Points against 27

Other Matches

Opponents	Venue (Attendance)	For	Against
Oldham	Oldham (1165)	15	11
Featherstone Rovers	Featherstone (842)	13	5
Wigan	Wigan (3714)	7	11

Individual Records

	Tries	Goals	Points
A Perez	1	–	10
G Delaunay	3	–	9
C Scicchitano	2	–	6
J Imbert	–	2	4
D Bernard	1	–	3
F Laforgue	1	–	3

Did not score: P Solal, J Guigue, S Rodriguez, P Fourcade, M Laville, Y Gresque, H Guirade, M Chantal, J Gine, C Zaluendo, D Verdieres, C Macalli, T Bernabe, G Laforge, JJ Cologni, M Ambert, P Marty, P Puech, M Caravaca.

EE CHRISTENSEN

Ernie Christensen was recognised as the foremost Australian Rugby League journalist of the 1960s and 1970s. During this period he covered virtually every international played by Australia for either the Sydney *Sun* newspaper or Australian Associated Press. From 1946 on, Christensen also edited the official Rugby League Year Book and chose the NSW Player-of-the-Year. He died soon after returning from the 1980 Moscow Olympics.

NSW PLAYER-OF-THE-YEAR (As chosen by E E Christensen)

Season	Player	Club
1946	Lionel Cooper	Eastern Suburbs
1947	Bobby Lulham	Balmain
1948	Len Smith	Newtown
1949	Clive Churchill	South Sydney
1950	Clive Churchill	South Sydney
1951	Keith Holman	Western Suburbs
1952	Clive Churchill	South Sydney
1953	Jack Rayner	South Sydney
1954	Roy Bull	Manly-Warringah
1955	Ken Kearney	St George
1956	Keith Holman	Western suburbs
1957	Norm Provan	St George
1958	Keith Holman	Western Suburbs
1959	Reg Gasnier	St George
1960	Johnny Raper	St George
1961	Reg Gasnier	St George
1962	Arthur Summons	Western Suburbs
1963	Ian Walsh	St George
1964	Johnny Raper	St George
	& Reg Gasnier	St George
1965	Ken Thornett	Parramatta
1966	Billy Smith	St George
1967	Les Johns	Canterbury-Bankstown
1968	Ron Coote	South Sydney
1969	Ron Coote	South Sydney
1970	Graeme Langlands	St George
1971	Graeme Langlands	St George
1972	Bob Fulton	Manly-Warringah
1973	Bob Fulton	Manly-Warringah
1974	Ron Coote	Eastern Suburbs
1975	Arthur Beetson	Eastern Suburbs
1976	Ron Coote	Eastern Suburbs
1977	Mick Cronin	Parramatta

(Award discontinued after 1977)

CLIVE CHURCHILL

Thirty-four Tests for Australia (1948–56). Also played three matches in one World Cup (1954) and 54 minor matches on three Kangaroo tours (1948–49, 1952–53 and 1956–57) and two New Zealand tours (1949 and 1953).

The fans dubbed Clive Churchill 'The Little Master'. That he was. Little, just 1.7m (5ft 7ins) tall, and weighing just 76kg (12 stone). However he was a master of his craft and rates arguably as Australia's greatest Rugby League fullback. Jersey Flegg, for three decades chairman of the Australian Board of Control (the forerunner of the Australian Rugby League) said of him: 'Churchill was the greatest all-round champion the Rugby League code has known'.

Clive Churchill

Churchill excelled in both attack (where he had an uncanny knack of chiming into the backline to provide opportunities for his wingers) and in defence (where he was a devastating tackler and could relieve pressure on his side with long, accurate kicks for touch). He was the complete footballer. He had his first taste of representative football in 1947, when chosen to play for Country Seconds in the annual clash with City. South Sydney scouts, who had already watched him play in the Newcastle competition, lured him to the NSW capital with an offer of £12 a win (and nothing for a loss).

Churchill made his first international appearance against New Zealand in the Second Test of the 1948 series, displacing goal-kicking star Noel Pidding. From that moment on, Churchill had a mortgage on the Test fullback spot and Pidding was forced to switch to the wing to regain a place in the Test line-up. At the end of that season Churchill made the first of six overseas tours as a player (he also made one as non-playing coach of the 1959–60 Australian Kangaroos). By the time he had played his last international, in 1956, Churchill had played a record 34 Tests—32 of them in succession. There were 13 against Great Britain, 12 versus France and nine against New Zealand. He also played against each of those countries in the 1954 World Cup in France.

Churchill may never have made such an impact on the international scene had it not been for a ban on poaching players from other countries. In 1949 he was offered £10 000 to play for the British club Workington Town. It was a princely sum for a fellow who was earning just £9 a week as a sports goods salesman. But the Board of Control refused to give Churchill a clearance and he was forced to remain in Sydney. The Little Master became the first man to captain Australia in three series against arch-rival Britain. And he was also the first in 28 years to skipper an Australian Ashes-winning combination (in 1950).

Churchill played in four Premiership-winning sides with South Sydney (1950, 1951, 1953 and 1954).

After he bowed out of the international arena as a player, he turned his talents to coaching, with considerable success. He coached Queensland and Australia and then steered his old club, South Sydney, to four Premierships in five seasons (1967, 1968, 1970 and 1971). The Rabbitohs were runners-up the other year (1969).

Just before his death from cancer in 1985, Churchill was honoured with an Order of Australia award and then heard that a new grandstand at the scene of some of his greatest triumphs, the Sydney Cricket Ground, was to be named after him.

CLIVE CHURCHILL MEDAL

After 'The Little Master' Clive Churchill died in 1985, the NSW Rugby League decided that, in his memory, a medal would be struck and presented to the Man-of-the-Match in the Sydney Premiership grand final.

The inaugural winner of the Clive Churchill Medal, in a low-scoring match in which Parramatta beat Canterbury-Bankstown 4–2, was another all-time great, Parramatta halfback Peter Sterling. In close voting the following year Manly-Warringah five-eighth Cliff Lyons won, although many keen judges believed British front-rower Kevin Ward should have been honoured. Internationals Paul Dunn (1988) and Bradley Clyde (1989) were almost unanimous choices. Ricky Stuart's success in 1990 was the start of a couple of months of triumph. He was chosen in the Kangaroo squad and while on tour made his Rugby League Test debut.

WINNERS OF THE CLIVE CHURCHILL MEDAL

Year	Winner	Club
1986	Peter Sterling	Parramatta
1987	Cliff Lyons	Manly-Warringah
1988	Paul Dunn	Canterbury-Bankstown
1989	Bradley Clyde	Canberra
1990	Ricky Stuart	Canberra
1991	Bradley Clyde	Canberra

CITY CUP See *Extinct Competitions*

BRIAN CLAY

Five Tests for Australia (1959–60). Also played three matches in one World Cup (1957) and 16 minor games for Australia on one Kangaroo tour (1959–60).

Brian 'Poppa' Clay had a brief period of international prominence. He played a major role in Australia's success in the 1957 World Cup and appeared in five of the six Tests on the 1959–60 Kangaroo tour of Britain and France. Clay was also an important cog in the St George juggernaut which swept all before it in the late 1950s and 1960s, and he represented New South Wales for many years. Clay's looks belied his power and football ability. He was short and balding (he lost most of his hair while still a teenager). However he was a dynamic footballer, whether playing at lock-forward or five-eighth. He was a real thinker in attack and his battering-ram defence was close to being the finest seen in the post-World War II era.

Brian Clay

Clay began his career with Newtown. After three seasons there and another with Griffith in the Riverina area of southern NSW (during which he represented Country Firsts as a centre) he joined St George. He was to play for the Dragons for a decade, at a time when they were almost unbeatable. Between 1957 and 1966 he figured in eight grand final-winning sides. He missed out in 1962 and 1963 because of broken arms.

In 1959, he and St George clubmate Johnny Raper were chosen as locks for the Kangaroo tour. However, first-choice five-eighth Tony Brown was injured and played in only the first international against France. Clay and Raper then took it in turns to fill his spot. Clay played the three Tests against Britain as five-eighth and Raper was stand-off in the final two French Tests (with Clay at lock). Clay retired after the 1956 grand final—his 200th game for St George. He died prematurely in 1987 from a heart attack.

CLAYTON CUP

The Clayton Cup has been awarded annually since 1937 to the most outstanding club side in the country districts of New South Wales. Riverina club, Young, was the first to win the award twice (1953 and 1955). Cobar, in the far west of the State, went one better by taking out the Cup in successive seasons (1971 and 1972). This feat was repeated in 1985 and 1986, by Tumbarumba, in southern New South Wales. Tumbarumba's captain-coach, Les Cleal, had also been at the helm of two other Clayton Cup winners, Sawtell (1978) and Scone (1979). When Tweed Heads Seagulls, the oldest country club in New South Wales, won in 1989 under captain-coach John Harvey the former Manly-Warringah star, it became the first to win the Clayton Cup three times. It had previously scored in 1963 and 1983.

THE CLAYTON CUP WINNERS

1937	West Tamworth
1938	Nimmitabel
1939	Wagga Magpies
1940	Henty
1941–1945	Not awarded
1946	Port Kembla
1947	Bombala
1948	Cootamundra
1949	Tumut
1950	Bathurst Railway
1951	North Tamworth
1952	Gundagai
1953	Young
1954	Orange CYMS
1955	Young
1956	Maitland
1957	Temora
1958	Coonamble
1959	Dubbo Macquarie
1960	Goulburn Workers
1961	Ballina
1962	Warialda
1963	Tweed Heads Seagulls
1964	Oberon
1965	Tullibigeal
1966	Picton Magpies
1967	Casino
1968	Darlington Point
1969	Tarcutta
1970	Delegate
1971	Cobar

Continued

THE CLAYTON CUP WINNERS *continued*

1972	Cobar
1973	Gunnedah
1974	Queanbeyan United
1975	Albury Blues
1976	Bombala
1977	Belconnen United
1978	Sawtell
1979	Scone
1980	Nawan
1981	Bellingen
1982	Warilla
1983	Tweed Heads Seagulls
1984	Bourke
1985	Tumbarumba
1986	Tumbarumba
1987	Lismore Marist Brothers
1988	Bega
1989	Tweed Heads Seagulls
1990	Singleton
1991	Mittagong

LES CLEAL

Although his brother Noel made a name for himself internationally, Les Cleal is just as revered as a footballer around the country areas of Australia. The displays of this big, tough forward as captain-coach of various sides was without equal in the bush. Four times he was captain-coach of a team which won the coveted Clayton Cup, awarded annually to the most outstanding side in the New South Wales country. Such is the competition for this honour that the winners invariably go through the season unbeaten.

Cleal's first Clayton Cup success was in 1978 with Sawtell on the NSW north coast. The following year he switched to Scone, north west of Newcastle and won again. His finest achievement was in 1985 and 1986 when he steered Tumbarumba in the Southern Alps to consecutive wins— only the second club to have achieved this. In those two seasons, Tumbarumba won all 32 games, scoring 1409 points to its opponents 202.

In between his Clayton Cup successes, Cleal made an attempt to break into the Sydney scene. He played with his brother at Eastern Suburbs in 1982—but soon became homesick for the bush and returned to the country the following season.

NOEL CLEAL

Eight Tests for Australia (1985–86). Also played for Rest-of-the-World against Great Britain (1988) and eight minor games for Australia on one Kangaroo tour (1986) and one New Zealand tour (1985).

Few players have had a more apt nickname than Noel Cleal. He was called 'Crusher'. And that's what he did to opponents—crushed them with stampeding runs from around the rucks. He had only a brief international career but he left his imprint on Sydney Premiership matches and State-of-Origin games for almost a decade.

Cleal spent his early years roving around the country. He represented Wide Bay in Queensland in 1976, NSW North Coast in 1978 and Northern Division and NSW Country the following year (including a match against Great Britain). He was still relatively green when he joined Eastern Suburbs as a centre in 1980, but Cleal so blossomed under the coaching of the great Bob Fulton that he made the NSW side in his second Sydney season. He was a member of Easts' side which reached the preliminary final in 1982 and was considered unlucky not to have been chosen for the Kangaroo tour of Britain and France.

When Fulton moved to Manly-Warringah in 1983 Cleal followed him and, after a switch to the second-row, had some of the best seasons of his career. In 1984 he was named second-rower of the year in the annual Dally M awards and was runner-up in the Rothmans Medal. The following year he finally made his Test debut, against New Zealand in Brisbane, before touring the Shaky Isles with the Australian side.

The highlight of his career should have been the 1986 Kangaroo tour of Papua New Guinea, Britain and France. However after playing in the Test against the Kumuls and the first two against Britain, his luck changed. In a brawling, spiteful match against Hull, 'Crusher' broke his arm. It spelled the end of his Test career. After moving to England in late 1988 to play out his career with Hull, he was chosen in a Rest-of-the-World team to play Britain in a match to celebrate the opening of the Rugby League Hall-of-Fame. In late 1990 he took over as Hull's coach-manager and steered his side to success in the 1991 Premiership.

MIKE CLEARY

Eight Tests for Australia (1962–65). Also played 25 minor matches for Australia on one Kangaroo tour (1963–64) and two New Zealand tours (1965 and 1969).

Mike Cleary is one of a select few men to represent Australia in three sports. He played six Rugby Union internationals in 1961 (against Fiji, South Africa and France). The following year, he represented Australia in the Commonwealth Games in Perth and won a bronze medal in the 100 yards sprint. After he turned professional, he played Tests against the three major Rugby League nations (one against Britain, three against New Zealand and four against France).

Cleary made three overseas tours, and although he played only eight Tests, it must be noted in his defence that he was playing in a vintage period for wingers, with such great names as Ken Irvine, Peter Dimond, Eddie Lumsden and Johnny King appearing on the playing fields at the same time as Cleary.

On the club scene, Cleary regularly topped the try-scoring lists for South Sydney. He was a member of three of Souths' Premiership-winning combinations (1967, 1968 and 1970). After he retired as a player, Cleary turned his talents to civic affairs. He was elected to the NSW Parliament and, in the early 1980s served as Minister of Sport in the Labor Government of the day.

GORDON CLIFFORD

Eight Tests for Australia (1956–58). Also played eight minor games for Australia on one Kangaroo tour (1956–57).

Gordon Clifford will forever be remembered as the man who brought an end to the Test career of Clive Churchill, the man they dubbed 'The Little

Master'. Churchill had played a record 34 Tests for Australia when he lost his fullback spot to 'Punchy' Clifford on the 1956–57 Kangaroo tour of Britain and France.

Churchill played the first two internationals on tour, before being dumped for the consistent, goal-kicking Clifford. Indeed, some critics had expected the fall even sooner. On the eve of Churchill's last Test, Clifford had turned in a superlative performance against Huddersfield, which prompted the famous Harry Sunderland to ponder: 'The Australian selectors must have gone home with puzzled thoughts, whether to prefer Clifford to Churchill for next Saturday's Test at Wigan. Clifford has done some great goalkicking in every match he has played'.

Clifford eventually played only eight Tests, bowing out after the 1958 series against the Englishmen. He was a stalwart for the Newtown club, playing more than 100 first-grade games for the Blues.

CLUB CHAMPIONSHIP See *Flowers Memorial Pennant*

ARTHUR CLUES⎯⎯⎯⎯⎯⎯⎯⎯⎯⎯⎯⎯⎯⎯⎯⎯⎯⎯⎯⎯⎯⎯⎯⎯

Three Tests for Australia (1946). Also played 14 internationals for Other Nationalities in Britain and France.

Arthur Clues had few peers in forward play. He was a constructive second-rower, achieving fame first as an Australian international (he played in all three Tests against the touring British Lions in 1946) and then as a grand clubman for the English team, Leeds. Many English critics rate him as the greatest second-rower of all time.

Clues played first-grade Rugby Union for Parramatta at the age of 17. He switched codes to join Western Suburbs in 1943 and was chosen for City Seconds the same year. By 1946 he was universally regarded as Australia's top second-rower. The tough but creative forward was the first Australian to join a British club after World War II and many Australian fans were angry about his departure, but the money in Britain was too good to refuse. He made one Challenge Cup Final appearance, at Wembley Stadium in 1947, however for Clues and Leeds it wasn't a happy day. Leeds was beaten 8–4 by Bradford Northern.

During his stay at Leeds, Clues was chosen 14 times to play for Other Nationalities in the International Championship. In these matches he formed a devastating second-row partnership with fellow-Australian Harry Bath, who played for Warrington. In 1954, after a dispute with Leeds, Clues transferred to Hunslet for a final three seasons before retirement. Unlike most Australian footballers he never returned home, preferring instead to open a sports store in Leeds after he hung up his boots.

BRADLEY CLYDE⎯⎯⎯⎯⎯⎯⎯⎯⎯⎯⎯⎯⎯⎯⎯⎯⎯⎯⎯⎯⎯⎯⎯

Eight Tests for Australia (1989–91). Also played three minor games for Australia on one New Zealand tour (1989) and on Papua New Guinea tour (1991).

Canberra scouts were well aware of Bradley Clyde's talents from an early age. He was playing with the local side Belconnen United, from where he gained selection in the NSW Under-16 side and the Australian Schoolboys Test team in 1986, and there was no way he was going to slip through their net. The tall, rangy youngster, who was equally at home as lock or in the second-row, joined the Raiders the following year, but he was still nursed along before making his first grade debut as an 18–year-old in 1988. There was no looking back. In 1989, he was sensational, playing for City Origin and New South Wales in the State-of-Origin clashes, before being chosen to tour New Zealand with the Australian line-up.

He played in all three Tests against the Kiwis. In the third encounter he turned in a blinder, topping the tackle count with 27 defensive hits, scoring the try which broke a second-half deadlock and narrowly missing two others. He was a unanimous choice as Man-of-the-Match.

Clyde also played a major role in the Raiders march towards their first Premiership, and his display in the grand final against Balmain earned him the Clive Churchill Medal as Man-of-the-Match. For his efforts in 1989 he also won the Dally M award as the best lock in the Premiership competition. The young champion was in great form the following year, with prospects of a Kangaroo tour, but midway through the season, on the eve of the Test against France, he suffered a crippling knee injury. Surgery meant that Clyde missed the remainder of the season, the Kangaroo tour and the first few weeks of the 1991 football year.

But once back in action there was no stopping him. He played all three Tests against New Zealand and was a vital cog in Canberra's late push to the grand final. Although the Raiders were beaten by Penrith, Clyde was in devastating form, taking out his second Clive-Churchill Medal in as many grand finals. The Australian Rugby League gave an indication of their future plans for Clyde when they named him vice-captain to Mal Meninga in the Australian squad which made an end-of-season tour of Papua New Guinea. Clyde did not disappoint them and was chosen as the official Man-of-the-Tour.

COACH-OF-THE-YEAR

For several seasons in the 1970s and 1980s there was a universally recognised award for the Coach-of-the-Year in the Sydney Premiership. At first he was chosen by journalists but later it was a vote of all first-grade coaches which decided the issue. Eventually however, arguments about the merits of the winners forced the sponsors to scrap the award.

The honour had been instituted in 1971 and the first winner was the former Australian captain Ian Walsh, who steered Parramatta from the wooden spoon (with a mere four wins in 1970) to the semi-finals, in just 12 months. Jack Gibson, the man with the magic touch, won three awards—by lifting Newtown (1973) and Eastern Suburbs (1975) to among the Premiership elite and for steering Parramatta to its second title (1982). In 1983, Eastern Suburbs mentor Laurie Freier created history by winning the award in his first year as a first-grade coach. His efforts were equalled by George Piggins, who was Coach-of-the-Year in 1986, his first year at the helm of South Sydney.

WINNERS OF THE COACH-OF-THE-YEAR TROPHY

Year	Coach	Club
1971	Ian Walsh	Parramatta
1972	Ron Willey	Manly-Warringah
1973	Jack Gibson	Newtown
1974	Don Parish	Western Suburbs
1975	Jack Gibson	Eastern Suburbs
1976	Terry Fearnley	Parramatta
1977	Harry Bath	St George
1978	Roy Masters	Western Suburbs
1979	Ted Glossop	Canterbury-Bankstown
1980	Ted Glossop	Canterbury-Bankstown
1981	Warren Ryan	Newtown
1982	Jack Gibson	Parramatta
1983	Laurie Freier	Eastern Suburbs
1984	Warren Ryan	Canterbury-Bankstown
1985	Roy Masters	St George
1986	George Piggins	South Sydney
1987	Arthur Beetson	Eastern Suburbs

EDDIE COLLINS

Played nine minor matches for Australia on one Kangaroo tour (1937–38) and one New Zealand tour (1935).

Lock-forward Eddie 'Babe' Collins did not play for Australia in Test matches. He had the misfortune to be playing at the same time as Wally Prigg, who held a mortgage on the lock spot in the international pack. However the fine play by Collins was rewarded by a visit to New Zealand in 1935 and a Kangaroo tour of England and France two years later.

Collins was renowned for his pace in the open and his devastating cover defence (especially around the base of the scrum). For almost a decade from 1932 he was a regular in the Queensland representative line-up. He is also remembered for some fine club displays, including two great tries in the last 15 minutes to give Northern Suburbs a 17–11 win over Brothers in the 1940 Brisbane Premiership final.

COLTS

Several times touring sides have played matches against NSW or Sydney Colts' teams and once a Colts v Other Nationalities clash was scheduled as the curtain-raiser to a Test match. For some of the young stars, the occasion proved to be too much, but many others went on to become all-time greats.

After the 1958 clash, British Test lock-forward Vince Karalius took his opposing lock aside and gave him his jersey. 'This is your first international jumper, son. But you'll earn many more in your own right,' said Karalius. How true—the youngster was Johnny Raper, destined to become possibly Australia's greatest-ever lock.

Playing with Raper that day were five others who would wear the green and gold for Australia—fullback Don Parish, winger Eddie Lumsden, halfback Bobby Bugden and forwards Brian Hambly and Ian Walsh. Eight of the 1964 side which beat France 39–15 also later played for Australia—Ron Coote, Bob McCarthy, Jim Morgan, Allan Thompson, John O'Neill, Brian Moore, Ron Saddler and Nick Yakich. Mark Harris had a horror game against the 1970 British tourists. However it did not stop him from earning his first Australian jumper by the end of that year, in the World Cup in England.

How the Colts' Teams have fared

Year	Opponents	For	Against
1958	Great Britain	11	19
1964	France	35	15
	Other Nationalities	25	16
1970	Great Britain	7	26

COMMONWEALTH BANK CUP

The Commonwealth Bank Cup is the major knockout competition for Australian schoolboy Rugby League teams. It replaced the Amco Shield in 1980 after that competition's sponsor quit football. Some 350 teams take part in the qualifying rounds with the later matches televised nationally.

The Amco Shield had its beginnings in 1975. That year saw Fairfield Patrician Brothers down Blacktown High School 16–8 in the final. Australian Rugby League president Kevin Humphreys said of the match: 'It was the greatest game of pure Rugby League I have ever seen. It did not have the stirring patriotism of a Test match or the intense excitement of a grand final, but the football of both sides showed Rugby League as it should be played'.

Results of the competitions have shown the strength of Rugby League in the west of Sydney—with teams from that area dominating play. The games have unearthed some great stars too. Future Test halfback Peter Sterling was one of the prominent players in the Fairfield Patrician Brothers lineup which won in 1978. Ben Elias, of Holy Cross, Ryde, was named Player-of-the-Series in both 1980 and 1981 and he went on to play for Australia. So, too, did Paul Langmack (Player-of-the-Series, 1982) and Greg Alexander (Player-of-the-Series 1983).

In an interesting aftermath of their schoolboy play, two Players-of-the-Series, a decade apart but both from St Gregory's, Campbelltown, Ivan Henjak (1980) and Jason Taylor (1989), ended up as Western Suburbs' first-grade halfback combination during the 1990 season.

WINNERS OF THE COMMONWEALTH BANK CUP
(and Amco Shield)

Year	Winner
1975	Fairfield Patrician Brothers
1976	Blacktown High
1977	Ashcroft High
1978	Fairfield Patrician Brothers
1979	St Gregory's, Campbelltown
1980	St Gregory's, Campbelltown
1981	Holy Cross, Ryde
1982	Fairfield Patrician Brothers
1983	Fairfield Patrician Brothers
1984	St Gregory's, Campbelltown
1985	Ashcroft High
1986	St Gregory's, Campbelltown
1987	Fairfield Patrician Brothers
1988	Parramatta Marist Brothers
1989	St Gregory's, Campbelltown
1990	St Gregory's, Campbelltown
1991	St Gregory's, Campbelltown

COMMONWEALTH BANK MAN-OF-THE-SERIES

Year	Result	School
1975	No Award	
1976	Steve White	Blacktown High

Continued

COMMONWEALTH BANK MAN-OF-THE-SERIES *continued*

Year	Result	School
1977	Alan Emery	Ashcroft High
1978	Peter Sterling	Fairfield Patrician Brothers
1979	Ivan Henjak	St Gregory's, Campbelltown
1980	Ben Elias	Holy Cross, Ryde
1981	Ben Elias	Holy Cross, Ryde
1982	Paul Langmack	Fairfield Patrician Brothers
1983	Greg Alexander	Fairfield Patrician Brothers
1984	Paul Osborne	Lewisham Christian Brothers
1985	David Rowles	Ashcroft High
1986	Damian Kenniff	St Gregory's, Campbelltown
1987	David Danes	Fairfield Patrician Brothers
1988	David Bayssari	Parramatta Marist Brothers
1989	Jason Taylor	St Gregory's, Campbelltown
1990	Tony Dicinoski	St John's, Woodlawn
1991	Damian Chapman	St Gregory's, Campbelltown

GREG CONESCU

Nine Tests for Australia (1984–88). Also played in Bicentennial international against the Rest-of-the-World (1988) and in 11 minor games on one Kangaroo tour (1982) and one New Zealand tour (1985).

Hooker Greg Conescu was one of the more notable discoveries of the famous Kiwi coach, Graham Lowe. Conescu, affectionately dubbed 'Turtle', was one of the young stars at Brisbane Norths moulded by Lowe into a Premiership-winning side in 1980. Conescu went on to become one of the stalwarts of Australian Rugby League in the 1980s. He made his State-of-Origin debut in 1981 and, although overlooked for the Queensland sides the following year, was one of three hookers who toured Britain and France with the Kangaroos at the end of that season.

Conescu made his Test debut, against the touring 1984 British Lions, while playing with Gladstone Brothers in the Queensland country. He toured New Zealand the following year, but was then overlooked by the national selectors until he teamed up with the Brisbane Broncos.

In 1988, he played all four Tests involving Australia (three against Britain, including the historic 100th Ashes encounter, and one versus Papua New Guinea), as well as the Bicentennial international against the Rest-of-the-World. However his world came crashing down at the start of the 1989 season, when Broncos coach Wayne Bennett passed him over in favour of another hooker destined to play for Australia, Kerrod Walters. Unwanted by other clubs because of the large transfer fee automatically imposed on internationals, Conescu called it a day.

MEL COOKE

Twenty Tests for New Zealand (1959–1964). Also played three matches in one World Cup (1960) and 29 minor games on three Kiwi tours (1959 and 1963 to Australia and 1961–62 to Britain and France).

Mel Cooke was one of the finest locks New Zealand ever produced. He played Rugby Union at school, as a halfback and five-eighth, but switched into the forwards once he was in the League ranks.

Cooke had his first taste of representative football in 1959, turning out for South Island against North Island and later for New Zealand on the tour of Australia. He was to play 52 matches for his country between then and 1964. His finest hour came in 1962 when he led New Zealand to upset wins over the touring British Lions, fresh from a resounding triumph over Australia. Cooke spent his final footballing years in Australia where he coached the Canberra side in a southern NSW competition. It was while playing there that Cooke made a brief return to the international scene, as captain of the Monaro representative team soundly beaten by the 1966 Lions.

LIONEL COOPER

Three Tests for Australia (1946).

A big, tough, bullocking winger, Lionel Cooper was a sensation on both sides of the world. Some of his records still stand almost four decades after his retirement. However, but for the eagle-eye of Test forward Ray Stehr who saw him playing Australian Rules in Darwin during World War II, Cooper may never have played the 13-a-side game.

In 1945, Cooper joined Eastern Suburbs, the Sydney club for which Stehr had played, and after just six games was chosen for New South Wales. The following year he played in all three Tests against the touring Great Britain side In his debut he scored a try 10 minutes before the end to help Australia snatch an 8-all draw. For his efforts he was named NSW Player-of-the-Year.

Lionel Cooper in action during a 1950 match at Odsal Stadium for the English club Huddersfield

Cooper went to England in 1947 to join the powerful Huddersfield line-up. He was a bargain buy, costing the Yorkshire club just £1000. With Huddersfield he set a host of try and point-scoring records. During his eight seasons in England he scored 432 tries, an average of 54 each year. His best season was 1951–52, when he led Britain's try-scorers with a bag of 71 three-pointers. Once during that season, against Keighley, Cooper went over for no fewer than 10 tries and kicking a couple of goals, too, brought his match tally to 34 points. The 10 tries remain a British record for a Championship game.

That season saw Cooper figure prominently on the international scene. In November he captained Other Nationalities in what has become known as 'The Battle of the Boulevard' against France at Hull. In a vicious match there were a host of players injured. One of them, fellow-Australian Arthur Clues, was hospitalised. However, for Cooper, the match was a triumph. He scored three tries, helping Other Nationalities to a 17–14 victory. It was France's only defeat in that year's International Championship. Two months later, in a London match, Cooper skippered a British Empire XIII to a crushing 26–2 victory over the touring New Zealand Kiwis.

Cooper was Huddersfield's reserve kicker, a job he did well in the 1953 Challenge Cup Final at Wembley, when he helped the club to a 15–10 success over St Helens. Cooper also appeared in two Championship Finals, with Huddersfield beating Warrington in 1949, but going down to Wigan the following year.

Cooper is remembered with affection at Huddersfield. Fans still point to 'Cooper's Corner' at the Fartown ground. It's the corner in which he scored most of his tries.

RON COOTE

Thirteen Tests for Australia (1967–74). Also played in 10 matches in two World Cups (1968 and 1970) and one World Championship (1975), one minor international (1970) and 16 minor games on one Kangaroo tour (1967–68) and one New Zealand tour (1969).

Ron Coote had to play out of position in his early Test matches. He was normally a lock-forward, a spot firmly held by the immortal Johnny Raper. However such was Coote's brilliance that a position had to be found for him in the Australian pack and the selectors switched him to the second-row. When Raper bowed out of representative football after the 1968 World Cup, Coote moved back to the position in which he played best.

Coote was still a teenager when he first made the South Sydney first grade team in 1964. It was the start of a great career. In his second season, he forced his way into the NSW side and only a broken jaw kept him out of the Australian team which toured New Zealand. A chipped knee-cap the following season also crushed his representative hopes. However in 1967, Coote was one of the first chosen for the Kangaroo tour of Britain and France. He missed the First Test, but was in the Australian line-up for the other five.

Next year he was one of the stars of the unbeaten Australian side in the World Cup, scoring five tries in just four matches. Two years later

Ron Coote in a typical break for Eastern Suburbs

he was captain of the squad which retained the Cup in England against all odds. Personal commitments forced him out of representative football for a couple of seasons, but in the mid-1970s, he returned to the Test arena and made his farewell to international football in the 1975 World Championship matches.

Coote continued playing club football with Eastern Suburbs until 1979. All told, he played 157 matches for Souths and a further 100 for Easts. He was a member of six Premiership-winning sides (with Souths in 1967, 1968, 1970 and 1971; with Easts in 1974 and 1975).

Father JOHN COOTES

Four Tests for Australia (1969–70). Also played three World Cup matches (1970), one minor international (1970) and four minor games on one New Zealand tour (1969) and one World Cup tour (1970).

Father John Cootes is the only clergyman to have played international football for Australia. The Roman Catholic priest from Newcastle turned out as a centre in two Test series and a World Cup competition in a period of just over 12 months.

He made his Test debut on the 1969 tour of New Zealand, retained his international jersey when the British Lions visited Australia the following year and then went to England with the victorious 1970 Australian World Cup squad. After the Cup was won, he also played in an international against France. Cootes then faded from the representative scene. He later quit the priesthood and worked for a time as a television sports reporter before setting up a furniture business.

CORBETT Family

No family can compare with the Corbetts when it comes to reporting Rugby League. For more than 50 years after the start of Rugby League in Australia there was always at least one member of the family covering the game for a major Sydney newspaper.

The first was WF Corbett, who joined *The Referee* in 1888, where in the ensuing years he reported boxing, swimming, bowls and Rugby. In 1913 he switched to the Sydney *Sun*, where one of his five sons, Claude, had already established himself. Claude was to become, arguably, Australia's most famous Rugby League writer. He covered four Kangaroo tours (the first in 1911) and, in his time, was the only newspaperman to receive life-membership of the NSW Rugby League.

For two seasons in the 1930s, the Corbetts achieved a distinction unique in the world of journalism. All four Sydney Rugby League matches were covered for *The Sun* by a member of the family—Claude, his brothers W F (Bill) and Jack, and his son Mac.

Claude died of cancer in 1944. Brother Bill continued writing until his death in 1970. In the meantime, Bill had donated the Claude Corbett Memorial Trophy in honour of his brother.

WINNERS OF THE CLAUDE CORBETT MEMORIAL TROPHY

(Awarded to the captain of the winning side in the Third Test of each Anglo-Australian series in Australia)

Year	Winner
1946	Gus Risman (GB)
1950	Clive Churchill (Aust)
1954	Clive Churchill (Aust)
1958	Alan Prescott (GB)
1962	Arthur Summons (Aust)
1966	Ian Walsh (Aust)
1970	Frank Myler (GB)
1974	Graeme Langlands (Aust)
1979	George Peponis (Aust)
1984	Wally Lewis (Aust)
1988	Ellery Hanley (GB)

In the Second Test at Edinburgh, on the 1911–12 Kangaroo tour, Claude Corbett served as touch judge (the only time in the history a newspaperman has filled this role). Early in the game Arthur 'Boller' Francis took a kick for goal. Corbett raised his flag, but the British judge waved it away. The referee spoke to both men before disallowing the goal. It was a crucial decision. Had it been allowed, Australia would have won 13–11. Instead, the game was an 11–all draw.

COUNTRY RUGBY LEAGUE

From humble beginnings, in which neither officials nor players were really conversant with the rules, Rugby League in the country areas of New South Wales has grown into a major sport involving more than 20 000 players and 200 clubs.

Although Tweed Heads' Seagulls became the first registered provincial Rugby League club in Australia in 1909 and Newcastle hosted a match against the touring Great Britain side the following year, the first real country football had its foundation at a meeting in the central western town of Orange on 10 April, 1912. It was at this meeting that the Central Western Rugby League was formed. The controlling authorities in Sydney donated a Challenge Cup for play in the district. They also sent a rule book, to clear up some of the finer points of the game.

The first club to apply for affiliation was from the tiny village of Glenbrook, but the first Cup match took place between two teams from Orange—Waratahs and Our Boys. Two years later the code spread to the north coast and then throughout the State. Sydney clubs helped in the initial propagation of the game. Glebe and Eastern Suburbs played an exhibition in the west in 1912 and South Sydney travelled north to Lismore in 1914 to play a team representing the fledgling Richmond River zone.

The country areas are divided into several Divisions, each with a number of so-called 'Groups' conducting different competitions. These Divisions get an occasion crack at international touring sides.

The Country Rugby League introduced a Divisional Championship in 1960 and Riverina took out the first title. The 1964 winner, Newcastle, went one better by following up with a State Cup triumph in which it beat four Sydney sides, including the great St George combination. Newcastle has since returned to the Sydney Premiership. (It was a founding member, playing in 1908 and 1909.) Canberra (the centre of the old Monaro Division) and Illawarra have also graduated from the country to the race for the Sydney Premiership.

Each year Country representative teams take on sides chosen from the ranks of the Sydney clubs. Over the years, the boys from the bush have only managed to win an occasional game. The most notable of these successes came in 1961 and 1962 when Country was coached by former British captain Phil Jackson and led by Tony Paskins who had made a name for himself in club games both in Sydney and England.

Because of the usual one-sided matches, the format was changed in 1984 with Country being allowed to select eight country-born players from the Sydney competition to bolster its ranks however City still won 38–11. It was closer the following year, 18–12, but in 1986 the City boys won easily, 34–18. It was then decided to make it a Place-of-Origin clash. The 1987 City side raced to a 29–6 lead at half-time. Country, in a do-or-die effort, fought back to eventually go down 30–22. Under lights for the first time, at the Sydney Football Stadium in 1988, City snatched a last-minute 20–18 victory. It was just as close in 1990 when City had to survive a last-minute conversion attempt by Country winger Ricky Walford, which, had it been successful, would have tied the match 28–all.

One can only wonder how the annual clashes would have finished if they had always been Place-of-Origin. A number of great post-World War II Test captains to have come from the country but who played for City include Clive Churchill, Ian Walsh, Graeme Langlands and Bob Fulton. Few players now make their representative debuts from the country—Sydney talent scouts quickly snapping up every exciting youngster. The last to be capped for the first time for Australia while playing in the country was

Steve 'Slippery' Morris from Dapto, who played against New Zealand in 1978.

Country Championship Honour Roll

Year	Winner	Year	Winner
1960	Riverina	1976	Illawarra
1961	Western Division	1977	Monaro
1962	Western Division	1978	Illawarra
1963	Western Division	1979	Newcastle
1964	Newcastle	1980	Southern Division
1965	Newcastle	1981	Newcastle
1966	Newcastle	1982	Riverina
1967	Northern Division	1983	Southern Division
1968	Newcastle	1984	Newcastle
1969	Newcastle	1985	Riverina
1970	Northern Division	1986	Western Division
1971	Illawarra	1987	Northern Rivers
1972	Illawarra	1988	Riverina
1973	Newcastle	1989	Northern Division
1974	Illawarra	1990	Northern Rivers
1975	Riverina	1991	Newcastle

Country Players-of-the-Year

Year	Winner	Year	Winner
1965	Laurie Moraschi (Griffith)	1979	Pat Smith (Maitland)
1966	Terry Pannowitz (Maitland)	1980	Perry Haddock (Erina)
1967	Allan Thomson (Lakes United)	1981	Terry Regan (Cessnock)
1968	Allan Thomson (Lakes United)	1982	Willy Tarry (Cessnock)
1969	John Cootes (Newcastle Western Suburbs)	1983	Paul Field (Cootamundra)
1970	Les Hutchings (Condobolin)	1984	Ross Gibson (Wyong)
1971	Dick Jeffery (Glen Innes)	1985	Peter Hawthorne (Griffith)
1972	Brian Burke (Maitland)	1986	Neil Moy (Parkes)
1973	John Donnelly (Gunnedah)	1987	Steve Walters (Lakes United)
1974	Mick Cronin (Gerringong)	1988	Chris Cumming (Aberdeen)
1975	Steve Hewson (Queanbeyan United)	1989	Mark Ryan (Moree)
1976	Peter Kennedy (Forbes)	1990	Paul Danes (Wagga Magpies)
1977	Barry Pearson (Illawarra Western Suburbs)	1991	Richard Jones (South Newcastle)
1978	Ray Brown (Griffith Waratahs)		

NSW Country v International Touring Sides

Year	Opponents	Venue	For	Against
1948	Great Britain	Wollongong (10 000)	16	30
1953	American Allstars	Wollongong (11 787)	35	9
1972	New Zealand	Queanbeyan (4000)	26	10
1988	XIII Catalan	Wyong (1000)	11	0

NSW COUNTRY TOURS OF NEW ZEALAND

1965

NSW Country's first tour of New Zealand was a lightning affair, with only two games being played, on the one weekend. The visitors, spearheaded by former Australian captain-coach Arthur Summons, overwhelmed the fine Canterbury provincial side but, backing up the next day, could not contain a powerful Auckland combination which had downed Test sides in previous years.

Record in New Zealand

Played 2, Won 1, Lost 1, Points for 37, Points against 28

Match Results

Opponents	Venue	For	Against
Canterbury	Christchurch	32	10
Auckland	Auckland	5	18

Individual Point-scorers

	Tries	Goals	Points
B Carlin	–	5	10
L Moraschi	2	–	6
B Beath	2	–	6
R Weir	2	–	6
R Horne	1	–	3
A Summons	1	–	3
T Pannowitz	1	–	3

1966

The NSW Country side played three matches in four days on its 1966 tour. As in the inaugural visit, the only side to beat the tourists was Auckland, which led 5–2 at half-time and only took command in the last 10 minutes when it piled on four tries. Stars of the tour were 18–year-old five-eighth Gary Banks and second-rower Allan Thomson, both of whom went on to play for Australia.

Record in New Zealand

Played 3, Won 2, Lost 1, Points for 36, Points against 35

Other matches

Opponents	Venue	For	Against
Northland	Whangarei	13	0
Auckland	Auckland	2	23
Canterbury	Christchurch	21	12

Individual Point-scorers

	Tries	Goals	Points
G Moran	–	6	12
N Nott	1	3	9
R Horne	2	–	6
T Pannowitz	1	–	3
L Hanigan	1	–	3
G Banks	1	–	3

1970

The immortal Johnny Raper led the Country side on its third visit to New Zealand. He was injured in the second of the three matches, a tough encounter with Auckland. In that match the Country players' performance slipped once they lost their skipper and inspiration and they went down 20–12.

Record in New Zealand

Played 3, Won 2, Lost 1, Points for 72, Points against 43

Match Results

Opponents	Venue	For	Against
Canterbury	Christchurch	38	12
Auckland	Auckland	12	20
Waikato	Huntly	22	11

Individual point-scorers

	Tries	Goals	Points
D Mount	1	11	25
T Pannowitz	3	1	11
L Simmons	3	–	9
T Scurfield	2	–	6
D Crampton	–	3	6
D Grimmond	1	–	3
G Lye	1	–	3
L Hutchings	1	–	3
K Brown	1	–	3
H Cameron	1	–	3

1983

Country made a lightning trip to New Zealand in 1983 for just one match—against South Island. Former Sydney star Robert 'Rocky' Laurie was captain of the side and, with three tries in one eight-minute period, starred in the 52–12 victory. Man-of-the-Match was second-rower Paul Field of Cootamundra.

Match Result

Opponents	Venue (Attendance)	For	Against
South Island	Christchurch (3000)	52	12

Individual point scorers

	Tries	Goals	Points
R Laurie	3	–	12
N Elwin	–	5	10
T McCartney	2	–	8
P Ford	2	–	8
K Kearney	1	1	6
R French	1	–	4
N Mitchell	1	–	4

City v Country

1928	Country	35	City	34
1929	City	16	Country	5
1930	Country	35	City	26
1931	City	17	Country	15
1932	City	27	Country	15
1933	City	47	Country	6
	City	17	Country	17
1934	City	28	Country	14
	City	32	Country	29
1935	City	20	Country	5
1936	City	41	Country	8
1937	Country	20	City	12
	Country	15	City	5
1938	City	42	Country	12
1939	City	38	Country	17
1940	City	28	Country	10
1941	City	44	Country	21
1942	Country	14	City	11
1943	City	37	Country	25
1944	City	17	Country	10
1945	City	41	Country	12
1946	City	31	Country	10
1947	City	33	Country	10
1948	City	28	Country	13
	City	6	Country	5
1949	City	23	Country	2
1950	City	51	Country	13
1951	City	24	Country	6
1952	City	23	Country	21
1953	Country	28	City	27

▶

City v Country

Year	Winner	Score	Opponent	Score
1954	City	50	Country	9
1955	City	31	Country	18
1956	City	32	Country	17
1957	City	53	Country	2
1958	City	55	Country	14
1959	City	37	Country	7
1960	City	20	Country	2
1961	Country	19	City	5
1962	Country	18	City	8
1963	City	35	Country	11
1964	City	27	Country	4
1965	City	32	Country	2
1966	City	18	Country	17
	Country	16	City	12
1967	City	18	Country	14
1968	City	34	Country	14
1969	City	27	Country	20
1970	City	22	Country	18
1971	City	17	Country	0
1972	City	35	Country	8
1973	City	33	Country	17
1974	City	23	Country	0
1975	Country	19	City	9
1976	City	47	Country	0
1977	City	36	Country	0
1978	City	30	Country	13
1979	City	29	Country	0
1980	City	55	Country	2
1981	City	38	Country	7
1982	City	47	Country	3
1983	City	30	Country	14
1984	City	38	Country	12
1985	City	18	Country	12
1986	City	34	Country	18
1987	City	30	Country	22
1988	City	20	Country	18
1989	City	16	Country	8
1990	City	28	Country	26
1991	City	22	Country	12

City v Country Records

Most points: 115 by Mick Cronin (3 tries, 41 goals, 91 points for City; 2 tries, 9 goals, 24 points for Country)
Most games: 11 by Mick Cronin (6 for City; 5 for Country)
Most points in a game: 25 (1 try, 11 goals) by Mick Cronin, for City in 1980
Most goals in a game: 12 by Noel Pidding, for City in 1950
Biggest win: 55–2, by City in 1980

COURTNEY GOODWILL TROPHY

The Courtney Goodwill Trophy has been in existence for more than half-a-century, but during most of this time only the keenest of fans were aware of its existence—even many officials were in the dark and only shrugged their shoulders when asked about it. The 'mystery' trophy was donated in 1936 to serve as a symbol of world Rugby League supremacy. Unfortunately the best side has not always held it and for a time it became a somewhat devalued honour.

The trophy was given by Christchurch (New Zealand) businessman Roy Courtney in memory of servicemen, including his brother, who died in World War I. Not only is it tall (1.2 metres), it is also heavy, weighing 152kg. At the time it was donated it was worth an incredible (for those days) £1000. Figures on the base of the trophy depict famous personalities from each of the four early Rugby League nations—Dally Messenger (Australia), Jim Lomas (Great Britain), AH Baskerville (New Zealand) and Jean Galia (France).

Initially, the trophy could only be won or lost in a Test series. The first recipient was Great Britain, who eventually lost it in the 1950 series to Australia, who, in turn, handed it over to France 12 months later. Over the next eight years each nation held it at least once.

In 1960, officials decided to give the trophy to the country which had the best Test record over a five-year period. Under this system, New Zealand, in 1965, became holders with a 66.7 percent success rate in 18 Tests. France, bottom in the first period, turned the tables in 1965–70, to carry off the trophy with nine wins in 14 Tests. After Australia won it for the second time under the new system, in 1985, it was decided to award the trophy to the winner of the next World Cup. Australia retained it with a 25–12 win over New Zealand in the final of the series at Auckland's Eden Park in late 1988.

HOW THE COURTNEY GOODWILL TROPHY HAS BEEN WON

(when decided in a Test series)

Year	Result				
1936	Great Britain	2	Australia		1
1936	Great Britain	2	New Zealand		1
1937	Great Britain	2	Australia		1
1946	Great Britain	2	Australia		1
1946	Great Britain	1	New Zealand		0
1947	Great Britain	3	New Zealand		0
1948	Great Britain	3	Australia		0
1950	Australia	2	Great Britain		1
1951	France	2	Australia		1
1951	New Zealand	1	France		0
1951	Great Britain	3	New Zealand		0
1952	Great Britain	2	Australia		1
1954	Australia	2	Great Britain		1
1955	France	2	Australia		1
1955	France	1	New Zealand		1
1956	Australia	2	France		0
1958	Great Britain	2	Australia		1
1958	Great Britain	1	New Zealand		1
1959	Great Britain	2	France		0
1959	Great Britain	2	Australia		1

(when decided over a five-year period)

Year	Winner	Runner-up
1965	New Zealand	Australia
1970	France	Australia
1975	Australia	Great Britain
1980	France	Australia
1985	Australia	Great Britain

(when decided in World Cup Final)

Year	Result			
1988	Australia	25	New Zealand	12

TEDDA COURTNEY

Eleven Tests for Australia (1908–11). Also played two internationals (1910) which for many years were recognised as Tests and 51 minor games on two Kangaroo tours (1908–09 and 1911–12).

There have been few players who could match the ferocious tackling of big Sydney forward Tedda Courtney. Courtney tamed many an opposition player during the early years of Rugby League. Reputations meant nothing to him as he threw himself into the rucks.

Courtney was one of the select band of Rugby Union players who backed the breakaway movement in 1907. He played in the second of the three matches in which New South Wales took on the New Zealand All Golds, and received his thanks by being awarded life membership of the NSW Rugby League the following year. He was also a part of history as a member of the Pioneers, the first Kangaroo squad to tour Britain (in 1908–09). Courtney's value to the side is evidenced by his 31 games on tour. Only three of his team-mates appeared in more matches. He was also leading try-scorer amongst the forwards, with 10 touchdowns.

Courtney appeared in five different Test series before World War I brought an end to his international career. He made a second Kangaroo tour in 1911–12, this time playing in 25 games. Courtney also made two tours of New Zealand with New South Wales sides.

The tough prop never managed a Sydney Premiership-winner's cap. He played a total of 304 matches for three clubs—Newtown, North Sydney and Western Suburbs and finished his career with Wests in 1924. In a unique feat, he played that last season in the same team as his son.

LES 'CHIC' COWIE

Six Tests for Australia (1949–53). Also played 30 minor games on one Kangaroo tour (1948–49) and two New Zealand tours (1949 and 1953).

Les 'Chic' Cowie is recognised as one of the greatest cover-defenders in the history of the game, but this talented lock-forward was also a top attacking player who had a brilliant understanding with his halves.

Cowie, a Queensland schoolboy star, joined South Sydney after his discharge from the armed forces at the end of World War II. In 11 seasons in the Sydney Premiership competition, he established himself as one of the code's finest. From 176 first-grade games he scored 65 tries—no mean feat for a modern-day lock—including four in one game, the 1956 final against Balmain. He appeared in two series against New Zealand and one against Britain. He toured with the Kangaroos in 1948–49 and was unlucky not to have been chosen for a second tour of the northern hemisphere four years later.

Cowie played for the Rabbitohs from 1947 to 1957. It was Souths' golden era, and Cowie was with them for five Premiership successes.

GARY COYNE

Two Tests for Australia (1991). Also played two minor games on one Papua New Guinea tour (1991).

Gary Coyne raced his way into the record books in 1991, when he became only the second forward in the history of the game to score four tries in one of the end-of-season play-off matches. Coyne went over four times in Canberra's 34–26 success over Manly-Warringah in the 1991 minor semi-final. The only other player to have achieved this feat was Souths' Chic Cowie in the 1956 final.

The big effort could not have come at a better time. When the Test selectors sat down two weeks later to choose a side to tour Papua New

Guinea, the 29-year-old Coyne's name was there. It made up for the disappointment of missing out on a Kangaroo spot 12 months earlier.

Coyne began his career with the Booval Swifts in the Ipswich competition before joining Wynnum-Manly in Brisbane, under coach Wayne Bennett. He was a member of the Wynnum side which won the 1984 Brisbane Premiership, Queensland State League and Woolies' Trophy. They almost repeated the feat the following year, winning the latter two but going down 10–8 to Souths in the Premiership grand final.

After an off-season stint with Avignon in France, Coyne joined the Canberra Raiders in 1986. He was one of their stalwarts, recognised for his jarring cover defence. With Canberra he reached the grand final four times in five years between 1987 and 1991, collecting his winner's medal in 1989 and 1990. By 1992, he had played nine State-of-Origin matches (1981–91).

BOB CRAIG

Seven Tests for Australia (1910–14). Also played one international (1910) which for many years was recognised as a Test and 28 minor games on one Kangaroo tour (1911–12).

Bob Craig was one of the greatest all-round sportsmen Australia has known. He was a brilliant swimmer (winning eight NSW freestyle championships between 1899 and 1906), a fine water polo player (appearing in four Sydney Premiership-winning sides) and a real Soccer star (helping Balmain to win the State's top event, the Gardiners' Cup, in 1905). However it was as a second-row forward on the Rugby field that Craig really excelled. As an amateur he was one of the successes of the 1908–09 Wallabies side which toured Britain and North America. On this tour he played in the Australian team which won the gold medal for Rugby at the 1908 London Olympic Games.

When he returned home, Craig was one of the 14 Wallabies to switch en masse to Rugby League and he soon established himself in the professional code. He played in three Test series against Britain, including one during the 1911–12 Kangaroo tour. On that visit Craig played in 31 of the 36 games (two more than any of his 27 team-mates). He also appeared in all three Tests, helping Australia bring back the Ashes. So impressed were they with Craig that the directors of Aston Villa Soccer club tried, in vain, to persuade him to stay in England and play for the famous team.

As well as his Kangaroo tour, Craig also visited New Zealand in 1913 with the New South Wales side. In club football, Craig was an important cog in the Balmain machine which powered its way to four Sydney Premierships (1915, 1916, 1917 and 1919) and a City Cup (1917).

JIMMY CRAIG

Seven Tests for Australia (1921–28). Also played 23 minor games on one Kangaroo tour (1921–22).

Jimmy Craig was the greatest all-round footballer ever to grace a Rugby League field in Australia, if not the world. Respected Rugby League historian George Crawford said of him: 'He was the master strategist. He could fit in anywhere, play in any position. There was none better as far as all-round play was concerned.' Indeed, Craig played in three different positions in Tests against Britain—halfback, centre and fullback—and he was equally at home as a five-eighth or on the wing.

Craig began his football in Balmain, working his way up through the local juniors, until called into the first-grade side in 1914. During the next few years he was one of the mainstays of a Balmain combination which won five Premierships in just six seasons (1915, 1916, 1917, 1919 and 1920). His first international was in 1921, on the Kangaroo tour of Britain, as a centre. Next year, on a tour of New Zealand with the New South Wales side, Craig added another position to his repertoire by packing down as a hooker (and winning an even share of the ball).

He left Balmain in 1922 and moved to Queensland where he was to form a formidable centre partnership with the great Tommy Gorman. That first year in Queensland, Craig, who was playing in Ipswich, captained the State side in its first-ever win over New South Wales (after 22 successive losses). He captained Australia in all three Tests against the touring 1924 British side. He was also to play all three internationals against the next tourists, four years later, this time under the captaincy of Gorman.

The great all-rounder returned to Sydney in 1930 and, as captain-coach, led Western Suburbs to its first Premiership, scoring a try and kicking two goals in Wests' 27–2 grand final win over St George.

CRAVEN MILD CUP see *Extinct Competitions*

GEORGE CRAWFORD————————————————————

George Crawford was not only one of Australia's most respected Rugby League journalists, but he was acclaimed as one of the country's top sporting historians. He watched Rugby League for more than six decades and covered all the top games for the Sydney papers the *Daily Telegraph* and *Sunday Telegraph* from the 1946 Lions tour of Australia, until poor eyesight forced him to quit reporting after the famous 1965 Sydney Premiership grand final between St George and South Sydney.

Crawford continued to write, until 1990, a twice-weekly column, 'Sportifacts', which detailed interesting records and incidents from all sports. It was so popular that readers' queries used to fill bags of mail.

Crawford's Greatest Teams
(1930–1990)

Australia	The World
Clive Churchill	Clive Churchill (Aust)
Brian Bevan	Brian Bevan (Aust)
Reg Gasnier	Reg Gasnier (Aust)
Dave Brown	Stanley Brogden (GB)
Ken Irvine	Billy Boston (GB)
Vic Hey	Vic Hey (Aust)
Peter Sterling	Alex Murphy (GB)
Johnny Raper	Johnny Raper (Aust)
George Treweek	Elie Brousse (Fr)
Norm Provan	Eduoard Ponsinet (Fr)
Duncan Hall	Ken Gee (GB)
Ian Walsh	Joe Egan (GB)
Roy Bull	Brian McTigue (GB)

MICK CROCKER

Fifteen Tests for Australia (1950–55). Also played two World Cup matches (1954) and in 17 minor games on one Kangaroo tour (1952–53) and one New Zealand tour (1953).

When raw 21–year-old Mick Crocker was drafted into the Queensland side in 1949, the experts predicted a bright future. How right they were. Within a year he was in the Test side and was to remain a cornerstone of the international line-up for the next five years.

Crocker—baptised Harold but known to everyone as Mick—was a product of Brisbane Souths. After his first interstate game he was to appear in the Maroon of Queensland for 17 successive encounters with the Blues, before accepting a big offer to move south, in 1954, to join Parramatta in the Sydney competition. He made his Test debut against the 1950 British Lions and then figured in the historic clashes with the Frenchmen a year later. Crocker toured Britain and France with the 1952–53 Kangaroos, visited New Zealand in 1953 and went back to France for the inaugural World Cup in 1954.

At the end of 1954, Crocker, then 27, announced his retirement, having suffered the ignominy of playing with a Parramatta side which was constantly on the receiving end of drubbings. Friends talked him into one last fling and despite missing much of the early season through a leg injury, Crocker forced his way back into the Test side for the final two 1955 clashes with France.

MICK CRONIN

Twenty-two Tests for Australia (1973–82). Also played 11 matches in two World Championships (1975 and 1977), two minor internationals (1975 and 1978), and 23 minor games on two Kangaroo tours (1973 and 1978).

Talent scouts could never understand Mick Cronin. For years he was the most valuable Rugby League centre in the world, but he continually rejected offers of big money to play in the Sydney Premiership competition. He preferred, instead, to turn out in his home town of Gerringong on the NSW south coast. It took some smooth talking from Parramatta coach Terry Fearnley to finally make Cronin change his mind and even after the Eels signed him in 1977, he continued to live at Gerringong and travel hundreds of kilometres a week for training sessions and matches.

Cronin first made headlines when he was a surprise selection in the Australian team for the 1973 Kangaroo tour of Britain and France. It was a selection ridiculed by many leading commentators, but Cronin made them eat crow. He finished as top-scorer on the tour, with 77 points (seven tries and 28 goals) in his 12 matches. From then on he was always one of the first chosen to play for Australia. By the time he quit the international scene in 1982, he had played 35 internationals for Australia.

Cronin rewrote the record books. When he retired in 1986 he was the greatest pointscorer in the history of the Sydney Premiership (with 1 749 points). As well, he scored the most in a Sydney season (282 in 1978), the most in a calendar year (547 from 52 games in 1978), the most points by a player from any country in World Series clashes (108), the most in the world in Tests (201), the most points in a Test series (54 against Great Britain in 1979) and the most successive successful kicks for goal in top-class Rugby League (26 in 1978). The Crow, as he was affectionately known, also won an unprecedented two straight Rothmans Medals as the best and fairest player in the Sydney premiership (1977 and 1978).

In 1986 Cronin suffered an awful injury in an accidental clash with a team-mate and almost lost the sight of one eye, but he returned to finish

Mick Cronin

his playing career in glory, with the Eels' 4–2 grand final victory over Canterbury-Bankstown. In 1990, Cronin was back with Parramatta—this time as coach trying to inspire the Eels out of a period in the doldrums.

CRONULLA-SUTHERLAND

One of the younger Sydney Premiership sides, Cronulla-Sutherland overcame severe financial problems to establish itself as among the best in the competition.

For a while in the early months of 1976, it seemed the Cronulla-Sutherland side which in a few short years had made such an impact on the Sydney Rugby League scene, would fold. The club was in dire financial straits. A lot of money had been outlaid to start building a new Leagues' Club complex at Cronulla's home ground, Endeavour Field. Officials suddenly found themselves without enough money to complete the project—let alone pay players. Only emergency aid from the Government, the NSW Rugby League and fans saved Cronulla.

The club had its beginnings in 1952 when a group of players banded together and formed a junior team, Cronulla-Caringbah, to play in the St George competition. That club soon proved to be one of the best in junior ranks. Cronulla entered the Sydney Second Division (known as the Interdistrict Competition) in 1963 and, in that season reached the grand final, where it went down to Kingsford 9–7.

In 1967, under the new name Cronulla-Sutherland, the club was promoted, with Penrith, to the top Premiership competition. However the Sharks, as the team became affectionately known, showed mediocre form until they persuaded English Test star Tommy Bishop to take over the reins as captain-coach. Bishop lured his old St Helens and Great Britain team-mate Cliff Watson to Cronulla and the pair proceeded to lift the Sharks from among the also-rans to the 1973 grand final.

Their effect on the club was never more evident than in the following season. Because of an ôfficial NSW Rugby League ceiling on player payments, Bishop left to take up a player-coach job in Brisbane and Watson went to Wollongong. Almost overnight, Cronulla found itself back near the bottom of the competition table.

Cronulla then tried a variety of coaches, including the immortal Johnny Raper. It was not until 1978 however, when Raper's former boss at St George, Norm Provan took over as mentor, that the Sharks again showed any real bite. Provan lifted them to the 1978 grand final (which they lost on replay to Manly-Warringah) and the final the following year. They had a star-studded side in this period. Among the classy line-up were Australian Test representatives Steve Rogers, Greg Pierce and Steve Kneen and New Zealand's Test brothers Dane and Kurt Sorensen.

Rogers topped the Premiership pointscoring (with 194 points) when Cronulla made the semi-finals in 1981. Generally the Sharks' form over the next decade was fairly ordinary, however, under respected coach Jack Gibson they underwent a rebuilding program with the accent on youth. When Gibson handed over to Allan Fitzgibbon in 1988 they were ready to fire. They rocketed from eighth place to take out the Minor Premiership. Only inexperience told in the play-offs—with Cronulla going down in the final. The two young three-quarters, Andrew Ettingshausen and Mark McGaw, both made their Test debuts in 1988, as did veteran second-rower Gavin Miller. Miller was pipped in the voting for the Rothmans Medal by Cronulla's halfback Barry Russell.

The Sharks again made the play-offs in 1989, after beating Brisbane 38–14 in a play-off for the fifth and final spot, but they went down to the eventual Premiers, Canberra, in the elimination semi-final. That year, Miller won every major individual prize, including the Rothmans Medal and the Dally M Award. Forward Danny Stains became the latest international from the Sharks ranks when he won a spot in the Australian side which toured New Zealand in 1989.

In early 1990, Cronulla were again going well. With eight rounds left to play the Sharks were in the top five and facing, what appeared to be, a simple run home—but they lost seven of those eight games and finished a dismal 10th. The only consolation was to see Ettingshausen and McGaw in the Kangaroos side which toured Britain and France. Sadly, after scoring a sensational individual try in the First Test and looking the class player of the Australian backline, McGaw was then badly injured and missed the rest of the tour.

Cronulla-Sutherland

Founded: 1952 (as Cronulla-Caringbah)
Entered Sydney Premiership competition: 1967
Home ground: Caltex Field (formerly named Endeavour Field) (Record crowd—21 956)
Colours: Blue, black and white
Nickname: The Sharks
Honours:
    Sydney Premiership—Runners-up, 1973, 1978
    Midweek Cup—1979
    Second Division Premiership—Runners-up, 1963
    Endeavour Cup—1971
    Under-23 Premiership—1975
*Most games in a career:*216 by Dane Sorensen
Most points in a career: 1235 by Steve Rogers
Most tries in a career: 84 by Andrew Ettingshausen
Most points in a season: 202 by George Taylforth, in 1970
Most tries in a season: 17 by Ray Corcoran, in 1971; by Chris Gardner, in 1983; and by Andrew Ettingshausen, in 1988
Rothmans Medal winners: Terry Hughes (1968), Ken Maddison (1973), Steve Rogers (1975), Barry Russell (1988), Gavin Miller (1989)
*Rugby League Week Player-of-the-Year:*Tommy Bishop (1970), Gavin Miller (1989)

LEE CROOKS

Fourteen Tests for Great Britain (1982–89). Also played 13 minor games on two tours of Australasia (1984 and 1988).

Lee Crooks was one of Britain's finest teenage talents. A ball-playing prop who kicked brilliantly both for goal and field position, Crooks captained the first-ever British Colts team to visit Australia, in 1982. At the time he had been a senior team player with Hull for two years (signing with the Humberside club as a 17–year-old). He had already tasted success in the Challenge Cup, after scoring a try and kicking three goals in Hull's 18–9 success over Widnes in the replayed final that year.

Crooks was to go on to establish himself as one of the finest forwards of the 1980s. Only persistent injuries stopped him from playing more than his 14 Tests, the latest against France in 1989. However this did not stop Leeds from outlaying a world record transfer fee of £172 500 ($362 000) to buy the big prop from Hull in June 1987.

Lee Crooks

When Crooks made his Test debut against the Kangaroos in October 1982, he became the youngest player to represent his country—at 19 years and 14 days. He went on to make two senior tours of Australasia (in 1984 and 1988). Such was his form on the first, that Western Suburbs, in dire need of a ball-distributor and on-field inspiration, eased the purse-strings in 1985. The Wests chiefs lured him to Lidcombe Oval in a vain effort to improve the Magpies sagging fortunes. Crooks spent two Australian seasons with Wests (with a period as captain) before linking up with Balmain in 1987.

By 1992, Crooks was still playing top-class club football in his home country, this time, with Castleford.

LES CUBITT

Four Tests for Australia (1919). Also played eight minor games for Australia on one Kangaroo tour (1921–22) and one New Zealand tour (1919).

Les Cubitt was one of the most exciting wingers of the period immediately after World War I and with opponents of the calibre of Harold Horder and Cec Blinkhorn, that's certainly saying something. But for the outbreak of the war, Cubitt may have chalked up a much more impressive record than his four Test appearances. He was just blossoming when the hostilities began, having been one of the stars of the New South Wales team which crossed the Tasman for a tour of New Zealand in 1913.

After the Armistice, Cubitt firmly established himself. He was one of the real successes of the 1919 tour of New Zealand, playing in all four Test matches. In four minor games, in which Australia ran up cricket scores, he scored no less than 19 tries, a feat unequalled on any subsequent international tour. He finished the tour as top-scorer with 72 points, eight more than Horder.

Cubitt achieved the ultimate when he was named as captain of the 1921–22 Kangaroos side to visit Britain although it proved to be a disappointing tour for him. Records were broken left, right and centre, but Cubitt suffered a severe cartilage injury, and managed to turn out in only four of the tourists' 36 games.

In club football, Cubitt played 106 first-grade games for Eastern Suburbs and was a member of that club's squad which won the 1913 Sydney Premiership.

FRANK CURRAN

Ten Tests for Australia (1935–36). Also played 25 minor games on two Kangaroo tours (1933–34 and 1936–37).

Rugged prop Frank Curran never gave an inch. He was at his very best when the going was at its toughest. Curran showed tremendous ability as a schoolboy in northern New South Wales, representing New England in a match against the NSW State side. His first major representative games were in the annual City-Country clashes in 1928, and for Far North Coast against the touring British side the same year.

It was not until he joined South Sydney in 1931 that he achieved his full potential. The following year he narrowly missed out on Test selection, but turned out against the touring Englishmen for Metropolis and New South Wales. Curran was a member of the 1933–34 Kangaroo touring side and made a second visit to the northern hemisphere four years later. On this second tour, he was one of the select few to take part in the pioneer Test series against France.

With Souths, Curran won two Sydney Premiership caps, after the Rabbitohs beat Eastern Suburbs 12–7 in the 1931 grand final and Western Suburbs 19–12 in the grand final 12 months later.

In the Third Test of the 1936 series against Great Britain, Curran was involved in one of the most unusual situations in Rugby League history. It was the first time Australia had gone into a Test without a specialist hooker. Australia's Percy Fairhall had been completely outhooked 49 scrums to 22 in the second international clash in Brisbane, so in the final (and deciding) Test the selectors threw caution to the wind and chose three prop-forwards, Curran, Mick Madsen and Ray Stehr. The success, or otherwise, of this ploy was never really tested as the two front-row combinations were soon disorganised as Stehr and Englishman Jack Arkwright were sent off early for fighting.

TONY CURRIE

Seven Tests for Australia (1988–89). Also played two minor games on one New Zealand tour (1989)

It needed the experience of Sydney Premiership football to hone the natural skills of classy Brisbane three-quarter Tony Currie. Currie had shown promise while playing for Wests and Redcliffe in the Brisbane competition and had been chosen as a replacement for State-of-Origin matches in 1982, 1984 and 1985. However when he moved to Canterbury-Bankstown in 1986 his career really blossomed. After a quiet first season, he burst into prominence and from 1987 on was a Queensland regular in the State-of-Origin clashes, playing either in the centre or on the wing. The 1988 season was a big one for Currie. As well as helping the Bulldogs to a Premiership success, he broke into international football, playing all three Tests against the visiting British Lions and in the World Cup qualifier against Papua New Guinea.

Moving back home in 1989 to join the Brisbane Broncos, Currie continued his good form in the interstate clashes and on Australia's tour of New Zealand, playing in five of the six matches including all three Tests. Currie looked a certainty to tour Britain and France with the 1990 Kangaroos when he started the following season in top form, but after only six matches he tore his Achilles tendon—an injury which sidelined him for the rest of the season.

D

LAURIE DALEY

Seven Tests for Australia (1990–91). Also played in three minor games on one Kangaroo tour (1990).

When the great Wally Lewis was injured and forced to leave the international stage in 1990, a young Laurie Daley was waiting in the wings to take over. Daley had been destined for greatness ever since Canberra talent scouts had spied him playing at nearby Junee as a 15–year-old, a year before he made the 1986 Country Under-18 side.

By 1987, the Raiders reckoned he was ready for the big time and brought him to the national capital. That season he played just two first-grade matches, but such was the Canberra faith in his ability that they had him on the reserve bench for the grand final against Manly. Daley was a regular first-grader in 1988, but missed the playoffs through injury. He really came of age in 1989, making the NSW State-of-Origin side and helping Canberra to its first Premiership. Then came the Lewis injury. Daley made his Test debut against France, in the World Cup qualifying match at Parkes, and then took on New Zealand in Wellington.

At the end of 1990, there was another Premiership for Daley and the Raiders, before he headed off to Britain and France with the Kangaroo touring side. Daley missed the First Test against Britain because of a broken hand. He also had to be nursed through the tour because of a nagging hamstring injury, which finally forced his retirement at half-time in the First Test against France.

Daley had a wretched year in 1991, plagued by several injuries which cost him his spot for the First Test encounter with New Zealand. But he made it onto the field for the remaining two encounters and then played a major role in Canberra's late surge to the grand final. For several weeks, he was unable to train because of a fracture in his ankle. But he took the field with painkillers and performed brilliantly. In the grand final he also had to contend with a hamstring tear—but he still survived only to see his beloved Raiders go down 19–12 to Penrith.

DALLY M AWARDS

Throughout each year a team of experts from the *Daily Mirror* newspaper (now merged into the *Daily Telegraph Mirror*) and Channel 10 have cast–votes for the best players and coaches in the Sydney Premiership competition. At the end of the season the finest footballers receive statuettes honouring their performances.

The awards are named after Dally Messenger, the great football pioneer. The major Dally M Award, for the best player, has been won twice by the same player on three occasions since it was instituted in 1980. Parramatta halfback Peter Sterling won in 1986 and 1987 and Cronulla-Sutherland forward Gavin Miller claimed the honours in 1988 and 1989. Michael Potter won his first Dally M when playing for Canterbury in 1984. Seven years later, by this time captain of St George, the classy fullback took it out a second time.

Dally M Player-of-the-Year

1980	Rocky Laurie (South Sydney)
1981	Steve Rogers (Cronulla-Sutherland)
1982	Ray Price (Parramatta)
1983	Terry Lamb (Western Suburbs)
1984	Michael Potter (Canterbury-Bankstown)
1985	Greg Alexander (Penrith)
1986	Peter Sterling (Parramatta)
1987	Peter Sterling (Parramatta)
1988	Gavin Miller (Cronulla-Sutherland)
1989	Gavin Miller (Cronulla-Sutherland)
1990	Cliff Lyons (Manly-Warringah)
1991	Michael Potter (St George)

BRIAN DAVIES

Twenty-seven Tests for Australia (1951–58). Also played six matches in two World Cups (1954 and 1958), one minor international (1951), one match against the Rest-of-the-World (1957) and in 31 minor games on two Kangaroo tours (1952–53 and 1956–57) and one New Zealand tour (1953).

Brian Davies rose to the top in Rugby League at an incredible pace. He played his first-ever game of Rugby League in 1948. Only two years later he was chosen to represent his State, Queensland, in a match against Britain and was a reserve for a Test against the tourists.

He found it hard to make it into the Test XIII because of the number of fine front and second-row forwards available, including such greats as Duncan Hall and Roy Bull. However Davies finally broke through and made his Test debut against France at the Sydney Cricket Ground in 1951. Twelve months later he toured with the Kangaroos, the first of four overseas jaunts (the others being to New Zealand in 1953, to France for the 1954 World Cup and the 1956–57 Kangaroo tour).

Davies was to figure in 33 Test and World Cup matches before bowing out of the international arena in 1958. In that final series he crowned a fine career by being chosen as captain-coach of the Australian Test side for the clashes with Britain. He was also in an Australian XIII which played France in Melbourne in 1951 and a World Cup side which beat the Rest-of-the-World 20–11 in 1957.

Brian Davies (right) joins Canterbury team-mates Kevin Brown (4) and Bill Petley to pound a Western Suburbs rival to the ground during the 1962 pre-season final. Canterbury won 14–10.

The year after he played his final Test he left the Brisbane Brothers club (with which he won two Premierships, in 1956 and 1958) to join Canterbury-Bankstown as captain-coach. He managed to lift the Berries from second-last to the semi-finals in 1960, but quit after ordinary results the following year.

JONATHAN DAVIES

Seven Tests for Great Britain (1990–91). Also played one minor international for Wales (1991) and seven minor games for Britain on one tour of New Zealand and Papua New Guinea (1990).

In late 1988, the Rugby Union world was stunned when Jonathon Davies accepted a four-year deal from Widnes worth around $650 000 to switch to the professional code. The 'Welsh Wizard' was his country's captain and a veteran of 27 full internationals at five-eighth. The rah-rahs couldn't believe it and the signing was headlines all over the world. For his first match, on January 15, the following year, a crowd of 11 871—almost double the Widnes average—turned up for what would have been, without Davies, a game with little appeal.

Davies was a quick success in the 13-a-side game. Although playing only half the season, he scored 123 points in 16 matches. In his first full season, 1989–90, he scored 260 and was named Players' Player by his peers.

He was a controversial choice for Great Britain's 1990 tour of Papua New Guinea and New Zealand, as he was suffering from a hamstring problem. But the selectors were obviously swayed by his versatility which had seen him play centre, wing and fullback as well as five-eighth for Widnes. Davies proved the critics wrong by playing in 11 of the 15 tour games (including all five Tests) and topping the pointscoring with 92 (6 tries and 34 goals). But he was overlooked for the first two Tests when the Australian Kangaroos toured later in the year. He did come on as a substitute in the third encounter.

Davies proved a great buy for Canterbury-Bankstown when the Bulldogs lured him to Sydney in the 1991 English off-season. His goal-kicking and spirited attack was a major factor in Canterbury shocking the pundits by finishing equal fifth. It was Davies 18 points (2 tries and five goals) in the last match, against Cronulla, which helped turn a 16–0 deficit into a 26–16 victory and force a playoff for the last semi-final spot. Davies cool kicking under pressure in the play-off against Western Suburbs kept Canterbury in contention until the final moments of the match.

Back home, Davies was chosen as captain of Wales for the international at Swansea against the 1991 touring Papua New Guinea side. He broke the Welsh international record with 24 points (two tries and eight goals) in the 68–0 thrashing of the Kumuls.

SID DEANE

Five Tests for Australia (1908–14). Also played in 24 minor games on one Kangaroo tour (1908–09).

Sid Deane was fine utility back who played alongside the great Dally Messenger on the 1908–09 Kangaroo tour. Such was the form of the North Sydney star that several English clubs made offers for him to stay on and play in the English competition.

Deane accepted the terms offered by Oldham, said to be the highest by any club in the history of the game, and for the next four seasons the clever, elusive Australian was one of the stars in a fine lineup which included fellow-Kangaroos Arthur 'George' Anlezark and Tom McCabe, English captain Jim Lomas and his British Test team-mates AE Wood and AE Avery. In 1909 Oldham was beaten 7–3 in the Championship Final by Wigan but had its revenge in the following two seasons, winning 13–7 in 1910 and 20–7 the next year. Deane was also in the side which went down 8–5 to Dewsbury in the 1912 Challenge Cup Final at Headingley, Leeds. He returned home and was rewarded with the captaincy of Australia in the three Tests against the touring 1914 British Lions, the series which included the famous Rorke's Drift Test.

DAN DEMPSEY

Seven Tests for Australia (1928–33). Also played 20 minor games on two Kangaroo tours (1929–30 and 1933–34).

There was no doubting the courage of Ipswich forward Dan Dempsey. His gritty spirit was never more evident than in the famous 1932 Test match against Great Britain, since dubbed 'The Battle of Brisbane'. The Queenslander was one of a host of Australian stars badly injured in that game and had to leave the field with a badly broken wrist. No replacements were allowed in those days, so he pleaded with Australian officials and doctors to be allowed to return to the game. 'Even if I can't tackle, I can at least get in the way of the Englishmen,' he argued. When the doctors refused to allow him to re-enter the fray, Dempsey broke down and wept.

Dempsey played in four different series against the British, two at home and two away. He was also a major influence in the Ipswich representative side which dominated the Bulimba Cup, the triangular series with Brisbane and Toowoomba, in the 1930s. After he retired as a player, he continued in the game as a coach and at one stage served as an Australian Test selector.

JIM DEVEREUX

Five Tests for Australia (1908–09). Also played in 29 minor games on one Kangaroo tour (1908–09).

It took a great player to outshine Dally Messenger, the man they dubbed 'The Master', but that is exactly what the clever North Sydney centre Jim Devereux did, in the first ever Anglo-Australian Test in 1908. At Park Royal in London, Devereux (at 60kg the smallest of the pioneer Kangaroos and Messenger's centre partner) turned in a sensational game, scoring three tries to help Australia to a 22–all draw. Four players of the modern era (Reg Gasnier, Ken Irvine, Michael O'Connor and Gene Miles) have also scored three tries in a single Ashes Test—but no one has yet bettered Devereux's effort.

In so many matches on tour (he played 31 of the 45 games), Devereux was brilliant and finished with 16 tries, more than any of his team-mates managed. His form attracted the attention of several English clubs and he eventually was persuaded to stay behind when the Kangaroos returned home, to play with Hull, together with Kangaroo team-mate Andy Morton.

Devereux stayed in England until the 1921–22 season. He scored the winning try for Hull when it beat Hull Kingston Rovers 16–14 in the 1921 Championship Final at Headingley. He also played halfback when Hull won the Challenge Cup in 1914, beating Wakefield Trinity 6–0 at Thrum Hall, Halifax (fellow Australian Herb Gilbert captained the side that day). And Devereux was also a member of the side which went down to Leeds in the 1910 Challenge Cup Final replay. On top of his two Test appearances against Britain, Devereux appeared as well in the first three clashes with New Zealand, in 1908.

PAT DEVERY

Three Tests for Australia (1946). Also played 11 internationals for Other Nationalities in Britain and France.

Pat Devery, one of the finest five-eighths of the post-World War II era, was a resident star on both sides of the world. He was discovered by a Balmain talent scout playing for the Royal Australian Navy in a match on the NSW north coast in 1944. Coming to Sydney later that year, he had one run in reserve grade before taking over the stand-off spot in the powerful Balmain first-grade side. He figured in three of Balmain's Premiership-winning teams (1944, 1946 and 1947). In 1945 he played only four matches because of wartime naval service.

After the War, Devery represented Australia in the three Tests against the touring 1946 British Lions. The next year, he captained New South

Wales, but it was to be his last season in Australian football, for he joined a host of stars lured to England by fat contracts. He teamed up with fellow expatriates Lionel Cooper and Johnny Hunter at Huddersfield as one of the highest paid players in the world.

Devery's record speaks for itself: in 50 matches for Balmain, he scored 32 tries and kicked 60 goals (a total of 216 points), and 223 appearances at Huddersfield netted him 98 tries and 398 goals (1090 points). He captained his English club to two Championship Finals, steering Huddersfield to a 13–12 success over Warrington in 1949 (scoring a try and kicking two goals), only to be beaten the following year 20–2 by Wigan. He was also a member of Huddersfield's Wembley Challenge Cup-winning side in 1953. Former Balmain and Australian Rugby League secretary, Harold Matthews, said of Devery: 'He was one of the greatest backs Australia has ever seen—and one of the most versatile. If he had not gone to Huddersfield, he would most certainly have held his Australian Test spot for many years. There have been few players since the War who could match his natural ability'.

MIKE DIMITRO

Mike Dimitro was an American gridiron player-cum-promoter who tried unsuccessfully to get Rugby League established in the United States. In 1953, Dimitro got together 21 gridiron players to make a Rugby League tour of Australasia. The American Allstars, as they were known, were schooled on the finer points of League before their first match, but their tour proved to be a gigantic disaster. They won only three of their 18 matches in Australia and three of their eight in New Zealand.

Undeterred, Dimitro had a hand in staging two exhibition matches in California between the Australian and New Zealand sides returning from the 1954 World Cup in France. Sadly, few spectators bothered to turn up. In the late 1960s, Dimitro tried to persuade the international authorities to let him stage a World Cup series in North America, but no one took him seriously.

PETER DIMOND

Ten Tests for Australia (1958–66). Also played in 18 minor games on one Kangaroo tour (1963–64).

Peter Dimond was just nine when he watched his 19–year-old brother, Bobby, leave for England as the youngest member of the 1948–49 Kangaroos. Ten years later, Peter took up the mantle Bobby had cast aside and pulled on his own green and gold Australian jersey. For the next decade, the big, tough winger-cum-centre was to spread havoc among opposing three-quarters throughout the world.

In 1958, he graduated from the NSW south coast to join Western Suburbs in the Sydney Premiership competition. After only a few matches, Dimond found himself in the NSW State side. He scored a hat-trick of tries against Queensland, but his second match, against the touring British side, was not so rewarding. Dimond was one of three players sent off for fighting. Suspension cost him a place in the First Test line-up, but he made the side for the final two encounters.

Peter Dimond is tackled heavily by Great Britain's Alan Buckley and Cliff Watson during the Third Test of the 1966 Ashes series at the Sydney Cricket Ground

The high point in Dimond's career came in 1963, when he was one of the stars of the highly successful Kangaroos side, which wrested the Ashes from Britain. He played in all six Tests against Britain and France and, in 24 tour matches, went over for 16 tries. Dimond's final Test appearance was in 1966 when, after a two-year absence from the international scene, he was recalled to play centre in the deciding Test against the touring British Lions. His tough play earned three cautions, but also helped pave the way for an Australian victory.

DANIEL DIVET

Nine Tests for France (1987–91). Also played in one minor international (1991) and four minor games on one tour of Australia (1990).

Second-rower Daniel Divet grew up in Sydney, but it was with his native France that he made a name for himself in international football. Divet emigrated to Australia with his parents when he was 10 months old and began playing Rugby League in the Manly-Warringah area. In 1987 he was a member of the Sea Eagles under-23 side, but then went back to France. He played six times for French junior sides before making the Test team against the visiting Papua New Guinea Kumuls in 1987. Divet toured Australia with the French side in 1990 and played both Tests against the Kangaroos a few months later. He was one of the few Frenchmen not disgraced in the drubbings.

When the Soviet Union played its first international, against France at Lyon in November 1991, Divet, a last-minute inclusion at lock, was the Man-of-the-Match and the inspiration behind France's 26–6 victory. He then followed up with a stirring performance in the World Cup qualifier against Papua New Guinea.

JOHN DONNELLY

One Test for Australia (1978). Also played three matches in one World Championship (1975).

John 'Dallas' Donnelly was a self-confessed larrikin who lived life to the full. When he died suddenly in February 1986, his former coach at Sydney's Western Suburbs, Roy Masters, said of him: 'He put 60 years of living into his 30'.

Donnelly, a big, no-nonsense prop-forward, began his football career in the New England town of Gunnedah from where, as a teenager, he represented NSW Country in the 1974 clash with Sydney. He joined Wests the following season and stayed with the Magpies until the end of his Australian career a decade later. He was granted life membership of the Magpies in recognition of the service he gave in more than 170 games (148 of them in first-grade).

Donnelly played in Australia's 1975 World Championship side in home matches against France, Wales and England and three years later turned out for his lone Test appearance, against New Zealand in Brisbane. After Donnelly left Wests he had a season playing for English Second Division side Southend Invicta.

Test front-rower John 'Dallas' Donnelly, one of Western Suburbs' stars of the late 1970s

Throughout his life Donnelly was plagued by epilepsy but kept this a secret until, late in his football career, he made his illness public in an effort to inspire fellow epileptics. The big fellow suffered an epileptic fit and drowned while surfing at Byron Bay on the NSW north coast, where he had planned to finish his career as captain-coach of the local side.

JOHN DORAHY

Two Tests for Australia (1978).

Utility back John Dorahy was a sensational club performer on both sides of the world. Only an uncustomary lapse under the pressure of semi-final football cost him a Kangaroo tour in 1978 and many more than his two

Test appearances. His nickname was 'Joe Cool', and he normally handled the pressure of big-time football very well.

Dorahy was one of Rugby League's survivors. He started his first grade career in the Wollongong competition in 1972 and finished with Halifax, in England 19 years later. His performance, as a 19–year-old with Country Firsts in 1973, attracted the attention of Western Suburbs officials, and he teamed up with the Magpies the following season, the first of six years at Lidcombe Oval. Twice he notched more than a century of points (183 in 1975 and 145 in 1979).

He could play anywhere in the backline, but it was at fullback that he made his Test debut against the touring New Zealand Kiwis in 1978. He seemed to have a Kangaroo spot at his mercy, but turned in a shocker as Wests, the Minor Premiers, bombed out of the semi-finals.

At the end of 1979, Dorahy was one of three Magpie internationals lured to Manly-Warringah. He had two ordinary seasons with the Sea-Eagles before returning home to join Illawarra in its first season in the Sydney Premiership fight. In the first two years back in the 'Gong he again topped the century (159 points in 1982 and 175 the following season). He had four years with the Steelers, but in 1983 he went to England to try his luck during the off-season with Hull Kingston Rovers. He was so successful that until 1986 he did not bother returning for the Sydney season.

John Dorahy, while playing for Western Suburbs

In 1984, Hull KR won both the Championship and the Premiership and Dorahy became the first Australian to win the Harry Sunderland Medal (as the Man-of-the-Match in the Premiership Final). Hull KR retained the Championship in 1985. As captain, Dorahy was a real inspiration as the side fought its way through to the final of the Challenge Cup in 1986. 'Joe Cool' had a chance to win the match in the last minute of play— Hull KR trailed 14–15 as he lined up a kick from the sideline—but the ball veered away at the last moment.

Dorahy eventually came home and had three more seasons in Sydney, this time with Norths (during which he took his Premiership points tally past 1000) before one last stab at English football. As captain-coach, he steered Halifax to the final of the Regal Trophy, but when he could not get the club back into First Division he and Halifax parted company.

MIKE DORE

Three Tests for Australia (1908–09).

Mike Dore was one of the founders of Rugby League in Queensland. The Brisbane halfback had played Rugby Union for Australia (against New Zealand at Dunedin in 1905) but saw a real future in the breakaway code. His decision to swap codes influenced many other Queensland players, including his elder brother, Edmund, who had played a Test against the 1904 British Isles tourists, to join the Rugby League ranks.

Mike Dore was a member of the first committee of the Queensland Rugby Football Association (the forerunner of the Queensland Rugby League). He was also an Australian selector, choosing himself for the first two Tests, against New Zealand, in 1908. Dore missed the 1908–09 Kangaroo tour when he could not get leave of absence from his job and was the only one of the five selectors who did not tour. Dore finished his international career with a third Test appearance against New Zealand, in 1909.

GREG DOWLING

Twelve Tests for Australia (1984–87). Also played in eight minor games on one Kangaroo tour (1986) and one New Zealand tour (1985).

There have been few front-rowers as tough as Brisbane's Greg Dowling. He had only a brief period in the international limelight, but he certainly left his mark.

Dowling made 12 Test appearances, however he is probably best remembered for a fiery encounter with New Zealand prop Kevin Tamati in a 1985 international at Lang Park. The pair were sent to the sin-bin for 10 minutes after a brawl in centre field. As they reached the gate into the stand Tamati appeared to elbow Dowling. The pair then slugged it out, trading punches before wrestling on the ground. A special committee convened to consider the incident suspended them for eight days—a mere slap on the wrist which allowed both players to appear in the Second Test in New Zealand 10 days later.

The big Queenslander would rather remember another sensational incident—this time in a 1984 State-of-Origin match at the Sydney Cricket Ground. In a torrential rainstorm, Dowling leaped in the air to freakishly catch a Wally Lewis bomb which bounced off the crossbar, and dived over for a try.

Dowling played 11 State-of-Origin matches in just four years before quitting representative football to concentrate on Premiership games for the Brisbane Broncos. When he retired at the end of his testimonial season (1991), he had played 77 first-grade games, but had missed many others because of a back injury.

Dowling also had a season in Britain (1985–86) with the great Wigan combination and was rewarded with a Cup-winners' medal in the John Player Trophy.

THE DRAFT_____

In 1990, the NSW Rugby League introduced one of the most controversial policies in the history of the game—the draft. It was designed to help weaker clubs, to encourage the growth of junior teams, to eliminate disruptive mid-season negotiations and to prevent clubs from buying up players just to stop them from playing with opposition sides. But it was all to no avail. After more than 12 months of legal battles, the Federal Court eventually ruled that it was illegal.

But it did operate for the 1991 season. While it was in operation, each club was entitled to nominate up to 57 players, contracted for the season for the first and reserve-grade sides and the President's Cup competition.

There were two drafts. The only players not subject to the draft were those who had played 10 consecutive seasons for a club or players whose father played for the club for at least five seasons.

The external draft was held on the first Wednesday in November, giving clubs the chance to select up to five players who had not previously played in the Premiership or a major overseas competition. The bottom club on the previous competition table received the first choice, the second last side the second choice and so on.

The internal draft, which drew the ire of the Players' Association, was held on the third Tuesday in November and then monthly during the season. It is made up of players not listed among the 57 contracted players for each club. These players nominated their terms and had to join the club which chose them in the draft. As with the external draft, choices were made in the reverse order in which clubs finished in the first-grade Premiership—the last-placed club getting first choice.

Players could refuse to move to a club located more than 100km from their current club. The players also had the right of appeal if they did not wish to join the club which chose them.

Even though the legality of the Draft was being tested in the Courts, the first Internal Draft went ahead on November 20, 1990. South Sydney (the bottom club), Eastern Suburbs (third last), Parramatta (eighth in the 1990 Premiership) and Balmain (fifth) declined the opportunity to participate.

And the honour of being the first Premiership player drafted went to Western Suburbs prop Pat O'Doherty, who was snapped up by the Gold Coast for $60 000. No club used up the five choices allowed it, but Wests nominated four including three Canterbury stars, Test forwards David Gillespie and Paul Langmack and hooker Joe Thomas.

All told, 23 players were chosen at a value of $1.4 million. Some 92 (value 4 million dollars) were not chosen and became free agents. More were chosen in subsequent drafts. And by the fourth, the Courts had upheld its legal status.

But the Players' Association appealed to the Federal Court, which decided the draft was an unreasonable restraint of trade. A subsequent hearing refused the NSWRL permission for a further appeal, to the High Court. And for 1992 it was a return to the free-for-all bargaining between players and clubs.

DUAL INTERNATIONALS

A number of Australian Rugby League internationals also represented their country while playing Rugby Union. In the modern era they include Michael O'Connor, Ricky Stuart, Ray Price, Phil Hawthorne, Rex Mossop, Arthur Summons and Ken Kearney. Hawthorne, Summons and Kearney captained Australia in League.

Only a few League stars have carried Australia's colours in completely different sports. Notable ones include Kangaroo fullback Vic Bulgin, who played in amateur golf series in South Africa and Canada, second-rower Dennis Tutty, who was a champion rower, winger Mike Cleary, who won an athletics medal at the 1962 Commonwealth Games and forward Dick Thornett, who made the Australian water polo side. Cleary and Thornett also played international Rugby Union for Australia.

Those who have represented Australia in both codes
(Figures in brackets: Number of RU Tests, number of RL Tests)

Arthur Analzark (1, 1)
Jack Barnett (5, 2)
John Brass (12, 3)
Alec Burdon (4, 2)
Peter Burge (3, 0*)
Mike Cleary (6, 8)
Bob Craig (1, 7)
Mike Dore (1, 3)
Jack Fihelly (3, 0*)
Herb Gilbert (1, 7)
Scott Gourley (0*, 1)
Bob Graves (1, 6)
Bill Hardcastle (2, 2)
Phil Hawthorne (21, 3)
Jack Hickey (2, 2)
Bob Honan (2, 2)
Ken Kearney (7, 25)
Steve Knight (6, 0*)
Jimmy Lisle (4, 6)
Dinny Lutge (4, 3)
Paddy McCue (4, 4)

Chris McKivat (4, 5)
Doug McLean (3, 1)
Doug McLean (10, 2)
Charles McMurtrie (0*, 0*)
Dally Messenger (2, 7)
Rex Mossop (5, 9)
Michael O'Connor (13, 17)
Clarrie Prentice (6, 5)
Ray Price (8, 22)
Geoff Richardson (9, 2)
Johnny Rosewell (2, 1)
Charlie 'Boxer' Russell (5, 3)
Kevin Ryan (5, 2)
Len Smith (0*, 2)
Bob Stuart (2, 0*)
Ricky Stuart (0*, 5)
Arthur Summons (10, 9)
Dick Thornett (11, 11)
Pat Walsh (3, 3)
George Watson (1, 1)

* Toured with Australian side without playing in a Test

(Jack Fihelly toured with the 1908–09 Rugby League Kangaroos but never played a match. Len Smith was a member of the 1939 Rugby Union Wallabies, who returned from Britain without playing a game except for an exhibition match in Ceylon. He played two Rugby League Tests for Australia.)

E

GRAHAM EADIE

Twelve Tests for Australia (1973–79). Also played eight matches in two World Championships (1975 and 1977), two minor internationals (1975 and 1977) and in eight minor games for Australia on one Kangaroo tour (1978).

Australia has produced some fine Rugby League fullbacks—and few were better than Graham Eadie. His international debut gave an indication of what was to follow. He was called in as a replacement for injured Australian captain Graeme Langlands in the Second Test on the 1973 Kangaroo tour of England. Eadie was the star of the match, kicking five goals to steer Australia to a 14–6 victory. After Langlands retired in 1975, Eadie took over the Test fullback spot and quickly established himself as the best in the world. All told, he played in 12 Tests (nine against Britain, two versus France and one against New Zealand) and eight World Championship matches before quitting representative football in 1979.

On the club scene 'Wombat', as Eadie was affectionately known, was also a dominant force. He played major roles in Manly-Warringah's Sydney Premiership successes in 1972, 1973, 1976 and 1978. Then, in his final season in Sydney football (1983) he became the first player to score 2000 points in all grades. He also became the highest pointscorer in first–grade history—with 1917 points from his 238 games. This was 74 more than the previous record holder, Eric Simms (South Sydney).

After less than three years of retirement, Eadie was lured back to the football field to play under former Test colleague Chris Anderson with the English club, Halifax. The Aussies inspired Halifax to the 1986 English Championship title and success in the 1987 Challenge Cup Final at Wembley, in which Eadie became only the second Australian ever to win the Lance Todd Trophy as Man-of-the-Match. Eadie was back at Wembley 12 months later, but it was not a repeat of 1987, with Halifax comprehensively beaten by Wigan. After that match Eadie took over as coach of Halifax, however after only a couple of months he was replaced, bringing the curtain down on a great career.

EASTERN SUBURBS

Eastern Suburbs has over the years been one of Sydney's most glamorous clubs. The Roosters have had periods of glory in which they have been virtually unbeatable but, by the same token, there have been times when they have languished at the bottom of the table. Easts have also numbered in their ranks two players who became legends in their lifetime—Dally Messenger and Dave Brown.

Messenger, the man they dubbed 'The Master', more than any other person, assured that the 1908 start of Rugby League in Australia was a success. Until the brilliant centre and goalkicker swapped from the Rugby Union ranks, the state of the fledgling sport was insecure. With Messenger, its future was assured–previously uncertain fans flocked to see him play.

Rugby League has never known—and possibly never will again—a scoring machine to equal Dave Brown. During the 1930s, he broke every record in the book. All stood for decades until the Sydney competition was enlarged, giving players more matches in which to boost their tallies.

The Eastern Suburbs club was formed on 24 January 1908, a little more than two weeks after the first club, Glebe, came into existence. A famous name at that inaugural meeting was Victor Trumper. Trumper, best known as a cricketer of world fame, was a leading light in the preparatory meetings which got Rugby League off the ground in Australia.

Easts had to wait until 1911 for their first Premiership success, but then there was no stopping them. They won again in 1912 and 1913 and, from 1914 to 1916, scored another treble—this time in the City Cup. The 1913 side was one of the best club combinations seen in Australian football–every player in the top side had represented New South Wales and 10 of the 13 were internationals. The team included such all-time greats as Dan Frawley, Dally and Wally Messenger, Les Cubitt, Pony Halloway, Bluey Watkins and Sandy Pearce. It can be speculated just how much better it would have been had the great Eastern Suburbs winger Albert Rosenfeld not decided to join the English club Huddersfield after the 1908–09 Kangaroo tour. Rosenfeld had captained Australia against New Zealand in 1908 and, when he went to Huddersfield, broke all try-scoring records. His 80 tries in one season remain a world's best to this day.

Easts next great era came in the late 1930s and early 1940s. In the eight seasons 1934 to 1941, Easts won four Premierships and were runners-up three times. The backbone of the Easts team in the early stage of this period was Dave Brown. In 1935, he scored a phenomenal 38 tries and 65 goals (244 points) in just 14 matches. In one game alone, he grabbed 45 points. Easts lost only one game that year, scoring 139 tries and 108 goals (633 points). No major club in the world has been able to match this record, an average of 42 a match.

From the late-1960s Easts struck a rich new lode. With money from the highly profitable local Leagues Club, the Roosters bought established Test and Rugby Union stars. Ron Coote and Elwyn Walters transferred from South Sydney and Arthur Beetson from Balmain. John Brass and Russell Fairfax left the Rugby Union ranks. Their presence, and the guidance of coach Jack Gibson, inspired the young players, and Easts became the strongest club in the competition.

Promise of what was going to happen was revealed in 1967. The previous year, without Gibson, Easts had been wooden spooners and only the third club in history to finish the season without a competition point (the others were Annandale in 1918 and South Sydney in 1946). In the 1968 competition Easts reached the semi-finals.

The highlight of Easts vintage run came in 1975 when the Premiership was hardly in doubt from the first match Easts played. The Roosters won the Minor Premiership by a margin of 10 points. Easts, perhaps a trifle overconfident, were upset by St George in the semi-finals but bounced back to humiliate the Dragons 38–0 in the grand final. Easts' form was such that eight of its players turned out for Australia in that year's World Championship games—wingers Mark Harris and Ian Schubert, centre John Brass, halves John Peard and Johnny Mayes, and forwards Ron Coote, Arthur Beetson and Ian Mackay. Schubert was a sensation. He played in three of the last four matches (being rested in the other) and scored in each game (including hat-tricks against both Wales and England).

Eastern Suburbs made the grand final in 1980. The following year the Roosters won the Pre-Season competition and when they added the Minor Premiership looked likely to carry off another JJ Giltinan Shield. However they faltered in the play-offs, falling in extra time in the semi-final to Newtown and to Parramatta in the final. The Roosters were also knocked out in the final by Parramatta in 1982. Then, despite big spending sprees, Easts failed to reach the semis for four straight seasons.

In 1987, Easts were surprisingly beaten in the final by Canberra, after a big year inspired by great form from players such as New Zealand Test star Hugh McGahan (an effort which helped him win the Adidas Golden Boot as the finest player in the world), English Test ace Joe Lydon and former Australian Test halfback turned winger, Steve Morris. Arthur Beetson, in the second last of his four years holding the reins at Easts, was named Coach-of-the-Year.

After that Easts form slumped dramatically. It was so bad, in fact, that in mid-1990 the Roosters sacked their coach, the former star player Russell Fairfax. Easts turned to their former saviour Jack Gibson to take over the role of club manager and appointed Queensland's former Test halfback Mark Murray in Fairfax's place.

EASTERN SUBURBS

Founded: 1908
Entered Sydney Premiership competition: 1908
Home Ground: Sydney Football Stadium (Record crowd: 20 685)
Colours: Red, white and blue
Nickname: The Roosters (formerly The Tricolours)
Honours:
   Sydney Premiership—Winners, 1911, 1912, 1913, 1923, 1935, 1936 (unbeaten), 1937 (unbeaten), 1940, 1945, 1974, 1975; Runners-up, 1908, 1919, 1922, 1928, 1931, 1934, 1938, 1941, 1960, 1972, 1980
   Midweek Cup—1975, 1978
   Pre-Season competition—1977, 1979, 1981
   Flowers' Memorial Pennant (Club Championship)—1930, 1931, 1934, 1935, 1936, 1937, 1945, 1970, 1974, 1975
   Reserve-grade Premiership—1908, 1909, 1910, 1911, 1935, 1937, 1949, 1980
   Third-grade Premiership—1914, 1917, 1924, 1929, 1930, 1931, 1932, 1941, 1947, 1970
   Under-23 Premiership—1976
   League Cup—1912
   President's Cup—1910, 1911, 1913, 1915, 1920, 1922, 1923, 1924, 1927, 1938, 1948, 1949, 1955, 1978

Most games in a career: 217 by Kevin Hastings
Most points in a career: 889 by Alan McKean

Most tries in a career: 100 by Bill Mullins
Most points in a season: 260 by Mike Eden, in 1983
Most tries in a season: 38 by Dave Brown, in 1935
Rothmans Medal winners: Kevin Junee (1970), Kevin Hastings (1981), Mike Eden (1983)
NSW Player-of-the-Year: Lionel Cooper (1946), Ron Coote (1974 & 1976), Arthur Beetson (1975)
Rugby League Week Player-of-the-Year: John Ballesty (1972), Arthur Beetson (1974), Kevin Hastings (1980, 1981 & 1982)

BEN ELIAS

Five Tests for Australia (1985–90). Also played in 1988 World Cup final and nineteen minor games for Australia on two Kangaroo tours (1986, 1990) and one New Zealand tour (1985).

Ben Elias was always destined for big things. As a schoolboy he was one of the stars of Ryde's Holy Cross side which won the Commonwealth Bank Cup televised schoolboy competition in 1981 (after being runners-up the previous two seasons). He was Player-of-the-Year in 1980 and 1981 and starred in the 1981 Australian Schoolboys Test side against New Zealand.

Elias was called into the Balmain first-grade side the following year and at 18 was being touted as a possible 1982 Kangaroo tourist, but the Tigers' officials decided to bring him along slowly. In 1985 Elias was given his big chance when he starred for New South Wales in the State-of-Origin series and made the Australian side which toured New Zealand. He was the centre of controversy when he replaced experienced Queenslander Greg Conescu in the Test line–up for the Third and final Test—and he paid the price for Australia's ignominious 18–0 loss. While he toured Britain and France with the 1986 Kangaroos, it was not until 1988 that the selectors gave him another chance in Australia's first XIII. He was recalled for the final of the World Cup against New Zealand in Auckland and was one of Australia's stars in an impressive 25–12 victory.

Elias had one of his finest moments in 1990 when he was skipper of New South Wales and the Blues broke an eight-match winning sequence by Queensland in State-of-Origin clashes. His inspired captaincy earned him the Man-of-the-Series award, and it helped him gain selection as vice-captain of the 1990 Kangaroo team to tour Britain and France. He went away as number two hooker to Kerrod Walters, but after Australia's surprise loss to Britain in the First Test, at Wembley Stadium, he was recalled for the remaining four internationals, winning the Man-of-the-Match in the Second Test against Britain. He was also named as one of the world's top five players in the biannual ratings issued by the respected British League magazine *Open Rugby*.

STEVE ELLA

Four Tests for Australia (1983–85). Also played one minor international (1982), for the Rest-of-the-World against Great Britain (1988) and 12 minor games for Australia on one Kangaroo tour (1982).

Two try-scoring feats on the 1982 Kangaroo tour ensured utility back Steve Ella a place in Rugby League history. In the first, he scored four tries against Wales at Cardiff, equalling the record for an Australian in a full international. Later, on the French leg of the tour, Ella went over for seven tries against Villeneuve. This equalled the Kangaroo record set by the immortal Cec Blinkhorn 50 years earlier.

The 21-year-old Ella, a cousin of the famous Ella brothers of Rugby Union fame, finished the tour with 21 tries (from just 13 matches), the second best of the Kangaroos. Ironically, Ella was lucky to even be playing at all. Three years earlier he had suffered an awful injury. It took several operations, 10 months in plaster and two years out of the game before Ella was fit again.

Ella made his Test debut against New Zealand in the second of two encounters in 1983. The day was soured when the Kiwis scored a shock 19–12 win at Brisbane's Lang Park but Ella scored one of the two tries for the home side. It was a better result when Australia toured the Shaky Isles two years later. Ella played in all three Tests. Australia won the first two but was whitewashed 18–0 by New Zealand in the third.

A series of injuries in the next couple of years (Ella missed 22 weeks of the 1987 season) brought an end to his international career.

ENDEAVOUR CUP See *Extinct Competitions*

ENGLAND

For Test matches, English and Welsh players combine to form Great Britain sides. The two countries have played matches as separate entities and for a long time they took part in a four-sided competition, with France and Other Nationalities, for what was known as The International Championship.

The British components also split for the 1975 World Championship. England was a little unlucky not to win that series, which went to Australia. The Australians did not beat England. They drew 10–all in Sydney and England won the return game, at Wigan, 16–13.

ENGLAND V AUSTRALIA
World Championships Matches
1975

At Sydney, 28 June 1975.
Crowd: 33 858
AUSTRALIA 10 (Coote, Anderson tries, Cronin 2 goals) drew with ENGLAND 10 (Dunn, Gill tries, Fairbairn 2 goals)
Australia: G Langlands (c), J Rhodes, R Fulton, M Cronin, M Harris, T Pickup, T Raudonikis, R Coote, L Platz, G Stevens, T Randall, J Lang, A Beetson. Replacements: C Anderson (for Harris) and J Donnelly (for Pickup)
England: G Fairbairn, K Fielding, J Walsh, L Dyl, G Dunn, R Millward, S Nash, S Norton, P Cookson, G Nicholls, M Morgan, J Bridges, M Coulman. Replacements: K Gill (for Millward) and E Chisnall (for Cookson)
Referee: J Percival (New Zealand)

At Wigan, 1 November 1975
Crowd: 9393
ENGLAND 16 (Grayshon, Holmes tries, Fairbairn 5 goals) d AUSTRALIA 13 (Schubert 3 tries, Cronin 2 goals)
Australia: G Eadie, I Schubert, J Brass, M Cronin, J Rhodes, J Peard, J Mayes, G Pierce, R Higgs, T Randall, I Mackay, G Piggins, A Beetson (c). Replacement: S Rogers (for Peard)
England: G Fairbairn, G Dunn, J Holmes, L Dyl, D Redfearn, K Gill, R Millward, S Norton, R Irving, J Grayshon, J Thompson, J Bridges, B Hogan. Replacement: M Adams (for Bridges)
Referee: J Percival (New Zealand)

ENGLAND V AUSTRALIA
International Matches
1908-09

At Everton, 18 November 1908
Crowd: 7000
AUSTRALIA 10 d ENGLAND 9

At Huddersfield, 2 January 1909
Crowd: 7000
ENGLAND 14 (G Tyson 2, W Batten, P Holroyd tries, J Lomas goal) d AUSTRALIA 9 (W Heidke, A Conlon, D Frawley tries)

At Glasgow, 3 February 1909
Crowd: 3000
AUSTRALIA 17 drew with ENGLAND 17

At Everton, 3 March 1909
Crowd: 4000
ENGLAND 14 d AUSTRALIA 7

1911

At Fulham, London, 18 October 1911
Crowd: 6000
AUSTRALIA 11 d ENGLAND 6

At Nottingham, 6 December 1911
Crowd: 3000
ENGLAND 5 d AUSTRALIA 0

1921

At Highbury, London, 10 October 1921
Crowd: 12 000
ENGLAND 5 d AUSTRALIA 4
(Charity match for Russian Famine Fund)

1933-34

At Paris, 31 December 1933
Crowd: 5000
AUSTRALIA 63 (Brown 3, Gibbs 3, Pearce 3, Prigg 2, Hey, Stehr, Mead, Why tries, Brown 9 goals) d ENGLAND 13
Australia: F McMillan (c), J Why, D Brown, V Hey, C Pearce, F Doonar, L Mead, W Prigg, S Pearce, J Gibbs, M Madsen, A Folwell, R Stehr

At Gateshead, 7 January 1934
Crowd: 15 576
ENGLAND 19 d AUSTRALIA 14

1975

At Leeds, 12 November 1975
Crowd: 7727
AUSTRALIA 25 (Lang 2, Peard, Randall, Cronin tries, Eadie 5 goals) d ENGLAND 0
Australia: G Eadie, J Rhodes, M Cronin, S Rogers, I Schubert, J Peard, T Raudonikis, G Pierce, T Randall, R Higgs, G Veivers, J Lang, A Beetson (c)
England: R Dutton, M Smith, N Stephenson, E Hughes, G Dunn, K Gill, R Millward, S Fearnley, M Adams, J Grayshon, J Thompson, J Bridges, H Beverley. Replacements: D Topliss (for Fearnley) and R Stone (for Adams)
Referee: F Lindop (Great Britain)

ANDREW ETTINGSHAUSEN————————————————

Fifteen Tests for Australia (1988–91). Also played in Bicentennial international against the Rest-of-the-World (1988) and nine minor games on one Kangaroo tour (1990) and one Papua New Guinea tour (1991).

There was never any doubt that Andrew Ettingshausen was going right to the top in Rugby League. An Australian schoolboy representative at 16, the player they dubbed 'ET' was in Cronulla-Sutherland's first-grade team a year later, where he soon began to impress the representative selectors. The tall three-quarter with the movie star looks was chosen for the President's XIII to play the Papua-New Guinea Test side in Port Moresby in 1985. From 1987 on, he was one of the first chosen in the NSW State-of-Origin teams.

ET made his Test debut against Britain in the 100th Anglo-Australian encounter, at the Sydney Football Stadium in 1988. He played in all three Tests against the tourists, but missed the romp against Papua-New Guinea before returning for the Bicentennial international against the Rest-of-the-World. His 17 tries for Cronulla that season equalled the club record. He also notched his century of first-grade games. He was again in great form the following year, notching a bag of five tries in the final round, against Illawarra.

His displays in 1990 could hardly be faulted. He came on as a replacement in the World Cup qualifier, against France in Parkes and against New Zealand at Wellington, before being chosen for the Kangaroo squad to tour Britain and France. He started the tour in a blaze of glory, notching a hat-trick of tries in the opening game against St Helens and another three in his next match, against Wigan. ET finished the tour as top tryscorer, with 15 touchdowns. His display on the wing in all five Tests was such that the respected British League magazine *Open Rugby* chose him as the best flankman in the world in its biannual ratings.

Despite the poor form of his club in the 1991 Premiership competition, Ettingshausen's Test selection was never in doubt. He was chosen on the wing for the First Test against the touring New Zealand Kiwis. And, after tyro Paul Hauff performed below par in that match, Ettingshausen was switched to fullback for the other two encounters. He was also in the Australian side which made an end-of-season tour of Papua New Guinea, playing in both Tests.

Dr HV EVATT————————————————————

Herbert Vere 'Doc' Evatt, for years Leader of the Opposition in the Australian Parliament and one of the first presidents of the United Nations, was, for two decades, patron of the NSW Rugby League—but he is remembered in the sport for much more than that.

In 1920, Evatt played a major role in forming the University club which played in the Sydney Premiership—no mean feat in an academy steeped in the Rugby Union tradition. As well, in 1946, it was largely his efforts which brought the British team to Australia for the first post-War tour. The visit was to have been cancelled because of lack of transport, but

Evatt, then a Minister in the Chifley Federal Government, intervened and persuaded the Royal Navy to take the team to Fremantle in Western Australia on the aircraft carrier HMS Indomitable, which was making the voyage anyway to collect vital food relief for Britain. The League tourists then travelled on to New South Wales overland. They won the Test series easily.

EXTINCT CLUBS

During the first eight decades of Rugby League in Australia several sides have come and gone. By the 1990s, a total of 21 clubs had competed in the first-grade Sydney Premiership competition. Three of those who disappeared were in the inaugural contest of 1908—Glebe, Newtown and Cumberland. Another, Newcastle, played just two seasons before dropping out, only to return to the fold 79 years later. Cumberland had only one season, playing eight matches for a lone victory. Glebe continued until 1929 and, although never winning a first-grade Premiership, it had one of the best records of any club in Sydney. Of 290 first-grade games, Glebe won 162 and drew another six. Newtown, Premiers in 1910, 1933 and 1943, were forced out of the competition in 1983 because of financial difficulties. Ironically, only two seasons earlier it had reached the grand final.

Other extinct clubs are Annandale and Sydney University. Annandale played between 1910 and 1920. It fared very ordinarily, winning only 23 of its 151 first-grade games. University, whose players were all amateurs, turned out between 1920 and 1937. The students did not have the experience to match the top sides and lost almost three-quarters of their games (44 wins in 226 matches). Several other extinct clubs, which never fielded first-grade sides, won titles in the third-grade competition—South Sydney Federal (twice), Mascot (twice), Sydney, Leichhardt and Kensington.

EXTINCT COMPETITIONS

Throughout the long history of Rugby League in Australia there have been various attempts to start new competitions. There was a State Championship and a State Cup, a City Cup, a spring knock-out (Ampol Cup) and contests for sides which missed the semi-finals of the Sydney Premiership (Channel 10 Challenge Cup, Thiess-Toyota Trophy and Endeavour Cup). There was even a contest for reserve-grade sides (League Cup).

The Cronulla-Sutherland club introduced the Endeavour Cup and its most memorable achievment was to experiment with some new rules—six-tackle football (instead of the old four-tackles) and no stoppages of play for injuries. Both were subsequently adopted internationally.

Ampol Cup

Year	Winner
1963	Western Suburbs

City Cup

Year	Winner	Year	Winner
1912	South Sydney	1918	Western Suburbs
1913	Glebe	1919	South Sydney
1914	Eastern Suburbs	1920	North Sydney
1915	Eastern Suburbs	1921	South Sydney
1916	Eastern Suburbs	1922	North Sydney
1917	Balmain	1923	Balmain	*Continued*

City Cup *continued*

Year		Winner	Year		Winner
1924	_____	South Sydney	1943	_____	Balmain
1925	_____	South Sydney	1944	_____	St George
1937	_____	Newtown	1945	_____	Newtown
1941	_____	Newtown	1959	_____	St George
1942	_____	Newtown			

Endeavour Cup

Year		Winner
1970	_____	Newtown

League Cup

Year		Winner	Year		Winner
1912	_____	Eastern Suburbs	1920	_____	Glebe
1913	_____	Balmain	1921	_____	Newtown
1914	_____	North Sydney	1922	_____	South Sydney
1915	_____	South Sydney	1923	_____	Balmain
1916	_____	South Sydney	1924	_____	Newtown
1917	_____	South Sydney	1925	_____	Newtown
1918	_____	South Sydney	1926	_____	Western Suburbs
1919	_____	South Sydney			

State Championships

Year		Winner
1939	_____	Canterbury-Bankstown
1941	_____	Newtown
1942	_____	Balmain
1944	_____	St George
1945	_____	Newtown

State Cup

Year		Winner
1964	_____	Newcastle
1965	_____	Western Suburbs

Thiess-Toyota Trophy

Year		Winner
1971	_____	Cronulla-Sutherland

F

FAMILIES IN RUGBY LEAGUE

Australia has known members of the same families who have excelled in the game. The first two legends were Dally and Wally Messenger. Dally played for Australia in the first three years after the game started down-under and had quit the Test scene by the time Wally played his two Tests in 1914. The first brothers to appear together in the same Test match were Viv and Billy Farnsworth, who played together in the 1911–12 series in Britain. It was to be another 52 years before brothers appeared in the same Test, when Ken and Dick Thornett turned out for the 1963 Kangaroos.

There were others who played for Australia at different times, either in Tests or on tour—Peter and Frank Burge, Bob and Peter Dimond, Joe and Ian Doyle, Jim and Alf Gibbs, Graham and Ray Laird, Steve and Chris Mortimer, Ray and Rex Norman, Alf and Frank O'Connor, Greg and Lew Platz, Norm and Peter Provan, Bill and Tom Tyquin, Kerrod, Kevin and Steve Walters and Graeme and Peter Wynn.

Four father-and-son combinations have played for Australia—Joe and Sandy Pearce, Doug McLean Snr and Doug McLean Jnr, Bill and Monty Heidke and Con and Bill Sullivan. Greg Pierce, captain of Australia in 1978, was the grandson of Arthur Folwell, who played Tests 45 years before. Gary Stevens, the Souths player who wore the green and gold for Australia between 1972 and 1975, was the grandson of Arthur Oxford, Souths' goal-kicking international of the immediate post-World War I era.

In 1990, three Walters brothers played State-of-Origin football for Queensland, a feat believed unique. Five-eighth Kevin Walters played two matches as a replacement. Test hooker Kerrod Walters was rake for the second and third clashes. He was injured an unable to play in the first clash. Instead, the hooker spot went to his brother Steve Walters. Kerrod and Kevin created further history by becoming the first twins to tour with the Kangaroos. When Kerrod Walters was suspended after being sent from the field in a club game the following year, Steve replaced him in the Queensland State-of-Origin side and performed so well that he was chosen as Test hooker, too. It was the first instance in the history of the game of three brothers all reaching Tests status.

Perhaps the most remarkable instance of families involved in Rugby League occurred in the 1980 Sydney Premiership grand final. Canterbury-Bankstown, which won the match, was spearheaded by two sets of brothers, the Mortimers and the Hughes. Chris and Peter Mortimer played in the centres, while brother Steve was halfback. Garry Hughes was five-eighth, Mark Hughes lock and Graeme Hughes second-row.

One of Australia's most remarkable footballing families was the Goldspinks, from the southern NSW town of Tumbarumba. In a 1977 charity match, family members came from around Australia to fill all 13 positions in one side. There were four Goldspinks as reserves, too. Those involved included fullback Barry, a Country and Riverina representative, and prop-forward Col, who played for Riverina against New Zealand and was a member of Canterbury-Bankstown's first-grade side for years. Missing was the most famous of all the Goldspinks, Kevin, who played second-row for Canterbury and Eastern Suburbs and toured Britain and France with the 1967 Kangaroos.

FAMOUS MATCHES

The Rorke's Drift Test

No team in the history of international Rugby League has shown the courage and determination to overcome all odds, to equal that of Britain's 1914 Third Test combination. Ten tired men (there were no replacements allowed in those days) held off 13 eager Australians for most of the second half to score a 14–6 victory and clinch the Ashes. Such was the stoic British display that one newspaper likened their play to the famous stand by 104 British soldiers against a 4000–strong Zulu horde at Rorke's Drift in 1879. The journalist's description will never be forgotten, for the decider of the 1914 series is universally remembered as 'The Rorke's Drift Test'.

The match was a controversial one even before the kick-off with Britain only taking the field under protest. The tourists had won the First Test 23–5 on the previous Saturday. Two days later, the Australians turned the tables with a 12–7 win (after Britain led 7–0 early in the game). Despite injuries, the tourists were unperturbed as the Third Test was not supposed to be played until they returned from a visit to New Zealand.

Then the Australian authorities dropped a bombshell. They rescheduled the Third Test for the following Saturday. The British were livid. Three Tests in eight days! With a limited squad carrying a long list of injuries, they would not agree.

The Australians, not to be dissuaded, cabled the British authorities at home to explain that the event would lose much of its crowd appeal if left until after the New Zealand section of the tour. The hierarchy in Leeds agreed, ordering tour manager John Clifford to go ahead with the game.

In a stirring dressing-room speech before the clash, Clifford told his charges they were 'playing for England's honour, playing for Right versus Wrong!'. What an honorable display they turned in.

Winger Frank Williams injured a leg in the first moments of the game. He stayed on but was a virtual passenger. Soon after, Huddersfield forward Douglas Clark broke a thumb—but he too, battled on. Britain led 9–0 at the interval. The second half had been under way for only a few minutes when Clark broke clear and headed for the try-line. The great Aussie halfback 'Pony' Halloway raced across to tackle him. Clark went to palm off but, wary of his injured thumb, decided to crash Halloway out of his path instead. Halloway ducked and Clark, off balance, crashed heavily to the ground. He badly smashed his collarbone and had to retire. Minutes later, Williams was again injured and forced off the field. Centre Hall followed soon after, with concussion.

Ten men and 30 minutes to go! Captain Harold Wagstaff and his men rose to the occasion. Magnificent defence kept the Australian 13 at bay and then Wagstaff cut through and sent the ball to forward Chick Johnson, who was playing as a makeshift winger. Johnson had fullback Howard Hallett to beat and did so by dribbling the ball past him Soccer-style. Hall came back for the final few minutes, but by then, the British had the game in their keeping.

At Sydney Cricket Ground, Saturday, 4 July 1914
Crowd: 34 420
GREAT BRITAIN 14 (W A Davies, A Johnson tries, A E Wood 4 goals) d AUSTRALIA 6 (W Messenger, S Deane tries)
Great Britain: Alf Wood, Frank Williams, Harold Wagstaff (c), Billy Hall, Avon Davies, WS Prosser, F Smith, J Chilcott, Dick Ramsdale, Duggie Clarke, D Holland, A P Coldrick, Albert Johnson
Australia: Howard Hallett, Bob Tidyman, Wally Messenger, Sid Deane (c), Dan Frawley, Charles 'Chook' Fraser, Arthur 'Pony' Halloway, Bill Cann, Bob Craig, Tedda Courtney, Con Sullivan, Sid 'Sandy' Pearce, Frank Burge
Referee: Tom McMahon

The 'Chimpy' Busch No-try Controversy

Of the many controversial decisions in the history of Rugby League, the most generally discordant must be 'Chimpy' Busch's disallowed try. The incident occurred in the Third (and deciding) Test at Swinton on the 1929–30 Kangaroo tour. Australia had won the initial encounter, at Hull, 31–8, and Britain had squared the series with a 9–3 victory at Leeds.

The Swinton match was traditionally a tough one, with neither side being able to score—at least, not until the brilliant Australian halfback Joe 'Chimpy' Busch dived over in the corner late in the proceedings. British lock-forward Butters dived vainly at Busch, hit the wooden corner post and tore an ear so badly that six stitches were required to sew up the gaping wound. However the touch judge, Albert Webster, ruled it had been Busch—not Butters—who had hit the post and landed out of bounds. Referee Bob Robinson, one of Britain's greatest-ever whistle-men, was right on the spot and noted: 'Fair try, Australia, but I can't give it to you. The linesman is the sole judge of touch'. The try was disallowed—and the match finished in a nil-all draw.

Even the partisan crowd was upset and many spectators wanted to sign a petition demanding Busch's try be allowed. British officials were also disturbed and offered to play an unprecedented Fourth Test. Australia snapped up the offer. It was in vain. The final encounter, another tough, tense affair, saw the Kangaroos beaten 3–0 and the Ashes remained where they had been for the previous nine years—in England.

At Swinton, Saturday, 4 January 1930
Crowd: 34 709
AUSTRALIA 0 drew with GREAT BRITAIN 0
Australia: Frank McMillan, Bill Spencer, Cec Fifield, Tommy Gorman (c), Bill Shankland, Eric Weissel,

Joe 'Chimpy' Busch, Jack Kingston, Vic Armbruster, George Treweek, Bill Brogan, Arthur 'Snowy' Justice, Herb Steinohrt
Great Britain: Jim Sullivan, Alf Ellaby, Arthur Atkinson, H Halsall, Stanley Smith, J Oster, Jonty Parkin (c), Fred Butters, Martin Hodgson, Albert Fildes, A G Thomas, N Bentham, Bill Burgess
Referee: Bob Robinson

The Battle of Brisbane

Anglo-Australian Test matches are always tough affairs. At times they become so tough they border on brutal. Such was the case in the Second Test of the 1932 series, a clash dubbed 'The Battle of Brisbane'.

The First Test, played in Sydney before 70 204 people, indicated Britain and Australia were evenly matched in football ability (the tourists scraped home 8–6). The Battle of Brisbane showed they were just as close in thuggery. The Australians, perhaps, came off a little worse than their opponents. The scoreboard of injuries read:

- Second-rower Dan Dempsey—a broken wrist
- Halfback Hec Gee—knocked out, with a badly gashed mouth
- Centre Eric Norman—severe concussion
- Prop-forward Frank O'Connor—split eye
- Fullback Frank McMillan—knocked out
- Five-eighth Eric Weissel—torn ligaments in an ankle

The fighting erupted when, with Australia leading 8–0, referee Simpson disallowed what seemed to be a legitimate try by British winger Alf Ellaby. From then on almost every tackle produced a foul—a punch, a kick or a combination of both. One journalist wrote: "It became the most desperate and rugged game imaginable. Players were left strewn like dead men on the field, or were carried off to touch lines to recover. These were chiefly Australians'.

There were only two or three instances of real football. The highlight was a brilliant move by Weissel who, ignoring his injured ankle, half-ran, half-hobbled 80 metres down the field only to be caught 10 metres from the line. From the ensuing play-the-ball, Gee was able to score. Australia won that Test 15–6 but, as one critic wrote: 'It wasn't clear who won the fight'.

At Brisbane Cricket Ground, Saturday, 18 June 1932
Crowd: 26 574
AUSTRALIA 15 (H Gee 2, J Wilson tries, E Weissel 2, S Pearce goals) d GREAT BRITAIN 6 (S Smith, E Pollard tries)
Australia: Frank McMillan, Cliff Pearce, Eric Norman, Fred Laws, Joe Wilson, Eric Weissel, Hec Gee, Frank O'Connor, Sid 'Joe' Pearce, Les Heidke, Mick Madsen, Dan Dempsey, Herb Steinohrt (c)
Great Britain: Jim Sullivan (c), Alf Ellaby, Arthur Atkinson, Stanley Brogden, Stanley Smith, E Pollard, L Adams, J F Thompson, L L White, Nat Silcock, Bill Horton, Martin Hodgson, Jack Feetham
Referee: J Simpson

Ron Roberts' Try Wins Ashes

Ron Roberts was notorious for his poor handling, but the tall, burly winger from St George held the one pass in his career which mattered most of all—and scored the try which earned Australia The Ashes previously held firmly in Britain's hands for 30 years.

It was in the Third Test of the 1950 series. The tourists had won the First Test, at the Sydney Cricket Ground, but Australia equalised in Brisbane.

The decider was also at the SCG and conditions that day were atrocious. Heavy rain had turned the field into a quagmire. More than 40 tonnes of sand were tipped on it, but that did little to provide a more solid footing. As the players ran on to start the game, the rain continued to bucket down.

It was to be a dour forwards' battle with only the series uncertainty to enthrall the 47 178 hardy spectators who had braved the rain. Half-time: 2–all. A goal apiece—and so it remained until 14 minutes from the end.

Then came one of the few try-scoring chances of the match. From a play-the-ball, Australian lock Mick Crocker tossed the ball to halfback Keith Holman who despatched it quickly along the backline. Australia got an overlap when centre Keith Middleton forced Englishman Jack Hilton to come in from the wing in defence. Middleton fired the ball to Roberts, who now had a clear run for the line. The ball was greasy with mud, but Roberts caught it perfectly and sailed in for the only try of the match. With the opposition line wide open again, he did drop a pass in the dying minutes of the game—but he had caught the important one.

There were emotional scenes as the final whistle blew. Eighty-year-old James J Giltinan, who had helped found the sport in Australia, wept openly. Ecstatic members of the public ran onto the field and carried the muddy Australians shoulder-high to their dressing room. Women embraced and kissed them—and some men knelt and kissed the slush on which Australia had regained The Ashes after so long a drought.

At Sydney Cricket Ground, Saturday, 22 July 1950
Crowd: 47 178
AUSTRALIA 5 (R Roberts try, C Churchill goal) d GREAT BRITAIN 2 (E Ward goal)
Australia: Clive Churchill (c), Ron Roberts, Keith Middleton, Doug McRitchie, Jack Troy, Frank Stanmore, Keith Holman, Les 'Chic' Cowie, Harold 'Mick' Crocker, Bernie Purcell, Jack Holland, Kev Schubert, Duncan Hall
Great Britain: J Ledgard, T Danby, E Ward (c), E Ashcroft, J Hilton, J Cunliffe, T Bradshaw, H Street, D Philips, F Higgins, E Gwyther, J Egan, K Gee
Referee: Tom McMahon

First Franco-Australian Test Down-Under

Australia, cock-a-hoop from the previous year's Ashes triumph over Britain, considered the band of Frenchmen making their country's first tour in 1951, rather as a schoolmaster might his pupil. The mercurial Frenchmen did not need long to shatter this illusion—just as long as it took them to play their first international, in Sydney.

The field was muddy, but the French team played as if it were a dry day, throwing the ball around with gay abandon. Led by eccentric fullback Puig-Aubert, France raced to an early 16–0 lead, with tries by wingers Contrastin and Cantoni and five goals by Puig-Aubert.

Despite a rally soon after the half-time break, which brought the home side back to 15–16, the unorthodox play of the new boys prevailed. The final whistle showed the pupil having outplayed the master to the tune of 26–15. France scored four tries to three and Puig-Aubert helped out with an individual goal-kicking record of seven. The tourists showed this bedazzling result was no flash-in-the-pan effort by going on to win the series two Tests to one.

At Sydney Cricket Ground, Saturday, 11 June 1951
Crowd: 60 160
FRANCE 26 (V Cantoni 2, R Contrastin, G Genoud tries, Puig-Aubert 7 goals) d AUSTRALIA 15 (J Graves, G Willoughby, H Crocker tries, J Graves 3 goals)
Australia: Clive Churchill (c), Johnny Bliss, Gordon Willoughby, Noel Hazzard, Johnny Graves, Frank Stanmore, Keith Holman, Noel Mulligan, Harold 'Mick' Crocker, Brian Davies, Denis Donoghue, Kev Schubert, Duncan Hall
France: Puig-Aubert (c), Vincent Cantoni, Gaston Combes, Joseph Crespo, Raymond Contrastin, Charles Galaup, Jean Dop, Rene Duffort, Edouard Ponsinet, Elie Brousse, Louis Mazon, Gabriel Genoud, Paul Bartoletti
Referee: Tom McMahon

The Abandoned International

The tenth of July 1954 was a black day in the history of Rugby League. That afternoon, a rain-drenched crowd of 27 000 witnessed possibly the most disgraceful international match ever played. So vicious, so unruly, so uncontrollable was the clash between Britain and New South Wales that referee Aub Oxford did what no other had done before or since— he walked off the field 56 minutes after the start, abandoned the match, and left the players to continue a brawl which had ranged from one end of the field to the other.

The climactic battle had its beginnings long before kick-off. Britain and Australia were level one Test all in the Ashes series and the decider was scheduled for the following Saturday. The NSW side contained most of those who would make up the Australian line-up. The tourists selected only three Test probables and, in a shock move, put forwards in the two wing positions and at fullback. This prompted many critics to suggest they planned to put the local stars out of action. The match certainly lived up to these pessimistic predictions.

'Whack! And it was on!' read the headline next day in the Sydney newspaper *Truth*. The first half was relatively quiet but the match exploded soon after the break when British five-eighth Ray Price was sent off for disputing one of Oxford's decisions.

The affair degenerated quickly. Its climax came after an exchange between NSW fullback Clive Churchill and British halfback Alf Burnell. A punch aimed at Churchill missed and hit winger Noel Pidding. Within seconds both teams were locked in a wild melee. Oxford, the touch judges and a couple of the calmer players tried in vain to separate the gladiators. When this proved fruitless, Oxford walked off, calling the match a no-contest, and quit refereeing for good.

The incident looked likely to wreck Anglo-Australian Rugby League relations, but cooler heads prevailed. Charlie Pawsey, who captained Great Britain on that day, addressed an official NSW Rugby League inquiry two days later. 'My team-mates wanted me to come along and say how sorry they were. I ask you to accept the apology, with all sincerity,' Pawsey said. The governing body did just that and officially, nothing more was said.

At Sydney Cricket Ground, Saturday, 10 July 1954
Crowd: 27 000
NEW SOUTH WALES V GREAT BRITAIN—Match abandoned
New South Wales: Clive Churchill (c), Noel Pidding, Harry Wells, Merv Lees, Brian Carlson, Dick Poole, Keith Holman, Peter Diversi, Norm Provan, Jack Rayner, Jack Evans, Ken Kearney, Roy Bull
Great Britain: G Gunney, J Wilkinson, J Henderson, D Greenall, B Briggs, R Price, A Burnell, K Traill, C Pawsey (c), T Harris, T McKinney, A Prescott
Referee: Aub Oxford

The Day the Kangaroos Broke All Records

The ninth of November 1963, goes down as the day English fans would most like to forget.

At Swinton that Saturday afternoon, the Kangaroos ripped apart their opponents and the record books:

- They became the first all-Australian side to win the Ashes in England (the only previous winners, the 1911–12 Kangaroos, had included New Zealanders).
- Their 50 points was Australia's highest tally in Tests against Great Britain.
- The 50–12 score provided the biggest winning margin.
- Two tries by the great centre Reg Gasnier took his total in Anglo-Australian Tests to nine, putting him on top of his country's individual try-scoring lists.
- His centre partner, Graeme Langlands, with 20 points (two tries and seven goals) became the top scorer in any single Test against Britain.

The match itself was little more than an exhibition. It was fairly even for the first 13 minutes but then Australia stacked on seven tries in 23 minutes to put the result beyond doubt. Although he did not score himself, lock Johnny Raper turned in a faultless display and had a hand in almost all the tries.

Admittedly, Britain was unlucky in losing centre Eric Ashton and five-eighth Frank Myler, thereby finishing with 11 men. Both casualties broke ribs—Ashton in the sixth minute and Myler almost 20 minutes later—in an era before replacements were permitted. Ashton explained: 'This was the best Australian side I have even seen. I doubt whether we could have beaten them with a full team today or any other day'.

The British Press aptly summed up the match: The *Sunday Mirror* described it as 'the great slaughter'. The *People* said: 'Matilda waltzed as she has never waltzed before.' The *Sunday Express* lamented: 'The day Britain died of shame'.

At Station Road, Swinton, Saturday, 9 November 1963
Crowd: 30 843
AUSTRALIA 50 (K Irvine 3, P Dimond 2, G Langlands 2, R Gasnier 2, E Harrison, N Kelly, R Thornett tries, G Langlands 7 goals) d GREAT BRITAIN 12 (J Measures, J Stopford tries, N Fox 3 goals)
Australia: Ken Thornett, Peter Dimond, Reg Gasnier, Graeme Langlands, Ken Irvine, Earl Harrison, Barry Muir, Johnny Raper, Ken Thornett, Ken Day, Noel Kelly, Ian Walsh (c), Paul Quinn
Great Britain: Ken Gowers, Mike Sullivan, Eric Ashton (c), Neil Fox, John Stopford, Frank Myler, Alex Murphy, Vince Karalius, Ron Morgan, Jim Measures, Cliff Watson, Len McIntyre, Bill Robinson
Referee: Dennis Davies

Fireworks After 1963 Test

Anglo-Australian Test matches are always fought with more than ordinary determination by both sides. Tempers invariably flare and spiteful attacks often follow. However after the match, everyone usually cools down—and the gladiators of minutes before become friends. This was not the case after the Third Test of the 1963 tour.

The visitors had already become the first all-Australian side to win the Ashes on British soil. In two great performances they had humbled the best of Britain—including a record-breaking 50–12 win in the second encounter. Now, all that remained was to score a clean sweep.

That was not to be. In a fiery clash, the home side won the Third Test 16–5, at Leeds. Three players were sent from the field by controversial referee Eric Clay. One of those dismissed, Queensland halfback Barry Muir, challenged jeering spectators to come out and fight him or 'shut up'— but it was after the match, when all normally would have been forgiven, that the fireworks really started.

Australian co-manager Jack Lynch, accepting the Ashes Trophy at the official presentation, lashed out at British Rugby League in general and referee Clay in particular. Said Lynch: 'Personally, I thought this trophy must have been made of solid gold because of the means that are used to retain it'.

On Clay: 'I thought his exhibition was disgraceful. It was too blatant, too obvious. This Clay—they call him the Sergeant Major—will probably be promoted to Field Marshall and be given a baton because of his great performance. We accept our defeats with good grace—the other side played well—but we do not have to accept what was done to us by the referee.' The Lynch speech was repeatedly interrupted by jeers and catcalls.

The usual Anglo-Australian cool eventually prevailed, with visiting Australian Rugby League president Bill Buckley diplomatically pouring oil on troubled waters: 'My firm conviction is that you only get beaten because the other fellow is too good. I think that is what happened in this match'.

Years later, after he retired, Clay laughed off the whole incident. 'A lot of players that day heaped abuse on me while the game was in progress,' he said. 'I did what had to be done. The players know it. And I know it. And that's all that counts'.

At Headingley, Leeds, Saturday, 30 November 1963
Crowd: 20 497
GREAT BRITAIN 16 (G Smith, J Stopford, D Fox, J Ward tries, D Fox 2 goals) d AUSTRALIA 5 (K Irvine try, G Langlands goal)
Great Britain: Ken Gowers, Geoff Smith, Keith Holden, Alan Buckley, John Stopford, David Bolton, Tommy Smales (c), Don Fox, Ken Roberts, Dick Huddart, Frank Collier, John Ward, Cliff Watson
Australia: Ken Thornett, Peter Dimond, Reg Gasnier, Graeme Langlands, Ken Irvine, Earl Harrison, Barry Muir, Johnny Raper, Dick Thornett, Brian Hambly, Paul Quinn, Ian Walsh (c), Noel Kelly
Referee: Eric Clay

The Mudbath Grand Final

Western Suburbs has over the years acquired a reputation for being the giant-killers of Sydney Rugby League. Its 1930 Premiership broke a sequence by South Sydney, which had won the preceding five titles and went on to win the next two. Wests did something similar in 1952 when Souths had won two, with three more to come. So, in 1963, it came as no surprise that the Magpies expected to play their role again and bring St George's seven years at the top to an end.

Wests had beaten the Dragons in both rounds of the season proper (the only two matches St George lost). They had made it three out of three with a 10–8 success in the major semi-final—but St George did not surrender grand finals meekly!

The field for the match was a quagmire. Sydney had been subjected to a long period of wet weather and the Sydney Cricket Ground was hit by a torrential downpour on grand final eve. The rain continued all Saturday. Despite the appalling conditions, a record 69 860 hardy souls crammed into the arena. Heaven only knows how many would have been there had it been fine.

The day seemed tailor-made for St George, whose style of football depended a great deal on the forward play of such seasoned internationals as captain-coach Norm Provan, Kevin Ryan, Ian Walsh and Elton Rasmussen. Wests, too, had a great six—including Provan's former Test second-row partner Kel O'Shea and legendary strongman Noel Kelly. Saints won the dour battle 8–3, thanks largely to a 2–1 scrum success rate and an 18–7 margin in penalties awarded.

Wests were particularly upset by some of referee Darcy Lawler's rulings. Not only did he hammer them in the penalties but he disallowed one Wests touchdown and awarded St George a try which was disputed. In the first instance, Magpie captain Arthur Summons had put through a magnificent kick which landed near the corner. Fellow-international Peter Dimond raced through and dived on the ball over the line but had it slide from his grasp and go 'dead'. Lawler ruled that Dimond had not touched the ball down. No try! On the other hand, St George winger Johnny King broke through but was tackled by fullback Don Parish near Wests' line. King, claiming he was not held, jumped up and, without playing the ball, ran over to score. Fair try, ruled Lawler.

As captain Provan and Summons, swathed in mud, walked from the field at the end of the match with their arms around each other a photographer, John O'Gready, snapped a prize-winning shot of the pair. This became the blue-print for the sculpture on the top of the Winfield Cup, one of the two trophies awarded to the Sydney Premiers each year.

It's now history how St George went on to win a world record 11 straight Premierships—most of them comfortably—but luck certainly provided that vital link between their successes of 1962 and 1964.

At Sydney Cricket Ground, Saturday, 24 August 1963
Crowd: 69 860 (Ground record)
ST GEORGE 8 (G Evans, J King tries, R Gasnier goal) d WESTERN SUBURBS 3 (G McDougall try)
St George: Graeme Langlands, Eddie Lumsden, Reg Gasnier, Billy Smith, Johnny King, Bruce Pollard, George Evans, Johnny Raper, Elton Rasmussen, Norm Provan (c), Kevin Ryan, Ian Walsh, Monty Porter
Western Suburbs: Don Parish, Johnny Mowbray, Rob McGuiness, Gil McDougall, Peter Dimond, Arthur Summons (c), Don Malone, Kevin Smyth, Johnny Hayes, Kel O'Shea, Dennis Meaney, Noel Kelly, Jack Gibson
Referee: Darcy Lawler

Referees 'Ban' English Players

In 1966, Balmain became the first Sydney club side to beat Great Britain. The Tigers downed the tourists 9–8 in a hard, fiery match at the Sydney Cricket Ground, succeeding where the mighty St George had failed four years previously.

Either team could have won with a good goalkicker. Balmain's kickers, especially, turned in woeful performances. Britain scored two tries to one and referee Les Samuelson caned the tourists in the penalties, 14–2. The British were also upset when winger Bill Burgess was ruled to have put his foot in touch for what would have been his second try of the match. The game, as such, was soon forgotten, but not so the troubled aftermath.

As the players left the field, English halfback Tommy Bishop and winger Burgess were involved in an incident with touch judge Rowland Morris.

He said Burgess had jostled him and, soon after, Bishop gave him a back-handed punch. When details were reported in the Press, it was expected that both players would receive stiff sentences. It wasn't to be. The members of the NSW League Judiciary Committee found the evidence conflicting. Bishop escaped scot free—after submitting an apology for being involved in an incident which had nothing to do with him. Burgess, charged with misconduct, was let off with a caution.

The Referees Association was incensed. The whistle-blowers passed a motion of no confidence in the Judiciary Committee and voted to refuse to officiate at any future match in which either Bishop or Burgess appeared. The decision had a 'Catch 22' ring about it. The British tour was over and it was to be four years before another. Even then, neither Bishop nor Burgess would be a certainty for the touring squad.

The active controversy soon died a natural death. Further apologies were offered and, within a few weeks, the whole episode—including the referees' threat—passed quietly into Rugby League history.

At Sydney Cricket Ground, Tuesday, 16 July 1966
Crowd: 22 369
BALMAIN 9 (H Browne try, S Williams 2, D Wilson goals) d GREAT BRITAIN 8 (A Buckley, W Burgess tries, C Clarke goal)
Balmain: Laurie Moraschi, Paul Cross, Kevin Yow Yeh, Harold Browne, Bob Mara, Paul Jones, David Bolton, Peter Provan, Dennis Tutty, Peter Oakley, George Piper, Dick Wilson, Bob Boland. Replacements: Sid Williams (for Bolton, half-time) and Garry Leo (for Oakley, half-time)
Great Britain: Frank Myler, Bill Burgess, Geoff Shelton, Alan Buckley, John Stopford, Alan Hardisty, Tommy Bishop, Dave Robinson, Terry Fogarty, Bill Bryant, Brian Edgar, Colin Clarke, Cliff Watson. Replacement: Harry Poole (for Watson, half-time)
Referee: Les Samuelson

Disputed Try Decides World Cup

Was Australia robbed of the 1972 World Cup final by an incredulous French referee? Australians are adamant: Yes! The British just smile and point to the score in the record books.

Ten points all—the only World Cup final to end in a draw. Even after 10 minutes extra each way the game was deadlocked but Britain's better showings in the preliminary rounds gave it the title.

The ruling which Australians say was wrong came in the twenty-fifth minute of the final, with the British trailing 5–2. Georges Jameau, one of France's most experienced and respected referees, disallowed an amazing touchdown by captain Graeme Langlands. It would have been one of the most spectacular tries ever recorded in international football. Australia's halfback Dennis Ward had made a break and, almost caught by the defence, punted high towards the tryline. Langlands, showing a great burst of acceleration and anticipation, shot through and, in one movement, leaped into the air, grabbed the ball and fell across the line. Jameau ruled him off-side—although checks of films and photographs of the incident indicate Langlands was well behind Ward when he kicked.

Only 4 500 people were at Lyon's Gerland Stadium that cold, grey November afternoon to see the final. It was not a classic match, but it was tough and tense to the very last and, if only for that controversial ruling, will be remembered for a long time to come.

At Stade Gerland, Lyon, Saturday, 11 November 1972
Crowd: 4 500

GREAT BRITAIN 10 (C Sullivan, M Stephenson tries, T Clawson 2 goals) drew with AUSTRALIA 10 (J O'Neill, A Beetson tries, R Branighan 2 goals)
Great Britain: Paul Charlton, Clive Sullivan (c), Chris Hesketh, John Walsh, John Atkinson, John Holmes, Steve Nash, George Nicholls, Brian Lockwood, Phil Lowe, David Jeanes, Mike Stephenson, Terry Clawson. Replacement: Bob Irving (for Jeanes)
Australia: Graeme Langlands (c), Ray Branighan, Geoff Starling, Mark Harris, John Grant, Bob Fulton, Dennis Ward, Gary Sullivan, Gary Stevens, Arthur Beetson, Bob O'Reilly, Elwyn Walters, John O'Neill
Referee: Georges Jameau (France)

Swansea Storm

International Rugby League returned to Wales in 1975, after a break of almost a quarter of a century. The locals soon saw how tough the professional game could be—with a vicious, brawling World Championship match between Australia and Wales. The venue for this glorified punch-up was the St Helen's ground at Swansea. Three major brawls erupted during the match, involving more than half the players. One spread over the touch-line and into the grand-stand, with several officials joining in. That the match was so violent came as no great surprise.

The Australians had a tough pack of forwards—led by probably the greatest of his era, Arthur Beetson, and the locals lacked nothing when it came to brute strength, with one of the willingest front-rows to tread a football field—Jim Mills, Tony Fisher and John Mantle. Beetson was prominent in the heavy work and was probably saved from an early dismissal by the fact that he never actually started any of the fighting.

The match, nevertheless, had moments in which both sides showed they could play top-class football. Its star was the 19–year-old blond Australian winger Ian Schubert, playing in only his second international. Amid all the tumult he helped himself to three tries, half of Australia's 18–6 winning score. Predictably, Schubert was named Man-of-the-Match.

At St Helen's Ground, Swansea, Sunday, 19 October 1975
Crowd: 11 112
AUSTRALIA 18 (I Schubert 3, J Peard tries, M Cronin 3 goals) d WALES 6 (D Watkins 3 goals)
Australia: Graham Eadie, Allan McMahon, Mick Cronin, Steve Rogers, Ian Schubert, John Peard, Johnny Mayes, John Quayle, Ray Higgs, Terry Randall, Greg Veivers, George Piggins, Arthur Beetson (c). Replacements: Ian Mackay (for Quayle, 19th min) and Jim Porter (for Mayes, 78th min)
Wales: David Watkins (c), Roy Mathias, Bill Francis, Frank Wilson, John Bevan, Glyn Turner, Peter Banner, Kel Coslett, Colin Dixon, Eddie Cunningham, John Mantle, Tony Fisher, Jim Fisher. Replacement: Peter Rowe (for Dixon, 49th min)
Referee: Jack Percival (New Zealand)

First Tied Grand Final

A nine–all draw in the 1977 Sydney Premiership grand final caught officialdom by surprise. St George and Parramatta had battled out the regular 80 minutes' play and an extra 10 minutes each way, but they remained locked together. The by-laws had no provision for a drawn grand final, so a hurried conference of the top brass had to decide that the contenders should replay their decider a week later.

Before the first match, most experts reckoned there was little between the two sides, although Parramatta, Minor Premiers and grand finalists the previous year, were expected to have too much guile and experience for the young St George side, nicknamed 'Bath's Babes' after their famous coach Harry Bath. However, at half-time, 'Bath's Babes' seemed home and hosed. They led 9–0 and Parramatta had not looked likely to score. In a second-half transformation, Parramatta came back with a vengeance.

The Eels drew level with a try just three minutes before the scheduled end of play and two points for a conversion would have given them the Premiership—but centre Mick Cronin, one of Australia's finest goal-kickers ever, sliced the ball wide of the posts.

When the match went in extra time, Parramatta continued attacking. Halfback John Kolc was pulled down a mere body-length from the line. Then front-rower Graham Olling was smothered near it with two men unmarked outside him. Saints held on and began to give as good as they took. A field goal attempt from fullback Tony Quirk hit the left upright with only a minute of extra time remaining and winger John Chapman missed a penalty attempt almost immediately after—and so, it remained 9–all. The gruelling 100 minutes took its toll on both sides—but the St George youngsters recovered best. A week later, they made no mistake with a violent 22–0 victory that caught the Parramatta hardheads unawares.

At Sydney Cricket Ground, Saturday, 17 September 1977
Crowd: 65 959
ST GEORGE 9 (E Goodwin try, E Goodwin 2, J Chapman goals) drew with PARRAMMATTA 9 (E Sulkowicz try, M Cronin 3 goals)
St George: Ted Goodwin, Steve Butler, Graham Quinn, Robert Finch, John Chapman, Rod McGregor, Mark Shulman, Rod Reddy, John Jansen, Robert Stone, Craig Young, Steve Edge (c), Bruce Starkey. Replacements; John Bailey (for Shulman) and Tony Quirk (for Goodwin)
Parramatta: Phil Mann, Jim Porter, Ed Sulkowicz, Mick Cronin, Graeme Atkins, Mark Levy, John Kolc, Ray Price, Ray Higgs (c), Geoff Gerard, John Baker, Ron Hilditch, Graham Olling. Replacement: Denis Fitzgerald (for Baker)
Referee: Gary Cook

Shock Kiwi Win Ends an Era

New Zealand brought about the end of an era when it scored a shock 19–12 victory over Australia at Brisbane's Lang Park in the return Test of the 1983 home-and-away series. The Kiwi victory ended a run of 16 Test wins by Australia. The previous defeat had been back in 1978, at the hands of France. Australia had also strung together 18 Test successes at home, stretching back to 1974. New Zealand's win was its first in Brisbane in 20 years.

The home side had no answer to the bruising running and tackling by the Kiwi pack. Lanky captain Graeme West and the tough brothers Kurt and Dane Sorensen were the pick of the New Zealand six—but the man who really demoralised the Australians was halfback Shane Varley, the Man-of-the-Match. He engineered one try (by centre James Leuluai) and had a hand in most other attacking movements.

Fullback Nick Wright also turned in a blinder. His tactical kicking regularly turned the Australians around. He also pulled off the best tackle of the match to bundle Australian centre Mal Meninga into touch, saving what seemed like a certain try. Meninga and fellow-Queenslander Gene Miles had dreadful games. Their size and speed were expected to be among the Australians' biggest assets, but they were held in check by Leuluai and Fred Ah Kuoi. Big Maori winger Joe Roparti regularly came in from the wing to put them to ground in no uncertain manner.

The only Australians to emerge from the Test with reputations untarnished were hooker Max Krilich and lock Ray Price. Krilich, the Australian skipper, was playing his last representative match and the loss was a bitter disappointment to him.

English referee Robin Whitfield explained the difference between the two sides: 'You could hear the New Zealanders talking non-stop, willing each other on to bigger and better things, but there was little talk from the Australians. They knew they were going down'.

At Lang Park, Brisbane, Saturday, 9 July 1983
Crowd: 15 000
NEW ZEALAND 19 (G West, J Leuluai, J Roparti tries, N Wright 3 goals) d AUSTRALIA 12 (E Grothe, S Ella tries, M Meninga 2 goals)
New Zealand: Nick Wright, Joe Ropati, James Leuluai, Fred Ah Kuoi, Dean Bell, Gordon Smith, Shane Varley, Gary Prohm, Kurt Sorensen, Graeme West (c), Dane Sorensen, Howie Tamati, Mark Broadhurst. Replacements: Ron O'Regan (for Varley) and Ian Bell (for Tamati)
Australia: Colin Scott, Kerry Boustead, Mal Meninga, Gene Miles, Eric Grothe, Wally Lewis, Steve Mortimer, Ray Price, Paul Vautin, Wally Fullerton Smith, Dave Brown, Max Krilich (c), Brad Tessmann. Replacements: Steve Ella (for Mortimer) and Ray Brown (for Tessmann).
Referee: Robin Whitfield (Great Britain)

Aussie Fright in 100th Test

In a major form reversal Great Britain matched Australia for much of the game in the 100th Test played between the two countries—only to finally go down gallantly, 17–6.

The British, on tour of Australia, had been thrashed in their two lead-up matches—36–12 by NSW Northern Division and 30–0 by reigning Sydney Premiers Manly-Warringah. However in the Test, the first ever at the Sydney Football Stadium, they led 6–0 at half-time and could very well have been much further ahead but for having two tries disallowed and missing a couple of relatively easy penalty kicks for goal.

The British snatched their half-time lead just three minutes from the break when skipper Ellery Hanley, playing at lock, bumped off tackles by halfback Peter Sterling and lock Bob Lindner to go over. Sterling dislocated his shoulder in the tackle but asked to stay on until the interval when, in a remarkable display, he recovered sufficiently to make a courageous return for the second half. It was the spark needed to ignite the Australians. In less than a quarter of an hour Sterling had helped send in big prop Sam Backo and centre Peter Jackson for what proved to be the winning tries.

The second impetus came after French referee Francis Desplas had erred in giving Australia an extra six tackles. Jackson was to get a bonus touch-down minutes from the end. Desplas slowed play, giving no less than 18 penalties in the first half. The Frenchman also disallowed a try to Andy Gregory, which would have brought the scores to 12–all and made a real game of it. This came from a pass from prop Kevin Ward, which Desplas ruled to be forward. Ward's whole-hearted effort was, however, rewarded when he was named Man-of-the-Match.

At Sydney Football Stadium, Saturday, 11 June 1988
Crowd: 24 480
AUSTRALIA 17 (P Jackson 2, S Backo tries, M O'Connor 2 goals, W Lewis field goal) d GREAT BRITAIN 6 (E Hanley try, P Loughlin goal)
Australia: Garry Jack, Andrew Ettingshausen, Michael O'Connor, Peter Jackson, Tony Currie, Wally Lewis (c), Peter Sterling, Bob Lindner, Paul Vauntin, Wally Fullerton Smith, Sam Backo, Greg Conescu, Phil Daley. Replacements: Steve Folkes (for Vauntin, 69th min) and Gary Belcher (for Sterling, 75th min)
Great Britain: Paul Loughlin, Phil Ford, Gary Schofield, David Stephenson, Martin Offiah, David Hulme, Andy Gregory, Ellery Hanley (c), Andy Platt, Mike Gregory, Paul Dixon, Kevin Beardmore, Kevin Ward. Replacements: Roy Powell (for Mike Gregory, 69th min) and Henderson Gill (for Loughlin, 78th min)
Referee: Francis Desplas (France)

Widnes Comeback in World Club Clash

England's Champion club Widnes came back from the dead to thrash the Sydney Premiers Canberra 30–18 for the 1989 World Club Championship.

Canberra had rushed to a 12–0 lead after only 11 minutes of the match at Old Trafford, Manchester, and looked like running away easy winners. Indeed, had all the Raiders chances in the first 25 minutes been taken, the match would have been out of Widnes' reach. However the English club fought back tenaciously to be only two points down at the break.

Canberra then lost all momentum when centre Laurie Daley was sin-binned for 10 minutes for a head-high tackle on former Welsh Rugby Union international Jonathan Davies just after the break. Daley caught Davies around the chin as the Welshman was crossing the line for a try. While Daley was off the field, Widnes ran in two more tries to take an unbeatable 12-point lead. The Raiders were also badly hit when captain Mal Meninga, the spearhead of Canberra's attack, was forced out of the game at half-time with a torn medial ligament.

At Old Trafford, Manchester, Wednesday, 4 October 1989
Crowd: 30 786
WIDNES 30 (M Offiah 2, J Davies, D Wright, P Hulme, R Eyres tries, J Davies 3 goals) d CANBERRA 18 (M Meninga, C O'Sullivan, S Walters tries, M Wood 2, C O'Sullivan goals)
Widnes: Alan Tait, Andy Currier, Jonathan Davies, Darren Wright, Martin Offiah, Tony Myler, David Hulme, Richard Eyres, Paul Hulme, Kurt Sorensen (c), Joe Grima, Phil McKenzie, Derrick Pyke. Replacements: Barry Dowd (for Myler, 44th min) and Richard Moriarty (for Grima, 61st min)
Canberra: Gary Belcher, Matthew Wood, Mal Meninga (c), Laurie Daley, John Ferguson, Chris O'Sullivan, Ricky Stuart, Bradley Clyde, Gary Coyne, Dean Lance, Steve Jackson, Steve Walters, Glenn Lazarus. Replacements: Paul Martin (for Meninga, half-time) and Mark Lowry (for Jackson, 66th min)
Referee: Francis Desplas (France)

Kiwi Shock in Historic Melbourne Test

New Zealand, written off by the critics as a second-rate side, caused one of the biggest upsets in Rugby League history by thrashing Australia 24–8 in the historic first Test ever played in Melbourne, in 1991. The Australians had been 5–1 on favourites to win the first Australian encounter held outside the two League strongholds of Sydney and Brisbane. And when the locals led 8–2 soon after half-time, a big win seemed on the cards. But the gallant Kiwis rallied and scored four tries against a side which fell into a succession of schoolboy errors.

It was only New Zealand's fourth win in a Test against Australia in 20 years. The victory was a triumph for Kiwi captain Gary Freeman, who had been dropped to Balmain's reserve-grade side several weeks earlier. His tactical kicking was superb. And his inspiration provided the spark for some of the young, inexperienced New Zealanders.

The best of these was centre Jarrod McCracken. Twelve months earlier he had been playing country football on the NSW north coast. But against the man rated the best player in the world, Mal Meninga, he shone like a shooting star and was a well-deserved Man-of-the-Match. McCracken was rewarded with a try after he backed up another tyro, Richard Blackmore, who had made a brilliant 60 metre dash down the right wing.

Said Freeman after the match: 'It was a real team effort. Everyone dug deep and showed a lot of character to come back in the second half.' Coach Bob Bailey agreed: 'The boys gave plenty and got the result. It was old-fashioned football. The Australians might not see much of it. But there is nothing wrong with the old ways.' His opposite number Bob Fulton had no excuses: 'We were outplayed by a more patient team which didn't make as many mistakes.'

The turning point in the match came when English referee John Holdsworth sent Australia's captain Meninga to the sin-bin 18 minutes into the second half. He had allegedly obstructed Freeman, who himself had just returned from the sin-bin. While Meninga was sidelined, New Zealand turned an 8–6 deficit into an 18–8 lead.

Australia should have had the match wrapped up before the interval after bombing at least three tries. But there was no doubting the courage of the Kiwis in coming back.

One of the few Australians to emerge with reputation untarnished was Test newcomer Steve Walters. Hooker Walters created football history. His two brothers Kevin and Kerrod had previously represented Australia. Never before had three brothers played Rugby League Tests for any country. Steve Walters made three great bursts from dummy half in the first half, including one in which he dived over to score Australia's only try.

The match saw the end of the Wally Lewis era. After 33 Tests and two other full internationals for Australia, Lewis was made one of the scapegoats for the defeat and dropped from the Test side. It was a sad finale to one of the great Test careers in history.

At Olympic Park, Melbourne, Wednesday, July 3, 1991
Crowd: 26 900 (Ground record)
NEW ZEALAND 24 (J McCracken, R Blackmore, C Friend, T Nikau tries, F Botica 4 goals) d AUSTRALIA 8 (S Walters try, M Meninga 2 goals)
New Zealand: Frano Botica, Jason Williams, Jarrod McCracken, Dave Watson, Richard Blackmore, Tony Kemp, Gary Freeman (c), Tawera Nikau, Dean Lonergan, Emosi Koloto, Brent Todd, Duane Mann, Peter Brown. Replacements: Clayton Friend (for Kemp, 55th min) George Mann (for Lonergan, 63rd min), Gary Mercer (for Koloto, 69th min) and Mike Patton (for Williams, 76th min)
Australia: Paul Hauff, Andrew Ettingshausen, Mal Meninga (c), Chris Johns, Dale Shearer, Wally Lewis, Allan Langer, Bradley Clyde, Bob Lindner, Ian Roberts, Steve Roach, Steve Walters, Martin Bella. Replacements: David Gillespie (for Roach, 34th min), Roach (for Gillespie, 53rd min), John Cartwright (for Lindner, 63rd min).
Referee: John Holdsworth (Great Britain)

Penrith Ends 25-year Drought

After 25 long years in the Sydney competition Premiership, Penrith finally broke through to become Premiers with a 19–12 victory over Canberra in the 1991 grand final. The Panthers shrugged off a woeful performance in the first half to crush the Raiders hopes of a third straight title.

It was a fairytale finish to the career of Penrith's internationsl hooker Royce Simmons. In the last of his 259 matches—a new record for Penrith (including 233 in first grade)—he received his first Premiership-winners' medal. And he scored two of Penrith's three tries—no mean feat for a player who was lucky to score that many in a couple of seasons. His first try, in which he spun out of a couple of tackles, including one from Test prop Glenn Lazarus, gave the Panthers a handy 6–0 lead after as many minutes. In his second, two minutes from full-time, he snapped up a sensational pass from fiery second-rower Mark Geyer, to give Penrith a seven point lead and seal the match.

'I saved my best for last,' Simmons said, fighting back tears after the game. 'We can now hold our heads high.' Ironically, Simmons beat the former record of 258 games, set by Tim Sheens, a former Penrith coach who was at the helm of the Raiders in the grand final.

Canberra looked certainties at half-time with a 12–6 lead. Penrith had been unable to cope with Canberra's switches of play from side to side. But for a couple of Canberra players ignoring supports, Canberra could well have been ahead by 20-odd points at the break.

Penrith coach Phil Gould gave his side a real tongue-lashing at half-time. He told them they were playing like losers. Captain Greg Alexander explained: 'Gus lifted us at half time. We were down. We were gone. But we kept fighting back.'

That fight-back saw Penrith hammer the Canberra line for much of the second-half. Canberra's defence was sensational. The best was a try-saving tackle on Penrith fullback Greg Barwick by captain Mal Meninga in which he swung him away from the line with brute strength. A few moments later Geyer gave a great pass to centre Brad Fittler who sent Izzard over for the equaliser. Penrith also had a try disallowed after an alleged illegal tackle. And stand-off Laurie Daley stole a ball in a tackle as Penrith was heading for an open line. The ball-stealing rule had caused a lot of controversy during the season, but on this occasion referee Bill Harrigan ruled with common sense and did not penalise him.

The Canberra dream run of eight straight wins faltered at the last hurdle largely because the two walking wounded, halves Ricky Stuart and Laurie Daley, did not provide the spark they did in the earlier play-offs. Both had extra needles at half-time to dull the pain—Stuart for his chronic groin injury and Daley for ankle and hamstring problems. It was revealed after the match that for the last five matches of the season Daley had played with a minor fracture to his ankle.

The Clive Churchill Medal (chosen by the former greats Johnny Raper, Reg Gasnier, Bob Fulton and Don Furner) went to Canberra's Bradley Clyde. He was the Raiders' best. But many commentators reckoned it was the great work of Penrith half Greg Alexander which turned the game. 'Brandy' was brilliant in attack. And his field goal six minutes from full-time gave the Panthers the narrow buffer which forced the Canberra players into attacking errors as they fought to catch up.

For Phil Gould it was a real triumph. The young coach's record showed two Premierships in just four years of coaching. He had previously steered Canterbury to victory in 1988 after being given the job as a caretaker awaiting the arrival back from Britain of the Bulldogs' favourite son Chris Anderson. The crowd of 41 815 was a record for the Sydney Football Stadium, beating the number who turned up to watch the Australian Rugby Union side beat the All Blacks six weeks earlier.

At Sydney Football Stadium, Sunday, September 22, 1991
Crowd: 41 815 (Ground record)
PENRITH 19 (R Simmons 2, B Izzard tries, G Alexander 3 goals & field goal) d CANBERRA 12 (M Wood 2 tries, M Meninga, M Wood goals)
Penrith: Greg Barwick, Graham Mackay, Brad Fittler, Col Bentley, Paul Smith, Steve Carter, Greg Alexander (c), Col Van Der Voort, Mark Geyer, Barry Walker, Paul Clarke, Royce Simmons, Paul Dunn. Interchange: Brad Izzard (for Bentley, 30th min), John Cartwright (for Walker, 33rd min) and Walker (for Dunn, 53rd min).
Canberra: Gary Belcher, Paul Martin, Mal Meninga (c), Mark Bell, Matthew Wood, Laurie Daley, Ricky Stuart, Bradley Clyde, David Barnhill, Gary Coyne, Brent Todd, Steve Walters, Glenn Lazarus. Interchange: Darren Fritz (for Clyde, 30th min), Clyde (for Fritz, 34th min), Fritz (for Lazarus, 55th min), Lazarus (for Coyne, 70th min), Michael Twigg (for Barnhill, 70th min) and Scott Gale (for Stuart, 75th min).
Referee: Bill Harrigan

FARNSWORTH BROTHERS

BILL FARNSWORTH

Four Tests for Australia (1910-1912). Also played in one international (1910), which for many years was regarded as a Test, and 11 minor games for Australia on one Kangaroo tour (1911-12).

VIV FARNSWORTH

Six Tests for Australia (1911-1920). Also played in two internationals (1910), which for many years were regarded as Tests, and 26 minor games for Australia on one Kangaroo tour (1911-12).

Two of Australia's first famous footballing brothers, Viv and Bill Farnsworth, wrought havoc among opponents on both sides of the world. Bill Farnsworth is still regarded as one of the greatest five-eighths ever to pull on a jumper. His brother, Viv, a centre, was renowned as one of the game's most fearsome tacklers.

They made their international debuts in 1910, against the touring British Lions. That same year they also figured in the Newtown line-up which won the Sydney Premiership. Both appeared for New South Wales again the following season and Viv was back in the State side in 1912 and 1920.

In 1911, the Farnsworths became the first brothers to tour together in a Kangaroo side—an achievement not repeated until 52 years later, by Ken and Dick Thornett. That first tour was a great one for the Farnsworths and for the rest of the Kangaroos, who became the first side to win the Ashes in England and, until 1982, remained the only combination to have gone through a Test series in Britain unbeaten.

Bill Farnsworth played in 13 matches on tour without once being in a losing side and Viv collected 19 tries in 29 games. Viv Farnsworth toured New Zealand with the NSW side in 1912 and then the brothers headed for England to play club football for Oldham. When Viv eventually returned to Australia he had three more Tests, against the touring 1920 British Lions.

Teams matched against the 1911-12 Kangaroos were always forewarned of Viv Farnsworth's tackling ability. One opposition player was ready to line up when he heard who his opposite number was. He immediately dressed and went home—or so the story goes!

FRANK 'BUMPER' FARRELL

Four Tests for Australia (1946-1948)

'Bumper' Farrell, the footballing policeman, was one of the most feared opponents in the years immediately before and after World War II. The war robbed this controversial character of the chance to run up a long list of international appearances, but he did play in Tests against both Great Britain and New Zealand. Farrell also turned out in more than 250 matches for his club side, Newtown, between 1937 and 1951 and he captained the Premiership-winning combination which thrashed North Sydney 34-7 in the 1943 grand final.

One of the most controversial incidents in the rough, tough footballer's career occurred in 1945. Farrell was accused of almost biting off the ear

Frank (Bumper) Farrell

of St George front-rower Bill McRitchie. McRitchie spent many weeks in hospital recovering. Farrell was exonerated in a vote of the NSW Rugby League general committee by 15 votes to 12. He claimed he had left his false teeth in the dressing room. After he retired as a player, Farrell continued in the administration of the Newtown club, of which he was president for many years.

JACK FIHELLY

Queenslander Jack Fihelly holds a unique place in Australian Rugby League history—he is the only player to complete a Kangaroo tour without playing a match. There was criticism of his selection in the 1908–09 Kangaroo side, largely because he was one of the five selectors and, according the *The Referee* newspaper, he was too light for international football. The Brisbane player was also named as Assistant Manager. Despite there being 45 games on tour, never once did he take the field.

Fihelly is also remembered as the man who got an Aborigine to write the war-cry used by the Pioneers and several subsequent Kangaroo squads. He did eventually make it into the Test arena. Two years later, Fihelly refereed the match between the touring Great Britain side and Combined NSW/Queensland, a game which today is recognised as the Second Test of the 1910 series.

OLSEN FILIPAINA

Twenty-six Tests for New Zealand (1978–86). Also played three games in one World Championship (1977) and 21 minor games for New Zealand on one tour of Australia (1978) and one tour of Britain and France (1985).

Olsen Filipaina was a Rugby League enigma. On the club scene he was often lethargic and predictable in his play. However, once he pulled on the black and white jumper for New Zealand he was one of the most feared backs in the game, whose bruising runs, bone-crunching tackles and accurate goal-kicking won many a game for the Kiwis.

Filipaina, from the Mangere East club in Auckland, burst upon the scene as a 20-year-old during the 1977 World Championship. The chunky centre, who was just 1.72m (5ft 9ins) but weighed a healthy 92kg (14 stone 7 lbs), played in all three of the Kiwis' matches and stamped himself as a hope for the future. His reputation was further enhanced by fine performances on the 1978 tour of Australia and Papua New Guinea and in the home series against the 1979 British Lions. It was then that Balmain snapped up his services. Filipaina played five seasons with the Tigers, but rarely set the world on fire in his 78 first-grade games. He then had a season with both Eastern Suburbs and North Sydney, spending much of the time in reserve grade.

When chosen to play in Tests for New Zealand he had a new lease of life, savouring the Kiwis shock successes over Australia at Brisbane's Lang Park in 1983 (19–12) and at Auckland's Carlaw Park in 1985 (18–0). His 108 points in Tests (six tries and 44 goals) is second only to the 132 scored by the great fullback of the 1950s, Des White. Only seven New Zealanders have played more Tests and World Series games.

Filipaina continued playing, out of the limelight, after his last Test series, against Australia in 1986. In 1990, having moved into the forwards, he captained Ryde-Eastwood to success in the inaugural Metropolitan Cup (Second Division) competition in Sydney.

BRAD FITTLER

Two Tests for Australia (1991). Also played in 11 minor games on one Kangaroo tour (1990) and one Papua New Guinea tour (1991).

When Penrith's Brad Fittler ran onto the field as a replacement in the NSW side during the second 1990 State-of-Origin clash, at Olympic Park, Melbourne, he created history. At 18 years and 114 days old, he became the youngest player to appear in a State-of-Origin match. Further history was made four months later when Fittler, a tough centre, was named in the Kangaroo squad to tour Britain and France, thus becoming only the fifth 18–year-old to be chosen as a Kangaroo (the others were Chook Fraser in 1911, Bobby Dimond in 1948, Steve Rogers in 1973 and Kerry Boustead in 1978).

Fittler was always destined to go to the top. He made the Australian schoolboys side in 1989 and, while still at school, made a meteoric rise into the Penrith first-grade side. After just three lower grade games he was thrown in at the deep end for Penrith's 1989 semi-final clash against Balmain, being preferred at five-eighth to the experienced Chris Mortimer. Fittler scored the Panthers' only try that day.

His senior representative career began in the 1990 Sydney Firsts side. On the Kangaroo tour, he did not get the chance to play in any of the Tests, but his brilliant form in the minor matches prompted coach Bob Fulton to name him as one of the tour successes.

Fittler played a major role in Penrith's march to glory in the early 1990s. He was in Penrith's first ever grand final side, in 1990 (scoring a try in

Penrith's 18–14 loss to Canberra) and was one of the stars in the Panthers' lineup which won the Premiership the following year, avenging the previous loss with a 19–12 victory over the Raiders.

At the end of that season he was one of those chosen for the Australian tour of Papua New Guinea. His tour form was such that he was chosen as lock for both the Tests in preference to several regular forwards. And he was the outstanding player in the second encounter at Port Moresby.

DENIS FLANNERY

Thirteen Tests for Australia (1950–1956). Also played in 24 minor games for Australia while on two Kangaroo tours (1952–53 and 1956–57).

Denis Flannery was a schoolboy sprint champion—and showed many an opposition winger a clean pair of heels once he turned his talents to Rugby League. The Ipswich flyer, who was the son-in-law of Test great and later Australian selector, Dan Dempsey, first played for Queensland at the Sydney Cricket Ground, in 1948 (scoring a try). With classy wingers of the calibre of Johnny Graves, Noel Pidding and Bobby Lulham around however, he had to wait until 1950 to make his Test debut, against the touring British Lions.

Except for 1954, when he was hampered by injuries, he was a Test regular for the next six years. He made two Kangaroo tours. On the first, in 1952–53, he went over for 23 tries in just 14 matches. His next tour saw him as the second top try-scorer with 12.

Flannery played 22 matches for Queensland (the last in 1956), scoring 16 tries. His best was in a 1955 mid-week match at the Sydney Cricket Ground when he bagged three tries to help the Maroons to a 30–28 victory.

HARRY 'JERSEY' FLEGG

'Jersey' Flegg was the most famous of all Australian Rugby League administrators. For three decades he was president of the NSW Rugby League (and for the last two he was also supremo on the Australian Board of Control, the forerunner of the Australian Rugby League).

Yorkshire-born Flegg emigrated to Australia as a child. When the sport was established in 1908, he was captain of Eastern Suburbs and the club's delegate to the controlling body. He became a State selector in 1909 and held the post for 19 years, also being a Test selector for most of that time. Flegg was elected NSW president in 1929 and held the position for 31 years. He also took over as chairman of the Board of Control in 1941.

The English and French Rugby Leagues each bestowed life membership honours on Flegg in the 1950s, as did three English clubs, Warrington, Wigan and Bradford Northern. Flegg was still active in Rugby League when he died in 1960, aged 82. A year after his death, a competition for junior players under the age of 18 was introduced in his memory.

As a youth, Harry Flegg had a magnificent head of red hair. He was given his nickname after he went with a party of schoolfriends to a reception for the Governor of NSW, Lord Jersey, who had red hair and a red beard.

Winners of the H 'Jersey' Flegg Memorial Trophy

Year	Winner	Year	Winner
1961	Manly-Warringah	1977	Penrith
1962	South Sydney	1978	South Sydney
1963	Canterbury-Bankstown	1979	Canterbury-Bankstown
1964	South Sydney	1980	Balmain
1965	Western Suburbs	1981	Western Suburbs
1966	South Sydney	1982	Balmain
1967	South Sydney	1983	Canterbury-Bankstown
1968	South Sydney	1984	St George
1969	South Sydney	1985	St George
1970	Parramatta	1986	Parramatta
1971	Canterbury-Bankstown	1987	Manly-Warringah
1972	South Sydney	1988	Manly-Warringah
1973	Balmain	1989	Canberra
1974	Manly-Warringah	1990	Parramatta
1975	St George	1991	Newcastle
1976	Canterbury-Bankstown		

FLOWERS MEMORIAL PENNANT

In 1930, the NSW Rugby League introduced a Sydney Club Championship. Each club was allotted four points for every point on the season's first-grade table, three for each reserve-grade point and two for each won in the minor grade. The Championship was named in memory of politician-cum-sporting enthusiast Fred Flowers, and a pennant given for the winner to fly at home games the following season.

Between 1988 and 1990, when Brisbane and the Gold Coast did not have President's Cup sides, only first and reserve-grade points counted towards the Club Championship. By far the most successful club since the introduction of the Championship is St George. In the first six decades, the Dragons won 18 times.

Flowers Memorial Pennant Winners

Year	Champion	Year	Champion
1930	Eastern Suburbs	1961	Western Suburbs
1931	Eastern Suburbs	1962	St George
1932	South Sydney	1963	St George
1933	South Sydney	1964	St George
1934	Eastern Suburbs	1965	St George
1935	Eastern Suburbs	1966	St George
1936	Eastern Suburbs	1967	South Sydney
1937	Eastern Suburbs	1968	South Sydney
1938	Canterbury-Bankstown	1969	South Sydney
1939	Canterbury-Bankstown	1970	Eastern Suburbs
1940	St George	1971	St George
1941	Balmain	1972	Manly-Warringah
1942	St George	1973	Newtown
1943	Balmain	1974	Eastern Suburbs
1944	Balmain	1975	Eastern Suburbs
1945	Eastern Suburbs	1976	Parramatta
1946	St George	1977	Parramatta
1947	Balmain	1978	Parramatta
1948	Western Suburbs	1979	Parramatta
1949	St George	1980	Parramatta
1950	Balmain	1981	Parramatta
1951	St George	1982	Parramatta
1952	South Sydney	1983	Manly-Warringah
1953	South Sydney	1984	St George
1954	South Sydney	1985	St George
1955	St George	1986	Parramatta
1956	St George	1987	Manly-Warringah
1957	St George	1988	Manly-Warringah
1958	St George	1989	South Sydney
1959	St George	1990	Canberra
1960	Western Suburbs	1991	Western Suburbs

FOLEY SHIELD

The Foley Shield is an important country competition for teams in North Queensland. It was instituted in 1948 in honour of Arch Foley, an official who worked hard to promote football in the area.

At present, six teams compete—Mt Isa, Cairns, Innisfail-Eacham, Herbert River, Mackay and Townsville. The finals always draw big crowds, usually in excess of 10 000. The most exciting final was without doubt that of 1982. Herbert River and Townsville were locked 22–all at full-time. After an extra 10 minutes each way, they were still even, 25–all. Another five minutes each way saw no addition to the score, so the two teams were named joint winners.

Foley Shield Winners

Year	Winner	Year	Winner
1948	Babinda	1971	Cairns
1949	Townsville	1972	Mt Isa
1950	Ayr	1973	Mt Isa
1951	Babinda	1974	Cairns
1952	Herbert River	1975	Innisfail
1953	Cairns	1976	Cairns
1954	Ayr	1977	Mt Isa
1955	Cairns	1978	Mt Isa
1956	Townsville	1979	Mt Isa
1957	Townsville	1980	Herbert River
1958	Cairns	1981	Mt Isa
1959	Mackay	1982	Townsville and Herbert River
1960	Innisfail	1983	Mt Isa
1961	Eacham	1984	Mackay
1962	Townsville	1985	Mt Isa
1963	Tully	1986	Cairns
1964	Innisfail	1987	Townsville
1965	Herbert River	1988	Mt Isa
1966	Cairns	1989	Innisfail-Eacham
1967	Townsville	1990	Innisfail-Eacham
1968	Innisfail	1991	Mackay
1969	Mt Isa		
1970	Cairns		

ARTHUR FOLWELL

Two Tests for Australia (1933). Also played 19 minor games for Australia on one Kangaroo tour (1933–34).

Arthur Folwell reached great heights as both a player and an administrator. He holds a special place in Rugby League record books as part of only two grandfather-grandson combinations to play Test football for Australia. Folwell was a big name on the playing field in the period between the two World Wars. A tough, fast-striking hooker, he reached the pinnacle of success in the early 1930s. He was a member of the 1933–34 Kangaroos combination and played two Tests in Britain.

When St George hooker Percy Fairall was convincingly beaten in the scrums in the first two Tests of the 1936 series, everyone expected Folwell to be recalled to the Test side. Instead, the selectors chose prop Mick Madsen as a spare-parts hooker for the Third Test, in Sydney. Madsen refused to play until he was convinced his good mate Folwell was suffering from influenza. Folwell, a fine sport, was bitterly disappointed at being overlooked, but lied to Madsen about his alleged flu to avoid any embarrassing incident. Unfortunately, Folwell missed success in the Sydney

Premiership. When his club, Newtown, beat St George 18–5 in the 1933 final, he was en route to England with the Kangaroos.

After he quit the playing ranks, he moved into administration. For a decade he was a vice-president of the NSW Rugby League and he served for some time as a selector for New South Wales and Australian Test teams. A grandson of Folwell, Greg Pierce, also wore the green and gold for Australia in the 1970s and captained the Test side in 1978.

FRANCE

Rugby was first played in France in the 19th Century, but that country remained one of the poor relations of the international Rugby community for more than 100 years. When League gained a firm footing in Great Britain, efforts to introduce the code across the Channel were only natural.

Strangely enough, it was an Australian who made the first overtures to the French. George Ball, manager of the 1921 Kangaroos, went to Paris to try to arrange a match. The French were only luke-warm to the idea. Their 'amateur' game already involved large under-the-table payments to top players. When Ball booked a ground, the Union chiefs brought pressure to bear on the local authorities and, suddenly, the ground became unavailable. Ten years later, the situation changed. England, Scotland, Ireland and Wales banned all Union games with French sides until the flouting of the amateur rules was stopped. The French were then more receptive to ideas put forward by the professional code.

In 1933, Kangaroo manager Harry Sunderland helped arrange the first Rugby League game in France. Also involved were Victor Breyer, editor of the *Echo des Sportes* newspaper, and French Rugby Union international Jean Galia. The first game was an exhibition between Australia and England at the Stade Pershing, Paris, on 31 December 1933. Icy, snowy conditions did not deter some 5000 Parisians from turning out to see Australia win 63–13. The great centre Dave Brown scored 27 points (3 tries and 9 goals) and was chaired from the field by the crowd. Rugby League in France had become a reality.

In March 1934, Galia got together a team of 17 former Rugby Union stars to tour Britain. English players Jonty Parkin and Joe Thompson coached the Frenchmen, who won only one of their six matches, but managed to score 116 points against 164. On his return home, Galia began organising a national competition.

English clubs visited France to help promote the game, and a number of overseas players joined the teams there—the most notable being Welshman Eddie Matthews and Albert Falwasser, a Maori. France soon made an impact on the international scene and in 1939 won its first International Championship (against England and Wales).

World War II almost spelled the end of Rugby League in France after the Vichy Government banned the sport because top officials were considered sympathetic to Britain. Nazi sympathisers burned down the League headquarters. After the war, Rugby League had to start almost from scratch, but again it was not long before the Chanticleers were again an international force. France made its first tour of Australasia in 1951. And what a tour it was! The Australians, who only a year before had regained the Ashes from Britain for the first time in almost three decades, had no answer to the brilliant, unorthodox play of the Frenchmen, who won two Tests to one.

It was at France's instigation that the World Cup was born. At first, the French suggestion fell on deaf ears, but eventually it was decided to hold the first Cup series in France in 1954. It was a great success, with the home side going down 12–16 to Britain in the final, played before 30 368 excited fans in Paris. It was ironic that France's poor form in the 1960s almost spelled an end to the World Cup. Australia refused to hold the series in 1965 because it felt the Frenchmen would be a box-office disaster. Not for another three years did Australian officials relent, and France's improvement was such that it was runner-up to Australia in the 1968 series. However, the form of the Frenchmen has generally fallen away since then.

France had another first when, in 1979, it was involved in the inaugural Test series with Papua New Guinea, while the Kumuls were on a full-scale tour of the northern hemisphere.

The game in France plummeted to real depths at the end of the 1980–81 season. The Championship Final between U S Villeneuve and XIII Catalan was abandoned after only four minutes, following one of the worst brawls in Rugby League history. The Cup Final, scheduled for the following week between A S Carcassonne and XII Catalan, was immediately cancelled and French president Rene Mauries resigned. Several officials and players, including Catalan's captain Jean-Jacques Cologni, were suspended for lengthy periods. For a while it was thought that XIII Catalan, France's most powerful club, would die, but with a new management and policy it returned with a vengeance to win four straight Championships (including the Championship-Cup double in 1985).

In the 1980s the local competition, plagued by defections to Rugby Union (the most prominent being Test star Jean-Marc Bourret), was bolstered by a number of Australians playing during the southern off-season. However France was still not regarded as strong enough to draw crowds in the major cities when it toured Australia in 1990, and for the first time, was forced to play a Test in the country, at Parkes.

The dawn of the 1990s also saw the absence of one of the fine newer clubs, Le Pontet. The Le Pontet side entered Poule B, the French Second Division, in 1980–81 and immediately won promotion to the top league. It reached the Championship final in 1985 only to be beaten by XIII Catalan. The following year (and again in 1988) it took out the coveted Championship-Cup double, the first club to achieve this twice. In 1989, Le Pontet swapped to Rugby Union after refusing to accept some disciplinary penalties imposed by the League hierarchy. Three of their Test players, Thierry Bernabe, Marc Palanques and David Fraisse refused to switch and joined other League clubs.

A GALLERY OF GREAT FRENCHMEN

Georges Aillieres

Gigantic forward Georges Aillieres had the misfortune to be playing during the 1960s, when French Rugby League stocks were at a real low, and so, he usually found his fine efforts going to waste. Ailleries made his

Test debut against New Zealand in 1961 and was a regular in the national side for almost a decade, playing in 31 Tests and three World Cup games. The highlight of his career came in 1968 when he led the Frenchmen who were runners-up to Australia in the World Cup. His son, Pierre Aillieres, also a huge prop forward, played Tests for France, too, and toured Australia with the 1990 squad.

Paul Barriere

One of the most dynamic of all France's Rugby League administrators, Paul Barriere played a major role in the sport's re-formation after World War II and served as French Rugby League president from 1946 to 1955. Barriere also had a hand in arrangements which led to the first World Cup series, in 1954.

Gilbert Benausse

One of France's finest five-eighths, Gilbert Benausse was also a great goal-kicker—though only in the latter half of his career did he concentrate on that art. He had played for both Carcassonne and France with the amazing Puig-Aubert and, therefore, had no need to be a front-line kicker. Benausse started his representative career as a 17–year-old. By the time he was 20 he was an international and, as such, was to make two tours of Australia (with the 1955 side and for the 1957 World Cup, in which he was France's leading point-scorer). In all, Benausse played 37 Tests, nine World Cup games and three European Championship matches—the most full internationals by any Frenchman.

Antoine Blain see alphabetical entry

Jean-Marc Bourret

Five-eighth Jean-Marc Bourret holds a unique position in Rugby folklore. He is the only professional Rugby League Test player to switch to so-called 'amateur' Rugby Union. The 23–year-old did so in December 1980, after a career in which he played 12 Tests for France, scoring 12 tries and kicking the field goal which gave France a shock 11–10 victory over Australia at Toulouse in 1978. The switch came only two weeks after he had scored all of France's points in a 6–5 win over the New Zealand Kiwis.

Elie Brousse

Rugby League historian George Crawford had no doubt about the finest Test second-row combination of all time—the French pair Elie Brousse and Edouard Ponsinet—and few would argue. All told, Brousse played 31 international matches for France (11 Tests and 20 matches in the International Championship, against England, Wales and Other Nationalities). He made his international debut in 1946 and called it a day after the three Tests against the 1952–53 Kangaroos. He was at his best on the 1951 tour of Australia, when he and Ponsinet laid the foundation for France's shock series win.

Raymond Contrastin

Team-mates called Raymond Contrastin the French equivalent of 'Bird's Head' because of his close cropped haircut and prominent, pointed nose. He could certainly fly like a bird down the wing. Contrastin first turned out against Australia in 1949 and when he retired from Test football in 1956 he had played in 33 internationals (19 Tests, Four World Cup matches and 10 European Championship games). He was at his peak during the 1954 World Cup, when he scored five tries in France's four games.

Daniel Divet see alphabetical entry

Jean Dop

Jean Dop is one of the immortals of French Rugby League. For almost a decade in the late 1940s and early 1950s, he was a regular in the French XIII and played 21 Tests. Dop had most of his games at halfback but performed creditably in other positions (including three Tests against Australia in 1955 at fullback). A volatile player, Dop often clashed not only with referees, but also with team-mates. He burst into prominence during the 1949 series against the Kangaroos. Although France was outplayed, Dop more than held his own against the Australian half, Keith Froome. Dop was to clash with Australia in three more series (in the successful 1951 and 1955 French touring sides and at home in 1956).

Patrick Entat

When the 1990 Kangaroo juggernaut rolled through France, one of the few players to emerge with reputation untarnished was Test halfback and skipper Patrick Entat. As the Australian scores rose, Entat never stopped trying. A schoolboy star, who began with Sporting Olympique Avignon club as an eight-year-old, Entat made his first impact on the international scene when he toured Australia with the French Juniors in 1983. Three years later he was called into the Test side and starred in France's 10–all draw with Britain, at Avignon. From then on he was a Test regular. He was French Player-of-the-Year in 1989 and a major force in the French line-up which shocked by beating Britain in England the following year. By 1992, Entat had played 17 Tests and had toured Australia again, with the 1990 senior side.

Jean Galia

More than any other single person, Jean Galia can claim responsibility for establishing Rugby League in France. A Rugby Union star, with 20 internationals to his credit, Galia, with Australian Harry Sunderland and others, arranged the first professional match in his country—a 'friendly' between Australia and England, in Paris, in 1933. France entered the international scene the following year, with Galia, an attacking forward, taking a team to Britain. Back home, he turned his hand to organising and coaching teams, and by the start of the 1934–35 season had got together 12 teams for the first domestic competition. As a player, Galia turned out in five internationals. He was still actively engaged in the code as an administrator when he died in 1949, at the age of 43.

Claude Mantoulan

One of the most brilliant of the French stars of the 1960s, Claude Mantoulan excelled at five-eighth or centre. He was no slouch at fullback, either. He was also a better-than-average goal-kicker, although for much of his international career he had to play second fiddle to Pierre Lacaze. Mantoulan first appeared on the Test scene during the 1959–60 series against the touring Australian Kangaroos. He was to go on to play 46 internationals (36 Tests, 5 World Cup matches and 5 European Championship games). He made two tours of Australasia (1960 and 1964), scoring 96 points on the second.

Jacques Merquey

A lightweight in size (weighing just 65kg), Jacques Merquey was a heavyweight in courage and brilliance. A centre in most of his Test match appearances, he was never outplayed even against big men like Australia's Harry Wells. He first achieved prominence as a 21–year-old on the 1951 tour of Australia. He returned as captain of the great 1955 French combination and as skipper of the 1957 World Cup team. He was honoured by being chosen as captain of the Rest-of-the-World side which took on the Cup winners, Australia. By the time he quit the international arena after playing against the 1959–60 Kangaroos, Merquey had appeared in 35 internationals (24 Tests, 7 World Cup matches and 4 European Championship games).

Edouard Ponsinet

Half of the pair which historian George Crawford claims was the finest second-row combination of all time, Eduoard Ponsinet was on the international scene for only four years—but in that short time he set the world alight. He made his international debut in 1948, against the touring New Zealand Kiwis, and finished after the clashes with the 1952–53 Australian Kangaroos and the 1953 International (European) Championship. All told, he played 18 internationals (four Tests against each of Australia and New Zealand and one against Great Britain, as well as three internationals against each of England, Wales and Other Nationalities). Ponsinet was dominant in the 1951 series against Australia, when he and second-row partner Elie Brousse wrought havoc, and helped the French tourists to a surprise success.

Puig Aubert

A piquant legend . . . the roly-poly, chain-smoking fullback figured prominently in the era of the great Test sides from France of the early 1950s. If Puig Aubert had any fault it was the casual attitude, which was also part of his charm. He took kicks for goal as if he were idly practising on some remote field, and he would often refuse to attempt a tackle on an opponent, as if demonstrating against the failure of team-mates to have done so first. 'Pipette', as he was called (a reference to his smoking—so heavy that he often smoked on the field), had a playing career which stretched from 1944 to 1957. He played in a then-record 46 internationals

(27 Tests, four World Cup matches and 15 European Championship games). The height of his success was the 1951 tour of Australasia, when he played in 25 of France's 29 matches, and scored a record 221 points—outdoing the English great, Jim Sullivan. Puig Aubert's performances in 1951 earned him his country's Champion of Champions title—the first time a footballer of any code had been so honoured. Puig Aubert played in eight French Championship finals, winning five (in 1945, 1946, 1950 and 1952 with A S Carcassonne and in 1957 with Catalan XIII), and nine Cup Finals, winning four (in 1946, 1947, 1951 and 1952 with A S Carcassonne).

The French legend's real name was Aubert Puig. But when, as a teenager he signed for A S Carcassonne, there were so many other better-known players with the surname Puig that a local newspaper editor printed his name back-to-front to avoid confusion. It stuck and, ironically, he became the most famous of them all. Even today, the great fullback still signs his cheques Puig Aubert.

Hugues Ratier

Unfortunately for a player of immense talent, Hugues Ratier was in the French Test side at a time when the Chanticleers fortunes were at a low ebb. Ratier played centre for his club, F C Lezignan, but in the international squad turned out on the wing. He made his Test debut as a 19-year-old in 1980 in the Perpignan clash with the touring Kiwis. The highlight of his career was when he captained France to its shock win over Great Britain at Headingley, Leeds, in 1990—the first success on British soil in 23 years. When Ratier led the Frenchman onto the field for the World Cup Test in Australia a few months later, it was the 29th (and last) time he wore his country's colours in a full international. It was his second tour of Australia, having the dubious honour of being France's lone scorer in Australia's 43–3 drubbing of the tourists in 1981.

Max Roussie

A brilliant, versatile player with an incredible turn of speed, Max Roussie starred in the early days of French Rugby League. He was at home in a variety of positions and took the field as fullback, centre, five-eighth and lock in international matches. All told he played 15 times for France (two Tests against Australia and 13 matches in the International Championship). A true character on and off the field, he would often turn out for matches barefoot, because he claimed this enabled him to move faster.

FRANCE V AUSTRALIA

TEST MATCHES

1938

First Test
At Stade Buffalo, Paris, Sunday, 2 January 1938
Crowd: 11 500
AUSTRALIA 35 (Gilbert 2, Dawson 2, Narvo, Norval, Reardon, Prigg, Beaton tries, Beaton 4 goals) d FRANCE 6 (Durant, Cussac tries)

Australia: L Ward, L Dawson, R McKinnon, J Beaton, A Norval, J Reardon, F Gilbert, W Prigg (c), E Lewis, H Narvo, L Heidke, H Pierce, F Curran.
France: M Chaud, C Lamarque, J Dauger, E Bosch, A Cussac, M Rousie, S Bes, J Davant, L Griffard, A Rousse, H Durand, J Domercq, C Petit.

Second Test

At Stade Municipal, Marseille, Sunday, 16 January 1938
Crowd: 24 000
AUSTRALIA 16 (Norval, McKinnon, Pierce, Prigg tries, Beaton 2 goals) d FRANCE 11 (Griffaud, Sanz, Cussac tries, Rousie goal)
Australia: L Ward, L Dawson, B Williams, J Beaton, A Norval, R McKinnon, F Gilbert, W Prigg (c), E Lewis, H Narvo, L Heidke, H Pierce, F Curran
France: M Guiral, H Sanz, M Rousie, C Estoveight, A Cussac, J Dauger, P Brinsolles, M Brunetaud, L Griffard, A Blain, M Nourrit, H Durrand, P Etchard

1949

First Test

At Stade Municipal, Marseille, Sunday, 9 January 1949
Crowd: 15 796
AUSTRALIA 29 (Tyquin 2, McMahon, O'Connell, de Belin, Gibbs, Hall tries, Froome 4 goals) d FRANCE 10 (Lespes, Nequer tries, Comes 2 goals)
Australia: C Churchill, P McMahon, D McRitchie, J Hawke, R Lulham, W O'Connell, K Froome, W Tyquin (c), F de Belin, N Mulligan, D Hall, K Schubert, J Gibbs
France: G Combes, J Crespo, A Kempe, R Casse, O Lespes, P Tailantou, G Calixte (c), E Brousse, U Negrier, L Mazon, M Martin, A Beraud
Referee: A S Dobson (Great Britain)

Second Test

At Stade Municipal, Bordeaux, Sunday, 23 January 1949
Crowd: 17 365
AUSTRALIA 10 (Hall, Mulligan tries, Froome 2 goals) d FRANCE 0
Australia: C Churchill, P McMahon, D McRitchie, J Hawke, R Lulham, W O'Connell, K Froome, W Tyquin (c), N Mulligan, F de Belin, J Gibbs, K Schubert, D Hall
France: J Barreteau, R Contrastin, R Caillou, J Crespo, F Trescazes, P Tailantou, J Dop, P Dejean, G Calixte (c), H Rui, U Negrier, M Martin, P Bartoletti
Referee: A Pascall (France)

1951

First Test

At Sydney Cricket Ground, Monday, 11 June 1951
Crowd: 60 160
FRANCE 26 (Cantoni 2, Contrastin, Genoud tries, Puig Aubert 7 goals) d AUSTRALIA 15 (Graves, Willoughby, Crocker tries, Graves 3 goals)
Australia: C Churchill (c), J Bliss, G Willoughby, N Hazzard, J Graves, F Stanmore, K Holman, N Mulligan, H Crocker, B Davies, D Donoghue, K Holman, D Hall
France: Puig Aubert (c), V Cantoni, G Combes, J Crespo, R Contrastin, C Galaup, J Dop, R Duffort, E Ponsinet, E Brousse, L Mazon, G Genoud, P Bartoletti
Referee: T McMahon (Australia)

Second Test

At Brisbane Cricket Ground, Saturday, 30 June 1951
Crowd: 35 000
AUSTRALIA 23 (Hall, Flannery, Holman tries, Pidding 6, Churchill goals) d FRANCE 11 (Merquey try, Puig Aubert 4 goals)
Australia: C Churchill (c), N Pidding, C Geelan, N Hazzard, D Flannery, F Stanmore, K Holman, H Crocker, B Drew, B Davies, D Hall, E Hammerton, A Thompson
France: Puig Aubert (c), V Cantoni, G Combes, J Crespo, R Contrastin, J Merquey, J Dop, R Duffort, E Brousse, E Ponsinet, L Mazon, G Genoud, P Bartoletti
Referee: T McMahon (Australia)

Third Test

At Sydney Cricket Ground, Saturday, 21 July 1951
Crowd: 67 009
FRANCE 35 (Crespo 3, Contrastin 2, Combes, Brousse tries, Puig Aubrt 7 goals) d AUSTRALIA 14 (Davies, Hall tries, Pidding 4 goals)
Australia: C Churchill (c), N Pidding, N Hazzard, J Hawke, D Flannery, W O'Connell, K Holman, H Crocker, B Drew, B Davies, D Hall, K Schubert, D Donoghue
France: Puig Aubert (c), R Contrastin, G Combes, J Merquey, V Cantoni, R Duffort, J Crespo, G Calixte, E Ponsinet, E Brousse, L Mazon, G Genoud, P Bartoletti
Referee: T McMahon (Australia)

1952-53

First Test
At Parc de Princes, Paris, Saturday, 27 December 1952
Crowd: 18 327
AUSTRALIA 16 (Ryan 2, Davies, Hazzard tries, Pidding 2 goals) d FRANCE 12 (Cantoni, Brousse tries,
Puig Aubert 3 goals)
Australia: C Churchill (c), T Ryan, C Geelan, N Hazzard, N Pidding, F Stanmore, K Holman, A Collinson,
B Davies, F Ashton, R Bull, K Kearney, D Hall
France: Puig Aubert (c), V Cantoni, J Merquey, A Carrere, R Contrastin, G Benausse, J Dop, C Duple,
R Bernard, E Brousse, L Mazon, G Genoud, J Dedieu
Referee: E Martung (France)

Second Test
At Stade Municipal, Bordeaux, Sunday, 11 January 1953
Crowd: 23 419
FRANCE 5 (Carrere try, Rives goal) d AUSTRALIA 0
Australia: C Churchill (c), N Pidding, N Hazzard, C Geelan, T Ryan, F Stanmore, K Holman, H Crocker,
F Ashton, B Davies, D Hall, K Kearney, R Bull
France: G Rives, R Contrastin, C Teisseire, A Carrere, V Cantoni, J Crespo, G Benausse, E Brousse,
E Ponsinet, F Montrucolis, H Berthomieu, G Genoud, F Rinaldi
Referee: E Martung (France)

Third Test
At Stade de Gerland, Lyon, Sunday, 25 January 1953
Crowd: 17 454
FRANCE 13 (Benausse try, Puig Aubert 5 goals) d AUSTRALIA 5 (Hall try, Holman goal)
Australia: C Churchill (c), R Contrastin, C Teisseire, A Carrere, V Cantoni, G Benausse, J Crespo, F Montrucolis,
B Davies, F Ashton, D Hall, K Kearney, R Bull
France: Puig Aubert (c), R Contrastin, C Teisseire, A Carrere, V Cantoni, G Benausse, J Crespo, F Montrucolis,
E Ponsinet, E Brousse, F Rinaldi, G Genoud, L Mazon
Referee: P Ribas (France)

1955

First Test
At Sydney Cricket Ground, Saturday, 11 June 1955
Crowd: 67 748
AUSTRALIA 20 (Holman 2, Wells, Kite tries, Davies 3, Holman goals) d FRANCE 8 (Ducasse, Berthomieu
tries, Duple goal)
Australia: C Churchill (c), D Flannery, H Wells, A Watson, R Kite, D Henry, K Holman, P Diversi, B Davies,
H Holloway, R Bull, K Kearney, D Hall
France: J Dop, A Ducasse, J Merquey (c), R Rey, M Voron, A Jiminez, F Levy, C Duple, J Pambrun,
G Delaye, J Vanel, R Moulis, H Berthomieu
Referee: D Lawler (Australia)

Second Test
At Brisbane Cricket Ground, Saturday, 2 July 1955
Crowd: 45 745
FRANCE 29 (Rey 2, Merquey 2, Ducasse tries, Benausse 6, Duple goals) d AUSTRALIA 28 (Laird 2, Crocker
2, Kite, Holloway tries, Davies 3, Churchill, Holman goals)
Australia: C Churchill (c), A Watson, K McCaffery, H Wells, R Kite, G Laird, K Holman, H Crocker,
H Holloway, B Davies, D Hall, K Kearney, R Bull
France: J Dop, A Ducasse, R Rey, J Merquey (c), M Voron, G Benausse, C Teisseire, F Levy, H Berthomieu,
F Montrucolis, A Carrere, J Audoubert, J Vanel
Referee: D Lawler (Australia)

Third Test
At Sydney Cricket Ground, Saturday, 23 July 1955
Crowd: 62 458
FRANCE 8 (Contrastin, Ducasse tries, Duple try) d AUSTRALIA 5 (Davies try, Churchill goal)
Australia: C Churchill (c), R Kite, R Poole, A Watson, D Flannery, G Laird, K Holman, H Crocker, H Holloway,
B Davies, R Bull, K Kearney, D Hall. (D Henry was chosen to play for Australia but at the last minute
was inexplicably replaced by R Poole)
France: J Dop, A Ducasse, J Merquey (c), R Rey, R Contrastin, G Benausse, C Duple, F Levy, H Berthomieu,
F Montrucolis, J Vanel, J Audoubert, J Fabre.
Referee: J Casey (Australia)

1956-57

First Test
At Parc de Princes, Paris, Thursday, 1 November 1956
Crowd: 10 789
AUSTRALIA 15 (Holman 2, McGovern tries, Churchill 2, Holman goals) d FRANCE 8 (Parent, Merquey
tries, Audy goal)

Australia: C Churchill, D Flannery, R Poole, A Watson, D McGovern, R Banks, K Holman, K O'Shea, N Provan, T Tyquin, B Davies, K Kearney (c), R Bull.
France: A Audy, M Voron, R Rey, J Merquey (c), A Savonne, A Ambert, G Lucia, J Rouqueirol, A Parent, R Medus, F Montrucolis, A Apelian, F Rinaldi.
Referee: P Ribas (France)

Second Test
At Stade Municipal, Bordeaux, Sunday, 23 December 1956
Crowd: 11 379
AUSTRALIA 10 (Flannery, Holman tries, Clifford 2 goals) d FRANCE 6 (Benausse 2, Audy goals)
Australia: G Clifford, D Flannery, A Watson, R Poole, D Adams, R Banks, K Holman, I Doyle, N Provan, K O'Shea, R Bull, K Kearney (c), B Orrock
France: A Audy, M Voron, R Rey, A Jiminez, A Ducasse, G Benausse, J Dop, C Duple, A Save, G Verdie, G Berthomieu, A Apelian, A Boldini

Third Test
At Stade de Gerland, Lyon, Thursday, 3 January 1957
Crowd: 5743
AUSTRALIA 25 (Poole, Moir, Kearney, Payne, Provan tries, Clifford 4, Banks goals) d FRANCE 21 (Savonne 2, Nedorezoff, Fabre, Merquey tries, Rives 3 goals)
Australia: G Clifford, D Flannery, T Payne, R Poole, I Moir, R Banks, K Holman, I Doyle, K O'Shea, N Provan, R Bull, K Kearney (c), W Marsh.
France: A Rives, A Savonne, A Jiminez, R Rey, J Nedorezoff, J Merquey (c), C Teisseire, C Duple, A Parent, G Berthomieu, J Fabre, L Michel, H Delhoste
Referee: J Barreau (France)

1959-60

First Test
At Parc de Princes, Paris, Saturday, 31 October 1959
Crowd: 9864
AUSTRALIA 20 (Lumsden 3, Wells tries, Barnes 4 goals) d FRANCE 19 (Quaglio try, Lacaze 6 goals & 2 field goals)
Australia: K Barnes (c), E Lumsden, H Wells, R Gasnier, K Irvine, A Brown, B Muir, B Hambly, R Mossop, J Paterson, D Beattie, I Walsh, G Parcell
France: P Lacaze, M Voron, J Merquey (c), A Jiminez, A Savonne, G Benausse, G Fages, S Tonus, J Aubert, R Eramouspe, A Quaglio, A Appelian, J Pano
Referee: G Jameau (France)

Second Test
At Stade Municipal, Bordeaux, Sunday, 20 December 1959
Crowd: 8848
AUSTRALIA 17 (Wells, Raper, Carlson tries, Barnes 4 goals) d FRANCE 2 (Mantoulan goal)
Australia: K Barnes (c), B Carlson, H Wells, R Gasnier, E Lumsden, J Raper, B Muir, B Clay, B Hambly, G Parcell, D Beattie, I Walsh, W Wilson
France: C Mantoulan, M Voron, J Foussat, A Jiminez (c), A Savonne, R Moulinat, R Jean, S Tonus, J Barthe, R Eramouspe, M Bescos, A Casas, H Conti
Referee: A Cassan (France)

Third Test
At Roanne, Wednesday, 20 January 1960
Crowd: 3437
AUSTRALIA 16 (Raper 2, Hambly, Gasnier tries, Barnes 2 goals) d FRANCE 8 (Velvaud, Gruppi tries, Lacaze goal)
Australia: K Barnes (c), E Lumsden, H Wells, R Gasnier, B Carlson, J Raper, B Muir, B Clay, B Hambly, J Paterson, E Rasmussen, I Walsh, W Wilson
France: P Lacaze, R Gruppi, J Foussat, G Velvaud, A Savonne, C Mantoulan, B Fabre, G Fages, S Tonus, P Laurent, M Bescos, A Casas, H Conti
Referee: G Jameau (France)

1960

First Test
At Sydney Cricket Ground, Saturday, 11 June 1960
Crowd: 49 868
AUSTRALIA 8 (Barnes 4 goals) drew with FRANCE 8 (Lacaze 4 goals)
Australia: K Barnes (c), E Lumsden, R Gasnier, R Boden, K Irvine, A Brown, B Muir, J Raper, E Rasmussen, J Paterson, D Beattie, N Kelly, G Parcell
France: P Lacaze, R Gruppi, A Jiminez (c), G Benausse, A Foussat, C Mantoulan, B Fabre, G Fages, J Barthe, R Eramouspe, F Rossi, A Casas, M Bescos
Referee: C Pearce (Australia)

Second Test
At Brisbane Exhibition Ground, Saturday, 2 July 1960
Crowd: 32 644
AUSTRALIA 56 (Bugden 3, Irvine 3, Morgan 2, Provan 2, Gasnier, Hambly tries, Barnes 10 goals) d FRANCE 6 (Lacaze 3 goals)
Australia: K Barnes (c), L Morgan, R Gasnier, H Wells, K Irvine, R Banks, R Bugden, J Raper, N Provan, B Hambly, R Mossop, W Rayner, E Rasmussen
France: P Lacaze, R Gruppi, A Jiminez (c), A Foussat, J Dubon, C Mantoulan, B Fabre, G Fages, J Barthe, R Eramouspe, A Quaglio, A Vadon, M Bescos
Referee: D Lawler (Australia)

Third Test
At Sydney Cricket Ground, Saturday, 16 July 1960
Crowd: 29 127
FRANCE 7 (Dubon try, Mantoulan 2 goals) d AUSTRALIA 5 (Bugden try, Barnes 2 goals)
Australia: K Barnes (c), K Irvine, R Gasnier, H Wells, L Morgan, R Boden, R Bugden, J Raper, B Hambly, N Provan, E Rasmussen, W Rayner, R Mossop
France: L Poletti, A Marty, C Mantoulan, B Fabre, J Dubon, A Jiminez (c), J Guiraud, J Barthe, R Eramouspe, A Quaglio, A Boldini, A Vadon, M Bescos
Referee: D Lawler (Australia)

1963–64

First Test
At Stade Municipal, Bordeaux, Sunday, 8 December 1963
Crowd: 4261
FRANCE 8 (Ailleres, Fabre tries, Villeneuve goal) d AUSTRALIA 5 (Langlands try & goal)
Australia: K Thornett, M Cleary, G Langlands, R Gasnier, P Dimond, E Harrison, B Muir, J Raper, R Thornett, B Hambly, P Quinn, I Walsh (c), N Kelly
France: A Carrere, J Etcheberry, B Fabre, C Mantoulan, F Roldos, J Villeneuve, G Fages (c), A Lacaze, G Ailleres, H Marracq, J Pano, J Graciet, L Faletti
Referee: A Cassan (France)

Second Test
At Stade de Minimes, Toulouse, Sunday, 22 December 22, 1963
Crowd: 6932
AUSTRALIA 21 (Irvine 2, Langlands, Thornett, Summons tries, Langlands 3 goals) d FRANCE 9 (Etcheberry try, Villeneuve 2, Lacaze goals)
Australia: K Thornett, K Irvine, R Gasnier, R Gasnier, P Dimond, A Summons (c), B Muir, J Raper, B Hambly, K Smyth, P Gallagher, N Kelly, G Wilson
France: A Carrere, J Etcheberry, B Fabre, C Mantoulan, F Roldos, J Villeneuve, G Fages, A Lacaze, G Ailleres, H Marracq, J Pano, J Graciet, L Faletti. Replacement: G Fages (for Fabre)
Referee: E Martung (France)

Third Test
At Parc de Princes, Paris, Saturday, 18 Januray 1964
Crowd: 5979
AUSTRALIA 16 (Muir 2, Rushworth, Irvine tries, Hambly 2 goals) d FRANCE 8 (Verge, Roldos tries, Villeneuve goal)
Australia: K Thornett, K Irvine, R Gasnier, B Rushworth, P Dimond, A Summons (c), B Muir, K Smyth, K Day, G Wilson, P Gallagher, N Kelly, B Hambly
France: A Carrere, F Roldos, B Fabre, G Benausse, D Pellerin, J Villeneuve, L Verge, J Barthe, H Marracq, H Larrue, J Pano, J Graciet, L Faletti
Referee: G Jameau (France)

1964

First Test
At Sydney Cricket Ground, Saturday, 13 June 1964
Crowd: 20 270
AUSTRALIA 20 (Cleary, Langlands, Gasnier, Irvine tries, Langlands 4 goals) d FRANCE 6 (Mantoulan 3 goals)
Australia: K Thornett, M Cleary, R Gasnier, G Langlands, K Irvine, J Lisle, W Smith, J Raper, R Thornett, K Day, R Crowe, I Walsh (c), B Hambly
France: A Carrere, M Boule, C Mantoulan, H Castel, A Bourreil, J Villeneuve, L Verge, H Chamorin, J Lapoterie, G Ailliere, J Pano (c), J Graciet, L Faletti. Replacement: E Duseigneur (for Pano)
Referee: C Pearce (Australia)

Second Test
At Lang Park, Brisbane, Saturday, 4 July 1964
Crowd: 20 076
AUSTRALIA 27 (Gasnier 3, Day, Cleary tries, Langlands 5, Johns goals) d FRANCE 2 (Villeneuve goal)

Australia: L Johns, M Cleary, R Gasnier (c), J Lisle, K Irvine, J Gleeson, W Smith, J Raper, K Thornett, K Day, R Crowe, N Kelly, K Ryan. Replacement: G Langlands (for Johns)
France: J P Lecompte, M Boule, C Mantoulan, G Savonne, J Lapoterie, J Villeneuve, L Verge, H Chamorin, G Aillieres, S Estieu, J Pano (c), J Graciet, F Mas
Referee: C Pearce (Australia)

Third Test
At Sydney Cricket Ground, Saturday, 18 July 1964
Crowd: 16 731
AUSTRALIA 35 (Cleary 2, Irvine 2, K Thornett, Gleeson, Wilson tries, Irvine 7 goals) d FRANCE 9 (Savonne try, Mantoulan 3 goals)
Australia: K Thornett, K Irvine, R Gasnier (c), J Lisle, M Cleary, J Gleeson, W Smith, J Raper, R Thornett, E Wilson, P Quinn, N Kelly, K Ryan
France: A Carrere, A Bourreil, C Mantoulan, J P Lecompte, G Savonne, J Villeneuve, L Verge, H Chamorin, G Aillieres, R Eramouspe, F Mas, P Azalbert, E Duseigneur. Replacements: M Boule (for Carrere) and P Plo (for Eramouspe)
Referee: C Pearce (Australia)

1967-68

First Test
At Stade Velodrome, Marseille, Sunday, 17 December 1967
Crowd: 5193
AUSTRALIA 7 (Johns try, Langlands, Johns goals) drew with FRANCE 7 (Bonnet try, Lacaze 2 goals)
Australia: L Johns, J King, G Langlands, J Greaves, K Irvine, A Branson, W Smith, J Raper (c), R Coote, E Rasmussen, P Gallagher, N Kelly, D Manteit. Replacement: R Lynch
France: P Lacaze, D Pellerin, G Andrieu, J P Lecompte, Y Reynard, C Mantoulan, R Garnung, G Bonnet, A Alesina, G Aillieres (c), G Ribot, Y Begou, C Sabatie. Replacement: J Capdouze
Referee: G Jameau (France)

Second Test
At Stade Albert Domec, Carcassonne, Sunday, 24 December 1967
Crowd: 4 193
FRANCE 10 (Capdouze 5 goals) d AUSTRALIA 3 (Greaves try)
Australia: L Johns, J King, J Greaves, G Langlands, J McDonald, A Branson, W Smith, J Raper (c), R Coote, R Lynch, E Rasmussen, N Gallagher, P Gallagher
France: P Lacaze, D Pellerin, G Andrieu, R Garrigue, P Surre, J Capdouze, R Garnung, G Bonnet, F de Nadai, G Aillieres (c), P Dubie, Y Begou, C Sabatie. Replacements: J Fabre and A Alesina
Referee: A Breysse (France)

Third Test
At Stade de Minimes, Toulouse, Sunday, 7 January 1968
Crowd: 5000
FRANCE 16 (Surre, Pellerin tries, Capdouze 5 goals) d AUSTRALIA 13 (Greaves 2, Langlands tries, Langlands, Johns goals)
Australia: L Johns, J King, J Greaves, G Langlands, J McDonald, A Branson, W Smith, J Raper (c), R Coote, A Thomson, E Rasmussen, N Kelly, P Gallagher
France: C Mantoulan, P Surre, R.Moliner, G Andrieu, D Pellerin, J Capdouze, R Garnung, G Bonnet, G Aillieres (c), F de Nadai, P Dubie, Y Begou, C Sabatie
Referee: G Jameau (France)

1973

First Test
At Stade Gilbert Brutus, Perpignan, Sunday, 9 December 1973
Crowd: 7630
AUSTRALIA 21 (Goodwin 2, Fulton 2, Starling tries, Branighan 2, Cronin goals) d FRANCE 9 (Molinier, Ruiz tries, Garrigue goal & field goal)
Australia: R Branighan, L Williamson, R Fulton, M Cronin, D Waite, T Pickup, T Raudonikis (c), G Starling, E Walters, G Pierce, J O'Neill, J Lang, A Beetson. Replacement: E Goodwin (for Williamson)
France: M De Matos, S Marsolan, M Molinier, A Ruiz, J C Marty, P Rives, R Garrigue (c), G Bonnet, J P Sauret, J J Cologni, C Thenegal, J Franc, C Carre. Replacements: M Frattini and S Gleyzes
Referee: G Jameau (France)

Second Test
At Stade de Minemes, Toulouse, Sunday, 16 December 1973
Crowd: 7060
AUSTRALIA 14 (Maddison, Cronin, Branighan, Fulton tries, Cronin goal) d FRANCE 3 (Franc try)
Australia: R Branighan, E Goodwin, M Cronin, G Starling, D Waite, R Fulton, T Pickup, P Sait, G Stevens, K Maddison, A Beetson (c), E Walters, R O'Reilly
France: J Calle, S Marsolan, M Molinier, A Ruiz, J C Marty, M Mazare, R Garrigue (c), G Bonnet, S Gleyzes, J P Sauret, C Carre, J Franc, V Serrano. Replacement: L Brunet and P Rives
Referee: M Caillol (France)

1978

First Test
At Stade Albert Domec, Carcassonne, Sunday, 26 November 1978.
Crowd: 7000
FRANCE 13 (Naudo try, Moya 5 goals) d AUSTRALIA 10 (Cronin, Eadie tries, Cronin 2 goals)
Australia: G Eadie, K Boustead, M Cronin, S Martin, C Anderson, R Fulton (c), T Raudonikis, R Price,
L Boyd, G Gerard, R Morris, G Peponis, C Young
France: F Tranier, J Moya, C Lamond, M Naudo, G Borrell, E Walligunda, Y Greseque, M Maique, C Zalduendo,
D Hermet, D Castanon, A Malacamp, H Daniel (c)
Referee: A Breysse (France)

Second Test
At Stade de Minemes, Toulouse, Sunday, 10 December 1978
Crowd: 6500
FRANCE 11 (Naudo try, Moya 3 goals, Walligunda, Bourret field goals) d AUSTRALIA 10 (Boustead, Rogers
tries, Cronin 2 goals)
Australia: G Eadie, K Boustead, S Rogers, M Cronin, C Anderson, R Fulton (c), T Raudonikis, R Price,
R Reddy, G Gerard, C Young, R Hilditch, I Thomson
France: F Tranier, J Moya, C Lamond, M Naudo, G Borrell, E Walligunda, J Castel, M Maique, C Zalduendo,
D Hermet, D Castanon, A Malacamp, H Daniel (c). Replacement: J M Bourret
Referee: P Laverny (France)

1981

First Test
At Sydney Cricket Ground, Saturday, 4 July 1981
Crowd: 16 277
AUSTRALIA 43 (Mortimer 2, McCabe 2, Brentnall, Ribot, Rogers, Boustead, Masterman tries, Cronin 8 goals)
d FRANCE 3 (Ratier try)
Australia: G Brentnall, K Boustead, S Rogers (c), M Cronin, J Ribot, W Lewis, S Mortimer, R Price,
P McCabe, L Boyd, R Hilditch, J Masterman, C Young. Replacements: P Sigsworth and R Morris
France: S Rodriguez, H Ratier, J Imbert, P Fourquet, B Imbert, G Alard, Y Greseque, J J Vila, J Gine,
D Hermet (c), D Castanon, C Macalli, M Chantal. Replacement: H Guiraud
Referee: K Steele (New Zealand)

Second Test
At Lang Park, Brisbane, Saturday, 18 July 1981
Crowd: 14 000
AUSTRALIA 17 (Fahey 2, Morris tries, Cronin 4 goals) d FRANCE 2 (Perez goal)
Australia: G Brentnall, T Fahey, S Rogers (c), M Cronin, J Ribot, W Lewis, S Mortimer, R Price, P McCabe,
L Boyd, R Hilditch, J Masterman, R Morris. Replacement: R Ayliffe
France: M Pillon, S Rodriguez, P Fourquet, J Imbert, H Ratier, G Alard, Y Greseque, J Roosebrouck (c),
C Zalduendo, J Gine, M Chantal, C Macalli, D Hermet. Replacement: A Perez (for Alard)
Referee: D Wilson (New Zealand)

1982

First Test
At Parc de Sports, Avignon, Sunday, 5 December 1982
Crowd: 8000
AUSTRALIA 15 (Grothe 2, Pearce tries, Meninga 3 goals) d FRANCE 4 (Perez 2 goals)
Australia: G Brentnall, K Boustead, S Rogers, B Kenny, M Meninga, W Lewis, P Sterling, W Pearce, L Boyd,
P McCabe, R Morris, M Krilich (c), C Young. Replacements: E Grothe (for Lewis) and R Brown (for
McCabe)
France: A Perez, P Solal, G Delaunay, J Guigue, P Fourcade, H Guiraud, Y Greseque, J Roosebrouck (c),
M Ambert, G Laforgue, M Chantal, C Macalli, H Daniel. Replacements: C Laumond and M Caravaca
Referee: R Whitfield (Great Britain)

Second Test
At Stade L'Egassiarial, Narbonne, Saturday, 18 December 1982
Crowd: 7000
AUSTRALIA 23 (Grothe 2, Meninga, Reddy, Kenny tries, Meninga 4 goals) d FRANCE 9 (Gresequ try, Kaminski
3 goals)
Australia: G Brentnall, K Boustead, S Rogers, M Meninga, E Grothe, B Kenny, P Sterling, W Pearce,
P McCabe, R Reddy, L Boyd, M Krilich (c), C Young. Replacements: S Ella and R Brown
France: J Guigue, P Solal, G Delaunay, C Laumond, E Kaminski, H Guiraud, Y Greseque, J Roosebrouck
(c), G Laforgue, J J Cologni, M Chantal, C Macalli, C Zalduendo. Replacements: M Laville (for Laumond)
and M Caravaca (for Cologni)
Referee: R Whitfield (Great Britain)

1986

First Test
At Stade Gilbert Brutus, Perpignan, Sunday, 30 November 1986
Crowd: 6000
AUSTRALIA 44 (O'Connor 3, Lindner 2, Miles 2, Sterling, Jack tries, O'Connor 4 goals) d FRANCE 2 (Dumas goal)
Australia: G Jack, D Shearer, B Kenny, G Miles, M O'Connor, W Lewis (c), P Sterling, R Lindner, B Niebling, L Davidson, P Dunn, R Simmons, G Dowling. Replacements: T Lamb (for Sterling) and P Sironen (for Niebling)
France: G Dumas, D Couston, R Palisses, A Maury, H Ratier, D Espugna, P Entat, D Verdes, S Titeux, G Laforgue (c), J L Rabot, T Bernabe, M Chantal. Replacements: S Bret (for Palisses) and F Laforgue (for Maury)
Referee: F Lindop (Great Britain)

Second Test
At Stade Albert Domec, Carcassonne, Saturday, 13 December 1986
Crowd: 3000
AUSTRALIA 52 (Shearer 4, Jack 3, Folkes, Niebling, O'Connor tries, O'Connor 6 goals) d FRANCE 0
Australia: G Jack, D Shearer, B Kenny, G Miles, M O'Connor, W Lewis (c), P Sterling, R Lindner, B Niebling, S Folkes, P Dunn, R Simmons, G Dowling. Replacements: T Lamb (for Dowling) and L Davidson (for Folkes)
France: P Wozniack, S Rodriguez, P Fourquet, F Laforgue, H Ratier, R Palisses, C Scicchitano, P Gestas, D Verdes, G Laforgue (c), S Titeux, T Bernabe, M Chantal. Replacements: G Dumas (for Rodriguez) and Y Storer (for Chantal)
Referee: F Lindop (Great Britain)

1990

Test
At Pioneer Oval, Parkes, Wednesday, 28 June 1990
Crowd: 12 384 (Ground record)
AUSTRALIA 34 (Mackay 3, McGaw 2, Daley, Meninga, Shearer tries, Belcher goal) d FRANCE 2 (Dumas goal)
Australia: G Belcher, M O'Connor, M Meninga (c), M McGaw, D Shearer, L Daley, A Langer, B Mackay, D Gillespie, P Sironen, S Roach, K Walters, M Bella. Replacements: M Carroll (for Sironen) and A Ettingshausen (for McGaw)
France: E Castel, H Ratier (c), J B Saumitou, G Delaunay, C Pons, G Dumas, P Entat, T Valero, D Divet, D Cabestany, T Buttignol, F Lope, J L Rabot. Replacement: J Ruiz (for Buttignol)
Referee: G Ainui (Papua New Guinea)

1990

First Test
At Parc de Sports, Avignon, Sunday, 2 December 1990
Crowd: 2200
AUSTRALIA 60 (Alexander 3, Ettingshausen 2, Belcher 2, P Sironen, D Shearer, D Gillespie, G Lazarus tries, G Alexander 7, Meninga goals) d FRANCE 4 (Fraisse try)
Australia: G Belcher, D Shearer, M Meninga (c), L Daley, A Ettingshausen, C Lyons, R Stuart, B Mackay, D Gillespie, P Sironen, S Roach, B Elias, G Lazarus. Replacements: G Alexander (for Stuart), D Hasler (for Daley), M Geyer (for Gillespie) and M Sargent (for Sironen)
France: M Rozes, C Pons, S Bret, D Bienes, A Bouzer, D Fraisse, P Entat (c), J Moliner, D Verdes, D Divet, C Calvo, T Valero, S Titeux. Replacements: M Tisseyre (for Calvo), P Marginet (for Bienes) and J Bouscayrol (for Pons)
Referee: J Holdsworth (Great Britain)

Second Test
At Stade Gilbert Brutus, Perpignan, Sunday, 9 December 1990
Crowd: 3428
AUSTRALIA 34 (Mackay 2, Shearer, Alexander, Ettingshausen, Meninga, Roach tries, Alexander 3 goals) d FRANCE 10 (Pons, Entat tries, M Tisseyre goal)
Australia: G Belcher, G Alexander, D Shearer, M Meninga (c), A Ettingshausen, C Lyons, R Stuart, B Mackay, R Lindner, P Sironen, S Roach, B Elias, G Lazarus. Replacements: D Gillespie (for Lindner), C Johns (for Alexander), D Hasler (for Stuart) and M Sargent (for Lazarus)
France: D Fraisse, C Pons, S Bret, G Delaunay, A Bouzer, J Moliner, P Entat (c), D Verdes, D Divet, F Lope, M Tisseyre, T Valero, T Buttignol. Replacements: D Bienes (for Bret) and P Marginet (for Fraisse)
Referee: J Holdsworth (Great Britain)

Top Point-scorers in Franco-Australian Tests
(As of 1 January 1992)

	T	G	Pts
Puig Aubert (F)	—	26	52
Keith Barnes (A)	—	26	52
Graeme Langlands (A)	4	15	42
Mick Cronin (A)	2	18	42
Ken Irvine (A)	9	7	41
Michael O'Connor (A)	4	10	36
Greg Alexander (A)	4	10	36
Pierre Lacaze (F)	—	16	32
Keith Holman (A)	6	4	26
Noel Pidding (A)	—	12	24
Dale Shearer (A)	6	—	24
Mal Meninga (A)	2	8	23
Jean Capdouze (F)	—	10	20
Reg Gasnier (A)	6	—	18
Claude Mantoulan (F)	—	8	16
Jose Moya (F)	—	8	16
Garry Jack (A)	4	—	16

FRANCO-AUSTRALIAN TEST RECORDS

Biggest win: 60–4 by Australia, First Test, at Avignon, 1990 (Biggest French win: 35–14, Third Test, at Sydney, 1951)
Biggest crowd: 67 009 at Sydney Cricket Ground, Third Test, 1951
Smallest crowd: 2200 at Avignon, First Test, 1990
Most points in a match: 26 by Greg Alexander, First Test, at Avignon, 1990 (Most for France: 16 by Pierre Lacaze, First Test, at Paris, 1959)
Most tries in a match: 4 by Dale Shearer (Aust), Second Test, at Carcassonne, 1986 (Most for France: 3 by Jo Crespo, Third Test, at Sydney, 1951)
Most goals in a match: 10 by Keith Barnes (Aust), Second Test, at   Brisbane, 1960 (Most for France: 8 by Pierre Lacaze, First Test, at Paris, 1959)
Most Test matches: 13 by Johnny Raper (Aust) (Most for France, 12 by Claude Mantoulan)

FRANCE V AUSTRALIA
WORLD CUP AND WORLD CHAMPIONSHIP MATCHES

1954

At Nantes, Thursday, 11 November 1954
Crowd: 14 000
FRANCE 15 (Merquey, Contrastin, Cantoni tries, Puig Aubert 3 goals) d AUSTRALIA 3 (O'Shea try)
Australia: C Churchill (c), N Pidding, A Watson, G Hawick, D Flannery, R Banks, K Holman, P Diversi, H Crocker, K O'Shea, B Davies, K Kearney, R Bull
France: Puig Aubert (c), V Cantoni, J Merquey, C Teissiere, R Contrastin, A Jiminez, J Crespo, R Guilhelm, J Pambrun, G Delaye, J Krawzyk, A Audobert, F Rinaldi
Referee: C Appleton (Great Britain)

1957

At Sydney Cricket Ground, Saturday, 22 June 1957
Crowd: 35 158
AUSTRALIA 26 (Carlson, Poole, O'Shea, Marsh tries, Carlson 7 goals) d FRANCE 9 (Benausse try & 3 goals)
Australia: B Carlson, A Watson, R Poole (c), H Wells, I Moir, B Clay, K McCaffery, D Schofield, N Provan, K O'Shea, B Davies, K Kearney, W Marsh
France: A Rives, G Husson, A Jiminez (c), J Foussat, M Voron, G Benausse, R Jean, F Levy, A Parent, R Medus, H Delhoste, A Appelian, R Ferrero
Referee: V Belsham (New Zealand)

1960

At Central Park, Wigan, Saturday, 24 September 1960
Crowd: 20 278
AUSTRALIA 13 (Raper, Kelly, Gasnier tries, Carlson 2 goals) d FRANCE 12 (Gruppi 2 tries, Lacaze 3 goals)
Australia: B Carlson, K Irvine, R Gasnier, H Wells, L Morgan, A Brown, B Muir (c), J Raper, B Hambly, E Rassmussen, B Beattie, N Kelly, R Mossop
France: L Poletti, J Dubon, C Mantoulan, R Rey, R Gruppi, J Merquey (c), G Fages, A Lacaze, R Eramouspe, J Barthe, A Quaglio, A Casas, A Boldini
Referee: E Clay (Great Britain)

1968

At Lang Park, Brisbane, Saturday, 8 June 1968
Crowd: 32 600
AUSTRALIA 37 (Williamson 2, Fulton 2, Greaves, Smith, Coote tries, Simms 5 goals, Smith 3 field goals) d FRANCE 4 (Capdouze 2 goals)
Australia: E Simms, B James, J Rhodes, J Greaves, L Williamson, R Fulton, W Smith, J Raper (c), R Coote, D Manteit, A Beeston, B Fitzsimmons, J Wittenberg
France: J Cros, A Ferren, M Mollinier, R Gruppi, J Ledru, J Capdouze, M Frattini, J P Clar, A Alesina, H Mazard, C Sabatie, Y Begou, V Serrano. Replacement: F De Nadai (for Sabatie)
Referee: J Percival (New Zealand)

Final
At Sydney Cricket Ground, Monday, 10 June 1968
Crowd: 54 290
AUSTRALIA 20 (Williamson 2, Greaves, Coote tries, Simms 4 goals) d FRANCE 2 (Capdouze goal)
Australia: E Simms, J Rhodes, G Langlands, J Greaves, L Williamson, R Fulton, W Smith, J Raper (c), R Coote, R Thornett, A Beeston, B Fitzsimmons, J Wittenberg
France: J Cros, D Pellerin, R Gruppi, J P Lecompte, J Ledru, J Capdouze, R Garrigues, J P Clar, H Marracq, F De Nadai, G Ailleres (c), Y Begou, C Sabatie
Referee: J Percival (New Zealand)

1970

At Odsal Stadium, Bradford, Sunday, 1 November 1970
Crowd: 6654
FRANCE 17 (Marsolan 2, Capdouze tries, Capdouze 2 goals & field goal, Garrigues field goal) d AUSTRALIA 15 (Cootes 2, Fulton tries, Simms 3 goals)
Australia: E Simms, R Branighan, J Cootes, R Fulton, L Williamson, D Pittard, W Smith, R Coote (c), P Sait, R McCarthy, R O'Reilly, E Walters, B McTaggart. Replacements: R Turner (for McTaggart) and G Sullivan (for Pittard)
France: J Cros, S Marsolan, M Molinier, R Gruppi, D Pellerin, J Capdouze, R Garrigues, J P Clar (c), R Biffi, F De Nadai, F Bonet, J Cabero, C Sabatie
Referee: W Thompson (Great Britain)

1972

At Stade de Minimes, Toulouse, Sunday, 5 November 1972
Crowd: 10 332
AUSTRALIA 31 (Harris 2, Sait 2, Fulton, O'Neill, Walters tries, Branighan 5 goals) d FRANCE 9 (Ruiz try, Bonal 3 goal)
Australia: G Langlands (c), R Branighan, M Harris, G Starling, J Grant, R Fulton, D Ward, P Sait, A Beeston, G Stevens, R O'Reilly, E Walters, J O'Neill
France: R Toujas, S Marsolan, M Molinier, A Ruiz, J Bonal, M Mazare, M Frattini, S Gleyzes, F De Nadai (c), V Serrano, J Garzino, J Franc, C Zalduendo. Replacements: B Guilhem (for Toujas) and M Anglade (for Zalduendo)
Referee: M Naughton (Great Britain)

1975

At Lang Park, Sunday, Brisbane, 22 June 1975
Crowd: 9000
AUSTRALIA 26 (Harris 2, Fulton 2, Pickup, Cronin tries, Cronin 4 goals) d FRANCE 6 (Calle 3 goals)
Australia: G Langlands(c), M Harris, M Cronin, R Fulton, T Pickup, T Raudonikis, R Coote, L Platz, T Randall, A Beeston, J Lang, J Donnelly. Replacements: C Anderson and J Quayle
France: F Tranier, A Dumas, A Ruiz, R Terrats, B Curt, J Calle, J Imbert, Anglade, S Gleyzes, M Maique, M Cassin, E Kaminski, F De Nadai. Replacements: J C Mayorgas and C Zalduendo
Referee: J Percival (New Zealand)

At Stade Gilbert Brutus, Perpignan, Sunday, 26 October 1975
Crowd: 10 440
AUSTRALIA 41 (Rogers 2, Rhodes, Peard, Platz, Higgs, Randall, Raudonikis, Eadie tries, Eadie 7 goals) d FRANCE 2 (Guilhem goal)
Australia: G Eadie, J Rhodes, S Rogers, J Brass, J Porter, J Peard, T Raudonikis, G Pierce, R Higgs, L Platz, T Randall, J Lang, A Beeston (c) Replacement: I Schubert (for Rhodes)
France: M Pillon, J F Grechi, A Ruiz, B Guilhem, P Chauvet, J Calle, J Imbert, R Terrats, J P Tremouille, J P Sauret, C Thenegal, A Gonzales, C Zalduendo. Replacements: P Clergeau (for Ruiz) and M Moussard (Zalduendo)
Referee: W Thompson (Great Britain)

1977

At Sydney Cricket Ground, Saturday, 11 June 1977
Crowd: 13 231
AUSTRALIA 21 (Eadie 2, McMahon, Fitzgerald, Veivers tries, Cronin 3 goals) d FRANCE 9 (Moya try, Calle 3 goals)
Australia: G Eadie, A McMahon, M Cronin, M Thomas, T Fahey, J Peard, T Raudonikis, R Reddy, T Randall, A Beetson (c), D Fitzgerald, N Geiger, G Veivers. Replacements: R Gartner and R Higgs
France: J Guigue, J Moya, R Terrats, J M Bourret, C Laskawiec, J Calle (c), E Alard, J Roosebrouck, J P Sauret, M Caravaca, M Cassin, E Garcia, M Chantal. Replacements: J Imbert and C Rodriguez
Referee: W Thompson (Great Britain)

1988

For qualifying game see entry above for *Second Test, Perpignan, 1986* (Australia 52 d France 0). France forfeited second qualifying game scheduled for Australia in 1987.

1992

For qualifying games see entry above for *Test, Parkes, 1990* (Australia 34 d France 2) and *Second Test, Perpignan, 1990* (Australia 34 d France 10)

FRANCE V AUSTRALIA
INTERNATIONALS

(Played after World Cups staged in Britain)

1960

At Stade de Minemes, Toulouse, Sunday, 16 October 1960
Crowd: 5304
AUSTRALIA 37 (Irvine 2, Kelly 2, Boden, Morgan, Brown, Bugden, Mossop tries, Carlson 5 goals) d FRANCE 12 (Benausse, Lacaze tries, Lacaze 3 goals)
Australia: B Carlson, K Irvine, R Gasnier, R Boden, L Morgan, A Brown, R Bugden, H Wells, R Mossop (c), G Parcell, N Kelly, W Rayner, D Beattie
France: L Poletti, J Dubon, A, Carrere, R Gruppi, R Benausse, A Jiminez, J Guiraud, R Lacans, C Combeau, G Verdie, A Lacaze, A Casas, R Majoral
Referee: A Cassan (France)

1970

At Stade Gilbert Brutus, Perpignan, Wednesday, 11 November 1970
Crowd: 14 700
AUSTRALIA 7 (Cootes try, Simms 2 goals) d FRANCE 4 (Capdouze 2 goals)
Australia: E Simms, L Williamson, R Branighan, J Cootes, M Harris, D Pittard, J Brown, R Fulton, R Coote (c), G Sullivan, B McTaggart, E Walters, R O'Reilly. Replacements: K Irvine (for Pittard) and W Smith (for Walters)
France: J C Cros, S Marsolan, M Molinier, J Gruppi, D Pellerin, J Capdouze, A Clere, J P Clar (c), F De Nadai, G Bonnet, F Bonet, J Cabero, C Sabatie. Replacements: D Hermet and C Clar
Referee: C Teissiere (France)

For details of French tours to Australia, New Zealand and England, see under *LES CHANTICLEERS*

The French Championship
(for the Max Rousie Shield)

Year	Champion	Year	Champion
1935	US Villeneuuve	1956	R C Albi
1936	XIII Catalan	1957	XIII Catalan
1937	Bordeaux	1958	R C Albi
1938	R C Albi	1959	U S Villeneuve
1939	R C Roanne	1960	R C Roanne
1941–1944*		1961	F C Lezignan
1945	A S Carcassonne	1962	R C Albi
1946	A S Carcassonne	1963	F C Lezignan
1947	R C Roanne	1964	U S Villeneuve
1948	R C Roanne	1965	Toulouse Olympique
1949	R C Marseilles	1966	A S Carcassonne
1950	A S Carcassonne	1967	A S Carcassonne
1951	Lyon	1968	S C Limoux
1952	A S Carcassonne	1969	XIII Catalan
1953	A S Carcassonne	1970	R C St Gaudens
1954	Bordeaux	1971	A S St Esteve
1955	Lyon	1972	A S Carcassonne

▶

The French Championship
(for the Max Rousie Shield) *continued*

Year	Champion	Year	Champion
1973	Toulouse Olympique	1983	XIII Catalan
1974	R C St Gaudens	1984	XIII Catalan
1975	Toulouse Olympique	1985	XIII Catalan
1976	A S Carcassonne	1986	Le Pontet
1977	XIII Catalan	1987	XIII Catalan
1978	F C Lezignan	1988	Le Pontet
1979	XIII Catalan	1989	A S St Esteve
1980	U S Villeneuve	1990	A S St Esteve
1981*		1991	R C St Gaudens
1982	XIII Catalan		

* There was no Rugby League during World War II. The 1981 Championship final, between XIII Catalan and U S Villeneuve, was abandoned after a brawl four minutes into the game.

Coupe de France
(for the Lord Derby Cup)

Finals

Year	Result			
1935	Lyon	22	XIII Catalan	7
1936	Cote Basque	15	U S Villeneuve	8
1937	U S Villeneuve	12	XIII Catalan	6
1938	R C Roanne	36	U S Villeneuve	12
1939	XIII Catalan	7	Toulouse Olymmpique	3
1940–1944*				
1945	XIII Catalan	23	A S Carcassonne	14
1946	A S Carcassonne	27	XIII Catalan	7
1947	A S Carcassonne	24	S O Avignon	5
1948	R C Marseille	5	A S Carcassonne	4
1949	R C Marseille	12	A S Carcassonne	9
1950	XIII Catalan	12	Lyon	5
1951	A S Carcassonne	22	Lyon	10
1952	A S Carcassonne	28	XIII Catalan	9
1953	Lyon	9	U S Villeneuve	8
1954	Lyon	17	XIII Catalan	15
1955	S O Avignon	18	R C Marseille	10
1956	S O Avignon	25	Bordeaux	12
1957	R C Marseille	11	XIII Catalan	0
1958	U S Villeneuve	20	S O Avignon	8
1959	XIII Catalan	7	S O Avignon	0
1960	F C Lezignan	7	A S Carcassonne	4
1961	A S Carcassonne	5	F C Lezignan	2
1962	R C Roanne	16	Toulouse Olymmpique	10
1963	A S Carcassonne	5	Toulouse Olymmpique	0
1964	U S Villeneuve	10	Toulouse Olymmpique	2
1965	R C Marseille	13	A S Carcassonne	8
1966	F C Lezignan	22	U S Villeneuve	7
1968	A S Carcassonne	9	Toulouse Olymmpique	2
1969	XIII Catalan	13	U S Villeneuve	8
1970	F C Lezignan	14	U S Villeneuve	8
1971	R C Marseille	17	F C Lezignan	2
1972	A S St Esteve	12	U S Villeneuve	5
1973	R C St Gaudens	22	A S Carcassonne	8
1974	R C Albi	21	F C Lezignan	11
1975	Pia	9	R C Marseille	4
1976	XIII Catalan	23	Toulouse Olymmpique	8
1977	A S Carcassonne	21	XIII Catalan	16
1978	XIII Catalan	18	F C Lezignan	7
1979	U S Villeneuve	15	A S Carcassonne	5
1980	XIII Catalan	18	A S Carcassonne	8
1981*				
1982	S O Avignon	18	A S Carcassonne	12
1983	A S Carcassonne	10	XIII Catalan	3
1984	U S Villeneuve	18	S C Limoux	7
1985	XIII Catalan	24	S C Limoux	7
1986	Le Pontet	35	A S St Esteve	10
1987	A S St Esteve	20	XIII Catalan	10
1988	Le Pontet	5	A S St Esteve	2
1989	S O Avignon	12	A S St Esteve	11
1990	A S Carcassonne	22	A S St Esteve	8
1991	R C St Gaudens	30	Pia	4

* There was no Rugby League during World War II. The 1981 final between A S Carcassonne and XIII Catalan was cancelled because of the brawl which caused the abandonment of the previous week's Championship final.

ARTHUR 'BOLLER' FRANCIS

Two Tests for Australasia (1911). Also played 22 minor games for Australia on one Kangaroo tour (1911–12).

Arthur 'Boller' Francis, a tough prop forward, was one of a handful of New Zealanders to tour with a Kangaroo side. Francis, a former All Black Rugby Union international, so impressed the locals on the tour of Australia in 1911 that he was invited, with three other Kiwis, to go on the 1911–12 Kangaroo tour of Britain. He was, however, the only one to play a Test, turning out in the first two encounters, at Newcastle and Edinburgh. Francis also topped the pointscoring on tour. In 24 games, his 125 points (9 tries and 49 goals) was almost double that of the next most successful tourist, Herb Gilbert. Ironically, in his two Test appearances Francis' goalkicking was very ordinary, with only one successful attempt in each game, but he did score a try in the 19–10 victory at Newcastle.

CHARLES 'CHOOK' FRASER

Eleven Tests for Australia (1911–1922). Also played 43 minor games for Australia on two Kangaroo tours (1911–12 and 1921–22) and one New Zealand tour (1919).

When 'Chook' Fraser went to England with the 1911–12 Australian side he was just 18 years old and the youngest to gain Kangaroo honours. By 1992, only four other 18–year-olds had made a Kangaroo tour—Bobby Dimond (1948), Steve Rogers (1973), Kerry Boustead (1978) and Brad Fittler (1990)—while Geoff Starling was the same age when he visited New Zealand with the 1971 Australian side.

Ten years later, Fraser made his second Kangaroo tour, during which he joined an elite who could boast appearances in four Anglo-Australian Test series. To cap a fine career he led the Australians in each of the three Tests, after tour skipper, Les Cubitt, was sidelined through injury.

Fraser was effective playing anywhere in the backline, although he excelled at fullback or five-eighth. He made his Test debut at Newcastle-on-Tyne, in 1911, as a fullback. In his other Tests (against the 1914 and 1920 Lions and while touring New Zealand in 1919 and Britain with the 1921–22 Kangaroos) he played seven times at fullback and three times at stand-off. Fraser also visited New Zealand with the great 1912 New South Wales side.

For much of the time he was with Balmain, that Sydney club was the undisputed champion side, winning five Premierships in six years (1915, 1916, 1917, 1919 and 1920). Fraser was also a member of the Balmain side which won in 1924. His 185 first-grade games stood as a club record for more than four decades, until beaten by that other great fullback Keith Barnes, who played 194.

DAN FRAWLEY

Seven Tests for Australia (1908–1914). Also played 32 minor games for Australia on two Kangaroo tours (1908–09 and 1911–12).

Dan Frawley was one of the fastest and most exciting of Australia's early footballers. He acquired his footballing skills in the Sydney dockside suburb of Woolloomooloo. According to local legend, when sent to collect meat from the local butcher, the young Frawley would run home side-stepping lampposts at full speed with the weekend joint under one arm. In other children's games, bone-testing spills on the hard Woolloomooloo streets soon taught him ways of falling without unduly hurting himself.

Frawley joined the professional ranks in 1908, after a short Rugby Union career. He had played in South Africa during the Boer War and was chosen in a side of Commonwealth Servicemen which played the national Test side. Frawley was an instant sensation in the pro ranks, touring Great Britain with the first Kangaroo side and playing in the first Test series against New Zealand, in 1909.

He figured in further clashes with the British in 1911–12 and 1914. However, the former appearances only came after an international uproar. Frawley had played with Warrington, the English club, after the 1909 Tests, and the Lancashire side claimed he was not eligible to line up with the 1911–12 Kangaroos. Because of the dispute, Frawley missed the First Test and other early games. The Warrington claims were eventually rejected. Frawley went on to score 18 tries in just 12 matches for the Kangaroos. Only two other players, each of whom had played more than twice as many games as Frawley, scored more points on tour.

Frawley made two tours of New Zealand with the fine 1912 and 1913 New South Wales sides. He was also a member of the Eastern Suburbs combination which won the Sydney Premiership in those two years.

In one match for Eastern Suburbs against South Sydney, Dan Frawley was playing on the wing, outside the man they dubbed 'The Master', Dally Messenger. That day, Messenger was trying to do too much himself and rarely passed the ball to Frawley. Upset, the Easts fans began a chant: 'Why don't they feed Frawley?' His father was in the crowd and eventually the chants of 'Feed Frawley' got on his goat. He turned to the barrackers and shouted: 'I'll have you know that I'm his father. And young Dan gets a pound of steak every day except Friday'.

Dan Frawley is the only player to have represented both Australia and Great Britain. He played seven Tests for Australia and made two Kangaroo tours but, in 1910, when the British side was visiting Australia, Frawley was called upon to play for the tourists in their 40–20 victory over Northern NSW at Newcastle. The British justified his selection by noting that Frawley was, at the time, registered with the Warrington club in England.

GARY FREEMAN

Twenty-seven Tests for New Zealand (1986–91). Also played in 1988 World Cup final and 12 minor games on one tour of Britain and France (1989) and one tour of Australia and Papua New Guinea (1986).

When New Zealand named Gary Freeman captain for the 1990 Tests against Papua New Guinea, it was due recognition of the great team efforts of the feisty halfback during his four years in the Kiwi international lineup. He had made has Test debut in the Second Test of the 1986 series against Australia as an inexperienced but tough little campaigner from Auckland— and he provided the spark needed for the Kiwis to challenge the Australians.

His efforts in the one-off Test in Brisbane the following season, in which the Kiwis shocked by winning 13–6, prompted Balmain to sign him for three years. At Leichhardt Oval, he initially found it hard to cement a first grade spot. Eventually his class prevailed and late in the year, with British captain Ellery Hanley, Freeman played a major role in Balmain's surge to the grand final.

In 1989, his hopes were shattered when he was suspended for 12 weeks after allegations of eye-gouging. The New Zealand selectors showed their faith however, by picking him for the home series against Australia despite lack of match play. That season he once again was instrumental in Balmain's run to the grand final, but, as they did 12 months before, the Tigers fell at the last hurdle.

The 1990 season was one of Freeman's best. His play for Balmain earned him a further three year contract, he played three Tests against the touring British Lions, a one-off international against Australia and was skipper of the Kiwis in their two Tests in Papua New Guinea.

By 1992, Freeman had played 27 Tests (10 against Australia, seven against Great Britain, six versus Papua New Guinea and four against France), as well as the 1988 World Cup final, against Australia. But 1991 was not a good year for the tough halfback. He had trouble keeping his first grade spot against competition from former Australia and Ireland Rugby Union Test star Brian Smith. Indeed, Freeman was chosen from reserve grade for the Tests against France and Australia. At the end of the season, he was released from the remainder of his contract with the Tigers to join up with Eastern Suburbs.

CLAYTON FRIEND

Twenty-three Tests for New Zealand (1982–91). Also played in 1988 World Cup Final, 14 minor games for New Zealand on one Australian tour (1982) and one tour of Britain and France (1985) and seven games for the Maoris on one British tour (1983).

The Test career of Kiwi halfback Clayton Friend is a story of one of the most remarkable comebacks in the history of the game. After two years in the wilderness in the early 1990s, unable to get a game with a senior club on either side of the world, Friend suddenly found the spark which not only got him back into the Test XIII but inspired his colleagues once he got there.

Friend, then 20, entered the international arena in 1982 when chosen for New Zealand's tour of Australia and Papua New Guinea. In Australia, he played only the minor games, but when New Zealand went into the Test against Papua New Guinea without its Sydney-based stars, he got his chance. He grabbed it with both hands, scoring a try in the Kiwis world-record 56–5 thrashing of the locals.

For the next six years Friend was a regular in the Kiwi lineup. He played a major role in a couple of the major upsets of Australia. When New Zealand won the Third Test, at Christchurch in 1985, 18–0, he was named Man-of-the-Match. And he basked in the glory of his country's 13–6 victory over Australia, in a one-off Test in Brisbane, two years later.

In 1986, Friend joined his Kiwi captain Mark Graham at North Sydney.

His best year was 1987, when his scheming play earned him second spot in the Dally M Awards.

Two years later his world began to fall apart. He was dropped from the Test side after the First Test against the touring Australians and at the end of the year Norths cut him from their playing ranks.

He was reduced to playing with Ryde-Eastwood which won the Metropolitan Cup, Sydney's 'Second Division' competition, in 1990. He then turned out with Carlisle in Britain's Division II before returning to Auckland in 1991 for a last-ditch effort to regain a Test spot.

His perseverance paid off. He came on late in the First Test, against France, as a replacement. Then, as the Kiwis struggled, with a fragile lead in the Second Test, he replaced captain and halfback Gary Freeman.

Friend sparked a Kiwi revival, scoring himself and setting up another try which put the match out of the reach of the tourists. He continued his good form in the three Tests against Australia.

BOB FULTON

Twenty Tests for Australia (1970–1978). Also played 15 matches in three World Cups (1968, 1970 and 1972) and one World Championship (1975), two minor internationals (1970 and 1975) and 22 minor games for Australia on two Kangaroo tours (1973 and 1978), one New Zealand tour (1971) and one World Cup tour (1970).

It is perhaps significant that Manly-Warringah's first three Sydney Premiership successes (1972, 1973 and 1976) occurred when Bob Fulton was at his inspired best and wearing Manly's maroon and white. Fulton was close to being the ultimate in a Rugby League player—a talented, dedicated professional with the ability to lift any side in which he was playing.

It was predictable therefore that shock waves resounded through Manly's northern beaches area after the 1976 grand final, when he decided to throw in his lot with Eastern Suburbs for the rest of his playing career. Ever since he had joined Manly as a baby-faced 17–year-old in 1966, Fulton had been the epitome of the Sea Eagles' quest for success. He rose from being just another promising country lad to one of the all-time greats of the sport. Indeed, the respected publication *Rugby League Week* named him, together with Johnny Raper, Reg Gasnier and Clive Churchill, as one of 'The Immortals' of post-World War II football.

Fulton's international debut was with the side which won the 1968 World Cup for Australia. Many keen judges felt, however, that he should have been in the Kangaroo squad which had toured Britain and France the previous year. In the next 11 seasons, Fulton achieved almost every possible honour in the international sphere—Kangaroo tours (1973 and 1978), a tour of New Zealand (1971), four World Series (1968, 1970, 1972 and 1975), home series against Great Britain (1970 and 1974) and New Zealand (1972 and 1978), the World Cup Man-of-the-Series (1970) and the captaincy of Australia (1978).

Perhaps, the highlight of his career came in a club match for Manly. In the 1973 grand final, the Sea Eagles were trying to win their second

Premiership on the trot. The match, against Cronulla-Sutherland, was delicately poised until Fulton's sheer individual brilliance snared two tries which turned the game. Manly ran out winners 10–7 in what is regarded as the most brutal grand final of all time—but the violence was completely overshadowed by Fulton's sensational play.

With Eastern Suburbs, Fulton had mixed success—as captain, then captain-coach and finally non-playing coach, however he did lift the Roosters to the 1980 grand final. Like the prodigal son, he returned to coach Manly in 1983. That first year he steered the Sea Eagles to the grand final and then, in 1987, he achieved the ultimate success, with Manly taking out the Premiership. Fulton thus became the first Manly personality to win Premierships as both a captain and a coach.

Fulton quit the club scene at the end of 1988 to take over the reins as Australia's Test coach. When he went to Britain and France with the 1990 Kangaroos he joined a select few to have made separate tours as both a player and a coach. The others were Arthur Hennessy (1929–30 coach), Clive Churchill (1959–60), Frank Stanton (1978 and 1982) and Don Furner (1986).

DON FURNER

One Test for Australia (1956). Also played in 10 minor games for Australia on one Kangaroo tour (1956–57).

As a player, Don Furner seemed destined to be the perpetual reserve. He was named a reserve forward in no fewer than seven Tests before he made his lone appearance, in the Second Test, at Bradford, on the 1956–57 Kangaroo tour. Then, just as his international career seemed finally assured, a leg injury put him out of further contention.

Furner was not so unlucky as a coach. His first five clubs, all in the NSW country, won Premierships. He also had some relative success with Eastern Suburbs in the early 1970s, coaching the Roosters into the 1972 Sydney Premiership grand final.

In 1982, when Canberra entered the Premiership race, the Raiders snapped him up as their mentor. He laid the foundation for a steady progress up the table. In 1987 (with co-coach Wayne Bennett), Furner steered the Canberra combination into the grand final. To get there the Raiders had thrashed South Sydney 46–12 in a semi-final and downed Eastern Suburbs 32–24 in the preliminary final—but Furner's boys faltered before Manly-Warringah, going down 18–8.

Furner also had a spell as coach of the Australian Test side. He was at the helm on the highly successful 1986 Kangaroo tour and for the historic 1988 matches, which included the 100th Anglo-Australian Test and the Bicentennial international between Australia and the Rest-of-the-World, both at the Sydney Football Stadium.

G

PETER GALLAGHER

Seventeen Tests for Australia (1963–1967). Also played 27 minor games for Australia on two Kangaroo tours (1963–64 and 1967–68).

Heavyweight Brisbane prop-forward, Peter Gallagher provided the backbone for the Australian pack in several Test series during the 1960s. He first caught the eyes of the critics during 1962, as a 25-year-old second-row forward, with impressive displays in the Brisbane and Queensland sides which stretched the British tourists. The following season, after switching up front, he played in all five home Tests (against New Zealand and South Africa) before being chosen for the Kangaroo tour of Britain and France.

Gallagher tore ligaments in his right knee after the First Test against Great Britain and aggravated the injury by a premature return to football. As a result, he was unable to return to the Test side until the second encounter with France, at Toulouse. Recurring injuries and business commitments interrupted the flow of Gallagher's Test career until the next Kangaroo tour, four years later. He finished his international stint with appearances in all six Tests (captaining Australia in the Second Test against Britain in the absence through injury of Kangaroo skipper, Reg Gasnier, and his deputy, Johnny Raper). His final tally of 17 Tests included four against Great Britain, six opposing New Zealand, five versus France and two against South Africa.

REG GASNIER

Thirty-six Tests for Australia (1959–1967). Also played three matches in one World Cup (1960), one minor international (1960) and 38 minor games for Australia on three Kangaroo tours (1959–60, 1963–64 and 1967–68) and two New Zealand tours (1961 and 1965).

Reg Gasnier, Australia's most brilliant post-World War II star, could have reached the top in any number of sports. He was a champion schoolboy Rugby Union player, a baseball star and an athlete who excelled in the

Reg Gasnier soaks his head in a bucket of water to wash the mud out of his eyes during a 1961 NSW-Queensland match at the Sydney Cricket Ground

long jump, high jump, sprints and high hurdles. As a cricketer he was on the verge of selection for the NSW Sheffield Shield side. Gasnier sacrificed further success in all those sports to concentrate on Rugby League. The decision paid huge dividends.

The great centre first turned out for St George's third-grade team in 1958, when he was 17 years old. Next year he was rapidly promoted to the Dragon's top side and his phenomenal rise into big-time football had begun. After just a handful of games, Gasnier was selected for the NSW State side and, a couple of weeks later, for Australia (against New Zealand). At one stage in 1959, he had played more representative games than he had first-grade matches for St George.

Gasnier's selection for the 1959–60 Kangaroo tour of Britain and France was a mere formality. At the start of the tour, however, he was laid up with a hamstring injury. When he did make the field the British had cause to regret his recovery. The first time he touched a ball, in a match against Widnes, he scored a 60–metre try. Later in the match, he bagged another two. Then, in his English Test debut, at Swinton, he went over for three more, to inspire a 22–14 victory. It was the first time the Kangaroos had ever won a Test at Swinton.

In 1962, Gasnier became the youngest player to have captained Australia. He was 23 years and 28 days old when he led his team out onto the Sydney Cricket Ground for the First Test against Britain, 58 days younger than Dave Brown, who was skipper in 1936. Gasnier displayed top form on his second Kangaroo tour, at the end of 1963. In the First Test, at Wembley Stadium, he and St George team-mate Graeme Langlands ran riot in the centres and touched down for two tries each in a 28–2 victory. Gasnier was also prominent in the record 50–12 Second Test win. He made his third and last tour of Britain and France in 1967 as captain. This was after he had recovered from a crippling knee injury which, for a time, looked as if it would finish his career.

Although Australia won the Ashes in 1967, the Kangaroo tour was a personal disappointment for Gasnier. He suffered a bad leg injury in the First Test against Britain and on his return to the Kangaroo line-up, against French Hopefuls at Avignon, he broke down completely. Only a few spectators were present on that cold, damp December day to witness the end of a glorious era.

In a tribute to Gasnier, the chairman of the Australian Rugby League, Bill Buckley, said: 'On his day, he was the greatest Rugby League player I have ever seen. Gasnier had an amazing change of pace and great anticipation. He was also particularly unselfish. He was without peer.'

ANDREW GEE

Played one minor match for Australia on one Papua New Guinea tour (1991).

The 1991 Brisbane Broncos Year Book said it all: 'It is not now a matter of if Andrew Gee will play for Australia, but when?' Less than a year later he had, chosen to tour Papua New Guinea with the Australian side.

The Year Book editor was not putting his reputation on the line. Gee, from Beaudesert near Brisbane, had played in Australian Schoolboys sides in 1985 and 1986 (touring Great Britain in the latter year). The crash-tackling second-rower was blooded in the Broncos senior side as an 19-year-old in 1989 and made the Queensland State-of-Origin side only a month after his 20th birthday. He immediately showed he had the class to mix it with the toughest players in the game.

Few of his contemporaries could match Gee's defensive record. He is one of the few players in the NSWRL Premiership to have finished a match with more than 50 tackles on more than one occasion. In one match, against Manly-Warringah, in 1990, he made an incredible 62 hits, despite being rested with 15 minutes of the match still to go.

Gee got his chance to wear the green and gold when Penrith Test forward John Cartwright pulled out of the 1991 squad to tour Papua New Guinea. It was not a happy tour. Walking from the ground after his debut for Australia against Island Zone, at Rabaul, Gee stepped in a pothole and suffered an ankle injury which finished his tour.

GEOFF GERARD

Six Tests for Australia (1978–1983). Also played eight minor games for Australia on one Kangaroo tour (1978).

When big, bearded prop-forward Geoff Gerard ran onto the field (to play Parramatta) at Penrith Park on 29 July 1989, he also ran into the record books. That Saturday afternoon he became the first player in the history

1978 Kangaroo forward Geoff Gerard in a typical tough burst in a club match for Parramatta

of the Sydney Premiership competition to play 300 first-grade games. Others had passed the magic figure in all grades, but Gerard was the first to do so in the top teams. Just under four months earlier he had passed another milestone, in a match against Newcastle. He eclipsed the previous record number of first-grade games—284 by another Test front-rower, Bob O'Reilly.

The 33–year-old Gerard had achieved his two big records in 16 seasons with Parramatta, Manly-Warringah and Penrith. Indeed, the record may have been even more pronounced had Gerard's many appearances as a replacement been included in the tally.

Gerard reached the pinnacle of his career while with Parramatta when he was chosen to tour Britain and France with the 1978 Kangaroos. He played in 13 of the 22 matches, including all five Tests. Gerard played in only one other international—against New Zealand at Auckland's Carlaw Park in 1983, while he was with the Manly Sea Eagles.

MARK GEYER

Three Tests for Australia (1990–91). Also played 10 minor games on one Kangaroo tour (1990).

Penrith talent scouts knew just how good the fiery young forward Mark Geyer was going to be, when they signed him from the St Mary's junior club in 1985. In his first full year with the club, 1986, Geyer made both the Sydney and NSW Under-19 sides. He became a regular first-grader the following year, and achieved his first representative selection—for City Seconds.

Geyer formed a lethal second-row combination with another tall Penrith forward, John Cartwright, but for a while his hotheaded play seemed to go against him when the major teams were selected. Geyer broke through for his first State-of-Origin match in 1989, and the following year made it into the Kangaroo side to tour Great Britain and France (as did Cartwright). It was in 1990 that Geyer also made his first grand final appearance, when Penrith lost 18–14 to Canberra. On the Kangaroo tour, Geyer blossomed. He shrugged off his bad-boy image and so impressed coach Bob Fulton that he eventually made his Test debut, coming on as a replacement midway through the second half of the First Test against France, at Avignon.

His fiery temper made headlines in 1991 when, in the second State-of-Origin match, he had a blow-up with Queensland captain Wally Lewis as the players were leaving the field for half-time. After the game, Geyer was cited for an illegal tackle on Queensland fullback Paul Hauff and suspended for six games—a decision which cost him a spot in the lineup for the First Test against the touring New Zealand Kiwis. But Geyer was in the green and gold for the final two encounters.

A ligament tear looked likely to put him out of Penrith's grand final side, but Geyer made a miraculous recovery to share in the Panthers' first Premiership. But the aggravation to the injury on grand final day meant he missed the end-of-season Papua New Guinea tour by Australia.

JIMMY GIBBS

Seven Tests for Australia (1933–37). Also played 34 minor games on two Kangaroo tours (1933–34 and 1937–38) and one New Zealand tour (1935).

Jim Gibbs was one of Australia's best forwards in the 1930s, but he very nearly pursued a Rugby Union career. He used to play both games in the industrial city of Newcastle. One Saturday in 1926 Gibbs found himself on the horns of a dilemma. He was picked for the South Newcastle League side and the Cook's Hill Union team who were listed to play at the same time that afternoon. Gibbs had to make a decision. He tossed a coin— and League won.

Gibbs eventually made his Test debut on the 1933–34 Kangaroo tour of Britain. He was a Test regular for the next four years, turning out in seven clashes against Britain and New Zealand. He made a second Kangaroo tour in 1937–38 as well as a tour of New Zealand in 1935.

JACK GIBSON

Jack Gibson was unlucky never to have played Test football for Australia. He was one of the best front-row forwards of his era but the selectors continually overlooked him. As a coach he came to receive the kudos he so richly deserved. In his first nine seasons as a mentor (with three Sydney clubs, Eastern Suburbs, St George and Newtown), his sides never once missed the semi-finals. Four times his charges made the grand final and two of the sides were Premiers. He later added three more Premierships with his fourth club, Parramatta.

Gibson began with Easts in 1967. The previous year, the Roosters had failed to win a match, but Gibson took them to the semi-finals, two years in succession. He swapped clubs and, in 1970 and 1971, coached St George into a final and a grand final. One of the more amazing examples of Gibson's ability to inspire players was in 1973 when he had the reins at Newtown and took them from also-rans to success in the pre-season Wills Cup and then to the Premiership final. His efforts won him his first Coach-of-the-Year award. Next season when Gibson switched back to Easts, Newtown played like a very ordinary combination while the Roosters won the Premiership. They won again the following year, helping Gibson to his second Coach-of-the-Year award.

The great coach's only real disappointment was at South Sydney in 1978 and 1979. Although the Rabbitohs won the 1978 pre-season competition, they became the first Gibson-coached outfit to miss out on a semi-final berth. However his methods laid the foundation for a Rabbitoh revival.

In 1981, Gibson took up the position of coach of Parramatta and, in that first season, steered the Eels to their first-ever Premiership. The Eels repeated the performance the following two seasons, while Gibson was in charge. Gibson's last club side was Cronulla-Sutherland. Although there is nothing in the record books to indicate a Gibson success, he put together a team of young hopefuls who were later to become a real force in Sydney football.

Jack Gibson

In 1989, Gibson was given the NSW State-of-Origin side. The players let him down and he had to suffer the indignity of a 3–0 whitewash at the hands of a Queensland side coached by his friend and protege Arthur Beetson. He had his revenge 12 months later however, with the Gibson-coached New South Welshmen winning the series 2–1, over Beetson's Queenslanders.

He quit while on top to answer an SOS from Easts to take over as manager, with former Test halfback Mark Murray as his coach for 1991 and 1992.

HERB GILBERT

Seven Tests for Australia (1911–1920). Also played in 29 minor games for Australia on one Kangaroo tour (1911–12) and one New Zealand tour (1919).

Herb Gilbert, a hard-running centre, starred in the early days of Rugby League in Australia. He first hit the limelight on the 1911–12 Kangaroo tour of Great Britain. He played in all three Tests on that visit and topped the try-scoring lists on tour with 20 touchdowns in 29 games.

Gilbert so impressed the British that the Hull club persuaded him to join its ranks. In 1914, he became the first overseas player to captain the winning side in the Challenge Cup, when Hull beat Wakefield Trinity 6–0 at Thrum Hall, Halifax. He missed the 1914 Tests against Britain because of his English sojourn, but he toured New Zealand in 1919 and the following year captained Australia in its Ashes success over the visiting Lions.

The star centre played with four Sydney clubs during his career: Eastern Suburbs, South Sydney, Western Suburbs and St George. He captained Wests and Saints who, in 1921, had their first season in the Premiership competition. After he retired as a player, Gilbert served for a time as a NSW State selector.

DAVID GILLESPIE

Seven Tests for Australia (1990–91). Also played in the 1988 World Cup Final and seven minor games for Australia on one Kangaroo tour (1990).

An awful injury at work in late 1986, which resulted in the amputation of a finger, cost tough Canterbury-Bankstown forward David Gillespie a certain Kangaroo tour and a possible Premiership. That year, Canterbury lost the grand final to Parramatta 4–2 and coach Warren Ryan claimed the difference was the absence of the powerhouse Gillespie, nicknamed 'Cement' by his team-mates. It was only his second season in regular top football. He had shown his potential the previous year when, in each of his first three full first-grade games, he had been nominated by his Canterbury colleagues as the player-of-the-match. Gillespie had joined Canterbury from the western NSW town of Narromine from where he had been chosen in the Australian Under-18 side which beat the touring 1983 British side.

The 1986 Kangaroos may have gone away without him. But Gillespie got a second chance four years later, touring with the 1990 squad. In the meantime, he had made his international debut in the Australian side which took out the 1988 World Cup Final at Auckland, and he won a Test jumper against France, at Parkes in 1990. On the 1990 Kangaroo tour, Gillespie played two Tests as a replacement and was in the starting lineup for the First Test against France, at Avignon, after second-rower Bob Lindner pulled out through injury. While away, Gillespie was also making headlines in the Australian newspapers as one of several internationals to switch clubs to join their old Canterbury coach Warren Ryan at Western Suburbs.

He had a good first season with the Magpies, helping them to a semi-final berth and playing in each of the three Tests against the touring New Zealand Kiwis.

JAMES J GILTINAN

James J Giltinan was the driving force behind the movement which led to the start of Rugby League in Australia. A prominent Sydney sportsman, he was well-known in Rugby Union, cricket and horse-racing circles.

In 1906, he had talks with dissident All Black winger George Smith, who had been converted to the professional code while touring Britain with the New Zealand Rugby Union side the previous year. Giltinan, upset about the plight of some Union players and disenchanted with less crowd-pleasing aspects of the amateur game, sounded out a number of top players. He eventually got together a group of enthusiasts who met in the sports store owned by Test cricketer Victor Trumper. Giltinan and his colleagues worked for months preparing a constitution for the game.

In 1908, the NSW Rugby League held its first meeting and Giltinan was elected secretary. His enthusiasm did not end there. He was at the inaugural meetings of many Sydney clubs and became joint honorary secretary of one of them, Newtown. However in one of the worst backhanders in sporting history, Giltinan, who was in England as manager of the first Kangaroos, was not given the chance to seek re-election to the NSW post in 1909. It was to be another 25 years before he received due recognition, when the 1933–34 Kangaroos, on their return home, played the Rest-of-NSW in a testimonial match. The NSW Rugby League also named the shield given to the Premiers after Giltinan.

James J Giltinan

JJ GILTINAN SHIELD See *Sydney Premiership*

GLEBE

Glebe is acknowledged as Australia's first Rugby League club. It was formed at a meeting on 9 January 1908. Newtown club's minutes claimed it was formed the day before (and there is NSW Rugby League receipt number one for its affiliation fees). However most historians discount this because all contemporary newspaper reports say the Newtown meeting actually took place on 15 January.

Although it never won a Premiership, Glebe was one of the best of the pioneer clubs. It came close to winning in 1911 when it took out the Minor Premiership, but it was beaten 11–8 in the grand final by Eastern Suburbs. In 21 seasons in the Sydney Premiership, Glebe finished in the top four no less than 13 times.

The Dirty Reds or Famous Reds, as they were known, played in the maroon colours of the Queensland side. Among the great players to turn out for the Reds were the legendary Frank Burge, Alec Burdon and Chris McKivat. Because of a lack of junior clubs and no home ground, Glebe was thrown out of the competition in 1929 by a 13–12 vote. Petitions by local residents and personal pleas by Glebe personalities failed to reverse the decision. All told, Glebe won 155 and drew five of its 278 matches—a fine success rate of 57 percent. Glebe won five reserve-grade Premierships.

JOHNNY GLEESON

Ten Tests for Australia (1964–1967). Also played 20 minor games on two Kangaroo tours (1963–64 and 1967–68) and one New Zealand tour (1965).

A great display in a 1963 end-of-season interstate match, gave snappy Queensland five-eighth Johnny Gleeson his chance at international football. Although Queensland were outplayed 31–5 that afternoon, Gleeson's fine display against the incumbent Test stand-off Earl Harrison, won him a place in the 1963–64 Kangaroos side. Gleeson didn't play in any of the six Tests on the tour. He had missed much of the early tour after being hospitalised following adverse reaction to pre-tour vaccinations and late in the tour he broke a leg. However the experienced gained in Britain and France set him in good stead for his debut in the Second Test against the touring 1964 Frenchmen, forming a great partnership with halfback Billy Smith. He toured New Zealand the following year, played against the visiting 1966 British and 1967 Kiwi sides, before bowing out of the international arena on his second Kangaroo tour (1967–68).

GOLD COAST

The far north coast of New South Wales saw some of the earliest Rugby League in Australia. The Tweed Heads' Seagulls, were the first country side formed in Australia, in 1909, just one year after the first Sydney Premiership clashes. By 1914 there were eight teams involved in a local competition. The area was one of the first to play host to visiting international sides, in the 1920s.

Across the border, the Gold Coast was one of the sides which took part in the first Queensland State League competitions in the 1980s. However the area really came of age when, in 1988, Gold Coast-Tweed was one of three new teams to join the Sydney competition (together with Brisbane and Newcastle). The Giants, as they were originally called, were backed by some of the greats of international Rugby League, including John Sattler, Ken Irvine, Bob McCarthy and Graeme Langlands, and they had the use of one of the best grounds in the competition, Seagulls' Stadium at Tweed Heads.

Because it got the go-ahead to join much later that the other two, the club found the early going very tough—it won just four matches in that opening season and was on the receiving end of two heavy defeats, 50–6 at the hands of Canberra and 47–12 by Penrith. There were some better performances the following year, especially at home, including a 29–6 thrashing of Manly-Warringah. Lock forward Bob Lindner became the club's first State-of-Origin player, but the Gold Coast still languished near the bottom of the competition, above only North Sydney and Illawarra.

At the end of the 1989 season, the Gold Coast dropped the mention of Tweed from its name, and switched nicknames to the Seagulls in recognition of the huge financial backing of the rich Seagulls' licenced club, which had the biggest poker-machine turnover in Australia. Despite this, 1990 was disastrous. Unable to attract name players, the Gold Coast proved to be easy pickings for the top clubs. Crowds were often around the 3 000 to 4 000 mark, and the Seagulls fought out the wooden spoon with South Sydney after several thrashings, including 46–2 by Balmain, 40–0 by Parramatta, 41–6 at the hands of Illawarra, 34–0 by Manly-Warringah and 32–2 to Cronulla-Sutherland.

Money was no object, so in the off-season they opened the purse strings to lure former Australian captain Wally Lewis south from the Brisbane Broncos (where he had a wretched testimonial year). 'King Wally' was reputed to have been getting $160 000 a year to play for the Seagulls. The club soon got a return—with a near record crowd turning up to watch his first match, a trial against Canterbury and the licenced club reporting record bar takings on the night of the game. But Lewis had a wretched season. He missed many games through injury and saw the Gold Coast pick up the wooden spoon with just two wins and one draw from the 22 games.

For 1992, Lewis was appointed captain-coach. And, after strong efforts, several big name-players such as Kiwi Test forward Brent Todd and State-of-Origin forward Steve Jackson were lured to the Seagulls.

Gold Coast

Founded: 1987
Joined Sydney Premiership competition: 1988
Home ground: Seagulls' Stadium, Tweed Heads (Record crowd: 13 423).
Colours: Red, black and white.
Nickname: The Seagulls (formerly The Giants).
Honours: Nil
Most games in a career: 61 by Billy Johnstone
Most points in a career: 142 by Mike Eden
Most tries in a career: 10 by Scott Mieni and Mark Ross
Most points in a season: 79 by Mike Eden, in 1988
Most tries in a season: 8 by Scott Mieni, in 1988

GOLDEN BOOT AWARD

In 1985, Harry Edgar, founder of *Open Rugby* magazine in the United Kingdom, instituted the Golden Boot Award for the finest player in the world. This was an extension of a regular system of player ratings in which the top five in each position were named. The new award was voted on by experts in all Rugby League countries. Later the Australian newspaper *Rugby League Week* and the television network Channel 10 joined *Open Rugby* in promoting the award.

Australia, as the dominant force in Rugby League, provided most of the early winners. The first players from other countries to achieve success, New Zealander Hugh McGahan and British captain Ellery Hanley, were, in fact, both playing club football in Australia at the time of their wins. Sponsorship problems meant that the award was not made in 1991.

WINNERS OF THE GOLDEN BOOT AWARD

1985	Wally Lewis (*Australia*)
1986	Brett Kenny (*Australia*)
1987	Garry Jack (*Australia*)
1988*	Peter Sterling (*Australia*)
	Hugh McGahan (*New Zealand*)
1989	Ellery Hanley (*Great Britain*)
1990	Mal Meninga (*Australia*)

Award shared

BARRY GOMERSALL

The critics dubbed referee Barry Gomersall -'The Grasshopper' because of his looks and his manner on the field. Thanks to some controversial State-of-Origin matches -'The Grasshopper' became one of the best known referees in the history of the game. Gomersall was catapulted from the obscurity of country matches in North Queensland into the Lang Park cauldron in 1982. He went on to control more State-of-Origin matches than any other referee—nine by the time he called it quits in 1988.

Southern journalists claimed he was biased towards the Queenslanders, and they attacked him for ignoring punch-ups until play (or the fracas) had stopped. He shrugged it all off: 'I honestly believe those who castigated me in the media thought it was their divine right to do so, and I say, good on them. They did wonders for the publicity of Rugby League.' Gomersall visited France and Britain in 1985 to referee two Tests and several club matches. The respected magazine *Open Rugby* described him as the best southern hemisphere referee to visit Europe.

TOM GOODMAN

Tom Goodman was one of the most respected of all Australian Rugby League journalists. Former Australian captain John Sattler once noted: 'If Tom Goodman criticised your play, you sat up and took notice. His was always constructive criticism'.

Goodman, in fact, was more than just a football journalist. For more than three decades, from the 1930s to the 1960s he covered all sports with distinction for the *Sydney Morning Herald*—notably cricket and League. In one 12 month period spent in Britain in the late 1940s he covered the 1947–48 Wallabies Rugby Union tour, the 1948 Olympic Games, the cricket tour by the great 1948 Australian side led by Don Bradman and the 1948–49 Kangaroo Rugby League tour. Illness restricted his appearances at football matches in later years. One of the last games he saw was the 100th Test between Australia and Great Britain at the Sydney Football Stadium, in 1988. He died the following year.

SID GOODWIN

Three Tests for Australia (1935). Also played one minor game for Australia on one New Zealand tour (1935).

If, for no other reason, Sid Goodwin deserves a place in the annals of Rugby League because of the record number of tries he scored in an interstate match in 1939. In the King's Birthday Holiday game at the Sydney Cricket Ground, Goodwin went over for six touchdowns, eclipsing the previous record of five, scored by the great Harold Horder 24 years earlier. Goodwin's record bag laid the foundation for a 54–13 NSW victory over Queensland. The Balmain winger had also starred in New South Wales' 50–15 win two days earlier.

Goodwin made the Balmain first-grade side in 1933 and played his first representative game the following season. He made only a brief appearance on the international scene, touring New Zealand in 1935. He played in all three Tests on the tour, scoring in two of them. The flyer was a member of Balmain's 1939 Premiership-winning side which thrashed South Sydney 33–4 in the final.

TOMMY GORMAN

Ten Tests for Australia (1924–1930). Also played 18 minor games for Australia on one Kangaroo tour (1929–30).

Tommy Gorman, the first Queenslander to lead a Kangaroo side, was one of the code's most inspiring captains. His regard for his team-mates was typified by decisions on the 1929–30 tour to defy the team manager's orders and play matches while nursing painful injuries. He did so because others badly needed rest.

Gorman was a classical, stylish centre with an ability to repeatedly make and slip through openings in defence. The Toowoomba star's form was such that he was an automatic selection for his State's side for 12 seasons. He made his Test debut in 1924, on the same day as English immortal Jim Sullivan. The Third Test of that series was, perhaps, Gorman's greatest. Britain was two up and eager to make it a whitewash, but Gorman had other ideas, figuring in three tries which contributed to a 21–11 victory for Australia. The great centre became Brisbane Brothers' first ever professional player when The Brethren signed him for the princely sum of £400 in 1926. It was money well spent. That season he inspired Brothers to the club's first Brisbane Premiership success.

Gorman continued as an administrator after his retirement from the football field. In the early 1960s, he drew a lot of comment by trying, unsuccessfully, to change the game's scoring system. He wanted tries to be worth five points instead of the three that they were then worth.

PHIL GOULD

There was always something inspirational about Phil Gould. In only his second first grade game, in 1978, the 20-year-old Gould was handed the captaincy of Penrith, when injuries and the forced retirement of international Mick Stephenson left the Panthers bereft of experienced players.

A decade later Gould was to show himself to be one of the greatest coaches in the history of the game.

'Gus' Gould was a hard-working backrow forward who played a century of first grade games for Penrith, Newtown, Canterbury and South Sydney. It was obvious he was destined for the coaching ranks, when George Piggins, in his first year as mentor of Souths, in 1986, relied heavily on Gould's advice. Gould had spent several years under master coach Warren Ryan, playing in the 1981 grand final with Newtown and sitting on the bench when the Bulldogs won in 1984 and 1985. And Ryan was quick to have him as Canterbury's reserve grade coach when Gould hung up his boots at the end of the 1986 season.

The reserves reached the semis that first year, and when Ryan and Canterbury parted company, Gould was given the firsts (although it was only really a stop-gap appointment until Canterbury's favourite son Chris Anderson returned from England). Gould caused a change of plans when he won a Premiership in his first season—at 30, the youngest coach ever to carry off the title. But after an unhappy 1989 season, he left to join Penrith. In his first season with the Panthers, Gould steered them into their first grand final and a year later they won the 1991 Premiership.

SCOTT GOURLEY

One Test for Australia (1991). Also played three minor matches on one Papua New Guinea tour (1991).

Robin Gourley was a fine front-rower who won two Premierships with the great St George 1960s combination (1965 and 1966). But his performances were nothing when compared with the efforts of his son Scott Gourley.

Although he played Rugby League as a schoolboy, Scott first made his mark in the amateur code, Rugby Union. He toured Britain, Europe, New Zealand, Japan and the Pacific islands with Wallaby and State sides and played five Tests for Australia.

In 1990, he was lured to League by a substantial three-year offer from his father's old club. He found the going tough at first, spending the first 10 weeks in reserve grade. But in 1991, he hit his straps displaying great ball skills, deceptive pace and a cast-iron defence. At the end of that season he became Australia's 36th dual international, when chosen in the Australian squad for the tour of Papua New Guinea. He made his Test debut in his third match in the green and gold, coming on as a replacement in the First Test, at Goroka.

MARK GRAHAM

Twenty-six Tests for New Zealand (1978–1988). Also played two matches in one World Championship (1977), the 1988 world cup

final, for the Rest-of-the-World against Australia in the Bicentennial international (1988) and for Oceania against Europe (1984).

Mark Graham is the only player to have captained two New Zealand touring sides to Britain and France (1980 and 1985), but he earns a place in the annals of Rugby League for much more than that. The 1.96m (6ft 5in), 102kg (16 stone) lock and second-rower was the inspiration behind a 1980s Kiwi revival that for the first time in years provided a Test team which managed to equal the might of Australia.

Graham first played League as a six-year-old at an Auckland convent school. He went on to captain the fine Otahuhu club side and, in 1977, made his international debut in the World Championships (first as a replacement against Great Britain, at Christchurch, and then in the first XIII for the Auckland match against France). The highlight of his international career came in 1985, when after losing the first two Tests against the Australians (the second by a controversial try in the last seconds of play), Graham and Kiwi coach Graham Lowe lifted the New Zealanders to a stunning 18–0 victory in the Third Test, at Rotorua. It was the first time in history that Australia had been held scoreless in a match against New Zealand.

Graham had a fine partnership with Lowe. He played under the master-coach with Norths in the Brisbane competition. Graham was the on-field inspiration when Norths won the 1980 Brisbane Premiership. Thanks to recurring injuries, he did not have the same success when he moved south to be skipper of North Sydney, but when he fired, so, too, did the Bears. The Kiwi great capped a fine career by being chosen to captain the Rest-of-the-World side in the Bicentennial international against Australia, in 1988. He finished his career, some say prematurely, with the English club Wakefield Trinity later that year.

BOB GRAVES

Six Tests for Australia (1908–1909). Also played 22 minor games for Australia on one Kangaroo tour (1908–09).

Tough forward Bob Graves was one of the pioneers of Australian Rugby League, both at the international and club level. He played in the three inaugural clashes between New South Wales and the New Zealand All Golds in 1907, and then turned out in the first three international series involving Australia. He played in all three Tests against New Zealand in 1908, scoring a try in Australia's lone victory, 14–9 in the Third Test. Graves was also a member of the first Kangaroo side which toured Britain in 1908–09, appearing in 23 games on tour, before bowing out of the international arena in the Tests against the touring Kiwis in 1909.

Graves was instrumental in assuring a successful start to the Sydney Premiership in 1908. One of the handful of officials who appeared on the stage of the formation meeting of the Balmain club, he also served as that club's first captain.

JOHNNY GRAVES

Seven Tests for Australia (1948–1951). Also played 20 minor games for Australia on one Kangaroo tour (1948–49) and one New Zealand tour (1949).

A flamboyant winger, Johnny 'Wacka' Graves was not only a speedster with an uncanny ability to score tries, but a champion goalkicker as well. He is remembered especially for his combination with South Sydney team-mate Clive Churchill in the late 1940s and early 1950s.

Graves began his international career in 1946, scoring two tries for Newcastle in an 18–13 upset of the touring British side. Next year, he joined Souths and, only four games later, made the NSW side. He donned the green and gold for Australia for the first time in 1948, in a series against New Zealand and went away with the Kangaroos a few months later. He returned as the side's top scorer, having bagged 16 tries and kicked 35 goals for 118 points. Graves made another tour, to New Zealand in 1949, and appeared in two more international series before bowing out of Test football in 1951. All told, he played in seven Test matches (three each against Britain and New Zealand and one against France), scoring five tries and kicking 14 goals (for 43 points).

Meanwhile, 'Wacka' was also a dominant force on the club scene. In 1950, when South Sydney won its first Premiership for 18 seasons, he scored two grand final tries against Western Suburbs. The next year he notched a grand final record of four tries in Souths' 42–14 disposal of challengers Manly-Warringah.

It was a close shave for Johnny Graves after the match against Huddersfield on the 1948–49 tour. During the match, Graves knocked out Johnny Hunter, an Australian who was the darling of the Huddersfield fans. Hunter was carried off on a stretcher and the crowd was calling for Graves' blood. At the end of the match, they climbed over the fence and headed for the Australian winger. The local secretary thought quickly and ordered the town band to strike up 'God Save The King'. As the fiercely patriotic English crowd stood to attention, Graves darted off the field to the sanctuary of the dressing room.

GREAT BRITAIN

Great Britain, where Rugby League was born in 1895 (see *History of Rugby League* entry), remained until the 1950s the mecca for the fans and players alike. It then gradually slipped into the shadow of Australia.

A host of top players were lured down-under by huge financial rewards available in the Sydney Premiership competition, subsidised by the Leagues' clubs poker-machine profits. Only a temporary transfer ban, imposed after the 1977 World Championships, halted the exodus. Ironically, all previous transfer bans had been aimed at protecting Australia from raids by English clubs. By the late 1980s, however, there was a regular two-way traffic in players, who would turn out for clubs on the other side of the world during the off–season. By then British clubs were able to offer as much, if not more, than some of their Australian counterparts.

In England, Australians Brett Kenny and Graham Eadie won the Lance Todd Trophy as Man-of-the-Match in Challenge Cup finals, and compatriots

John Dorahy, Les Boyd and Greg Mackey won the equivalent award in Premiership finals, the Harry Sunderland Medal. In Australia, British Test captain Ellery Hanley established himself as the highest paid footballer in the world by turning out, in 1989, for Western Suburbs for a reputed $6000 a match.

There are several major competitions in Britain:

Challenge Cup

It is probably the most coveted League trophy in the world. Every footballer (and not just those from England) hopes to play in at least one Challenge Cup final at London's famous Wembley Stadium in May. The qualifying competition for the Cup, which was first instituted in 1896, actually begins eight months before, in September, with amateur clubs competing to chose two of their number to join the big boys of Division One, Two and Three. A preliminary round and four more matches and a club can find itself at Wembley.

English Championship

Teams play two rounds of home-and-away football and the club with the most points is declared Champion. There are three divisions, with promotion and relegation after the conclusion of each season. In 1991–92 they were:

Division One—Bradford Northern, Castleford, Featherstone Rovers, Halifax, Hull, Hull Kingston Rovers, Leeds, St Helens, Salford, Swinton, Wakefield Trinity, Warrington, Widnes, Wigan.

Division Two—Carlisle, Leigh, London Crusaders, Oldham, Rochdale Hornets, Ryedale-York, Sheffield Eagles, Workington Town.

Division Three—Barrow, Batley, Bramley, Chorley, Dewsbury, Doncaster, Highfield, Huddersfield, Hunslet, Keighley Cougars, Nottingham City, Scarborough Pirates, Trafford Borough, Whitehaven.

Premiership

At the conclusion of the Championship the top clubs in each division take part in a knock-out series to decide the respective Premiers. The final is usually held a week after the Cup final.

Regal Trophy

This is an early season knock-out competition with the final in mid-January. It has built in stature since it was introduced, as the John Player Trophy, in 1972.

Yorkshire and Lancashire Cups

These knockout competitions were once regarded as immensely important, but in recent years they have become sadly devalued. They are held early in the season.

Charity Shield

This is contested as the first match of the new season between the winners of the previous season's Challenge Cup and Premiership.

GREAT BRITAIN V AUSTRALIA
TEST MATCHES See *Ashes* entry

GREAT BRITAIN V AUSTRALIA—
WORLD CUP AND WORLD CHAMPIONSHIP MATCHES————

1954

At Stade de Gerland, Lyon, Sunday, 31 October 1954
Crowd: 10 250
GREAT BRITAIN 28 (Brown 2, Jackson 2, Kitchen, Rose tries, Ledgard 5 goals) d AUSTRALIA 13 (Wells 2, Kearney tries, Pidding 2 goals)
Australia: C Churchill (c), N Pidding, A Watson, H Wells, I Moir, K McCaffery, K Holman, P Diversi, B Davies, N Provan, R Bull, K Kearney, D Hall
Great Britain: J Ledgard, D Rose, P Jackson, M Sullivan, F Kitchen, G Brown, G Helme, D Valentine (c), D Robinson, B Watts, R Coverdale, S Smith, J Thorley
Referee: R Guidicelli (France)

1957

At Sydney Cricket Ground, Monday, 17 June 1957
Crowd: 57 955
AUSTRALIA 31 (McCaffery 2, Moir 2, O'Shea, Wells, Clay tries, Carlson 4, Davies goals) d GREAT BRITAIN 6 (Jones 3 goals)
Australia: B Carlson, M Moir, H Wells, R Poole (c), A Watson, B Clay, K McCaffery, D Schofield, N Provan, K O'Shea, B Davies, K Kearney, W Marsh
Great Britain: G Moses, W Boston, E Ashton, A Davies, M Sullivan, L Jones, J Stevenson, D Turner, J Grundy, J Whiteley, A Prescott (c), T Harris, S Little
Referee: V Belsham (New Zealand)

1960

At Odsal Stadium, Bradford, Saturday, 8 October 1960
Crowd: 33 026
GREAT BRITAIN 10 (Boston, Sullivan tries, Rhodes 2 goals) d AUSTRALIA 3 (Carlson try)
Australia: K Barnes (c), R Boden, R Gasnier, H Wells, B Carlson, A Brown, B Muir, B Hambly, R Mossop, E Rasmussen, D Beattie, N Kelly, G Parcell
Great Britain: A Rhodes, W Boston, E Ashton (c), A Davies, M Sullivan, F Myler, A Murphy, V Karalius, B Shaw, D Turner, J Wilkinson, J Shaw, B McTigue
Referee: E Martung (France)

1968

At Sydney Cricket Ground, Saturday, 25 May 1968
Crowd: 62 256
AUSTRALIA 25 (Coote, Smith, Raper tries, Simms 8 goals) d GREAT BRITAIN 10 (Brooke, Sullivan tries, Risman 2 goals)
Australia: E Simms, J Rhodes, J Greaves, G Langlands, J King, A Branson, W Smith, J Raper (c), R Thornett, R Coote, J Wittenberg, F Jones, A Beetson
Great Britain: B Risman (c), I Brooke, M Shoebottom, C Burwell, C Sullivan, R Millward, T Bishop, C Renilson, R Haigh, R French, C Watson, K Ashcroft, M Clark
Referee: J Percival (New Zealand)

1970

At Headingley, Leeds, Saturday, 24 October 1970
Crowd: 15 084
GREAT BRITAIN 11 (Hynes try & field goal, Dutton 3 goals) d AUSTRALIA 4 (Simms, Fulton field goals)
Australia: E Simms, M Harris, R Branighan, R Fulton, L Williamson, D Pittard, W Smith (c), G Sullivan, P Sait, R McCarthy, R O'Reilly, E Walters, J O'Neill. Replacement: R Turner

Continued

1970 *continued*

Great Britain: R Dutton, A Smith, F Myler (c), S Hynes, J Atkinson, M Shoebottom, K Hepworth, M Reilly, J Thompson, D Laughton, C Watson, A Fisher, D Hartley
Referee: F Lindop (Great Britain)

Final

At Headingley, Leeds, Saturday, 7 November 1970
Crowd: 18 776
AUSTRALIA 12 (Cootes, Williamson tries, Simms 2 goals & field goal) d GREAT BRITAIN 7 (Atkinson try, Dutton goal, Hynes field goal)
Australia: E Simms, M Harris, J Cootes, P Sait, L Williamson, R Fulton, W Smith, R Coote (c), R Costello, R McCarthy, R O'Reilly, R Turner, J O'Neill. Replacements: R Branighan and E Walters
Great Britain: R Dutton, A Smith, F Myler (c), S Hynes, J Atkinson, M Shoebottom, K Hepworth, M Reilly, D Laughton, J Thompson, C Watson, A Fisher, D Hartley. Replacements: R Haigh and C Hesketh
Referee: F Lindop (Great Britain)

1972

At Stade Gilbert Brutus, Perpignan, Sunday, 29 October 1972
Crowd: 6300
GREAT BRITAIN 27 (Sullivan, Lowe, Atkinson, O'Neill, Stephenson tries, Clawson 6 goals) d AUSTRALIA 21 (Fulton 3, Raudonikis tries, Langlands 4 goals, McCarthy field goal)
Australia: G Langlands (c), S Knight, G Starling, R Branighan, M Harris, R Fulton, T Raudonikis, G Sullivan, J Elford, R McCarthy, A Beetson, E Walters, J O'Neill. Replacements: D Ward (for Beetson) and P Sait (for Branighan)
Great Britain: P Charlton, C Sullivan (c), C Hesketh, J Walsh, J Atkinson, D O'Neill, S Nash, G Nicholls, B Lockwood, P Lowe, D Jeanes, M Stephenson, T Clawson. Replacement: J Holmes (for J Walsh)
Referee: C Teissiere (France)

Final

At Stade de Gerland, Lyon, Saturday, 11 November 1972
Crowd: 4500
AUSTRALIA 10 (O'Neill, Beetson tries, Branighan 2 goals) drew with GREAT BRITAIN 10 (Sullivan, Stephenson tries, Clawson 2 goals)
There was no further score after extra time (10 minutes each) way was played. Britain was awarded the Cup because of its better record in preliminary matches.
Australia: G Langlands, R Branighan, G Starling, M Harris, J Grant, R Fulton, D Ward, G Sullivan, G Stevens, A Beetson, R O'Reilly, E Walters, J O'Neill
Great Britain: P Charlton, C Sullivan (c), C Hesketh, J Walsh, J Atkinson, J Holmes, S Nash, G Nicholls, B Lockwood, P Lowe, D Jeanes, M Stephenson, T Clawson. Replacement: B Irving (for Jeanes)
Referee: G Jameau (France)

1975

Great Britain split into England and Wales for 1975 series.

1977

At Lang Park, Brisbane, Saturday, 18 June 1977
Crowd: 25 200
AUSTRALIA 19 (Eadie 2, Randall tries, Cronin 5 goals) d GREAT BRITAIN 5 (Millward try, Fairbairn goal)
Australia: G Eadie, A McMahon, M Cronin, M Thomas, T Fahey, J Peard, T Raudonikis, G Pierce, A Beetson (c), T Randall, G Veivers, N Geiger, D Fitzgerald. Replacement: R Higgs (for Raudonikis)
Great Britain: G Fairbairn, K Fielding, W Francis, L Dyl, S Wright, R Millward (c), S Nash, P Hogan, G Nicholls, E Bowman, S Pitchford, D Ward, J Thompson. Replacement: P Smith (for Ward)
Referee: M Caillol (France)

Final

At Sydney Cricket Ground, Saturday, 25 June 1977
Crowd: 24 457
AUSTRALIA 13 (McMahon, Gartner, Kolc tries, Cronin 2 goals) d GREAT BRITAIN 12 (Pitchford, Gill tries, Fairbairn 3 goals)
Australia: G Eadie, A McMahon, M Cronin, R Gartner, M Harris, J Peard, J Kolc, G Pierce, R Higgs, A Beetson (c), T Randall, N Geiger, G Veivers. Replacement: D Fitzgerald (for Veivers)
Great Britain: G Fairbairn, S Wright, J Holmes, L Dyl, W Francis, R Millward (c), S Nash, P Hogan, E Bowman, G Nicholls, S Pitchford, K Elwell, J Thompson. Replacements: K Gill (for Wright) and P Smith (for Hogan)
Referee: W Thompson (Great Britain).

1988

For qualifying matches see *Third Test, at Wigan, 1986* (Australia 24 d Great Britain 15) and *Third Test, at Sydney, 1988* (Great Britain 26 d Australia 12)

1992

For qualifying match see *Third Test, at Leeds, 1990* (Australia 14 d Great Britain 0)

THE BRITISH CLUBS

(and some of the Australians who have played with them)

BARROW: *Founded* late 1870s; *Home ground* Craven Park; *Colours* royal blue; *Nickname* Shipbuilders; (Cavill Heugh, Chris Johns).

BATLEY: *Founded* 1880; *Home ground* Mount Pleasant; *Colours* cerise and fawn; *Nickname* Gallant Youths.

BRADFORD NORTHERN: *Founded* 1863 (as Bradford); *Home ground* Odsal Stadium; *Colours* white, red, amber and black; *Nickname* Northern; (Albert Rosenfeld).

BRAMLEY: *Founded* 1879; *Home ground* McLaren Field; *Colours* amber and black; *NicKname* Villagers.

CARLISLE: *Founded* 1980; *Home ground* Gillford Park (Harraby); *Colours* royal blue, red and white; (Tony Catton).

CASTLEFORD: *Founded* 1926; *Home ground* Wheldon Road; *Colours* amber and black; *Nickname* Tigers; (Gary Belcher, Graeme Bradley, Ian French, Ron Gibbs, Jeff Hardy, Chris Johns, Steve Larder, James Sandy).

CHORLEY: *Founded* 1989; *Home ground* Victory Park; *Colours* black and white.

DEWSBURY: *Founded* 1875; *Home ground* Mount Pleasant (Batley); *Colours* red, amber and black.

DONCASTER: *Founded* 1951; *Home ground* Tattersfield; *Colours* blue and gold; *Nickname* Dons.

FEATHERSTONE ROVERS: *Founded* 1908; *Home ground* Post Office Road; *Colours* blue and white; *Nickname* Colliers; (Allan McMahon).

HALIFAX: *Founded* 1873; *Home ground* Thrum Hall; *Colours* royal blue and white; *Nickname* Thrum Hallers; (Chris Anderson, Greg Austin, Martin Bella, Peter Coyne, John Dorahy, Graham Eadie, Paul Langmack, Keith Neller, Grant Rix, Dan Stains, Fred Tottey, Lionel Williamson).

HIGHFIELD: *Founded* 1922 (as Wigan Highfield, later London Highfield, Liverpool Stanley, Liverpool City, Huyton and Runcorn Highfield); *Home ground* St Helens; *Colours* red, green and yellow (Simon Chappell, John Cogger).

HUDDERSFIELD: *Founded* 1864 (as Huddersfield Athletic Club); *Home ground* Fartown; *Colours* claret and gold; *Nickname* Fartowners; (Lionel Cooper, Pat Devery, Johnny Hunter, Ray Markham, Ernie Mills, Albert Rosenfeld, Pat Walsh).

HULL: *Founded* 1865; *Home ground* The Boulevard; *Colours* black and white; *Nickname* Airlie Birds; (Noel Cleal, Craig Coleman, Jim Devereux, Steve Folkes, Herb Gilbert, Keith Gittoes, Greg Mackey, Andy Morton, John Muggleton, Wayne Portlock, Peter Sterling, George Watt).

HULL KINGSTON ROVERS: *Founded* 1883; *Home ground* Craven Park; *Colours* red, white and blue; *Nickname* Robins; (Arthur Beetson, Chris Close, John Dorahy, Gavin Miller, Bryan Niebling, Michael Porter).

HUNSLET: *Founded* 1895; *Home ground* Elland Road (Leeds); *Colours* myrtle, white and flame; (Paul Carr, Arthur Clues).

KEIGHLEY COUGARS: *Founded* 1889; *Home ground* Lawkholme Lane; *Colours* emerald green and scarlet; *Nickname* Cougars.

LEEDS: *Founded* 1889; *Home ground* Headingley; *Colours* royal blue and amber; *Nickname* Loiners; (Sam Backo, Joe 'Chimpy' Busch, Arthur Clues, Andrew Ettingshausen, Eric Grothe, Eric Harris, Cavill Heugh, Vic Hey, Ken Kearney, Cliff Lyons, Mark McGaw, Keith McLellan, Bob McMaster, Steve Martin, Jeff Moores, Frank O'Rourke, Ken Thornett, Ted Verrenkamp).

LEIGH: *Founded* 1887; *Home ground* Hilton Park; *Colours* red and white; (Trevor Allan, Mick Bolewski, Rex Mossop).

LONDON CRUSADERS: *Founded* 1980 (as Fulham); *Home ground* Crystal Palace National Stadium; *Colours* black, white and red; *Nickname* Crusaders; (Shane Buckley, Frank Rolls).

NOTTINGHAM CITY: *Founded* 1984; (as Mansfield Marksmen); *Home ground* Harvey Hadden Stadium; *Colours* green and yellow: *Nickname* The Outlaws.

OLDHAM: *Founded* 1876; *Home ground* Wattersheddings; *Colours* red and white; *Nickname* Roughyeds; (Arthur 'George' Anlezark, Brett Clark, John Cogger, Bruce Clark, Sid Deane, Bill and Viv Farnsworth, Ashley Gilbert, Tom McCabe, Chris O'Sullivan, Stuart Raper, Paul Taylor).

ROCHDALE HORNETS: *Founded* 1871; *Home ground* Spotland; *Colours* red, white and blue; *Nickname* Hornets; (Brett Clark, Dave Gallagher).

RYDALE YORK: *Founded* 1868 (as York); *Home ground* Rydale Stadium; *Colours* yellow and black; *Nickname* Wasps; (Anthony Marshall, Jeff Moores, Dean Revell).

ST HELENS: *Founded* 1890; *Home ground* Knowsley Road; *Colours* red and white; *Nickname* Saints; (Brett Clark, Mal Meninga, Michael O'Connor, Phil Veivers).

SALFORD: *Founded* 1879; *Home ground* The Willows; *Colours* red and white; *Nickname* Red Devils; (Garry Jack, Peter Tunks).

SCARBOROUGH PIRATES: *Founded* 1990; *Home ground* McCain Stadium; *Colours* Purple and gold; *Nickname* Pirates.

SHEFFIELD EAGLES: *Founded* 1984; *Home ground* Owlerton Stadium; *Colours* red, white, gold and black; *Nickname* Eagles; (Mark Geyer, Bruce McGuire, Ian Russell, Peter Tunks).

SWINTON: *Founded* 1867; *Home ground* Station Road; *Colours* royal blue and white; *Nickname* Lions; (Chris O'Sullivan).

TRAFFORD BOROUGH: *Founded* 1954 (as Blackpool Borough—later Springfield Borough and Chorley Borough); *Home ground* Moss Lane, Altrincham; *Colours* blue and crimson; *Nickname* Griffins; (Brian Bevan, Steve Mavin).
WAKEFIELD TRINITY: *Founded* 1873; *Home ground* Belle Vue; *Colours* red, white and blue; *Nickname* Dreadnoughts; (Steve Ella, Geoff Gerard, Brian Jackson, Wally Lewis, Chris Mortimer, Chris Perry, Ray Price, Albert Rosenfeld).
WARRINGTON: *Founded* 1875; *Home ground* Wilderspool; *Colours* primrose, blue and white; *Nickname* Wires; (Harry Bath, Brian Bevan, Phil Blake, Les Boyd, Dave Brown, Les Davidson, Dan Frawley, Johnny Grant, Bob Fulton, Bob Jackson, Les Davidson, Larry O'Malley, Chris O'Sullivan, Steve Roach, Bill Shankland, David Wright).
WHITEHAVEN: *Founded* 1948; *Home ground* The Recreation Ground; *Colours* chocolate, blue and gold; *Nickname* Havens; (Gary McFarlane).
WIDNES: *Founded* 1873; *Home ground* Naughton Park; *Colours* black and white; *Nickname* Chemics; (Chris Anderson, Noel Cleal, Phil McKenzie).
WIGAN: *Founded* 1872; *Home ground* Central Park; *Colours* cherry and white; *Nickname* Riversiders; (Greg Dowling, Steve Ella, John Ferguson, Kerry Hemsley, Brett Kenny).
WORKINGTON TOWN: *Founded* 1944; *Home ground* Derwent Park; *Colours* royal blue and white; *Nickname* Towners; (Rupert Mudge, Tony Paskins, Bevan Wilson).

LANCE TODD TROPHY
(For Man-of-the-Match in Wembley Challenge Cup Final)

Year	Winner	Club
1946	Billy Stott	Wakefield Trinity
1947	Willie Davies	Bradford Northern
1948	Frank Whitcombe	Bradford Northern
1949	Ernest Ward	Bradford Northern
1950	Gerry Helme	Warrington
1951	Cec Mountford	Wigan
1952	Billy Iveson	Workington Town
1953	Peter Ramsden	Huddersfield
1954	Gerry Helme	Warrington
1955	Jack Grundy	Barrow
1956	Alan Prescott	St Helens
1957	Jeff Stevenson	Leeds
1958	Rees Thomas	Wigan
1959	Brian McTigue	Wigan
1960	Tommy Harris	Hull
1961	Dick Huddart	St Helens
1962	Neil Fox	Wakefield Trinity
1963	Harold Poynton	Wakefield Trinity
1964	Frank Collier	Widnes
1965	Ray Ashby	Wigan
	Brian Gabbitas	Hunslet
1966	Len Killeen	St Helens
1967	Carl Dooler	Featherstone Rovers
1968	Don Fox	Wakefield Trinity
1969	Malcolm Reilly	Castleford
1970	Bill Kirkbride	Castleford
1971	Alex Murphy	Leigh
1972	Kel Coslett	St Helens
1973	Steve Nash	Featherstone Rovers
1974	Derek Whitehead	Warrington
1975	Ray Dutton	Widnes
1976	Geoff Pimblett	St Helens
1977	Steve Pitchford	Leeds
1978	George Nicholls	St Helens
1979	David Topliss	Wakefield Trinity
1980	Brian Lockwood	Hull Kingston Rovers
1981	Mick Burke	Widnes
1982	Eddie Cunningham	Widnes
1983	David Hobbs	Featherstone Rovers
1984	Joe Lydon	Widnes
1985	Brett Kenny*	Wigan
1986	Bob Beardmore	Castleford
1987	Graham Eadie*	Halifax
1988	Andy Gregory	Wigan
1989	Ellery Hanley	Wigan
1990	Andy Gregory	Wigan
1991	Denis Betts	Wigan

* Australian
(NB. David Topliss, the Hull captain, won the Man-of-the-Match award in the 1982 Cup Final replay at Elland Road, Leeds)

HARRY SUNDERLAND MEMORIAL TROPHY

(For Man-of-the-Match in British Premiership Final)

Year	Winner	Club
1965	Terry Fogarty	Halifax
1966	Albert Halsall	St Helens
1967	Ray Owen	Wakefield Trinity
1968	Gary Cooper	Wakefield Trinity
1969	Bev Risman	Leeds
1970	Frank Myler	St Helens
1971	Bill Ashurst	Wigan
1972	Terry Clawson	Leeds
1973	Mike Stephenson	Dewsbury
1974	Barry Philbin	Warrington
1975	Mel Mason	Leeds
1976	George Nicholls	St Helens
1977	Geoff Pimblett	St Helens
1978	Bob Haigh	Bradford Northern
1979	Kevin Dick	Leeds
1980	Mal Aspey	Widnes
1981	Len Casey	Hull
1982	Mick Burke	Widnes
1983	Tony Myler	Widnes
1984	John Dorahy*	Hull Kingston Rovers
1985	Harold Pinner	St Helens
1986	Les Boyd*	Warrington
1987	Joe Lydon	Wigan
1988	David Hulme	Widnes
1989	Alan Tait	Widnes
1990	Alan Tait	Widnes
1991	Greg Mackey*	Hull

* Australian

MAN-OF-STEEL AWARD

(English Player-of-the-Year)

1977	David Ward	Leeds
1978	George Nicholls	St Helens
1979	Doug Laughton	Widnes
1980	George Fairbairn	Wigan
1981	Ken Kelly	Warrington
1982	Mick Morgan	Carlisle
1983	Allan Agar	Featherstone Rovers
1984	Joe Lydon	Widnes
1985	Ellery Hanley	Bradford Northern
1986	Gavin Miller*	Hull Kingston Rovers
1987	Ellery Hanley	Wigan
1988	Martin Offiah	Widnes
1989	Ellery Hanley	Wigan
1990	Shaun Edwards	Wigan
1991	Garry Schofield	Leeds

* Australian

BRITAIN'S WINNING CLUBS

Year	Championship	Challenge Cup
1897	—	Batley
1898	—	Batley
1899	—	Oldham
1900	—	Swinton
1901	—	Batley
1902	Broughton Rovers	Broughton Rovers
1903	Halifax	Halifax
1904	Bradford Northern	Halifax

Continued

BRITAIN'S WINNING CLUBS *continued*

Year	Championship	Challenge Cup
1905	Oldham	Warrington
1906	Halifax	Bradford Northern
1907	Halifax	Warrington
1908	Hunslet	Hunslet
1909	Wigan	Wakefield Trinity
1910	Oldham	Leeds*
1911	Oldham	Broughton Rovers
1912	Huddersfield	Dewsbury
1913	Huddersfield	Huddersfield
1914	Salford	Hull
1915	Huddersfield	Huddersfield
1916–1919	No competitions	
1920	Hull	Huddersfield
1921	Hull	Leigh
1922	Wigan	Rochdale Hornets
1923	Hull Kingston Rovers	Leeds
1924	Batley	Wigan
1925	Hull Kingston Rovers	Oldham
1926	Wigan	Swinton
1927	Swinton	Oldham
1928	Swinton	Swinton
1929	Huddersfield	Wigan
1930	Huddersfield	Widnes
1931	Swinton	Halifax
1932	St Helens	Leeds
1933	Salford	Huddersfield
1934	Wigan	Hunslet
1935	Swinton	Castleford
1936	Hull	Leeds
1937	Salford	Widnes
1938	Hunslet	Salford
1939	Salford	Halifax
1940	—	—
1941	—	Leeds
1942	—	Leeds
1943	—	Dewsbury **
1944	—	Bradford Northern **
1945	—	Huddersfield **
1946	Wigan	Wakefield Trinity
1947	Wigan	Bradford Northern
1948	Warrington	Wigan
1949	Huddersfield	Bradford Northern
1950	Wigan	Warrington
1951	Workington Town	Wigan
1952	Wigan	Workington Town
1953	St Helens	Huddersfield
1954	Warrington	Warrington *
1955	Warrington	Barrow
1956	Hull	St Helens
1957	Oldham	Leeds
1958	Hull	Wigan
1959	St Helens	Wigan
1960	Wigan	Wakefield Trinity
1961	Leeds	St Helens
1962	Huddersfield	Wakefield Trinity
1963	Swinton	Wakefield Trinity
1964	Swinton	Widnes
1965	Halifax	Wigan
1966	St Helens	St Helens
1967	Wakefield Trinity	Featherstone Rovers
1968	Wakefield Trinity	Leeds
1969	Leeds	Castleford
1970	St Helens	Castleford
1971	St Helens	Leigh
1972	Leeds	St Helens
1973	Dewsbury	Featherstone Rovers
1974	Salford	Warrington
1975	St Helens	Widnes
1976	Salford	St Helens
1977	Featherstone Rovers	Leeds
1978	Widnes	Leeds
1979	Hull Kingston Rovers	Widnes
1980	Bradford Northern	Hull Kingston Rovers
1981	Bradford Northern	Widnes

BRITAIN'S WINNING CLUBS

Year	Championship	Challenge Cup
1982	Leigh	Hull
1983	Hull	Featherstone Rovers
1984	Hull Kingston Rovers	Widnes
1985	Hull Kingston Rovers	Wigan
1986	Halifax	Castleford
1987	Wigan	Halifax
1988	Widnes	Wigan
1989	Widnes	Wigan
1990	Wigan	Wigan
1991	Wigan	Wigan

* Won on replay after final was drawn
** Final played on home-and-away basis

OTHER BRITISH WINNERS

Year	Premiership	Regal Trophy (formerly John Player Trophy)
1965	St Helens	—
1966	St Helens	—
1967	Leeds	—
1968	Leeds	—
1969	Leeds	—
1970	Leeds	—
1971	Wigan	
1972	Leeds	Halifax
1973	Warrington	Leeds
1974	Warrington	Warrington
1975	Leeds	Bradford Northern
1976	St Helens	Widnes
1977	St Helens	Castleford
1978	Bradford Northern	Warrington
1979	Leeds	Widnes
1980	Widnes	Bradford Northern
1981	Hull Kingston Rovers	Warrington
1982	Widnes	Hull
1983	Widnes	Wigan
1984	Hull Kingston Rovers	Leeds
1985	St Helens	Hull Kingston Rovers
1986	Warrington	Wigan
1987	Wigan	Wigan
1988	Widnes	St Helens
1989	Widnes	Wigan
1990	Widnes	Wigan
1991	Hull	Warrington

AUSTRALIANS WHO HAVE PLAYED IN A CHALLENGE CUP FINAL

On the winning team: Albert Rosenfeld (Huddersfield, 1913 and 1915), Herb Gilbert (Hull, 1914), Jim Devereux (Hull, 1914), Eric Harris (Leeds, 1932 and 1936), Frank O'Rourke (Leeds, 1932), Ray Markham (Huddersfield, 1933), Vic Hey (Leeds, 1941 and 1942), Brian Bevan (Warrington, 1950 and 1954), Harry Bath (Warrington, 1950 and 1954), Tony Paskins (Workington Town, 1952), Rupert Mudge (Workington Town, 1952), Johnny Hunter (Huddersfield, 1953), Pat Devery (Huddersfield, 1953), Lionel Cooper (Huddersfield, 1953), Keith McLellan (Leeds, 1957), Chris Anderson (Widnes, 1975; Halifax, 1987), John Ferguson (Wigan, 1985), Brett Kenny (Wigan, 1985), James Sandy (Castleford, 1986), Ian French (Castleford, 1986), Graham Eadie (Halifax, 1987), Grant Rix (Halifax, 1987), Keith Neller (Halifax, 1987).

On the losing team: Jim Devereux (Hull, 1910 and 1911), George Anlezark

(Oldham, 1912), Sid Deane (Oldham, 1912), Bill Shankland (Warrington, 1933 and 1936), Ray Markham (Huddersfield, 1935), Arthur Clues (Bradford Northern, 1947), Tony Paskins (Workington Town, 1955), Rupert Mudge (Workington Town, 1955), Mark Cannon (Wigan, 1984), Kerry Hemsley (Wigan, 1984), Peter Sterling (Hull, 1985), John Muggleton (Hull, 1985), John Dorahy (Hull Kingston Rovers, 1986), Peter Johnston (Hull Kingston Rovers, 1986), Gavin Miller (Hull Kingston Rovers, 1986), Phil Veivers (St Helens, 1987 and 1991), Brett Clark (St Helens, 1987), Graham Eadie (Halifax, 1988), Keith Neller (Halifax, 1988), Martin Meredith (Halifax, 1988), Robert Grogan (Halifax, 1988), Tony Anderson (Halifax, 1988), Paul Vautin (St Helens, 1989), Michael O'Connor (St Helens, 1989), Bob Jackson (Warrington, 1990).

BRITISH RUGBY LEAGUE RECORDS

Club
Highest score: Huddersfield d Swinton Park 119–2, 1914
Most points in a season in all matches: 1436, by Leigh, 1985–86
Most points in a League season: 1005, by St Helens, 1958–59
Most points in a Division Two season: 1156 by Leigh, 1985–86
Unbeaten in a League season: Hull, 1978–79 (Division Two)

Individual
Most points in a match: 53, by George West (Hull Kingston Rovers), versus Brookland Rovers, 1905
Most points in a season: 496, by Lewis Jones (Leeds), 1956–57
Most points in a career: 6220, by Neil Fox (Wakefield Trinity, Bradford Northern, Hull Kingston Rovers, York, Bramley, Huddersfield), 1955–80
Most tries in a match: 11, by George West (Hull Kingston Rovers), versus Brookland Rovers, 1905
Most tries in a season: 80, by Albert Rosenfeld (Huddersfield), 1913–14
Most tries in a career: 834*, by Brian Bevan (Warrington and Blackpool Borough), 1945–1959
Most goals in a match: 22, by Jim Sullivan (Wigan), versus Flimby and Fothergill, 1925
Most goals in a season: 221, by David Watkins (Salford), 1972–73
Most goals in a career: 2867, by Jim Sullivan (Wigan), 1921–1946
Most field goals in a match: 5, by Danny Wilson (Swinton, versus Hunslet, 1983; Peter Wood (Runcorn Highfield), versus Batley, 1984; Paul Bishop (Warrington) versus Wigan, 1986
Most field goals in a season: 29, by Lyn Hallett (Cardiff City), 1983–84
Most field goals in a career: 85, by Norman Turley (Warrington, Runcorn Highfield, Swinton, Blackpool Borough, Rochdale Hornets, Barrow, Workington Town), 1974–88
* including 38 in so-called friendly matches

A GALLERY OF BRITISH GREATS

Jack Arkwright

Big, tough prop-forward Jack Arkwright is the only player ever to be sent off twice in the same match on a tour of Australia. In the match against Southern New South Wales on the 1936 Lions tour, Arkwright was given his marching orders early in the game. The local captain, Jack Kingston, persuaded the referee to reverse his decision. However, a few minutes later, Arkwright was sent off again—for punching Kingston. Arkwright is well-remembered for his on-field battles with another tough nut, Australian Ray Stehr. In the Third Test of the 1936 series, both men were ordered off after a skirmish. In club football, for Warrington, Arkwright played in one Challenge Cup final (1936) and two Championship finals (1935 and 1937), but was on the losing side on each occasion.

Eric Ashton

The record of Eric Ashton during 15 seasons of football with Wigan is almost without equal. When he retired, in 1969, the lanky centre had played more than 500 games for the club, scored in excess of 300 tries in club and international football and landed almost 500 goals. Ashton led Wigan to six Challenge Cup Finals at Wembley, winning three (in 1958, 1959 and 1965). He had been a Test regular for six years in the late 1950s and early 1960s and captain of Great Britain for much of that time (leading Britain to success in the 1960 World Cup and to victory in the Ashes series, down-under, two years later). Indeed, on his two tours to Australasia—the other was in 1958—Ashton scored 51 tries. Both before and after he retired as a player, Ashton excelled as a coach with Wigan and nearby St Helens. He was awarded an MBE in 1966.

Billy Batten

In the early years of Rugby League, few three-quarters were the equal of Billy Batten. He also has the record of being the elder half of the first father-son combination to play Test football for Great Britain (Eric Batten

British great, Billy Batten

played in Australia in 1946). Batten senior appeared in 12 Tests for Britain (eight against Australia and four versus New Zealand) and would have played in more but for a clash with selectors, who refused to choose him for the 1920 tour of Australia after he spurned a mid-week trial match. With his first club, Hunslet, he won two Championships and one Challenge Cup (including the double in 1908). He was transferred to Hull in 1913, for a record fee of £600 (doubling the previous record), and continued his success—the Challenge Cup (1914), Championships (1920 and 1921) and a Yorkshire Cup and Championship.

Tommy Bishop see *alphabetical* entry

Billy Boston

Big, burly Billy Boston was one of the world's greatest wingers. He had been a sensation in Welsh Rugby Union (where he once scored 126 tries in a season). In 1953, he accepted a £3000 offer from Wigan to turn professional and was an instant hit in the pro ranks. In his first season (1953–54) he was chosen to tour Australia and New Zealand. He toured a second time eight years later with what is regarded as possibly the greatest British side to go down-under. On the first trip, Boston set a try-scoring record of 36. All told, Boston played 31 internationals. He totalled 563 tries in Rugby League (second only to Brian Bevan)—including 482 for Wigan, a club best. Boston's best year was 1956–57 when he scored 60. Twice (in 1955 and 1962) he scored seven tries in a match, and against New Zealand, in Auckland, on the 1962 tour, he equalled the then-Test record of four tries in a match.

Stanley Brogden

Seven different clubs enjoyed the success generated by the impeccable talents of Stanley Brogden, who gave up a promising Soccer career to follow his father into Rugby League. He made his first-team debut with Bradford Northern in 1927 and before he had turned 19 had achieved county and international selection, playing centre and wing. In August 1929, a record transfer fee of £1000 was paid for Brogden to join Huddersfield. He later turned out for Leeds (after another record transfer fee, of £1200), Hull, Rochdale Hornets, Salford and Whitehaven. Brogden played 16 Tests for Britain and made two tours of Australia (1932 and 1936).

Douglas 'Duggy' Clark

Duggy Clark cost Huddersfield only £30 on joining the famous club in 1909. It was one of the bargains of the century, for Clark, in 16 seasons of senior football, established himself as one of the finest forwards in the game. He earned three Cup-winner's medals and appeared in five Championship finals (three of which Huddersfield won), made two tours of Australasia (1914 and 1920) and played in eight Anglo-Australian Tests (including the famous 'Rorke's Drift Test in which he continued for most of the game despite a broken thumb and a broken shoulder). He also took on the Kiwis in three Tests. After finishing his football career, Clark gained world-wide recognition as a professional wrestler.

Lee Crooks see Alphabetical entry

Joe Egan

Joe Egan deserves a place in Rugby League's records not just for his ability as a hooker. He was also one of the finest ball distributors the game has known. He first gained representative honours in 1942 and from then until his retirement from big time football in November 1950, his position as his country's hooker was never questioned. Egan's career highlights included two tours of Australasia (1946 and 1950), coaching of a British World Cup side and the honour (as captain of Wigan in 1948) of being the first Rugby League skipper to receive the coveted Challenge Cup from a reigning British monarch.

Alf Ellaby

A badly ricked knee, which forced Alf Ellaby to give up a promising Soccer career, did not hamper him on the Rugby League field. The tall footballer swapped codes to join St Helens in 1926 and went on to become one of the greatest wingers the game has known. In his first season he went over for 55 tries, including 50 in club games—a record for St Helens which stood until the 1950s. He made two tours of Australia (in 1928 and 1932) and both times he was leading tryscorer (totalling 41 tries in just 28 appearances). Ellaby's career included 21 internationals (including nine full-scale Tests against Australia and four against New Zealand) and 20 county appearances for Lancashire. And he scored 446 tries.

Neil Fox

An incredible 828 games. A total of 2575 goals and 358 tries for 6220 points. That is the staggering record of burly centre Neil Fox. Playing for Wakefield Trinity, he rewrote the club's record books. In each of 13 consecutive seasons after he first joined Trinity as a schoolboy, in 1956, he scored more than 100 points. In four of those seasons he topped 300 points and notched a mammoth 407 in 1961–62. In the period from March 1958 to May 1960 he scored in every one of the 95 games in which he played. Fox also holds two Wembley Cup Final records. Three field goals in one match, for Wakefield in 1962, was a first and his 20 points against Hull (from seven goals and two tries) was an individual record tally. His big scoring was not restricted to club games. Fox kicked 96 goals and scored 15 tries in his 29 Test appearances (eight versus Australia, four against New Zealand and 17 versus France). And on the 1962 tour of Australasia he scored a phenomenal 162 points in only 13 matches.

Bernard Ganley

Even though he played only three Tests (all against France), Bernard Ganley was one of the game's greatest goalkickers. His club performances for Oldham broke all records. During a career which stretched from 1950 to 1961, he booted 1377 goals. This included a then-world record 219 in the 1957–58 season—the period in which he made his Test appearances.

Ken Gee

Rugby League historian George Crawford rated Britain's Ken Gee as the greatest prop-forward he ever saw (during the 1930–1990 period), and his partnership with Joe Egan, hooker both for Wigan and Great Britain, ensured many a vital scrum win over 21 years in top-flight football (1933–1954). A Rugby colossus, Gee weighed 108kg (17 stone) and his play was characterised by bulldozing runs through the rucks. He played 17 Tests, three Challenge Cup Finals (winning in 1948 and 1951) and three Championship Finals (winning all three, in 1934, 1947 and 1952). Because he was en route to Australia with the Lions he missed Wigan's 1946 and 1950 Championship Final successes. Gee was also a fine goalkicker who headed the season's listing in 1949–50 with 133 goals.

Andy Gregory see Alphabetical entry

Mike Gregory

When Britain sent a side devastated by injury dropouts to the Southern Hemisphere in 1990, few people gave them much chance against the strong Kiwi lineup, but skipper Mike Gregory inspired the side to its first series win in Australasia in more than a decade. The Warrington back-rower had starred on the 1988 Lions tour of Australia and played a gallant game for the Rest-of-the-World against Australia at the end of that visit. By 1992, he had played in 20 Tests.

Ben Gronow

'Big Ben' Gronow had played four Rugby Union internationals for Wales when, in 1910, Huddersfield lured him to the professional ranks with a £120 signing-on fee. A huge man, Gronow went on to become one of League's greatest all-round forwards. His point-scoring feats during the next two decades made him a living legend (he even had his own fan club—a rarity in those days). Gronow's play was rewarded by three Challenge Cup-winners' and three Championship-winners' medals. He was a member of the Huddersfield side which won the 'grand slam' in the 1913–14 season—the Northern Union Cup and Championship and the Yorkshire Cup and Championship. He played the first of his seven Tests in 1911 and made two Lions tours to Australasia (scoring 136 points in only 16 tour games).

Ellery Hanley see Alphabetical entry

Alan Hardisty

Castleford's Alan Hardisty was one of the finest five-eighths of the post-World War II era. He played 12 Tests for Great Britain between 1964 and 1970. The pocket-sized dynamo—he weighed only 70kg (11st)—was at his zenith in 1966, on the first of two Lions tours of Australasia. In the First Test he scored a glorious individual try which turned the match, eventually won 17–13 by Britain. In the third and deciding encounter he scored an intercept try and then was awarded the first-ever penalty try in an Ashes Test—but Britain went down 19–14. Hardisty's second trip in 1970 was not as successful, and he played in only one Test. Hardisty led Castleford to two Challenge Cup Final victories at Wembley (1969 and 1970) and when he switched to Leeds in the twilight of his career reached Wembley again (1972) and triumphed in the Championship the same year.

Tommy Harris

The fact that Tommy Harris played 22 Tests and three World Cup matches for Great Britain is proof of what a great hooker he was. He signed with Hull in 1949, after a fine Rugby Union career. He toured Australasia twice (in 1954 and 1958), making his Test debut against New Zealand on the former trip. He was a member of the British squad for both the 1957 and 1960 World Cups, bowing out of international football in the match against New Zealand in the latter series. Perhaps his finest moment was in the 1960 Challenge Cup final. Twice he had to leave the field for treatment for concussion, but both times he returned to thr fray. Although Hull was beaten by Wakefield Trinity, Harris was honoured with the Lance Todd Trophy as the Man-of-the-Match.

Martin Hodgson

Widely regarded as the greatest second-row forward to have played for Britain, Martin Hodgson was also a fine goalkicker. His Test debut was in the second encounter with the Kangaroos in 1929 and he made 15 more international appearances before bowing out in 1937. In 12 games against Australia he was never on the losing side. The Swinton star toured Australasia twice (in 1932 and 1936). Hodgson holds the record for the longest goal in English club football. On April 13, 1940, in a Lancashire Cup tie against Rochdale Hornets, he booted one from 77 yards, 2 feet out (71.02m).

Dick Huddart see Alphabetical entry

Lewis Jones see Alphabetical entry

Vince Karalius

They called him 'The Wild Bull of the Pampas'. Wild he was, but Vince Karalius was also one of the finest locks the world has known. Few players earned more respect from opponents, especially Australians with whom he clashed in two Test series (1958 and 1963) and one World Cup (1960). Karalius signed with St Helens in 1951. His first representative match was with a League XIII against the touring Kiwis in 1955 but not until chosen to tour Australasia three years later did he show what a great player he was. He was one of the stars of the side, playing two Tests each against Australia and New Zealand. Because of his fiery play, Karalius was often in trouble with referees. On that 1958 tour he was one of four players sent off in a violent match against New South Wales. A four-match suspension cost him a spot in the First Test, a match which would have been his Test debut and, significantly, the only clash which the Australians won. Karalius' form on the club scene was a carbon copy of his influence on the representative arena. Three times he made the trip to Wembley (twice as captain of his club) and each time he went home with a Cup-winners' medal. In 1956 and 1961 he was in successful St Helens sides and in 1964 captained Widnes to victory. The Challenge Cup magic did not desert Karalius when he retired as a player. In 1975, he coached Widnes to a Cup Final win over Warrington.

Brian McTigue see Alphabetical entry

Roger Millward see Alphabetical entry

Alex Murphy

Some critics rate Alex Murphy as the sport's finest halfback. His record speaks for itself: twenty-four Tests (nine each against Australia and France and six against New Zealand); a member of the successful 1960 World Cup side; and, on the club scene, 22 medals for successes in every major British competition. In 1955, only hours after Murphy turned 16, St Helens signed him up for just £80. He made his first-team debut before turning 17 and next year became the regular top half. At just 18 he was chosen to tour Australasia with the 1958 Lions. Britain was outclassed in the First Test, but everything went its way in the other two. Murphy so eclipsed veteran half Keith Holman that the Australian selectors never again chose him to play in the green and gold. Murphy continued as Britain's half until 1966 and then dropped out of the international limelight. A lot of good football was left in him however and, in 1971, as captain-coach of Leigh, he led his side to an unexpected but overwhelming 24–7 victory over Leeds in the Cup Final. Early next season (by which time he had moved to captain-coach of Warrington), Murphy was recalled to the Test arena to play a strong New Zealand touring side. He steered Warrington to a Cup success, too, in 1974. Warrington, as well as taking out the Cup won the Championship, the Player's No 6 Trophy and the Captain Morgan Trophy. Murphy coached England in the 1975 World Championship. The Australians won the series, but England drew with them in Sydney and prevailed in an exciting return clash at Wigan.

Martin Offiah

There has been no more exciting player in the modern era than Martin Offiah, a 21-year-old London-born speedster of Nigerian parents. He burst upon the scene during the 1987–88 season, scoring 44 tries for Widnes, the best by anyone in the Championship. He was top-scorer the next two seasons, too, with 60 and 45 apiece. Offiah was a sensation on the 1988 Lions tour of Australasia, scoring 19 tries in his 11 tour appearances. He made another two trips down under. The first, in 1989, was to play for Eastern Suburbs in the Sydney Premiership competition and the second was with the Lions, in 1990. He joined mid-tour, after recovering from an injury, and played in the three New Zealand Tests. He was also in the British lineup which gave the Kangaroos a real shock later that year. By early 1991, Offiah's tally of full internationals was 20. In the latest, against France at Headingley, he went over for five tries.

Jonathan Parkin

Jonty Parkin, the man they called 'The Wakefield Wizard', was a halfback unmatched by contemporaries. His brilliance was acclaimed on both sides of the world. He made three tours of Australia, two as captain (each of which saw Britain win the Ashes contest). Parkin played 16 Tests and 21 internationals in all. He scored seven tries in one match for Dewsbury, while a guest player during World War I. He represented Wakefield from 1913 to 1930 when, after a dispute, he switched to Hull Kingston Rovers, paying the £100 transfer fee himself. Rugby League rules were altered to prevent this happening again.

Alan Prescott

The Second Test of the Ashes series in 1958 is remembered by Rugby League fans as 'Prescott's Test'. In a stoic performance, British skipper Alan Prescott led his side to victory to square the series (which was won in the Third Test two weeks later). Britain had lost five-eighth David Bolton with a broken collarbone in the 17th minute and there were three others with severe injuries when Prescott broke his right arm just before half-time. There were no replacements in those days, so Prescott continued to the end, proving an inspiration to the 12 British who went on to win 25–18. It proved to be the last of the big prop's 25 Tests (Prescott also played three World Cup games). He was deceptively fast for a big man, a legacy of his early career on the wing with Halifax. It was at St Helens that he switched to prop, playing his first Test in 1951 against the touring New Zealand Kiwis. In club games he led St Helens to a Championship final win over Hunslet in 1959 and a Challenge Cup success in 1956 (scoring a try and winning the Lance Todd Trophy as Man-of-the-Match).

Mal Reilly see Alphabetical entry

Gus Risman

Augustus John Risman remains a Rugby League legend. No other player has been able to match his versatility over so many seasons of top-class football. A schoolboy wonder, poached by England's Salford club in 1929 when he was 17, Risman continued to thrill crowds for an amazing 26 years. He was still playing good football when he finally hung up his boots, at the age of 42, in 1954. Risman played in every position in the backline and, in doing so, notched no fewer than 4054 points (1679 goals and 232 tries). He made three tours of Australia (in 1932, 1936 and 1946). The last saw him as the captain of the team nicknamed 'The Indomitables', after the aircraft carrier which took them south on what was really an improvised tour. Indomitable they were, becoming the first British touring side never to lose a Test match in Australia. In all, Risman captained Great Britain in seven of his 17 Tests. During World War II, he made five appearances in Rugby Union internationals for Wales (a shaky peace had been made between the codes) and, as such, earned the distinction of captaining Wales in both League and Union. Risman's son, Bev, a fullback, also skippered Britain's Rugby League team, in the 1968 World Cup series in Australasia.

John Henry Rogers

The brilliant Welsh halfback John Henry Rogers had never seen a game of Rugby League before the one in which he made his professional debut in March, 1913. It proved to be no handicap. From the first day he began to establish himself as one of the code's top players. He was a tiny—66.5kg (10 stone)—20–year-old when he accepted Huddersfield's £100 to join its ranks. After only one year in Rugby League, he was selected for the first of two tours he was to make of Australasia. The second (in 1920) was somewhat unlucky as Rogers broke a leg in a New Zealand match, but he recovered to make the Test sides the following year when the Kangaroos visited England.

Garry Schofield see alphabetical entry

Jim Sullivan

Many critics rate Jim Sullivan as Britain's greatest Rugby League player—and statistics tend to justify this claim. A record 56 Tests and internationals for Britain, Wales and Other Nationalities. A record number of goals (2867). And the second greatest tally of points (6206). A record number of goals in one match (22 against Flimby and Fothergill, in 1925). Between 1921 and the outbreak of World War II, Sullivan played 18 consecutive seasons and topped the century of goals each time. The enormity of this feat can be gauged by the fact that no player in modern Rugby League has kicked 100 goals in more than five straight seasons. Sullivan played for Wigan from 1921 to 1946, by which time he was 40 years old. The classy fullback toured Australasia three times (in 1924, 1928 and 1932). On the last tour, as captain of the Lions, he notched 223 points. He was selected again for the 1936 tour, but declined for family reasons. After World War II, Sullivan also proved himself to be a great coach, steering Wigan and neighbouring St Helens to many successes.

Mick Sullivan

A tempestuous winger, Mick Sullivan was the most capped British player of all time. Between his international debut in the inaugural World Cup in 1954 and his final Test, against Australia, in 1963, he played 46 Test and World Cup games (19 v France, 16 v Australia and 11 v New Zealand). In doing so, he crossed for 40 tries. He was at his best on the 1958 tour of Australasia, when he scored a record 38 tries. In an era in which short tours are the norm, this is a record which almost certainly will never be broken. His record was helped by a great performance in the last match of the tour, against Western Australia, in which he scored seven tries—another record. In the Third Test, in which Britain retained the Ashes,

Sullivan scored a hat-trick of tries—one of the handful of players to have done so in an Anglo-Australian Test. In England, Sullivan played for Huddersfield, Wigan, St Helens and York. With Wigan he collected two Challenge Cup-winners medals, scoring a try in each of the victories— over Workington Town in 1958 and Hull a year later. Sullivan also played one year with Junee in the rebel Murrumbidgee League in southern New South Wales.

Derek Turner

Few English Rugby League players have won more honours that Derek 'Rocky' Turner. In a career spanning 16 seasons in the 1950s and 1960s, some 547 club matches brought Turner a host of medals—two Wembley Challenge Cup winners (he was captain both times, of Wakefield Trinity in 1960 and 1962), two English Championship winners (Oldham in 1956 and Wakefield in 1962), three Lancashire Cup winners and three Yorkshire Cup winners—and, after his playing days were over, he coached Castleford and Leeds to Championship and Challenge Cup successes. Turner began his playing career in 1951, was a Yorkshire regular from 1954 and a first choice for Britain after his debut against Australia in 1956. He played 24 Tests and World Cup matches (12 v France, 7 v Australia and 5 v New Zealand) and made two tours down-under—with the 1957 World Cup side and the 1962 Lions.

Dave Valentine

The name of Huddersfield lock forward Dave Valentine is firmly written in the annals of Rugby League as the captain of the side which won the first World Cup, in France in 1954. Valentine, who had just returned from a tour of Australasia was one of only three of the tourists who agreed to play. The others shied off because of allegedly poor match payments. Valentine and his British team shocked everyone by winning. Valentine had been capped three times for Scotland in Rugby Union before switching codes. In League he played 15 times for Britain in Tests and World Cup matches between 1948 and 1954 (9 v Australia, 4 v New Zealand and 2 v France). Valentine was a member of Huddersfield's side which won the Challenge Cup in 1953 (beating St Helens 15–10) and the Championship Final in 1949 (downing Warrington 13–12).

Harold Wagstaff

One of Rugby League's immortals, Harold Wagstaff, in 1906, became the youngest-ever player to turn out in a senior side—at 15 years and 175 days, for Huddersfield. He went on to figure in possibly the finest club three-quarter combination known to the game—Wagstaff, Rosenfeld, Gleeson and Moorhouse. They scored almost 200 tries between them in one season just before World War I Wagstaff captained Huddersfield to three Challenge Cup and three Championship wins, including the then-elusive double, in 1913. In the Cup, Wagstaff's side beat Warrington 9–5 in 1913, St Helens 37–3 in 1915 and Wigan 21–10 in 1920. The Championship successes were 13–5 over Wigan (1912), 29–2 over Wigan (1913) and

35–2 over Leeds (1915). The brilliant centre played the first of his 12 Tests in 1911 and captained his country on its 1914 and 1920 tours of Australasia. His League role did not end when he retired. Such was his reputation that when the New Zealand side toured Britain in 1926, Wagstaff was co-opted as 'an advisor' to the Kiwis.

Ernest Ward

A journalist described Ernest Ward as 'poetry in motion'. How apt! He was a big man (1.83m and 83kg) but his play at centre or fullback had the virtues of a smaller one. Ward was fast and a master of the change of pace and dummy pass. Bradford Northern signed him soon after his 16th birthday, in 1936. He played in 20 Test matches (12 v Australia and 8 v New Zealand) and made two Australasian tours (the second, in 1950, as Britain's captain). On the club scene, Ward played in five Challenge Cup finals and was on the winning side three times (1944, 1947 and 1949). In 1949, he won the Lance Todd Trophy as Man-of-the-Match. A prolific goal-kicker he once booted 17, in Britain's 96–0 win over Southern Queensland at Mackay, in 1946.

Kevin Ward see Alphabetical entry

David Watkins

It took $32 000 to lure David Watkins, one of the all-time greats of Rugby Union, to the professional game, in 1967. A brilliant five-eighth, he had been capped 21 times for Wales and six times for the British Lions (including twice on the 1966 tour of Australia). What was then a huge outlay of money was well spent, although, for a time, the Salford chiefs must have wondered whether they had made a mistake. Watkins found it tough at five-eighth in the pro ranks, but switched to centre with enormous success. His elusive running, great acceleration and superb touch-kicking baffled opponents. He also discovered a new gift—the art of goal-kicking. In the 1972–73 season, he scored in every game in which Salford played. He booted 221 goals to smash Bernard Ganley's world record of 219. Watkins also went over for 17 tries, to take his points tally to 493—just three short of Lewis Jones' record for a season. The following season, Watkins again scored in every game in which Salford played (182 goals and 24 tries). In the history of British Rugby League, the feat of scoring in every game has been performed by just 12 players. Watkins is one of only two men to have done it twice. In total, he scored in 92 consecutive matches. Watkins made his League Test debut in 1971, against France, and later played against the Kiwis. Three years on, he toured Australasia. A bad injury late in the tour seemed to spell an end to his football career, but he confounded the doctors by returning to lead Wales in its vain bid for the 1975 World Championship. All told, he played six Tests for Britain and 14 internationals for Wales.

Cliff Watson see Alphabetical entry

GREATEST AUSTRALIAN SIDE

The respected football magazine *Rugby League Week* gathered a distinguished group of experts together in 1982 to pick the greatest Australian team in the history of the game. The experts were famous journalists George Crawford and Tom Goodman, former players turned media figures Frank Hyde and Jack Reardon and ex-representative footballers and officials Herman Peters, Herb Steinohrt, Dick Dunn and Alex Mackie.

The eight came up with the following side:

Clive Churchill
Harold Horder
Dally Messenger
Reg Gasnier
Ken Irvine
Vic Hey
Duncan Thompson
Johnny Raper
Norm Provan
George Treweek
Duncan Hall
Sandy Pearce
Mick Madsen

Of course, in 1982, the great five-eighth and Kangaroo captain Wally Lewis had played in just two Tests (against France), and another all-time great, Peter Sterling, had not played the first of his 18 Tests. So who knows what may have been the selections had the experts sat down today?

For the record, there were 10 players short-listed for each position. Those who missed out on the final 13 were:

- Fullbacks: Keith Barnes, Jimmy Craig, Graham Eadie, Chook Fraser, Howard Hallett, Les Johns, Graeme Langlands, Frank McMillan, Ken Thornett.
- Wingers: Brian Bevan, Cec Blinkhorn, Kerry Boustead, Brian Carlson, Lionel Cooper, Johnny King, Ian Moir, Noel Pidding, Alan Ridley, Albert Rosenfeld.
- Centres: Jack Beaton, Dave Brown, Mick Cronin, Herb Gilbert, Tommy Gorman, Graeme Langlands, Cliff Pearce, Steve Rogers, Harry Wells.
- Five-eighths: Bobby Banks, Brian Clay; Pat Devery, Bob Fulton, Greg Hawick, Ernie Norman, Wally O'Connell, Frank Stanmore, Eric Weissel.
- Halfbacks: Joe 'Chimpy' Busch, Jimmy Craig, Pony Halloway, Keith Holman, Chris McKivat, Barry Muir, Tom Raudonikis, Billy Smith, Arthur Summons, Viv Thicknesse.
- Locks: Frank Burge, Ron Coote, Les 'Chic' Cowie, Mick Crocker, Noel Mulligan, Ray Price, Waly Prigg, Paul Sait, Billy Tyquin, Jack Watkins.
- Second-rowers: Harry Bath, Frank Burge, Mick Crocker, Noel Mulligan, Herb Narvo, Kel O'Shea, Rod Reddy, Dick Thornett.
- Props: Arthur Beetson, Roy Bull, Brian Davies, Noel Kelly, Jack Rayner, Kevin Ryan, Ray Stehr, Herb Steinohrt.
- Hookers: George Bishop, Ken Kearney, Max Krilich, Noel Kelly, George Peponis, Kevin Schubert, Ian Walsh, Elwyn Walters, George Watt.

ANDY GREGORY

25 Tests for Great Britain (1981–90). Also played one match against Rest-of-the-World (1988), for Rest-of-the-World against Australia in Bicentennial international (1988) and in 13 minor games for Great Britain on two tours of Australasia (1984 and 1988).

When Great Britain shocked the football world by downing Australia 26–12 in the Third Test of the 1988 series (Britain's first win in 16 clashes) one little fellow stood head and shoulders above the rest—pint-sized Wigan halfback Andy Gregory. He was deserved winner of the Man-of-the-Match award. It was his 15th, and finest, Test appearance.

He had had a disappointing first tour of Australia four years earlier during which he lost his Test spot, but he regained it in 1986. When he quit Test football after the 1990 Ashes series, Gregory had played 25 full internationals, one minor international against France in Venice (1982), and matches for and against the Rest-of-the-World. He was also a vital cog in the Wigan side which won four straight Challenge Cups between 1988 and 1991. In the 1988 and 1990 finals he won the Lance Todd Trophy as Man-of-the-Match. And most critics consider he was unlucky, in 1991, not to have become the first player to win three times.

Gregory had a spell in Australia in 1989 with the lowly-rated Illawarra. He played nine Premiership matches and also helped inspire the Steelers side to the final of the midweek Panasonic Cup, where they gave the star-studded Brisbane Broncos a real fright before going down 22–20. 'It was terrible to lose, but it was still one of the best nights of my life,' said Gregory.

FRED GRIFFITHS

One Test for South Africa (1963). Also played four minor games for South Africa on one Australasian tour (1963).

Fred Griffiths was one of several fine South African Rugby Union players to make a name for themselves overseas in the League code. The tough, goal-kicking fullback was a star for Wigan in the British competition and later made a real impact as captain-coach of North Sydney. He spent five seasons at Wigan (1958 to 1963). He played in the 1960 Championship winning side and, in 1959, kicked six goals to help Wigan to a 30–13 Challenge Cup final success over Hull.

Griffiths had planned to return to South Africa but changed his mind when Norths offered him the job of captain-coach. He was an instant success in the Sydney Premiership. In 1963, he took Norths from last to fifth, the following year to the semi-finals for the first time in 10 years and in 1965 to the preliminary final. Twice he topped the Sydney Premiership pointscoring lists. His 181 points (one try and 89 goals) in 1965 remained a North's club record until topped in 1991, by another foreign import, New Zealander Daryl Halligan (196 points). In his four seasons in Sydney, Griffiths scored 590 points, at an incredible average of almost nine a match. In 1963 he played centre for the South African Test side touring Australasia, and the following year he captained an Other Nationalities side which played NSW Colts in a special one-off representative match.

ERIC GROTHE

Eight Tests for Australia (1982–84). Also played 10 minor games on one Kangaroo tour (1982).

One can only speculate on just what records block-busting winger Eric Grothe would have set had he not been plagued by knee ligament troubles. In the couple of seasons when he was free of injury, Grothe set the Rugby League world on fire.

Eighteen years old, standing 1.83m (6ft) and weighing 89kg (14 stone), 'The Guru', as he was affectionately known, was Parramatta's Rookie-of-the-Year in 1978 after scoring 16 tries in 17 matches for the Eels' Under-23 Premiership team. He missed much of the next couple of years through injury, but, in 1981, Grothe made the NSW State-of-Origin side and, the following year, the Kangaroo squad for the tour of Britain and France. Grothe had a sensational tour. He played two Tests against both countries and was second on the try-scoring lists with 21 touchdowns in his 14 games. His best effort was five tries in the match against Roanne, won by Australia 65–0. He played against New Zealand in 1983 and the British Lions the following year. That was his last appearance in the international arena as chronic injury cut into his play in subsequent years. In 1990, doctors advised him to retire to avoid permanent damage.

In club matches, Grothe played a major role in Parramatta's Premiership supremacy in the 1980s. He was a member of Eels sides which won the title in 1981, 1982, 1983 and 1986. In 1985 he had a season in England with Leeds.

H

DUNCAN HALL

Twenty-two Tests for Australia (1948–1954). Also played one match in one World Cup (1954) and 36 minor games for Australia on two Kangaroo tours (1948–49 and 1952–53).

For many years Duncan Hall was one of Brisbane's best-known bookmakers, but there was no gamble about his choice as a Test front-row forward years before, in the early 1950s. A tough, clever player, Hall had few equals. Indeed, when a team of experts sat down in 1982 to pick the greatest Australian team ever, Hall was chosen as one of the two props. The Queenslander had started as a second-rower and made his Test debut in that position against Great Britain on the 1948–49 Kangaroo tour. However, in France, he was tried as a prop and was an instant success.

The highlights of his career were in 1950 and 1954 when he played a major role in the defeat of Great Britain. Hall would have been an even more important cog in the Australian Test machine, but for a severe nasal problem which made breathing difficult for most of his career. A knee injury forced his retirement in 1956 and Hall switched his talents to administration. He managed the Australian team which won the 1977 World Championship.

Hall's son, Duncan junior, followed his father into the Test arena—but in the amatuer Rugby Union code.

HOWARD HALLETT

Six Tests for Australia (1911–1914). Also played 26 minor games for Australia on one Kangaroo tour (1911–12).

Howard Hallett is still recognised as one of the top few fullbacks Australia has ever produced, but it was only luck which resulted in him being used in that position. A former Australian Rules footballer with a prodigious punt, he was selected as a centre for the 1911–12 Kangaroo side to tour Great Britain. However when Webby Neill, the first-choice fullback, had trouble gaining long distances with a ball made heavy by the muddy conditions in England, Hallett was tried in his place. So steady was Hallett's play that the fans soon dubbed him -'The Rock of Gibraltar'.

On the club scene, Hallett was a driving force in the early successes of South Sydney. He played a then-record 181 first-grade games for the Rabbitohs, from 1909 to 1924. During this period he featured in three Premiership-winning sides (1909, 1914 and 1918) and six sides which were runners-up (1910, 1916, 1917, 1920, 1923 and 1924). Such was the support for Hallett after his 16 seasons that, as soon as he hung up his boots, he was asked to take over as Souths' non-playing coach, and, in his very first year in this new job, Hallett steered to Rabbitohs to the 1925 Premiership—the start of a run of five straight successes.

ARTHUR 'PONY' HALLOWAY

Ten Tests for Australia (1908–1919). Also played 48 minor games for Australia on two Kangaroo tours (1908–09 and 1911–12) and one New zealand tour (1919).

Pony Halloway, a pioneer of Australian Rugby League, is recalled as its first great halfback. His Test record would have been even better if he had not shared part of the era with another scrum-base champion, Chris McKivat, and for the fact that World War I put a stop to several prospective international tours.

Halloway was a Rugby Union star when, in 1907, he threw in his lot with those organising the breakaway professional teams to meet A H Baskerville's New Zealand All Golds, en route to England for the code's first international series. The fine little halfback's performances in the early period of the new game earned him a berth on the boat to England with the first Kangaroo side.

Halloway made another tour of Britain (1911–12) and two trips to New Zealand (one with New South Wales, in 1912, and the second as captain of the first full Australian side to cross the Tasman Sea, in 1919). He also played in Australia against New Zealand (1909), Great Britain (1914) and the New Zealand Maoris (1909).

On the club scene, Halloway began his Rugby League career with Glebe without any tangible club successes. From 1912 to 1914, he played with Sydney's Eastern Suburbs which won two Premierships and a City Cup. Then he switched to Balmain, where he played until 1920 (captaining the side from 1916 and forming a devastating scrum-base combination with Test five-eighth Chook Fraser). Between 1915 and 1920, Balmain won five of the six Premierships decided. Halloway's record was seven Premierships in nine seasons! Halloway later played north of the border (at Ipswich), captaining the Queensland side in matches against his old State. When he finally hung up his boots, Halloway turned his talents to coaching. He returned to Sydney to be mentor of the Eastern Suburbs side which won three Premierships and a City Cup in the 1930s.

A story is told about Pony Halloway's stoic play. It is said that at work one Saturday morning, he chopped off most of one of his fingers. He played that afternoon for Balmain—with his hand wrapped in a bloody bandage.

BRIAN HAMBLY

Eighteen Tests for Australia (1959–1965). Also played three matches in one World Cup (1960), for the Rest-of-the-World against Britain (1960), and 40 minor games for Australia on two Kangaroo tours (1959–60 and 1963–64), one New Zealand tour (1965) and one World Cup trip (1960).

The Australian Test sides of the early 1960s owed a real debt to the tough forward Brian Hambly. He never received the acclaim given to many of his contemporaries, but his value was enormous. He was the complete forward, a great ball carrier, equally at home in the front or second row, and when needed, he would also play lock.

Hambly first showed his potential on the representative scene in 1958, when as a young South Sydney star he turned out for NSW Colts against the touring British side (together with two other future greats, Johnny Raper and Ian Walsh). He then tried his hand in the southern NSW country town of Wagga, from where he gained selection in the 1959–60 Kangaroo side. It was the first of four overseas tours. He was back in Britain a year later for the World Cup, made a second Kangaroo tour in 1963–64 and finally visited New Zealand in 1965. In all, Hambly played in eight different Test series, appearing against all the major Rugby League nations—Great Britain (5 times), France (9) and New Zealand (4).

On the club scene, Hambly played a major role in the first real success for Parramatta. He joined the club in 1961. The following year, Parramatta reached the semi-finals of the Sydney Premiership for the first time, and a year later reached the final. Hambly was also a member of the Parramatta side which reached the final of the Pre-Season competition in 1963.

Hambly bowed out of Test football in the 1965 series against New Zealand. He continued playing for Parramatta for two more seasons, coaching the Eels in the last year, and bringing his total matches for the club past the century.

ERNIE HAMMERTON

One Test for Australia (1951). Also played 11 minor games for Australia on one Kangaroo tour (1956–57)

Ernie Hammerton played only one Test for Australia (in the Second Test against the great 1951 touring Frenchmen). The South Sydney hooker had the misfortune to be playing at the same time as two of the all-time great rakes, Kev Schubert and Ken Kearney. Hammerton was given his Test chance when Schubert was injured and made his only overseas tour, as Kearney's understudy in the 1956–57 Kangaroos squad. However Hammerton played a major role in the great success of the South Sydney sides of the early 1950s. He was in the Premiership-winning lineup five times in six years (1950, 1951, 1953, 1954 and 1955).

After his retirement as a player, Hammerton served for many years as chairman of the panel of Test selectors during the period in which Australia were almost unbeatable.

MICHAEL HANCOCK

Five Tests for Australia (1989–1990). Also played in 8 minor games on one Kangaroo tour (1990) and one New Zealand tour (1989).

Michael Hancock rose from being just a promising first-grader to become the best winger in Australia over just a few months in 1989. He joined the select few who have represented their country as teenagers when, at the age of 19, he was chosen in the Australian squad which toured New Zealand.

The winger from Stanthorpe near the NSW border had represented Toowoomba and Queensland Country in 1987 before joining the Brisbane Broncos the following year for their first season in the Sydney Premiership. He was one of the stars in the Queensland State-of-Origin whitewash of New South Wales in 1989. In New Zealand he played in all six tour games, including the three Tests. A bad hamstring injury midway through the 1990 season robbed him of the chance to play in the State-of-Origin clashes and the World Cup Test against France. Once he was fit again, Hancock came back with a vengeance to regain his Test spot for the one-off Test against New Zealand at Wellington and make the Kangaroo squad for the tour of Britain and France.

He played in the First Test at Wembley Stadium. But then, two minutes before the end of the match against Second Division club Halifax—Hancock's sixth game in Britain—he tore ankle ligaments, an injury which put him out of the rest of the tour.

During 1991, a season in which he again played State-of-Origin football, Hancock took his career tally of tries for the Broncos to a club record 35. But despite his good form in both the Premiership and the interstate clashes he was unable to reclaim his Test spot.

ELLERY HANLEY

Thirty-four Tests for Great Britain (1984–91). Also played for the Rest-of-the-World against Australia (1988), for Britain against the Rest-of-the-World (1988), for Europe against Oceania (1984) and 16 minor games for Britain on two tours of Australia and New Zealand (1984 and 1988).

When the *Rothmans Rugby League Yearbook* celebrated its tenth year of publication in 1990, it commemorated the event by naming the outstanding British player of the 1980s. There was no criticism of the selection—Great Britain captain Ellery Hanley. In the world of Rugby League perhaps only Australia's Wally Lewis and Peter Sterling could challenge Hanley as the greatest player of the decade. Three times during the eighties, Hanley was named Britain's Player-of-the-Year. In 1989, he won the Adidas Gold Boot award as the greatest Rugby League player in the world—and he was the highest paid. When Western Suburbs signed him for 13 games in 1989 it was estimated that he was earning $6000 a match. Two years before, he had set the Sydney scene alight with some outstanding displays which helped guide Balmain to the grand final.

Hanley began his career as a centre and five-eighth with Bradford Northern, from where he made his Test debut against France, in 1984,

Great Britain Captain Ellery Hanley evades Kangaroo second-rower Paul Sironen in a 1990 Ashes clash

before making his first tour down-under. He was top try scorer on that tour, with 12 touchdowns in his 17 games. In 1985 he switched to Wigan for a then-world record transfer fee of more than $200 000. He never looked back. By 1992, Hanley, who by then had moved to lock forward, had played in 34 Tests, the last 19 of them as captain. Injury cost him at least seven more caps. He captained Wigan during one of its great periods in football history, winning three Championships (1987, 1990 and 1991) and an unprecedented four straight Challenge Cup Finals (1988 to 1991). In the 1989 success Hanley won the coveted Lance Todd Trophy as Man-of-the-Match. He was also Man-of-the-Match in the First Test against the touring 1990 Kangaroos, the first British win against the Australians on home soil since 1978.

The chance of having a hand in coaching lured Hanley to Leeds in late 1991. But there was much bickering about the size of his transfer fee before Wigan allowed him to go.

BILL HARDCASTLE

Two Tests for Australia (1908). Also played one minor international for Australia (1908) and six minor games on one Kangaroo tour (1908–09).

Bill Hardcastle holds a unique place in the annals of the Rugby game. He is the only man to have represented two countries in Rugby Union and one in Rugby League. In Union, Hardcastle was capped seven times for New Zealand, as well as playing provincial games for both Wellington and North Island, before he moved across the Tasman in 1898. In Sydney, he turned out with the Glebe amateur side and played Test matches against the 1899 Great Britain side and his former country four years later.

By the time the great Rugby split came in 1907, Hardcastle had moved to Ipswich in Queensland. It was from there that he gained selection for Tests in the first series played in Australia—against the 1908 New Zealand All Golds, who stopped over on their journey home from the tour of Britain. At the end of the season he was chosen for the Kangaroo tour of Britain. Unfortunately, injury kept him off the field for most of the tour and he played only six unimportant games.

ERIC HARRIS

English fans dubbed Eric Harris 'The Toowoomba Ghost'. He was certainly a will-o-the-wisp. Fast and elusive, he was one of the most thrilling of the scores of Australian stars to have turned out with English clubs. A winger, with dazzling acceleration, Harris spent 10 seasons in the 1930s with Leeds and would have stayed on with the Yorkshire club but for the outbreak of World War II Harris scored 391 tries for Leeds, including a club record of 64 in the 1935–36 season. He made two Challenge Cup Final appearances. In 1932, Harris scored Leeds' only try when it downed Swinton 11–8 at Central Park, Wigan. Four years later, he also scored in Leeds' 18–2 win over Warrington, at Wembley Stadium.

After his return home in 1940, Harris linked up with Brisbane Western Suburbs and the following year won selection in the Queensland side for the annual series against New South Wales, but, because of the War, a Test jumper eluded him.

Such was the ability of Eric Harris that, some 30 years after he finished playing with Leeds, a loyal fan wrote a song lauding his exploits. Sung to the tune of 'The British Grenadiers' it went:

Some talk of Vollenhoven,
And some of Ellaby,
Of Sullivan and Cooper,
And such great wings as these.
But of all the game's great wingmen,
The one Leeds' fans like the most,
With a too! ooo! ooo! ooo!
Was the Toowoomba Ghost.

MARK HARRIS

One Test for Australia (1972). Also played 10 matches in two World Cups (1970 and 1972) and two World Championships (1975 and

1977), one minor international (1970) and two minor games on one World Cup tour (1970).

Mark Harris is one of the select few players to have appeared in four different World Series. He was a member of the Australian squads for the 1970 and 1972 World Cups and was in the teams for the World Championships in 1975 and 1977. Only two other players, Arthur Beetson and Bob Fulton, can boast a record to equal that of Harris. Strangely enough, Harris made only one Test appearance—against the touring 1972 New Zealand Kiwis, but he was playing in an era of few Tests.

Harris, then a big, raw 22–year-old, first hit the international headlines on the 1970 World Cup tour. He played a major role in Australia's success in the final against Britain at Headingley, Leeds. Then, in post-Cup matches, he starred in an international against France, at Perpignan, before running riot against the France B side. The Australian selectors had a habit of turning to Harris for vital matches. Such was the case for his last international appearance—the final of the 1977 World Championships, at the Sydney Cricket Ground. He had been overlooked for most of the lead-up games, but came up trumps in the final.

In club football, Harris was a member of the Eastern Suburbs side which won the 1974 Sydney Premiership, but tragedy struck 12 months later. In the preliminary final against Manly-Warringah, Harris broke a leg and had to miss Easts' 38–0 thrashing of St George in the grand final as well as the second-half of the 1975 World Championships, in New Zealand, France and Britain. Harris quit Easts at the end of the 1979 season after 195 first-grade games—at the time, the second highest number in the history of the club. He had two more club seasons, playing out his career with 33 matches for North Sydney.

EARL HARRISON

Nine Tests for Australia (1963). Also played in 13 games on one Kangaroo tour (1963–64).

A rugged, hard-tackling five-eighth from Gilgandra in the central-west of New South Wales, Earl Harrison had only one year on the international scene, but in that brief time he played an important role in one of Australia's greatest performances. Harrison was a member of the great 1963–64 Kangaroo squad, which became the first all-Australian side to win the Ashes on British soil. He had made his Test debut earlier in the year against the touring New Zealand and South African sides. On the tour he proved to be a perfect link between halfback Barry Muir and the rampaging three-quarter line of Reg Gasnier, Graeme Langlands, Ken Irvine and Peter Dimond. Back home, Harrison quickly faded from the representative scene, although he did turn out for Western Division against the touring 1964 Frenchmen.

GREG HARTLEY

Few officials have matched the flamboyance of Greg Hartley, Australia's leading referee of the late 1970s. He was a real showman on the field, with dramatic gestures part and parcel of his style. It was so dramatic that he earned the nickname 'Hollywood' Hartley, but he was also respected by the players—as several polls showed.

Hartley may have made his mark as a footballer but for a bad injury sustained while playing for Newtown in 1967. A kick in the stomach, which ruptured his pancreas and spleen, forced his early retirement. The previous year, Hartley had been a member of the NSW Country Firsts side which shocked with a 16–6 win over the star-studded City combination.

Hartley refereed his first grand final in 1978, and was criticised in some quarters for allegedly allowing seven tackles—one too many—in a scoring movement by the eventual Premiers, Manly-Warringah. He toured Britain at the end of that season, at the same time as the Kangaroos, and controlled several British club and representative matches. In 1979, Hartley was a Test referee in the Ashes series between Australia and Britain and again in charge of the Sydney grand final.

During 1981, Hartley had the unique distinction of refereeing Tests in five different countries—Australia, New Zealand, Papua-New Guinea, England and France. In early 1982, he quit the football field to become a radio commentator. He teamed up with former Manly-Warringah first-grade forward, Peter 'Zorba' Peters, and the pair became Sydney's top-rating callers of the weekend matches.

DES HASLER

Twelve Tests for Australia (1985–1991). Also played in Bicentennial match against Rest-of-the-World (1988) and 23 minor games for Australia on two Kangaroo tours (1986 and 1990) and two New Zealand tours (1985 and 1989).

Penrith let one of Australia's greatest utility players slip through its fingers in the early 1980s. Des Hasler had played just 11 first-grade games when Manly-Warringah lured him away in 1984. He had been showing great potential and starred for Penrith's third grade side which had reached the Premiership final in 1982. Hasler never looked back at Manly. In his first season with the Sea Eagles he was runner-up in the Rothmans Medal, awarded to the best and fairest player in the Sydney Premiership.

In 1985 he was chosen in the Australian side to tour New Zealand. A sensation in the minor matches, Hasler was the centre of a storm when he was one of four New South Welshmen who replaced entrenched Queensland Test players (in his case, halfback Mark Murray) for the final encounter. It was a disastrous debut, with the Australians suffering an ignominious 18–0 defeat. Hasler made his second overseas tour with the 1986 Kangaroos. He played in the Test against Papua-New Guinea, but suffered a crippling shoulder injury in the second match of the English leg of the tour, which cost him any chance of a spot in the remaining five internationals.

The Manly's star's utility value (he could play, five-eighth, centre and lock as well as half) made him one of the first players chosen in Test squads, with subsequent matches against Papua New Guinea (1988) and New Zealand (1989, 1990 and 1991). He also made his second Kangaroo tour in 1990, coming on as a replacement in four of the five Tests. He would have been a certainty for the 1991 tour of Papua New Guinea but for an injury.

KEVIN HASTINGS

Experts have long pondered the reasons why Kevin Hastings never played for Australia. The plucky Eastern Suburbs halfback was one of the finest players in the land in the early 1980s. But he never got within a coo-ee of a green and gold jumper. Some said he was too slow, however the great Easts' coaches Bob Fulton and Arthur Beetson thought otherwise—and so did the independent judges of individual awards. Hastings won the 1981 Rothmans Medal, as the best and fairest player in the Sydney competition. He was also named Player-of-the-Year by the respected football magazine, *Rugby League Week*, three years in a row—1980, 1981 and 1982.

Hastings was widely tipped to make the Kangaroo squad at the end of 1982, but the selectors instead went for Peter Sterling (Parramatta), Steve Mortimer (Canterbury-Bankstown) and Mark Murray (Brisbane Valleys). Hastings did make it into the record books however. He is the only player to turn out in more than 200 first grade games for the Roosters. When he quit in 1987 he had played 217 senior games. Most were at half but in the last couple of years Hastings played both lock-forward and hooker. He was also one of the most durable players. A rare five-year sequence of not missing a match through injury was broken in 1982 only by a severe case of concussion.

PAUL HAUFF

One Test for Australia (1991).

Few players have had a more dramatic debut in first grade football than Brisbane fullback Paul Hauff. Called into the senior side, in April 1990, after Test star Dale Shearer was injured, the 19-year-old Hauff demoralised the Newcastle Knights in front of their home crowd, with three slashing tries (equalling the club record). When shearer returned the following week he was switched to the centres. The Broncos fullback spot from then on belonged to Hauff.

Such was the form of the tall (197cm or 6ft 6in), gangling fullback during the rest of the 1990 season that some keen critics expected him to be chosen in the Kangaroo squad for the tour of Britain and France. It was not to be but Hauff got his chance in 1991. With Test custodian Gary Belcher injured, he was chosen in the Queensland State-of-Origin side and played so well that he was included in the Australian side to play the First Test against the touring New Zealand Kiwis.

Sadly, Hauff blotted his copybook by fumbling a kick which led to a Kiwi try which turned the game. He was made one of the scapegoats for the shock loss and dropped for the final two encounters.

GREG HAWICK

Six Tests for Australia (1952–1958). Also played three matches in two World Cups (1954 and 1957), one minor international (1951), one match against Rest-of-the-World (1957) and 19 minor games

for Australia on one Kangaroo tour (1952–53) and one New Zealand tour (1953).

On one Tuesday afternoon in June 1957, Greg Hawick, a crack five-eighth then playing for a country side in Wagga Wagga, kicked himself into the record books. He booted 15 goals in New South Wales' 69–5 thrashing of Queensland. It is an interstate record which, now that State-of-Origin rules ensure close matches, will possibly last forever. It was a feat which ensured Hawick's return to the Australian lineup for the second World Cup, after three years in the representative wilderness.

Although he turned out for an Australian XIII against France in Melbourne in 1951, Hawick, one of the most versatile players Australia has known, did not make his Test debut until more than a year later, on the Kangaroo tour of Britain and France. In that first Test appearance Hawick played at five-eighth, but in eight subsequent Test and World Cup appearances he was also to play halfback, centre and even lock forward. In all, Hawick made three overseas trips. In addition to the Kangaroo tour, he went to New Zealand in 1953 and to France for the inaugural World Cup, in 1954.

On the club scene, Hawick was an important cog in the South Sydney machine which won the Sydney Premiership in 1950, 1951, 1953 and 1954.

JOHNNY HAWKE

Six Tests for Australia (1948–1950). Also played 24 minor games for Australia on one Kangaroo tour (1948–49) and one New Zealand tour (1949).

When Canberra five-eighth Johnny Hawke was chosen to play for New South Wales in the 1948 King's Birthday Holiday match in Brisbane, his employer was not amused. He sacked Hawke for taking the time off work. Hawke was rewarded later in the year when chosen in the Kangaroo squad to visit Britain and France, and the St George club was only too willing to find the country star new employment in Sydney.

Hawke, nicknamed 'Feathers' by his Kangaroo team-mates, played four of the five Tests on the Kangaroo tour, as a centre. He made 23 appearances on tour, second only to forward Jack Rayner's 24 games. Hawke was to play two more Tests, against New Zealand (at Auckland's Carlaw Park in 1949) and France (in the deciding Third Test at the Sydney Cricket Ground in 1951).

Perhaps Hawke's finest hour was, however, in a club match. In 1949, the Saints had finished third on the Sydney Premiership table. However, ably led by Hawke, they beat Minor Premiers, South Sydney, 16–12 in the semi-final and Balmain 18–7 in the final. In the grand final, Souths had a second chance, but Hawke, the St George skipper, dictated play so well that his backs were able to run over the Rabbitohs for much of the match. St George won 19–12.

PHIL HAWTHORNE

Three Tests for Australia (1970).

Phil Hawthorne was one of the most famous names in Rugby Union when he accepted the lure of big money to switch to League in 1968. He went on to join the select lineup of stars who played for Australia in both codes.

As an amateur, five-eighth Hawthorne had formed a fine combination with the great half Ken Catchpole. Hawthorne was capped 21 times in five years (between 1962 and 1967) before he took the bait after the 1966–67 Wallaby tour, the 1967 home Test against Ireland and the away game against New Zealand. A broken jaw in 1969 did not help Hawthorne's rise to the top in his new code, but the following year he played all three Tests against the touring British Lions, capping his international career by leading the Australians in the final encounter. It was a disappointing day for Hawthorne, as the British regained The Ashes.

NOEL HAZZARD

Thirteen Tests for Australia (1951-1954). Also played 17 minor games for australia on one Kangaroo tour (1952-53).

There have been few centres as tough and durable as Queenslander Noel Hazzard. It was said that he was so strong he could lift a 44–gallon drum of petrol over his head. He continued playing until the ripe old age of 48, in Queensland country football.

Hazzard was at his prime in the early 1950s. While playing at Bundaberg, he made his Test debut against the great 1951 French tourists, appearing in all three clashes. He played in all Tests in the next three series in which Australia was involved—against New Zealand at home and against Great Britain and France on the 1952–53 Kangaroo tour (on which he turned out in 23 of the 40 tour games). He played the last of his 13 Tests in the second encounter with Dicky Williams' 1954 British Lions.

BILL HEIDKE

Four Tests for Australia (1908-1910). Also played in 24 minor games on one Kangaroo tour (1908-09).

Bill Heidke was one of the pioneers of Rugby League in Queensland. The Bundaberg back was chosen to play at fullback in a Test against New Zealand in the first season, 1908, but had to withdraw for business reasons, but later that year he toured Britain with the first Kangaroo side. A big, tough player, who was at his best in the centres, Heidke was described by an English journalist as being 'as strong as a lion'. Heidke was one of the stars of that pioneering tour, playing in two Tests, the first on the wing.

Back home he turned out for Australia against the 1909 New Zealand Kiwis and in the Second Test, at Brisbane, against the touring British Lions the following year. In a fitting finale to his career he captained his country in that match. The fine player's son, Les 'Monty' Heidke, in 1932, became the second player to follow his father into the Australian Test team. Joe Pearce had achieved that distinction only two weeks before Heidke.

LES 'MONTY' HEIDKE

Nine Tests for Australia (1932-38). Also played 17 minor games on one Kangaroo tour (1937-38).

Les Heidke

Monty Heidke is one of a handful of players to emulate their fathers by playing Test football for Australia. However the Ipswich forward played more than twice as many Tests as did Bill Heidke, one of the pioneers of Rugby League. Heidke junior made his Test debut, against the touring Lions, in Brisbane in 1932 and was one of the first chosen for the Kangaroo squad to visit Britain the following year. Unfortunately, he suffered an infection of the leg and had to leave the ship at Fremantle, Western Australia, and return home.

His Test career was far from over however. In 1936, playing in the second-row, he was one of the stars in the Ashes series against Britain. In the First Test at the Sydney Cricket Ground he played a major part in two of Australia's four tries, handling twice in one brilliant move which saw winger Alan Ridley score and later booting a loose ball downfield for five-eighth Vic Hey to dive over. Heidke, by then a front-rower, eventually made it to Britain, with the 1937–38 Kangaroos, and took part in the first series against France. The Second Test, at Marseilles in January 1938, was Heidke's last.

ARTHUR HENNESSY

Two Tests for Australia (1908). Also played seven minor games on one Kangaroo tour (1908–09).

Arthur Hennessy was one of the founders of Rugby League in Australia. The fine hooker was a highly respected Rugby Union star who had played for New South Wales in the amateur code. He helped organise the first League matches, against the 1907 New Zealand All Golds, en route to Britain. Hennessy was one of the three selectors of the NSW side and captained the Blues in the three matches, all of which were won by the New Zealanders. When they returned from Britain the following year, Hennessy played in two of the three Tests.

The man described as the best hooker of the early years of League in Australia was also a major figure in the formation of the South Sydney club. He missed the Rabbitohs' first Premiership, while on tour with the 1908–09 Kangaroos, but was in the squad which won the second Premiership after Balmain forfeited the 1909 final. The Kangaroo tour was a real disappointment for Hennessy. *The Referee* newspaper had attacked his role in selecting himself for the visit, claiming he was too slow. Hennessy had no chance to prove the critics wrong. In the second match of the tour, against Bradford Northern, he broke his jaw, and in his comeback game, against Widnes towards the end of the tour, he fractured his cheekbone. All told, he managed to appear in just seven minor games.

A real thinker, Hennessy made his name as a coach. It was he who devised Souths' tactics of running the ball instead of kicking, as was the normal practice in Rugby Union. As coach of the NSW side which toured New Zealand in 1913, he introduced a steak-only diet on match days. The non-kicking game almost paid dividends on the 1929–30 Kangaroo tour. Hennessy was the first coach to go away with the Australians and the Kangaroos went within a whisker of bringing home The Ashes.

DARCY HENRY

Two Tests for Australia (1955–56).

Darcy Henry was one of the lightest players ever to pull on a green and gold jumper for Australia. When he made his Test debut in the first clash with the visiting 1955 Frenchman, the diminutive five-eighth weighed only 67kg (10st 8lb). It is believed that, of all Australia's Test players, only Arthur 'Snowy' Justice, the hooker with the 1928–29 Kangaroos, and Allan Langer, the half who made his Test debut in 1988, were lighter.

Henry was also a reluctant representative. The young man from Forbes in central-western New South Wales tried four times to return home after coming to Sydney with the Western Division to play Parramatta in the 1955 Country Week matches. First he was selected for the Country trials (and scored 5 tries), then for Country Firsts before making the State side for two matches against Queensland.

Henry was the centre of controversy in the Third Test against France, when he was chosen as five-eighth and then sacked only moments before taking the field, without any reason given. He played only one more Test, against New Zealand the following year, but he was later an important member of the fine Western Suburbs combination which gave the great St George side several frights in the late 1950s and early 1960s.

VIC HEY

Six Tests for Australia (1933–1936). Also played 23 minor games on one Kangaroo tour (1933–34).

Although Vic Hey played only six Tests and was seen in his home country for just six seasons at his peak, some critics still rate him as Australia's greatest five-eighth. He was so clever in attack—and his powerful defence was a bonus. Hey was a schoolboy star. He sprang into prominence when he entered first-grade for Sydney's Western Suburbs club in 1933. After a mere handful of games he was chosen for the New South Wales side and at the end of the season was one of five backs from Wests to make

Vic Hey

the Kangaroo side. It was, however, a close thing. He was only chosen after one of the original selections, Ernie Norman, failed a fitness test. Hey played in all three Tests on tour, combining well with Wests' halfback Les Mead.

Hey played against the traditional foe when Britain toured in 1936. By this time he was living in the Queensland city of Toowoomba. However at the end of that Southern Hemisphere season he left for Britain to play club football with Leeds. He led Leeds to many successes, including two consecutive Challenge Cup wins, beating Halifax 19–2 in 1941 and again 15–10 a year later. Hey also appeared in a Championship Final, when Leeds went down 8–2 to Hunslet in 1938. He was later captain-coach of Dewsbury and Hunslet before deciding to return home to steer Parramatta through its second and third season in the Sydney Premiership. He quit playing in 1949 but continued as Parramatta's coach for another four seasons. He was also to later coach Canterbury-Bankstown and Western Suburbs.

The crowning glory in Hey's coaching career came in the Test arena. He was the Test coach in Australia's great victories over Britain in 1950 and 1954—the former being the first Australian success in an Anglo-Australian series in three decades.

RAY HIGGS

One Test for Australia (1974). Also played eight matches in two World Championships (1975 and 1977) and one minor international (1975).

Fellow players dubbed Ray Higgs 'Bulldog'. It was an apt nickname, for the tough second-rower from Queensland's Sunshine Coast displayed the tenacity of a bulldog in every match in which he appeared.

Higgs smashed his way into the headlines in 1974, after 12 months out of football while concentrating on business affairs. He was selected for Queensland Country, then the State side and, after another player withdrew, the Australian Test team for the Lang Park clash against Great Britain. The following year he linked up with Parramatta and played a vital role in the Eels push to two successive Sydney Premiership grand finals. In 1976, his powerhouse displays for Parramatta won him the coveted Rothmans Medal, as the best and fairest player in the Premiership competition. Higgs also starred in Australia's World Championship sides which triumphed in both the 1975 and 1977 series. After an internal dispute, Higgs switched to Manly-Warringah in 1978 before returning to the Queensland country, from where he made his last sortie into representative football—an interstate clash in 1980.

HISTORY OF RUGBY LEAGUE

The sixth of August 1823—the day Rugby began. William Webb Ellis, a pupil at the elite Rugby School in England, fed up with the slow play in a Soccer match, picked up the ball and ran with it in his arms. What a scandal! The teachers at Rugby School threw up their hands in horror. At least, that was their original reaction. After saner contemplation, they realised the merits and potential of Ellis' rash move. With a few modifications in rules, a new sport was born, and it soon spread world-wide as the 15–a–side game now known as Rugby Union.

Naturally enough for a sport started in a school for the sons of rich gentlefolk, it was strictly an amateur sport. While this was all right for the university and public school players, who could afford any expenses and who had no trouble in getting time off to play, in the north of England it was a different matter. There, the players were miners, factory workers and labourers. They could not take time off work to play, and any injury spelled financial disaster. The clubs from the north sought permission to compensate players out of pocket through playing Rugby. But the answer from the controlling body in London was a firm *NO!* The annual meeting of the Rugby Union in 1893 rejected a Yorkshire move towards financial compensation by 282 votes to 136.

It was a costly decision, for moves aimed at breaking away began soon after. At a meeting in the George Hotel, Huddersfield, on August 19, 1895, the break finally came. The clubs involved were:

From Yorkshire—Batley, Bradford, Brighouse Rovers, Halifax, Huddersfield, Hull, Hunslet, Leeds, Liversedge, Manningham and Wakefield Trinity.

From across the border in Lancashire—Broughton Rovers, Leigh, Oldham, Rochdale Hornets, St Helens, Tyldesley, Warrington, Widnes and Wigan.

The rebels had no plans to start a new game. It was just a breakaway Rugby Union competition, with compensation allowed for so-called 'broken time', ie time lost through playing or through injury. A maximum broken time payment of six shillings was set.

The first season ended with the rebel clubs showing a small financial loss. But, by that time, their number had grown rapidly to 59. The administrators soon realised that by sticking to old Rugby Union rules they were ensuring their code would never be more than a mere copy of—and less important than—the game run by the parent body they had rejected. And so, changes were made.

The Challenge Cup was introduced in 1896 and the bold move paid off so handsomely that modern finals have drawn more than 100 000 fans. The method of scoring was first altered in 1897, with three points for a try and two for a goal—no matter what kind. The values remained unchanged until 1972, when a field goal was again reduced—this time to just one point. In 1983 the value of a try was increased to four. Line-outs and loose rucks were abolished.

The major change came in 1898, when professionalism was allowed for the first time, eventually leading to an undreamed of situation. Today, top players in both Australia and Britain receive hundreds of thousands of dollars for playing. However, Rugby League in France, New Zealand and Papua New Guinea remains virtually an amateur sport. Another huge change came in 1906, when the number of players in a team was reduced from 15 to 13, after 12-a-side trials had proved failures. This led to a more open, exciting style of play which helped attract bigger crowds.

Australia and New Zealand entered the Rugby League scene in 1907. When a small group of Rugby Union rebels sat down in a Sydney sports store that year, they not only paved the way for the introduction of a new sport in Australia, but decided on a new name for it—one eventually adopted by the rest of the world. Rugby League! The breakaway code was known in Great Britain as the Northern Rugby Football Union. The British persisted with this name until 1922 when they switched and joined the Australians.

The Australian split was the result of widespread unrest over the non-payment of compensation for injuries received on the Rugby field. This came to a head in 1907, when top forward Alec Burdon broke a shoulder and was incapacitated for a long time, with a loss of earnings and medical costs which caused him great financial stress. The Rugby Union authorities refused his claim for compensation and the revolution began.

Burdon was one of the group which met in a room over the sports store owned by Test cricketer Victor Trumper. Others included James J Giltinan, a sporting identity well-known in cricket and horse-racing circles, and Harry Hoyle, a politician who later became the NSW Minister for Railways.

Initially, the breakaway was not popular. The Press and a large section of the general public were openly hostile. The Rugby Union threatened life suspensions of anyone associated with the new movement. But it was all to no avail. A group of top players was gathered together to play three matches against the New Zealand All Golds, en route to Britain for the first-ever international Rugby League tour. The matches were played under Rugby Union rules, as neither side knew the new ones of the breakaway English code. The three matches were a great success, yielding 200 pounds profit. With this cash, the NSW Rugby League was formed and a constitution drafted.

The League held its inaugural meeting in 1908, with Hoyle becoming the first president, Trumper treasurer and Giltinan the secretary. A few months later the first competition matches were played with nine teams involved—Balmain, Cumberland, Eastern Suburbs, Glebe, Newcastle, Newtown, North Sydney, South Sydney and Western Suburbs. At the end of the 1908 season, the League threw caution to the wind and sent a touring side to Britain. Giltinan managed the 36 players.

The tour almost proved a disaster. The Australians played 45 games, of which they won 18 and drew six, but were hit financially by a crippling cotton mills strike which laid idle a large percentage of the working people of northern England. The out-of-work fans had little enough money for food, rent and clothing—let alone spare cash to pay their way through the turnstiles. The tourists often had to make do on short rations, and they rarely had any spending money. However the tour proved to be a real turning point for Australian Rugby League. Visiting Great Britain at the same time was the Australian Wallabies Rugby Union side. Secret overtures made to the lilywhites were accepted.

When they returned home, the bulk of the Wallabies switched codes en masse, accepting a guarantee of 100 pounds per man to take the field in a series of matches against the Kangaroos. The teams for those matches were:

Kangaroos—Webby Neill, Charlie Hedley, Frank Cheadle, Bill Heidke, Dally Messenger, Albert Broomham, Arthur 'Pony' Halloway, Arthur Butler, Bill Cann, Alec Burdon, Sandy Pearce, Bill Noble, James Davis and Tedda Courtney.

Wallabies—Bill Dix, Edward Mandible, John Hickey, Bill and Viv Farnsworth, Charles 'Boxer' Russell, Arthur McCabe, Chris McKivat, Charles McMurtrie, Jack 'Jumbo' Barnett, Ken Gavin, Bob Craig, Peter Burge and Albert 'Son' Burge.

The series attracted huge crowds and Rugby League's future was assured.

In 1934, following troubles within the French Rugby Union, League seized the opportunity to spread its wings to another country.

Later attempts to promote the code in South Africa and Italy were failures, although a South African competition did get underway and a national side toured Australasia in 1963 (losing badly to Australia, but upsetting New Zealand in their only encounter). Papua New Guinea was admitted to the International Rugby League in 1974 and played it first international the following year against England (going down 40–12) and its first Test on the 1979 tour of France and England (beaten by France, 15–9).

A World Cup competition was introduced in 1954. These competitions (including two World Championships) have been held at irregular intervals since then, with Australia and Great Britain dominating. Of the nine played by the 1990s, Australia won six and Britain three.

As the 1990s dawned attempts were being made to nurture the sport in the Soviet Union. Three Soviet clubs visited England in 1990 for specialised coaching and the following year a club competition began behind what had been, for four decades, the Iron Curtain. In October 1991, the Soviet Union played its first international, losing 26–6 to France, at Lyon. And with the abolition of Apartheid in South Africa, new efforts were being made to rekindle the interest there.

LANDMARKS IN THE HISTORY OF RUGBY LEAGUE⸻

1893 — A Yorkshire proposal that players be compensated for genuine loss of time was defeated 282 votes to 136 at the annual meeting of the English Rugby Union.

1895 — Twelve of the leading clubs resigned their membership of the Yorkshire Rugby Union (29 July). They and 10 others from Yorkshire and Lancashire formed the Northern Rugby Union (August 29) allowing payment of players on a compensation basis only.

— The first 10 matches (with all clubs except Huddersfield and Oldham competing) took place on 7 September.

1897 — The first Challenge Cup competition was held, with Batley beating St Helens 10–3 in the final at Headingley, Leeds.

— The value of field goals and penalty goals was reduced to two points.

1898 — Professionalism was made legal (19 July).

1903 — A proposal that the size of teams be reduced to 12 players was supported by the majority of the clubs. But the voting (52–24) was less that the 75 per cent required by the rules.

1906 — The number of players in a side was reduced to 13. The first 13-a-side matches took place on 1 September. Play-the-ball was introduced to replace loose mauls.

1907 — Top Australian forward Alec Burdon broke his shoulder in a Rugby Union match. Refusal to pay compensation for medical expenses and time lost at work prompted a series of meetings which led to the start of Rugby League in Australia.

— Three matches were arranged (17, 21 and 24 August) between New South Wales and the New Zealand All Golds, en route to Britain for the first-ever international tour.

1908 — On January 9, Glebe became the first Rugby League club formed in Australia. It was quickly followed by Newtown, South Sydney, Balmain, Eastern Suburbs, Western Suburbs, North Sydney, Cumberland and Newcastle.

— The first Test match took place at Headingley, Leeds, on 25 January, with Britain beating the touring New Zealand side 14–6. They had played a non-Test international at Wigan two weeks earlier. England won that match 18–16.

— At the end of the All Golds tour, Edgar Wrigley became the first overseas player to sign with a British club—joining Huddersfield.

— The All Golds played in Queensland's first matches on their way back to New Zealand.

— The first Australian interstate matches were held. New South Wales beat Queensland in all three.

— South Sydney won the first Sydney Premiership. Eastern Suburbs was runner-up.

— The first Kangaroo tour of Britain began with a match against Mid Rhonda at Tonypandy on 3 October. Australia won 20–6.

— On 18 November, the first non-Test Anglo-Australian international was played at Everton. Australia won 19–9 before a crowd of 7000.

— The first Anglo-Australian Test match was played on 12 December, at Park Royal, London. Australia and Great Britain drew 22–all. Britain won the remaining two Tests to take out the first Ashes series.

1909 __ Back in Australia, the Kangaroos played four matches against a team drawn from the Wallabies Rugby Union side which had been touring Britain at the same time as the League stars. The games were shared two a piece.

__ Tweed Heads Seagulls became the first provincial club formed in Australia.

__ The first inter-city match in Queensland was played on 9 October, with Brisbane downing Ipswich 43–10.

__ Valleys won the first Brisbane Premiership.

1910 __ The first match by a Great Britain side in Australia was played on 4 June, in Sydney, against New South Wales. A fortnight later, the tourists won the first Anglo-Australian Test match in Australia at the RAS Showground in Sydney, 27–20.

__ The first match in New Zealand for a British side was at Auckland, on 20 July, against a Maori XIII. Britain won its first Test in New Zealand 10 days later, 52–20.

1911 __ The first Rugby League game played on the Sydney Cricket Ground took place on June 22.

__ Billy and Viv Farnsworth became the first brothers to play for Australia against Great Britain.

1913 __ The Northern Rugby Union banned English clubs from signing Australian and New Zealand players, unless they had lived in England for two years.

1914 __ The match dubbed the Rorke's Drift Test was played at the Sydney Cricket Ground. Because of injuries during the game, Britain finished with only 10 men, but still won 14–6.

1920 __ Brisbane forward Bill Richards became the first Australian to be sent off in a Test match—charged with tripping British winger Squire Stockwell during the Third Test, at the RAS Showground in Sydney.

__ Oldham's Joseph Platt retired as secretary of the Northern Rugby Football Union, having held the post since its inception.

1921 __ St George entered the Sydney Premiership competition.

1922 __ The Northern Rugby Football Union changed its name to the Rugby Football League, following the advice offered by the NSW Rugby League three years earlier.

1924 __ New South Wales and Queensland formed the Australian Board of Control.

__ The final of the Sydney Premiership, in which South Sydney beat Balmain 3–0, was the first Rugby League match broadcast on radio (Ironically, the commentator was the Balmain secretary Bob Savage).

1927 __ Seven of the New Zealand touring side, who had gone on strike during the just-completed visit to Britain, were, on 2 March, suspended for life by the NZ Rugby Football League.

__ The first radio broadcast of an English match took place when Swinton and Oldham met in the Cup Final at Wigan on 7 May.

1928 __ Australia first wore its now traditional green and gold colours, in the First Test against Great Britain, in Brisbane, on 23 June.

— Western Suburbs became the first Sydney club to use an animal for its nickname and logo. Wests, previously known as 'The Fruitpickers' became 'The Magpies'.

1929 — The first Challenge Cup Final staged at Wembley Stadium was played on 4 May, Wigan beating Dewsbury 13–2.

1929 — Glebe, the first club formed in Australia, was sacked from the Sydney Premiership.

1930 — A fourth Test was played between Great Britain and Australia, at Rochdale on 15 January, the only time a four-Test series has taken place. The extra Test followed a controversial draw in the third, and would-be deciding, game. The British won the Fourth Test 3–0.

1933 — The first Rugby League game in France saw Australia beat England 63–13 at the Stade Pershing, Paris, on 31 December.

1934 — France made its first tour of England in March. On 15 April, the two countries played their first international, in Paris. England won 32–21.

1935 — Canterbury-Bankstown entered the Sydney Premiership competition.

1938 — The first Franco-Australian Test match was played in Paris on 2 January. The Australians triumphed 35–8.

1940 — Rugby League was banned in France by the wartime Vichy Government because the French Rugby League authorities were considered sympathetic to Britain.

1945 — The first chairman of the Northern Rugby Football Union, HH Waller, was the sole survivor of the 1895 breakaway when the 50th anniversary of the League's formation was celebrated on 29 August.

1947 — The British Rugby League Council imposed another ban on the transfer of players between clubs in Australia and England.

— Manly-Warringah and Parramatta entered the Sydney Premiership competition.

1948 — The International Board of Rugby League was formed at a meeting in Bordeaux, France, on 23 January.

1950 — Australia won the Ashes for the first time in 30 years when it beat Britain 5–2 in the third and deciding Test, at the Sydney Cricket Ground, on 22 July.

1951 — France opened its first tour of Australia on 23 May, with a 37–12 victory over Monaro, at Canberra. The Frenchmen went on to win the first Test series in Australia, two games to one. The First Test between Great Britain and New Zealand, at Swinton on 10 November, was the first Rugby League match televised.

1953 — The American Allstars side opened its tour of Australia on 27 May, with a 34–25 victory against a combined Southern NSW and Monaro side at Canberra. It was one of only three wins in 18 matches on a disappointing tour.

1954 — A world record attendance for a Rugby League match was set when 102 569 fans turned up at Odsal Stadium, Bradford, on 5 May, to see the Warrington-Halifax Cup Final replay.

— The only international match ever abandoned was played at the Sydney Cricket Ground on 10 July, between Great Britain and New South Wales. Referee Aubrey Oxford walked off midway through the second half, during a brawl involving most of the 26 players.

— The first Rugby League World Cup was held in France during October and November. Britain beat France in the final.

1956 — The first referees' strike occurred in Brisbane on the weekend of 1–2 September. They were protesting against 'lenient' treatment of players ordered from the field. Strike-breaking referees were brought in, but the clubs would not play under their control.

— Tiger Black of 2KY made the first Test radio broadcast from England back to Australia.

1957 — Australia celebrated 50 years of Rugby League by staging and winning the second World Cup.

— The first match played in South Africa took place on 20 July when France and Great Britain, returning home from the World Cup, played an exhibition at Benoni.

1961 — Channel 9 made the first live telecast of an Australian match (between Balmain and North Sydney, at North Sydney Oval).

1963 — South Africa, making its one and only overseas tour, to Australia and New Zealand, was soundly beaten two Tests to nil by Australia, but upset New Zealand 4–3 in their only Test.

1965 — The Australian attendance record was set when 78 056 fans were counted through the turnstiles to see South Sydney and St George fight out the grand final of the Sydney Premiership. Many thousands more scaled the walls of the Sydney Cricket Ground after its gates were closed. The figure will not be bettered as all major matches are now played at the Sydney Football Stadium which has a ground capacity of just under 42 000.

1967 — Penrith and Cronulla-Sutherland entered the Sydney Premiership competition.

1970 — Head-high tackles were outlawed.

1971 — The six-tackle rule was introduced in the Sydney Premiership competition.

1971 — The value of a field goal was reduced from two points to one.

1972 — The first drawn final of a World Cup saw Australia and Great Britain locked 10–all at the end of their game at Lyon, France. An extra 10 minutes each way was played with no change in the score. Britain as awarded the Cup because of a better record in the preliminary matches.

1974 — Papua New Guinea was admitted to the International Board of Rugby League.

1975 — The six-tackle rule was accepted by all countries. Differential penalties for scrum offences were introduced.

— Decision was made that all future Test matches would have neutral referees.

1977 — St George and Parramatta were involved in the first drawn grand final of the Sydney Premiership competition. Their scores were still equal (9-all) after extra time. The decider was played a week later and St George won 22–0.

1979 — Papua New Guinea made its first tour of France and Britain, losing to France in the only two Tests played.

1980 — The first State-of-Origin match was played, at Lang Park, Brisbane. Queensland won 20–10.

1982 — The Kangaroos became the first Australian side to go through a tour of Britain and France unbeaten.

— Illawarra and Canberra entered the Sydney Premiership competition.

1983 — Wide-ranging rule changes were introduced—the value of a try was raised to four points; lock-forwards were required to always bind into the scrum; halfbacks had to roll the ball into the scrum; referees could send players to the sin-bin for minor or technical offenses; and, after the sixth tackle the player had to hand the ball over to an opponent.

— Newtown and Western Suburbs were sacked from the Sydney Premiership because of financial problems. Wests took the NSW Rugby League to court and won the right to stay in the competition. The NSWRL changed its constitution to become an incorporated body with the right to sack teams. In future, all clubs would have to re-apply each year for a place in the competition.

1985 — Brisbane five-eighth Wally Lewis became the first winner of the Adidas Golden Boot as the best player in the world.

1988 — Brisbane, Newcastle and the Gold Coast entered the Sydney Premiership competition.

— The 100th Anglo-Australian Test match was played at the Sydney Football Stadium.

— Western Suburbs relocated its headquarters to Orana Park, Campbelltown (later renamed the Campbelltown Sports Ground).

— Billy Batten, Brian Bevan, Billy Boston, Alex Murphy, Jonty Parkin, Gus Risman, Albert Rosenfeld, Jim Sullivan and Harold Wagstaff became the first nine players inducted into the British Rugby League Hall of Fame, at Oulten, near Leeds.

1989 — Canberra became the first side based outside the Sydney metropolitan area to win the Sydney Premiership.

1990 — A salary cap was imposed on all teams in the Sydney Premiership. Canberra and Parramatta were forced to sack players after exceeding the cap.

— Papua New Guinea scored its first Test victory over Great Britain, winning 20–18 at Goroka.

— The players' draft was introduced in the Sydney Premiership.

1991 — The Courts first ruled the Draft to be legal, but three Appeal judges overturned that decision.

— Canberra, in dire financial straits, was also fined for exceeding the salary cap.

— Penrith celebrated its 25th anniversary by winning its first Premiership.

— Australia made its first full tour of Papua New Guinea at the end of the domestic season.

— The Soviet Union played its first international, losing 26–6 to France, at Lyon.

1992 — First World Sevens tournament was held in Sydney.

WHEN LEAGUE AND AUSTRALIAN RULES NEARLY AMALGAMATED

In the early years of Rugby League in Australia there were moves for the new game to amalgamate with Australian Rules and produce a code of super football. JJ Giltinan, one of the League's founders and manager of the 1908–09 Kangaroos, first proposed the merger when he passed through Melbourne on his way back from the tour of Britain. Five top officials travelled to Melbourne in 1914 to confer with the Rules' hierarchy. After hours of discussion, a loose framework of rules for a new game was drawn up. The Melbournites agreed in principle to the inclusion of a cross-bar on the goalposts and there was an agreement on modification of League's knock-on and offside rules.

The outbreak of World War I brought all negotiations to a halt, but the amalgamation scheme was revived in 1933. NSW Rugby League secretary Horrie Miller conferred with Con Hickey, secretary of the Australian National Football League. They agreed in principle that 'the laws of the game of both codes might be open to improvement and that the present isolation and administration are not economically sound'. The two men proposed a single game which could be 'just as common to the whole of Australia as the Laws of Cricket'.

Plans were made for further conferences among experts on the codes, but the talks did not eventuate. The two games remain separate and distinct.

JACK HOLLAND

Seven Tests for Australia (1948–1950). Also played 25 minor games for Australia on one Kangaroo tour (1948–49) and one New Zealand tour (1949).

Jack 'Dutchy' Holland had a perfect goalkicking record in Test football. The rugged St George forward took only one kick at goal during his international career—in the Second Test of the 1950 series against Great Britain—and it soared over the cross-bar. It was the only two points Holland ever notched in the Test arena. The no-nonsense Holland had made his Test debut two years earlier against the visiting New Zealanders. In the next 12 months he was to make two overseas tours—with the Kangaroos to Britain and France and across the Tasman to New Zealand. Undoubtedly the highlight of his career was the three Tests against the 1950 touring Lions, which saw Australia win the Ashes for the first time in 30 years. In club football Holland also achieved the ultimate as a member of the fine St George combination which won the Sydney Premiership in 1949, beating South Sydney in the grand final 19–12.

KEITH HOLMAN

Thirty-two Tests for Australia (1950–1958). Also played three matches in two World Cups (1954 and 1957), two minor internationals (1954) and 18 minor games on two Kangaroo tours (1952–53 and 1956–57) and one New Zealand tour (1953).

Keith Holman was one of the greatest halfbacks to represent Australia. He appeared in 32 Tests (in 12 series), made two Kangaroo tours, toured New Zealand and played in the first two World Cups. When he played in all three Tests against Britain in 1958 (his last international appearances), Holman took his tally of Anglo-Australian internationals to 14, a record which beat that of Clive Churchill and Sandy Pearce. Holman was only 1.68m (5ft 6in) tall and 73kg (11st 7lb), an ideal type of halfback for international clashes. He was rugged, determined and the fiercest of tacklers.

As a club player, Holman received the rare honour of being made a life member of Western Suburbs while still a player, yet, early in his career, no club, including Wests, wanted him. In 1947, he tried out with several Sydney teams, and when none expressed any interest, he went to the country town of Dubbo for a season. In 1948, Wests finally acquired his services, but Holman still attracted little attention, spending all but one match in reserve grade. He was the Magpies' top half in 1949. Then, in the following season, he made his meteoric rise into international football, being chosen for the Test side even though he had been overlooked for the City-Country and NSW-Queensland representative clashes. From then, until the 1958 series, he remained as Australia's top halfback.

Keith Holman

As well as his 14 Tests against Great Britain, Holman played 12 against France and six versus New Zealand. In all these he scored 14 tries and kicked six goals (for 54 points). Holman was named NSW Player-of-the-Year three times (in 1951, 1956 and 1958).

After he retired as a player, Holman switched to refereeing and graduated to control the Test matches when New Zealand toured in 1972. In that same year, he was awarded the MBE for his services to Rugby League. He also had a brief career as a coach, guiding his beloved Magpies to success in the midweek Amco Cup in 1977.

When Australia and New Zealand played exhibition games in the United States in 1954, Keith Holman was named Man-of-the-Series. For this he was awarded the Dick Hyland Trophy, named after the man who captained the 1924 US gold medal-winning Olympic Rugby Union team. Holman however never received the trophy, and to this day no one knows what happened to it.

HAROLD HORDER

Thirteen Tests for Australia (1914–1924). Also played in 24 minor matches on one Kangaroo tour (1921–22) and one New Zealand tour (1919).

Harold Horder was a genius in attack—fast, elusive, with a bewildering side-step and swerve. Many critics rate him as Australia's greatest Test winger. Horder was a phenomenal goalkicker, too. On the King's Birthday Holiday weekend in 1915, he scored 60 points for New South Wales in two matches against Queensland, five tries and eight goals on Saturday and seven goals on Monday.

Horder's first taste of international football came as an 18–year-old when he toured New Zealand with the 1913 NSW side. His best effort on tour was a five-try scoring spree against Auckland. Next year, he played for the Metropolis XIII against the touring Englishmen and followed that up with his first Test appearance. He toured New Zealand again in 1919. And try-scoring was the order of the day—Horder scored two tries in each of the First and the Third Tests and three in the Fourth Test. His 52 points on tour was second only to the 64 scored by the great Frank Burge. Then came the 1921–22 Kangaroos. That was an incredibly successful trip for Horder. He starred in all three Tests and topped the visitors' scoring with 127 points (35 tries and 11 goals) in 25 games.

On the club scene, when North Sydney carried all before it in 1921, Horder finished the season with a personal tally of 164 points (18 tries and 55 goals) from just 18 outings. He was a member of Norths' Premiership side the following season, too, but when, in 1923, he and his try-scoring partner on the other wing, Cec Blinkhorn, switched to South Sydney (from where Horder had originally come), Norths' form slumped and they missed the semi-finals. During a career which stretched over 15 seasons, Horder amassed a remarkable (especially for those days when there were fewer matches) 1725 points, scoring 307 tries and kicking 268 goals.

DICK HUDDART

Sixteen Tests for Great Britain (1958–1963). Also played in 28 minor games for Britain on two Australian tours (1958 and 1962).

The great English lock-forward Vince Karalius was in awe of his St Helens' team-mate Dick Huddart. Said Karalius: 'He is the best attacking forward I have ever seen in my life'. And few would disagree. Huddart's runs from the rucks would send opponents bouncing off him like fallen nine-pins. The big, fast Cumbrian second-rower first attracted attention at Whitehaven and the tall (1.9m) 21–year-old was one of the young Turks who came of age on the 1958 Lions tour down-under. His 17 tries on tour ensured his swap to the powerful St Helens lineup. He was to go on to play 16 Tests for Britain (seven each against Australia and New Zealand and two against France) and make a second trip to Australasia (in 1962, when he scored 13 tries).

On the club scene, he won the Lance Todd Trophy as Man-of-the-Match in the 1961 Challenge Cup Final, against neighbours Wigan. After the series against the 1963 Kangaroos he decided to cash in on his talents and move to Australia. St George paid a $12 500 transfer fee for the champion— a huge figure by Australian standards in those days. At the time, the Dragons were in the latter stages of their world record 11 straight Premierships. Injuries to a troublesome knee forced Huddart to miss St George's Premiership successes in 1964 and 1965, but the following year he played every match and tasted victory as St George thrashed Balmain 23-4 in the grand final.

HULL

One of Britain's most famous clubs, Hull, sent a team to Australasia in 1983—only the second club to make such a tour—but there were not enough players to cover injuries and the tour was almost a disaster. As it was, Hull won only one of its four games and, except for a game against Auckland, failed to draw decent crowds.

Record in New Zealand

Played 2, Drawn 1, Lost 1, Points for 32, Points against 44

Match Results

Opponents	Venue (Attendance)	For	Against
Auckland	Auckland (11 500)	28	28
Maoris	Huntly (3000)	4	16

Record in Australia
Played 2, Won 1, Lost 1, Points for 32, Points against 44

Match Results

Newcastle	Newcastle (3860)	2	22
NSW Southern Division	Dapto (1500)	24	22

GRAEME HUGHES

Graeme Hughes was a fine all-round sportsman who represented New South Wales in both Sheffield Shield cricket and Rugby League. He decided to concentrate on League but unfortunately, he was plagued by injuries throughout his career and never achieved his full potential. Hughes played grade football for Canterbury-Bankstown for almost a decade in the late 1970s and early 1980s, until forced into premature retirement by a knee injury in 1984. In the meantime he had tasted grand final success in 1980 (with his brothers Mark and Garry, all products of a local junior club, Lakemba Brothers).

Once off the football field Graeme Hughes was to become even better known as a commentator for the Ten Network. The pinnacle of this new career was in 1990 when he called all matches on the British leg of the Kangaroo tour.

HUGH McINTOSH SHIELD

The Hugh McIntosh Shield was one of the first major trophies in Australian Rugby League. McIntosh, one of the country's most famous sporting promoters, is remembered as the man who built the Sydney Stadium and promoted the 1908 world heavyweight boxing championship between Jack Johnson and Tommy Burns. The Hugh McIntosh Shield was donated in 1914 and awarded to the Sydney Premiers. When Balmain won the Premiership three years in a row during World War I, it won the Shield outright.

Winners of the Hugh McIntosh Shield

Year	Winner
1914	South Sydney
1915	Balmain
1916	Balmain
1917	Balmain

FRANK HYDE

Frank Hyde was a top-class footballer in the 1930s and early 1940s. World War II robbed him of the chance to represent his country—although he did play for New South Wales. He was a member of Balmain's 1939 Premiership-winning side and steered North Sydney to the final in 1943, as captain-coach.

Hyde is best remembered as a radio and television commentator. For more than 20 years he broadcast club, representative and Test football for the Sydney radio station 2SM. His audience was greater than that of all the other stations put together for much of that period. For more than a decade, Hyde also appeared on a sports show on Sydney television station Channel 9.

During his long association with the code, Hyde figured as a club official, non-playing coach and referee. He was a pioneer organiser of supporters' tours to coincide with the Kangaroo and New Zealand sorties by the Australian sides and even recorded a best-selling sing-along record album.

I

ILLAWARRA

In late 1980, the NSW Rugby League took one of its most momentous decisions. It decided to accept an application by Illawarra to join the Sydney Premiership. Until then only teams in Sydney or its close environs had taken part in what most critics regard as the world's most important club competition. The League chiefs allowed Illawarra to quit the 'country' and join the big league in 1982.

Illawarra, covering the industrial cities of Wollongong and Port Kembla, just south of Sydney, had been one of the most successful of all the divisions under the control of the Country Rugby League. It had the best record of any against touring international teams (11 wins and one draw in 20 games) and it had won the Country Divisional Championship five times (1971, 1972, 1974, 1976 and 1978). The area had also produced Test players of the calibre of Brian Carlson, Mick Cronin, Bobby and Peter Dimond, Bob Fulton, Garry Jack, Graeme Langlands, Ian Moir, Noel Mulligan, Paul Quinn, Kev Schubert and Craig Young.

The last success in the Country Championship was the highlight of one of Illawarra's best seasons in country football. As well as winning the Country title (beating Newcastle 32–15 in the final, at Newcastle), it downed the New Zealand Kiwis 15–10 and reached the quarter-finals of the Amco Cup (the midweek knockout competition which, at the time, included country divisional sides). Coach that year was former British Test halfback Tommy Bishop, who capped a fine year by coaching Western Suburbs to success in the Illawarra Premiership.

Despite having the services of several fine coaches, including Allan Fitzgibbon, Brian Smith, Terry Fearnley and Ron Hilditch, Illawarra has never managed to make any real impact since joining the Sydney Premiership. The first year, the Steelers, as they are known, finished in front of only one other side. Three times since then they have earned the wooden spoon (1985, 1986 and 1989). Their best season was 1984, when they finished eighth out of 13. Centre Brian Hetherington made the NSW side that year.

In 1989, there was an almost fairytale run in the midweek competition, the Panasonic Cup. Bolstered by top English players Andy Gregory and Steve Hampson, Illawarra beat, in turn, Western Suburbs (12–0), Cronulla-Sutherland (40–0) and North Sydney (12–all, on countback) to reach the final. There the Steelers went down narrowly to a star-studded Brisbane Broncos outfit, 22–20.

In 1990, Illawarra won only six of its first 15 matches, but came home under a wet sail, to lose only one of its last seven games. Among the stars were young lock Ian Russell and the Steeler's captain, prop Chris Walsh, who both finished in the top five in the voting for the Rothmans Medal. Winger Rod Wishart was one of the season's top scorers.

The following year, the Steelers looked likely to reach the semi-finals for the first time when, midway through the season they were in fourth spot. But a poor run home saw their hopes fade.

Wishart achieved the distinction of becoming the club's first Test player, when he was called up for the last two clashes with New Zealand. He also toured Papua New Guinea at the end of the season.

Former NSW State-of-Origin winger Alan McIndoe topped the 1991 Sydney tryscoring lists with 19 touchdowns, taking his career total for Illawarra to a record 57.

Illawarra
Founded: 1981
Entered Sydney Premiership: 1982
Home ground: Wollongong Showground (Record crowd: 15 296)
Colours: Scarlet and white
Nickname: The Steelers
Honours:
   Sydney Premiership—Nil
   President's Cup—1984
   SG Ball Cup—1989
   Harold Matthews Cup—1987
Most first-grade games: 145 by Michael Bolt
Most points in a career: 463 by John Dorahy
Most tries in a career: 57 by Alan McIndoe
Most points in a season: 175 by John Dorahy, in 1983
Most tries in a season: 19 by Alan McIndoe, in 1991

INTER-DISTRICT COMPETITION see *Second Division*

INTERNATIONAL FOOTBALL

Australia has played a host of internationals other than Test matches and World Cup and World Championship games. Often, like the games against Wales, they take place on Kangaroo tours. Others, as with several against France occur, after World Cup contests. Twice, in 1957 and 1988, Australia has played a team chosen from the best players in the Rest-of-the-World.

Only two players, the St George team-mates from the early 1960s, Reg Gasnier and Graeme Langlands, have played 40 or more internationals for Australia. Gasnier has the most Tests to his credit—36. Langlands however, by virtue of 11 World Cup and Championship games in 1968, 1972 and 1975, has the biggest overall total—45. Langlands is also the highest point-scorer for Australia in international football.

Most Full International Matches for Australia

	Tests	World Series Games	Other Internationals *	Total
Graeme Langlands	34	11	—	45
Reg Gasnier	36	3	1	40
Johnny Raper	33	6	—	39
Clive Churchill	34	3	—	37
Bob Fulton	19	15	2	36
Keith Holman	32	3	—	35
Ken Irvine	31	2	—	35
Mick Cronin	22	11	2	35
Wally Lewis	33	1	2	36
Brian Davies	27	6	1	34
Tom Raudonikis	23	9	1	33
Ken Kearney	25	6	1	32
Harry Wells	21	8	2	31
Mal Meninga	34	—	1	35
Arthur Beetson	14	14	1	29
Barry Muir	26	3	—	29
Noel Kelly	25	3	1	29
Billy Smith	18	8	1	27
Kerry Boustead	25	—	1	26
Roy Bull	22	3	—	25
Steve Rogers	21	3	1	25
Brian Carlson	17	6	2	25
Graham Eadie	14	8	2	24
Duncan Hall	22	1	—	23
Ian Walsh	22	—	—	22
Ray Price	22	—	—	22
Garry Jack	20	1	1	22
Brian Hambly	18	3	—	21
Ron Coote	10	9	1	20
Craig Young	20	—	—	20
Steve Roach	19	1	1	21

* Matches played against France, England and Wales which were not Test matches and games against the Rest-of-the-World.

Top Australian Point-scorers in All Test and World Series Matches

	T	G	FG	Pts
Mick Cronin	9	140	—	307
Graeme Langlands	20	73	—	206
Michael O'Connor	17	65	—	198
Mal Meninga	15	85	—	220
Noel Pidding	6	61	—	140
Ken Irvine	33	11	—	121
Keith Barnes	—	59	—	118
Brian Carlson	16	21	—	90
Eric Simms	2	42	—	87
Reg Gasnier	28	—	—	84
Bob Fulton	24	—	6	79
Dave Brown	7	26	—	73
Les Johns	2	30	—	66
Keith Holman	14	6	—	54
Harold Horder	11	10	—	53
Kerry Boustead	15	—	—	46
Graham Eadie	7	12	—	45
Wally Lewis	11	—	2	45
Dally Messenger	4	16	—	44
Garry Jack	11	—	—	44
Johnny Graves	5	14	—	43

Top Australian Point-scorers in All Matches
(including Kangaroo and New Zealand tour games)

	T	G	Pts
Graeme Langlands	39	195	507
Mick Cronin	19	209	495
Brian Carlson	74	84	393
Noel Pidding	30	150	382
Dave Brown	31	143	379
Mal Meninga	41	177	500
Michael O'Connor	46	109	310
Ken Irvine	96	19	320
Keith Barnes	—	140	280
Greg Alexander	26	60	226
Reg Gasnier	65	3	201

Australia's International Footballers

(The years in brackets specify the period in which the player represented Australia. Internationals are clashes with the Rest-of-the-World, or matches with Wales, England or France which were not Tests or World Series games. Tour games refer to all other matches while on tour)

Abercrombie, Jim (1908–09): 2 Tests, 30 tour games
Adams, Don (1956): 5 Tests, 13 tour games
Alexander, Greg (1986–89): 6 Tests, 26 tour games
Ambrum, George (1972): 2 Tests
Anderson, Chris (1975–82): 8 Tests, 3 World Championship matches, 1 International, 23 tour games
Anderson, Tommy (1908–09): 1 Test, 5 tour games
Anderson, Vic (1909): 1 Test
Andrews, Ned (1950): 1 Test
Anlezark, Arthur (1908–09): 1 Test, 16 tour games
Armbruster, Vic (1924–30): 8 Tests, 16 tour games
Armstrong, Jim (1946): 1 Test
Asher, Albert (NZ) (1910): 2 Internationals
Ashton, Ferris (1952–53): 8 Tests, 21 tour games
Ayliffe, Royce (1981): 1 Test
Aynsley, Cec (1924–28): 4 Tests

Backo, Sam (1988–89): 6 Tests, 1 International, 3 tour games
Bailey, Bill (1908–09): 3 Tests
Bailey, Ron (1946): 2 Tests
Baird, Eddie (1908): 1 Test
Banks, Gary (1966): 1 Test
Banks, Bob (1953–62): 13 Tests, 2 World Cup matches, 16 tour games
Barnes, Keith (1959–66): 14 Tests, 3 World Cup matches, 16 tour games
Barnett, Jack (1910): 2 Tests
Beath, Barry (1965–71): 7 tour games
Beaton, Jack (1936–38): 8 Tests, 22 tour games
Beattie, Dud (1959–62): 12 Tests, 3 World Cup matches, 1 International, 23 tour games
Beavan, Ray (1961): 4 tour games
Beetson, Arthur (1966–77): 14 Tests, 14 World Cup & Championship matches, 1 International and 10 tour games
Belcher, Gary (1988–91): 15 Tests, 21 tour games
Bella, Martin (1986–91): 8 Tests, 26 tour games
Bennett, Jim (1924): 3 Tests
Bennett, Wayne (1971): 2 tour games
Benton, Henry (1948–49): 10 tour games
Berecry, Tom (1911–12): 1 Test, 12 tour games
Bichell, Henry (1935): 2 tour games
Bishop, George (1929–30): 2 Tests, 13 tour games
Blair, Alf (1924): 1 Test
Blinkhorn, Cec (1921–24): 4 Tests, 26 tour games
Bliss, Johnny (1951): 1 Test
Boden, Ron (1959–60): 2 Tests, 1 World Cup match, 1 International, 1 tour game
Bolewski, Henry (1914): 1 Test
Bolewski, Mick (1908–09): 4 Tests, 30 tour games
Boustead, Kerry (1978–84): 25 Tests, 2 Internationals, 18 tour games
Boyd, Les (1978–82): 17 Tests, 20 tour games
Brackenreg, Herb (1909–10): 3 Tests, 2 Internationals
Bradstreet, Bill (1966): 1 Test
Branighan, Ray (1970–75): 8 Tests, 8 World Cup & Championship matches, 1 International, 12 tour games
Branson, Tony (1967–71): 6 Tests, 3 World Cup matches, 12 tour games
Brass, John (1970–75): 3 Tests, 3 World Championship matches
Brentnall, Greg (1980–83): 13 Tests, 13 tour games
Broadfoot, Neville (1920–22): 1 Test, 4 tour games
Brogan, Bill (1929–30): 3 Tests, 17 tour games
Broomham, Albert (1909–12): 5 Tests, 2 Internationals, 19 tour games
Brosnan, Eddie (1948–49): 1 Test, 17 tour games
Brown, Tony (1958–60): 7 Tests, 3 World Cup matches, 1 International
Brown, Dave (1933–36): 9 Tests, 31 tour games
   9 tour games
Brown, Dave (1983–84): 5 Tests
Brown, Edwin (1921–22): 4 tour games
Brown, Johnny (1970): 3 tour games
Brown, Ray (1982–83): 5 Tests, 10 tour games
Buckley, Edward (1910): 1 Test
Bugden, Bob (1959–60): 2 Tests, 5 tour games
Bulgin, Vic (1948–49): 23 tour games
Bull, Roy (1949–1956): 22 Tests, 3 World Cup matches, 36 tour games
Buman, Allan (1965–67): 2 Tests
Burdon, Alex (1908–09): 2 Tests, 24 tour games
Burge, Frank (1914–22): 13 Tests, 24 tour games
Burge, Peter (1911–12): 4 tour games
Burke, Peter (1959–60): 14 tour games
Busch, Joe (1928–30): 6 Tests, 15 tour games

Butler, Arthur (1908–09): 3 Tests, 23 tour games
Byrne, Hugh (1928): 1 Test

Campbell, Keith (1971): 1 Test, 1 tour game
Cann, Bill (1908–14): 8 Tests, 1 International, 8 tour games
Caples, Harry (1921–22): 2 Tests, 22 tour games
Carlson, Brian (1952–61): 17 Tests, 6 World Cup matches, 2 Internationals, 42 tour games
Carne, Willie (1991): 4 Tests, 8 tour games
Carroll, Mark (1990): 1 Test, 6 tour games
Carson, Bill (1962): 2 Tests
Carstairs, George (1921–22): 2 Tests, 15 tour games
Cartwright, John (1990–91): 4 Tests, 8 tour games
Cavanagh, Noel (1965): 3 tour games
Chapman, Darrell (1959–60): 18 tour games
Cheadle, Frank (1908–09): 5 Tests, 7 tour games
Christie, Bill (1932): 1 Test
Churchill, Clive (1948–56): 34 Tests, 3 World Cup matches, 54 tour games
Clay, Brian (1957–60): 5 Tests, 3 World Cup matches, 16 tour games
Cleal, Noel (1985–86): 8 Tests, 8 tour games
Cleary, John (1963–64): 14 tour games
Cleary, Mike (1962–69): 8 Tests, 25 tour games
Clifford, Gordon (1956–57): 8 Tests, 8 tour games
Close, Chris (1980–85): 3 Tests, 6 tour games
Clues, Arthur (1946): 3 Tests
Clyde, Bradley (1989–91): 8 Tests, 3 tour games
Collins, Eddie (1935–38): 9 tour games
Collinson, Arthur (1952–53): 3 Tests, 17 tour games
Conescu, Greg (1982–88): 9 Tests, 1 International, 9 tour games
Conlon, Albert (1908–09): 3 Tests, 7 tour games
Conlon, Ross (1984): 1 Test
Connell, Cyril (1956–57): 2 Tests, 14 tour games
Connell, Geoff (1967): 1 Test
Cooper, Lionel (1946): 3 Tests
Coote, Ron (1967–75): 13 Tests, 7 World Cup matches, 3 World Championship matches, 1 International, 16 tour games
Cootes, John (1969–70): 4 Tests, 3 World Cup matches, 1 International, 2 tour games
Corowa, Larry (1978–79): 2 Tests, 7 tour games
Costello, Ron (1969–71): 3 Tests, 1 World Cup match, 4 tour games
Courtney, Tedda (1908–1914): 11 Tests, 2 Internationals, 51 tour games
Cowie, Les (1949–53): 6 Tests, 30 tour games
Coyne, Gary (1991): 2 Tests, 2 tour games
Craig, Bob (1910): 7 Tests, 1 International, 28 tour games
Craig, Jimmy (1921–28): 7 Tests, 23 tour games
Crear, Steve (1977): 1 tour game
Crema, Angelo (1966): 1 Test
Crippen, Arch (1936): 3 Tests
Crocker, Mick (1950–55): 15 Tests, 17 tour games
Cronin, Mick (1973–82): 22 Tests, 11 World Championship matches, 2 Internationals, 23 tour games
Crowe, Ron (1961–66): 5 Tests, 5 tour games
Cubitt, Les (1919–22): 4 Tests, 8 tour games
Curran, Frank (1933–38): 10 Tests, 25 tour games
Currie, Tony (1988–89): 7 Tests, 2 tour games

Daley, Laurie (1990–91): 7 Tests, 3 tour games
Daley, Phil (1986–88): 3 Tests, 7 tour games
Darmody, Steve (1911–12): 7 tour games
Davidson, Les (1986–87): 4 Tests, 11 tour games
Davies, Brian (1951–58): 27 Tests, 6 World Cup matches, 2 Internationals, 31 tour games
Davis, James (1908–09): 3 Tests, 6 tour games
Dawson, Les (1937–38): 5 Tests, 19 tour games
Day, Ken (1961–64): 9 Tests, 17 tour games
Deane, Sid (1908–14): 5 Tests, 24 tour games
De Belin, Fred (1948–50): 8 Tests, 16 tour games
Delamere, Bill (1959–60): 19 tour games
Dempsey, Dan (1928–34): 7 Tests, 20 tour games
Denman, Jeff (1969): 3 tour games
Denny, Henry (1933–34): 8 tour games
Devereux, Jim (1908–09): 5 Tests, 29 tour games
Devery, Pat (1946): 3 Tests
Dickens, Harry (1909): 1 Test
Dimond, Peter (1958–66): 10 Tests, 18 tour games
Dimond, Bobby (1948–49): 15 tour games
Diversi, Peter (1954–55): 2 Tests, 2 World Cup matches
Dobbs, Alf (1908–09): 6 tour matches
Donnelly, John (1975–78): 1 Test, 3 World Championship matches
Donoghue, Denis (1951): 2 Tests
Donohoe, Col (1952–53): 2 Tests, 15 tour matches
Doonar, Frank (1933–34): 11 tour matches

Dorahy, John (1978): 2 Tests
Dore, Mickey (1908): 3 Tests
Dowling, Garry (1980): 2 Tests, 3 tour games
Dowling, Greg (1984–87): 12 Tests, 8 tour games
Doyle, Ian (1956–57): 7 Tests, 12 tour games
Doyle, Joe (1933–34): 1 Test, 20 tour games
Drake, Frank (1961–62): 2 Tests, 6 tour games
Drew, Bernie (1951–53): 3 Tests, 4 tour games
Duffin, George (1909): 1 Test
Duncan, Rees (1952–53): 2 Tests, 18 tour games
Dunn, Paul (1986–88): 6 Tests, 1 World Cup match, 6 tour games

Eadie, Graham (1973–1979): 12 Tests, 8 World Championship matches, 2 Internationals, 8 tour games
Eather, Trevor (1946): 1 Test
Edwards, Arthur (1928): 1 Test
Elford, John (1972): 2 Tests, 2 World Cup matches
Elias, Ben (1985–90): 5 Tests, 1 World Cup match, 9 tour games
Ella, Steve (1982–85): 4 Tests, 2 Internationals, 12 tour games
Ettingshausen, Andrew (1988–91): 15 Tests, 1 International, 9 tour games

Fahey, Terry (1975–81): 3 Tests, 3 World Championship matches
Fairall, Percy (1935–38): 5 Tests, 15 tour games
Farnsworth, Bill (1910–12): 4 Tests, 1 International, 11 tour games
Farnsworth, Viv (1910–20): 6 Tests, 2 Internationals, 26 tour games
Farrar, Andrew (1988): 1 World Cup match
Farrell, Frank (1946–48): 4 Tests
Ferguson, John (1985): 3 Tests, 2 tour games
Fewin, Harry (1920): 1 Test
Fifield, Cec (1929–30): 4 Tests, 18 tour games
Fihelly, Jack (1908–09): *
Finch, Harry (1929–30): 10 tour matches
Fittler, Brad (1990–91): 2 Tests, 11 tour games
Fitzgerald, Denis (1975–77): 5 World Championship matches, 1 tour game
Fitzsimmons, Brian (1967–71): 3 Tests, 1 World Cup match, 5 tour games
Flannery, Denis (1950–57): 13 Tests, 2 World Cup matches, 24 tour games
Folkes, Steve (1986–88): 5 Tests, 5 tour games
Folwell, Arthur (1933–34): 2 Tests, 19 tour games
Francis, Arthur (NZ) (1911–12): 2 Tests, 22 tour games
Fraser, Charles (1911–22): 11 Tests, 43 tour games
Frauenfelder, Eric (1924): 3 Tests
Frawley, Dan (1909–12): 7 Tests, 32 tour games
Frawley, Mick (1909): 1 Test
Freestone, Jim (1928): 1 Test
Froome, Keith (1948–49): 8 Tests, 16 tour games
Fullerton Smith, Wally (1983–88): 8 Tests, 1 International, 4 tour games
Fulton, Bob (1968–1978): 20 Tests, 11 World Cup matches, 4 World Championship matches, 2 Internationals, 22 tour games
Furner, Don (1956–57): 1 Test, 10 tour matches

Gallagher, Noel (1967–68): 2 Tests, 12 tour games
Gallagher, Peter (1963–68): 17 Tests, 27 tour games
Gardner, Fred (1933–34): 1 Test, 19 tour games
Gartner, Russel (1977): 2 World Championship matches
Gasnier, Reg (1959–68): 36 Tests, 3 World Cup matches, 1 international, 38 tour games
Gee, Andrew (1991): 1 tour game
Gee, Hec (1932): 3 Tests
Geelan, Col (1951–53): 8 Tests, 16 tour games
Gehrke, Bob (1961): 5 tour games
Geiger, Nick (1977): 4 World Championship matches
Gerard, Geoff (1978–83): 6 Tests, 8 tour games
Geyer, Mark (1990–91): 3 Tests, 10 tour games
Gibbs, Alf (1948–49): 5 Tests, 14 tour games
Gibbs, Jimmy (1933–38): 7 Tests, 34 tour games
Gibbs, John (1978): 3 tour games
Gil, Alan (1961–62): 6 tour games
Gilbert, Fred (1935–38): 4 Tests, 20 tour games
Gilbert, Herb (1911–19): 7 Tests, 29 tour games
Gill, Charlie (1952–53): 7 Tests, 23 tour games
Gillespie, David (1988–91): 7 Tests, 1 World Cup match, 10 tour games
Gillett, George (NZ) (1911–12): 5 tour games
Glasheen, Mick (1933–34): 2 tour games
Gleeson, Johnny (1964–68): 10 Tests, 20 tour games
Glover, Neville (1978): 2 Tests
Goldspink, Kevin (1967–68): 13 tour games
Goodwin, Ted (1972–73): 4 Tests, 6 tour games
Goodwin, Sid (1935): 3 Tests, 1 tour game
Gorman, Tommy (1924–30): 10 Tests, 18 tour games
Gourley, Scott (1991): 1 Test, 3 tour games
Grant, John (1972): 3 World Cup games

Grant, Bob (1970–72): 2 Tests, 2 tour games
Graves, Bob (1908–09): 6 Tests, 22 tour games
Graves, Johnny (1948–50): 7 Tests, 20 tour games
Gray, Bert (1920–22): 4 Tests, 4 tour games
Greaves, Johnny (1966–68): 8 Tests, 4 World Cup matches
Grice, John (1946): 2 Tests
Griffiths, Frank (1937–38): 10 tour games
Griffiths, Ron (1949): 3 tour games
Grothe, Eric (1982–84): 8 Tests, 10 tour games

Hagan, Bob (1962–63): 2 Tests
Hall, Duncan (1948–1955): 22 Tests, 1 World Cup match, 36 tour games
Hallett, Howard (1911–14): 6 Tests, 26 tour games
Halloway, Arthur (1908–1919): 10 Tests, 48 tour games
Hambly, Brian (1959–65): 18 Tests, 3 World Cup matches, 1 International, 40 tour games
Hamilton, Bill (1973): 8 tour matches
Hammerton, Ernie (1951): 1 Test, 11 tour games
Hancock, Michael (1989–90): 5 Tests, 8 tour games
Hancock, Rohan (1980–82): 3 Tests, 13 tour games
Hand, Nevyl (1948–49): 2 Tests, 12 tour games
Hanigan, Les (1967–68): 2 Tests, 11 tour games
Hansen, Kevin (1949–52): 1 Test, 6 tour games
Hardcastle, Bill (1908–09): 2 Tests, 1 International, 6 tour games
Hardy, Nelson (1928): 3 Tests
Harris, Mark (1970–77): 1 Test, 5 World Cup matches, 5 World Championship games, 1 International,
    2 tour games
Harrison, Earl (1963–64): 9 Tests, 13 tour games
Hasler, Des (1985–91): 12 Tests, 1 International, 23 tour games
Hauff, Paul (1991): 1 Test
Hawick, Greg (1952–57): 6 Tests, 3 World Cup matches, 2 Internationals, 19 tour games
Hawke, Johnny (1948–51): 6 Tests, 24 tour games
Hawthorne, Phil (1970): 3 Tests
Hazelton, Charlie (1937–38): 1 Test, 15 tour games
Hazzard, Noel (1951–54): 13 Tests, 17 tour games
Hedley, Charlie (1908–09): 3 Tests, 17 tour games
Heidke, Bill (1908–10): 4 Tests, 24 tour games
Heidke, Monty (1932–38): 9 Tests, 17 tour games
Henderson, Arthur (1929–30): 7 tour games
Hennessy, Arthur (1908–09): 2 Tests, 7 tour games
Henry, Darcy (1955–56): 2 Tests
Hey, Vic (1933–36): 6 Tests, 23 tour games
Hickey, Jack (1910): 2 Tests
Higgs, Ray (1974–77): 1 Test, 8 World Championship matches, 1 International
Hilditch, Ron (1978–81): 3 Tests, 8 tour games
Hines, Ray (1935): 3 Tests, 2 tour games
Holland, Jack (1948–50): 7 Tests, 25 tour games
Holloway, Henry (1955): 3 Tests
Holman, Keith (1950–58): 32 Tests, 3 World Cup matches, 2 Internationals, 18 tour games
Holmes, Jack (1929–30): 12 tour games
Honan, Bob (1969): 2 Tests, 3 tour games
Hopkins, Bruce (1948–49): 13 tour games
Horder, Harold (1914–22): 13 Tests, 24 tour games
Hornery, Alan (1953): 5 tour games
Horrigan, Jack (1948–49): 1 Test, 19 tour games
Hunt, Johnny (1924): 2 Tests
Hutchinson, Jack (1946): 1 Test

Irvine, Ken (1959–70): 31 Tests, 2 World Cup matches, 2 Internationals, 68 tour games
Ives, Clarrie (1921–24): 1 Test, 6 tour games

Jack, Garry (1984–88): 20 Tests, 1 World Cup match, 1 International, 10 tour games.
Jackson, Peter (1988–91): 8 Tests, 6 tour games
James, Brian (1968): 1 World Cup match
Jarvis, Pat (1983): 1 Test
Johns, Chris (1990–91): 6 Tests, 13 tour games
Johns, Les: (1963–69): 14 Tests, 29 tour matches
Johnson, Frank (1948–49): 7 tour games
Johnston, Brian (1987): 1 Test
Johnston, Rick (1919–22): 8 Tests, 12 tour games
Johnston, Ian (1949–57): 1 Test, 13 tour games
Jones, Fred (1968–72): 3 World Cup matches
Jones, Lou (1908–09): 1 Test, 5 tour matches
Jorgensen, Joe (1946): 3 Tests
Junee, Kevin (1967–68): 10 tour games
Justice, Arthur (1928–30): 5 Tests, 11 tour games

Kadwell, Harry (1929–30): 8 tour games
Kay, Reg (1946): 3 Tests
Kearney, Ken (1952–57): 25 Tests, 6 World Cup matches, 1 International, 30 tour games

Kelly, Bill (1914): 1 Test
Kelly, Noel (1959–68): 25 Tests, 3 World Cup matches, 1 International, 43 tour games
Kennedy, Clem (1946): 1 Test
Kenny, Brett (1892–1986): 17 Tests, 16 tour games
Kerwick, Joe (1919): 3 tour games
King, Johnny (1966–70): 13 Tests, 2 World Cup matches, 13 tour games
Kingston, Jack (1928–30): 3 Tests, 24 tour games
Kiss, Les (1986): 4 Tests, 3 tour games
Kite, Ross (1955–58): 5 Tests
Kneen, Steve (1978): 6 tour games
Knight, Stephen (1972): 2 World Cup matches
Kolc, John (1977): 1 World Championship match
Krilich, Max (1978–1983): 13 Tests, 14 tour games

Laing, Bert (NZ) (1921–22): 10 tour matches
Laird, Graham (1955): 2 Tests
Laird, Ray (1970): 1 Test
Lamb, Terry (1986–88): 7 Tests, 1 World Cup match, 18 tour games
Lang, John (1973–80): 3 Tests, 5 World Championship matches, 1 International, 11 tour games
Langer, Alan (1988–91): 7 Tests, 1 World Cup match, 1 International, 10 tour games
Langlands, Graeme (1963–75): 34 Tests, 7 World Cup matches, 4 World Championship matches, 45 tour
  games
Langmack, Paul (1986): 10 tour games
Latta, Reg (1919–24): 5 Tests, 23 tour games
Laws, Fred (1928–34): 6 Tests, 28 tour games
Lazarus, Glenn (1990–91): 8 Tests, 11 tour games
Leis, Jim (1980): 3 tour games
Levison, Jack (1909): 1 Test
Lewis, Eric (1935–38): 9 Tests, 19 tour games
Lewis, Wally (1981–91): 33 Tests, 1 World Cup match, 19 tour games
Lindner, Bob (1986–91): 16 Tests, 11 tour games
Lisle, Jimmy (1962–65): 6 Tests, 17 tour games
Little, Jack (1932–34): 4 tour games
Lulham, Bobby (1948–49): 3 Tests, 16 tour games
Lumsden, Eddie (1959–63): 15 Tests, 27 tour games
Lumsden, Jack (1952): 1 Test
Lutge, Dinny (1908–09): 5 tour games
Lye, Graeme (1969): 3 tour matches
Lynch, Ron (1961–70): 12 Tests, 15 tour games
Lyons, Cliff (1990–91): 6 Tests, 7 tour games

McCabe, Paul (1981–83): 6 Tests, 10 tour matches
McCabe, Tom (1908–09): 2 Tests, 21 tour games
McCaffery, Ken (1953–57): 5 Tests, 3 World Cup matches, 1 International, 15 tour games
McCarthy, Bob (1969–74): 10 Tests, 5 World Cup matches, 12 tour games
McCoy, Matt (1949): 2 Tests, 5 tour games
McCrohon, Ken (1956): 1 Test
McCue, Paddy (1911–14): 4 Tests, 20 tour games
McDonald, John (1966–70): 13 Tests, 15 tour games
McDonald, Trevor (1959): 1 Test
McGaw, Mark (1988–91): 3 Tests, 1 World Cup match, 1 International, 6 tour games
McGovern, Des (1952–57): 7 Tests, 21 tour games
McGrath, Ted (1921–22): 16 tour matches
McGregor, Doug (1909–10): 2 Tests
McGuire, Bruce (1989–91): 2 Tests, 4 tour matches
McIndoe, Alan (1988): 1 International
Mackay, Ian (1975): 3 World Championship matches
Mackay, Brad (1990): 6 tests, 8 tour matches
McKean, Allan (1970): 1 Test
McKinnon, Don (1982): 10 tour matches
McKinnon, Ross (1935–38): 6 Tests, 28 tour games
McKivat, Chris (1910–12): 5 Tests, 2 Internationals, 29 tour games
McLean, Doug (1908): 1 Test
McLean, Doug (1937–38): 2 Tests, 8 tour games
MacLennan, Gordon (1937–38): 16 tour games
McMahon, Allan (1975–78): 5 World Championship matches, 15 tour games
McMahon, Pat (1948–49): 9 Tests, 23 tour matches
McMillan, Frank (1929–33): 9 Tests, 41 tour games
McMurtrie, Charlie (1911–12): 7 tour games
McRitchie, Doug (1948–49): 6 Tests, 10 tour games
McTaggart, Barry (1970): 1 World Cup match, 1 International, 2 tour games
Maddison, Ken (1973): 4 Tests, 9 tour matches
Madsen, Mick (1929–36): 9 Tests, 37 tour games
Maher, Pat (1928–30): 1 Test, 12 tour games
Mahon, Bill (1935): 1 Test, 3 tour games
Manteit, Dennis (1967–69): 3 Tests, 1 World Cup match, 12 tour games
Marsh, Bill (1956–58): 5 Tests, 3 World Cup matches, 1 International, 15 tour games
Martin, Steve (1978–80): 1 Test, 15 tour games

Masterman, Jeff (1981): 2 Tests
Maxwell, Col (1948–49): 1 Test, 11 tour games
Mayes, Johnny (1975): 3 World Championship matches
Mead, Les (1933–34): 1 Test, 14 tour games
Meninga, Mal (1982–91): 34 Tests, 1 International, 28 tour games
Messenger, Dally (1908–10): 7 Tests, 2 International, 29 tour games (also played 3 Tests for New Zealand)
Messenger, Wally (1914): 2 Tests
Middleton, Keith (1950): 3 Tests
Miles, Gene (1983–1988): 14 Tests, 2 Internationals, 19 tour games
Miller, Gavin (1988): 1 Test, 1 World Cup match, 1 International
Moir, Ian (1954–58): 8 Tests, 4 World Cup matches, 1 International, 14 tour games
Moore, Brian (1967–68): 11 tour games
Morgan, Jim (1970): 2 Tests
Morgan, John (1965): 2 Tests, 5 tour games
Morgan, Lionel (1960): 2 Tests, 1 World Cup match, 1 International, 1 tour game
Morris, Ray (1933): *
Morris, Rod (1977–82): 14 Tests, 23 tour games
Morris, Steve (1978): 2 Tests
Mortimer, Chris (1986): 1 Test, 9 tour games
Mortimer, Steve (1981–84): 8 Tests, 9 tour games
Morton, Andy (1908–09): 1 Test, 23 tour games
Mossop, Rex (1958–60): 9 Tests, 3 World Cup matches, 1 International, 22 tour games
Muggleton, John (1982): 3 Tests, 14 tour games
Muir, Barry (1959–64): 22 Tests, 3 World Cup games, 1 International, 23 tour games
Mulligan, Noel (1946–51): 10 Tests, 21 tour games
Murphy, Jim (1971–72): 1 Test, 2 tour games
Murray, Joe (1911–12): 7 tour games
Murray, Mark (1982–85): 6 Tests, 1 International, 11 tour games

Narvo, Herb (1937–38): 4 Tests, 18 tour games
Neill, Webby (1911–12): 9 tour games
Neumann, Fred (1932–34): 1 Test, 9 tour games
Newham, Edgar (1946): 2 Tests
Nicholson, Harry (1909–10): 2 Tests
Niebling, Bryan (1984–87): 13 Tests, 5 tour games
Noble, Bill (1909–12): 6 Tests, 13 tour games
Nolan, Fred (1937–38): 2 Tests, 9 tour matches
Norman, Ernie (1932–38): 12 Tests, 21 tour games
Norval, Andy (1937–38): 3 Tests, 12 tour games

O'Connell, Wally (1948–51): 10 Tests, 19 tour games
O'Connor, Alf (1924): 3 Tests
O'Connor, Frank (1932–34): 4 Tests, 14 tour games
O'Connor, Michael (1986–89): 16 Tests, 1 World Cup match, 1 International, 15 tour games
O'Donnell, Claude (1919): 4 Tests, 2 tour games
Oliphant, Greg (1978): 2 Tests, 4 tour games
Olling, Graham (1977–78): 4 Tests, 8 tour games
O'Malley, Larry (1908–09): 5 Tests, 31 tour games
O'Neill, John (1970–75): 2 Tests, 7 World Cup matches, 1 World Championhsip match, 5 tour games
O'Reilly, Bob (1970–74): 9 Tests, 7 World Cup matches, 1 International, 11 tour games
Orr, Warren (1973–74): 2 Tests, 8 tour games
Orrock, Bryan (1956–57): 2 Tests, 3 tour games
O'Shea, Kel (1954–58): 15 Tests, 5 World Cup matches, 1 International, 8 tour games
Owen, Bill (1961–62): 1 Test, 6 tour games
Oxford, Arthur (1919–24): 5 Tests, 1 tour game

Pannowitz, Terry (1965): 4 tour games
Papakura, Riki (NZ) (1910): 2 Internationals
Parcell, Gary (1959–62): 6 Tests, 3 World Cup matches, 16 tour games
Parish, Don (1959–61): 3 Tests, 17 tour games
Parkinson, Dave (1946): 3 Tests
Paten, Bill (1919–24): 2 Tests, 1 tour game
Paterson, Jim (1959–61): 8 Tests, 22 tour games
Paul, Albert (1952–53): 4 Tests, 25 tour games
Payne, Tom (1956–57): 1 Test, 12 tour games
Pearce, Cliff (1928–34): 7 Tests, 24 tour games
Pearce, Joe (1932–38): 11 Tests, 2 Internationals, 23 tour games
Pearce, Sandy (1908–22): 14 Tests, 49 tour games
Pearce, Wayne (1982–88): 18 Tests, 1 World Cup match, 1 International, 10 tour games
Peard, John (1975–78): 8 World Championship matches
Pegg, Len (1948–49): 2 Tests, 13 tour games
Peponis, George (1978–80): 8 Tests, 8 tour games
Peters, Herman (1921–22): 4 tour matches
Pickup, Tim (1972–75): 7 Tests, 4 World Championship matches
Pidding, Noel (1948–54): 16 Tests, 3 World Cup matches, 23 tour games
Pierce, Greg (1973–78): 3 Tests, 5 World Championship matches, 11 tour games
Pierce, Harry (1937–38): 5 Tests, 13 tour games
Piggins, George (1975): 3 World Championship matches

Pittard, Denis (1969–70): 2 Tests, 2 World Cup matches, 1 International, 3 tour games
Platz, Greg (1978): 1 Test
Platz, Lew (1975): 6 World Championship matches
Poole, Dick (1955–57): 10 Tests, 3 World Cup matches, 1 International, 11 tour games
Pope, Norm (1956): 1 Test
Porter, Jim (1975): 2 World Championship matches
Potter, Norm (1919–24): 7 Tests, 12 tour games
Prentice, Clarrie (1919–22): 5 Tests, 26 tour games
Price, Ray (1978–84): 22 Tests, 16 tour games
Prigg, Wally (1929–38): 19 Tests, 70 tour matches
Provan, Norm (1954–60): 14 Tests, 4 World Cup matches, 1 International, 12 tour games
Provan, Peter (1963): 1 Test
Purcell, Bernie (1950–57): 1 Test, 7 tour games

Quayle, John (1975): 2 World Championship matches, 2 tour games
Quinn, Graham (1980): 1 Test, 5 tour games
Quinn, Paul (1963–65): 7 Tests, 20 tour games

Randall, Terry (1973–77): 11 World Championship matches, 5 tour games
Raper, Johnny (1959–68): 33 Tests, 6 World Cup matches, 35 tour games
Rasmussen, Elton (1959–68): 15 Tests, 2 World Cup matches, 35 tour games
Raudonikis, Tom (1972–80): 20 Tests, 1 World Cup match, 8 World Championship matches, 1 International,
23 tour games
Rayner, Bill (1960): 2 Tests, 1 International
Rayner, Jack (1948–49): 5 Tests, 27 tour games
Reardon, Jack (1937–38): 4 tests, 22 tour games
Reddy, Rod (1977–82): 16 Tests, 1 World Championship match, 2 Internationals, 19 tour games
Rhodes, Johnny (1968–75): 4 World Cup matches, 6 World Championship matches, 1 International,
2 tour games
Ribot, John (1981–85): 9 tests, 16 tour games
Richards, Bill (1920–22): 4 Tests, 14 tour games
Richardson, Geoff (1974): 2 Tests
Ridley, Alan (1930–34): 5 Tests, 32 tour games
Riley, John (1959–60): 1 Test, 13 tour games
Ritchie, Ray (1957): 1 International
Roach, Steve (1985–91): 19 Tests, 1 World Cup match, 1 International, 17 tour matches
Roberts, Ian (1990–91): 6 Tests, 3 tour games
Roberts, Ron (1949–50): 2 Tests, 5 tour games
Robinson, Jack (1919–20): 5 Tests, 3 tour games
Robison, Harry (1937–38): 14 tour games
Robson, Ian (1969): 3 tour games
Rogers, Steve (1978–83): 21 Tests, 3 World Championship matches, 30 tour games
Rooney, Jack (1952–53): 2 Tests, 17 tour games
Root, Eddie (1929–30): 15 tour games
Rosenfeld, Albert (1908–09): 4 Tests, 13 tour games
Rosewell, John (1908–09): 1 Test, 1 tour game
Rushworth, Barry (1963–64): 1 Test, 18 tour games
Russell, Charles (1910–12): 3 Tests, 22 tour games
Ryan, Felix (1919–22): 4 Tests, 25 tour games
Ryan, Kevin (1963–64): 2 tests, 4 tour games
Ryan, Tommy (1952–53): 4 Tests, 16 tour games

Sait, Paul (1970–74): 7 Tests, 7 World Cup matches, 2 World Championship matches, 10 tour games
Salvatori, Craig (1991): 2 Tests, 1 tour game
Sargent, Mark: 3 Tests, 6 tour games
Sattler, John (1967–71): 4 Tests, 12 tour games
Savory, Charles (NZ) (1911–12): 5 tour games
Schofield, Don (1957): 2 World Cup matches
Schubert, Ian (1975–82): 4 World Championship matches, 1 International, 25 tour games
Schubert, Kevin (1948–53): 19 Tests, 39 tour games
Schultz, Bill (1919–22): 7 Tests, 26 tour games
Scott, Colin (1983): 1 Test
Sellars, Les (1929–30): 8 tour games
Shankland, Bill (1929–30): 4 Tests, 19 tour matches
Shearer, Dale (1986–91): 16 Tests, 19 tour games
Shields, Mick (1935): 2 tour games
Sigsworth, Phil (1981): 1 Test
Simmons, Royce (1986–87): 10 Tests, 5 tour games
Simms, Eric (1968–70): 8 World Cup matches, 1 International, 2 tour games
Sinclair, Jack (1961): 1 Test, 4 tour games
Sironen, Paul (1986–90): 11 Tests, 1 World Cup match, 16 tour games
Smith, Billy (1964–70): 18 Tests, 8 World Cup, 1 International, 15 tour games
Smith, George (1962): 1 Test
Smith, Len (1948): 2 Tests
Smyth, Kevin (1963–64): 2 Tests, 16 tour matches
Spence, Bill (1910): 1 Test
Spencer, Bill (1929–30): 4 Tests, 18 tour games
Stains, Dan (1989): 3 tour games

Stanmore, Frank (1949–52): 10 Tests, 21 tour games
Stanton, Frank (1963–64): 18 tour games
Starling, Geoff (1971–73): 7 Tests, 4 World Cup matches, 11 tour games
Stehr, Ray (1933–38): 11 Tests, 44 tour games
Steinohrt, Herb (1928–32): 9 Tests, 18 tour games
Sterling, Peter (1982–88): 18 Tests, 12 tour games
Stevens, Gary (1972–75): 5 Tests, 3 World Cup matches, 3 World Championship matches, 5 tour games
Stewart, Wayne (1972): 1 Test
Strudwick, Ross (1975): 1 World Championship match
Stuart, Bob (1911–12): 2 tour games
Stuart, Ricky (1990): 5 Tests, 4 tour games
Sullivan, Bob (1954): 1 Test
Sullivan, Con (1910–14): 5 Tests, 2 Internationals, 9 tour games
Sullivan, Gary (1970–72): 4 World Cup matches, 1 International, 2 tour matches
Summons, Arthur (1961–64): 9 Tests, 18 tour games
Sweeney, Tom (1919): 2 Tests, 4 our games

Tessmann, Brad (1983): 1 Test
Thicknesse, Viv (1933–36): 7 Tests, 16 tour games
Thomas, Mark (1977): 3 World Championship matches, 1 tour game
Thompson, Alan (1949–51): 3 Tests, 4 tour matches
Thompson, Alan (1978–80): 7 Tests, 14 tour games
Thompson, Bill (1948–49): 1 Test, 14 tour games
Thompson, Duncan (1919–24): 9 Tests, 23 tour games
Thompson, Roy (1937–38): 7 tour games
Thomson, Allan (1967–68): 3 Tests, 13 tour games
Thomson, Ian (1978): 3 Tests, 13 tour games
Thornett, Dick (1963–68): 11 Tests, 2 World Cup matches, 18 tour games
Thornett, Ken (1963–64): 12 Tests, 10 tour games
Thorogood, Clarrie (1919): 2 Tests, 1 tour game
Tidyman, Bob (1914): 2 Tests
Toovey, Geoff (1991): 2 Tests, 3 tour games
Townsend, Dick (1919–22): 3 Tests, 13 tour games
Treweek, George (1928–30): 7 Tests, 18 tour games
Trewhella, David (1989): 3 tour games
Troy, Jack (1950): 2 Tests
Tubman, Bob (1908–10): 2 Tests
Tunks, Peter (1985–87): 6 Tests, 3 tour games
Turner, Ron (1970–74): 1 Test, 3 World Cup matches
Tutty, Dennis (1967): 1 Test
Tyquin, Bill (1948–49): 6 Tests, 10 tour games
Tyquin, Tom (1956–57): 6 Tests, 13 tour games
Tyrrell, Tom (1952): 2 Tests, 16 tour games

Upton, Jack (1929–30): 19 tour games

Vautin, Paul (1982–88): 13 Tests, 3 tour games
Veivers, Greg (1975–77): 6 World Championship matches, 1 tour game
Veivers, Mick (1962–66): 6 Tests, 3 tour games
Vest, Dick (1919–22): 7 Tests, 27 tour games

Waite, David (1973): 6 Tests, 9 tour games
Walker, Bruce (1978): 8 tour games
Walsh, Ian (1959–66): 25 Tests, 39 tour games
Walsh, Pat (1908–09): 3 Tests, 25 tour games
Walters, Elwyn (1967–74): 12 Tests, 7 World Cup matches, 1 International, 18 tour games
Walters, Kerrod (1989–91): 8 Tests, 11 tour games
Walters, Kevin (1990–91): 2 Tests, 11 tour games
Walters, Steve (1991): 3 Tests
Ward, Dennis (1969–73): 2 Tests, 4 World Cup matches, 8 tour games
Ward, Laurie (1935–38): 8 Tests, 2 Internationals, 24 tour games
Watkins, Jack (1914–22): 7 Tests, 13 tour games
Watson, Alex (1954–57): 14 Tests, 5 World Cup matches, 18 tour games
Watt, George (1946): 3 Tests
Watt, Harry (1924): 3 Tests
Wearing, Benny (1928): 1 Test
Weier, Lloyd (1965–66): 3 Tests, 5 tour games
Weiss, Col (1969–70): 3 Tests, 3 tour games
Weissel, Eric (1928–32): 8 Tests, 17 tour games
Wellington, Gary (1965): 3 tour games
Wells, Harry (1952–60): 21 Tests, 8 World Cup matches, 1 International, 34 tour games
Westaway, Roy (1946): 2 Tests
White, Noel (1946): 1 Test
Whittle, Gordon (1935–38): 14 tour games
Why, Jack (1933–34): 2 Tests, 15 tour games
Willey, Ron (1952–53): 17 tour games
Williams, Bert (1937–38): 3 Tests, 12 tour games
Williams, Percy (1937–38): 2 Tests, 2 Internationals, 14 tour games
Williams, Robert (1911–12): 2 Tests, 18 tour games

Williamson, Lionel (1968–74): 5 Tests, 6 World Cup matches, 1 International, 10 tour games
Willoughby, Gordon (1951–52): 2 Tests
Wilson, Billy (1959–63): 10 Tests, 14 tour games
Wilson, Graham (1963–64): 3 Tests, 16 tour matches (also played 1 Test for New Zealand)
Wilson, Joe (1932): 3 Tests
Wishart, Rod (1991): 4 Tests, 2 tour games
Wittenberg, John (1966–69): 6 Tests, 4 World Cup matches, 3 tour games
Woodhead, Charlie (1909–10): 4 Tests
Woodward, Frank (NZ) (1911–12): 7 tour games
Woolley, Fred (1909): 2 Tests
Wright, David (1975): 1 World Championship match
Wynn, Graeme (1980): 5 tour matches
Wynn, Peter (1985): 3 Tests

Yakich, Nick (1965): 4 tour games
York, Colin (1928): 2 Tests
Young, Craig (1978–84): 20 Tests, 21 tour games

* Kangaroo tourists who did not play in a game.

INTERSTATE FOOTBALL see *State-of-Origin Matches*

KEVIN IRO

Seventeen Tests for New Zealand (1987–91). Also played in 1988 World Cup Final, for Rest-of-the-World against Australia (1988) and four minor games for New Zealand on one tour of Britain (1989).
Few players have had such a dramatic introduction to Test football as Kevin Iro. He was a 19-year-old unknown from the Mt Albert club in Auckland when he burst upon the international scene in 1987.

In his Test debut, against Papua-New Guinea, at Port Moresby, he scored 20 points (3 tries and 4 goals) to set a new record for a Kiwi newcomer. Nine days later he showed it was no fluke, starring in a one-off Test against Australia at Brisbane's Lang Park. The Kiwis were given little chance against the star-studded Australian lineup. But they shocked with a 13–6 victory. Iro and his experienced centre partner Dean Bell wrought havoc among the Australian backline, leaving the reputations of their opposite numbers, Gene Miles and Brett Kenny, in tatters.

It did not take former New Zealand coach, Graham Lowe, long to snap up the youngster's services for the Wigan club, in England. And with him went his elder brother, Tony. Kevin Iro capped a fine 12 months by scoring two tries in Wigan's 32–12 triumph over Halifax in the 1988 Challenge Cup Final at Wembley. He scored two more when Wigan successfully defended the trophy 12 months later with a 27–0 whitewash of St Helens and a further two in 1990, when Wigan triumphed 36–14 over Warrington. The six are a record tally for Cup Finals. But Iro drew a blank when Wigan made it four Cups in a row, beating St Helens 13–8 in 1991.

When his contract with Wigan ran out in mid-1991, Iro joined his brother and former coach, Lowe, at Manly-Warringah in the Sydney Premiership competition. The 188cm (6 ft 2 in) centre needed a knee operation before he could turn out with the Sea Eagles. But after three blockbusting club games he found himself back in the Test lineup for the final two encounters of the series against Australia. He was a major force with Manly, helping them to the Premiership semi-finals.

KEN IRVINE

Thirty-one Tests for Australia (1959–1968). Also played two matches in one World Cup (1960), two minor internationals (1960 and 1970) and 68 minor games on three Kangaroo tours (1959–60, 1963–64 and 1967–68), and two New Zealand tours (1961 and 1965) and one World Cup tour (1960).

Ken Irvine was perhaps the fastest winger international Rugby League has known. So fast, that for years while he was playing top-class football, he also held the world professional athletics record for 100 yards (10.3 seconds, set in March 1963). At the very least, Irvine was the greatest try-scorer Australian Rugby League has known. When he finished representative football he was only four short of becoming the first man to score a century of tries for Australia in all matches. He scored more in Tests than any other footballer (31). He also led the try-scoring lists against each of the other League playing nations: 12 against Britain (in only nine matches), nine against New Zealand, six against France and four against South Africa. These tries, two more in World Cup games, and 11 goals helped put him among the elite who have scored more than 100 points for Australia in Test and World Series matches.

Ken Irvine dives over for one of the 54 tries he scored on three Kangaroo tours

Irvine had been playing first-grade football for North Sydney for just one year when he made his first overseas tour, with the 1959–60 Kangaroos. He returned to England 12 months later for the World Cup, his second tour before he had turned 21. He made two more Kangaroo tours of England and France and visited New Zealand twice during his decade of international football.

Irvine appeared in 31 Tests (9 against Great Britain, 10 each versus New Zealand and France and two against South Africa). He also played World Cup games against France and New Zealand as well as two post-Cup matches against France. The second clash was unusual. It was after the 1970 World Cup In England, and Australia was so plagued with injuries that Irvine, who was travelling with the side as a journalist, was seconded into the side which beat France 7–4 at Perpignan.

England has cause to remember Irvine. As well as his record 12 tries (the best for either country), Irvine thwarted a British attempt at a clean-sweep of the Ashes series in 1962. The Englishmen had won the first two Tests and were leading 17–13 in the third, when Irvine scored a try seconds before the end of the game. Although he was not a recognised kicker, he tried for the conversion and surprised even himself by landing a great goal from the sideline to give Australia a one-point victory.

Irvine's 176 first-grade games for North Sydney is fourth highest for the club and his 169 tries is a Norths' record. His Norths' teammates were nowhere near his calibre however and the best Irvine managed in the Sydney Premiership for the Bears was a semi-final appearance in 1964 and a loss in the preliminary final 12 months later. When he switched to Manly-Warringah to play out his career it was a different matter. He starred in the Sea Eagles' first two Premiership-winning sides (in 1972 and 1973), and Irvine's 42 tries brought his tally to 211—a record for the Sydney Premiership.

The dashing winger lost a seven year fight with leukemia in 1990, and died at the age of just 50.

ITALY

In the 1950s there was a concerted effort to establish Rugby League in Italy. A group of dissident Rugby Union players started the ball rolling by organising a tour of Britain in 1950. The side failed to win any of its six games, but the impetus saw the establishment of teams in Turin, Milan, Treviso, Venice and several smaller towns. There was a second tour four years later. The British Rugby League was at the forefront of these early efforts. But it was the Australians who eventually brought international Rugby League to Italy. The 1959–60 Kangaroos, returning home from Britain and France, played two matches against sides representing Italy.

The local teams contained mainly eager, young hopefuls and proved no match for the Australians. They played before crowds of just over 3000 in the cities of Padua and Treviso. For the latter game, sawdust had to be spread on the field to soak up the snow and slush. Beaten 37–15 and 67–22, the Italians, disheartened, soon lost interest and the game there died out.

In 1982, a new attempt was made to get the game underway again in

Italy. A game was arranged in Venice between Great Britain and France, and about 2000 turned up to watch France win a close match 8–7.

ITALY TO GREAT BRITAIN

1950

Twenty-seven disgruntled Italian Rugby Union players got together for a trail-blazing tour of England and Wales in 1950. The Italians, skippered by Vincenze Bertolotte, played six games and, predictably for such an inexperienced group, failed to win a match. There were however, a couple of good performances, including one high-scoring match against Leeds.

Record in Great Britain

Played 6, Lost 6, Points for 145, Points against 294

Match results

Opponents	Venue (Attendance)	For	Against
Wigan	Wigan (14 000)	28	49
St Helens	St Helens (14 000)	38	74
South Wales	Swansea (2500)	11	39
Huddersfield	Huddersfield (3750)	12	28
Leigh	Leigh (6500)	15	58
Leeds	Leeds (8500)	41	56

1954

Italy made a second tour of Britain in 1954 and, as on the first occasion, was beaten in all matches. These included clashes with amateur international sides representing England and France.

Record in Great Britain

Played 7, Lost 7, Points for 109, Points against 291

International Results

Italy	6	France	20	(Huddersfield, 2950)
Italy	11	England	18	(Halifax, 2000)

Other Matches

Opponents	Venue (Attendance)	For	Against
Bradford Northern	Bradford (7000)	18	67
York	York (4000)	17	54
Hunslet	Hunslet (3300)	23	40
Keighley	Keighley (3500)	27	57
Leigh	Leigh (5000)	7	35

Italy's International Matches

Year	Venue	Result				Attendance
1954	Huddersfield	France	20	Italy	6	2950
1954	Halifax	England	18	Italy	11	2000
1960	Padua	Australia	37	Italy	15	3500
1960	Treviso	Australia	67	Italy	22	3105

J

GARRY JACK

Twenty Tests for Australia (1984–88). Also played in 1988 World Cup Final, Bicentennial match against the Rest-of-the-World (1988) and 10 minor games for Australia on one Kangaroo tour (1986) and one New Zealand tour (1985).

Over the years there have been many individual awards for excellence in Rugby League. One of the most recent has achieved universal recognition—the Adidas Golden Boot, instituted in 1985 to annually honour the finest player in the world. The third winner, in 1987, was Garry Jack—and no-one disputed the fact that the Balmain fullback was, indeed, the best in all the Rugby League countries.

Jack had stepped into the breach left by Greg Brentnall's early retirement in 1983. That year, Jack did not play a single representative match, but, in 1984, he was one of the first chosen for every game—including the Tests against the touring Great Britain side. In the next four years he played 20 successive Tests (nine versus Britain, seven against New Zealand, and two each against France and Papua-New Guinea) as well as the 1988 World Cup final against New Zealand and the Bicentenary international against the Rest-of-the-World, scoring 11 tries in the process, which was no mean feat for a fullback.

The great custodian was at his prime on the 1986 Kangaroo tour of Papua-New Guinea, Britain and France. He played in 13 of the 21 matches including all six Tests, and scored 52 points (third only to Michael O'Connor and Terry Lamb, the two Kangaroo goalkickers). Jack also played a major role in Balmain's almost fairytale finish to the 1988 Sydney Premiership season. Balmain was forced to play-off for the fifth semi-final spot. In sudden-death matches Balmain (and Jack) made its way through to the grand final, only to go down 24–12 to Canterbury-Bankstown.

Jack was badly injured in a trial match at the start of the 1989 season. By the time he had returned, his Australian understudy, Gary Belcher, had stolen a march and took over his Test spot for the tour of New Zealand. Jack's 1990 form was superb. Many keen critics tipped him to make another

Kangaroo tour, but the selectors ignored his great displays and chose only one fullback, Belcher, with halfback Greg Alexander called upon to supply the last line of defence in the minor matches.

PETER JACKSON

Seven Tests for Australia (1988–91). Also played six minor games on one New Zealand tour (1989) and one Papua New Guinea tour (1991).

Peter Jackson is the only player to have represented Australia in both Rugby League and Rugby Union at junior level. While at The Southport School, an exclusive private academy on the Gold Coast, he played for the Australian Under-17s against New Zealand's Junior All Blacks. Two season's later he was in the Australian Under-18 side which played Great Britain's Rugby League Colts touring side.

Jackson was to go on to play Tests for Australia in the 13-a-side code. He got his start with Souths in the Brisbane competition, under coach Wayne Bennett, combining in the centres with future Australian captain Mal Meninga to help the Magpies win the 1985 Premiership. In 1986, Jackson played his first State-of-Origin match. A year later, Bennett took Jackson with him to Canberra, where they were reunited with Meninga. The Raiders went from second-last in 1986, to that year's grand final.

The following season, Jackson really exploded on the representative scene, playing all three Tests against the touring British Lions and the one-off international against Papua New Guinea. An ankle injury early in 1989, hampered Jackson, who had linked up with the Brisbane Broncos. But he still toured New Zealand with the Australian side, although Meninga and fellow-Queenslander Dale Shearer were preferred as the centre partnership for the Tests.

Jackson had an unhappy season in 1990. But with a change of clubs, this time to North Sydney, he was one of the stars of 1991. Norths reached the semi-finals for the first time in almost a decade. And after warming the bench in the First Test, Jackson was recalled as five-eighth for the remaining two encounters with the visiting New Zealand Kiwis. He was one of the first chosen for Australia's end-of-season tour of Papua New Guinea, although he missed the First Test because of a severe virus.

CHRIS JOHNS

Six Tests for Australia (1990–91). Also played 13 minor games on one Kangaroo tour (1990) and one Papua New Guinea tour (1991).

Chris Johns is the only Queensland-based player to have turned out in State-of-Origin matches for New South Wales. Johns played all three games in the Blues' loss to Queensland in 1989.

Johns surprised the fans by accepting an offer to leave St George and join the Brisbane Broncos for their first season in the Sydney competition (1988). The move gave him a new lease of life after four seasons with the Dragons, much of which was spent in reserve grade. Despite a star-studded backline, Johns had no trouble holding his first grade centre spot with the Broncos. And, although he was overlooked for the 1990 State-of-Origin matches, his form in Brisbane's surge towards the preliminary final won him a berth in the Kangaroo side to tour Britain and France. On tour, Johns was a model of consistency and was rewarded with his Test debut, coming on as a replacement in the Second Test against France, at Perpignan.

Johns played all three Tests against the 1991 New Zealand Kiwis (albeit the last two as a replacement) before being chosen for Australia's end-of-season tour of Papua New Guinea.

LES JOHNS

Fourteen Tests for Australia (1964–69). Also played 29 minor games on two Kangaroo tours (1963–64 and 1967–68) and two New Zealand tours (1965 and 1969).

Les Johns was a footballing freak. He had the ability to turn the tide of a game in seconds. Only a string of injuries prevented him from establishing himself as one of the all-time great full-backs, in the mould of a Clive Churchill or a Howard Hallett.

Johns was first noticed as a 19–year-old playing for South Newcastle club and was chosen to represent Newcastle in the Country Championships and Country Seconds in the annual clash with City. He was again selected for Country next year, this time for the Firsts, but had to pull out through injury. He was replaced by another great talent, Graeme Langlands.

In 1962, Johns made the headlines with a great performance in the Newcastle side which beat the British tourists, one of the best international combinations ever to visit Australia. Next year, he joined Canterbury-Bankstown and immediately established himself as a star of the Sydney competition. He was chosen to play in the Tests against the touring New Zealand Kiwis, but injury forced him out. As a result he found himself playing second-fiddle to Ken Thornett on the ensuing Kangaroo tour of Britain and France. Johns did manage a Test against the Frenchmen in 1964, but had to retire at half-time with a damaged ankle. His only real run of top-line success was on the 1967–68 Kangaroo tour, when he played in all six Tests, and on two visits to New Zealand (1965 and 1969), when he appeared in all Tests, too.

The fine Canterbury fullback was named NSW Player-of-the-Year for 1967.

ALEC 'RICK' JOHNSTON

Eight Tests for Australia (1919–21). Also played in 12 minor games for Australia on one Kangaroo tour (1921–22) and one New Zealand tour (1919).

Rick Johnston had a brief stay in the international arena—just four years between 1919 and 1922, but the fine five-eighth was a real force during that time. He teamed up with two of the greatest halfbacks in the history of the game, Pony Halloway and Duncan Thompson. Johnston, who was sometimes nicknamed Ricketty, made his Test debut on the 1919 tour of New Zealand. In the first three encounters with the Kiwis he played outside the veteran Halloway (his former club partner at Balmain) before young Thompson joined him for the Fourth Test. The latter pair was reunited for the 1920 series against the touring British Lions (in which Johnston led the side for the First Test, at Brisbane) and on the 1921–22 Kangaroo tour of Britain.

Johnston played for three Sydney clubs. He was a member of Balmain's Premiership-winning sides in 1915, 1916 and 1917. He was with Newtown when he toured New Zealand. By the time of the Kangaroo tour, he had switched clubs again, joining St George midway through its first season in the Sydney Premiership competition (1921). He was later to coach St George and, in 1946, was given the task of preparing the Australian Test sides for the first post-War Ashes series against Britain.

FRED JONES

Three appearances for Australia in one World Cup (1968). Also chosen in squad for 1972 World Cup.

Hooker Fred Jones played only three internationals for Australia, all in the 1968 World Cup. Unfortunately he had to play second fiddle to the fine rake Elwyn Walters for much of his representative career, including the 1972 World Cup. Jones was, nevertheless, one of the best hookers Australian football has known. In club football, for Manly-Warringah, he played 298 Premiership games, at the time the second greatest number in the Sydney competition. He was rewarded with two Premiership successes when the Sea Eagles beat Eastern Suburbs 19–14 in the 1972 grand final and Cronulla-Sutherland 10–7 the following year. He was also in the sides which lost grand finals to South Sydney in 1968 and 1970 (with Jones winning the scrums in the former match over his old nemesis Walters).

LEWIS JONES

Twelve Tests for Great Britain (1954–57). Also played two internationals for Wales (1953), three matches for Great Britain in one World Cup (1957) and one game for the Rest-of-the-World against Australia (1957).

The game has known few pointscorers the equal of Lewis Jones. He was a top Rugby Union player when, in November 1952, he accepted the then-record signing-on fee of £6000 to join Leeds in the professional ranks. He was an instant success, playing either fullback, centre or five-eighth.

His Test debut came on the 1954 Lions tour of Australasia. Jones played in all six Tests and set one record for the number of points scored by a tourist (278) and another for the most goals in an Anglo-Australian Test match (10 in the Second Test, in Brisbane). Possibly the most outstanding of all Jones' records was set during the 1956–57 English season, when he amassed a phenomenal 496 points (194 goals and 36 tries)—a target which remains to this day.

In 1964, at the age of 33, Jones emigrated to Australia to join the Wentworthville club as captain-coach. It was largely because of his talents that Wentworthville held a virtual mortgage of the Sydney Second Division Premiership for several years.

JOE JORGENSON

Three Tests for Australia (1946).

Joe Jorgenson assured himself of a place in Rugby League when, in the 1940s, he introduced a revolutionary method of kicking for goal. He cultivated the idea of place-kicking from a mound instead of a divot, finding that he could gain more height that way. The purists of yesteryear shuddered, but Jorgenson showed it worked. In representative matches for New South Wales, Jorgenson notched 74 points, a tally which had been previously bettered only by the immortals Dave Brown, Dally Messenger, Harold Horder and Alan Ridley. Within a few years Jorgenson's way of kicking was the norm and the old method obsolete. Jorgenson was more than just a goalkicker however. He was a fine three-quarter (centre or wing) known for his bone-jarring tackles.

In 1945, he became the first post-War Australian player to receive an offer to play in England, but he turned down Huddersfield's £1000 pounds bait. The hope of playing for Australia in Test football kept him with the Balmain club. That hope was fulfilled 12 months later when Jorgenson played in all three Tests against the touring Lions, skippering his team in two of the three encounters.

On the club scene, he had already tasted Sydney Premiership success, in 1944 (kicking three goals in Balmain's 12–8 victory over Newtown). And he was on the winning side again in 1946 and 1947. In the former match he scored two tries in Balmain's 13–12 win over St George. And the following year he scored all of the Tigers' points (one try and five goals) when they beat Canterbury-Bankstown 13–9.

ARTHUR 'SNOWY' JUSTICE

Five Tests for Australia (1928–30). Also played in 11 minor games for Australia on one Kangaroo tour (1929–30).

When Snowy Justice first tried out for top-grade football, officials of the St George club scoffed. 'You're too small,' they told the would-be hooker. Small he was, just 1.68m (5ft 6ins) and 60.5kg (9st 7lb). But his heart was big, and he proved it by eventually playing 150 games for the Dragons' first-grade side without missing one through injury. He played every State match for New South Wales from 1925 to 1930 and he played five Tests between 1928 and 1930. His career was at its zenith when he toured Britain with the 1929–30 Kangaroos. His inclusion in that squad began a great St George tradition—every Kangaroo side since has also contained at least one player from the Dragons' lineup. Justice played with St George from 1922 to 1932.

After he hung up his boots, he continued with the club in a variety of official positions until his death in 1977. He also served for a time as chairman of the NSW Judiciary Committee.

K

KANGAROOS

Kangaroos is the title traditionally given to Australian Rugby League teams which tour Great Britain and France, but fans sometimes loosely refer to the sides which visit New Zealand and Papua New Guinea by the same name. By 1992, Australian Test sides had made five tours of Britain alone and 12 to Britain and France. There also had been 11 full tours of New Zealand and one of Papua New Guinea. Once the Kangaroos stopped off in New Zealand and twice in Papua New Guinea on their way to the northern hemisphere.

AUSTRALIA TO GREAT BRITAIN AND FRANCE 1908-09

The first Kangaroo tour of Britain, in 1908-09, was almost a disaster due to small gate-takings. With a crippling cotton mills strike in northern England, most fans could not afford to pay their way through the turnstiles. There was also some criticism of what the Australians wanted to charge as entrance fees. The team of 35 included three added after an outcry at their original omission. These three included Albert Rosenfeld who, in English club football, was later to become one of the game's immortals. Dally Messenger, who had toured Britain the previous year, with the pioneering New Zealand All Golds, was again a sensation and topped the scoring with 155 points.

Record in Great Britain

Played 46, Won 18, Lost 22, Drawn 6, Points for 561, Points against 484

Test Match Results

Australia	22	Great Britain	22	(Park Royal, 2000)
Australia	5	Great Britain	15	(Newcastle, 22 000)
Australia	5	Great Britain	6	(Birmingham, 9000)

Other International Results

Australia	9	England	14	(Huddersfield, 7000)
Australia	17	England	17	(Glasgow, 3000)
Australia	7	England	14	(Everton, 4000)

Other Matches

Opponents	Venue (Attendance)	For	Against
Mid Rhonda	Tonypandy (7500)	20	6
Bradford Northern	Bradford (4000)	12	11
Rochdale Hornets	Rochdale (3000)	5	0
York	York (2500)	5	5
Salford	Salford (6100)	9	9
Runcorn	Runcorn (2700)	9	7
Warrington	Warrington (5000)	3	10
Northern League	Everton (6000)	10	9
Hull Kingston Rovers	Hull (7000)	16	21
Lancashire	Wigan (4000)	20	6
Barrow	Barrow (6500)	21	5
Halifax	Halifax (6000)	8	12
Swinton	Swinton (1500)	10	9
Treherbert	Treherbert (4000)	6	3
Wakefield Trinity	Wakefield (3000)	13	20
Leeds	Leeds (12 000)	14	10
Oldham	Oldham (11 800)	5	11
Widnes	Southport (1200)	55	3
Widnes	Widnes (1000)	13	2
Wigan	*Wigan (4000)	10	7
Batley	Batley (2000)	5	12
Welsh League	Merthyr Tydfil (6000)	13	14
Ebbw Vale	Ebbw Vale (5000)	9	8
Cumberland League	Whitehaven (4000)	52	10
Leigh	Leigh (6000)	11	14
Dewsbury	Dewsbury (2000)	0	15
Yorkshire	Hull (3500)	24	11
Hunslet	Hunslet (6000)	12	11
Aberdare	Aberdare (5000)	37	10
Wigan	Wigan (9100)	8	16
Keighley	Keighley (1000)	8	8
Hull	Hull (10 000)	8	9
Cumberland	Carlisle (2000)	2	11
Broughton Rovers	Broughton (12 000)	12	14
St Helens	St Helens (1500)	0	9
Warrington	Warrington (7000)	8	8
Huddersfield	Huddersfield (9700)	3	5
Barrow	Barrow (6000)	3	11
Merthyr Tydfil	Merthyr Tydfil (4000)	13	15
Lancashire	Wigan (4000)	14	19

* *Friendly match*

Individual Records

	Matches	Tests	Tries	Goals	Points
H Messenger	31	2	9	64	155
J Devereux	31	2	16	3	54
D Frawley	24	2	13	1	41
A Morton	24	1	4	10	32
E Courtney	31	3	10	—	30
A Conlon	8	1	5	6	27
P Walsh	28	3	8	—	24
A Butler	20	2	4	5	22
S Deane	26	2	7	—	21
A Rosenfeld	14	1	7	—	21
T McCabe	22	1	6	—	18
L O'Malley	34	3	5	—	15
A Halloway	31	1	5	—	15
J Abercrombie	32	2	2	3	12

Individual Records

	Matches	Tests	Tries	Goals	Points
W Heidke	26	2	4	—	12
M Bolewski	33	3	3	—	9
A Burdon	26	2	3	—	9
L Bailey	3	—	3	—	9
R Graves	23	1	2	—	6
W Cann	9	—	2	—	6
L Jones	5	—	2	—	6
P Moir	4	—	2	—	6
S Pearce	33	3	1	—	3
A Anlezark	17	1	1	—	3
W Hardcastle	6	—	1	—	3
C Hedley	18	1	—	1	2
F Cheadle	7	—	—	—	-
A Hennessy	7	—	—	—	-
J Davis	6	—	—	—	-
A Dobbs	6	—	—	—	-
D Lutge (c)	5	—	—	—	-
T Anderson	5	—	—	—	-
W Noble	3	—	—	—	-
J Rosewell	1	—	—	—	-
J Fihelly	—	—	—	—	-

1911–12

At the very least, the 1911–12 Kangaroos have the record of being the first (and, for 70 years, the only) tourists to go three Tests without a loss. An indication of their mastery comes from the Third Test victory. The Australians were without a regular goalkicker, but notched nine tries to win 33–8.

Of the five losses on tour only one was not close—and that was against the Huddersfield combination dubbed by critics 'The Team of All Talents'. The Kangaroos ranks encompassed four New Zealanders and several Australians still considered to be among the all-time greats: fullback Howard Hallett, utility back 'Chook' Fraser, brothers Viv and Bill Farnsworth and halfback and captain Chris McKivat. McKivat played in 32 of the 36 games, despite injuries.

Record in Great Britain

Played 36, Won 29, Lost 5, Drawn 2, Points for 673, Points against 287

Test Match Results

Australia	19	Great Britain	10	(Newcastle, 5317)
Australia	11	Great Britain	11	(Edinburgh, 8000)
Australia	33	Great Britain	8	(Birmingham, 4000)

Other International Results

Australia	28	Wales	20	(Ebbw Vale, 7000)
Australia	11	England	6	(Fulham, 4000)
Australia	3	England	5	(Nottingham, 3000)

Other Matches

Opponents	Venue (Attendance)	For	Against
Midlands/ Southern England	Coventry (2000)	20	11
Yorkshire	Sheffield (2000)	33	13
Broughton Rovers	Broughton (12 000)	18	8
Lancashire	Blackburn (5000)	25	12
Widnes	Widnes (5000)	23	0
St Helens	St Helens (12 000)	16	5
Hunslet	Hunslet (4000)	3	3

Continued

Other Matches *continued*

Opponents	Venue (Attendance)	For	Against
Northern League	Everton (6000)	16	3
Wigan	Wigan (25 000)	2	7
Swinton	Swinton (4000)	28	9
Hull	Hull (10 000)	26	7
Oldham	Oldham (10 500)	8	14
Leigh	Leigh (7000)	13	12
Wakefield Trinity	Wakefield (5000)	24	10
Cumberland	Maryport (6000)	5	2
Barrow	Barrow (6400)	44	8
Runcorn	Runcorn (2000)	23	7
Huddersfield	Huddersfield (17 000)	7	21
Salford	Salford (4000)	6	3
York	York (1500)	16	8
Wales/West England	Bristol (1000)	23	3
Rochdale Hornets	Rochdale (4500)	18	6
Runcorn	Runcorn (1500)	54	6
Halifax	Halifax (10 000)	23	5
Warrington	Warrington (8500)	34	6
Leeds	Leeds (1200)	8	6
Hull Kingston Rovers	Hull (7000)	5	2
Barrow	Barrow (1500)	22	5
Batley	Batley (2000)	5	13
Northern League	Wigan (2000)	20	12

Individual Records

	Matches	Tests	Tries	Goals	Points
A Francis (NZ)	24	2	9	49	125
H Gilbert	29	3	20	2	64
D Frawley	12	2	18	4	62
V Farnsworth	29	3	19	—	57
T Berecry	13	1	16	—	48
H Hallett	29	3	14	1	44
W Cann	22	3	10	6	42
C McKivat (c)	32	3	13	1	41
C Russell	24	2	9	5	37
R Craig	31	3	7	2	25
C Fraser	21	1	—	12	24
P McCue	23	3	7	—	21
S Darmody	7	—	—	9	18
A Broomham	20	1	5	—	15
R Williams	20	2	3	—	9
C McMurtrie	7	—	3	—	9
E Courtney	25	2	3	—	9
A Halloway	13	—	1	1	5
C Savory (NZ)	5	—	1	1	5
W Farnsworth	14	2	1	—	3
W Noble	12	2	1	—	3
C Sullivan	10	1	1	—	3
J Murray	7	—	1	—	3
F Woodward (NZ)	7	—	1	—	3
P Burge	4	—	1	—	3
W Neill	9	—	—	1	2
G Gillett (NZ)	5	—	—	1	2
R Stuart	2	—	—	—	—

1921-22

A record-breaking tour! The 1921–22 visit was the first financial success—the Kangaroos went home with a £6000 profit—a fortune in those days. Four tourists scored more than 100 points each, a feat never repeated. Winger Cec Blinkhorn notched 39 tries, still the most by any Kangaroo. Frank Burge crossed for 33 (in just 23 matches), more than any forward before or since. Winger Harold Horder and halfback Duncan Thompson were the other century toppers. The Kangaroos ran up a score never to be beaten when they downed Bramley 92–7.

The Ashes, however, belonged to Britain. The Australians were a trifle unlucky. They disputed a British try in the 6–5 loss in the First Test. In the third and deciding encounter they hung on, to go down by just 6–0, despite losing captain 'Chook' Fraser with a broken leg in the first half (replacement of injured players was not allowed in those days).

Record in Great Britain

Played 36, Won 27, Lost 9, Points for 763, Points against 253

Test Match Results

Australia	5	Great Britain	6	(Leeds, 31 700)
Australia	16	Great Britain	2	(Hull, 21 504)
Australia	0	Great Britain	6	(Salford, 22 000)

Other International Matches

| Australia | 4 | England | 5 | (Highbury, 12 000)* |
| Australia | 21 | Wales | 16 | (Pontypridd, 13 000) |

* Gate takings donated to the Russian Famine Fund

Other Matches

Opponents	Venue (Attendance)	For	Against
Salford	Salford (9000)	48	3
Keighley	Keighley (5500)	29	5
Hull Kingston Rovers	Hull (13 000)	26	4
Bradford Northern	Bradford (3000)	53	3
Widnes	Widnes (14 000)	28	4
Broughton Rovers	Broughton (17 000)	18	6
Wigan	Wigan (29 000)	14	6
Leeds	Leeds (14 600)	11	5
Wakefield Trinity	Wakefield (6000)	29	3
Batley	Batley (6000)	33	7
Warrington	Warrington (16 000)	5	8
York	York (5000)	3	9
Bramley	Bramley (1200)	92	7
Rochdale Hornets	Rochdale (12 000)	16	2
Swinton	Swinton (6000)	0	9
Huddersfield	Huddersfield (12 000)	36	2
St Helens	St Helens (6000)	16	8
Oldham	Oldham (15 000)	16	5
Lancashire League	Everton (17 000)	29	6
Barrow	Barrow (8000)	24	15
Yorkshire	Wakefield (6000)	24	5
Lancashire	Warrington (7500)	6	8
Dewsbury	Dewsbury (6000)	6	13
Leigh	Leigh (5000)	17	4
Hull	Hull (13 000)	21	10
Widnes	Widnes (12 000)	17	8
Halifax	Halifax (12 000)	35	6
Hunslet	Hunslet (3000)	19	10
Cumberland	Workington (5000)	25	12
Oldham	Oldham (6000)	5	15
St Helens Recreation	St Helens (4000)	16	5

Individual Records

	Matches	Tests	Tries	Goals	Points
H Horder	25	3	35	11	127
C Blinkhorn	29	3	39	—	117
F Burge	23	3	33	6	111
D Thompson	26	3	3	49	107
J Craig	24	1	10	14	58
R Norman	21	—	2	13	32
G Carstairs	17	2	7	2	25
R Vest	26	3	7	—	21
H Caples	24	2	7	—	21
R Latta	22	1	7	—	21
F Ryan	24	2	6	—	18
C Prentice	25	3	3	2	13
W Richards	15	1	4	—	12

Continued

263

Individual Records *continued*

	Matches	Tests	Tries	Goals	Points
B Laing (NZ)	10	—	4	—	12
A Johnston	12	1	3	1	11
C Fraser	23	3	2	1	8
E McGrath	16	—	1	2	7
R Townsend	13	1	2	—	6
B Gray	5	1	2	—	6
N Broadfoot	4	—	2	—	6
H Peters	4	—	2	—	6
N Potter	10	—	1	—	3
W Schultz	24	2	1	—	3
J Watkins	11	2	1	—	3
E Brown	4	—	1	—	3
L Cubitt (c)	4	—	1	—	3
J Ives	6	—	1	—	3
S Pearce	21	2	—	—	—

1926-27

The Kangaroo tour that never was! The Australian Board of Control considered it a mere formality when asking that an Australian side be invited to Britain in 1926. However the New Zealanders also sought an invitation, and Britain chose the Kiwis. The Australian hierarchy protested, but to no avail. The British authorities shrugged off the complaint, noting that New Zealand had beaten the 1924 Lions two Tests to one while Australia managed to win only one of its three clashes with the same tourists. As it turned out, New Zealand was no match for the locals in 1926–27 and the Kiwi tour was a financial flop—little compensation for the Australians who had to wait another three years for their next visit.

1929-30

Australia did not win the Ashes on the 1929–30 tour, but morally the Kangaroos were victors, having been robbed of success in the Third Test by a bad touch judge decision which disallowed a try which the referee and most critics saw as being fairly scored. The game went into the record books as a nil-all draw but the outcry over the 'no-try' caused officials to schedule an unprecedented Fourth Test to decide the Ashes. Great Britain won narrowly. Kangaroo captain Tommy Gorman was an inspiration to his side, regularly taking the field carrying injuries to enable other players to be rested. The 1929–30 side was the first to take a non-playing coach. The job went to the first man to have captained New South Wales, Arthur Hennessy, who had also toured as a player with the first Kangaroo squad.

Record in Great Britain

Played 35, Won 24, Lost 9, Drawn 2, Points for 708, Points against 347

Test Match Results

Australia	31	Great Britain	8	(Hull, 20 000)
Australia	3	Great Britain	9	(Leeds, 31 402)
Australia	0	Great Britain	0	(Swinton, 33 809)
Australia	0	Great Britain	3	(Rochdale, 16 743)

Other International Matches

Australia	26	Wales	10	(Wembley, 16 000)

Other Matches

Opponents	Venue (Attendance)	For	Against
Rochdale Hornets	Rochdale (6521)	36	3
York	York (4729)	32	11
Batley	Batley (6000)	27	5
Widnes	Widnes (6400)	37	13
Broughton Rovers	Broughton (5883)	21	8
Lancashire	Warrington (24 000)	29	14
Wakefield Trinity	Wakefield (9786)	3	14
Keighley	Keighley (3000)	15	9
Castleford	Castleford (4000)	51	2
Huddersfield	Huddersfield (18 500)	18	8
Leigh	Leigh (8000)	19	16
Barrow	Barrow (10 000)	13	10
Leeds	Leeds (10 500)	7	8
Hull	Hull (10 000)	35	2
Oldham	Oldham (18 000)	18	10
Bradford Northern	Bradford (7000)	26	17
St Helens	St Helens (9500)	18	18
Yorkshire	Wakefield (7011)	25	12
Halifax	Halifax (8440)	58	9
Swinton	Swinton (9000)	5	9
Northern League	Wigan (9987)	5	18
Cumberland	Workington (3000)	5	8
Glamorgan/Monmouthshire	Cardiff (3000)	39	9
St Helens Recreation	St Helens (9000)	22	8
Warrington	Warrington (12 826)	8	17
Hunslet	Hunslet (12 000)	3	18
Hull Kingston Rovers	Hull (12 500)	10	5
Northern League	Newcastle (9890)	32	22
Wigan*	Wigan (8000)	10	9
Salford	Salford (8000)	21	5

* Match abandoned 10 minutes before fulltime, but awarded to Kangaroos.

Individual Records

	Matches	Tests	Tries	Goals	Points
E Weissel	20	3	5	56	127
W Shankland	23	4	24	16	104
H Finch	10	—	16	18	84
W Spencer	22	4	23	—	69
J Kingston	26	2	18	—	54
J Upton	19	—	10	—	38
A Ridley	7	—	11	—	33
C Fifield	22	4	8	—	24
G Treweek	22	4	6	—	18
V Armbruster	19	3	6	—	18
F Laws	15	1	2	5	16
H Kadwell	8	—	2	5	16
J Holmes	12	—	5	—	15
W Prigg	16	2	4	—	12
G Bishop	15	2	4	—	12
P Maher	12	—	4	—	12
E Root	15	—	3	—	9
A Edwards	9	—	3	—	9
F McMillan	26	4	—	4	8
T Gorman (c)	22	4	2	—	6
W Brogan	20	3	2	—	6
A Justice	13	2	2	—	6
J Busch	19	4	2	—	6
M Madsen	17	2	1	—	3
L Sellars	8	—	1	—	3
H Steinohrt	21	3	—	—	—
D Dempsey	10	1	—	—	—
A Henderson	7	—	—	—	—

1933–34

Dave Brown's tour. How else could it be described? Brown, a 20–year-old, broke a number of records while in Britain—his 285 points (19 tries and 114 goals) almost doubling Dally Messenger's previous Kangaroo record tally. More remarkable was that Brown was not a recognised

THE "KANGAROOS" - AUSTRALIAN TEAM, 1933-4

R. STEHR S. PEARCE. A. RIDLEY. P. MADSEN. F. CURRAN. H. DENNY. C. PEARCE.
M. GLASHEEN. R. MORRIS. W. PRIGG. F. O'CONNOR. L. HEIDKE. J. DOYLE. J. GIBB. J. LITTLE.
C. SMITH. J. WHY. F. LAWS. H. SUNDERLAND. F. McMILLAN. W. WEBB. F. NEUMANN. A. FOLWELL. D. BROWN.
(V. CAPT.) (MNGR.) (CAPT.) (MNGR.)
V. THICKNESSE. F. GARDNER. L. MEAD. F. GILBERT. V. HEY. F. DOONAR.

The Kangaroos, 1933-34

goalkicker before the tour and was only tried after five matches (he landed seven goals in his first as kicker). The Kangaroos failed to win a Test, but all three were close encounters. Another highlight of the tour was playing the first Rugby League match in France. Australia and England clashed in Paris on New Year's Eve, with Australia winning 63–13. Centre Ray Morris was taken off the ship at Malta on the way to England with an ear infection. He died in hospital a few days later.

Record in Great Britain and France

Played 37, Won 27, Lost 10, Points for 754, Points against 295

Test Match Results

Australia	0	Great Britain	4	(Manchester, 33 000)
Australia	5	Great Britain	7	(Leeds, 29 688)
Australia	14	Great Britain	19	(Swinton, 10 990)

Other International Matches

Australia	51	Wales	19	(Wembley, 10 000)
Australia	63	England	13	(Paris, 5000)
Australia	14	England	19	(Gateshead, 15 576)

Other Matches

Opponents	Venue (Attendance)	For	Against
St Helens Recreation	St Helens (8880)	13	9
Leigh	Leigh (4590)	16	7
Hull Kingston Rovers	Hull (7831)	20	0
Bramley	Bramley (1902)	53	6
Yorkshire	Leeds (15 281)	13	0
Oldham	Oldham (10 309)	38	6
Barrow	Barrow (12 221)	24	5
Lancashire	Warrington (16 576)	33	7
Wigan	Wigan (15 712)	10	4
Castleford	Castleford (4250)	39	6
Halifax	Halifax (10 358)	16	5
Bradford Northern	Bradford (3380)	5	7
Warrington	Warrington (16 440)	12	15
Hunslet	Hunslet (6227)	22	18
Salford	Salford (15 742)	9	16
Widnes	Widnes (6691)	31	0
Wakefield Trinity	Wakefield (5596)	17	6
Bradford Northern	Bradford (9397)	10	7
Northern League	York (3158)	5	7
Swinton	Swinton (13 341)	4	10
Keighley	Keighley (3680)	14	7
Huddersfield	Huddersfield (7522)	13	5
London Highfield	London (10 541)	20	5
Broughton Rovers	Broughton (5527)	19	0
Leeds	Leeds (5295)	15	7
St Helens	St Helens (5735)	20	11
Rochdale Hornets	Rochdale (3602)	26	4
Cumberland	Whitehaven (5802)	16	17
York	York (7000)	15	7
Hull	Hull (16 341)	19	5
Oldham	Oldham (4000)	38	5

Individual Records

	Matches	Tests	Tries	Goals	Points
D Brown	32	3	19	114	285
A Ridley	27	2	25	—	75
W Prigg	32	3	16	—	48
S Pearce	24	2	12	4	44
F Gardner	20	1	13	2	43
V Hey	26	3	14	—	42
J Gibbs	19	2	10	—	30

Continued

267

Individual Records *continued*

	Matches	Tests	Tries	Goals	Points
J Why	17	2	8	—	24
F O'Connor	16	2	7	—	21
J Doyle	21	1	7	—	21
C Pearce	27	3	6	1	20
L Mead	15	1	2	5	16
F Laws	16	1	1	5	13
R Stehr	26	2	4	—	12
F McMillan (c)	21	2	1	3	9
V Thicknesse	18	2	3	—	9
W Smith	16	1	3	—	9
M Madsen	25	3	2	—	6
A Folwell	21	2	2	—	6
F Doonar	11	—	2	—	6
F Gilbert	4	—	2	—	6
D Dempsey	12	11	—	3	—
F Newmann	9	—	1	—	3
M Glasheen	2	—	1	—	3
F Curran	12	—	—	—	—
H Denny	8	—	—	—	—
J Little	4	—	—	—	—
M Heidke*	—	—	—	—	—
R Morris**	—	—	—	—	—

* Quit team in Perth with infected leg.
** Died of an ear infection in hospital in Malta.

The great second-rower Joe Pearce became the first son of a Kangaroo to tour Britain when he went in 1933–34. Joe's father, Sandy Pearce, had visited the 'Old Country' with the first Australian tourists in 1908. Queensland forward Monty Heidke, whose father had also been on that first tour, should have shared the honour with Pearce, but he sailed only as far as Fremantle, Western Australia, before being forced to quit the team with an infected leg. It is perhaps sobering to realise that such an injury today would be cleared up with antibiotics in little more than the time it takes to fly to Britain in a jumbo jet.

1937–38

One point decided the Ashes on the 1937–38 Kangaroo tour. Great Britain won the First Test 5–4 and the Second Test 13–3 and Australia reversed that result in the Third Test. Captain Wally Prigg became the first player to make three Kangaroo tours. As on his second tour, he shared the honour of most games—29 of the 38, and with 13 tries, he became the only forward to head the list of try-scorers on a Kangaroo tour—a record which remains to this day. For the first time, a Kangaroo squad toured France. The Australians also played two Tests and one minor match in New Zealand en route to Britain. The great second-rower Joe Pearce broke a leg in one of the New Zealand games. Herb Narvo, a surprising omission from the original team, was sent as a replacement and played in four Tests. Two former Eastern Suburbs players, Dave Brown and Bill Shankland, played for Warrington which beat the Kangaroos 8–6. Vic Hey and Eric Harris, two other Australian stars, were in the Leeds lineup which triumphed 21–8.

Record in New Zealand
Played 3, Won 1, Lost 2, Points for 32, Points against 40

Test Results

Australia	12	New Zealand	8	(Auckland, 12 000)
Australia	15	New Zealand	16	(Auckland)

Other Match

Opponents	Venue	For	Against
Maoris	Ngaruawhia	5	16

Record in Great Britain

Played 25, Won 13, Drawn 1, Lost 11, Points for 293, Points against 232

Test Match Results

Australia	4	Great Britain	5	(Leeds, 31 949)
Australia	3	Great Britain	13	(Swinton, 31 724)
Australia	13	Great Britain	3	(Huddersfield, 9403)

Other Matches

Opponents	Venue (Attendance)	For	Against
Leigh	Leigh (5000)	11	9
York	York (5200)	15	6
Newcastle	Newcastle (4000)	37	0
Lancashire	Warrington (16 250)	5	7
Halifax	Halifax (14 500)	2	12
Yorkshire	Bradford (7570)	8	4
Wakefield Trinity	Wakefield (8696)	17	10
Rochdale Hornets	Rochdale (2400)	6	0
Widnes	Widnes (4201)	13	13
Hull	Hull (15 000)	22	12
Bradford Northern	Bradford (5749)	19	6
Salford	Salford (12 000)	8	11
Wigan	Wigan (9800)	25	23
Oldham	Oldham (15 000)	10	6
Liverpool Stanley	Liverpool (1500)	28	9
Huddersfield	Huddersfield (9383)	7	17
Swinton	Swinton (4113)	3	5
Warrington	Warrington (12 637)	6	8
Leeds	Leeds (5000)	8	21
St Helens/St Helens Recs	St Helens (2000)	15	17
Barrow	Barrow (8153)	8	12
Broughton Rovers	Broughton (3000)	0	13

Record in France

Played 10, Won 9, Lost 1, Points for 267, Points against 80

Test Match Results

Australia	35	France	6	(Paris, 11 500)
Australia	16	France	11	(Marseille, 24 000)

Other Matches

Opponents	Venue (Attendance)	For	Against
R C Roanne	Roanne	20	13
South-West France	Bordeaux (10 000)	12	11
Albi	Albi	47	3
XIII Catalan	Perpignan (8000)	53	2
Cote Basque	Bayonne	33	8
South of France	Toulouse (15 000)	0	15
Villeneuvois S A	Villeneuve (18 000)	26	3
South-East France	Lyon	25	8

Individual Records

	Matches	Tests	Tries	Goals	Points
J Beaton	27	5	6	53	124
R McKinnon	29	4	10	10	50
P Williams	16	2	2	19	44
W Prigg (c)	29	5	13	—	39
J Reardon	26	4	13	—	39
L Dawson	23	4	11	—	33
H Narvo	22	4	10	—	30
C Hazelton	15	—	9	—	27
A Norval	15	3	8	—	24
F Gilbert	16	3	5	4	23
H Pierce	18	5	7	—	21
E Collins	7	—	7	—	21
B Williams	5	3	5	—	15
E Norman	21	2	4	—	12
F Curran	17	4	4	—	12
E Lewis	23	5	3	—	9
R Stehr	18	1	3	—	9
H Robinson	14	—	3	—	9
D McLean	8	—	3	—	9
L Ward	27	5	2	—	6
J Gibbs	17	2	2	—	6
F Griffiths	10	—	2	—	6
R Thompson	7	—	1	1	5
L Heidke	21	4	1	—	3
G MacLennan	16	—	1	—	3
P Fairhall	14	—	1	—	3
G Whittle	12	—	1	—	3
F Nolan	9	—	1	—	3
S Pearce	2	—	—	—	—

1948–49

The selection of the 1948–49 Kangaroos provided what was probably the greatest shock in the history of the game. Len Smith, captain-coach of the Test side which beat New Zealand on the day the tourists were chosen, was not among the 26. His omission caused a public outcry. In the absence of Smith, Col Maxwell led the side away, but he played in only one Test. The great Australian referee Tom McMahon went along in an unofficial capacity, controlled the game against Yorkshire and incurred the wrath of local fans by sending off their hooker for repeated scrum infringements. Britain made a clean sweep of the Tests.

Record in Great Britain

Played 27, Won 15, Lost 12, Points for 348, Points against 275

Test Match Results

Australia	21	Great Britain	23	(Leeds, 36 529)
Australia	7	Great Britain	16	(Swinton, 36 354)
Australia	9	Great Britain	23	(Bradford, 43 500)

Other International Matches

Australia	12	Wales	5	(Swansea, 9161)

Other Matches

Opponents	Venue (Attendance)	For	Against
Huddersfield	Huddersfield (26 053)	3	22
Belle Vue Rovers	Manchester (7535)	14	9
Hull	Hull (16 616)	13	3
Wakefield Trinity	Wakefield (20 040)	26	19

▶

Other Matches

Opponents	Venue (Attendance)	For	Against
Leigh	Leigh (12 968)	24	12
Salford	Salford (16 627)	13	2
Castleford	Castleford (14 004)	10	8
Cumberland	Whitehaven (8818)	4	5
St Helens	St Helens (20 175)	8	10
Dewsbury	Dewsbury (13 614)	14	4
Hull Kingston Rovers	Hull (7614)	12	17
Wigan	Wigan (28 554)	11	16
Barrow	Barrow (13 143)	11	5
Leeds	Leeds (13 542)	15	2
Warrington	Warrington (26 879)	7	16
Bradford Northern	Bradford (13 287)	21	7
Workington Town	Workington (13 253)	7	10
Swinton	Swinton (6041)	21	0
Yorkshire	Leeds (5301)	2	5
Halifax	Halifax (6520)	10	8
Oldham	Oldham (14 798)	27	7
Lancashire	Wigan (11 788)	8	13
Widnes	Widnes (10 761)	18	8

Record in France

Played 10, Won 9, Lost 1, Points for 279, Points against 71

Test Match Results

Australia	29	France	10	(Marseille, 15 796)
Australia	10	France	0	(Bordeaux, 17 365)

Other Matches

Opponents	Venue (Attendance)	For	Against
Pyrenees	Toulouse (6806)	43	3
XIII Catalan	Perpignan (12 254)	5	20
A S Carcassonne	Carcassonne (7990)	13	8
Languedoc	Beziers (2300)	38	0
Cannes	Cannes (1100)	60	7
French XIII	Romans (4385)	30	8
Lyon/Roanne	Lyon (4514)	29	10
Cavaillon	Avignon (4500)	22	5

Individual Records

	Matches	Tests	Tries	Goals	Points
J Graves	20	2	16	35	118
K Froome	16	3	3	39	87
J Horrigan	20	1	16	8	64
P McMahon	22	5	12	—	36
R Lulham	18	3	12	—	36
J Hawke	23	4	11	—	33
D Hall	21	4	10	—	30
L Cowie	20	—	10	—	30
R Dimond	15	—	9	—	27
B Hopkins	13	—	1	10	23
N Mulligan	21	5	6	—	18
W O'Connell	21	5	6	—	18
W Tyquin	14	4	6	—	18
J Rayner	24	2	5	1	17
F de Belin	15	3	4	—	12
J Holland	19	1	3	—	9
D McRitchie	14	4	3	—	9
V Bulgin	16	—	1	2	7
A Gibbs	19	5	2	—	6
E Brosnan	17	—	2	—	6
W Thompson	15	2	2	—	6
N Hand	13	1	2	—	6
C Maxwell (c)	12	1	2	—	6
K Schubert	22	5	1	—	3
L Pegg	13	—	1	—	3
F Johnson	7	—	1	—	3
C Churchill	21	5	—	1	2
H Benton	10	—	—	—	—

1952-53

The 1952–53 Kangaroos did not come back with the Ashes, but they had a great tour otherwise. The Australians won more matches in Britain than any previous side (23 out of 27), losing to only one club (St Helens). They also scored more points than any other previous side to visit Britain (816) and drew record gate receipts, in the First Test. This was the only Kangaroo tour in which every player scored.

Record in Great Britain

Played 27, Won 23, Drawn 1, Lost 3, Points for 816, Points against 248

Test Match Results

Australia	6	Great Britain	19	(Leeds, 34 305)
Australia	5	Great Britain	21	(Swinton, 32 421)
Australia	27	Great Britain	7	(Bradford, 30 509)

Other Matches

Opponents	Venue (Attendance)	For	Against
Keighley	Keighley (7431)	54	4
Hull	Hull (15 364)	28	0
Barrow	Barrow (16 045)	26	2
Whitehaven	Whitehaven (9253)	15	5
Oldham	Oldham (19 370)	7	7
Halifax	Halifax (18 773)	39	7
Wigan	Wigan (16 223)	23	13
St Helens	St Helens (17 205)	8	26
Featherstone Rovers	Featherstone (3700)	50	15
Bradford Northern	Bradford (28 987)	20	6
Warrington	Warrington (21 478)	34	10
Leigh	Leigh (8409)	34	5
Swinton	Swinton (10 269)	31	8
Hunslet	Hunslet (3273)	49	2
Workington Town	Workington (11 341)	27	15
Doncaster	Doncaster (2452)	41	13
Huddersfield	Huddersfield (25 494)	27	9
Wakefield Trinity	Wakefield (7239)	58	8
Hull Kingston Rovers	Hull (5817)	31	6
Lancashire	Warrington (5863)	36	11
Leeds	Leeds (29 335)	45	4
Yorkshire	Huddersfield (3737)	55	11
Dewsbury	Dewsbury (2405)	22	7
Widnes	Widnes (7411)	18	7

Record in France

Played 13, Won 10, Lost 3, Points for 301, Points against 125

Test Match Results

Australia	16	France	12	(Paris, 18 327)
Australia	0	France	5	(Bordeaux, 23 419)
Australia	5	France	13	(Lyon, 17 545)

Other Matches

Opponents	Venue (Attendance)	For	Against
French XIII	Nantes (4320)	45	2
U S Villeneuve	Villeneuve (2262)	18	11
Albi	Albi (4900)	31	22
French XIII	Perpignan (9301)	19	13
A S Carcassonne	Carcassonne (4881)	18	5
French XIII	Nimes (3518)	39	7
R.C. Marseille	Marseille (11 133)	14	10
Cannes	Cannes (780)	62	0
Paris-Lyon XIII	Roanne (5532)	10	12
Selection du Midi	Toulouse (7107)	24	13

Individual Records

	Matches	Tests	Tries	Goals	Points
N Pidding	22	4	18	87	228
R Willey	17	—	5	63	141
B Carlson	19	3	29	3	93
T Ryan	20	4	24	—	72
D Flannery	14	1	23	—	69
D McGovern	10	—	17	—	51
C Churchill (c)	23	6	4	17	46
K Holman	10	5	10	8	46
A Paul	21	1	9	4	35
C Geelan	20	4	10	—	30
F Ashton	22	5	9	—	27
R Duncan	18	—	9	—	27
K McCaffery	12	—	9	—	27
D Hall	25	6	8	—	24
B Davies	24	6	8	—	24
A Collinson	20	3	8	—	24
T Tyrrell	17	1	8	—	24
G Hawick	16	2	8	—	24
N Hazzard	23	6	6	—	18
H Wells	14	2	5	—	15
J Rooney	17	—	5	—	15
F Stanmore	21	5	4	—	12
C Gill	20	1	4	—	12
C Donohoe	16	1	4	—	12
H Crocker	17	2	3	—	9
R Bull	17	4	2	—	6
K Kearney	20	4	1	—	3
K Schubert	19	2	1	—	3

Western Suburbs five-eighth Frank Stanmore captained the 1952–53 Kangaroos in seven matches in England and France. and the Kangaroos won all seven—a rare feat in those days.

1956-57

Injuries hit the 1956–57 Kangaroos at vital stages of their tour. Although they won four of their six Tests, they left the Ashes in Britain. The tour saw the end of the Test career of 'The Little Master', Clive Churchill, who was dropped after the First Test in Britain. His successor at fullback, Gordon Clifford, was the tour topscorer with 94 points. It was the first time not one player reached a century on tour. The English League XIII which played the Kangaroos at Leigh contained three Australian greats, Brian Bevan, Harry Bath and Arthur Clues.

Record in Great Britain

Played 19, Won 10, Lost 9, Points for 335, Points against 296

Test Match Results

Australia	10	Great Britain	21	(Wigan, 22 473)
Australia	22	Great Britain	9	(Bradford, 23 334)
Australia	0	Great Britain	19	(Swinton, 13 515)

Other Matches

Opponents	Venue (Attendance)	For	Against
Liverpool City	Liverpool (4712)	40	12
Leeds	Leeds (24 459)	13	18
Hull XIII	Hull (17 172)	37	14
Barrow	Barrow (9880)	25	11
Whitehaven	Whitehaven (10 917)	11	14
Bradford Northern	Bradford (2743)	23	11

Continued

Other Matches *continued*

Opponents	Venue (Attendance)	For	Against
Warrington	Warrington (15 613)	17	21
English League XIII	Leigh (7811)	19	15
York	York (6842)	20	18
Oldham	Oldham (8458)	2	21
Huddersfield	Huddersfield (12 127)	20	10
Hunslet	Hunslet (4451)	27	11
St Helens	St Helens (15 579)	2	44
Halifax	Halifax (2254)	3	6
Wigan	Wigan (15 854)	32	4
Wakefield Trinity	Wakefield (3381)	12	17

Record in France

Played 9, Won 8, Drawn 1, Points for 207, Points against 110

Test Match Results

Australia	15	France	8	(Paris, 10 789)
Australia	10	France	6	(Bordeaux, 11 379)
Australia	25	France	21	(Lyon, 5743)

Other Matches

Opponents	Venue (Attendance)	For	Against
French Army	Limoges (3153)	11	11
R C Albi	Albi (3789)	25	20
A S Carcassonne	Carcassonne (3493)	26	12
XIII Catalan	Perpignan (7900)	20	14
S O Avignon	Avignon (5061)	38	11
R C Marseille	Marseille (2938)	37	7

Individual Records

	Matches	Tests	Tries	Goals	Points
G Clifford	12	4	2	44	94
C Connell	14	—	10	17	64
K Holman	17	6	10	5	40
I Moir	16	2	13	—	39
D Flannery	16	5	12	—	36
D Adames	15	2	11	—	33
C Churchill	15	2	—	13	26
B Purcell	7	—	—	12	24
R Poole	17	6	7	—	21
I Johnston	9	—	7	—	21
D McGovern	9	3	6	—	18
K O'Brien	11	—	6	—	18
B Davies	12	3	5	1	17
R Banks	18	6	5	—	15
W Marsh	17	2	5	—	15
N Provan	15	3	3	—	9
T Payne	13	1	3	—	9
K Kearney (c)	19	6	2	1	8
R Bull	21	6	2	—	6
I Doyle	16	4	2	—	6
T Tyquin	16	3	2	—	6
K O'Shea	14	6	2	—	6
D Furner	11	1	—	3	6
A Watson	18	5	1	—	3
E Hammerton	11	—	—	—	—
B Orrock	5	2	—	—	—

1959–60

The 1959–60 Kangaroos went within an ace of becoming the first all-Australian side to win the Ashes in Britain. They won the First Test 22–14 and lost the Second 11–10, only after several disputed decisions went against them. Britain won the third and deciding encounter 18–12. The tour saw the Ashes debuts of two all-time greats of Rugby League, Reg Gasnier and Johnny Raper. Gasnier's emergence in the First Test was sensational. The St George star scored three tries. The Kangaroos played two promotional matches in Italy at the end of the tour.

Record in Great Britain

Played 24, Won 15, Lost 9, Points for 495, Points against 390

Test Match Results

Australia	22	Great Britain	14	(Swinton, 34 964)
Australia	10	Great Britain	11	(Leeds, 30 311)
Australia	12	Great Britain	18	(Wigan, 26 089)

Other Matches

Opponents	Venue (Attendance)	For	Against
Leeds	Leeds (14 629)	44	20
Rochdale Hornets	Rochdale (10 155)	27	14
Warrington	Warrington (17 112)	30	24
Lancashire	St Helens (15 743)	22	30
Salford	Salford (11 008)	22	20
Yorkshire	York (7338)	15	47
Widnes	Widnes (9381)	45	15
Oldham	Oldham (17 630)	25	14
Leigh	Leigh (11 932)	17	18
St Helens	St Helens (29 156)	15	2
Cumberland XIII	Whitehaven (7463)	13	8
Barrow	Barrow (8488)	9	12
Hull XIII	Hull (15 944)	29	9
Bradford Northern	Bradford (4126)	29	8
Halifax	Halifax (8274)	17	5
Featherstone Rovers	Featherstone (7671)	15	23
Wigan	Wigan (24 466)	9	16
Swinton	Swinton (4237)	25	24
Wakefield Trinity	Wakefield (17 615)	10	20
Huddersfield	Huddersfield (2349)	21	7
Hunslet	Hunslet (8169)	12	11

Record in France

Played 11, Won 9, Lost 2, Points for 277, Points against 120

Test Match Results

Australia	20	France	19	(Paris, 9864)
Australia	17	France	2	(Bordeaux, 8848)
Australia	16	France	8	(Roanne, 3437)

Other Matches

Opponents	Venue (Attendance)	For	Against
French Army	Nantes (993)	15	2
U S Villeneuve	Villeneuve (1458)	11	5
R C Albi	Albi (5845)	10	19
Carcassonne/Lezignan	Carcassonne (6364)	9	32
XIII Catalan	Perpignan (8198)	32	8
Montpellier	Montpellier (3741)	44	13
R C Marseille	Marseille (1366)	38	7
Avignon/Cavaillon	Avignon (2806)	65	5
Lyon/Grenoble	Grenoble *	—	—

* Cancelled due to heavy snow

Record in Italy

Played 2, Won 2, Points for 104, Points against 37

International Results

Australia	37	Italy	15	(Padua, 3500)
Australia	67	Italy	22	(Traviso, 3105)

Individual Records

	Matches	Tests	Tries	Goals	Points
K Barnes (c)	22	6	–	101	2028
B Carlson	24	5	19	49	155
E Lumsden	27	6	25	—	75
R Gasnier	19	6	20	—	60
D Parish	12	—	7	17	55
K Irvine	21	1	17	—	51
J Raper	18	3	14	—	42
H Wells	23	6	11	—	33
B Hambly	22	6	9	2	31
P Burke	14	—	9	—	27
W Delamere	19	—	5	—	15
R Boden	13	—	5	—	15
B Clay	21	5	4	1	14
J Paterson	20	2	4	—	12
E Rasmussen	19	2	4	—	12
A Brown	9	1	4	—	12
R Bugden	5	—	4	—	12
I Walsh	23	6	3	1	11
D Chapman	18	—	3	—	9
N Kelly	14	—	2	1	8
B Muir	20	6	1	2	7
R Mossop	25	4	2	—	6
G Parcell	20	4	2	—	6
W Wilson	19	5	2	—	6
J Riley	14	—	2	—	6
D Beattie	20	4	—	—	—

The St George stars Brian Clay and Johnny Raper were both chosen as lock-forwards for the 1959–60 Kangaroo tour of Britain and France. It was the first time two players from the one club had been selected in the same single position for an international tour. When Clay and Raper appeared together, one played five-eighth and the other lock.

1963-64

The 1963–64 Kangaroos became the first all-Australian combination to bring the Ashes back from Britain (the previous 'burglars' had included New Zealanders). What's more, their 50–12 Second Test success was the highest score ever in such a series and the 38 points margin was also a record. Graeme Langlands' 20 points towards it equalled the highest individual score ever. In the previous Test he had scored 13, the most points for a Test debut against Britain.

Record in Great Britain

Played 22, Won 16, Lost 5, Drawn 1, Points for 379, Points against 201

Test Match Results

Australia	28	Great Britain	2	(Wembley, 13 946)
Australia	50	Great Britain	12	(Swinton, 30 843)
Australia	5	Great Britain	16	(Leeds, 20 497)

Other Matches

Opponents	Venue (Attendance)	For	Against
Warrington	Warrington (2090)	28	20
Huddersfield	Huddersfield (13 677)	6	5
Yorkshire	Hull (10 324)	5	11
Leeds	Leeds (16 641)	13	10

▶

Other Matches

Opponents	Venue (Attendance)	For	Against
Lancashire	Wigan (15 068)	11	13
St Helens	St Helens (21 284)	8	2
Featherstone Rovers	Featherstone (7898)	17	23
Oldham	Oldham (11 338)	12	4
Leigh	Leigh (9625)	33	7
Hull XIII	Hull (10 481)	23	10
Rochdale Hornets	Rochdale (8190)	3	0
Hunslet	Hunslet (4450)	17	13
Wakefield Trinity	Wakefield (15 821)	29	14
Cumberland XIII	Workington (8029)	21	0
Barrow	Barrow (10 157)	18	5
Castleford	Castleford (7887)	12	13
Wigan	Wigan (11 737)	18	10
Widnes	Widnes (6509)	20	9
Swinton	Swinton (11 957)	2	2

Record in France

Played 14, Won 12, Lost 2, Points for 328, Points against 111

Test Match Results

Australia	5	France	8	(Bordeaux, 4261)
Australia	21	France	9	(Toulouse, 6932)
Australia	16	France	8	(Paris, 5979)

Other Matches

Opponents	Venue (Attendance)	For	Against
Celtic de Paris	Paris (200)	30	2
Basque-Bearnaise	Bayonne (4261)	18	5
South-West France	Villeneuve (1266)	41	11
Pyrenees	St Gaudens (2059)	14	10
Rouergue	Albi (3780)	13	2
Languedoc	Carcassonne (6143)	16	12
XIII Catalan	Perpignan (4524)	11	15
France Sud	Marseille (889)	51	11
Vaucluse	Avignon (2009)	35	4
France B	Lyon*	—	—
Roanne	Roanne (2969)	38	2
Les Espoirs (Colts)	Limoges (2617)	19	12

* *Cancelled because of heavy snow and frozen ground*

Kangaroo captain Arthur Summons, surrounded by other players, shows Lord Mayor Harry Jensen the Ashes Cup won on the 1963–64 tour

Individual Records

	Matches	Tests	Tries	Goals	Points
G Langlands	25	5	17	78	207
K Irvine	28		29	2	91
L Johns	14	—	3	29	67
P Dimond	24	6	16	—	48
R Gasnier	19	6	15	—	45
M Cleary	21	1	14	—	42
B Hambly	24	5	2	12	30
B Rushworth	19	1	9	—	27
R Thornett	22	4	6	—	18
B Muir	20	6	5	—	15
K Day	18	2	5	—	15
A Summons (c)	16	2	5	—	15
K Smyth	18	2	4	—	12
F Stanton	18	—	4	—	12
E Harrison	17	4	3	—	9
K Thornett	16	6	3	—	9
J Gleeson	9	—	3	—	9
N Kelly	22	6	2	—	6
P Gallagher	21	3	2	—	6
J Raper	18	5	2	—	6
J Lisle	13	—	2	—	6
P Quinn	20	3	1	—	3
G Wilson	18	2	1	—	3
I Walsh	18	4	1	—	3
J Cleary	14	—	1	—	3
K Ryan	4	—	—	—	—

1967-68

The 1967–68 Kangaroos retained the Ashes but otherwise provided some low points. For the first time, the Kangaroos failed to win a Test in France. The Australian Rugby League was forced to pay a sizable bill to the Ilkley Hotel in Yorkshire for damage—including repairs to doors allegedly battered with an axe. Some players were found guilty of misconduct and fined—although their names were never made public. The tour also signalled the end of the career of the great centre and Kangaroo captain, Reg Gasnier, who broke down in a match at Avignon.

Record in Great Britain

Played 20, Won 12, Lost 7, Drawn 1, Points for 293, Points against 196

Test Match Results

Australia	11	Great Britain	16	(Leeds, 20 019)
Australia	17	Great Britain	11	(White City, 17 445)
Australia	11	Great Britain	3	(Swinton, 13 515)

Other Matches

Opponents	Venue (Attendance)	For	Against
Warrington	Warrington (11 642)	16	7
Yorkshire	Wakefield (19 370)	14	15
Hull Kingston Rovers	Hull (11 252)	15	27
Lancashire	Salford (9369)	14	2
Wigan	Wigan (22 779)	6	12
Rochdale Hornets	Rochdale (2676)	25	2
St Helens	St Helens (17 275)	4	8
Wakefield Trinity	Wakefield (10 056)	33	7
Castleford	Castleford (6137)	3	22
Oldham	Oldham (3329)	18	8
Widnes	Widnes (9828)	33	11
Barrow	Barrow (8418)	10	10
Cumberland	Workington (7545)	15	17

►

Other Matches

Opponents	Venue (Attendance)	For	Against
Swinton	Swinton (5640)	12	9
Leeds	Leeds (5522)	7	4
Halifax	Halifax (5285)	22	2
Bradford Northern	Bradford (14 173)	7	3

Record in France

Played 7, Won 4, Lost 2, Drawn 1, Points for 105, Points against 53

Test Match Results

Australia	7	France	07	(Marseille, 4193)
Australia	3	France	10	(Carcassonne, 4971)
Australia	13	France	16	(Toulouse, 4898)

Other Matches

Opponents	Venue (Attendance)	For	Against
Les Espoirs (Colts)	Avignon (1116)	17	7
XIII Catalan	Perpignan (3000)	37	7
France B	Albi (2949)	13	6
South-West France	St Gaudens (1205)	15	0

Individual Records

	Matches	Tests	Tries	Goals	Points
G Langlands	19	6	5	43	1018
J McDonald	17	5	5	13	41
K Irvine	14	1	8	5	34
B Moore	11	—	10	—	30
J King	18	6	9	—	27
R Coote	18	5	7	—	21
L Johns	14	6	2	7	20
L Hanigan	11	—	6	—	18
J Greaves	14	5	6	—	18
W Smith	15	5	3	3	15
K Junee	10	—	4	1	14
D Manteit	14	3	4	—	12
A Branson	17	5	3	—	9
J Gleeson	11	3	2	1	8
R Lynch	14	3	2	—	6
A Thomson	14	1	2	—	6
K Goldspink	13	—	2	—	6
E Walters	8	—	2	—	6
P Gallagher	15	6	1	—	3
R Gasnier (c)	6	1	1	—	3
E Rasmussen	18	6	—	—	—
N Kelly	17	5	—	—	—
N Gallagher	14	2	—	—	—
J Raper	12	5	—	—	—
R Saddler	12	—	—	—	—
J Sattler	9	—	—	—	—

1973

The year 1973 heralded in the era of streamlined Kangaroo tours. The Australians played just 19 games in Britain and France—a 33 percent drop on the number of matches on the tour before. The tour was a financial flop, with gate takings falling short of costs. However, if the Kangaroos failed financially, such was not the case on the field. They lost only two matches in Britain (the First Test and the clash with St Helens) and went through France unbeaten. The star of the tour was five-eighth-cum-centre Bob Fulton. He scored 20 tries—more than 20 percent of the tourists' touchdowns.

Record in Great Britain

Played 16, Won 4, Lost 2, Points for 362, Points against 141

Test Match Results

Australia	12	Great Britain	21	(Wembley, 10 100)
Australia	14	Great Britain	6	(Leeds, 16 286)
Australia	15	Great Britain	5	(Warrington, 10 019)

Other Matches

Opponents	Venue (Attendance)	For	Against
Salford	Salford (11 200)	15	12
Wakefield Trinity	Wakefield (5863)	13	9
Dewsbury	Dewsbury (5864)	17	3
Castleford	Castleford (2424)	16	10
Widnes	Widnes (5163)	25	10
Oldham	Oldham (3020)	44	10
Cumbria	Whitehaven (3666)	28	2
Bradford Northern	Bradford (5667)	50	14
Hull Kingston Rovers	Hull (5150)	25	9
Huddersfield	Huddersfield (1331)	32	2
Leigh	Leigh (2507)	31	4
St Helens	St Helens (10 400)	7	11
Featherstone Rovers	Featherstone (5069)	18	13

Record in Great Britain

Played 3, Won 3, Points for 59, Points against 24

Test Match Results

Australia	21	France	9	(Perpignan, 7630)
Australia	14	France	3	(Toulouse, 7060)

Other Match

Australia	21	France B	12	(Bordeaux, 2 523)

Individual Records

	Matches	Tests	Tries	Goals	Points
M Cronin	12	2	7	28	77
G Langlands (c)	8	1	4	27	66
R Fulton	14	5	20	1*	61
G Eadie	10	2	4	9	30
R Branighan	13	5	7	2	25
G Starling	14	5	8	—	24
E Goodwin	9	3	7	—	21
K Maddison	13	4	6	—	18
D Waite	13	4	4	—	12
R McCarthy	8	2	3	—	12
W Orr	8	—	4	—	12
A Beetson	15	5	3	—	9
T Raudonikis	10	4	3	—	9
E Walters	14	5	2	—	6
T Pickup	14	4	2	—	6
P Sait	13	4	2	—	6
J Lang	8	1	2	—	6
S Rogers	6	—	2	—	6
R O'Reilly	13	4	1	—	3
G Stevens	8	3	1	—	3
G Pierce	8	1	1	—	3
D Ward	8	—	1	—	3
W Hamilton	8	—	1	—	3
T Randall	5	—	1	—	3
L Williamson	9	3	—	—	—
J O'Neill	6	1	—	—	—

* field goal worth one point

1978

After one of the most successful tours of Great Britain, the 1978 Kangaroos wound up the French section of their tour with egg on their faces—they lost both Tests there. The refereeing in the first international, at Carcassonne, came in for some criticism, but coach Frank Stanton admitted there were no excuses for the Australian defeat in the second encounter. However, the tour was a resounding financial success, with the players receiving record bonuses.

Record in Great Britain

Played 16, Won 13, Lost 3, Points for 375, Points against 119

Test Match Results

Australia	15	Great Britain	9	(Wigan, 17 644)
Australia	14	Great Britain	18	(Bradford, 26 477)
Australia	23	Great Britain	6	(Leeds, 29 627)

Other International Result

Australia	8	Wales	3	(Swansea, 4250)

Other Matches

Opponents	Venue (Attendance)	For	Against
Blackpool Borough	Blackpool (3000)	39	1
Cumbria	Barrow (5964)	47	4
Britain Under-24	Hull (6418)	30	8
Bradford Northern	Bradford (15 755)	21	11
Warrington	Warrington (10 056)	12	15
Leeds	Leeds (9488)	25	19
Widnes	Widnes (12 202)	10	11
Hull	Hull (10 723)	34	4
Salford	Salford (6155)	14	2
Wigan	Wigan (10 645)	28	2
St Helens	St Helens (16 352)	26	4
York	York (5155)	29	2

Record in France

Played 6, Won 3, Lost 3, Points for 116, Points against 73

Test Match Results

Australia	10	France	20	(Carcassonne, 7000)
Australia	10	France	11	(Toulouse, 6500)

Other Matches

Opponents	Venue (Attendance)	For	Against
XIII Catalan	Perpignan (2270)	26	15
Cote d'Azur	Avignon (645)	29	7
Les Espoirs (Colts)	Albi (1600)	5	20
Midi-Pyrenees	Villeneuve (1627)	36	7

Individual Records

	Matches	Tests	Tries	Goals	Points
M Cronin	17	5	4	65	142
S Rogers	14	4	8	22	68
R Fulton (c)	15	5	9	2*	29
A McMahon	11	—	9	1	29
G Eadie	13	5	8	—	24
K Boustead	15	5	6	—	18
G Peponis	8	2	6	—	18
L Corowa	7	—	6	—	18

Continued

Individual Records *continued*

	Matches	Tests	Tries	Goals	Points
I Schubert	11	—	5	—	15
T Raudonikis	15	5	4	—	12
C Anderson	13	5	4	—	12
R Reddy	13	3	4	—	12
A Thompson	13	2	4	—	12
S Martin	11	1	4	—	12
B Walker	8	—	4	—	12
G Gerard	13	5	3	—	9
L Boyd	10	3	3	—	9
C Young	16	5	2	—	6
R Price	12	5	2	—	6
R Morris	12	2	2	—	6
G Olling	10	2	2	—	6
M Krilich	9	2	2	—	6
S Kneen	6	—	2	—	6
R Hilditch	9	1	1	—	3
J Gibbs	3	—	1	—	3
I Thomson	15	2	—	—	—
G Oliphant	4	—	—	—	—
G Pierce	4	—	—	—	—

* two field goals worth one point

1982

The 1982 Kangaroos were nicknamed 'The Invincibles'—because they were the first to go through a tour unbeaten. They won all 23 games, in Papua-New Guinea, Great Britain and France and produced some remarkable football, scoring 752 points (at an average of 33 per match) and 176 tries (including 69 in just seven matches in France) compared with their opponents nine. The 99 points in the three Tests against Britain is a record for Anglo-Australian encounters. Queensland centre Mal Meninga scored 48 points (two tries and 21 goals) in these Tests—second only to the 54 scored by fellow Australian Mick Cronin in Australia three years earlier. Steve Ella scored seven tries in the match against the French club, US Villeneuve, equalling the Kangaroo record. This is the only tour in which two hookers from the same club—Manly-Warringah's Max Krilich and Ray Brown—toured together.

Record in Papua New Guinea
Played 1, Won 1, Points for 38, Points against 2

Test Match Results

Australia	38	Papua New Guinea	2	(Port Moresby, 15 000)

Record in Great Britain
Played 15, Won 15, Points for 423, Points against 80

Test Match Results

Australia	40	Great Britain	4	(Hull, 32 500)
Australia	27	Great Britain	6	(Wigan, 23 126)
Australia	32	Great Britain	8	(Leeds, 17 328)

Other International Match

Australia	37	Wales	7	(Cardiff, 5617)

Other Matches

Opponents	Venue (Attendance)	For	Against
Hull Kingston Rovers	Hull (10 742)	30	10
Wigan	Wigan (12 158)	13	9
Barrow	Barrow (6217)	29	2
St Helens	St Helens (8190)	32	0
Leeds	Leeds (11 511)	31	4
Leigh	Leigh (7680)	44	4
Bradford Northern	Bradford (10 506)	13	6
Cumbria	Carlisle (5748)	41	2
Fulham	Fulham (10 432)	22	5
Hull	Hull (16 049)	13	7
Widnes	Widnes (9790)	19	6

Record in France

Played 7, Won 7, Points for 291, Points against 20

Test Match Results

Australia	15	France	4	(Avignon, 6000)
Australia	23	France	9	(Narbonne, 5000)

Other Matches

Opponents	Venue (Attendance)	For	Against
R C Roanne	Roanne (2000)	65	0
U S Villeneuve	Villeneuve (3579)	67	2
Les Espoirs (Colts)	Toulouse (2000)	42	3
XIII Catalan	Perpignan (4000)	53	2
Midi-Pyrenees	Pamiers (1000)	26	0

Exhibition Match

Opponents	Venue	For	Against
Western Australia	Perth	57	5

Individual Records

	Matches	Tests	Tries	Goals	Points
M Meninga	14	6	10	68	166
J Ribot	14	2	25	20	115
S Ella	13	—	21	3	69
E Grothe	14	4	21	1	65
S Rogers	16	6	10	7	44
W Lewis	14	3	3	9	27
J Muggleton	14	1	9	—	27
K Boustead	13	6	9	—	27
P Sterling	12	5	8	—	24
C Anderson	12	—	8	—	24
P McCabe	13	3	7	—	21
S Mortimer	9	1	6	1	20
B Kenny	12	6	6	—	18
W Pearce	13	5	5	—	15
M Murray	10	—	4	1	14
D McKinnon	10	—	3	1	11
L Boyd	14	—	3	—	9
G Brentnall	13	6	3	—	9
I Schubert	12	—	3	—	9
G Conescu	14	—	2	1	8
R Reddy	12	5	2	—	6
R Price	9	3	2	—	6
M Krilich (c)	12	6	1	—	3
C Young	11	5	1	—	3
G Miles	11	—	1	—	3
R Brown	14	—	—	—	—
R Morris	12	—	—	—	—
R Hancock	10	1	—	—	—

1986

Four years after the first unbeaten tour, the 1986 Kangaroos had a lot to live up to—and they did, in fine style. They won all 21 matches, scoring 800 points (at an average of 38 per match) to their opponents 138. Michael O'Connor set two Test records (22 points against Papua-New Guinea and 20 against Great Britain) and equalled a third (20 against France). Dale Shearer equalled the record four tries in a Test (against Papua New Guinea), and Terry Lamb became the first player to appear in every match on a Kangaroo tour of Britain and France (nine full games and 11 as a replacement). The Australians were particularly savage in France. In the two Tests they scored 92 points to just two by the French. They also whitewashed the France B side by 50–0.

Record in Papua New Guinea

Played 1, Won 1, Points for 62, Points against 12

Test Match Result

Australia	62	Papua New Guinea	12	(Port Moresby, 17 000)

Record in Great Britain

Played 13, Won 13, Points for 452, Points against 105

Test Match Results

Australia	38	Great Britain	16	(Manchester, 50 583)
Australia	34	Great Britain	4	(Leeds, 30 808)
Australia	24	Great Britain	15	(Wigan, 20 169)

Other Matches

Opponents	Venue (Attendance)	For	Against
Wigan	Wigan (30 622)	26	18
Hull Kingston Rovers	Hull (6868)	46	10
Leeds	Leeds (10 974)	40	0
Cumbria	Barrow (4233)	48	12
Halifax	Halifax (7193)	36	2
St Helens	St Helens (15 370)	32	8
Oldham	Oldham (5678)	22	16
Widnes	Widnes (10 268)	20	4
Hull	Hull (8216)	48	0
Bradford Northern	Bradford (10 663)	38	0

Record in France

Played 7, Won 7, Points for 286, Points against 21

Test Match Results

Australia	44	France	2	(Perpignan, 5500)
Australia	22	France	0	(Carcassonne, 5000)

Other Matches

Opponents	Venue (Attendance)	For	Against
President's XIII	Paris (800)	36	4
Le Pontet	Avignon (2500)	42	5
Midi-Pyrenees	Toulouse (1500)	12	2
France B	Albi (2000)	50	0
Selection Aquitaine	Villeneuve (500)	50	8

Individual Records

	Matches	Tests	Tries	Goals	Points
M O'Connor	14	6	15	66	190
T Lamb	20	5	19	20	116
G Jack	13	6	13	—	52
M Meninga	14	4	9	7	50
G Alexander	10	—	10	5	50
D Shearer	13	4	12	—	48
G Miles	14	6	8	—	32
B Kenny	14	5	8	—	32
W Lewis (c)	12	6	7	—	28
R Lindner	11	6	7	—	28
G Belcher	10	—	6	—	24
C Mortimer	10	1	5	—	20
D Hasler	9	1	5	—	20
N Cleal	8	3	5	—	20
S Roach	9	2	4	—	16
P Langmack	10	—	3	—	12
P Sterling	10	5	3	—	12
B Elias	10	—	3	—	12
L Kiss	5	2	3	—	12
B Niebling	11	6	2	—	8
R Simmons	11	6	1	—	4
G Dowling	11	5	1	—	4
M Bella	10	—	1	—	4
S Folkes	6	1	1	—	4
L Davidson	14	3	—	—	—
P Dunn	12	5	—	—	—
P Sironen	11	2	—	—	—
P Daley	7	—	—	—	—

1990

It was another tour of records in 1990, even though the Kangaroos did lose one match, the First Test against Britain. They also just won the second encounter, with a length of the field try in injury time. Utility player Greg Alexander scored the fastest century of points in any country when he notched 106 in five matches in France. His 46 against France B at Lyon was a world record for an international clash—and his 26 points in the First Test was an Franco-Australian best. That Test win of 60–4 was also a record against France.

Record in Great Britain

Played 13, Won 12, Lost 1, Points for 347, Points against 103

Test Match Results

Australia	12	Great Britain	19	(Wembley, 52 274)
Australia	14	Great Britain	10	(Manchester, 46 615)
Australia	14	Great Britain	0	(Leeds, 32 500)

Other Matches

Opponents	Venue (Attendance)	For	Against
St Helens	St Helens (15 260)	34	4
Wakefield Trinity	Wakefield (7083)	36	18
Wigan	Wigan (25 101)	34	6
Cumbria	Workington (6750)	42	10
Leeds	Leeds (16 037)	22	10
Warrington	Warrington (10 480)	26	6
Castleford	Castleford (9033)	28	8
Halifax	Halifax (8730)	36	18
Hull	Hull (13 500)	34	4
Widnes	Widnes (12 666)	15	8

Kangaroo second-rower Paul Sironen tries to burst out of a tackle by Great Britain captain Ellery Hanley during a 1990 Ashes clash

Record in France

Played 5, Won 5, Points for 256, Points against 49

Test Match Results

Australia	60	France	4	(Avignon, 2200)
Australia	34	France	10	(Perpignan, 3428)

Other Matches

Opponents	Venue (Attendance)	For	Against
President's XIII	Paris (1500)	46	18
France B	Lyon (2000)	78	8
Languedoc/Roussillon	Carcassonne (800)	38	9

Individual Records

	Matches	Tests	Tries	Goals	Points
G Alexander	17	4	14	50	156
M Meninga (c)	11	5	8	16	64
A Ettingshausen	12	5	15	—	60
D Shearer	13	5	9	1	38
B Fittler	8	—	8	—	32
G Belcher	11	5	6	2*	27
M Sargent	11	3	6	1	25
Kevin Walters	8	—	5	—	20
B Mackay	12	4	4	—	16
C Johns	11	1	4	—	16
M Geyer	11	1	4	—	16
A Langer	11	1	4	—	16
M Hancock	6	1	4	—	16
C Lyons	8	4	3	—	12
D Hasler	13	4	3	—	12
P Sironen	10	5	3	—	12
G Lazarus	13	5	2	—	8
S Roach	10	5	2	—	8
R Lindner	10	4	2	—	8
B Elias	10	4	2	—	8
Kerrod Walters	8	1	2	—	8
M Carroll	6	—	2	—	8

▶

Individual Records

	Matches	Tests	Tries	Goals	Points
D Gillespie	10	3	1	—	4
R Stuart	9	5	1	—	4
J Cartwright	9	1	1	—	4
M McGaw	6	1	1	—	4
M Bella	11	1	—	—	—
L Daley	6	3	—	—	—

* including one field goal worth one point

Most points on Kangaroo Tours

Player	Tours	Matches	Tries	Goals	Points
Graeme Langlands	3	52	26	148	374
Dave Brown	1	32	19	114	285
Mal Meninga	3	38	27	91	280
Brian Carlson	2	43	48	52	248
Noel Pidding	1	22	18	87	228
Mick Cronin	2	29	11	93	219
Greg Alexander	2	27	24	53	206
Keith Barnes	1	22	—	101	202
Ken Irvine	3	63	44	7	176
Michael O'Connor	1	14	13	59	170
Dally Messenger	1	31	9	64	155
Ron Willey	1	17	5	63	141

Most points per game on a Kangaroo Tour

Player	Tour	Matches	Points	Average per game
Michael O'Connor	1986	14	170	12.41
Mal Meninga	1982	14	166	11.86
Noel Pidding	1952–53	22	228	10.36
Keith Barnes	1959–60	22	202	9.18
Greg Alexander	1990	17	156	9.18
Dave Brown	1933–34	32	285	8.91
Harry Finch	1929–30	10	84	8.40
Mick Cronin	1978	17	142	8.35
Ron Willey	1952–53	17	141	8.29
Graeme Langlands	1963–64	25	207	8.28
Graeme Langlands	1973	8	66	8.25
John Ribot	1982	14	115	8.21
Gordon Clifford	1956–57	12	94	7.83
Eric Weissel	1929–30	20	127	6.35

Most Tries Per Game on a Kangaroo Tour

Player	Tour	Matches	Tries	Average per game
John Ribot	1982	14	25	1.79
Des McGovern	1952–53	10	17	1.70
Denis Flannery	1952–53	14	23	1.64
Steve Ella	1982	13	21	1.62
Harry Finch	1929–30	10	16	1.60
Alan Ridley	1929–30	7	11	1.57
Brian Carlson	1952–53	19	29	1.53
Dan Frawley	1911–12	12	18	1.50
Eric Grothe	1982	14	21	1.50
Frank Burge	1921–22	23	33	1.43
Bob Fulton	1973	14	20	1.43
Harold Horder	1921–22	25	35	1.40
Cec Blinkhorn	1921–22	29	39	1.34
Andrew Ettingshausen	1990	15	12	1.25

AUSTRALIA TO NEW ZEALAND

1919

After two tours of the Dominion in the early 1900s by New South Wales, a full Test side finally made the trip across the Tasman in 1919. The standard there was not the equal of the Australians—although New Zealand did manage one Test victory. The visitors won their last three minor games, 67–4, 73–7 and 93–5, with centre Les Cubitt scoring 17 tries in these three encounters alone.

Record in New Zealand

Played 9, Won 8, Lost 1, Points for 443, Points against 101

Test Match Results

Australia	44	New Zealand	21	(Wellington, 8000)
Australia	10	New Zealand	26	(Christchurch, 7000)
Australia	34	New Zealand	23	(Auckland, 24 300)
Australia	32	New Zealand	2	(Auckland, 15 000)

Other Matches

Opponents	Venue (Attendance)	For	Against
Auckland Province	Auckland (15 000)	32	8
Waikato	Huntly (1500)	58	5
Hawke's Bay	Napier (1200)	67	4
Hawke's Bay	Napier (1000)	73	7
Wellington	Wellington (1000)	93	5

Individual Records

	Matches	Tests	Tries	Goals	Points
L Cubitt	8	4	24	—	72
F Burge	7	4	10	17	64
H Horder	6	4	12	8	52
A Oxford	4	3	1	18	39
R Vest	5	1	11	—	33
J Robinson	7	3	10	1	32
R Norman	5	1	4	8	28
C Fraser	5	2	4	5	22
H Gilbert	5	1	6	—	18
A Halloway	8	3	4	2	16
F Ryan	5	3	4	—	12
J Watkins	8	4	3	1	11
C Prentice	6	2	2	2	10
T Sweeney	6	2	1	2	7
R Latta	2	—	2	—	6
J Kerwick	3	—	1	1	5
W Schultz	6	2	1	—	3
A Johnston	5	4	1	—	3
C Thorogood	3	2	1	—	3
W Paten	2	1	1	—	3
C O'Donnell	6	4	—	1	2
N Potter	3	—	—	1	2
R Townsend	3	2	—	—	—
D Thompson	2	2	—	—	—

1935

The immortal Dave Brown led a strong Australian combination on the 1935 tour. New Zealand took the First Test 22–14 and this shook the Australians who rallied to record easy wins in the other two full internationals. Bert Cooke and Lou Brown were among the New Zealand stars in the series.

Record in New Zealand

Played 6, Won 5, Lost 1, Points for 173, Points against 81

Test Match Results

Australia	14	New Zealand	22	(Auckland)
Australia	29	New Zealand	22	(Auckland)
Australia	31	New Zealand	8	(Auckland)

Other Matches

Opponents	Venue	For	Against
Auckland	Auckland	16	6
Combined XIII	Taranaki	47	31
Auckland	Auckland	36	6

Individual Records

	Matches	Tests	Tries	Goals	Points
D Brown (c)	5	3	10	22	74
R McKinnon	5	2	2	6	18
R Hines	5	3	4	—	12
W Mahon	4	1	4	—	12
E Collins	2	—	3	—	9
S Goodwin	4	3	3	—	9
F Curran	4	3	2	—	6
P Fairall	4	3	2	—	6
W Prigg	6	3	1	—	3
R Stehr	6	3	1	—	3
E Norman	5	3	1	—	3
L Ward	5	3	1	—	3
H Bichel	2	—	1	—	3
F Gilbert	2	—	1	—	3
V Thicknesse	5	3	—	—	—
S Pearce	4	3	—	—	—
E Lewis	3	2	—	—	—
M Shields	2	—	—	—	—
G Whittle	2	—	—	—	—

1937

The Kangaroos played two Tests against New Zealand on the way to England and France in 1937. The sides shared the honours after New Zealand made the most of the sloppy, muddy conditions at Auckland to win the second clash 16–15. Two great Maoris turned out at fullback for New Zealand, Steve Watene in the first encounter and George Nepia in the second. (See 1937–38 Kangaroo tour)

1949

A fine New Zealand side shared the series with the touring Australians in 1949. A 26–21 defeat in the First Test was the only loss the tourists suffered. They ran up big scores in most games. Stars such as Clive Churchill and Chic Cowie were to provide the nucleus of the Australian side which a year later surprised by downing the touring British Lions.

Record in New Zealand

Played 10, Won 9, Lost 1, Points for 299, Points against 123

Test Match Results

Australia	21	New Zealand	26	(Wellington, 7737)
Australia	31	New Zealand	10	(Auckland, 12 361)

Other Matches

Opponents	Venue (Attendance)	For	Against
South Auckland	Huntly (1823)	33	7
West Coast	Greymouth (3676)	39	14
South Islane	Christchurch (2900)	38	8
Southern Provinces	Wanganui (1500)	17	15
Maoris	New Plymouth (1827)	33	0
Auckland	Auckland (12 831)	36	18
Northern Provinces	Whangerei (1164)	39	9
Auckland Colts	Auckland (1953)	30	16

Individual Records

	Matches	Tests	Tries	Goals	Points
J Graves	7	7	12	8	52
M McCoy	7	2	8	14	52
I Johnston	5	1	8	12	48
K Froome (c)	5	2	2	11	28
P McMahon	8	2	7	—	21
R Roberts	6	1	6	—	18
V Bulgin	7	—	3	4	17
L Cowie	8	2	5	—	15
F Stanmore	5	—	3	—	9
N Mulligan	7	2	2	—	6
J Rayner	7	2	1	—	3
R Bull	6	1	1	—	3
J Hawke	6	1	1	—	3
C Churchill	5	2	1	—	3
W O'Connell	5	2	1	—	3
F de Belin	5	1	1	—	3
W Thompson	5	—	1	—	3
K Schubert	7	2	—	—	—
K Hansen	6	—	—	—	—
A Thompson	4	—	—	—	—
R Griffiths	3	—	—	—	—

1953

The 1953 tourists were the first full Australian side to use air travel for an overseas trip, but they were an unlucky combination. They won every match except the first two Tests and the second, which gave New Zealand the Trans-Tasman Cup, was a hotly disputed 12–11 result. The Australians claimed both tries by the home team should have been disallowed, as should have the final goal by New Zealand fullback Des White. The managers reported back to the Australian hierarchy that the referee had agreed White's kick had missed by about two metres but could not overrule both touch judges who awarded the goal.

Record in New Zealand

Played 9, Won 7, Lost 2, Points for 366, Points against 98

Test Match Results

Australia	5	New Zealand	25	(Christchurch, 5509)
Australia	11	New Zealand	12	(Wellington, 5394)
Australia	18	New Zealand	16	(Auckland, 16 033)

Other Matches

Opponents	Venue (Attendance)	For	Against
West Coast	Greymouth (2003)	17	11
South Island	Dunedin (2956)	66	9
Taranaki	New Plymouth (1950)	62	3
South Auckland	Huntly (1044)	63	11
Auckland	Auckland (8556)	26	4
Northland	Whangarei (1051)	98	7

Individual Records

	Matches	Tests	Tries	Goals	Points
N Pidding	8	3	8	18	60
D McGovern	6	1	19	1	59
B Carlson	6	2	16	5	58
B Drew	5	1	9	2	31
K McCaffery	6	3	8	—	24
F Ashton	5	1	4	5	22
H Wells	7	3	7	—	21
A Watson	5	—	6	1	20

▶

Individual Records

	Matches	Tests	Tries	Goals	Points
R Banks	7	3	4	2	16
G Hawick	6	2	2	3	12
K Holman	4	1	2	2	10
B Davies	7	3	3	—	9
R Bull	6	3	2	—	6
C Gill	7	3	1	1	5
A Paul	5	—	1	1	5
A Hornery	5	—	1	1	5
C Churchill (c)	8	3	1	—	3
H Crocker	5	3	—	—	—
L Cowie	5	1	—	—	—
K Kearney	4	3	—	—	—

1961

Australia was hard hit by injuries on the 1961 tour of New Zealand but still managed to retain the Trans-Tasman Trophy in a very close series. The two Tests were played in appalling conditions on a muddy Carlaw Park in Auckland. New Zealand won the first 12–10. Fullback Gary Phillips kicked the first field goal in a Test in New Zealand to give his side the edge. The second international encounter was just as close, with Australia winning 10–8. Captain Brian Carlson was picked to tour as a utility back and showed his versatility by turning out as lock-forward in one match.

Record in New Zealand

Played 9, Won 7, Lost 2, Points for 215, Points against 68

Test Match Results

Australia	10	New Zealand	12	(Auckland, 11 485)
Australia	10	New Zealand	8	(Auckland, 12 424)

Other Matches

Opponents	Venue (Attendance)	For	Against
Maoris	Rotorua (1787)	25	13
Wellington	Wellington (707)	66	3
National Coaching School	Christchurch (2793)	9	4
West Coast	Greymouth (2125)	27	7
Taranaki	Hawera (600)	34	0
Waikato	Hamilton (886)	26	8
Auckland	Auckland (5148)	8	13

Individual Records

	Matches	Tests	Tries	Goals	Points
D Parish	7	2	4	23	58
K Irvine	8	2	10	1	32
F Drake	7	1	8	—	24
R Gasnier	6	2	7	—	21
E Lumsden	8	2	6	—	18
B Muir	7	2	4	2	16
J Sinclair	5	1	3	—	9
J Paterson	6	2	2	—	6
R Gehrke	5	—	2	—	6
B Carlson (c)	3	1	—	3	6
R Crowe	7	2	1	1	5
A Summons	6	2	1	—	3
W Owen	6	—	1	—	3
A Gil	6	—	1	—	3
I Walsh	5	2	1	—	3
R Beavan	4	—	1	—	3
E Rasmussen	7	2	—	1	2
D Beattie	7	1	—	—	—
R Lynch	6	2	—	—	—
K Day	1	—	—	—	—

1965

The Australians were unlucky not to win the series when they ventured across the Tasman in 1965. The tourists had a fine 13–8 win over New Zealand on the muddy Carlaw Park field in the First Test. In the Second Test, also played in the mud, they were beaten 7–5. They should have scored a winning try but the slippery ball scooted from five-eighth Jim Lisle's hands as he was about to cross the line. The elusive Lisle was one of the stars of the tour. Another was second-rower Jim Morgan, who played in seven of the eight matches.

Record in New Zealand

Played 8, Won 7, Lost 1, Points for 159, Points against 58

Test Match Results

Australia	13	New Zealand	8	(Auckland, 13 295)
Australia	5	New Zealand	7	(Auckland, 11 383)

Other Matches

Opponents	Venue (Attendance)	For	Against
Wellington	Wellington (1745)	34	16
Canterbury	Christchurch (2654)	19	4
West Coast	Greymouth (1682)	16	6
Taranaki	New Plymouth (900)	29	11
Waikato	Huntly (1800)	25	4
Auckland	Auckland (7000)	18	2

Individual Records

	Matches	Tests	Tries	Goals	Points
L Johns	7	2	1	17	37
R Gasnier	5	2	4	3	18
N Yakich	4	—	6	—	18
K Irvine	7	2	5	—	15
J Lisle	6	2	5	—	15
W Smith	7	2	3	—	9
G Langlands	4	2	1	2	7
J Morgan	7	2	2	—	6
J Gleeson	5	—	2	—	6
B Beath	5	—	2	—	6
N Cavanagh	3	—	—	2	4
L Weier	7	2	1	—	3
B Hambly	6	2	1	—	3
M Cleary	5	2	1	—	3
T Pannowitz	4	—	1	—	3
G Wellington	3	—	1	—	3
P Quinn	5	2	—	—	—
M Veivers	5	2	—	—	—
A Buman	3	1	—	—	—
I Walsh (c)	3	1	—	—	—

1969

Australia had to be content with a drawn series on its lightning tour of New Zealand. Six games (including two Tests) were played in just 13 days. The strenuous itinerary told on the tourists. They easily won the First Test 20–10, but lost the second encounter, a week later 18–14. This success ended a run of 15 Test losses against all countries by New Zealand.

Record in New Zealand

Played 6, Won 4, Lost 2, Points for 137, Points against 78

Test Match Results

Australia	20	New Zealand	10	(Auckland, 13 375)
Australia	14	New Zealand	18	(Auckland, 9848)

Other Matches

Opponents	Venue (Attendance)	For	Against
North Island Colts	Rotorua (953)	17	13
South Island	Christchurch (3376)	24	15
Wellington	Wellington (1415)	48	7
Auckland	Auckland (6520)	14	15

Individual Records

	Matches	Tests	Tries	Goals	Points
L Johns	4	2	—	21	42
D Manteit	3	—	5	—	15
J Cootes	4	2	3	2	13
R Coote	5	2	4	—	12
M Cleary	2	—	4	—	12
D Ward	5	2	1	2	7
J McDonald	5	2	2	—	6
G Langlands	5	2	—	3	6
R Costello	4	1	2	—	6
R Honan	5	2	1	—	3
J Wittenberg	5	2	1	—	3
D Pittard	4	2	1	—	3
R McCarthy	4	2	1	—	3
J Sattler (c)	4	2	1	—	3
C Weiss	4	1	1	—	3
E Walters	4	2	—	—	—
J Denman	3	—	—	—	—
G Lye	3	—	—	—	—
I Robson	3	—	—	—	—
B Fitzsimmons	3	—	—	—	—

1971

Australia, winners of the World Cup the previous year, received a real shock on the short tour of New Zealand in 1971. The Australians played three matches in just six days and managed to win only one of them. The mud at Carlaw Park, Auckland, proved to be their downfall. They suffered their then-second biggest defeat by New Zealand. Auckland also beat the tourists, 15–14 after leading 10–nil early in the game. So tough was the tour that nine of the 18 players returned home nursing bad injuries.

Record in New Zealand

Played 3, Won 1, Lost 2, Points for 52, Points against 53

Test Match Result

Australia	3	New Zealand	24	(Auckland, 13 917)

Other Matches

Opponents	Venue (Attendance)	For	Against
NZ Second XIII	Huntly (3572)	35	14
Auckland	Auckland (11 000)	14	15

Individual Records

	Matches	Tests	Tries	Goals	Points
K Campbell	2	1	1	7	17
R Fulton	3	1	5	—	15
R McCarthy	3	1	2	—	6
L Williamson	3	1	1	—	3
R O'Reilly	3	1	1	—	3
G Starling	2	—	1	—	3
W Bennett	2	—	1	—	3
R Branighan	3	1	—	1	2
R Grant	3	1	—	—	—
T Raudonikis	2	—	—	—	—
J Murphy	2	—	—	—	—
P Sait	2	1	—	—	—
J Sattler (c)	1	1	—	—	—
G Langlands	1	1	—	—	—
A Branson	1	1	—	—	—
R Costello	1	1	—	—	—

1980

Australia easily beat New Zealand in the two Tests on the 1980 tour, but it had its colours lowered by South Island, which was helped by a 10–1 penalty count in the second half. The Maoris also managed a 10–all draw. New Zealand failed to cross Australia's line in the two Tests. Star of the tour was Parramatta fullback Garry Dowling, who only made the tour after Graham Eadie declared himself unavailable.

Record in Great Britain

Played 7, Won 5, Lost 1, Drawn 1, Points for 158, Points against 48

Test Match Results

Australia	17	New Zealand	6	(Auckland, 12 321)
Australia	15	New Zealand	6	(Auckland, 9706)

Other Matches

Opponents	Venue (Attendance)	For	Against
Maoris	Hastings (5000)	10	10
Central Districts	Wellington (4000)	23	0
New Zealand XIII	Christchurch (6000)	51	7
South Island	Christchurch (3000)	11	12
Auckland	Auckland (14 000)	21	7

Individual Records

	Matches	Tests	Tries	Goals	Points
M Cronin	5	2	2	28	62
R Reddy	5	2	5	—	15
G Brentnall	7	2	4	—	12
G Quinn	6	1	3	—	9
G Wynn	5	—	1	3	9
C Close	5	—	3	—	9
C Anderson	6	2	2	—	6
L Boyd	6	2	2	—	6
A Thompson	5	2	2	—	6
G Dowling	5	2	2	—	6
T Raudonikis	6	2	1	—	3
C Young	5	2	1	—	3
S Martin	5	—	1	—	3
R Hancock	4	—	1	—	3
G Peponis (c)	3	2	1	—	3
K Boustead	1	1	1	—	3
R Morris	6	2	—	—	—
J Leis	5	—	—	—	—
J Lang	4	—	—	—	—

1985

The Test series was decided on both sides of the Tasman in 1985. Australia won the First Test at Brisbane's Lang Park, 26–20, in a fiery match which saw opposing props Greg Dowling (Australia) and Kevin Tamati (New Zealand) suspended after a fight on their way to the sin-bin. Australia then toured New Zealand and were lucky to win the Second Test after winger John Ribot scored and converted a try 90 seconds from full-time. However the Kiwis avenged this defeat with an 18–0 victory in the third encounter. It was the first time in history that Australia had failed to score a point in a Test against New Zealand. The visit was also remarkable for the big name players who refused to tour for personal reasons, including Brett Kenny and Steve Mortimer.

Record in New Zealand

Played 6, Won 5, Lost 1, Points for 192, Points against 44

Test Match Results

Australia	10	New Zealand	6	(Auckland, 19 132)
Australia	0	New Zealand	18	(Auckland, 15 327)

Other Matches

Opponents	Venue (Attendance)	For	Against
South Island	Christchurch (6800)	56	0
Central Districts	Wellington (5500)	24	4
Northern Districts	Whangerei (1500)	52	6
Auckland	Auckland (18 000)	50	10

Individual Records

	Matches	Tests	Tries	Goals	Points
M O'Connor	4	—	2	13	34
M Meninga	5	2	3	9	30
J Ribot	6	2	4	2	20
G Jack	5	2	5	—	20
D Hasler	5	1	5	—	20
C Close	4	2	5	—	20
N Cleal	4	1	4	—	16
J Ferguson	5	2	2	—	8
S Ella	5	2	2	—	8
W Lewis (c)	4	2	1	—	4
B Elias	4	1	1	—	4
W Fullerton Smith	4	—	1	—	4
W Pearce	5	2	—	—	—
S Roach	5	2	—	—	—
P Tunks	5	1	—	—	—
G Conescu	4	1	—	—	—
G Dowling	4	1	—	—	—
M Murray	3	1	—	—	—
P Vautin	3	2	—	—	—
P Wynn	3	2	—	—	—

1989

A shock 26–24 win by Auckland prevented the 1989 Australian side from becoming the first to go through a full New Zealand tour unbeaten. The Test series was won easily by the tourists, although the Kiwis made a real match out of the third and final encounter. There was a great deal of criticism about the timing of the tour by some Australian clubs which were without their stars at a vital stage of the Sydney Premiership. It was later agreed that all future tours be conducted at the end of the season, after the Sydney grand final.

Record in New Zealand

Played 6, Won 5, Lost 1, Points for 158, Points against 74

Test Match Results

Australia	26	New Zealand	6	(Christchurch, 15 000)
Australia	26	New Zealand	6	(Rotorua, 26 000)
Australia	22	New Zealand	14	(Auckland, 15 000)

Other Matches

Opponents	Venue (Attendance)	For	Against
President's XIII	Palmerston North (5000)	50	18
Auckland	Auckland (9000)	24	26
Wellington	Wellington (5000)	28	10

Individual Records

	Matches	Tests	Tries	Goals	Points
M O'Connor	5	2	4	15	46
D Shearer	5	3	5	—	20
G Alexander	5	2	5	—	20
M Meninga	3	3	5	—	20
M Hancock	6	3	3	—	12
G Belcher	5	3	3	—	12
A Currie	5	3	2	—	8
S Backo	6	3	1	—	4
K Walters	5	3	1	—	4
B Clyde	4	3	1	—	4
D Hasler	4	2	1	—	4
W Lewis (c)	3	3	1	—	4
P Sironen	3	2	1	—	4
P Vautin	6	3	—	—	—
S Roach	5	3	—	—	—
B McGuire	5	2	—	—	—
P Jackson	3	—	—	—	—
D Stains	3	—	—	—	—
M Bella	3	—	—	—	—
D Trewhella	3	—	—	—	—

AUSTRALIA TO PAPUA NEW GUINEA ————————

1991

Australia made its first full tour of Papua New Guinea at the end of the 1991 domestic season. The players were treated as super-heroes with huge crowds mobbing them wherever they went. Every match drew a capacity gate. The Kumuls were no match for the slick Australian professionals, losing both Tests by big margins. Vice-captain Bradley Clyde was named official Man-of-the-Tour.

Record in Papua-New Guinea

Played 5, Won 5, Points for 208, Points against 42

Test Match Results

Australia	58	Papua New Guinea	2	(Goroka, 13 000)
Australia	40	Papua New Guinea	6	(Port Moresby, 14 500)

Other Matches

Opponents	Venue (Attendance)	For	Against
Northern Zone	Lae (10 300)	40	6
Island Zone	Rabaul (10 000)	42	25
Highland Zone	Mount Hagen (11 000)	28	3

Individual Records

	Matches	Tests	Tries	Goals	Points
Gary Belcher (Canberra)	5	2	3	10	32
Willie Carne (Brisbane)	5	2	8	—	32
Rod Wishart (Illawarra)	4	2	4	4	24
Mal Meninga (Canberra) (c)	3	2	2	6	20
Brad Fittler (Penrith)	5	2	4	—	16
Bradley Clyde (Canberra) (v/c)	4	2	3	—	12
Andrew Ettingshausen (Cronulla—Sutherland)	4	2	3	—	12
Scott Gourley (St George)	4	1	3	—	12
Peter Jackson (North Sydney)	4	1	3	—	12
Cliff Lyons (Manly-Warringah	5	2	3	—	12
Chris Johns (Brisbane)	5	2	2	—	8
Glenn Lazarus (Canberra)	5	2	1	—	4
Ian Roberts (Manly-Warringah)	4	2	1	—	4
Geoff Toovey (Manly-Warringah)	5	2	1	—	4
Kevin Walters (Brisbane)	5	2	1	—	4
Martin Bella (Manly-Warringah)	5	2	—	—	—
Gary Coyne (Canberra)	4	2	—	—	—
Andrew Gee (Brisbane)	1	—	—	—	—
Mark McGaw (Cronulla-Sutherland)	1	—	—	—	—
Bruce McGuire (Canterbury-Bankstown)	1	—	—	—	—
Steve Roach (Balmain)	1	—	—	—	—
Craig Salvatori (Eastern Suburbs)	1	—	—	—	—
Kerrod Walters (Brisbane)	4	2	—	—	—
Steve Walters (Canberra)*	—	—	—	—	—

* Did not play—injured at training before first game.

KB CUP see *Midweek Cup*

KEN KEARNEY

Twenty-five Tests for Australia (1952–58). Also played six matches in two World Cups (1954 and 1957), one match against the Rest-of-the-World (1957) and 30 minor games on two Kangaroo tours (1952–53 and 1956–57) and one New Zealand tour (1953).

If appearances were anything to go by, 'Killer' Ken Kearney would never have made it in Rugby League. A slow, tubby figure in long, baggy shorts, his image was unlike that of a football star. However Kearney was a real champion at winning the ball and scheming what to do with it. He played in seven Rugby Union internationals in 1947 and 1948—two versus New Zealand at home and one each against England, Scotland, Wales, Ireland and France on the Wallaby tour. After changing codes, he appeared in another 25, 22 of them in succession. He also played in two World Cups and was captain-coach of Australia in nine Tests.

As a Wallaby tourist, chosen from the Parramatta Union side, Kearney was spotted by the British club, Leeds, and turned professional in 1948. He returned to Australia four years later and hooked for St George until a series of injuries forced him to retire in 1962.

Kearney was just as successful on the club scene as he was internationally. He was captain of the mighty St George side in the first six years of their world record 11 straight Premiership victories of the 1950s and 1960s (and coach for five of those years). After he quit playing he had disappointing runs as coach of two other Sydney sides, Parramatta and Cronulla-Sutherland.

BILL KELLY

One Test for Australia (1914). Also played 10 minor games for New Zealand on two tours of Australia (1912 and 1913).

Bill Kelly was a great centre three-quarter and an even greater coach.

He played international Rugby League for New Zealand as an amateur, making tours of Australia in 1912 and 1913 and playing against the 1912 and 1913 New South Wales sides which visited the Shaky Isles. His form impressed scouts from Balmain Rigby League club, who persuaded him to turn professional in 1914 and play in the Sydney competition. Only four months after his first Sydney game, he was selected to play for Australia in the First Test against the touring British Lions. Kelly was made one of the scapegoats for a 23–5 win by Britain and was never chosen for in international sides again.

Kelly was the captain-coach of the Balmain side which, in 1915, won the Sydney Premiership for the first time in the club's history. The side, which included other great stars such as Chook Fraser, Jimmy Craig, Pony Halloway, Ricketty Johnston and Changa Schultz, went through the season unbeaten. Kelly later had some success as coach of other Sydney clubs— St George, Canterbury-Bankstown, Newtown and University.

NOEL KELLY

Twenty-five Tests for Australia (1959–67). Also played three matches in one World Cup (1960), one minor international (1960) and 43 minor games for Australia on three Kangaroo tours (1959–60, 1963–64 and 1967–68) and one World Cup tour (1960).

Noel Kelly is one of a select few players who have made three Kangaroo tours. He was an ultra-tough forward, equally at home as either hooker or prop-forward. Veteran Australian sporting journalist Tom Goodman said of Kelly: 'Rugged, determined and knowledgeable, he was one of the best combinations of hooker and player Australia has had in the modern era'.

'Ned' Kelly arrived on the representative scene in 1959, when he made his Test debut against the touring New Zealand side. He played in all three Tests and was later chosen, with Ian Walsh, as one of the hookers on the Kangaroo tour of Britain and France. Walsh, however, filled the hooker's spot in the Tests on tour, after Kelly had suffered an injury. On his other two visits to Britain with Kangaroo sides, Kelly appeared in all internationals. With the great 1963–64 side, he played prop alongside Walsh—and in 1967–68, after Walsh had retired, he was back as hooker again. In all, Kelly played in 25 Tests, against every Rugby League nation (eight against both Great Britain and France, seven against New Zealand and two against South Africa).

Kelly's fiery play often got him into trouble with referees, but there was no doubting his ability, both as a player and a leader. He was captain of Sydney's Western Suburbs side for several years. His knowledge of the finer points of the game was also never in dispute. He had spells as coach of two Sydney sides, Wests (while still a player) and North Sydney.

BRETT KENNY

Seventeen Tests for Australia (1982–87). Also played in 16 minor games for Australia on two Kangaroo tours (1982 and 1986).

When 19–year-old Brett Kenny played seven first-grade games for Parramatta in 1980, keen judges sat up and took notice. The Eels' secretary, former international Denis Fitzgerald, even picked him ahead of Peter Sterling (the former schoolboy champion destined to become one of the game's all-time greats) as the rookie most likely to make it to the top. Kenny didn't disappoint him. Six years later he was awarded the Adidas Golden Boot as the finest player anywhere in the world.

The five-eighth-cum-centre made his bold bid for international recognition in mid-1982. He was added to the NSW side for the third and deciding State-of-Origin clash, and, despite the Blues' loss, his performance was good enough to win him a place in the Kangaroo touring side later that year. On tour he grabbed his opportunity. When vice-captain Wally Lewis went to Western Australia with half the Kangaroo squad for an exhibition match, Kenny took over his five-eighth spot for the Test against Papua New Guinea—and he played so well that he remained at pivot for all the other Tests on tour. In subsequent years, however, Kenny was moved to inside centre to allow the great Queenslander Lewis to return to five-eighth. Kenny was back in Britain and France with the Kangaroos again four years later. And in 12 matches he averaged a try for every appearance.

His 17–Test international career (eight versus Great Britain, four each against New Zealand and France and one versus Papua New Guinea) came to an end in 1987 after, first, a series of niggling injuries and, then, an awful cruciate tear. The latter kept him sidelined for most of the 1988 season, too. However he was back playing, albeit only in club matches, in 1989, and even though his form was as good as ever, he declined to be considered for representative matches. Kenny also had a stint in England in 1985 with Wigan and won the coveted Lance Todd Trophy as Man-of-the-Match in the Wembley Challenge Cup Final.

Parramatta star Brett Kenny steers a pass around St George's Brad McKay in a 1990 clash

JOHNNY KING

Thirteen Tests for Australia (1966–70). Also played two matches in one World Cup (1968) and in 13 minor games on one Kangaroo tour (1967–68).

Winger Johnny King has a record unequalled in the Sydney Premiership competition—he scored a try in six successive grand finals—and in the seventh he went close on a number of occasions. King was one of the stars of the mighty St George side which won a world record 11 straight titles. King made the first-grade side in 1960 and was with the Dragons for the last seven of the record run. All told he played 191 first-grade games for St George.

Strangely enough, it took the Australian Test selectors a long time to fully recognise his talents. King first played for New South Wales in 1962, in the second of two clashes with the touring Great Britain side, scoring his team's only try. He was chosen as a reserve for the Third Test, but did not get a run. Although he turned out for the State side in 1963 and 1964, the Test spot continued to elude him. When he was transferred to Melbourne in his employment the following year all seemed lost, but he returned a few months later, and in 1966 finally got to wear the green and gold, against the touring British Lions. He made the Kangaroo touring side the following year and the World Cup squad in 1968, before bowing out against the 1970 Lions.

Another brush with fame came in 1974. King was non-playing coach of the NSW Western Division side, which shocked the critics by winning the midweek Amco Cup in its inaugural season, beating Penrith in the final.

ROSS KITE

Five Tests for Australia (1955–58).

St George winger Ross Kite certainly showed his potential when, as a 22–year-old, he played his first interstate game against Queensland, in 1954. It was at the Brisbane Exhibition Ground and Kite went over for four tries in New South Wales' 46–7 thrashing of the Maroons. It was the start of a fine sequence for Kite in NSW-Queensland clashes. In eight appearances for the Blues he scored 14 tries.

Kite, a winger noted for his skillful kicking over the defence, made his Test debut the following year against the great French combination led by Jacques Merquey. Despite a game for New South Wales against the 1956 Kiwis, it seemed that the selectors had forgotten him, until, after moving to Wagga in the south of the State, he bounced back in 1958. A great game for Riverina against the touring British side, saw him recalled to the Test side for his final two internationals.

KIWIS

The Kiwis is the traditional name given to New Zealand Rugby League teams making overseas tours. They made the first by any national side when, in 1907–08, as the All Golds (a play on the All Blacks Rugby Union name and the fact that the Kiwis were professionals) toured Australia and Great Britain. By 1992, the Kiwis had made a further 22 visits to Australia and/or Papua New Guinea and 10 to Great Britain and/or France.

NEW ZEALAND TO AUSTRALIA AND PAPUA NEW GUINEA
1907-08

AH Baskerville's pioneering All Golds played three matches in Australia on their way to Britain for the first international Test series and 10 more (including three Tests) on their way home. A narrow win in the First Test and a more decisive one in the Second gave the tourists victory over Australia in the inaugural series.

Record in Australia

Played 13, Won 9, Lost 3, Drawn 1, Points for 276, Points against 131

Test Match Results

New Zealand	11	Australia	10	(Sydney)
New Zealand	29	Australia	12	(Brisbane)
New Zealand	8	Australia	14	(Sydney)

Other Matches

Opponents	Venue	For	Against
New South Wales	Sydney	12	8
New South Wales	Sydney	19	5
New South Wales	Sydney	5	3
Newcastle	Newcastle	53	6
Newcastle	Newcastle	34	8
New South Wales	Sydney	10	18
New South Wales	Sydney	10	13
Queensland	Brisbane	34	12
Brisbane	Brisbane	43	10
Queensland	Brisbane	12	12

Team members (Test match appearances in brackets): H F Rowe (3), H S Turtill (1), D McGregor (—), G W Smith (—), J A Leverty (—), E Wrigley (2), R J Wynward (3), W T Wynyard (3), L B Todd (—), W H Tyler (3), J C Gleeson (—), E Tyne (2), A F Kelly (—), W M Trevarthen (3), H R Wright (1), W Johnston (2), T W Cross (2), A Lile (2), C J Pearce (3), D G Fraser (—), W H Mackrell (1), C A Byrne (2), D Gilchrist (2), E Watkins (—), C Dunning (1), A Callum (—), A H Baskerville (c) (1), H J Palmer (—), J Barber (3)

1909

Australia won its first Test series when New Zealand toured in 1909. The Kiwis showed mixed form and won only two of the six games played in Sydney, the heartland of Australian Rugby League.

Record in Australia

Played 10, Won 5, Lost 5, Points for 181, Points against 181

Test Match Results

New Zealand	19	Australia	11	(Sydney)
New Zealand	5	Australia	10	(Brisbane)
New Zealand	5	Australia	25	(Sydney)

Other Matches

Opponents	Venue	For	Against
New South Wales	Sydney	21	26
New South Wales	Sydney	20	27
New South Wales	Sydney	20	8
Metropolis	Sydney	18	27
Newcastle	Newcastle	6	3
Queensland	Brisbane	40	25
Queensland	Brisbane	27	19

Team members (Test match appearances in brackets): J Barber (3), E Buckland (3), C Byrne (3), A Carlaw (2), D Fraser (—), P George (—), G Hooker (2), T H Houghton (1), A P House (3), B King (3), H Knight (2), A Lile (3), R McDonald (3), H F Rowe (3), G Spencer (1), J Spencer (3), C Sullivan (1), W M Trevarthan (3)

1911

The Kiwis did not play any Tests on their 1911 tour. Had they done so, it seems certain they could have been soundly beaten for New South Wales won all three clashes and Queensland, for the first time, managed a win. However George Gillett, Charlie Savory, Frank Woodward and ex-All Black Rugby Union forward 'Boller' Francis so impressed on tour that they were invited to join the Kangaroos on their second tour of Britain later in the year.

Record in Australia

Played 8, Won 4, Lost 4, Points for 143, Points against 178

Match Results

Opponents	Venue (Attendance)	For	Against
New South Wales	Sydney (48 200)	10	35
New South Wales	Sydney (41 726)	7	39
New South Wales	Sydney (35 000)	10	26
Newcastle	Newcastle	21	20
Queensland	Brisbane	24	13
Queensland	Brisbane	13	23
Queensland	Brisbane	18	14
Hunter River	Newcastle	40	8

Team members: G A Gillett, C Siddells, R Shrange, E Buckland, F Woodward, F Morse, G Smith, H Cottrall, D Mason, C Savory, A R H Francis, S Feary, C Dunning, E K Asher, S Keen, R McDonald, J Rukutai, G Seager, A Stanaway, E Hughes, H Milne

1912

The Kiwis had a mixed tour in 1912. Generally, they were not in the same class as the NSW combinations—but they did win one clash when a couple of local stars were absent. One of the best in the New Zealand side was Boller Francis who had toured Great Britain with the Kangaroos only a few months before.

Record in Australia

Played 7, Won 4, Lost 3, Points for 84, Points against 83

Match Results

Opponents	Venue (Attendance)	For	Against
New South Wales	Sydney (28 912)	8	27
New South Wales	Sydney (18 000)	12	7
Queensland	Brisbane	15	8
Combined XIII	Brisbane	10	13

▶

Match Results

Opponents	Venue (Attendance)	For	Against
Queensland	Brisbane	16	10
New South Wales	Sydney (20 000)	3	14
Newcastle	Newcastle	20	4

Team members: A Hardgrave, A H Francis, W Curran, A Carlaw, C Webb, C Bradley, J Gilmour, S Weston, C Moir, J Barber, D Kenealy, J Rukutai, C King, T Brownlee, H Hayward, W Dervan, D Evans, R Irvine, C Dunning, W Kelly

1913

The New Zealanders ventured deeper into the country for the first time on the 1913 tour of Australia, to play a side at Orange, in the central-west of New South Wales. The tourists also played at Ipswich and Toowoomba in Queensland. The Kiwis' matches against New South Wales (once again, no Tests were played) were a mixed bag. There were two close contests but the other two were a romp for the locals.

Record in Australia

Played 99, Won 5, Lost 4, Points for 199, Points against 161

Match Results

Opponents	Venue (Attendance)	For	Against
New South Wales	Sydney (35 000)	15	17
New South Wales	Sydney	12	31
New South Wales	Sydney	10	34
New South Wales	Sydney	17	11
Queensland	Brisbane	39	5
Ipswich	Ipswich	29	12
Toowoomba	Toowoomba	32	6
Northern NSW	Newcastle	17	40
Orange	Orange	28	5

Team members: W Miller, W Mitchell, W Kelly, R Probestal, G Bradley, C Manning, H Devrall, R Reke, L Campbell, A Asher, K Ifwerson, A Carlaw, A Jackson, C King, C Byrne, J Auld, A Shadbolt, S Walters, R Mitchell, J Clark, H Hayward, J Hogan

1919

New Zealand had a disappointing tour of Australia in 1919. The Kiwis were beaten in all six matches they played against the two State sides and only wins against country teams managed to lend some respectability to their final record.

Record in Australia

Played 11, Won 5, Lost 6, Points for 211, Points against 187

Match Results

Opponents	Venue (Attendance)	For	Against
New South Wales	Sydney (46 157)	18	23
New South Wales	Sydney (38 884)	9	20
Northern NSW	Tamworth	21	13
Newcastle	Newcastle	11	8
New South Wales	Sydney	31	39
New South Wales	Sydney	19	22
Ipswich	Ipswich	11	8
Queensland	Brisbane (11 146)	13	26
Queensland	Brisbane (12 335)	13	16
Rockhampton	Rockhampton	23	0
Toowoomba	Toowoomba	42	12

Team members: N McCarthy, A McGregor, W Cloke, K Ifwerson, W Davidson, T A McClymont, A Matthews, W Walsh, B Laing, I Stewart, W Mitchell, W Wilson, J Clark, W Williams, J Rukutai, W Somers, E Waddell, E Herring, S Walters, H Tancred, J Parker, J Brown

1921

The New Zealand side found itself out of its depth when touring Australia in 1921. The locals had some fine players who were unlucky not to beat the British in England later that year. The New Zealanders won just one match against the State sides—and suffered the degradation of a 56–9 drubbing by New South Wales.

Record in Australia

Played 7, Won 3, Lost 4, Points for 131, Points against 164

Other Matches

Opponents	Venue	For	Against
New South Wales	Sydney	9	56
Queensland	Brisbane	25	12
Queensland	Brisbane	16	21
Queensland	Brisbane	3	8
Toowoomba	Toowoomba	18	30
Wide Bay	Bundaberg	33	23
Newcastle	Newcastle	27	14

Team members: G Paki, F Delgrosso, C Polson, C Wooley, B Laing, W Davidson, T A McClymont, N Bass, S Walters, H Avery, W Williams, W Somers, H Tancred, I Meadows, H Nunn, W Wilson, J Saunders, A Shadbolt, C McElwie, P Burrows

1925

The coming of age of Queensland football was never more evident than on the 1925 Kiwi tour of Australia. The New Zealanders lost all four matches in the northern State. Three wins in four games against New South Wales helped bolster their record.

Record in Australia

Played 12, Won 5, Lost 7, Points for 224, Points against 230

Match Results

Opponents	Venue	For	Against
New South Wales	Sydney	5	7
Universities	Sydney	13	15
Newcastle	Newcastle	29	11
New South Wales	Sydney	21	13
New South Wales	Sydney	17	10
Lismore	Lismore	21	20
Queensland	Brisbane	19	43
Ipswich	Ipswich	21	22
Queensland	Brisbane	20	29
Toowoomba	Toowoomba	14	16
New South Wales	Sydney	19	18
Southern Districts	Cootamundra	25	26

Team members: C Dufty, C Gregory, L Brown, H Brisbane, F Delgrosso, J Kirwan, J Parkes, B Laing, M Weatherill, J Sanders, W Wilson Hall, C Webb, H Avery, E Herring, J O'Brien, H Dixon, E Carroll, H Thomas, N Mouat, F Henry, J Ellis, A Green

1930

Queensland, once again, provided a none-too-pleasant interlude for the Kiwis, when they toured in 1930. They played four matches in the northern State and tasted victory in just one—and then only narrowly. The NSW side also quickly disposed of the visitors. Successes in the country again gave some semblance of respectability to their record.

Record in Australia

Played 12, Won 5, Lost 7, Points for 224, Points against 230

Match Results

Opponents	Venue	For	Against
New South Wales	Sydney	5	16
Western Districts	Parkes	20	16
New South Wales	Sydney	2	29
New England	Tamworth	34	19
Queensland	Brisbane	11	14
Ipswich	Ipswich	3	10
Queensland	Brisbane	6	32
Brisbane	Brisbane	19	17
Metropolis	Sydney	22	34
Metropolis	Sydney	17	34
Southern Districts	Cootamundra	24	30
Newcastle	Newcastle	25	22
Universities	Sydney	18	12

Team members: C Gregory, H Brisbane, L Seagar, J Amos, J Dodds, M Weatherill, J Calder, R Stephenson, T Timms, L Barchard, C Dufty, A Eckhoff, C Dobbs, N Griffiths, J Pearce, G Tittleton, E Abbott, E Meyer, R Trauvetter, J Jones, S Watene, S Clarke

1938

The 1938 Kiwi visit to Australia was an uninspiring tour. The New Zealand lineup was devoid of big names and failed in three of the four games against the State sides.

Record in Australia

Played 12, Won 5, Lost 7, Points for 224, Points against 230

Match Results

Opponents	Venue	For	Against
New South Wales	Sydney	12	25
New South Wales	Sydney	37	18
NSW North Coast	Lismore	23	2
Queensland	Brisbane	11	31
Toowoomba	Toowoomba	12	11
Queensland	Brisbane	12	21
NSW Country XIII	Tamworth	26	15
Newcastle	Newcastle	30	19
Sydney	Sydney	19	19

Team members: G Midgley, J Smith, W Tittleton, W Glynn, J Cootes, J Satherley, G McNeil, A Kay, J McLeod, G Orman, J Broderick, A Gault, J Anderson, J Hemi, D Herring, R Chase, W McNeight, R Brown, H Tetley, W Brimble, R Grotte

1948

New Zealand showed the benefit of a recent tour of Britain and France when it came to Australia in 1948. The Kiwis shared the Test series and only lost one other match.

Record in Australia

Played 8, Won 6, Lost 2, Points for 118, Points against 99

Test Match Results

New Zealand	21	Australia	19	(Sydney, 55 866)
New Zealand	4	Australia	13	(Brisbane, 23 013)

Other Matches

Opponents	Venue (Attendance)	For	Against
New South Wales	Sydney (43 505)	17	23
NSW Country	Wollongong (10 000)	30	16
Northern Division	Armidale (4000)	13	7
Queensland	Brisbane (20 812)	11	10
Rockhampton	Rockhampton (3176)	12	2
Newcastle	Newcastle (8000)	10	9

Individual Records

	Matches	Tests	Tries	Goals	Points
W Clarke	6	2	—	21	42
M Rich	4	—	—	8	16
D Redmond	6	2	3	—	9
A Graham	6	2	2	—	6
A Laird	3	—	2	—	6
C McBride	7	2	2	—	6
D Barchard	5	2	2	—	6
A Hambleton	5	2	2	—	6
J Forrest	4	2	1	—	3
A Wiles	3	1	1	—	3
R Cunningham	5	1	1	—	3
J Newton	4	2	1	—	3
C Hurndell	6	2	1	—	3
D Anderson	3	—	1	—	3
J Duke	4	—	1	—	3
M Roberston	6	2	—	—	—
W McKenzie	3	—	—	—	—
P Smith (c)	5	2	—	—	—
J Johnson	4	—	—	—	—
V Belsham	4	—	—	—	—
R Aynsley	3	—	—	—	—

1952

New Zealand shocked by taking the series in 1952, after Australia had scored a convincing win in the First Test. The touring party contained several players now regarded as among the all-time greats of New Zealand Rugby League—fullback Des White (who scored 107 points in just nine matches on the tour), utility back Cyril Eastlake and five-eighth George Menzies.

Record in Australia

Played 13, Won 10, Lost 3, Points for 368, Points against 159

Test Match Results

New Zealand	13	Australia	25	(Sydney, 56 326)
New Zealand	49	Australia	25	(Brisbane, 29 249)
New Zealand	19	Australia	9	(Sydney, 44 916)

Other Matches

Opponents	Venue (Attendance)	For	Against
Riverina/Western	Young (3351)	22	5
New South Wales	Sydney (49 442)	26	15
Monaro/Southern	Goulburn (1802)	21	8
Newcastle	Newcastle (14 000)	7	9
Northern/North Coast	Tamworth (4732)	55	12
Queensland	Brisbane (9995)	20	5

▶

Other Matches

Opponents	Venue (Attendance)	For	Against
Central Queensland	Rockhampton (3500)	35	4
Central Western Queensland	Barcaldine (2400)	66	17
North Queensland	Townsville (7953)	25	10
Toowoomba	Toowoomba (5901)	10	15

Individual Records

	Matches	Tests	Tries	Goals	Points
D White	9	3	1	52	107
R Moore	4	—	—	20	40
A Atkinson	9	3	10	—	30
F Mulcare	9	3	8	—	24
C Eastlake	10	3	7	—	21
B Hough	7	—	6	—	18
R McKay	8	3	5	—	15
T Baxter	10	3	4	—	12
T Hardwick (c)	11	3	4	—	12
G Davidson	8	3	2	3	12
J Haig	9	3	3	1	11
J Edwards	9	3	3	—	9
G Menzies	8	2	3	—	9
J Ratima	4	—	3	—	9
W McLennan	11	3	3	—	9
H Kreyl	6	—	2	—	6
L Blanchard	8	3	2	—	6
R Roff	5	—	2	—	6
A Riechelmann	4	—	1	—	3
R Neilson	5	—	1	—	3
W McKenzie	5	1	—	—	—
C Harris	2	—	—	—	—
J Russell-Green	4	—	—	—	—
R O'Donnell	4	—	—	—	—

1956

Australia won its first Test series against New Zealand in more than three decades when the Kiwis toured in 1956. The home side took all three Tests. The first two encounters were close, tough affairs and only in the Third Test did Australia really exert its authority to beat the travel-weary New Zealanders 31–14. Winger Don 'Bandy' Adams was the star of this match. His bumping runs netted him three of Australia's seven tries.

Record in Australia

Played 15, Won 9, Lost 6, Points for 352, Points against 253

Test Match Results

New Zealand	9	Australia	12	(Sydney, 46 766)
New Zealand	2	Australia	8	(Brisbane, 28 361)
New Zealand	14	Australia	31	(Sydney, 46 735)

Other Matches

Opponents	Venue (Attendance)	For	Against
Western Division	Lithgow (6620)	19	16
New South Wales	Sydney (35 492)	26	17
Newcastle	Newcastle (12 500)	5	20
Brisbane	Brisbane (14 367)	26	8
Toowoomba	Toowoomba (6142)	33	25
Queensland	Brisbane (28 261)	40	26
Central Queensland	Rockhampton (5800)	60	22
North Queensland	Townsville (4000)	53	8
Wide Bay	Maryborough (1326)	29	5
Northern Division	Narrabri (2040)	15	14
Southern Division	Wollongong (6804)	10	25
Southern NSW	Cootamundra (6000)	11	16

Individual Records

	Matches	Tests	Tries	Goals	Points
D White	10	3	—	43	86
W Sorensen	12	3	10	5	40
R Percy	8	—	12	—	36
V Bakalich	7	3	7	—	21
A Greene	6	—	6	—	18
C Eastlake	11	3	2	6	18
K Roberts	5	—	5	—	15
P Creedy	3	—	1	5	13
R Griffiths	7	—	4	—	12
T Hadfield	8	1	4	—	12
R Ackland	3	—	4	—	12
F Mulcare	7	3	3	—	9
J Murray	7	—	3	—	9
H Maxwell	10	3	3	—	9
J Lasher	7	—	3	—	9
J Bond	6	—	2	—	6
G Menzies	9	3	2	—	6
G Moncur	6	—	1	—	3
T Baxter (c)	9	2	1	—	3
S Belsham	9	3	1	—	3
C Johnson	8	3	1	—	3
J Yates	4	—	1	—	3
J Butterfield	10	3	1	—	3
D McRae	9	3	—	—	—
J Riddell	9	3	—	—	—
O Butt	5	—	—	—	—

1959

Cliff Johnson's 1959 Kiwis lost only two matches on their Australian tour—
but they were the two which counted—the first two Tests, which gave
Australia the Trans-Tasman Cup. Of the rest of the games, only the clashes
with New South Wales and Toowoomba provided New Zealand with any
headaches and in the country centres, especially those in Queensland,
the tourists ran up cricket scores.

Record in Australia

Played 15, Won 13, Lost 2, Points for 488, Points against 205

Test Match Results

New Zealand	8	Australia	9	(Sydney, 38 613)
New Zealand	10	Australia	38	(Brisbane, 30 994)
New Zealand	28	Australia	12	(Sydney, 31 629)

Other Matches

Opponents	Venue (Attendance)	For	Against
Western Division	Forbes (4000)	51	3
Newcastle	Newcastle (9203)	25	6
Northern Division	Gunnedah (4556)	26	11
Riverina	Narranderra (4000)	37	13
New South Wales	Sydney (35 444)	23	22
Southern Division	Wollongong (5741)	27	10
Brisbane	Brisbane (16 888)	36	8
Toowoomba	Toowoomba (5000)	21	19
Queensland	Brisbane (17 811)	34	19
Central Queensland	Rockhampton (4801)	48	19
Wide Bay	Bundaberg (3331)	62	0
Ipswich	Ipswich (3875)	52	16

Team members: B Reidy, G Phillips, T Hadfield, N Denton, M Paterson, E Anderson, R Griffiths, G Turner,
C Eastlake, G Kennedy, G Menzies, B Campbell, N Roberts, W Snowden, R Percy, M Cooke, T Kilkelly,
R Ackland, D Hammond, C Johnson (c), B Hallaway, H Maxwell, J Ratima, P Turner, W Schultz, J Butterfield

1963

The brilliant forward play of captain Mel Cooke was not enough to carry New Zealand to victory in the Test series on its 1963 tour of Australia. Cooke's inspired play was rewarded with success in the Brisbane clash which squared the series but in the decider, in Sydney, Australia won 14–0. The Kiwis had the dubious distinction of becoming the first international side to go down to a Sydney club team. St George beat them 22–7, with the immortal Reg Gasnier scoring three tries.

Record in Australia

Played 16, Won 12, Lost 4, Points for 258, Points against 157

Test Match Results

New Zealand	3	Australia	7	(Sydney, 48 330)
New Zealand	16	Australia	13	(Brisbane, 30 748)
New Zealand	0	Australia	14	(Sydney, 46 567)

Other Matches

Opponents	Venue (Attendance)	For	Against
Western Division	Parkes (3400)	36	11
New South Wales	Sydney (49 960)	5	2
Southern Division	Wollongong (7385)	14	8
Riverina	Temora (4463)	29	10
Newcastle	Newcastle (16 511)	24	6
North Coast	Grafton (3803)	28	2
Brisbane	Brisbane (12 630)	16	15
Toowoomba	Toowoomba (3850)	22	0
Queensland	Brisbane (16 612)	14	10
North Queensland	Townsville (5974)	18	12
Central Queensland	Rockhampton (5400)	10	15
Wide Bay/Burnett	Gympie (2869)	16	10
St George	Sydney (19 160)	7	22

Individual Records

	Matches	Tests	Tries	Goals	Points
J Fagan	8	2	1	22	47
G Phillips	5	1	—	20	40
N Denton	7	1	7	4	29
B Reidy	11	3	9	—	27
K McCracken	11	2	8	—	24
K George	8	—	2	6	18
G Kennedy	10	3	3	1	11
R Bailey	10	3	3	—	9
R Griffiths	7	—	3	—	9
M Cooke (c)	11	3	2	—	6
B Lee	7	3	2	—	6
C McMaster	6	—	2	—	6
J Fisher	6	—	2	—	6
F White	6	—	1	—	3
J Sparnon	3	—	1	—	3
J Bond	10	3	1	—	3
G Woollard	6	—	1	—	3
R Ackland	10	3	1	—	3
D Hammond	6	1	1	—	3
D Ellwood	8	—	—	—	—
W Snowden	9	2	—	—	—
R Sinel	7	1	—	—	—
H Emery	13	3	—	—	—
S Edwards	10	2	—	—	—
J Butterfield	8	2	—	—	—
G Blackler	6	1	—	—	—

1967

The young 1967 Kiwi side was no match for an experienced Australian lineup destined to beat Britain in England that year. The New Zealanders lost all three Tests.

Record in Australia

Played 17, Won 11, Lost 6, Points for 369, Points against 216

Test Match Results

New Zealand	13	Australia	22	(Sydney, 33 416)
New Zealand	22	Australia	35	(Brisbane, 30 122)
New Zealand	9	Australia	13	(Sydney, 27 530)

Other Matches

Opponents	Venue (Attendance)	For	Against
Newcastle	Newcastle (13 246)	7	14
Riverina	West Wyalong (5500)	21	19
Western Division	Lithgow (2500)	22	6
New South Wales	Sydney (27 048)	15	14
Southern Division	Wollongong (6157)	15	9
Brisbane	Brisbane (4671)	31	10
Wide Bay	Gympie (1467)	19	6
Queensland	Brisbane (13 142)	6	15
Central Queensland	Rockhampton (1400)	33	0
Toowoomba	Toowoomba (4620)	35	9
Far North Queensland	Cairns (2312)	45	3
North Queensland	Townsville (4587)	22	10
Ipswich	Ipswich (2165)	37	8
Northern Division	Armidale (4500)	17	23

Individual Records

	Tries	Goals	Points
R Tait	2	36	78
D Ellwood	2	33	72
L Mills	8	—	24
H Tatana	3	5	24
E Baker	5	—	15
K Dixon	5	—	15
W White	5	—	15
A Kriletich	4	—	12
R Sinel	4	—	12
L Morgan	4	—	12
R Orchard	4	—	12
C O'Neil	3	—	9
O Danielson	3	—	9
R Christian	3	—	9
W Southorn	3	—	9
R Irvine	3	—	9
W Noonan	2	—	6
R Carey	2	—	6
B Castle (c)	2	—	6
G Smith	2	—	6
G Woolard	1	—	3
P Schultz	1	—	3
G Brown	1	—	3
R Bailey	1	—	3
W Deacon	—	—	—
R Ballantyne	—	—	—

1972

The Kiwis came to Australia as uncrowned world champions. The previous year their Test side had shocked Australia in a one-off Test 24–3 and had gone on to beat both Britain and France on those nations' home grounds. The Kiwis were in for a rude shock. Not only were they no match for the Australians in the two Tests but they suffered the humiliation of a defeat by a very ordinary NSW Country representative side in the only other match of the quick tour. It was the first time a New Zealand side had failed to win a match on a visit to Australia.

Record in Australia

Played 3, Lost 3, Points for 28, Points against 93

Test Match Results

| New Zealand | 11 | Australia | 36 | (Sydney, 29 714) |
| New Zealand | 7 | Australia | 31 | (Brisbane, 24 000) |

Other Match

Opponents	Venue (Attendance)	For	Against
NSW Country	Queanbeyan (4000)	10	26

Individual Records

	Tries	Goals	Points
R Orchard	1	4	11
W Collicoat	—	4	8
P Orchard	1	—	3
M Eade	1	—	3
J Whittaker	1	—	3

Did not score: M Brereton, R Christian (c), D Williams, J O'Sullivan, D Sorensen, K Stirling, A Kriletich, B Bolton, J Greengrass, A Thompson, D Gailey, R Paul, J Fisher, S Dowsett

1978

The Kiwis had another bad tour in 1978. They were no match for the slick, professional Australians who, in the 3–0 Test rout, kept the visitors to just three tries (including a penalty try) and scored 95 points to 25. The Brisbane Test provided a record winning margin of 31 points. So little appeal did the Kiwis have that only 6 541 people turned up to watch the final Test—the smallest crowd since the beginning of Test football in Australia, 70 years before.

Record in Australia

Played 6, Won 2, Lost 4, Points for 90, Points against 135

Test Match Results

New Zealand	2	Australia	24	(Sydney, 16 577)
New Zealand	7	Australia	38	(Brisbane, 14 000)
New Zealand	16	Australia	33	(Sydney, 6541)

Other Matches

Opponents	Venue (Attendance)	For	Against
Newcastle	Newcastle (3500)	12	19
Riverina	Wagga Wagga (3000)	25	18
Northern Division	Moree (5000)	28	3

Individual Records

	Tries	Goals	Points
N Wright	5	37	89
C Jordan	1	23	49
A Coll	8	—	24
G Prohm	7	—	21

Continued

Individual Records *continued*

	Tries	Goals	Points
O Filipaina	7	—	21
M O'Donnell	3	6	21
W Winter	6	—	18
D Williams	2	3	12
S Varley	4	—	12
S McGregor	4	—	12
T Fepuleai	4	—	12
I Bell	4	—	12
F Ah Kuoi	3	—	9
D O'Hara	3	—	9
J Smith	3	—	9
M Eade	2	—	6
M Graham	2	—	6
K Stirling (c)	1	—	3
A Rushton	1	—	3
J Wright	1	—	3

Did not score: L Proctor, W Henry, G Taylor, R Baxendale, B Edkins

1982

The Kiwis put on a much improved performance on their 1982 tour. They were bolstered by several stars playing in the Sydney competition—captain Mark Graham, Fred Ah Kuoi, Olsen Filipaina and Mark Broadhurst. Some others were fresh from a season in England. New Zealand held the great Australian combination to three points in the First Test but was outclassed in the second encounter a fortnight later. The Kiwis played their first-ever Test against Papua New Guinea, winning easily 56–5.

Record in Australia

Played 8, Won 3, Lost 5, Points for 145, Points against 147

Test Match Results

New Zealand	8	Australia	11	(Brisbane, 14 000)
New Zealand	2	Australia	20	(Sydney, 16 775)

Other Matches

Opponents	Venue (Attendance)	For	Against
Gold Coast	Burleigh Heads (3000)	39	10
Toowoomba	Toowoomba (2000)	15	19
Central Queensland	Rockhampton (2500)	30	11
Queensland	Brisbane (12 000)	16	31
Northern Division	Tamworth (3000)	6	42
Riverina	Wagga Wagga (4500)	29	3

Record in Papua New Guinea

Played 3, Won 3, Points for 135, Points against 30

Test Match Result

New Zealand	56	Papua New Guinea	5	(Port Moresby, 13 000)

Other Matches

Opponents	Venue	For	Against
Highlands Zone	Goroka	54	20
Islands Zone	Rabaul	25	5

Individual Records

	Tries	Goals	Points
G Smith	2	32	70
L Hudson	4	17	46
G Kemble	7	—	21

Individual Records

	Tries	Goals	Points
K Fisher	6	—	18
H McGahan	6	—	18
J Leuluai	6	—	18
D O'Hara	6	—	18
G Prohm	4	—	12
B Gall	2	—	6
C Friend	2	—	6
P Mellars	2	—	6
J Whittaker	2	—	6
O Wright	2	—	6
G West (c)	2	—	6
H Tamati	2	—	6
W Dwyer	2	—	6
M Broadhurst	2	—	6
M Gillespie	1	—	3
D Field	1	—	3
K Tamati	1	—	3

Did not score: O Filipaina, F Ah Kuoi, M Graham, S Varley, A Coll, G Stokes, J Griffin

1983

The Kiwis played one Test in Brisbane in 1983—the second in a home-and-away series. There were no other matches played on the lightning trip across the Tasman. New Zealand shocked by easily beating Australia 19–12, breaking a sequence of 18 straight home wins. (For scorers see *New Zealand* entry).

1985

For the second time the Kiwis came to Australia for an only Test. Australia won 26–20 in a brawling match at Brisbane's Lang Park. (For scorers see *New Zealand* entry).

1986

After playing a Test in Auckland, the New Zealand Kiwis made a short six-match tour of Australia to complete the Trans-Tasman series. Australia won the series three Tests to nil. The Kiwis then travelled to Papua New Guinea where, without their Sydney-based stars, they suffered a shock loss in the Second Test. One of the regional sides also beat the Kiwis.

Record in Australia

Played 6, Won 3, Lost 3, Points for 138, Points against 105

Test Match Results

New Zealand	12	Australia	29	(Sydney, 34 302)
New Zealand	12	Australia	32	(Brisbane, 22 811)

Other Matches

Opponents	Venue (Attendance)	For	Against
Western Division*	Orange	—	—
Newcastle	Newcastle (6300)	22	17
Riverina	Wagga Wagga (5000)	14	16
Wide Bay	Kingaroy (2326)	32	7
North Queensland	Mackay (5000)	46	4

* *cancelled because of snow*

Record in Papua New Guinea

Played 4, Won 2, Lost 2, Points for 104, Points against 80

Test Match Results

New Zealand	36	Papua New Guinea	26	(Goroka, 11 000)
New Zealand	22	Papua New Guinea	24	(Port Moresby, 15 000)

Other Matches

Opponents	Venue	For	Against
Islands Zone	Rabaul	26	6
Southern Zone	Port Moresby	20	26
Northern Zone*	Lae	—	—

* cancelled

Individual records

	Tries	Goals	Points
J Roparti	2	4	16
P Brown	1	6	16
D Williams	4	—	16
G Freeman	3	—	12
B Todd	3	—	12
O Filipaina	1	4	12
D O'Hara	2	—	8
M Crequer	2	—	8
J Leuluai	2	—	8
D Lonergan	2	—	8
W Wallace	1	—	4
M Elia	1	—	4
A Shelford	1	—	4
O Wright	1	—	4
S Stewart	1	—	4
T Ropati	—	1	2

Did not score: G Kemble, G Mercer, S Cooper, B Harvey, J Goulding, D Bell, G Prohm, H McGahan, M Graham (c), K Sorensen

1987

New Zealand ventured across the Tasman for a single Test in 1987. And the Kiwis shocked the locals with an impressive 13–6 victory in Brisbane over a side which had swept all before it the previous year. (For scorers see *New Zealand* entry).

1990

New Zealand played two Tests in Papua New Guinea in 1990. There was to have been a full tour, but the Australian clubs refused to allow their New Zealand players time off for the minor matches. The Kiwis won both Tests, 36–6 and 18–10.

1991

New Zealand had hoped for a full tour of Australia in 1991, but opposition from Sydney clubs who would lose their Kiwi stars forced it to be scrapped. Instead, three midweek Tests were played. Despite this compromise, some clubs still refused to release New Zealand players who had been signed from the Rugby Union ranks and had never played League in New Zealand.

Record in Australia

Played 3, Won 1, Lost 2, Points for 36, Points against 92

Test Match Results

New Zealand	24	Australia	8	(Melbourne, 26 900)
New Zealand	0	Australia	44	(Sydney, 34 911)
New Zealand	12	Australia	40	(Brisbane, 29 139)

Individual Records

	Tries	Goals	Points
F Botica	—	6	12
J McCracken	2	—	8
R Blackmore	2	—	8
C Friend	1	—	4
T Nikau	1	—	4

Did not score: G Freeman (c), D Watson, J Williams, T Kemp, D Lonergan, E Koloto, P Brown, D Mann, E Todd, G Mann, M Patton, G Mercer, K Iro, E Failmolo.

NEW ZEALAND TO GREAT BRITAIN AND FRANCE

1907-08

AH Baskerville's 'All Golds' were the first international side to make an overseas tour. The party included four Rugby Union All Blacks and Australian star Dally Messenger, who topped the pointscoring with 146—101 more than the next most successful tourist. The New Zealanders shocked by winning the series, two Tests to one, after losing the first encounter, at Leeds. The tourists played matches in Australia en route to Britain and again on the way home (see *New Zealand to Australia and Papua New Guinea*, above).

Record in Great Britain

Played 35, Won 19, Lost 14, Drawn 2, Points for 414, Points against 294

Test Match Results

New Zealand	6	Great Britain	14	(Leeds, 8000)
New Zealand	18	Great Britain	6	(Chelsea, 15 000)
New Zealand	8	Great Britain	5	(Cheltenham, 5000)

Other International Match Results

New Zealand	8	Wales	9	(Aberdare, 15 000)
New Zealand	16	England	17	(Wigan, 10 000)

Other Matches

Opponents	Venue (Attendance)	For	Against
Bramley	Bramley	25	6
Huddersfield	Huddersfield (8130)	19	8
Widnes	Widnes	26	11
Broughton Rovers	Broughton (24 000)	20	14
Wakefield Trinity	Wakefield	5	5
Leeds	Leeds	8	2
St Helens	St Helens	24	5
Merthyr Tydfil	Tonypandy	27	9
Keighley	Keighley	9	7
Wigan	Wigan	8	12
Barrow	Barrow	3	6
Hull	Hull	18	13
Leigh	Leigh	9	15
Oldham	Oldham (20 000)	7	8
Runcorn	Runcorn	0	9

Continued

Other Matches *continued*

Opponents	Venue (Attendance)	For	Against
Dewsbury/Batley	Dewsbury	18	8
Swinton	Swinton	11	2
Rochdale Hornets	Rochdale	19	0
Bradford Northern	Bradford	2	7
Halifax	Halifax	4	9
Yorkshire	Wakefield	23	4
Warrington	Warrington	7	9
Hunslet	Hunslet	11	11
Salford	Salford (10 000)	9	2
Hull Kingston Rovers	Hull	6	3
Cumberland	Workington	9	21
Lancashire	Oldham	4	20
York	York	3	5
Ebbw Vale	Ebbw Vale	3	2
St Helens	St Helens	21	10

Team members (Test match appearances in brackets): H F Rowe (1), H S Turtill (3), D McGregor, G W Smith (3), J A Lavery, E Wrigley (3), H H Messenger (3), J R Wynyard (3), L B Todd (3), W H Tyler (2), J C Gleeson, E Tyne, A F Kelly (1), W M Trevarthen (3), H R Wright (c) (3), W Johnston (3), T W Cross (3), A Lile, C J Pearce (3), D G Fraser, W H Mackrell, C A Byrne, D Gilchrist (3), E L Watkins, C Dunning (1), A Callum, A H Baskerville, H J Palmer, J Barber

1926-27

Both Australia and New Zealand applied to tour Great Britain in 1926. The Australians thought an invitation would be a mere formality but the British authorities, pointing out that New Zealand had beaten the 1924 Lions and the Australians hadn't, asked the Kiwis to visit. The tour turned out to be a disaster. New Zealand was thoroughly outplayed in all three Tests, a game against Wales and in many of the minor games. The Kiwis did not lose financially, but the British who had offered guarantees ended up £900 in the red (a significant amount in those days).

Record in Great Britain

Played 34, Won 17, Lost 17, Points for 562, Points against 554

Test Match Results

New Zealand	20	Great Britain	28	(Wigan)
New Zealand	11	Great Britain	21	(Hull)
New Zealand	17	Great Britain	32	(Leeds)

Other International Match Result

New Zealand	8	Wales	34	(Pontypridd, 18 000)

Other Matches

Opponents	Venue	For	Against
Dewsbury	Dewsbury	13	9
Leigh	Leigh	23	16
Halifax	Halifax	13	19
Rochdale Hornets	Rochdale	11	9
Barrow	Barrow	19	16
Widnes	Widnes	15	5
York	York	19	11
Warrington	Warrington	5	17
Bramley	Bramley	35	12
Hull	Hull	15	13
Bradford Northern	Bradford	38	17
Oldham	Oldham	10	15
Leeds	Leeds	13	11
St Helens Recs	St Helens	14	28
Salford	Salford	18	10
Huddersfield	Huddersfield	10	12
Wigan Highfield	Wigan	14	2

▶

Other Matches

Opponents	Venue	For	Against
Batley	Batley	17	19
Keighley	Keighley	21	3
Swinton	Swinton	14	16
St Helens	St Helens	12	22
Wigan	Wigan	15	36
Yorkshire	Wakefield	16	17
Hunslet	Hunslet	12	13
Pontypridd	Pontypridd	17	8
Broughton Rovers	Broughton	32	8
Wakefield Trinity	Wakefield	29	24
Hull Kingston Rovers	Hull	15	20
Lancashire	Leigh	3	28
Cumberland	Workington	18	3

Team members (Test appearances in brackets): C Dufty (2), E C Gregory (2), J Sanders (1), L Brown (3), J Parkes (1), W L Desmond (1), B Davidson (3), J Kirwan (3), H Brisbane (3), S G Webb, H Cole (2), F Delgrosso (3), A Wilson Hall (2), H Avery (c) (3), N Mouat (1), L C Petersen (1), F Henry (2), J Wright (1), H E Thomas (2), W W Devine (2), A J Carroll (2), L T Mason (3), E Herring (3), A Singe (1), G Gardiner (1), J Menzies (1)

1939

The 1939 tour was the shortest on record. The outbreak of World War II brought it to a close almost before it had begun. The 26 New Zealanders arrived in Britain on August 29, played two matches and then left for home.

Record in Great Britain

Played 2, Won 2, Points for 41, Points against 13

Match Results

Opponents	Venue	For	Against
St Helens	St Helens	19	3
Dewsbury	Dewsbury	22	10

Team members: J R Banham, G W Beadle, G R Bellaney, L Brown, J J Campbell, T H Chase, J Clark, J G Cootes, C H Davison, J Hemi, R D Jones, A G Kay, R K King (c), B Leatherbarrow, A McInnerney, H Mataira, H M Milliken, L D Mills, G G Mitchell, G A Orman, P Ririnui, V J Scott, J Smith, D Solomon, I G Stirling, W H Tittleton

1947–48

The first tour after World War II made up for the disappointments of the previous two visits. The Kiwis were unlucky to have been beaten 11–10 in the First Test (after a disputed last-minute try by Britain) and won the second encounter despite being badly out-hooked in the scrums. However Britain clinched the series with a fine win, before more than 42 000 spectators, in the decider at Odsal Stadium. After leaving Britain, the Kiwis shared the two-match Test series on their first visit to France.

Record in Great Britain

Played 27, Won 16, Lost 10, Drawn 1, Points for 391, Points against 240

Test Match Results

New Zealand	10	Great Britain	11	(Leeds, 28 445)
New Zealand	10	Great Britain	7	(Swinton, 28 531)
New Zealand	9	Great Britain	25	(Bradford, 42 680)

Other International Match Result

New Zealand	28	Wales	20	(Swansea, 18 333)

Other Matches

Opponents	Venue (Attendance)	For	Against
St Helens	St Helens (22 000)	11	5
Swinton	Swinton (18 000)	6	8
York	York (4500)	29	0
Castleford	Castleford (10 000)	17	3
Hull Kingston Rovers	Hull (12 000)	7	13
Bradford Northern	Bradford (17 500)	17	7
Leigh	Leigh (15 000)	10	5
Wigan	Wigan (22 000)	10	8
Oldham	Oldham (17 239)	18	8
Hunslet	Hunslet (5553)	10	18
Batley	Batley (3510)	18	19
Leeds	Leeds (8864)	23	16
Warrington	Warrington (20 682)	5	7
Halifax	Halifax (5276)	21	5
Huddersfield	Huddersfield (8872)	7	12
Hull	Hull (16 113)	7	13
Widnes	Widnes (11 900)	0	7
Dewsbury	Dewsbury (7270)	24	5
Workington Town	Workington (10 722)	12	7
Barrow	Barrow (5565)	2	2
Wakefield Trinity	Wakefield (11 959)	30	3
Bramley	Bramley (3100)	31	3
Belle Vue Rovers	Belle Vue (3800)	19	3

Record in France

Played 8, Won 4, Lost 3, Drawn 1, Points for 118, Points against 104

Test Match Results

New Zealand	11	France	7	(Paris, 12 000)
New Zealand	7	France	25	(Bordeaux, 22 000)

Other Matches

Opponents	Venue (Attendance)	For	Against
XIII Catalan	Perpignan (18 000)	10	7
Languedoc/Pyrenees	Toulouse (18 000)	0	15
Centre Lyonnaise	Lyon (15 000)	10	20
Provence	Avignon (10 000)	36	7
France B	Carcassonne (25 000)	41	20
Basques de France	Bayonne (12 000)	3	3
Antibes*	Antibes	54	7

* Exhibition match

Team members (Test and international appearances in brackets): H D Anderson (2), R Aynsley (3), D A Barchard (1), R J Clark (2), W S Clarke (6), R Cunningham (2), W G Davidson (1), J A Forrest (6), A C Gillman (1), A H Graham, J S Haig (3), C C Hancox, T H Hardwick (3), C C Hurndell, J J Johnson (4), L D Jordan (6), C J McBride (6), R G McGregor (5), A J McInnerney (1), A W McKenzie, K H Mountford (6), J Newton (6), R G Nuttall, L R Pye (2), M W Robertson (6), P A Smith (c) (6)

1951–52

Britain made a clean-sweep of the 1951 series, but the Kiwis were unlucky not to win the Second Test, at least. They scored five tries to four and lost 20–19 after a last-minute British penalty goal. To complete an unhappy tour they also lost both Tests to France.

Record in Great Britain

Played 28, Won 18, Lost 10, Points for 482, Points against 348

Test Match Results

New Zealand	15	Great Britain	21	(Bradford, 37 475)
New Zealand	19	Great Britain	20	(Swinton, 27 065)
New Zealand	12	Great Britain	16	(Leeds, 18 649)

Other International Match Results

New Zealand	15	Wales	3	(Abertillery, 8568)
New Zealand	2	Empire XIII	26	(Chelsea, 2000)

Other Matches

Opponents	Venue (Attendance)	For	Against
Rochdale Hornets	Rochdale (4137)	13	9
Halifax	Halifax (14 476)	12	18
Workington Town	Workington (8935)	17	15
Oldham	Oldham (15 174)	18	21
Castleford	Castleford (6643)	10	9
Huddersfield	Huddersfield (9859)	34	12
Warrington	Warrington (18 889)	19	13
Batley	Batley (5087)	20	13
Bramley	Bramley (2096)	24	20
St Helens	St Helens (18 210)	33	10
Leigh	Leigh (8168)	31	5
Barrow	Barrow (13 319)	5	9
Bradford Northern	Bradford (28 672)	8	13
Wigan	Wigan (13 538)	15	8
York	York (4173)	15	12
Wakefield Trinity	Wakefield (8855)	26	18
Leeds	Leeds (17 039)	19	4
Lancashire	Warrington (7313)	12	13
Belle Vue Rovers	Belle Vue (3321)	5	7
Hull	Hull (8000)	28	8
Salford	Salford (9535)	27	12
Yorkshire	Wakefield (2958)	10	3
Cardiff	Cardiff (1475)	18	10

Record in France

Played 12, Won 7, Lost 4, Drawn 1, Points for 181, Points against 93

Test Match Results

New Zealand	7	France	17	(Paris, 23 459)
New Zealand	3	France	8	(Bordeaux, 8954)

Other Matches

Opponents	Venue (Attendance)	For	Against
Bearn/Gasogne	Pau	13	12
Languedoc/Pyrenees	Toulouse (4022)	23	15
U S Villeneuve	Villeneuve (1887)	5	5
XIII Catalan	Perpignan (8575)	20	10
A S Carcassonne	Carcassonne (6519)	7	9
Tarn et Garonne	Montauban	20	3
Selection Guyenne	Limoges (3617)	13	0
Lyon/Paris	Lyon (10 514)	7	9
Provence	Cavaillon	18	0
R C Marseille	Marseille (8170)	26	5

Team members (Test and international appearances in brackets): A J Atkinson (7), T O Baxter (5), A N Berryman, D A Barchard (1), D L Blanchard (2), G Burgoyne, R Cranch, J J Curtain, W G Davidson (6), J F Dodd, C A Eastlake (7), J R Edwards (5), K H English, J A Forrest (1), J S Haigh (6), W B Hough (5), C R Johnson (7), D Jolly, C J McBride (7), W R McLennan (6), G Menzies (1), F G Mulcare (6), B E Robertson (2), M W Robertson (c) (4), W Sorensen (1), D White (6)

1955-56

On the 1956–57 tour, the Kiwis showed indifferent form until the Third Test against Britain when they upset a side so confident it had not even bothered to have a training run. The patchy form returned in France, where the locals won the series two Tests to one.

Record in Great Britain

Played 26, Won 13, Lost 11, Drawn 2, Points for 435, Points against 418

Test Match Results

New Zealand	6	Great Britain	25	(Swinton, 21 613)
New Zealand	12	Great Britain	27	(Bradford, 24 442)
New Zealand	28	Great Britain	13	(Leeds, 10 438)

Other Matches

Opponents	Venue (Attendance)	For	Against
Blackpool Borough	Blackpool (12 502)	24	24
York	York (8242)	16	20
Halifax	Halifax (12 492)	17	18
Yorkshire	Hull (7407)	33	17
Wigan	Wigan (19 386)	15	17
Hull	Hull (10 167)	17	12
Barrow	Barrow (7098)	13	17
Workington Town	Workington (11 043)	26	16
Lancashire	Warrington (6859)	17	15
Leeds	Leeds (15 738)	18	16
Featherstone Rovers	Featherstone (4042)	7	6
Huddersfield	Huddersfield (10 618)	16	25
St Helens	St Helens (11 327)	8	16
Oldham	Oldham (14 422)	15	13
Leigh	Leigh (3536)	13	14
Warrington	Warrington (14 462)	15	22
Castleford	Castleford (2442)	31	7
Rochdale Hornets	Rochdale (9475)	17	16
Bradford Northern	Bradford (5271)	11	6
Salford	Salford (4239)	21	5
Wakefield Trinity	Wakefield (4907)	27	16
British XIII	Bradford (3403)	11	24
Keighley	Keighley (3881)	11	11

Record in Great Britain

Played 11, Won 5, Lost 5, Drawn 1, Points for 167, Points against 177

Test Match Results

New Zealand	7	France	24	(Toulouse, 10 184)
New Zealand	29	France	22	(Lyon, 7051)
New Zealand	3	France	24	(Paris, 14 752)

Other Matches

Opponents	Venue (Attendance)	For	Against
Paris	Rennes (1428)	6	12
Sud-Ouest	Nantes (3161)	19	11
Gironde XIII	La Rochelle (2187)	29	11
Anee Francaise	Bordeaux (3378)	10	7
Bigorre	Tarbes (4003)	11	11
Provence	Cavaillon (821)	11	14
Marseilles XIII	Toulon (2805)	22	11
Lyon XIII	Grenoble (2928)	18	30

Team members (Test appearances in brackets): A Atkinson (3), V Bakalich (5), T Baxter (c) (6), S Belsham (3), D Blanchard (4), J Bond (1), P Creedy (3), N Denton, I Grey (2), D Haggie (4), B Hawes (1), T Kilkelly (1), G McDonald (3), R McKay (5), W McLennan (5), L McNichol (1), H Maxwell (6), G Menzies (2), R Moore (4), R Percy (4), J Riddell (2), K Roberts (3), B Robertson (1), W Sorensen (5), J Yates

1961-62

The young, enthusiastic 1961–62 Kiwis were not expected to unduly concern the World Cup champions Britain—but they certainly did. In the First Test, a second-half rout saw them down the locals 29–11, with fullback Jack Fagan booting seven goals. The British recovered to win the other two Tests, but their pride had been sorely dented. In France, New Zealand at last won a series. The Kiwis romped home 23–2 in the Second Test— the only encounter which did not end in a draw.

Record in Great Britain

Played 20, Won 8, Lost 12, Points for 320, Points against 328

Test Match Results

New Zealand	29	Great Britain	11	(Leeds, 16 479)
New Zealand	10	Great Britain	23	(Bradford, 20 049)
New Zealand	19	Great Britain	35	(Swinton, 22 558)

Other Matches

Opponents	Venue (Attendance)	For	Against
Liverpool/Widnes	Widnes (9050)	6	9
Manchester XIII	Swinton (6926)	7	19
Castleford/Featherstone Rovers	Castleford (5744)	31	20
Leeds XIII	Leeds (7085)	24	9
Oldham/Rochdale Hornets	Oldham (8795)	8	10
Yorkshire	Hull (6650)	11	21
Barrow	Barrow (6647)	36	11
Lancashire	Warrington (9332)	13	15
Halifax/Huddersfield	Huddersfield (7251)	31	11
Rugby League XIII	Manchester (5271)	20	22
Warrington	Warrington (9332)	13	15
Hull XIII	Hull (8125)	6	17
Wigan	Wigan (25 483)	6	28
Cumberland XIII	Whitehaven (5033)	10	9
St Helens	St Helens (21 680)	10	25
Leigh	Leigh (6584)	15	4
Wakefield Trinity	Wakefield (16 558)	7	20

Record in France

Played 9, Won 6, Lost 1, Drawn 2, Points for 150, Points against 57

Test Match Results

New Zealand	6	France	6	(Bordeaux, 2375)
New Zealand	23	France	2	(Perpignan, 9020)
New Zealand	5	France	5	(Paris, 3307)

Other Matches

Opponents	Venue (Attendance)	For	Against
U S Villeneuve	Villeneuve (900)	8	2
R C St Gaudens	St Gaudens (1565)	38	8
Pyrenees XIII	Toulouse (2897)	14	16
Languedoc XIII	Carcassonne (6412)	15	8
Sud-Ouest	Cavaillon (1145)	13	6
R C Roanne	Roanne (2922)	28	4

Team members (Test appearances in brackets): A Amer, G Bailey, R Bailey (6), J Bond (6), J Butterfield (5), B Castle (1), M Cooke (6), R Cooke (4), R Duffy, S Edwards (6), H Emery (5), J Fagan (4), G Farrar, J Ford, T Hadfield (3), D Hammond (c) (6), R Harrison (2), W Harrison (2), R Hart (1), G Kennedy (3), B Lee (3), K McCracken (2), J Patterson (1), B Reidy (6), W Snowden (6), N Tiller

1965

The 1965 Kiwi tour was a real financial flop. Spectators refused to come to watch a side whose performances rarely rose above the mediocre. The Kiwis were beaten in nearly half of the British games, including two of the three Tests (the third was drawn). In France it was no better. The New Zealanders lost half of their matches and were thoroughly outplayed in all three internationals.

Record in Great Britain

Played 23, Won 13, Lost 9, Drawn 1, Points for 274, Points against 259

Test Match Results

New Zealand	2	Great Britain	9	(Swinton, 8497)
New Zealand	9	Great Britain	15	(Bradford, 15 849)
New Zealand	9	Great Britain	9	(Wigan, 7919)

Other Matches

Opponents	Venue (Attendance)	For	Against
Other Nationalities	London	15	7
Bradford Northern	Bradford (8373)	15	28
Warrington	Warrington (8162)	14	7
Halifax	Halifax (6730)	24	12
Oldham	Oldham (13 021)	5	2
Wigan	Wigan (12 853)	17	12
Widnes	Widnes (9450)	3	8
Hull Kingston Rovers	Hull (7540)	21	11
St Helens	St Helens (11 270)	7	28
Leeds	Leeds (5782)	28	13
Yorkshire	Castleford (14 814)	8	15
Leigh	Leigh (4840)	10	5
Barrow	Barrow (5081)	20	10
Whitehaven	Whitehaven (3208)	7	12
Castleford	Castleford (5702)	7	6
Hull	Hull (6591)	11	8
Lancashire	St Helens (8781)	21	10
Rochdale Hornets	Rochdale (7075)	10	4
Swinton	Swinton (8345)	7	14
Wakefield Trinity	Wakefield (7484)	4	16

Record in France

Played 8, Won 3, Lost 4, Drawn 1, Points for 67, Points against 80

Test Match Results

New Zealand	3	France	14	(Marseille, 3431)
New Zealand	2	France	6	(Perpignan, 9000)
New Zealand	5	France	28	(Toulouse, 7000)

Other Matches

Opponents	Venue	For	Against
Provence	Avignon	16	11
Midi Selection	Montpellier	23	10
L'Aude Selection	Carcassonne	11	2
Pyrenees Selection	St Gaudens	5	7
French Under-24s	Bayonne	2	2

Individual Records

	Matches	Tests	Tries	Goals	Points
R Tait	19	4	4	31	74
J Fagan	19	5	—	34	68
G Kennedy	25	6	3	8	25
R Bailey	24	6	8	—	24
H Emery	22	6	7	—	21
G Mattson	15	1	5	—	15
B Reidy	17	4	5	—	15
W Deacon	19	6	4	—	12
R Orchard	18	4	4	—	12
K Dixon	14	2	4	—	12
R Strong	11	—	3	—	9
P Schultz	18	3	3	—	9
L Brown	9	—	3	—	9
R Christian	19	6	2	—	6
P White	10	—	2	—	6
D Hammond	19	4	2	—	6
C O'Neil	15	2	1	—	3
W Schultz	16	4	1	—	3
B Langton	13	2	1	—	3
J Walshe	9	—	1	—	3
R Irvine	18	4	1	—	3
E Moore	17	3	1	—	3
J White	8	—	—	—	—
R Scholfield	9	—	—	—	—
S Edwards	19	4	—	—	—
W Snowden (c)	14	2	—	—	—

1971

The British fans, remembering the poor form of the previous Kiwi tourists did not rush to matches in which the 1971 New Zealand side appeared. The biggest Test crowd was a paltry 5479, but the Kiwis were good. For the first time, they won the series against both Britain and France.

Record in Great Britain

Played 22, Won 12, Lost 10, Points for 452, Points against 306

Test Match Results

New Zealand	18	Great Britain	13	(Salford, 3764)
New Zealand	17	Great Britain	14	(Castleford, 4108)
New Zealand	3	Great Britain	12	(Wigan, 5479)

Other Matches

Opponents	Venue (Attendance)	For	Against
Southern Amateurs*	London	67	6
Southern Amateurs*	London	66	0
Rochdale Hornets	Rochdale (2374)	23	8
St Helens	St Helens (8169)	8	18
Hull Kingston Rovers	Hull (5746)	10	12
Widnes	Widnes (5787)	18	15
Castleford	Castleford (5889)	8	25
Warrington	Warrington (6295)	2	13
Barrow	Barrow (4839)	25	15
Whitehaven	Whitehaven (3105)	21	8
Swinton	Swinton (3280)	15	26
Wigan	Wigan (11 987)	24	10
Huddersfield	Huddersfield (3495)	10	11
Leigh	Leigh (3819)	5	10
Salford	Salford (7127)	30	31
Wakefield Trinity	Wakefield (5367)	23	12
Oldham	Oldham (1882)	24	13
Bradford Northern	Bradford (6277)	30	23
York	York (2803)	5	11

* Exhibition games

Record in France

Played 6, Won 5, Drawn 1, Points for 117, Points against 43

Test Match Results

New Zealand	27	France	11	(Perpignan)
New Zealand	24	France	2	(Carcassonne)
New Zealand	3	France	3	(Toulouse)

Other Matches

Opponents	Venue	For	Against
Littoral Province	Avignon	14	9
Albi Selection	Albi	29	9
Bordeaux Selection	Bordeaux	20	9

Individual Records
(does not include two exhibition games)

	Matches	Tests	Tries	Goals	Points
H Tatana	21	6	5	65	145
P Orchard	19	5	27	—	81
M Brereton	20	6	11	—	33
D Williams	18	6	7	2*	23
R Orchard	18	6	3	5	19
R Christian (c)	17	6	5	—	15
J Whittaker	19	6	5	—	15
W Deacon	13	—	—	6	12
J Greengrass	14	4	4	—	12

Continued

Individual Records *continued*
(does not include two exhibition games)

	Matches	Tests	Tries	Goals	Points
B Lowther	11	2	3	—	9
A Kriletich	20	6	3	—	9
M McLennan	11	—	2	—	6
J O'Sullivan	13	—	2	—	6
R McGuinn	14	2	2	—	6
M Eade	13	1	2	—	6
D Sorensen	9	—	2	—	6
G Woollard	19	5	2	—	6
G Smith	16	2	2	—	6
D Gailey	14	5	1	—	3
K Stirling	13	6	1	—	3
G Cooksley	10	—	1	—	3
R Williams	10	—	1	—	3
J Fisher	16	6	—	—	—
S Dowsett	4	—	—	—	—
W Burgoyne	11	—	—	—	—

* field goals worth one point

1980

The Kiwis didn't manage to repeat their success of the previous tour to the Northern Hemisphere, but they drew the series against both Britain and France. A poor refereeing display in the First Test against France probably cost them victory in that match and the series. Attendances for the British Tests were a vast improvement on the 1971 figures. Star of the tour was five-eighth Fred Ah Kuoi.

Record in Great Britain

Played 14, Won 7, Lost 6, Drawn 1, Points for 202, Points against 143

Test Match Results

New Zealand	14	Great Britain	14	(Wigan, 7000)
New Zealand	12	Great Britain	8	(Bradford, 10 946)
New Zealand	2	Great Britain	10	(Leeds, 8089)

Other Matches

Opponents	Venue (Attendance)	For	Against
Blackpool Borough	Blackpool (1300)	23	5
Hull	Hull (15 945)	33	10
Cumbria	Whitehaven (4000)	3	9
St Helens	St Helens (6022)	6	11
Bradford Northern	Bradford (4553)	10	15
Hull Kingston Rovers	Hull (9516)	20	12
Leeds	Leeds (6923)	25	5
Warrington	Warrington (5680)	7	11
Britain Under-24s	Fulham (2397)	18	14
Widnes	Widnes (7500)	7	14
Leigh	Leigh (4000)	22	5

Record in France

Played 7, Won 6, Lost 1, Points for 119, Points against 34

Test Match Results

New Zealand	5	France	6	(Perpignan, 6000)
New Zealand	11	France	3	(Toulouse, 1956)

Other Matches

Opponents	Venue (Attendance)	For	Against
R C Roanne	Roanne (3500)	16	11
Provence	Avignon (3200)	24	5
France Under-24s	Pamiers (1300)	5	4
Lenguedoc Selection	Lezignan (3800)	28	5
Aquitane Selection	Tonneins (2000)	30	0

Individual Records

	Tests	Tries	Goals	Points
G Smith	—	2	22	50
G Kemble	1	3	18	45
D O'Hara	5	8	—	24
B Edkins	1	—	9	18
A Coll	3	5	—	15
J Leuluai	3	5	—	15
M Graham (c)	5	5	—	15
M O'Donnell	5	1	6	15
B Green	—	5	—	15
G Prohm	4	4	—	12
N Tupaea	—	3	—	9
B Dickison	3	3	—	9
B Gall	—	3	—	9
K Fisher	1	3	—	9
F Ah Kuoi	5	2	—	6
J Whittaker	4	2	—	6
S Varley	—	2	—	6
W Kells	—	2	—	6
R Muru	—	1	—	3
A Rushton	4	1	—	3
K Tamati	5	1	—	3
H Tamati	3	1	—	3
R Baxendale	3	1	—	3
G West	5	1	—	3
M Broadhurst	5	—	—	—
P Te Ariki	—	—	—	—

1985

The Kiwis were hot favourites to take out the series against Britain following their good form against the Australians, but the home side surprised by sharing the honours. In the match against St Helens, the Kiwis ran up 46 points—a record for any New Zealand touring side in Britain. The nine goals by Olsen Filipaina in that same match was also a record.

Record in Great Britain

Played 12, Won 8, Lost 3, Drawn 1, Points for 249, Points against 153

Test Match Results

New Zealand	24	Great Britain	22	(Leeds, 12 591)
New Zealand	8	Great Britain	25	(Wigan, 15 506)
New Zealand	6	Great Britain	6	(Leeds, 22 209)

Other Matches

Opponents	Venue (Attendance)	For	Against
Wigan	Wigan (13 009)	8	14
Britain Under-21s	Bradford (2285)	16	12
Hull Kingston Rovers	Hull (6585)	20	10
Cumbria	Whitehaven (5500)	32	6
Yorkshire	Bradford (3745)	8	18
St Helens	St Helens (7897)	46	8
Leeds	Leeds (4713)	16	10
Widnes	Widnes (5200)	32	12
Lancashire*	Oldham	—	—
Hull	Hull (8500)	33	10

* Cancelled due to frozen field

Record in France

Played 7, Won 7, Points for 192, Points against 41

Test Match Results

New Zealand	22	France	0	(Marseille, 1500)
New Zealand	22	France	0	(Perpignan, 5000)

Other Matches

Opponents	Venue (Attendance)	For	Against
Invitation XIII	Paris (1500)	20	8
Midi-Pyrenees	Toulouse (3000)	18	12
Languedoc/Rousillon	Carcassonne (5000)	66	1
Rest-of-the-World	Narbonne (700)	22	10
Aquitane/Cote d'Azur	Talence (1930)	22	10

Team Members (Test appearances in brackets): D Bell (5), M Bournville, S Cooper (1), R Cowan (1), M Crequer, M Elia (1), O Filipaina (5), C Friend (5), G Gibb, M Graham (c) (2), H McGahan (5), V O'Callaghan, R O'Regan (1), J Ropati, A Shelford, D Sorensen (5), K Sorensen (5), S Stewart (1), H Tamati (2), R Taylor, B Todd (1), W Wallace (3), D Williams (2), O Wright (3)

1989

Unfortunately, it was the events off the field for which the 1989 Kiwis will be remembered. Winger David Ewe, flown over at the end of the English leg of the tour as a replacement, lasted just a couple of weeks before being sent home in disgrace. He countered a charge of a sexual romp in a hotel foyer but admitted to having drunk too much and was suspended from representative football for two years. Then three other Kiwis, hooker Wayne Wallace, fullback Darrell Williams and halfback Phil Bancroft, were arrested in Spain and fined $400 for assaulting a police officer. On the field, the Kiwis came close to being only the second New Zealand side to win the series in England. They easily accounted for France.

Record in Great Britain

Played 12, Won 8, Lost 4, Points for 300, Points against 183

Test Match Results

New Zealand	24	Great Britain	16	(Manchester, 18 723)
New Zealand	6	Great Britain	26	(Leeds, 13 073)
New Zealand	6	Great Britain	10	(Wigan, 20 346)

Other Matches

Opponents	Venue (Attendance)	For	Against
St Helens	St Helens (6940)	26	27
Castleford	Castleford (5963)	22	20
Wigan	Wigan (15 083)	14	24
Bradford Northern	Bradford (3598)	26	8
Leeds	Leeds (9218)	34	4
Cumbria	Whitehaven (3000)	28	2
Hull	Hull (5898)	44	8
Widnes	Widnes (9905)	26	18
Featherstone Rovers	Featherstone (2830)	44	20

Record in France

Played 5, Won 5, Points for 218, Points against 30

Test Match Results

New Zealand	16	France	14	(Carcassonne, 3500)
New Zealand	34	France	0	(Carcassonne, 6000)

Other Matches

Opponents	Venue (Attendance)	For	Against
Midi-Pyrenees	Toulouse (1000)	36	12
Selection de L'Aude	Carcassonne (500)	70	0
France B	Albi (1500)	62	4
Provence-Cote d'Azur*	Avignon	—	—

* *Cancelled after New Zealand side delayed in traffic jam*

Individual Records

	Tries	Goals	Field goals	Points
P Bancroft	—	50	—	100
D Watson	17	—	—	68
K Shelford	5	14	1	49
G Freeman	8	—	—	32
H McGahan (c)	7	—	1	29
M Elia	7	—	—	28
K Sherlock	1	10	—	24
M Kuiti	6	—	—	24
K Iro	5	—	—	20
W Taewa	5	—	—	20
M Edwards	2	5	—	18
T Kemp	4	—	—	16
F Leota	4	—	—	16
D Williams	3	—	—	12
D Clark	2	—	—	8
G Mercer	2	—	—	8
T Nikau	2	—	—	8
W Wallace	1	—	—	4
J Goulding	1	—	—	4
B Tuuta	1	—	—	4
E Faimalo	1	—	—	4
S Stewart	1	—	—	4
D Mann	1	—	—	4
G Mann	1	—	—	4
D Bell	1	—	—	4
D Ewe	—	1	—	2

Did not score: T Ropati, A Shelford, B Todd

MAX KRILICH

Thirteen Tests for Australia (1978–83). Also played in 14 minor games on two Kangaroo tours (1978 and 1982).

Manly Hooker Max Krilich evades a tackle during a Sydney Premiership game against Western Suburbs

Max Krilich knew the meaning of patience. The fine Manly-Warringah hooker had to be content to stand in the wings for a long, long time as Fred Jones held centre stage at Brookvale Oval. Jones set a Sydney record of 298 Premiership games. Krilich stayed in his shadow playing 100 reserve grade games before he got the chance to establish himself as the club's number one hooker. He was then able to prove to the world what a great rake he was. At the age of 28, he finally made his Test debut, in the Third Test against the touring 1978 New Zealand Kiwis, before touring, himself, with the Kangaroos squad which visited Britain and France.

Although he was, for a while, ignored by the Test selectors after that tour he continued to turn in consistently good performances for Manly. Once again he was rewarded for his patience. In 1982, the selectors recalled Krilich to the Test scene—and they made him captain of the side to take on the New Zealanders. Even though he had to fight with Ray Brown for the Manly hooker's spot, he was an automatic selection to captain the Kangaroos at the end of that season (and, remarkably, Brown made the side, too). It's now history how Krilich led the Kangaroos into the record books—unbeaten in 23 games in Papua New Guinea, Britain and France, the first time an Australian squad had gone through such a tour without losing a game.

Krilich quit football after leading the Australian side against New Zealand in 1983. After 16 seasons (and 215 first-grade games for Manly), he was forced out of the game by a bad neck injury.

KUMULS

The Kumuls is the name given to Papua New Guinea touring sides. Kumul is Pidgin English for Bird of Paradise, the national symbol. The Kumuls made a tour of New South Wales in 1971, but their first major overseas trip was in 1979 when they visited England and France. They made their first tour of New Zealand four years later.

PAPUA NEW GUINEA TO AUSTRALIA AND/OR NEW ZEALAND

1971

The first tour of the Kumuls came before Papua New Guinea had been accepted as a full member of the International Board. They played against minor sides, with the toughest match being against the NSW Country champions, Illawarra.

Record in Australia

Played 3, Won 1, Lost 2, Points for 45, Points against 41

Match Results

Opponents	Venue	For	Against
Second Division	Sydney	10	15
Illawarra	Wollongong	9	18
Group 12	Gosford	26	8

1983

The first visit to New Zealand was, at that time, the most successful tour ever made by the Kumuls. Although they lost their last two games, against New Zealand and the Maoris, the early tour form was first class. The Test, won 60–20 by New Zealand, was one of several records. The 60 points was the then-highest ever scored by a Test side—and the six tries (24 points) notched by Kiwi second-rower Hugh McGahan was a try-scoring and pointscoring record, too.

Record in New Zealand

Played 7, Won 4, Lost 3, Points for 234, Points against 213

Test Match Result

| Papua New Guinea | 20 | New Zealand | 20 | (Auckland, 7 000) |

Other Matches

Opponents	Venue	For	Against
Northland	Whangerei	42	26
Waikato	Huntly	28	24
Northern Selection	Tokoroa	20	21
Wellington	Wellington	62	16
Eastern Districts	Gisborne	30	10
Maoris	Auckland	32	56

Team members: L Ngala (c), O Aiya, K Ario, T Gau, R Heni, J Joseph, J Katsir, J Kelly, P Kila, S Kimia, M Kitimum, D Koki, R Loitive, F Matmillo, L Minadi, K Nil, D Noifa, I Segeyaro, A Taumaku, J Tep, E Togili, J Wagambi, W Waluka, S Wemas.

1988

The Kumuls made a tour of Australasia in 1988 to complete their away games in the World Cup, but they were no match for the home Test sides. However, several members of the squad impressed, and one, Darai Kovae, was later chosen to play for the Rest-of-the-World in the Bicentennial International against Australia.

Record in Australia

Played 4, Won 1, Lost 3, Points for 54, Points against 136

Test Match Result

| Papua New Guinea | 8 | Australia | 70 | (Wagga Wagga, 11 685) |

Other Matches

Opponents	Venue (Attendance)	For	Against
Southern Division	Nowra (800)	18	26
NSW Country	Bathurst (1000)	10	28
Central Coast	Gosford (1000)	18	12

Record in New Zealand

Played 4, Won 3, Lost 1, Points for 166, Points against 92

Test Match Result

| Papua New Guinea | 12 | New Zealand | 66 | (Auckland, 14 000) |

Other Matches

Opponents	Venue	For	Against
Midlands	Tokoroa	58	0
Waikato	Huntly	38	12
Northland	Whangerei	58	14

Team members: E Numapo (c), L Atoi, D Ben Moide, Y Bom, T Evei, J Gispe, D Haili, S Kaeta, S Karara, T Kila, M Kombra, G Kouru, H Kouru, D Kovae, A Krewanty, A Kuno, N Lapan, M Matmillo, M Morea, T Rombuk, I Rop, A Tivelit, I Wanega.

PAPUA NEW GUINEA TO BRITAIN AND FRANCE————————

1979

The first major overseas tour by the Kumuls was regarded as a success even though the tourists won only three of their 10 matches. In France they played two Tests. In the first, at Albi, they were beaten 16–9 after leading 9–8 with only 10 minutes to go. In the Second Test, at Carcassonne, they had trouble containing the French superstar Jean-Marc Bourret, who scored three tries in France's 15–2 victory.

Record in France

Played 7, Won 2, Lost 5, Points for 81, Points against 89

Test Match Results

| Papua New Guinea | 9 | France | 16 | (Albi, 4500) |
| Papua New Guinea | 2 | France | 15 | (Carcassonne, 3500) |

Other Matches

Opponents	Venue (Attendance)	For	Against
Ile de France	Paris (1000)	42	15
Provence	Avignon (2000)	2	7
France Under-24s	Toulouse (2500)	14	4
XIII Catalan	Perpignan (3000)	7	11
Pyrenees	Rodez (200)	5	21

Record in Great Britain

Played 3, Won 1, Lost 2, Points for 52, Points against 56

Match Results

Opponents	Venue (Attendance)	For	Against
St Helens Amateurs	St Helens (4000)	17	19
Britain Amateurs	Hull (3000)	12	28
Cumbria	Barrow (2000)	23	9

Team members: S Sapu (c), P Akis, H Aope, N Bangkoma, L Geni, F Giheno, Z Gomia, J Joseph, V Kapani, V Karava, P Kila, D Koki, P Combinari, K Kuveu, D Laiwa, A Limi, P Monama, K Posu, C Sirosi, R Som, D Tamtu, D Tinemau, M Tore, J Wanimara, J Watabar.

1987

The Kumuls second trip to the Northern Hemisphere was in 1987 and included Tests which were part of the home-and-away World Cup series, due for completion the next year. The tourists were no match for Great Britain, but performed creditably against France.

Record in Great Britain

Played 8, Won 3, Lost 4, Drawn 1, Points for 90, Points against 163

Test Match Results

| Papua New Guinea | 0 | Great Britain | 42 | (Wigan, 9121) |

Other Matches

Opponents	Venue (Attendance)	For	Against
Featherstone Rovers	Featherstone (3315)	22	16
Lancashire	St Helens (4202)	22	22
Swinton	Swinton (2132)	6	13
Cumbria	Whitehaven (3750)	4	22
Yorkshire	Leeds (1780)	4	28
Britain Amateurs	Halifax (3000)	20	16
Fulham	Chiswick (1216)	12	4

Record in France

Played 4, Won 1, Lost 2, Drawn 1, Points for 78, Points against 55

Test Match Results

Papua New Guinea	4	France	21	(Carcassonne, 3500)

Other Matches

Opponents	Venue (Attendance)	For	Against
Midi-Pyrenees	Toulouse (2000)	12	12
Tarn Selection	Albi (1354)	48	4
XIII Catalan	Perpignan (2439)	14	18

Team members: B Numapo (c), B Ako, L Atoi, D Gaius, J Gispe, D Haili, R Heni, M Ipu, E Kamiak, J Kapia, T Kila, M Kitimun, M Kombra, D Kovae, A Krewanty, N Lapan, A Lomutopa, M Matmillo, M Morea, C Mou, T Rombuk, K Saea, A Taumaku, J Tep, B Waketsi.

1991

The Kumuls travelled to Britain and France in 1991 for their away games in the World Cup. Sadly, the tourists were no match for the professional British lineups and had to send for former Test Captain Bal Numapo and fellow international Michael Matmillo to bolster their side for the French leg of the tour.

Record in England

Played 5, Lost 5, Points for 23, Points against 232

Test Match Result

Papua New Guinea	4	Great Britain	56	(Wigan, 4193)

Other Matches

Opponents	Venue (Attendance)	For	Against
Wales	Swansea (11 422)	0	68
Great Britain Under 21s	Leeds (2500)	0	58
Combined Humberside	Hull (2500)	14	16
Cumbria	Workington (2000)	5	34

Record in France

Played 4, Won 1, Lost 3, Points for 60, Points against 115

Test Match Result

Papua New Guinea	14	France	28	(Carcassonne, 2000)

Other Matches

Opponents	Venue	For	Against
Midi-Pyrenees	Toulouse	4	35
President's XIII	Villeneuve-sur-Lot	16	32
Provence XIII	Carpentras	26	20

Team members: S Haru (c), M Angra, P Boge, T Daki, J Gispe, L Hoffman, C Itam, S Karara, T Karu, J Kola, J Kouoru, N Lapan, M Matmillo, D Moi, J Naipao, K Ngaffin, B Numapo, K Paglipari, L Palangat, K Sinemau, M Tiri, J Unagi, J Uradok, R Wagambie, I Wanega, J Yawing.

L

LABOR DAILY CUP

The Labor Daily Cup was one of the trophies awarded to the winners of the Sydney Premiership before the J J Giltinan Shield. Donated by the *Labor Daily* newspaper, the first winner was Western Suburbs, in 1934. The Cup was won outright by Eastern Suburbs, which won the Premiership in each of the next three seasons.

Winners of The Labor Daily Cup

1934	Western Suburbs
1935	Eastern Suburbs
1936	Eastern Suburbs
1937	Eastern Suburbs

TERRY LAMB

Seven Tests for Australia (1986). Also played 1988 World Cup Final and 15 minor games on one Kangaroo tour (1986).

Terry Lamb made history in 1986 when he became the first footballer to play in every match on a Kangaroo tour of Britain and France. He turned out in each of the 20 games (albeit some as a replacement). In doing so, he scored 19 tries and 20 goals (116 points) to be leading tryscorer and second to Michael O'Connor (190) in the point-scoring lists. Lamb, a very tough five-eighth who was known for his ability to support the man making a break, was unlucky to have been playing at the same time as the great Wally Lewis. As a result he made only seven Test appearances— all in the one year. However he did manage to make the side for the World Cup final against New Zealand in 1988.

Lamb began with Western Suburbs, but when the Magpies looked like being kicked out of the competition in 1984 he switched to Canterbury-Bankstown. That same year he topped the Sydney try-scoring lists with 17 touch-downs. He also won the Rothmans Medal as the best-and-fairest player in the Premiership competition. The fine stand-off missed the 1985 grand final through injury. He gained consolation in the JJ Giltinan Shield in 1988, scoring a try and kicking four goals in Canterbury's 24–12 victory over Balmain. In 1986, the year he topped the Sydney pointscoring with 210 (12 tries, 76 goals and 10 field goals), Lamb scored Canterbury's lone goal in its close 4–2 grand final loss to Parramatta in the lowest scoring finish to the Premiership on record.

Even though his representative days were over, Lamb continued for several seasons as a vital force in the Sydney Premiership. In 1991, he became one of a select few players to have scored more than 1000 points in the competition. An unabashed Lamb said on achieving the milestone: 'It's nice to score 1000 points but it's no big deal. I just go out there to try to do my best.'

JOHN LANG

Three Tests for Australia (1973–78). Also played five games in one World Championship (1975), one minor international (1975), and 11 minor games on one Kangaroo tour (1973) and one New Zealand tour (1980).

Queenslander John Lang had the misfortune to be playing at the same time as two hookers who captained Australia—Max Krilich and George Peponis. So, while Lang was on the top rung of football ability for almost a decade, he only turned out in three Tests and five World Championship matches, playing second-fiddle to the others on far too many occasions.

However Lang was a fine rake. He made his Test debut, against France, on the 1973 Kangaroo tour and clashed with the visiting British Lions the following year. His big effort was in 1975 when he was a lynch-pin in the Australian World Championship side which won the first home-and-away series ever conducted. In 1978, the selectors tried three different hookers in each of the Tests against New Zealand in an effort to decide who to take to England for that year's Kangaroo tour. Lang's fine effort in the second encounter seemed to assure himself of one spot—but the selectors went for Peponis and Krilich. Lang made a second overseas tour—to New Zealand in 1980—but played only the minor games (Peponis was the Test hooker), before bowing out of the major League.

Lang had a great record in the Brisbane Premiership. A victory by Easts in 1991 was the fifth in which he was involved. He had played in winning teams in 1972, 1977 and 1978. And he was the Tigers' coach when Easts won in 1983 and 1991.

ALLAN LANGER

Seven Tests for Australia (1988–91). Also played in 1988 World Cup Final, for Australia in the Bicentennial international against the Rest-of-the-World (1988), for the Rest-of-the-World against Great Britain (1988), and 10 minor games for Australia on one Kangaroo tour (1990).

Allan Langer was only a pint-sized player, weighing just 66.5kg (10st 7lb) and standing only 1.68m (5ft 6ins) high, so when the great halfback of the 1970s, Tom Raudonikis, Langer's coach at Ipswich, predicted he would turn out to be one of the greatest players of the modern era, there were a few raised eyebrows—even though Langer had been an Australian schoolboy representative in 1982. However he proved Raudonikis right with some big-hearted displays in both club and representative football. He made the Queensland State-of-Origin team in 1987 as a fresh-faced 20–year-old and was such an instant sensation that he won the Man-of-the-Match award in the third and deciding clash at Brisbane's Lang Park.

Langer continued his good form in 1988 (winning the Man-of-the-Match award again, in the opening clash) and it was a mere formality that after the great Peter Sterling was injured in the Third Test against Great Britain, Langer should take over for the Test against Papua-New Guinea, the Bicentennial international against the Rest-of-the-World and the World Cup Final against New Zealand in Auckland. Against Papua-New Guinea (a match won 70–8 by Australia) Langer was once more Man-of-the-Match, after scoring two tries and having a hand in several others. Another great Test half, Arthur Summons, noted after the game: 'That's the best I've seen from a halfback in years'. Langer was yet again Man-of-the-Match in the World Cup Final, scoring two tries in Australia's 25–12 victory.

Australian halfback Allan Langer makes a break during the opening match of the 1990 Kangaroo tour against St Helens

The young halfback was already in great form in 1989 when he broke a leg in the second State-of-Origin match, at the Sydney Football Stadium, putting him out of action for most of the remainder of the season and forcing him to miss the Test series against New Zealand. He was back with a vengeance the following year, regaining his Test spot for the one-off clashes with France and New Zealand, before touring Britain and France with the Kangaroos. He was one of the scapegoats for Australia's shock loss in the First Test against Britain, playing with the second-string combination for the rest of the tour.

But Langer was not content to call it a day. In 1991, he produced some of the best football of his career. In the pre-season Challenge Cup he won the Man-of-the-Match award an unprecedented four times in a row.

He starred in Queensland's 2–1 victory in the State-of-Origin series to ensure that he returned to the Test arena against the New Zealand Kiwis. In the second clash, in which Australia scored a record 44–0 victory, Langer was the unanimous choice as Man-of-the-Match. Unfortunately, he had to miss Australia's tour of Papua New Guinea at the end of the season when he was recovering from an operation on his nose.

GRAEME LANGLANDS

Thirty-four Tests for Australia (1963–74). Also played 11 matches in two World Cups (1968 and 1972) and one World Championship (1975) and 45 minor games for Australia on three Kangaroo tours (1963–64, 1967–68 and 1973) and three New Zealand tours (1965, 1969 and 1971).

If for no other reason, Graeme 'Changa' Langlands will be remembered as the only player to score more than 100 points in Anglo-Australian Test matches. He broke the century in his 12th and last Test against Britain, at the Sydney Cricket Ground, in 1974.

However Langlands deserves a place in the annals of Rugby league for many more reasons. He was the complete player: a brilliant fullback, a penetrating centre, a great goalkicker, a superb on-field tactician, an inspiring captain and a shrewd coach. Langlands burst into the limelight in 1962, while playing as a fullback in Wollongong, south of Sydney. That year he represented Country against City, New South Wales against Queensland and Southern NSW against the touring Great Britain side.

St George scouts were quick to spot his potential and the following year he was wearing the famed red and white of the Dragons. There was no looking back. With a surfeit of fine fullbacks at that time, the representative selectors switched Langlands to the centre—in which position he made his Test debut, against New Zealand. Langlands was to be a regular for Australia for more than a decade. On his first Kangaroo tour, in 1963–64, 21-year-old Langlands began breaking records. The highlight came in Australia's 50–12 drubbing of Britain in the Second Test. Langlands' 20 points (two tries and seven goals) was the most scored by an Australian against Britain in one match.

Langlands made two more Kangaroo tours, his last, in 1973, as captain-coach. He missed two of the Tests against Britain because of injury, but his tactics helped Australia to a two Tests to one triumph. Despite severe criticism in the local press of his play and coaching methods, he was able to repeat the performance in Australia the following year.

Langlands played in 34 Tests (12 against Great Britain, 13 against New Zealand, seven against France and two against South Africa). He was also a member of two World Cup sides, the successful 1968 combination and the 1972 lineup which lost on points average to Great Britain, after what seemed to be a fair—and spectacular—try by Langlands in the final was disallowed by a French referee.

In 1975 he was captain-coach of the Australian side which won the World Championship after a series of home-and-away games. He had to relinquish the captaincy of Australia's World Cup-winning squad in 1970, after breaking a bone in his left hand in the Sydney Premiership final just before the team was due to leave for England.

For St George, Langlands played 227 matches, the fourth highest by any of the Dragon stars. He appeared at fullback in four Premiership-winning sides (1963, 1964, 1965 and 1966). His last grand final appearance was a sad affair. It was against Eastern Suburbs in 1975. Langlands had taken painkillers to mask an injury, but they ended up leaving him with rubbery legs. Easts won 38–0—and Langlands' embarrassing display was vividly highlighted by his decision to play in white boots.

LANG PARK

Brisbane's Lang Park was the first major stadium in Australia controlled by the Rugby League authorities. The Queensland Rugby League secured a 40–year lease on the ground, built on the site of a former cemetery close to the centre of the city, in 1953.

Work began on the site in earnest in 1955 and was finished in time for the first game to take place on 12 April, 1958. The first major clash was a Queensland-New South Wales match in May 1959, when 26 328 spectators turned up. Ground capacity has since been enlarged to accommodate crowds of more than 40 000—although the police now order the gates to be shut long before that limit is reached. The record attendance is 45 047 for the Second Test of the 1966 Ashes series between Australia and Great Britain. Since 1988, Lang Park has also been the home ground of the Brisbane Broncos. The biggest club crowd was the 33 245 who turned up to see Brisbane play Parramatta on 20 August, 1989.

REG 'WHIP' LATTA

Five Tests for Australia (1921–24). Also played 23 minor games for Australia on one Kangaroo tour (1921–22) and one New Zealand tour (1919).

Whip Latta was, as his nickname implied, a fast, explosive player who caused opponents their fair share of pain. Latta, a lock or second-row, played for Balmain for more than a decade during and after World War I. Latta was a vital member of a great side which swept almost all before it. He was in the Balmain Premiership-winning sides of 1917, 1919, 1920 and 1924 (scoring the winning try in Balmain's 3–0 victory over Souths in the '24 final).

He made his debut for Australia on the 1919 tour of New Zealand, but was unable to make it into the Test lineup. This honour was achieved in the Second and Third Tests of the 1921–22 Kangaroo tour. He then played all three Tests against the visiting 1924 Lions. During the Kangaroo tour, Latta helped firemen at Harrogate get into a burning hotel. The Press (with a little assistance from the vivid imaginations of Latta's Kangaroo team-mates) so embellished the story that Latta was lauded locally as a hero who helped rescue trapped children.

DARCY LAWLER

Darcy Lawler was one of the most controversial of all Australian Test referees. He was regularly the target of criticism by touring sides, especially the

1958 and 1962 Lions. However the Australian officials continued to use him and Lawler showed no sign of being worried by the objections. For almost a decade, from 1954, he controlled most Tests in Australia. In all, he refereed three series against Great Britain and two each against France and New Zealand—a total of 16 Tests. In addition, he was in charge of three of the 1957 World Cup matches.

In the Sydney Premiership, Lawler refereed eight grand finals. Ironically, all featured St George. His first was in 1953, when South Sydney triumphed 31–12. He then controlled all of the finals from 1956 to 1963 (with the exception of 1962), each of them won by the Dragons.

FRED LAWS

Six Tests for Australia (1928–33). Also played 28 minor games for Australia on two Kangaroo tours (1929–30 and 1933–34).

A souvenir booklet on the 1933–34 Kangaroos described Fred Laws as 'one of the finest tacklers in the world'. Many keen judges suggest he was *THE* finest. At the very least, many an opposing player was left sick and sorry after being hit around the legs by one of Laws' tackles.

He was so tough that team-mates dubbed him 'Tiger'. Tiger Laws was a regular in the Queensland State side from 1927 (when he was 22 years old) until 1935. He forced his way into the Test arena for the first time when the British Lions toured in 1928. At the time, he was chosen as a five-eighth, but in later Tests he also turned out in the centres. His lack of size however—he was only 5ft 9ins (1.75m) and 12st 6lb (89kg)— put him at a disadvantage in the three-quarters.

Laws made two Kangaroo tours, in 1929–30 and 1933–34. On the second occasion he was vice-captain to Frank McMillan. He was also the centre of controversy on that visit. There seemed to have been some bias against Queenslanders, particularly Laws, in the selection of the teams for the first two Tests. It was alleged that co-manager Harry Sunderland, a Queenslander, threatened to resign after Laws was omitted from the second encounter, but all Sunderland would officially say was: 'There were some players I would have played more often had I had the deciding vote.'

Fred Laws

GLENN LAZARUS

Eight Tests for Australia (1990–91). Also played 11 minor games on one Kangaroo tour (1990) and one Papua New Guinea tour (1991).

Glenn Lazarus was a vital cog in Canberra's 'Green Machine' which powered to successive Premierships in 1989 and 1990. A tough, no-nonsense prop, Lazarus, in the space of a few years, evolved from being a young toiler to one of the finest front-rowers in the world. The representative selectors showed they were aware of his ability when they chose the 22–year-old for the President's XIII to play the touring Great Britain side in 1988, his first season in senior football. That same year he was named Discovery-of-the-Year by the Rugby League Writers' Association.

He made his State-of-Origin debut in 1989 and the following season first trod the Test arena as a second-half replacement in the one-off Test against New Zealand in Wellington.

A month later, Lazarus was named in the Kangaroo squad for the tour of Britain and France. On tour he really came of age. He was a replacement for Martin Bella in Australia's shock loss in the First Test against Britain, but for the remaining Tests, Lazarus was one of the first chosen and was named by the respected British League magazine *Open Rugby* as the best prop in the world in its biannual ratings.

Lazarus had patchy form in 1991 thanks largely to a chronic injury to his sternum. His only representative matches were for Country Origin and for NSW in the first State-of-Origin clash. But showing better form after shrugging off the injury near the end of the season he was once more in the green and gold for the tour of Papua New Guinea.

LEAGUE CUP See *Extinct Competitions*

WALLY LEWIS

Thirty-three Tests for Australia (1981–91). Also played in 1988 World Cup final, the Bicentennial international against the Rest-of-the-World (1988), for Oceania against Europe (1984) and 19 minor games for Australia on two Kangaroo tours (1982 and 1986) and two New Zealand tours (1985 and 1989).

They called him 'King Wally', for Wally Lewis was a right royal Rugby League player—and, in his native Queensland, he was treated with the respect normally reserved for a monarch. At the very least, Lewis was one of the all-time greats of football. Indeed, in 1985, he was honoured with the Adidas Golden Boot award as the finest player in the world.

Lewis was a member of the great Australian Schoolboys Rugby Union side which toured Europe, Britain and Japan in 1977–78. However, unlike other famous team-mates, the Ella brothers (Mark, Glen and Gary), Michael O'Connor, Michael Hawker and Tony Melrose, instead of remaining in the amateur code he went straight to senior Rugby League where he was to become a legend at five-eighth.

Lewis made his Test debut against France in 1981 and was an instant hit, combining with another fine newcomer, Steve Mortimer. The following

Wally Lewis

year he was named vice-captain of the Kangaroo side which toured Britain and France. While overseas he lost his Test spot to Parramatta star Brett Kenny, but it was only a temporary aberration and Kenny was later moved to the centres to make way for Lewis. He was never dropped again.

Lewis was especially dominant for Queensland in the Maroons' State-of-Origin matches against New South Wales. He played (as a lock forward) in the historic first game in 1980. When he was forced to miss one of the clashes in 1988 he had played a record 22 straight matches (every clash which had taken place until that time). In that period, Queensland had lost only two series—and it was Lewis' clever play (including his brilliant long passes and accurate tactical kicking) which swung many a match. King Wally led Queensland on its historic tour of England in 1983. It was only a matter of time before he took over the reins of the great Australian side. He was skipper from the 1984 series against Great Britain, and he was at the helm on his second Kangaroo tour in 1986. Only a broken arm robbed him of his Test spot, and the captaincy, in 1990, for the one-off Tests against France and New Zealand.

The year 1990 was to have been Wally's most memorable season. It was his testimonial year—but everything went wrong. As well as the broken arm, he was relieved of his captaincy of the Brisbane Broncos—there was also a lot of controversy concerning him failing a fitness test which would have enabled him to have toured with the Kangaroos for a third time.

Lewis, quoting sources in the media, suggested a conspiracy to keep him from breaking records held by the famous Clive Churchill and Reg Gasnier. At the end of the season, Lewis was unable to come to terms with the Broncos for another season of football. Instead he switched to the Gold Coast for a reputed $160 000 a season. His popularity was never more evident than when a near record crowd of 13 189 turned up to watch his debut in the Seagulls colours—and it was only a trial match!

He did not give up hope of regaining his Test spot. In 1991, he captained Queensland to victory in what was to be his last State-of-Origin series. He finished with a record number of appearances (29) and the most Man-of-the-Match awards (8).

Lewis was included in the First Test side to play New Zealand that season, but when the Kiwis scored a shock win he was one of the scapegoats who were dropped. He had played in 33 Tests (15 against New Zealand, 11 versus Great Britain, five against France and two versus Papua New Guinea). He also captained Australia in its 1988 Bicentennial international against the Rest-of-the-World at the Sydney Football Stadium and in the World Cup final against New Zealand in Auckland the same year. When, in 1987, he was inducted into Australia's Sporting Hall of Fame, he became only the tenth Rugby League Player to have been so honoured—and the only one of his era.

LIGHTWEIGHT FOOTBALLERS

Although many small men have played big-time football in Australia, there are no official records to judge just who was the lightest of them all.

Rugby League historian George Crawford reckoned that, on the international scene, it would probably have been Arthur 'Snowy' Justice, the St George hooker. He was only 10st (63.4kg) when he first played for Australia, against Great Britain in 1928. Other Test lightweights include Johnny Hunt, the Queensland five-eighth of the 1920s, and his NSW counterpart of the 1950s, Darcy Henry, who both weighed 10st 8lb (67kg). John Kolc, the Parramatta halfback who played in the 1977 World Championship final, was only 5ft 3ins (1.6m) tall and weighed the same as Hunt and Henry. Brisbane Broncos half Allan Langer was only a shade heavier when he first played for Australia, in 1988.

In club ranks there were a number of smaller players, including Joey Murphy (Glebe) and Tiger Gillespie (South Sydney and Newtown), who both tipped the scales at 9st (57.2kg)—yet, according to Crawford, even they could have not matched George McGowan, who played for South Sydney from 1916 to 1920. He was just 7st 7lb (47.6kg).

BOB LINDNER

Sixteen Tests for Australia (1986–91). Also played 11 minor games on two Kangaroo tours (1986 and 1990).

Bob Lindner showed just what a force he was going to be when he made his State-of-Origin debut for Queensland in 1984. In his first match the 21–year-old Brisbane lock went over for a fine try—stamping himself as a star of the future. Because of a crippling knee injury sustained in the second State-of-Origin match the following year however, he had to wait more than two years for his first Test appearance—against Papua-New Guinea at the start of the 1986 Kangaroo tour. While on tour, Lindner played in all three Tests against Britain and the two against France.

In 1987, Lindner left the Wynnum-Manly club in Brisbane to try his luck with Parramatta in the Sydney Premiership competition. It was an unhappy two seasons in the south, although his performances in State-of-Origin matches and Tests against New Zealand in 1987 and Great Britain the following year belied his ordinary club form.

After moving to the Gold Coast, Lindner's Test career was interrupted he broke a leg in the second State-of-Origin match in 1989. The 27–year-old was in cracking representative form again in 1990 after finding a happy niche as one of only a couple of experienced campaigners in a young Western Suburbs lineup. He starred in the one-off 1990 Test against New Zealand before being chosen in the Kangaroo squad to tour Britain and France. Lindner had a sensational tour. He was switched to the second-row after the First Test against Britain and forged a formidable combination with big Paul Sironen. He missed the First Test against France through injury and, not fully recovered, came off early in the second encounter. Nevertheless, his consistently good form won him the award as Player-of-the-Tour.

Lindner had a wretched year in 1991. The season had hardly begun when he broke his leg in a match against Cronulla. He made an incredibly quick recovery and was back playing less than two months later. He came on as a replacement in the third State-of-Origin match and was one of the first chosen for the First Test against the New Zealand Kiwis. Midway through the second half disaster struck—Lindner broke his leg for the second time in 10 weeks. It was the end of the season for him.

LIONS

The Lions is the name given to touring Rugby League teams from Great Britain. The first Lions visited Australia and New Zealand in 1910 and another 17 tours had followed by 1992. The Lions also made a tour of Papua-New Guinea and New Zealand in 1990. Until the late 1970s Britain had been highly successful, with only the 1950 tourists losing their series against both Australia and New Zealand. In 1979, Australia inflicted the first clean-sweep, with the home side scoring 87 points to 18 in the three Tests and holding the Lions tryless in the first and third encounters. The 1988 Lions took part in the 100th Test between Australia and Britain— a match which was the first Test at the new Sydney Football Stadium.

Great Britain to Australia and New Zealand
1910

The 1910 Lions are the only such team to have been given a guarantee to tour Australia. They were promised £6000 but that first tour was so successful that no side since has sought a similar financial safeguard. There has always been a great deal of confusion about which games played in 1910 were, in fact, Test matches. Great Britain played five internationals while on tour. The first was against Australia, the next against the Kangaroos, the third against Combined New South Wales and Queensland and the last two against Australasian sides which included two New Zealanders, winger Albert 'Opai' Asher and fullback Riki Papakura. For years, Australia recognised the clashes with Australia and Australasia as Test matches. At the same time, Britain claimed the games with Australia and one of the Combined XIIIs were the Tests. Eventually, however, the Australians fell into line with Britain. The one New Zealand Test was a pushover for Britain—winning by 32 points, still the biggest margin in Anglo-New Zealand internationals.

Record in Australia

Played 14, Won 9, Lost 4, Drawn 1, Points for 340, Points against 247

Test Match Results

| Great Britain | 27 | Australia | 20 | (Sydney, 42 000) |
| Great Britain | 22 | Australia | 17 | (Brisbane, 18 000) |

International Results

| Great Britain | 13 | Australasia | 13 | (Sydney, 50 000) |
| Great Britain | 15 | Australasia | 32 | (Sydney, 50 000) |

Other Matches

Opponents	Venue (Attendance)	For	Against
New South Wales	Sydney (37 000)	14	28
New South Wales	Sydney (36 500)	20	27
New South Wales	Sydney (30 000)	23	10
Metropolis	Sydney	34	25
Newcastle	Newcastle	24	8
Northern NSW	Newcastle	40	20
Queensland	Brisbane	33	9
Queensland	Brisbane	15	4
Kangaroos	Sydney (30 000)	10	22
New South Wales	Sydney (35 000)	50	12

Record in New Zealand

Played 4, Won 4, Points for 187, Points against 47

Test Match Results

| Great Britain | 52 | New Zealand | 20 | (Wellington, 20 000) |

Other Matches

Opponents	Venue	For	Against
Maoris	Auckland	29	0
Auckland	Auckland	52	9
Rotorua	Rotorua	54	18

Team members: J Lomas (c), J Sharrock, F Young, C Jenkins, F Farrar, J Leytham, W Batten, J Bartholomew, B Jenkins, J Riley, F Smith, J Thomas, J Davies, T Newbould, T Helm, G Ruddick, F Shugars, R Ramsdale, E Curzon, W Winstanley, F Boylen, H Kershaw, W Jukes, W Ward, F Webster, A Avery.

1914

The 1914 series was completed within eight days. The First Test, won 23–5 by Britain, was played on the last Saturday in June. The Second, won by Australia, came two days later. The Third, which has gone down in sporting annals as the 'Rorke's Drift' Test, took place (against the tourists' wishes) on the following Saturday. The 'Rorke's Drift' Test saw the British triumph 14–6, even though they were three men short because of injuries for much of the second half. The tourists later played one Test in Auckland, narrowly downing the Kiwi combination.

Record in Australia

Played 12, Won 9, Lost 3, Points for 341, Points against 134

Test Match Results

Great Britain	23	Australia	5	(Sydney, 40 000)
Great Britain	7	Australia	12	(Sydney, 38 000)
Great Britain	14	Australia	6	(Sydney, 41 000)

Other Matches

Opponents	Venue (Attendance)	For	Against
South Australia	Adelaide	101	0
Metropolis	Sydney (45 000)	10	38
New South Wales	Sydney (49 000)	3	11
Queensland	Brisbane	18	10
Ipswich	Ipswich (2000)	45	8
Queensland	Brisbane	22	8
Northern Districts	Newcastle	35	18
Western Districts	Bathurst (1200)	42	3
New South Wales	Melbourne (12 000)	21	15

Record in New Zealand

Played 6, Won 6, Points for 194, Points against 62

Test Match Results

Great Britain	16	New Zealand	13	(Auckland, 24 600)

Other Matches

Opponents	Venue (Attendance)	For	Against
Wellington	Wellington	14	7
Hawke's Bay	Napier (4000)	30	7
Taranaki	Eltham (2000)	43	11
Auckland	Auckland (13 000)	34	12
Wanganui	Wanganui (3000)	57	12

*Team members:*H Wagstaff (c), A Wood, G Thomas, A Francis, S Moorhouse, J Robinson, F Williams, W Davies, B Jenkins, W Hall, J O'Gara, W Prosser, J Rogers, F Smith, L Clampitt, D Clark, F Longstaff, W Roman, D Holland, J Smales, W Jarman, J Chilcott, J Guerin, A Coldrick, A Johnson, R Ramsdale.

1920

Australia scored its first Ashes win at home when it beat the Lions in the first two Tests of the 1920 series. However, the tourists made amends with a 23–13 success in the third encounter. After two Australians withdrew through injury two days before the First Test in Brisbane, replacement players Alf 'Smacker' Blair and Jack 'Junker' Robinson raced north by ship, car and train. However floods south of Brisbane meant they missed the match and were replaced by Queenslanders Harry Fewin and Nev Broadfoot, who each played their one and only Test. The Lions suffered their first defeat in three tours of New Zealand when Auckland surprised them 24–16.

Record in Australia

Played 15, Won 12, Lost 3, Points for 377, Points against 228

Test Match Results

Great Britain	4	Australia	8	(Brisbane, 28 000)
Great Britain	8	Australia	21	(Sydney, 60 000)
Great Britain	23	Australia	13	(Sydney, 32 000)

Other Matches

Opponents	Venue (Attendance)	For	Against
Metropolis	Sydney (67,859)	27	20
Orange	Orange (2000)	50	8
New South Wales	Sydney (60 000)	6	42
New South Wales	Sydney (60 000)	18	10
Queensland	Brisbane (20 000)	25	15

Continued

Other Matches *continued*

Opponents	Venue (Attendance)	For	Against
Wide Bay	Bundaberg (3500)	34	13
Central Queensland	Rockhampton (5000)	26	15
Ipswich	Ipswich (5000)	40	12
Toowoomba	Toowoomba (4000)	48	28
Tamworth	Tamworth (2000)	27	10
Newcastle	Newcastle (3000)	17	10
Newcastle	Newcastle (3000)	24	3

Record in New Zealand

Played 10, Won 9, Lost 1, Points for 373, Points against 104

Test Match Results

Great Britain	23	New Zealand	7	(Auckland, 34 000)
Great Britain	19	New Zealand	3	(Christchurch, 10 000)
Great Britain	23	New Zealand	10	(Wellington, 5000)

Other Matches

Opponents	Venue (Attendance)	For	Against
Auckland	Auckland (35 000)	16	24
Rotorua	Rotorua	58	15
District XIII	Hamilton	49	10
King Country	Taumarunui	47	3
North Island	Napier	46	5
Canterbury	Christchurch (1500)	29	14
West Coast	Greymouth (2000)	55	13

Team members: H Wagstaff (c), G Thomas, A Wood, W Stone, S Stockwell, C Stacey, J Bacon, D Hurcombe, E Davies, J Doyle, E Jones, J Parkin, R Lloyd, J Rogers, J Cartwright, A Milnes, J Bowers, W Cunliffe, G Skelhorne, B Gronow, A Johnson, W Reid, G Rees, H Hilton, D Clark, F Gallagher

1924

The immortal Jim Sullivan made his Test debut on the 1924 tour of Australasia. In that first international he booted five goals, the first just two minutes after the start of play. The British wrapped up the Ashes with wins in the first two Tests against Australia. It was a different story in New Zealand where the locals scored shock wins in the first two encounters.

Record in Australia

Played 18, won 14, Lost 4, Points for 466, Points against 258

Test Match Results

Great Britain	22	Australia	3	(Sydney, 50 005)
Great Britain	5	Australia	3	(Sydney, 33 842)
Great Britain	11	Australia	21	(Brisbane, 39 000)

Other Matches

Opponents	Venue (Attendance)	For	Against
Victoria	Melbourne	45	13
Cootamundra	Cootamundra	31	4
Newcastle	Newcastle	43	18
New England	Tamworth	34	17
New South Wales	Sydney (42 000)	10	5
New South Wales	Sydney (37 000)	18	33
Ipswich	Ipswich	17	0
Queensland	Brisbane (40 000)	10	25
Toowoomba	Toowoomba (10 000)	20	23
New south Wales	Sydney (26 042)	43	5
Orange	Orange	42	23
Lismore	Lismore	28	19
Central Queensland	Rockhampton	34	20
Maryborough	Maryborough	22	3
Universities XIII	Sydney	31	23

Record in New Zealand

Played 9, Won 7, Lost 2, Points for 272, Points against 117

Test Match Results

Great Britain	8	New Zealand	16	(Auckland, 22 000)
Great Britain	11	New Zealand	13	(Wellington, 6000)
Great Britain	31	New Zealand	18	(Dunedin, 14 000)

Other Matches

Opponents	Venue (Attendance)	For	Against
South Auckland	Hamilton	28	16
Auckland	Auckland (19 000)	24	11
Lower Waikato	Ngaruawahia	30	12
Provincial XIII	Auckland	28	13
West Coast	Greymouth	65	8
Canterbury	Christchurch	47	10

Team members: J Parkin (c), J Sullivan, E Knapman, F Evàns, J Ring, C Pollard, W Bentham, S Rix, T Howley, C Carr, J Bacon, W Mooney, S Whitty, D Hurcombe, B Gronow, H Bowman, J Darwell, R Sloman, W Cunliffe, J Bennett, J Price, D Rees, J Thompson, W Burgess, A Brough, F Gallagher

1928

The British tourists won close series in both Australia and New Zealand on the 1928 tour Down-Under. In Australia, the Ashes were theirs after the first two Tests—both evenly matched games which could have gone either way. In New Zealand, they lost the First Test but came back to win the decider by just one point.

Record in Australia

Played 16, Won 11, Lost 4, Drawn 1, Points for 324, Points against 219

Test Match Results

Great Britain	15	Australia	12	(Brisbane, 39 300)
Great Britain	8	Australia	0	(Sydney, 44 548)
Great Britain	14	Australia	21	(Sydney, 37 000)

Other Matches

Opponents	Venue (Attendance)	For	Against
South West NSW	Cootamundra (2000)	14	14
New South Wales	Sydney (55 000)	15	20
New South Wales	Sydney (48 000)	22	9
New South Wales	Sydney (38 000)	7	22
Far North Coast	Lismore (3000)	20	9
Queensland	Brisbane (25 000)	7	21
Ipswich	Ipswich (2000)	26	13
Central Queensland	Rockhampton	27	11
North Queensland	Townsville	30	16
Wide Bay	Bundaberg	61	13
Toowoomba	Toowoomba (12 000)	17	12
Newcastle	Newcastle (4000)	19	17
Western NSW	Parkes (3000)	22	9

Record in New Zealand

Played 9, Won 7, Lost 2, Points for 263, Points against 99

Test Match Results

Great Britain	13	New Zealand	17	(Auckland, 20 000)
Great Britain	13	New Zealand	5	(Dunedin, 12 000)
Great Britain	6	New Zealand	5	(Christchurch, 21 000)

Other Matches

Opponents	Venue (Attendance)	For	Against
South Auckland	Hamilton	31	5
Auckland	Auckland (15 000)	14	9
Auckland	Auckland (25 000)	26	15
Buller Region	Westport	72	3
West Coast	Greymouth	62	13
Invercargill	Invercargill (11 000)	26	27

Team members: J Parkin (c), J Sullivan, W Gowers, A Ellaby, E Gwynne, A Frodsham, T Askin, J Oliver, J Brough, M Rosser, J Evans, L Fairclough, W Rees, B Evans, W Williams, N Bentham, O Dolan, H Bowman, J Thompson, W Burgess, A Fildes, W Horton, R Sloman, F Bowen, B Halfpenny, H Young

1932

Jim Sullivan made his third (and last) tour of Australia as captain of the 1932 Lions—and he was chaired from the field by his team-mates after he played a major role in Britain's victory in the Third (and deciding) Test. Sullivan had been involved in two memorable incidents in the first international. He first missed a goal from right in front of the posts and then had a magnificent goal disallowed because Martin Hodgson was offside when the kick was taken. Luckily, two points decided the outcome in his team's favour. For the first time, New South Wales failed to win at least one game against the British.

Record in Australia

Played 18, Won 15, Lost 2, Drawn 1, Points for 483, Points against 172

Test Match Results

Great Britain	8	Australia	6	(Sydney, 70 204)
Great Britain	6	Australia	15	(Brisbane, 26 500)
Great Britain	18	Australia	13	(Sydney, 50 053)

Other Matches

Opponents	Venue (Attendance)	For	Against
Metropolis	Sydney (42 644)	29	5
Western NSW	Orange (8000)	50	9
New South Wales	Sydney (30 104)	18	5
Far North Coast	Lismore (4965)	44	8
Queensland	Brisbane (13 034)	15	10
Brisbane	Brisbane (4843)	15	18
Wide Bay	Gympie (2500)	56	17
Central Queensland	Rockhampton (4000)	63	21
North Queensland	Townsville (7000)	20	2
Far North Queensland	Cairns (5000)	53	8
Ipswich	Ipswich (3022)	19	2
Toowoomba	Toowoomba (10 861)	7	7
New South Wales	Sydney (19 744)	22	5
Newcastle	Newcastle (5500)	22	15
Riverina	Wagga Wagga (8000)	18	6

Record in New Zealand

Played 8, Won 8, Points for 299, Points against 87

Test Match Results

Great Britain	24	New Zealand	9	(Auckland, 25 000)
Great Britain	25	New Zealand	14	(Christchurch, 8000)
Great Britain	20	New Zealand	18	(Auckland, 20 000)

Other Matches

Opponents	Venue (Attendance)	For	Against
North Auckland	Whangarei (3000)	56	5
South Auckland	Taupiri (1600)	64	11
Auckland	Auckland (12 000)	19	14
West Coast	Greymouth (1500)	32	8
North Island	Wellington (3000)	59	8

Team members: J Sullivan (c), A Risman, B Hudson, S Smith, A Ellaby, J Woods, A Atkinson, S Brogden, W Dingsdale, G Robinson, I Davies, E Pollard, B Evans, L Adams, J Thompson, N Silcock, W Williams, J Wright, L White, J Lowe, A Fildes, N Fender, W Horton, M Hodgson, J Feetham, F Butters

1936

A feast of the ball from the scrums was the major factor of the Lions' 1936 Ashes success. Australia won the First Test but a change of hookers swung the balance. Swinton's Tommy Armitt replaced Harry Field (York), won the scrums 51–25 in the second encounter and was even more dominant in the decider, after the Australian selectors sprung a shock by naming three prop-forwards and no hooker in the front row. For the second straight tour Britain won all matches on the New Zealand leg of the tour.

Record in Australia

Played 17, Won 14, lost 3, Points for 401, Points against 204

Test Match Results

Great Britain	8	Australia	24	(Sydney, 63 920)
Great Britain	12	Australia	7	(Brisbane, 29 486)
Great Britain	12	Australia	7	(Sydney, 53 546)

Other Matches

Opponents	Venue (Attendance)	For	Against
Sydney	Sydney (52 894)	15	13
Southern Division	Leeton	35	13
New South Wales	Sydney	14	18
Western Division	Parkes	33	16
Queensland	Brisbane	19	4
Wide Bay	Maryborough	35	8
Mackay	Mackay	40	17
North Queensland	Townsville	39	3
Ipswich & West Moreton	Ipswich	23	3
Toowoomba	Toowoomba	10	8
Brisbane	Brisbane	35	13
Northern Division	Armidale	19	15
Newcastle	Newcastle	16	21
Western Division	Lithgow	36	14

Record in New Zealand

Played 8, Won 8, Points for 210, Points against 56

Test Match Results

| Great Britain | 10 | New Zealand | 8 | (Auckland, 25 000) |
| Great Britain | 23 | New Zealand | 11 | (Auckland, 16 000) |

Other Matches

Opponents	Venue	For	Against
Auckland	Auckland	22	16
Wellington	Wellington	48	8
South Island	Christchurch	17	3
Taranaki	New Plymouth	35	4
South Auckland	Huntly	21	6
North Auckland	Whangarei	34	0

Team Members: J Brough (c), W Belshaw, J Morley, B Hudson, S Smith, A Edwards, F Harris, A Atkinson, A Risman, G Davies, E Jenkins, S Brogden, W Watkins, T McCue, H Field, T Armitt, J Woods, J Miller, H Jones, A Troup, J Arkwright, M Hodgson, G Exley, H Beverley, H Ellerington

1946

The first British tourists after World War II were nicknamed 'The Indominatables'—after the aircraft-carrier which brought them to Australia—and the side captained by the great Gus Risman was one of the best to tour. An inexperienced Australian team held the Lions to a draw in the First Test but proved to be no match in the remaining two. The series saw the Test debuts of two Australians who were later to star in British club football, winger Lionel Cooper and five-eighth Pat Devery.

Record in Australia

Played 20, Won 16, Lost 3, Drawn 1, Points for 638, Points against 198

Test Match Results

Great Britain	8	Australia	8	(Sydney, 64,527)
Great Britain	14	Australia	5	(Brisbane, 40 500)
Great Britain	20	Australia	7	(Sydney, 35 294)

Other Matches

Opponents	Venue (Attendance)	For	Against
Southern Divison	Junee (7000)	36	4
Monaro	Canberra (5000)	45	12
New South Wales	Sydney (51 634)	14	10
South Coast	Wollongong (13 300)	12	15
New South Wales	Sydney (47 084)	21	7
Western Division	Orange (10 000)	33	2
Newcastle	Newcastle (20 000)	13	18
Northern Division	Tamworth (10 000)	61	5
Queensland	Brisbane (25 000)	24	25
Wide Bay	Bundaberg (6000)	16	12
Central Queensland	Rockhampton (6500)	35	12
North Queensland	Townsville (5000)	55	16
Southern Queensland	Mackay (6000)	94	0
Brisbane	Brisbane (15 722)	21	15
Ipswich	Ipswich (9500)	34	5
Toowoomba	Toowoomba (5500)	29	12
North Coast	Grafton (7500)	53	8

Record in New Zealand

Played 7, Won 5, Lost 2, Points for 145, Points against 78

Test Match Results

Great Britain	8	New Zealand	13	(Auckland, 11 000)

Other Matches

Opponents	Venue (Attendance)	For	Against
South Island	Christchurch (8000)	24	12
West Coast	Greymouth (4000)	8	17
Maoris	Wellington (8000)	32	8
Auckland	Auckland (12 000)	9	7
South Auckland	Huntly (3000)	42	12
Auckland	Auckland (12 400)	22	9

Team members: A Risman (c), M Ryan, J Jones, E Batten, J Lewthwaite, E Ward, J Kitching, B Knowleden, EH Ward, A Johnson, A Bassett, W Horne, W Davies, T McCue, D Jenkins, K Gee, F Hughes, J Egan, G Curran, F Whitcombe, R Nicholson, L White, D Phillips, T Foster, H Murphy, I Owens

The Australian Test team had trouble getting into the ground for the Second Test in 1946. By the time the players arrived at the Brisbane Exhibition Ground, a record crowd of 40 500 was on hand and the gates had been shut. Thousands of fans milled around the main gate, hoping to storm in once it was opened to admit the players. Eventually, the players were sneaked in through a tiny back gate.

1950

Australia won back the Ashes for the first time in almost three decades when the Lions toured in 1950. The home team was narrowly beaten, in atrocious conditions, in the First Test but came back. The decider was also played in deep mud and excited fans got down on their knees after the game to kiss the slush. The series was the first in which 'The Little Master', Clive Churchill, captained Australia and also saw the Test debut of another all-time great, halfback Keith Holman. New Zealand later continued it post-War unbeaten Test record against the Lions.

Record in Australia

Played 19, Won 15, Lost 4, Points for 603, Points against 178

Test Match Results

Great Britain	6	Australia	4	(Sydney, 47 215)
Great Britain	3	Australia	15	(Brisbane, 35 000)
Great Britain	2	Australia	5	(Sydney, 45 178)

Other Matches

Opponents	Venue (Attendance)	For	Against
Western Australia	Perth (7000)	87	4
Monaro	Canberra (4600)	37	10
Newcastle	Newcastle (22 274)	21	10
Riverina	Cootamundra (6943)	23	13
New South Wales	Sydney (70 419)	20	13
North Coast	Kempsey (7542)	37	7
Queensland	Brisbane (22 118)	14	15
North Queensland	Townsville (9500)	39	18
Central Queensland	Rockhampton (7000)	88	0
Wide Bay/Burnett	Gympie (4633)	84	9
Toowoomba	Toowoomba (7000)	44	12
Brisbane	Brisbane (15 084)	18	8
Ipswich	Ipswich (4946)	18	13
Northern Division	Gunnedah (5313)	41	4
New South Wales	Sydney (24 788)	10	0
Southern Division	Wollongong (8647)	11	18

Record in Australia

Played 6, Won 4, Lost 2, Points for 161, Points against 88

Test Match Results

| Great Britain | 10 | New Zealand | 16 | (Christchurch) |
| Great Britain | 13 | New Zealand | 20 | (Auckland) |

Other Matches

Opponents	Venue	For	Against
Southern Provinces	Wellington	40	15
West Coast	Greymouth	21	15
Auckland	Auckland	26	17
South Auckland	Huntly	51	5

Individual records in Australia

	Matches	Tests	Tries	Goals	Points
E Ward (c)	9	3	6	44	106
J Ledgard	9	2	2	37	80
T Danby	11	2	26	—	78
J Hilton	6	2	18	—	54
J Cunliffe	11	1	11	7	47
W Horne	5	—	2	13	32
K Traill	10	—	7	—	21
J Featherstone	9	—	7	—	21
G Ratcliffe	8	2	6	—	18
A Pepperell	9	—	6	—	21
A Daniels	4	—	5	—	15
E Ashcroft	7	3	5	—	15
F Higgins	8	3	4	—	12
R Ryan	9	1	4	—	12
F Osmond	8	—	4	—	12
M Ryan	9	1	3	1	11
J Egan	8	3	3	—	9
D Phillips	7	1	3	—	9
R Pollard	5	—	2	—	6
R Williams	7	2	2	—	6
D Naughton	8	—	2	—	6
E Gwyther	9	3	2	—	6
T Bradshaw	7	3	1	—	3
H Street	9	3	1	—	3
K Gee	7	3	1	—	3
H Murphy	9	1	—	—	—

Wigan created a British record when it had eight players selected for the 1950 tour of Australasia.
Back row: Gordon Racliffe, Jack Cunliffe, Joe Egan, Jack Hilton,

1954

The 1954 series was one of records. Australia ran up a record score in the First Test, which it won 37–12 and Noel Pidding notched an individual record of 19 points (a try and eight goals) in the match. Welshman Lewis Jones went one better when he kicked 10 goals in the Second Test. One record everyone would like to forget, though, is that the second match against New South Wales, a vicious, brawling affair, is the sport's only international encounter ever abandoned. Referee Aub Oxford walked off midway through the second half when the players wouldn't stop fighting. Billy Boston, a 19-year-old winger touring after only a handful of games for Wigan, set a tour tryscoring record with 36 touchdowns and equalled the record for the number of tries scored in a single Test with four in the First Test against New Zealand, at Auckland.

Record in Australia

Played 22, Won 13, Lost 7, Abandoned 1, Drew 1, Points for 627, Points against 427

Test Match Results

Great Britain	12	Australia	37	(Sydney, 65 885)
Great Britain	38	Australia	21	(Brisbane, 46 355)
Great Britain	16	Australia	20	(Sydney, 67 577)

Other Matches

Opponents	Venue (Attendance)	For	Against
Western Division	Bathurst (5218)	29	11
Newcastle	Newcastle (22 825)	10	11
Riverina	Wagga Wagga (10 732)	36	26
Sydney	Sydney (50 889)	25	32
Southern Division	Wollongong (15 435)	17	17
New South Wales	Sydney (55 518)	11	22
Brisbane	Brisbane (18 070)	34	4
Queensland	Brisbane (24 713)	34	32
Wide Bay	Maryborough (5912)	60	14
Southern Queensland	Mackay (5860)	28	7
Far North Queensland	Cairns (6545)	39	18
North Queensland	Townsville (8360)	39	13
Central Queensland	Rockhampton (4667)	21	13
Toowoomba	Toowoomba (13 310)	25	14
Northern NSW	Grafton (6380)	44	14
New South Wales *	Sydney (27 869)	6	17
New South Wales	Sydney (20 295)	15	35
Southern NSW	Canberra (3253)	66	21
Coalfields	Maitland (9585)	22	28

* Match abandoned

Record in New Zealand

Played 10, Won 8, Lost 2, Points for 292, Points against 106

Test Match Results

Great Britain	27	New Zealand	7	(Auckland, 22 097)
Great Britain	14	New Zealand	20	(Greymouth, 4240)
Great Britain	12	New Zealand	6	(Auckland, 6186)

Other Matches

Opponents	Venue (Attendance)	For	Against
Maoris	Whangarei (1728)	14	4
Wellington	Wellington (3103)	61	18
South Island	Dunedin (1154)	32	11
Canterbury	Christchurch (1544)	60	14
North Island	New Plymouth (2448)	42	7
South Auckland	Hamilton (1683)	26	14
Auckland	Auckland (4949)	4	5

Team Members: R Williams (c), J Cunliffe, E Cahill, W Boston, A Turnbull, E Ashcroft, P Jackson, L Jones, D Greenall, F Castle, T O'Grady, R Price, G Helme, A Burnell, J Bowden, J Henderson, A Prescott, J Wilkinson, T Harris, T McKinney, B Briggs, G Gunney, C Pawsey, N Silcock, K Traill, D Valentine

1958

Great Britain overcame almost insurmountable odds to retain the Ashes in the 1958 series against Australia. The British side was soundly beaten in the First Test, but came back in Brisbane, in what has been dubbed 'Prescott's Test', because of the heroic decision by Lions' captain Alan Prescott to stay on the field with a broken arm to direct his side's winning tactics. In the decider, in Sydney, the tourists scored a record 40 points. Another milestone on the tour went to St Helens winger Mike Sullivan who scored 38 tries to beat the mark set four years earlier by Billy Boston. He was helped by seven tries in the final match against Western Australia, which like games against NSW Colts and Coalfields, was played on the way home after the New Zealand leg of the tour.

Record in Australia

Played 21, Won 19, Lost 1, Drawn 1, points for 810, Points against 378

Test Match Results

Great Britain	8	Australia	15	(Sydney, 68 777)
Great Britain	25	Australia	18	(Brisbane, 33 563)
Great Britain	40	Australia	17	(Sydney, 68 720)

Other Matches

Opponents	Venue (Attendance)	For	Against
Southern Division	Wollongong (10 673)	36	18
Western Division	Orange (5005)	24	24
Newcastle	Newcastle (21 126)	35	16
Northern Division	Tamworth (6107)	27	17
Sydney	Sydney (48 692)	20	15
Riverina	Leeton (6000)	29	10
New South Wales	Sydney (52 963)	19	10
Brisbane	Brisbane (14 956)	34	29
Queensland	Brisbane (22 964)	36	19
Central Queensland	Rockhampton (7600)	61	19
Wide Bay	Bundaberg (3480)	50	25
Far North Queensland	Cairns (4851)	78	8
North Queensland	Townsville (6321)	78	17
Toowoomba	Toowoomba (7500)	36	19
North Coast	Lismore (5541)	56	15
NSW Colts	Sydney (9783)	19	11
Coalfields	Maitland (6766)	30	23
Western Australia	Perth (3127)	69	23

Record in New Zealand

Played 9, Won 8, Lost 1, points for 386, Points against 108

Test Match Results

Great Britain	10	New Zealand	15	(Auckland, 18 000)
Great Britain	32	New Zealand	15	(Auckland, 20 000)

Other Matches

Opponents	Venue (Attendance)	For	Against
Maoris	Huntly (5000)	59	7
Taranaki	New Plymouth (1200)	67	8
Wellington	Wellington (4000)	62	20
Canterbury	Christchurch (6000)	41	21
West Coast	Greymouth (4500)	19	2
Combined XIII	Palmerston North (3000)	72	3
Auckland	Auckland (5000)	24	17

Individual records in Australia

	Matches	Tests	Tries	Goals	Points
E Fraser	13	3	5	82	179
E Ashton	13	2	20	13	86
I Southward	12	3	13	20	79
M Sullivan	12	3	20	—	60
A Murphy	14	3	15	3	54
F Carlton	6	—	16	—	48
R Huddart	17	2	15	—	45
M Martyn	12	2	15	—	45
A Davies	15	2	11	—	33
B McTigue	12	2	3	11	31
J Challinor	9	1	7	—	21
J Whiteley	10	2	7	—	21
F Pitchford	10	—	7	—	21
D Bolton	8	2	6	—	18
W Wookey	7	—	6	—	18
P Jackson	9	2	4	—	12
T Harris	11	3	3	—	9
B Edgar	11	1	2	—	6
D Goodwin	8	—	2	—	6
V Karalius	12	2	2	—	6
A Terry	10	2	2	—	6
A Ackerley	12	—	1	3	
G Moses	13	—	1	—	3
H Archer	7	—	—	—	—
A Prescott (c)	9	2	—	—	—
K Jackson	6	—	—	—	—

1962

A last-minute goal in the Third Test, by Australian winger Ken Irvine, prevented the 1962 Lions from creating a record as the first side to win all three Tests in Australia. The goal gave Australia an 18–17 win. Many critics regard the Lions side, led by centre Eric Ashton, as the best British touring side ever. However the tourists blotted their copybook by going down in both Tests in New Zealand, apparently over-complacent after their triumphant spell in Australia.

Record in Australia

Played 21, Won 18, Lost 3, Points for 679, Points against 303

Test Match Results

Great Britain	31	Australia	12	(Sydney, 70 174)
Great Britain	17	Australia	10	(Brisbane, 34 766)
Great Britain	17	Australia	18	(Sydney, 42 104)

Other Matches

Opponents	Venue (Attendance)	For	Against
Western Australia	Perth (2842)	39	12
Riverina	Wagga Wagga (5191)	34	7
Sydney	Sydney (57 142)	21	13
Western Division	Bathurst (10 000)	24	10
New South Wales	Sydney (60 016)	33	26
Newcastle	Newcastle (22 750)	18	23
North Coast	Lismore (5240)	33	13
Brisbane	Brisbane (22 650)	16	14
Queensland	Brisbane (29 102)	22	17
Toowoomba	Toowoomba (10 491)	36	12
Central Queensland	Rockhampton (5000)	55	8
Far North Queensland	Cairns (4769)	33	31
North Queensland	Townsville (8278)	47	14
Wide Bay/Burnett	Maryborough (4376)	84	20
New South Wales	Sydney (28 042)	20	5
Southern Division	Wollongong (10 527)	10	18
St George	Sydney (57 895)	33	5
Northern Division	Tamworth (9000)	56	13

Record in New Zealand

Played 9, Won 6, Lost 3, Points for 319, Points against 161

Test Match Results

| Great Britain | 0 | New Zealand | 19 | (Auckland, 14 976) |
| Great Britain | 8 | New Zealand | 27 | (Auckland, 16 411) |

Other Matches

Opponents	Venue (Attendance)	For	Against
Waikato	Huntly (3461)	59	20
Maoris	Wellington (3091)	35	5
Canterbury	Christchurch (2500)	26	5
New Zealand XIII	Christchurch (3000)	31	7
West Coast	Greymouth (2758)	66	8
Bay of Plenty	Rotorua (1852)	81	4
Auckland	Auckland (1044)	13	46

Individual records in Australia

	Matches	Tests	Tries	Goals	Points
N Fox	14	3	8	62	148
L Gilfedder	13	1	8	33	90
E Ashton (c)	16	3	19	14	85
W Boston	14	3	19	—	57
F Carlton	12	—	13	—	39
M Sullivan	14	3	11	—	33
I Southward	9	—	11	—	33
R Huddart	16	3	10	—	30
A Murphy	11	3	9	—	27
G Cooper	8	—	6	—	18
D Turner	10	2	6	—	18
P Small	8	—	5	—	15
D Fox	4	—	5	—	15
B Edgar	12	3	4	—	12
G Round	13	3	4	—	12
D Bolton	12	1	3	—	9
J Taylor	6	—	3	—	9
W Sayer	13	3	2	—	6
N Herbert	13	3	1	—	3
B McTigue	12	3	1	—	3
K Noble	9	—	1	—	3
J Shaw	10	—	1	—	3
R Evans	9	—	—	—	—
H Poynton	8	2	—	—	—
J Wilkinson	9	—	—	—	—
E Fraser	7	—	—	—	—

1966

Britain had little luck in losing the 1966 series against Australia. The tourists took the First Test 17–13, but in the second encounter had to play one man short for the last 36 minutes (after second-rower Bill Ramsey was sent off) but still only went down 6–4, in the first try-less Test in 33 years. Similar misfortune struck in the Third Test when prop Cliff Watson was ordered from the field 34 minutes from the end. Australia won this sensational decider 19–14 to retain the Ashes. The British stocks picked up in New Zealand where they won all eight matches.

Record in Australia

Played 22, Won 13, Lost 9, Points for 506, Points against 307

Test Match Results

Great Britain	17	Australia	13	(Sydney, 57 962)
Great Britain	4	Australia	6	(Brisbane, 45 057)
Great Britain	14	Australia	19	(Sydney, 63 503)

Other Matches

Opponents	Venue (Attendance)	For	Against
Northern Territory	Darwin (2965)	17	7
Far North Queensland	Cairns (4557)	48	7
North Queensland	Townsville (6000)	15	17
Central Queensland	Rockhampton (2860)	5	10
Sydney	Sydney (38 831)	15	14
Newcastle	Newcastle (13 125)	5	2
North Coast	Kempsey (3500)	52	20
New South Wales	Sydney (38 907)	13	18
Southern Division	Wollongong (11 677)	8	17
Northern Division	Tamworth (9242)	13	15
Brisbane	Brisbane (18 638)	17	19
Queensland	Brisbane (23 270)	38	29
Wide Bay/Burnett	Bundaberg (5515)	30	22
Ipswich	Ipswich (2697)	44	10
Toowoomba	Toowoomba (6220)	38	10
Western Division	Parkes (8000)	38	11
Riverina	Narrandera (6030)	34	20
Balmain	Sydney (22 369)	8	9
Monaro	Cooma (6000)	33	12

Record in New Zealand

Played 8, Won 8, Points for 265, Points against 78

Test Match Results

Great Britain	25	New Zealand	8	(Auckland, 14 494)	
Great Britain	22	New Zealand	14	(Auckland, 10 657)	

Other Matches

Opponents	Venue (Attendance)	For	Against
Waikato	Huntly (2933)	47	8
Wellington	Wellington (1142)	28	9
West Coast	Greymouth (2212)	27	5
Canterbury	Christchurch (1192)	53	6
Maoris	New Plymouth (539)	51	17
Auckland	Auckland (4726)	12	11

Individual records

	Matches	Tests	Tries	Goals	Points
K Gowers	15	3	—	67	134
A Keegan	15	2	1	62	127
B Jones	15	—	24	—	72
J Stopford	16	1	16	1	50
W Burgess	17	5	14	—	42
I Brooke	18	5	13	—	39
G Wriglesworth	16	4	11	—	33
A Hardisty	16	4	10	—	30
W Aspinall	20	1	10	—	30
F Myler	16	3	7	—	21
F Myler	16	3	7	—	21
W Bryant	17	2	7	—	21
H Poole (c)	16	2	6	—	18
A Buckley	18	3	5	—	15
C Dooler	15	—	5	—	15
W Ramsey	15	4	5	—	15
T Fogerty	15	1	5	—	15
G Shelton	13	—	4	—	12
K Roberts	17	2	4	—	12
D Robinson	22	5	4	—	12
T Bishop	15	5	3	1	11
C Clarke	16	1	3	1	11
B Edgar	16	3	3	—	9
C Watson	14	5	3	—	9
P Flanagan	16	4	3	—	9
J Mantle	11	3	3	—	9
G Crewdson	13	—	—	—	—

1970

Britain staged a remarkable comeback to win the Ashes on the 1970 tour. Australia thrashed the Lions 37–15 in the First Test, but the tourists won the second 28–7, despite being one man short for the last 24 minutes of the game, and scored five tries to one in the decider. A clean sweep of the matches in New Zealand enabled the 1970 squad to finish with a better record than any of its predecessors—just one loss in 24 games.

Record in Australia

Played 17, Won 15, Lost 1, Drawn 1, Points for 496, Points against 213

Test Match Results

Great Britain	15	Australia	37	(Brisbane, 42 807)
Great Britain	28	Australia	7	(Sydney, 60 962)
Great Britain	21	Australia	17	(Sydney, 61 258)

Other Matches

Opponents	Venue (Attendance)	For	Against
Northern Territory	Darwin (3000)	35	12
North Queensland	Townsville (7890)	23	20
Central Queensland	Rockhampton (7290)	30	2
Wide Bay	Wondai (3344)	45	7
Queensland	Brisbane (17 071)	32	7
Toowoomba	Toowoomba (6549)	37	13
Brisbane	Brisbane (10 117)	28	7
New South Wales	Sydney (31 509)	17	17
Monaro	Queanbeyan (9500)	34	11
Western Division	Bathurst (4400)	40	11
Sydney Colts	Sydney (14 046)	26	7
Newcastle	Newcastle (22 655)	49	16
Riverina	Wagga Wagga (11 000)	12	11
Southern Division	Wollongong (7796)	24	11

Record in New Zealand

Played 7, Won 7, Points for 257, Points against 75

Test Match Results

Great Britain	19	New Zealand	15	(Auckland, 15 948)
Great Britain	23	New Zealand	9	(Christchurch, 8600)
Great Britain	33	New Zealand	16	(Auckland, 13 137)

Other Matches

Opponents	Venue (Attendance)	For	Against
Northern XIII	Tokoroa (3546)	42	17
Wellington	Wellington (859)	60	8
West Coast	Greymouth (676)	57	2
Auckland	Auckland (6074)	23	8

Individual Records

	Tests	Tries	Goals	Points
T Price	1	5	51	117
R Millward	5	12	22	80
R Dutton	2	1	18	39
S Hynes	4	11	1	35
A Hardisty	1	10	—	30
A Smith	5	9	—	27
J Atkinson	6	8	—	24
M Shoebottom	3	6	—	18
P Lowe	1	6	—	18
D Laughton	5	5	—	15
P Flanagan	1	5	—	15
R Irving	2	4	—	12
C Hesketh	1	3	—	9
C Sullivan	4	3	—	9
K Hepworth	5	3	—	9
F Myler (c)	6	2	—	6

Individual Records

	Tests	Tries	Goals	Points
D Hartley	4	2	—	6
J Thompson	4	2	—	6
B Seabourne	1	2	—	6
C Watson	6	2	—	6
M Reilly	6	1	—	3
A Fisher	5	1	—	3
D Edwards	1	—	—	—
J Ward	1	—	—	—
D Chisnall	1	—	—	—
D Robinson		—	—	—

1974

Critics on both sides of the world gave the 1974 Lions little chance of success. The rich Sydney clubs had plundered many of Britain's top forwards. In those days international sides had no right to draft players turning out with foreign clubs into their Test lineups, so Britain was left with a shortage of top-class players and sparse reserve talent. A host of tour injuries which forced forward Colin Dixon to play in the centre in one Test against New Zealand, and coach Jim Challinor to play his first game in five years (against South Island in New Zealand), didn't help. The underdogs surprised everyone. They narrowly lost two Tests to one against Australia—and in New Zealand they pulled up after a loss in the First Test to win the series.

Record in Australia

Played 20, Won 15, Lost 5, Points for 500, Points against 235

Test Match Results

Great Britain	6	Australia	12	(Brisbane, 35 116)
Great Britain	16	Australia	11	(Sydney, 48 006)
Great Britain	18	Australia	22	(Sydney, 55 505)

Other Matches

Opponents	Venue (Attendance)	For	Against
Darwin	Darwin (6500)	41	2
North Queensland	Cairns (7588)	30	5
Central Queensland	Rockhampton (12 000)	38	0
Wide Bay	Maryborough (3200)	24	12
Ipswich	Ipswich (3778)	36	8
Queensland	Brisbane (26 000)	13	12
Toowoomba	Toowoomba (4160)	42	16
Brisbane	Brisbane (7880)	15	20
North Coast	Grafton (6007)	19	9
Northern Division	Tamworth (10 640)	38	14
Western Division	Orange (6185)	25	10
New South Wales	Sydney (16 112)	9	13
Illawarra	Wollongong (10 000)	26	22
Monaro	Queanbeyan (10 584)	34	7
Riverina	Wagga Wagga (8000)	36	10
Newcastle	Newcastle (20 339)	24	14
Southern Division	Gosford (6500)	10	16

Record in New Zealand

Played 8, Won 6, Lost 2, Points for 175, Points against 78

Test Match Results

Great Britain	8	New Zealand	13	(Auckland, 20 000)
Great Britain	17	New Zealand	8	(Christchurch, 10 000)
Great Britain	20	New Zealand	0	(Auckland, 20 000)

Other Matches

Opponents	Venue (Attendance)	For	Against
North Island Country	Huntly (2800)	37	17
Maoris	Rotorua (7000)	19	16
Wellington	Wellington (5000)	39	11
South Island	Greymouth (2500)	33	2
Auckland	Auckland (10000)	2	11

Individual Records

	Matches	Tests	Tries	Goals	Field goals	Points
J Gray	15	5	2	52	1	111
R Millward	10	3	8	18	—	60
D Redfearn	17	5	18	2	—	58
T Clawson	13	4	—	24	—	48
J Bevan	16	3	15	—	—	45
L Dyl	17	5	14	—	—	42
D Eckersley	11	1	3	12	—	33
J Atkinson	8	—	8	—	—	24
D Willicombe	11	—	8	—	—	24
K Gill	13	3	8	—	—	24
D Watkins	6	1	2	12	—	30
J Butler	15	—	6	—	—	18
W Ramsay	5	2	2	5	—	16
S Nash	14	6	5	—	1	16
P Rose	12	1	5	—	—	15
S Norton	14	2	5	—	—	15
M Richards	10	3	5	—	—	15
P Charlton	16	6	4	—	—	12
C Hesketh (c)	17	6	4	—	—	12
G Nicholls	18	6	4	—	—	12
C Dixon	17	6	4	—	—	12
E Chisnall	17	4	3	—	—	9
A Bates	15	2	2	—	—	6
J Mills	15	3	2	—	—	6
K Ashcroft	13	—	2	—	—	6
J Thompson	18	6	1	—	—	3
J Challinor	1	—	1	—	—	3
K Bridges	8	1	—	—	—	3
J Bates	2	—	—	—	—	—

1979

For the first time in the history of Rugby League Tests between Australia and Great Britain, Australia won a series three Tests to nil, when the Lions toured down-under in 1979. However this was not the only record set by the locals. The points scored in the three clashes, 87, were four better than the previous best, set by the 1963 Kangaroos. Australia's Mick Cronin scored a record 54 points (2 tries & 24 goals) to top the previous best in any Test series—48 by Britain's Lewis Jones in 1956, against France. Australia let in only two tries, both in a second-half fightback by Britain in the Second Test.

Record in Australia

Played 18, Won 14, Lost 4, Drawn 1, Points for 352, Points against 246

Test Match Results

Great Britain	0	Australia	35	(Brisbane, 23 000)
Great Britain	16	Australia	24	(Sydney, 26 857)
Great Britain	7	Australia	21	(Sydney, 16 844)

Other Matches

Opponents	Venue (Attendance)	For	Against
North Queensland	Mackay (6200)	29	5
Central Queensland	Rockhampton (3307)	20	11
Wide Bay	Maryborough (2969)	27	7

▶

Other Matches

Opponents	Venue (Attendance)	For	Against
North Coast	Tweed Heads (4871)	33	6
Northern Division	Tamworth (7000)	20	11
Queensland	Brisbane (5000)	25	19
Toowoomba	Toowoomba (5500)	16	19
Brisbane	Brisbane (3500)	10	7
Southern Division	Campbelltown (4000)	10	10
Newcastle	Newcastle (14 570)	25	12
Riverina	Wagga Wagga (5000)	37	10
Illawarra	Wollongong (3994)	18	13
Western Division	Orange (4500)	19	12
New South Wales	Sydney (8902)	19	17
Monaro	Queanbeyan (6500)	21	7

Record in New Zealand

Played 9, Won 8, Lost 1, Points for 212, Points against 69

Test Match Results

Great Britain	16	New Zealand	8	(Auckland, 12 000)
Great Britain	22	New Zealand	7	(Christchurch, 7000)
Great Britain	11	New Zealand	18	(Auckland, 10 000)

Other Matches

Opponents	Venue (Attendance)	For	Against
Maoris	Whangarei (5000)	15	13
Northern Districts	Huntly (2000)	58	5
Central Districts	New Plymouth (900)	14	5
Wellington	Wellington (2000)	39	3
West Coast	Greymouth (900)	19	0
Auckland	Auckland (15 000)	18	10

Individual Records

	Matches	Tests	Tries	Goals	Field goals	Points
J Woods	17	4	12	67	1	171
S Evans	19	5	16	—	—	48
G Fairbairn	10	5	3	18	1	46
R Mathias	17	1	10	—	—	30
D Barends	16	2	10	—	—	30
E Hughes	17	6	8	—	—	24
K Mumby	13	—	1	8	—	19
J Joyner	14	5	6	—	—	18
G Stephens	15	5	6	—	—	18
P Glynn	15	—	6	—	—	18
J Grayshon	14	5	6	—	—	18
M Adams	16	6	—	8	1	17
P Hogan	14	4	5	—	—	15
L Casey	14	5	4	—	—	12
M Smith	11	3	4	—	—	12
T Martyn	5	—	—	3	—	9
J Holmes	13	6	2	3	—	9
M James	13	—	3	—	—	9
R Millward	3	—	—	4	—	8
D Watkinson	12	1	2	—	—	6
J Mills	5	1	2	—	—	6
G Nicholls	13	6	2	—	—	6
S Nash	6	—	2	—	—	6
D Topliss	7	1	2	—	—	6
T Skerrett	12	4	1	—	—	3
A Redfearn	10	1	1	—	—	3
G Liptrot	11	—	1	—	—	3
B Lockwood	12	1	1	—	—	3
D Ward	11	6	—	—	—	—
S Norton	9	2	—	—	—	—
D Laughton (c)	5	1	—	—	—	—
J Burke	9	—	—	—	—	—
C Stone	12	—	—	—	—	—

1984

Great Britain experienced its worst tour in history when it went down-under in 1984, being white-washed in both the series in Australia and New Zealand for the first time, as well as being given a fright by the fledgling Rugby League nation, Papua New Guinea. Britain was plagued by injuries to its stars and four players, Garry Schofield, Lee Crooks, Ray Ashton and Harry Pinner, had to fly home early. In the First Test against Australia, Brian Noble, at 23, went into the record books as the youngest ever British skipper.

Record in Australia

Played 15, Won 11, Lost 4, Points for 399, Points against 254

Test Match Results

Great Britain	8	Australia	25	(Sydney, 30 190)
Great Britain	6	Australia	18	(Brisbane, 26 534)
Great Britain	7	Australia	20	(Sydney, 18 756)

Other Matches

Opponents	Venue (Attendance)	For	Against
Northern Territory	Darwin (7830)	40	13
Riverina	Wagga Wagga (3000)	22	18
North Coast	Wauchope (4000)	56	6
Western Division	Dubbo (5000)	36	30
North Sydney	Sydney (4067)	14	8
Newcastle	Newcastle (10 000)	28	18
Wide Bay	Bundaberg (2336)	28	18
Central Queensland	Rockhampton (5671)	44	12
North Queensland	Townsville (6036)	38	20
Toowoomba	Toowoomba (4051)	16	18
Northern Rivers	Tweed Heads (3537)	24	12
Northern Division	Tamworth (6750)	32	18

Record in New Zealand

Played 8, Won 4, Lost 4, Points for 179, Points against 127

Test Match Results

Great Britain	0	New Zealand	12	(Auckland, 8500)
Great Britain	12	New Zealand	29	(Christchurch, 3824)
Great Britain	16	New Zealand	32	(Auckland, 7500)

Other Matches

Opponents	Venue (Attendance)	For	Against
Northern Districts	Whangarei (1600)	42	8
Maoris	Huntly (2392)	19	8
Central Districts	Wellington (2051)	38	6
South Island	Christchurch (2581)	36	14
Auckland	Auckland (6123)	16	18

Record in Papua New Guinea

Played 1, Won 1, Points for 36, Points against 20

Test Match Results

| Great Britain | 36 | Papua New Guinea | 20 | (Mt Hagen, 7510) |

(Match against Combined XIII at Port Moresby was cancelled because of a visit by Prince Charles)

Individual Records

	Matches	Tests	Tries	Goals	Field goals	Points
M Burke	13	7	2	36	—	80
J Lydon	14	4	4	26	—	68
E Hanley	17	7	12	3	—	54
D Drummond	17	7	11	—	—	44

▶

Individual Records

	Matches	Tests	Tries	Goals	Field goals	Points
G Schofield	11	4	7	6	—	40
D Hobbs	16	6	2	15	—	38
K Beardmore	11	1	7	—	—	28
G Clarke	10	—	7	—	—	28
J Basnett	10	—	6	—	—	24
B Noble (c)	14	7	6	—	—	24
W Proctor	11	1	6	—	—	24
M Smith	13	2	6	—	—	24
D Foy	8	1	5	—	—	20
A Goodway	13	7	5	—	—	20
K Mumby	16	7	5	—	—	20
A Gregory	15	5	3	—	1	13
N Holding	11	4	3	—	1	13
L Crooks	10	2	1	3	—	10
S Donlan	11	2	2	—	—	8
T Flanagan	10	2	2	—	—	8
M Adams	18	7	1	—	—	4
R Ashton	7	—	1	—	—	4
B Case	13	4	1	—	—	4
J Joyner	12	3	1	—	—	4
A Myler	10	5	1	—	—	4
K Rayne	13	3	1	—	—	4
M Worrall	9	2	1	—	—	4
C Burton	12	5	—	—	—	—
R Duane	1	—	—	—	—	—
M O'Neill	11	—	—	—	—	—
H Pinner	7	—	—	—	—	—

1988

Britain showed a great improvement on the 1988 tour. At the Sydney Football Stadium in the First Test (the 100th between the two adversaries), the tourists gave the home side a real scare. They led 6–0 at half-time, but faded to go down 17–6. They went one better in the third encounter. Despite being devastated by injuries—including two withdrawals on the eve of the match—the tourists showed their bulldog spirit to run out winners 26–12—and this score flattered the Australians. It was Britain's first Test win over Australia in a decade. Unfortunately, the Lions went down 12–10 in the lone Test against New Zealand—a match which had the added importance of deciding which country would meet Australia in the final of the World Cup.

Record in Papua New Guinea

Played 2, Won 2, Points for 78, Points against 40

Test Match Results

Great Britain	42	Papua New Guinea	22	(Port Moresby, 12 500)

Other Match

Opponents		Venue (Attendance)	For	Against
Highlands Zone		Lae (4000)	36	18

Record in Australia

Played 13, Won 8, Lost 5, Points for 330, Points against 241

Test Match Results

Great Britain	6	Australia	17	(Sydney, 24 480)
Great Britain	14	Australia	34	(Brisbane, 27 130)
Great Britain	26	Australia	12	(Sydney, 15 944)

Other Matches

Opponents	Venue (Attendance)	For	Against
North Queensland	Cairns (7000)	66	16
Newcastle	Newcastle (8970)	28	12
Northern Division	Tamworth (2192)	12	36
Manly-Warringah	Sydney (11 131)	0	30
Combined Brisbane	Brisbane (1800)	28	14
Central Queensland	Rockhampton (5000)	64	8
Toowoomba	Toowoomba (4500)	28	14
Wide Bay	Gympie (2500)	14	0
Western Division	Orange (3520)	28	26
President's XIII	Queanbeyan (6037)	16	24

Record in New Zealand

Played 3, Won 1, Lost 2, Points for 48, Points against 60

Test Match Result

Great Britain _____ 10   New Zealand _____ 12   (Auckland, 8525)

Other Matches

Opponents	Venue (Attendance)	For	Against
Wellington	Wellington (4428)	24	18
Auckland	Auckland (12 000)	14	30

Individual Records

	Matches	Tests	Tries	Goals	Points
P Loughlin	13	5	1	43	90
M Offiah	13	4	19	—	76
P Ford	13	5	9	1	38
E Hanley (c)	11	5	8	—	32
D Stephenson	11	4	1	13	30
H Gill	12	5	7	—	28
K Fairbank	10	—	6	—	24
A Currier	5	—	3	5	22
G Schofield	5	2	5	1	22
M Ford	7	—	5	—	20
M Gregory	10	5	5	—	20
P Medley	5	1	3	—	12
L Crooks	5	—	—	5	10
C Gibson	10	—	2	—	8
P Dixon	8	3	1	—	4
D Hulme	13	5	1	—	4
R Eyres	3	—	1	—	4
P Groves	8	—	1	—	4
R Powell	14	4	1	—	4
K Ward	10	5	—	—	—
K Breadmore	9	4	—	—	—
B Case	8	2	—	—	—
S Edwards	1	1	—	—	—
A Gregory	8	5	—	—	—
R Haggerty	7	—	—	—	—
P Hulme	7	3	—	—	—
J Joyner	3	—	—	—	—
A Platt	5	2	—	—	—
H Waddell	13	2	—	—	—
I Wilkinson	6	—	—	—	—
D Wright	8	2	—	—	—

1990

Great Britain made a trail-blazing tour of Papua New Guinea and New Zealand in 1990. It was the first time a visit south had not included Australia and, as a result, the tourists suffered a huge financial loss. The Lions had to endure extreme heat, riots and tear-gas from police trying to restore order among the fans in Papua New Guinea. They also suffered the humiliation of their first defeat by the young Rugby League nation. In New Zealand they made amends. Written off before the tour began because of the long list of withdrawals by established Test players including the great Ellery Hanley, the British rose to the occasion under new skipper Mike Gregory to win the series against the experienced New Zealanders.

Record in Papua New Guinea

Played 5, Won 4, Lost 1, Points for 172, Points against 60

Test Match Results

Great Britain	18	Papua New Guinea	20	(Goroka, 11 598)
Great Britain	40	Papua New Guinea	8	(Port Moresby, 7837)

Other Matches

Opponents	Venue (Attendance)	For	Against
Southern Zone	Port Moresby (7000)	40	18
Northern & Highland Zones	Lae (3500)	24	10
Island Zone	Rabaul (5000)	50	4

Record in New Zealand

Played 10, Won 6, Lost 4, Points for 179, Points against 161

Test Match Results

Great Britain	11	New Zealand	10	(Palmerston North, 10 000)
Great Britain	16	New Zealand	14	(Auckland, 7500)
Great Britain	18	New Zealand	21	(Christchurch, 5000)

Other Matches

Opponents	Venue (Attendance)	For	Against
President's XIII	Napier (4000)	23	22
Canterbury	Christchurch (3000)	10	18
Auckland	Auckland (10 000)	13	24
Kiwi Colts	Huntly (2000)	22	10
Wellington	Wellington (800)	22	30
Maoris	Rotorua (4500)	20	12
Taranaki Invitation XIII	New Plymouth (2000)	24	0

Individual Records

	Matches	Tests	Tries	Goals	Field goals	Points
J Davies	11	5	6	34	—	92
P Eastwood	10	2	9	18	—	72
G Schofield	9	5	7	—	1	29
C Gibson	11	5	6	—	—	24
D Betts	10	5	4	—	—	16
R Simpson	5	—	3	—	—	12
B Goulding	9	5	2	—	1	9
J Devereaux	5	—	2	—	—	8
D Fox	9	1	2	—	—	8
D Lyon	2	—	2	—	—	8
P Dixon	10	5	2	—	—	8
K Fairbank	7	1	2	—	—	8
M Offiah	4	3	1	—	—	8
M Dermott	8	2	1	—	1	5
C Bibb	8	1	1	—	—	4
S Irwin	9	3	1	—	—	4
D Powell	11	5	1	—	—	4
G Steadman	4	—	1	—	—	4
A Tait	4	2	1	—	—	4
D Bishop	6	—	1	—	—	4
P Clarke	7	1	1	—	—	4
G Price	6	1	1	—	—	4
K Skerrett	5	3	1	—	—	4
I Smales	6	1	1	—	—	4
R Powell	14	5	1	—	—	4
K England	10	5	—	—	—	—
J Lydon	6	3	—	—	—	—
M Gregory (c)	9	5	—	—	—	—
L Jackson	7	3	—	—	—	—
I Lucas	6	—	—	—	—	—
A Sullivan	—	—	—	—	—	—

JIMMY LISLE

Six Tests for Australia (1962–65). Also played 17 minor games for Australia on one Kangaroo tour (1963–64) and one New Zealand tour (1965).

Former Rugby Union Test star Jimmy Lisle holds the record for the fastest entry into the Rugby League Test ranks in the modern era—after just two first-grade and two representative matches. It's a record which is unlikely to be beaten, although former Rugby Union All Black Matthew Ridge made the New Zealand Test lineup after just four games with Manly-Warringah.

Lisle played three Tests for Australia in the amateur code in 1961. He turned out against Fiji in Sydney and Melbourne before playing South Africa at Johannesburg on a lightning trip across the Indian Ocean. He played centre inside the brilliant winger Mike Cleary. The following year the pair switched codes to join South Sydney. Lisle was laid-low early in the season by a hamstring injury, but after one first-grade game he found himself at five-eighth in the NSW team to play Queensland, and the following week in the Sydney side which took on the touring Great Britain side. Two weeks later he was in the side for the First Test. Although dropped to make way for Queensland veteran Bob Banks in the second encounter in Brisbane, Lisle returned for the Third Test, the only match won by Australia.

Another injury restricted Lisle to just seven appearances for Souths in 1963. Country stand-off Earl Harrison grabbed his chance and took over Lisle's Test spot, keeping it on the Kangaroo tour of Britain and France, in which Lisle played only the minor games. However Lisle was back as number one five-eighth for the 1964 series against the touring Frenchmen and on the 1965 tour of New Zealand.

In club matches, Lisle's greatest moment was in 1965, when, as skipper, he helped steer the Rabbitohs to the Sydney Premiership grand final where, before a record crowd of 78 056, they went down gallantly 12–8 to the great St George lineup.

LOTTO CHALLENGE see *Challenge Cup*

GEORGE LOVEJOY

George Lovejoy was the most famous of all Brisbane Rugby League callers. His radio bosses gave him the title 'The Greatest Name of All in the Greatest Game of All'. At one stage he had the highest listening audience per capita of any caller in Australia. He began in radio in Bundaberg soon after World War II but, after moving to Brisbane, began calling the Premiership matches in 1950. He continued for the next three decades until other business commitments forced him to quit. The controversial caller was once banned from the Ipswich ground by the local football authorities. So Lovejoy broadcast from the roof of a house adjacent to the ground. Years later, he and fellow-commentator Billy J Smith broadcast from a tower erected next to Brisbane's Lang Park after a rival station was given exclusive rights to call the Premiership matches.

GRAHAM LOWE

New Zealander Graham Lowe has a special niche in the annals of Rugby League as one of the code's greatest coaches. In the 1980s he turned the Kiwis from a team of easy-beats to the only Test side capable of challenging the superiority of the Australians.

In his late twenties he had a dream run with the Otahuhu club in Auckland, with three lower grade Premierships in his first four years of coaching, followed by successive A-grade titles. In 1979, he moved to Brisbane because his five-year-old daughter, an asthma sufferer, needed a warmer climate. In Brisbane he took wooden spooner Norths to fifth spot in his first year and to the Premiership 12 months later, with players such as halfback Mark Murray and hooker Greg Conescu, who were later to reach Test status.

Meanwhile, he had the reins of the Kiwis. Australia had regularly run up cricket scores against them. But in 1983, in a dramatic match at Brisbane's Lang Park, Lowe's side finally triumphed 19–12. Two years later, the Kiwis went with an ace of winning their first full series in 32 years. A last minute try, against the run of play, gave the Australians a 10–6 win in the Second Test, in Auckland (after they had won the first encounter, in Brisbane, 26–20). In the Third Test, at Auckland however, Lowe had his revenge. The Kiwis annihilated the Australians 18–0. It was their second biggest loss ever and the first time in 56 Tests that Australia had been held scoreless.

Lowe joined Wigan in 1986 and in three years at Central Park guided them to one Championship (1987), two Challenge Cups (1988 and 1989) and two John Player Trophies (1987 and 1989). In 1990, he was called in to rescue an ailing and strife-torn Manly-Warringah side in the Sydney Premiership. In his first year, Lowe took the Sea Eagles from 12th spot to the semi-finals.

At the start of 1991, Lowe suffered a life-threatening illness. But he recovered to steer Manly into third spot, even though the Sea Eagles were without many of their stars (away on Test duty and out through injury) during the home-and-away games. That was the year in which Queensland broke with tradition and appointed Lowe as the first non-Queenslander to coach its State-of-Origin side. In a tight series the Maroons triumphed two games to one.

EDDIE LUMSDEN

Fifteen Tests for Australia (1959–63). Also played 27 minor games on one Kangaroo tour (1959–60) and one New Zealand tour (1961).

Eddie Lumsden was the best of a fine footballing family. He was so good that he held a virtual mortgage on a Test wing spot in the early 1960s.

Lumsden joined St George in 1957, from the NSW coalfields town of Kurri Kurri. The previous season he had played for Country Seconds (the Firsts had two Test wingers, Brian Carlson and Don 'Bandy' Adams). With St George he was an immediate success, representing both Sydney and New South Wales in his first season.

He played his first Test in 1959, against the touring New Zealand Kiwis. When he bowed out of representative arena four years later Lumsden had appeared in 15 Tests (five against each of Britain and New Zealand, four versus France and one against South Africa) and had made overseas tours with the 1963–64 Kangaroos and to New Zealand in 1965. He topped the try-scoring lists on the Kangaroo visit with 25 touch-downs in 27 matches (which, incidentally, was the most played by an Australian on that tour).

Lumsden was no less brilliant with St George staying with the Dragons for 10 years. During this period he was in nine of St George's grand final-winning sides. He missed out in 1960 through injury. He set a club record of 164 tries in all grades while with the Dragons. He later became a Test selector.

DINNY LUTGE

Three Tests for Australia (1908). Also played five minor games on one Kangaroo tour (1908–09).

The giant North Sydney forward Dinny Lutge holds a special place in Rugby League history as the captain of the first Kangaroo side to tour Great Britain, in 1908–09. He and 1911–12 captain Chris McKivat are the only Kangaroo skippers to have been chosen by team-mates, Lutge getting the vote after the P & O ship Macedonia had sailed out of Sydney Harbour. However Lutge had a wretched tour. An injury to one of his legs kept him out of all but five of the tourists' 46 matches—and Dally Messenger led Australia in the Tests. Lutge did, however, play three Tests against the visiting New Zealand side in 1908, scoring a try in two of the clashes.

RON LYNCH

Twelve Tests for Australia (1961–70). Also played 15 minor games for Australia on one Kangaroo tour (1967–68) and one New Zealand tour (1961).

Had Ron Lynch been playing in any other era, he may have been remembered as one of the all-time great lock-forwards. Unfortunately he was around at the same time as the brilliant Johnny Raper and was forever in the shadow of that football genius. Lynch's first tussle with Raper was in the 1960 City-Country clash. Lynch, from the western NSW town of Forbes, so impressed the selectors that day that they gave him a spot in the second-row for New South Wales' games against Queensland and France (Raper, of course, was lock).

At the start of the following season, Lynch joined Parramatta in the Sydney Premiership competition. The move heralded the start of his international career. He made the Australian side which toured New Zealand that year and made his Test debut on Auckland's Carlaw Park. He was to be in and out of the Australian Test sides for the next decade, playing in seven different series. His 12 Tests included six against Britain, four versus New Zealand and two against France. His biggest disappointment came in 1963, when a shoulder injury in the last game of the season ruled him out of contention for the Kangaroo tour of Britain and France. However he was rewarded with a spot in the next Kangaroo side, four years later. Lynch bowed out of international football when vice-captain in the First Test of the 1970 series against the British tourists. It was a sad farewell. He suffered a fractured cheek-bone and had to quit the match. Once recovered, he was never able to regain his Test spot.

Lynch gave long and efficient service to Parramatta, for which he played 202 games. He was the Eels' player-coach in 1970. He finished his career with the Penrith club.

CLIFF LYONS

Six Tests for Australia (1990–91). Also played for the Rest-of-the-World against Great Britain (1988) and seven minor games for Australia on one Kangaroo tour (1990) and one Papua New Guinea tour (1991).

For several years it seemed as if the Australian selectors were purposely ignoring the talents of five-eighth Cliff Lyons. The fine playmaker had starred for both North Sydney and Manly-Warringah. It seemed that because he was overshadowed in his four State-of-Origin matches (1987–88) by the genius of Wally Lewis, Lyons would never wear the green and gold for Australia. All that changed in 1990. Lyons' form in the Sydney Premiership was so outstanding that he was named the Dally M Player-of-the-Year. A few weeks later when the Kangaroo squad to tour Britain and France was picked, Lyons was among the chosen few.

After Australia lost the First Test, at Wembley Stadium, Lyons got his chance. He grabbed it with both hands, dispelling any fears that he was not a big match player. He was one of the stars in the second encounter which Australia won with a try in injury time. He also starred in the Third Test victory which retained the Ashes. In France Lyons was no less authoritative, and was named Man-of-the-Match in the Second Test, at Perpignan.

Cliff Lyons with the star of NSW Rugby League TV commercials, Tina Turner

Back home, Lyons struggled to find form for much of 1991. He was outplayed by Wally Lewis in the State-of-Origin matches and was overlooked for the Tests against New Zealand. But when the chips were down around semi-final time he regained much of his zip and was chosen for Australia's end-of-season tour of Papua New Guinea.

On the club scene, Lyons achieved the ultimate success in 1987. Not only did his brilliant play lay the foundation for Manly's 18–8 grand final victory over Canberra, but he was rewarded with the Clive Churchill Medal as the Man-of-the-Match.

M

KEN McCAFFERY

Five Tests for Australia (1953–55). Also played three matches in two World Cups (1954 and 1957), one match against the Rest-of-the-World (1957) and 15 minor games for Australia on one Kangaroo tour (1952–53) and one New Zealand tour (1953).

The great English forward Derek 'Rocky' Turner once described Ken McCaffery as the finest Australian footballer of the post-World War II era. Indeed, McCaffery had an abundance of talent, but recurring injuries prevented him from proving just how correct Turner was in his assessment. McCaffery could play virtually any position in the backline. He began his career as a halfback (having the misfortune to be playing at the same time as that other great scrum-worker Keith Holman) and then starred as a centre.

He started in Sydney with Eastern Suburbs, but McCaffery did not step into the limelight until 1950, when he switched to Toowoomba. In the north, he came under the guidance of top coach Duncan Thompson, who put polish on his play. McCaffery made the State side a year after moving to Queensland and, 12 months later, he was chosen as a utility back in the Kangaroo squad. His real moment of glory came during the 1957 World Cup series. Keith Holman was injured in the first match. McCaffery took his place at halfback and played a major role in the Australian success in the series.

After he retired as a player, McCaffery continued in the game. He was secretary of the Canterbury-Bankstown Leagues Club and later secretary of North Sydney football club.

BOB McCARTHY

Ten Tests for Australia (1969–74). Also played five matches in two World Cups (1970 and 1972) and 12 minor games for Australia on one Kangaroo tour (173), two New Zealand tours (1969 and 1971) and one World Cup tour (1970).

Bob McCarthy was one of the most dynamic footballers Australia has produced. His tank-like charges wide of the rucks struck fear into the hearts of club and international opponents alike. The big second-rower began his first-grade career with South Sydney in 1963. He was an instant sensation. Critics enthused about his style of play and were particularly vocal in 1967 when he was left out of the Kangaroo squad to tour Britain and France. McCarthy had been outstanding in Souths' thrust to the Premiership that year.

Bob McCarthy

He had to wait until the 1969 tour of New Zealand before the national selectors finally gave him the nod. From then on, except for times when he was injured, McCarthy was one of the first chosen for Test and World Cup matches. He played against the 1970 and 1974 British Lions and in the 1970 and 1972 World Cups in Europe, as well as touring New Zealand again in 1971 and Britain and France, with the Kangaroos, two years later. He was vice-captain of the Kangaroo squad, but missed the Ashes-winning Third Test after damaging a collarbone while captaining Australia in the second clash with Britain.

On the club front, McCarthy appeared in a record 206 first-grade games (including six grand finals) for South Sydney, before moving to Canterbury-Bankstown in 1976. After 37 games for the Bulldogs, he returned to his original club in 1978 to finish his career, but injuries restricted him to just five first-grade appearances in that, his final, season.

After he retired, McCarthy turned his talents to coaching. In his first season, in 1980, he guided Souths to the Brisbane grand final. A year later Souths took out the Brisbane Premiership. When the Gold Coast joined the Sydney Premiership, in 1988, McCarthy was appointed the club's first coach but he and the Seagulls parted company in 1990 after indifferent results.

McCarthy was also honoured off the field. In 1977, he was awarded an MBE for his services to Rugby League.

JARROD McCRACKEN

Five Tests for New Zealand (1991).

Jarrod McCracken had the right pedigree for Test football. His father Ken McCracken had played eight internationals for New Zealand as a centre in the early 1960s and lost little in comparison with the Australian greats Reg Gasnier and Graeme Langlands.

Jarrod showed he was every bit as good as his father, if not better, at an early age. In 1989, he linked up with North Sydney under the New Zealand rookie scheme and, despite being knocked about by injuries, showed great promise. That year he toured Papua New Guinea with the Junior Kiwis, scoring a try in the first 'Test', won 34–8 by New Zealand. He was supposed to remain with North Sydney the following year but succumbed to wanderlust and ended up with some mates on the NSW North Coast where he played for Coffs Harbour.

McCracken was spotted by Canterbury-Bankstown supremo Peter Moore, who wanted him to play with the Bulldogs in 1991. But the NZRL said no. It was only the threat of court action which forced the authorities to relent. The big, blonde centre was an instant hit in the Sydney Premiership and after only a handful of games was chosen for New Zealand for the two Tests against the touring French side. In the first encounter he scored a try the first time he touched the ball, went on to bag a second and was named Man-of-the-Match.

A few weeks later McCracken was one of the first chosen when the Kiwis began a three-Test series in Australia. In the First Test, at Melbourne's Olympic Park, New Zealand scored an upset 24–8 victory over a complacent Australian side. McCracken repeatedly tore through the Australian defence and his bone-jarring tackles stopped many an Australian movement. He was predictably named Man-of-the-Match.

The second encounter, in Sydney, was not such a happy occasion. New Zealand trailed 8–0 but was still in the match until an ugly brawl in the 27th minute prompted British referee John Holdsworth to send off McCracken and Australian five-eighth Peter Jackson. The dismissals turned the game. Without McCracken on the field, the Australians had a field day, breaking through down the centre time and time again to run away to a record 44–0 victory. Both Jackson and McCracken were later found guilty of misconduct by an International Board judiciary panel—but escaped with a caution, allowing them to play in the Third Test, won by Australia.

McCracken's fine club form was one of the reasons why Canterbury defied the critics to finish the 1991 season in a play-off for the fifth and last semi-final spot in the Premiership race.

PADDY McCUE

Four Tests for Australia (1911–14). Also played 20 minor games for Australia on one Kangaroo tour (1911–12).

Patrick 'Paddy' McCue was one of the great 1908–09 Wallabies Rugby Union side to swap codes after the tour and take on the Rugby League Kangaroos in an historic series of matches. The Wallabies won two of the four matches and McCue went on to become a big name in the professional code.

As a lilywhite, McCue had played two Tests as a backrower and prop against the 1907 All Blacks before being picked for the pioneering Wallaby side. On tour he played Tests against both England and Wales as well as picking up a gold medal for Rugby in the London Olympic Games. He was to be back in England three years later as vice-captain of the 1911–12 Kangaroos, playing in all three Tests on tour. He bowed out of international football in the First Test against the 1914 Lions. In the meantime, he had captained two NSW representative sides to New Zealand (in 1912 and 1913).

On the club scene, McCue was a member of Newtown's side which won the 1910 Sydney Premiership.

JOHN McDONALD

Thirteen Tests for Australia (1966–70). Also played 15 minor games for Australia on one Kangaroo tour (1967–68) and one New Zealand tour (1969).

There were few more exciting players in the 1960s than centre John McDonald. The Toowoomba flyer had a deceptive swerve and change of pace which regularly left opposing three-quarters groping. He was also a fine cover-defender.

McDonald played his first international against Great Britain in 1966. It was not a happy baptism into the tough grind of Test football. He suffered a serious ankle injury, which, for a time, looked like threatening his career. Twelve months later McDonald was back with a vengeance against the touring New Zealand side. He missed the First Test, but in the second encounter he dazzled his opponents, scoring two tries and kicking six goals. His 18 points was a record against New Zealand, beating the 16 scored by Noel Pidding in 1952. McDonald was just as dominant in the Third Test, scoring two more tries and two goals. At the end of that season he was one of the first chosen for the Kangaroo touring side. He continued in top form in Britain and France, finishing as the team's second top-scorer with 41 points.

McDonald had a second overseas tour, to New Zealand in 1969. By that time, he was playing in the Sydney competition, with Manly-Warringah. He captained Australia in one match on that tour (against Auckland), playing despite a bad thigh injury. The classy centre had one more season in international football, playing in all three Tests against the 1970 British Lions. It was a sad finish to his career. In the final Test he was switched to the wing. He was all at sea and had a disastrous showing in a game which saw Britain regain the Ashes.

HUGH McGAHAN

Thirty-two Tests for New Zealand (1982–90). Also played for Oceania against Europe (1984) and 23 minor games for New Zealand on two Kiwi tours of Great Britain (1985 and 1989) and one tour of Australia and Papua New Guinea (1982) and eight games for Maoris on one British tour (1983).

When rangy lock-forward Hugh McGahan was overlooked by the New

Zealand Test selectors for the home-and-away series against Australia in 1983, he was devastated. The youngster had made his Test debut as a replacement against the Australians the previous year and in his first full Test, against Papua-New Guinea in Port Moresby, he had scored two tries. McGahan was determined to prove the selectors had erred—and he did so with a vengeance. Soon after the 1983 clashes with Australia he was recalled for the Auckland Test against the Kumuls. He went over for a world record six tries and was never dropped again, going on the play in 32 Tests, a total bettered by only three other Kiwis. In those games he captained his country 17 times and scored a record 16 tries.

McGahan joined Eastern Suburbs in the Sydney Premiership competition in 1985. Two years later he returned from a long spell on the sidelines, injured, to lead New Zealand to its historic 13–6 upset win over Australia at Brisbane's Lang Park. That same year he led Easts into the semi-final playoffs. These performances earned him a shared win in the Adidas Golden Boot Award, as the world's finest player, with Parramatta halfback Peter Sterling. It was the first time a non-Australian had been so honoured. McGahan was also the first winner from the forwards. Sadly, he accepted his award while on crutches, the legacy of an operation to reconstruct his right knee. This also prevented McGahan from leading his country in the 1988 World Cup Final at Auckland's Eden Park.

In 1989, McGahan made the last of his three overseas tours, captaining the Kiwis on their swing through England and France. The Kiwis lost the series against Britain two Tests to one (going down in the decider, at Wigan, by just 10–6). However they won the two French Tests. McGahan bowed out of the international arena at the age of 28, after the series against the touring 1990 British Lions and the one-off Test against Australia to commemorate New Zealand's 150th anniversary, but he continued his club career with Easts until the end of the 1991 season.

MARK McGAW

Three Tests for Australia (1990). Also played in 1988 World Cup Final, for Australia in the Bicentennial international against the Rest-of-the-World (1988) and six minor games on one Kangaroo tour (1990) and one Papua New Guinea tour (1991).

Team-mates gave Mark McGaw the nickname 'Sparkles' for that is what he did on the football field. He sparkled with the intensity of a shooting star.

Although he started his first grade career at Cronulla-Sutherland in 1984 as a fullback, it was as a centre that McGaw became a superstar. Ironically, it was in partnership with another Cronulla junior who had started out as a fullback, Andrew Ettingshausen. The two youngsters were so impressive early in their careers that they were named in the 1986 Kangaroo train-on squad even though they had yet to play State-of-Origin football. Both were considered unlucky not to have made the final touring team.

McGaw made his debut for New South Wales the following year and wore the green and gold for the first time in 1988 in the Bicentennial international against the Rest-of-the-World. Later that season he played in Australia's side which won the World Cup final, against New Zealand.

McGaw was overlooked for the 1989 tour of the Shaky Isles, but was one of the first picked for the home Test against France and the one-off Test against New Zealand, in Wellington, in 1990. He was in sensational form in the early matches on the 1990 Kangaroo tour, and he was one of only a handful of Australians to come out of the First Test loss at Wembley Stadium with reputations untarnished. Indeed, he scored one of the most brilliant individual tries of modern Rugby League, darting and weaving his way for 50 metres through the British defence. In the next game, against Castleford, tragedy struck. McGaw ruptured a medial ligament, an injury which put him out of the rest of the Kangaroo tour, including two Tests against each of Britain and France.

Back home, McGaw rarely sparkled during the 1991 season. He was chosen for City Origin but was overlooked for the State-of-Origin matches until the last encounter—and then he only got a start because Ettingshausen pulled out injured. He was also flown to Papua New Guinea midway through Australia's tour of its northern neighbour nation as a standby for the injured Ettingshausen.

DES McGOVERN

Seven Tests for Australia (1952–56). Also played 21 minor games for Australia on two Kangaroo tours (1952–53 and 1956–57) and one New Zealand tour (1953).

There have been few more courageous displays than that of Toowoomba winger Des McGovern in the Third Test against Britain on the 1956–57 Kangaroo tour. McGovern badly dislocated his shoulder when tackled going for a try in the third minute of the match. No replacements were allowed in those days, so McGovern, although suffering intense pain, battled on for the remaining 77 minutes of the game. The injury was so bad that he did not play in any of the subsequent matches in France. McGovern, nicknamed 'Wheatbags' because of his ability to lift such bags with ease, was always a tough customer. In the Second Test he had kept Billy Boston, one of the biggest, bruising backline runners in history, well in check.

The fine Queensland winger made his Test debut against the touring New Zealand Kiwis in 1952 and was an automatic selection for the Kangaroo squad at the end of that year. Although he did not play Tests on tour, he turned in a couple of extraordinary performances. Against Featherstone Rovers he scored six tries (including three in an eight-minute period), snapping up awkward passes on each occasion. Against the French side Cannes he notched five tries—all in the first 15 minutes. On the New Zealand tour in 1953, McGovern played in only one Test but was the leading tryscorer with 19 touchdowns in just six games. The 1956–57 Kangaroo tour was not a really happy one. Not only did he miss the matches at the end—but he was also laid low by a knee injury which forced him out of the early games.

BRUCE McGUIRE

Two Tests for Australia (1989). Also played four minor games on one New Zealand tour (1989) and one Papua New Guinea tour (1991).

Bruce McGuire was one of the unsung heroes of the Sydney football scene. During the late 1980s he was as good as any forward in the competition. But he seemed always to be in the shadow of his high-profile Balmain international team-mates, Steve Roach, Paul Sironen, Wayne Pearce and Ben Elias.

McGuire, a tough, hard-tackling second-rower had a handful of first-grade games for the Tigers in 1986 and 1987. But when the fine coach Warren Ryan took over the reigns the following year, McGuire blossomed. By the end of the season, he had improved so much that he was in Australia's shadow squad to cover any possible injuries in the run-up to the World Cup Final in New Zealand.

The following year he got his big chance. When Queensland thrashed New South Wales 36–6 in the first State-of-Origin clash, McGuire was called in for the last two matches and acquitted himself so well that he found himself in the Australian team for the three-week tour of New Zealand. He played in two of the three Tests as well as the three minor games.

During these two years, McGuire was one of the lynchpins in the Balmain thrust to successive grand finals (the Tigers went down to Canterbury). In 1990, he played for both Country Origin and in the three State-of-Origin matches, but missed out on the Tests against France and New Zealand and the Kangaroo tour of Britain and France.

McGuire switched clubs, to Canterbury-Bankstown, in 1991 and at the end of the season was rushed to Papua New Guinea as a replacement in the injury-plagued Australian lineup.

BRAD MACKAY

Six Tests for Australia (1990). Also played eight minor games on one Kangaroo tour (1990).

Few players have made such a sensational Test debut as St George utility player Brad Mackay. Mackay was called in as a late replacement for injured Test lock Bradley Clyde for the one-off Test, at Parkes, against the touring 1990 Frenchmen. He celebrated his arrival on the international scene with a hat-trick of tries, which helped him carry off the Man-of-the-Match award. Despite this great first game in the green and gold, Mackay had to be content with a place on the reserves bench for the Test against New Zealand to celebrate that nation's 150th anniversary. However when he came on late in the match, he went over for another try.

Mackay kept up a great St George tradition by being chosen for the 1990 Kangaroo tour of Britain and France. Every Kangaroo side to have toured since St George entered the Premiership in 1921 has contained at least one Saints player. The utility star was overlooked for the First Test against Britain. But after Australia's shock defeat at Wembley, he was chosen at lock for the remaining four Tests—two each versus Britain and France. Mackay was one of Australia's most consistent players and, in the second encounter against France, scored two tries—a just reward for backing up team-mates.

The 1991 season is one Mackay would rather forget. Broken fingers kept him out of all but one representative match (the third State-of-Origin clash)—just when he should have been consolidating his position in the Australian lineup.

ROSS McKINNON

Six Tests for Australia (1935-38). Also played 28 minor games on one Kangaroo tour (1937-38) and one New Zealand tour (1935).

Ross McKinnon was a superb footballer and just as great a coach. A fast, elusive five-eighth, with a devastating tackle, he showed great potential as a schoolboy, representing Sydney. He continued that form in the Premiership competition as an 18–year-old, when he turned out for the University club in 1933. That year he played his first State game for New South Wales.

McKinnon missed most of the following season through injury, but in 1935 he made his Test debut while a member of the Australian side touring New Zealand. He switched to Eastern Suburbs (and moved out into the centres) in 1936 and continued his good form. He had trouble staying in the Australian side because of competition from such all-time greats as Dave Brown, Vic Hey and Ernie Norman, but with the departure of Brown and Hey to English clubs, he was able to cement his centre spot on the 1937–38 Kangaroo tour, playing in two of the three encounters with Great Britain and both the Tests against France. With 50 points (from 10 tries and 10 goals) he was also second in the pointscoring lists behind Jack Beaton.

After he hung up his boots, McKinnon achieved fame as a coach. Such was his reputation that several international touring sides took advantage of his know-how to help them prepare for Tests against Australia.

CHRIS McKIVAT

Five Tests for Australia (1910-12). Also played two internationals (1910) which for many years were regarded as Tests and 29 minor games on one Kangaroo tour (1911-12).

Not only was Chris McKivat one of Australia's greatest halfbacks, but he was also one of his country's finest captains. That was never more evident than when he led the 1911–12 Kangaroos to a well-deserved win over Britain. He drove the tourists, but tempered the aggression with subtle psychology—and his players responded. That tour was the second McKivat had made to Britain. The first was in 1908, when he was playing Rugby Union, with the Australian Wallabies touring side. Although not tour captain, McKivat was the skipper in the major matches, including the Tests against England and Wales and the game against Great Britain which won Australia the gold medal for Rugby at the London Olympic Games.

McKivat and most of his team-mates turned professional after that tour (McKivat pocketing £200, the others £100) and took part in a unique series in Australia. It matched the Wallabies against the Rugby League Kangaroos, who had been touring Britain at the same time as their amateur counterparts.

McKivat appeared in seven internationals against British Rugby League sides and scored an average of one try per game. He was known for his unselfish play—except on one occasion. It was in a match against Coventry during the 1911–12 tour. A local businessman had offered an overcoat as a prize for the first try-scorer. McKivat won it after a brilliant solo effort marked by a series of dummy passes, sidesteps and sprints through gaps he created in the defence. 'It's cold in England. And overcoats don't grow on trees,' McKivat explained later.

After retiring as a player, McKivat successfully turned his talents to coaching. While under his guidance, North Sydney won its only two Premierships, in 1921 and 1922.

ALLAN McMAHON

Five matches for Australia in two World Championships (1975 and 1977). Also played 15 games on one Kangaroo tour (1978), one World Championship tour of England (1975) and one World Championship tour of New Zealand (1977).

Allan McMahon was too good a fullback to keep out of the Australian team. Balmain had signed up the young star in 1975 from the Wollongong competition, from where the 20–year-old had made the Country team. However, with Graham Eadie having a mortgage on the custodian's spot in the NSW and Australian Test sides, the representative selectors switched McMahon to the wing, where he played all his international football. He made his international debut against Wales, at Swansea in the 1975 World Championships. He was later to star for Australia's winning World Championship side in 1977.

McMahon suffered a serious thigh injury in 1978 and played only nine games for Balmain. Although the selectors still chose him for the Kangaroo squad, he had to play second fiddle to Kerry Boustead and Chris Anderson when the Test sides were chosen.

Allan McMahon in his Balmain playing days

A broken collarbone almost brought his playing days to an end in 1981. However he managed two final seasons, first with Newtown and then with the Canberra Raiders in their second season in the Premiership race.

Even after hanging up his boots, McMahon still had a lot to give to Rugby League. In 1985, he first tried his hand at coaching, steering Canberra's reserve grade side to the club's first grand final appearance in any grade. When Newcastle entered the Sydney Premiership in 1988, McMahon was the Knights' coach. They were 14th the first season, but McMahon had a long range plan. In 1989 he moved them up to seventh—and in 1990 he saw the knights bow out after a play-off with Balmain for the fifth and last semi-final spot.

After a good start to the 1991 season, the Knights slumped badly and before the season was over, McMahon decided to quit.

PAT McMAHON

Nine Tests for Australia (1948–49). Also played 23 minor games on one Kangaroo tour (1948–49) and one New Zealand tour (1949).

Toowoomba winger Pat McMahon played nine Tests in the space of just 16 months in the late 1940s. He may have played more but for the number of fine flankmen around at the time including Noel Pidding, Johnny 'Wacka' Graves, Ron Roberts and Bob Lulham. McMahon made his interstate debut at the Sydney Cricket Ground in 1946. He was to play another 10 matches for the Maroons in the next six seasons.

His first Test appearance was against the touring New Zealand Kiwis in 1948, and at the end of that season he toured Britain and France with the Kangaroos, playing in all five Tests. In the second encounter with the British, at Headingley, Leeds, he scored what many believe to have been the try of the tour. Five-eighth Wally O'Connell, centre Doug McRitchie and opposite winger Johnny Hawke combined well before sending to McMahon, who dived over in the corner. Hawke converted from the sideline to bring Australia to within two points of the British, with just five minutes to go. At full-time there was no change with Britain in front 23–21. McMahon ended his Test career on the 1949 tour of New Zealand, although he continued in the Queensland side until 1951.

TOM McMAHON

Two of Australia's greatest referees, although not related, shared the same name, Tom McMahon. The elder of the two was Australia's first great whistle-man. He had control of the first Anglo-Australian Test on Australian soil, at the RAS Showground in Sydney in 1910. He was also in charge of two other internationals that year which, for many years, were regarded as Test matches. McMahon also refereed all three Tests when the British next toured, in 1914, and was involved in two of the three Tests in 1920 and 1924. His eight Tests remains a record almost seven decades later. When McMahon retired after the 1926 season a Sydney report noted: 'He was always as cool as the Chief Justice when adjudicating in the midst of the stormiest battles. He was always consistent and always firm'.

TOM McMAHON

During a career spanning two decades, the younger of the two international referees called Tom McMahon (see entry above for elder McMahon) controlled Tests between Australia and every other Rugby League nation (three against each of Great Britain and France and one against New Zealand).

McMahon started as a junior referee in 1930. He progressed quickly, controlling his first interstate game three years later. When the British Lions toured in 1936 and the New Zealand Kiwis in 1938, McMahon had charge of several of their matches. However he had to wait until the British were back after the War, in 1946, before officiating in his first Test. He went to Britain, in a private capacity, with the 1948 Kangaroos and, taking charge of the Australia v Yorkshire match at Headingley, Leeds, became the first Australian to control a game in Britain. McMahon bowed out of refereeing after the 1951 season, during which he controlled the three Tests against the visiting Frenchmen.

The next year he whistled up another talent, coaching. Under his guidance, Western Suburbs that season shocked the sages by downing a fine South Sydney side to win the Premiership. With a 100 percent coaching record, McMahon then retired.

FRANK McMILLAN

Nine Tests for Australia (1929–1933). Also played 41 minor games on two Kangaroo tours (1929–30 and 1933–34).

Frank McMillan was one of the greatest of Australia's attacking fullbacks, renowned for his flair and skillful play. A fair-haired lightweight (hence his nickname, 'Skinny'), McMillan played his first Test on the 1929–30 Kangaroo tour of Britain, where he was pitted against the great Jim Sullivan. Many critics rate McMillan's performances in the four Tests on that tour as far superior to his immortal rival's. McMillan made the Test sides for two more series against the British. In 1932, he played (and was knocked out) in the infamous Battle of Brisbane match. Battle it was, with some

Frank McMillan

of the worst thuggery ever seen on a football field. Five Australians, including McMillan, suffered severe injuries in the match. The fine fullback also captained the Kangaroos on their 1933–34 tour of Britain and France, playing in 21 of the 37 games.

On the Sydney scene, McMillan was a vital cog in the Western Suburbs machine which won the club's first Premiership, in 1930, with only two losses in the season. He also played a major role when the Magpies won their second Premiership four years later.

PETER 'MICK' MADSEN

Nine Tests for Australia (1929–1936). Also played 37 minor games on two Kangaroo tours (1929–30 and 1933–34).

When, in 1982, the respected Rugby League Week magazine asked eight experts to pick the greatest Australian side of all time, there was a surprise name in the pack—front-rower Mick Madsen. The selection of Madsen— baptised Peter, but known to everyone as Mick—should not have come as such a shock. There were few tougher and more talented props in the history of the game. He was so strong that he was able to carry a 140kg bale of wool on one shoulder.

Madsen, from Toowoomba, made his Test debut in 1929, on the first of two Kangaroo tours he made to Britain, turning out in the first two encounters, at Hull and Leeds. He played all three Tests when Britain toured Australia in 1932, including the infamous Battle of Brisbane. He was also a dominant figure in all three Tests on the 1933–34 Kangaroo tour. The big fellow made his final appearance in the international arena in the deciding Test of the 1936 series, in Sydney. Strangely, he was chosen as hooker. He refused to play until he was convinced that his good mate, Arthur Folwell, who was expected to fill the hooker's role, was suffering from influenza. Folwell, a fine sport, was bitterly disappointed at not being chosen, but lied to Madsen about his alleged flu to avoid any embarrassing incident.

Peter ('Mick') Madsen

MAHER CUP

The Maher Cup, a battered trophy valued at only $32, was, over the years, contested by relatively insignificant teams from towns in southern New South Wales. However, because of the long list of colourful incidents associated with its history, the 'Old Pot' became one of the best known of all Australian sporting prizes.

The Cup was donated by a Ted Maher, in 1919, for Rugby Union competition, but only one match was played under Union rules. During the next 50–odd years, League teams in the Riverina area took turns at challenging whoever held it, at an average of fortnightly intervals. The last match for the Cup was held on June 6, 1971, when Tumut beat Young 43–4. The 'Old Pot' has since been kept in Tumut, being brought out for special reunions.

One early match, at Barmedman, finished after sunset and by the light of burning wheat stubble. At half-time, a local politician, Martin Flannery, had addressed his constituents. Flannery became so carried away that he talked for well over an hour—so long that, when the players returned to the field, the wheat stubble had to be lit to enable them to see their opponents and the ball. The West Wyalong team was once involved in an incident concerning the local jail. Supporters of their defeated opponents locked the Cup up in a cell and only after an argument which continued in bitterly cold conditions until three am did they relinquish the prisoner.

A 1929 game between Barmedman and Young was played on a field infested with rabbits. Players had as much difficulty in avoiding the bunnies and their burrows as they did with their opponents. Cootamundra, led by international Herb Narvo, became so engrossed in a Maher Cup match that they failed to notice the nearby river was beginning to flood. Swirling waters cut them off and only the arrival of high-wheeled trucks enabled them to reach safety.

At least that's the way the Maher Cup stories go—and who would be such a spoilsport as to question them?

MANLY-WARRINGAH

Manly-Warringah fans had a long, frustrating wait for their side's first Premiership. Loyal fans must have wondered whether the Sea Eagles would ever get to reign as Sydney's champion side. So often, the Sea Eagles (or the Seagulls, as they had been known in their early days) went within an ace of victory, only to falter in the final match. Some critics even suggested the club did not have the fighting spirit necessary for Premiership success. Manly finally triumphed in 1972, beating Eastern Suburbs in the grand final. There was no lack of fortitude that day—nor next year, when Manly downed Cronulla-Sutherland to make it two in a row.

Manly, with Parramatta, joined the Sydney first-grade competition in 1947. The first sides were a blend of eager youngsters who had been playing junior football the year before and a sprinkling of ex-North Sydney men who lived in the Manly-Warringah area (players were supposed to live in the club's district in those days). Unlike newly promoted clubs of the past, Manly did not experience humiliations associated with joining the top competition. In their first match, the Seagulls held Western Suburbs to just 15–13. That year they also beat Parramatta, Canterbury-Bankstown and Newtown (the last named by an incredible 33–0).

Looking at the first Manly outfit you can see why it wasn't disgraced. The distinguished members included two three-quarters who within a few years were to wear the green and gold for Australia, Johnny Bliss and Gordon Willoughby, and a raw prop who was to become one of Australia's greatest, Roy Bull.

Within five seasons, Manly had managed to reach the 1951 grand final. However the young club came up against a great South Sydney combination and was trounced 42–14, at the time the biggest winning margin in a grand final. Manly had some excuses. Captain-coach Wally O'Connell was sidelined with injury, Willoughby played in the centre with an injured leg heavily bandaged, and international hooker Kev Schubert had an off-day and was thoroughly outraked by Test star Ernie Hammerton. The pick of the side was halfback Ken Arthurson, who later made an indelible name for himself at Manly as a coach and top official before going on to become chairman of the Australian Rugby League.

The next four times the seasiders made grand finals, they also faced historic lineups, St George downed Manly in 1957 (31–9) and 1959 (20–0) to record two of its world-record 11 straight Premiership successes. Then Manly fell twice (1968 and 1970) to a South Sydney team which at the time provided the nucleus of Australia's Test sides. Two years after the second of those disappointments, everything changed for Manly. A side built around Manly regulars, including centre Bob Fulton and hooker Fred Jones, and bolstered by imported stars, such as Castleford (England) lock Mal Reilly and former South Sydney Test men Ray Branighan and John O'Neill, broke through. The coach in those balmy days was the ex-Kangaroo fullback Ron Willey, a Manly star of the 1950s. After two Premiership successes, Willey was riding high, but when Western Suburbs scored a shock win over his team in the semi-finals of 1974, he and Manly parted company.

The club was again a semi-finalist in 1975, but missed the Premiership. However, the Sea Eagles were flying highest in 1976. The English influence was never more evident than from the forwards Steve 'Knocker' Norton and Phil Lowe and halfback Gary Stephens, who helped engineer the victory. Manly did it the hard way for its Premiership in 1978. Beaten in the semi-finals by Cronulla, the club bounced back to beat Parramatta (in a replay) and Western Suburbs to reach the grand final. This, too, required a replay before Manly had its revenge over Cronulla.

It was therefore not unexpected when Manly had a large number of its players picked in the 1978 Kangaroo squad. Seven of the Sea Eagles were chosen to make the trip to Britain and France—fullback Graham Eadie, centre Alan Thompson, five-eighth Steve Martin, halfback John Gibbs and forwards John Harvey, Ian Thomson and Max Krilich. Another Manly star, Terry Randall, would almost certainly have joined them on the list had he not made himself unavailable for personal reasons. As it transpired, Harvey also turned down the tour for personal reasons. His place was taken by Bruce Walker—from Manly. Manly was well-represented on the next tour, too. Five of the grand final side made the Kangaroo squad—

John Ribot, Paul McCabe, Les Boyd, Ray Brown and Max Krilich. Krilich was the Kangaroo captain. He and Brown became the first two hookers from the same club to tour with an Australian side.

Manly, the Minor Premiers in 1983 made it straight through to the grand final with a 19–10 victory over Parramatta in the semi-final. However the Eels then turned the tables, taking out the big match 18–6. During this era Manly had a wealth of internationals, as well as its Kangaroos. They included the elusive wingers Kerry Boustead and Ian Schubert, powerhouse centre Chris Close, utility back Phil Sigsworth and forwards Noel 'Crusher' Cleal, Dave Brown, Paul Vautin and Geoff Gerard. Manly was a semifinalist in the next three years and provided three Kangaroos in 1986—winger Dale Shearer, halfback Des Hasler and prop Phil Daley. Another Kangaroo winger Michael O'Connor was signed from St George just before the team went away. In 1987, the Sea Eagles were once again Premiers. After the home-and-away games they had finished six points clear of their nearest rivals, Eastern Suburbs, and in the grand final faced a young and enthusiastic Canberra side, running out winners 18–8.

The man behind the victory was Manly's favourite son, Bob Fulton. He'd played in the sides which won Manly's first three Premierships. Now he was the coach. Putting the Fulton tactics into play were five-eighth Cliff Lyons, whose guile helped him win the Clive Churchill Medal as the Man-of-the-Match, and the English Test forward Kevin Ward, whose rugged and clever play must have almost stolen the medal from Lyon's grasp. There was also another overseas international, Kiwi Darrell Williams.

From champions to chumps. In 1988, the Sea Eagles slipped and were beaten in the elimination semi-final by Balmain. Then, in a bitter season, which saw the sacking of coach Alan Thompson (who holds the record for the number of first-grade games for Manly) and the eventual departure under a cloud of internationals Paul Vautin and Dale Shearer, Manly slumped to twelfth spot on the table at the end of 1989. However the bold signing of former New Zealand Test coach, Graham Lowe, from top English club Wigan turned it all around. Manly were again competitive and it took a sensational display by Brisbane in the semi-finals to eliminate the Sea Eagles.

Among Lowe's clever signings was the goalkicking New Zealand All Black fullback Matthew Ridge, who after just five games for Manly made the Kiwi Rugby League Test side and the New Zealand Test winger Tony Iro. Martin Bella, who switched from North Sydney, made the Australian Test lineup. Cliff Lyons won the Dally M award for Player-of-the-Year and half Geoff Toovey stamped himself as one of the future greats of Australian football.

There was an even bigger signing in 1991. Lowe persuaded blockbusting New Zealand Test centre Kevin Iro to join Manly after his contract with Wigan had expired. The Sea Eagles finished third, despite a lot of injuries and the loss during the Australia-New Zealand Test series of several stars—Iro, Hasler, Bella and second-rower Ian Roberts. Ridge finished the season second in the pointscoring charts, with 184 points (six tries, 79 goals and two field goals). Toovey, Bella, Lyons and Roberts all made the Australian squad for the end-of-season tour of Papua New Guinea.

MANLY-WARRINGAH

Founded: 1946
Entered Sydney Premiership: 1947
Home ground: Brookvale Oval (record crowd—27 655)
Colours: Maroon and white
Nickname: The Sea Eagles (formerly, The Seagulls)
Honours:
   Sydney Premiership—Winners, 1972, 1973, 1976, 1978, 1987; Runners-up, 1951, 1957, 1959, 1968, 1970, 1982, 1983
     Midweek Cup—1982, 1983
     Flowers' Memorial Pennant (Club Championship)—1972, 1983, 1987, 1988
     Pre-Season Competition—1980
     Reserve-grade Premiership—1954, 1960, 1969, 1973, 1988
     Third-grade Premiership—1952
     President's Cup—1946, 1970
     Flegg Memorial Trophy—1961, 1974, 1987, 1988
Most first-grade games: 263 by Alan Thompson
Most points in a career: 1917 by Graham Eadie
Most tries in a career: 129 by Bob Fulton
Most points in a season: 242 by Graham Eadie, in 1975
Most tries in a season: 27 by Phil Blake, in 1983
Rothmans Medal winners: Graham Eadie (1974), Mal Cochrane (1986)
NSW Player-of-the-Year: Roy Bull (1954), Bob Fulton (1972 & 1973)
Rugby League Week Player-of-the-Year: John Mayes (1973), Bob Fulton (1975), Phil Sigsworth (1983)
Dally M Player-of-the-Year: Cliff Lyons (1990)
Sun Herald Best-and-Fairest Player: Rex Mossop (1958), Dennis Ward (1968)

MAORIS

Many of New Zealand's finest footballers have been Maoris. Few Test sides are chosen without at least one representative of the country's native race. Most international touring sides play a match against a Maori XIII. Three Maoris sides have toured Australia and another has visited Britain. The first to go to Australia was in 1908, less than a year after a full New Zealand side made the first-ever overseas tour. The second was 12 months later and the latest in 1956. The Maoris made a trail-blazing tour of Britain in 1983, winning all eight matches.

Maoris to Australia

1908

Less than a year after the New Zealand 'All Golds' made the first-ever overseas Rugby League trip, a squad of Maoris travelled to Australia for a short tour. The 1908 Maoris were no match for the Australian and New South Wales lineups, but won six of the other nine games. There should have been two other matches, against Australia. However the Maoris refused to take part because they claimed they were owed gate money from earlier games.

Record in Australia

Played 12, Won 6, Lost 6, Points for 197, Points against 180

Match Results

Opponents	Venue	For	Against
New South Wales	Sydney	9	18
New South Wales	Sydney	16	30
Metropolis	Sydney	23	20
Newcastle	Newcastle	15	2
Queensland	Brisbane	19	16
Queensland	Brisbane	13	5
Queensland	Brisbane	5	6

Continued

383

Match Results *continued*

Opponents	Venue	For	Against
Queensland	Warwick	9	11
Queensland	Toowoomba	14	23
Newcastle	Newcastle	30	16
Australia	Sydney	10	20
Metropolis	Sydney	34	13

1909

The Maoris showed a tremendous improvement in the short interval between their first and second tours of Australia. On their return in 1909, they played Australia four times, won once and lost the other three games by small margins. They also downed a tough NSW combination in all three clashes.

Record in Australia

Played 10, Won 5, Lost 5, Points for 161, Points against 166

Match Results

Opponents	Venue	For	Against
New South Wales	Sydney	24	21
New South Wales	Sydney	14	11
Australia	Sydney	16	14
Newcastle	Newcastle	6	7
Queensland	Brisbane	11	21
Queensland	Brisbane	36	25
Australia	Brisbane	13	16
Australia	Brisbane	16	23
New South Wales	Sydney	12	8
Australia	Sydney	13	20

1956

Internationals Henry Maxwell and Bill Sorensen headed a strong Maori squad which toured Australia in 1956. Unlike their predecessors, they played neither national nor State sides. They did beat a Sydney Metropolis team (which included Ray Ritchie, Ian Johnston, Peter Burke and Henry Holloway who wore the green and gold for Australia), but went down to the full representative combinations from both Sydney and Brisbane.

Record in Australia

Played 14, Won 6, Lost 8, Points for 296, Points against 257

Match Results

Opponents	Venue (Attendance)	For	Against
NSW North Coast	Kempsey (7126)	10	8
Brisbane	Brisbane (9756)	23	32
Central Queensland	Rockhampton (6000)	38	24
Ipswich	Ipswich (2000)	11	21
Wide Bay	Bundaberg (2630)	31	6
Northern Division	Armidale (3000)	15	17
Newcastle	Newcastle (9918)	15	19
Western Division	Wellington (2000)	0	5
Southern Division	Wollongong (4000)	16	17
Group 9	Young (3000)	19	21
Metropolis	Sydney (13 148)	22	20
Monaro	Goulburn (1200)	67	13
Sydney	Sydney (11 619)	7	37
Riverina	Griffith (2460)	22	17

Maoris to Great Britain
1983

The Maoris, with several Kiwi representatives in their ranks (including two future Test captains, Hugh McGahan and Dean Bell), made a trail-blazing tour of northern England in 1983. The eight matches were against amateur sides, including one against a Great Britain representative team. Andrew Berryman, who had starred as a player on the 1956 tour of Australia, was the coach of the Maori side.

Record in Great Britain

Played 8, Won 8, Points for 238, Points against 85

International Match Result

| Maoris | 23 | Great Britain | 14 | (Hull, 3000) |

Other Matches

Opponents	Venue (Attendance)	For	Against
Humberside League	Hull (2076)	18	13
Heavy Woolen League	Dewsbury (3100)	28	8
Halifax League	Halifax (2110)	40	10
Barrow League	Barrow (1600)	46	12
Cumberland League	Whitehaven (2600)	40	6
York League	York (2300)	16	6
Oldham League	Oldham (1439)	28	16

RAY MARKHAM

Because of the eagle-eye of one of Britain's finest players, Stanley Brogden, Newcastle winger Ray Markham never played for Australia. Brogden was a member of the 1932 British Lions side which toured Australia, and Markham turned in a dazzling display against the British in the match against Newcastle (won by the tourists 22–15).

After the tour, Brogden persuaded his British club Huddersfield to snap up the young star's services. Markham was an immediate success and his efforts would have most certainly made all the Huddersfield record books but for two other great Aussie wingers who played at Fartown— Albert Rosenfeld (whose 80 tries is a British season record) and Lionel Cooper (whose 10 tries in a Championship match is also a British best). Markham scored tries at the rate of more than one a match in his career of over 300 games for Huddersfield. His best effort was nine tries in a 1935 match against Featherstone Rovers. He appeared in two Wembley Challenge Cup Finals, in the side which beat Warrington 21–17 in 1933 and on the losing side against Castleford two years later.

BILL MARSH

Five Tests for Australia (1956–58). Also played three matches in one World Cup (1957), one match against the Rest-of-the-World (1957) and 15 minor games on one Kangaroo tour (1956–57).

Bill Marsh was a tough front-row forward who starred for Australia in the late 1950s. While playing for Cootamundra in southern New South Wales, Marsh attracted the attention of the selectors with a big-hearted game for

Country against City in 1956—and he showed enough in a mid-week interstate game for New South Wales to gain selection on the Kangaroo tour at the end of the season. It was on tour that he made his Test debut, playing one international against both Britain and France. Back home, having switched to the Balmain club in Sydney, he was an automatic choice for the 1957 World Cup squad. He played in all matches for the victorious Australians, including the game against the Rest-of-the-World.

Marsh bowed out of the international arena in the series against the touring 1958 British Lions. That same year he captained the Balmain side which went close to putting the fine St George combination out of the Premiership run in a hard-fought clash in the preliminary final. It was the closest Marsh got to a Premiership success.

STEVE MARTIN

One Test for Australia (1978). Also played 15 minor games on one Kangaroo tour (1978) and one New Zealand tour (1980).

They called Steve Martin 'Whiz', because this classy utility back had an acceleration which really made him whiz through the opposition. Martin had a short international career as a player, and as the 1990s got underway he was carving out a new career as a coach.

Martin burst onto the international scene in 1978. He was halfback in Manly-Warringah's Premiership-winning side and one of seven from the Sea Eagles' ranks to make the squad for the Kangaroo tour of Britain and France. His ability to play anywhere in the backline came in handy—and it was in the centres that he got his chance to play against France, at Carcassonne. It was to be his only Test appearance. He toured New Zealand two years later, but did not make the Test sides. Martin switched to Balmain in 1982 to join his old Manly coach, Frank Stanton, for three years.

His first taste of Sydney coaching came in 1988, when he took over North Sydney's reserve–grade side (Stanton was coach of the Firsts). Martin helped lift the Bears from 11th to within one point of the semi-finals in

Steve Martin in his Manly playing days

his first year and to the Premiership in 1989. It was Norths first taste of success in any grade for 20 years. It came as no surprise that when Stanton quit at the end of 1989, Martin replaced him as first grade mentor.

With a few judicious signings, including international centre Peter Jackson, veteran Souths' forward Mario Fenech and goal-kicking New Zealand Rugby Union winger Daryl Halligan, Martin was able to mould a well-balanced team. And in 1991, the Bears made the semi-finals for the first time in almost a decade.

ROY MASTERS

Few people had heard of the Tamworth schoolteacher Roy Masters when he was chosen to coach the Australian schoolboys side which toured Britain in 1972. However, his performance in that triumphant experiment, grooming future Test players Ian Schubert, Craig Young, Les Boyd and Royce Ayliffe, brought Masters to the notice of Sydney clubs, which until then had usually looked to ex-star players for their coaches.

In 1977, Masters guided Western Suburbs Under-23 team to Premiership success and next year took over the Magpies' first-grade side. Masters' shrewd and psychological approach to the game lifted what appeared at the start of the season to be a very ordinary outfit to the Minor Premiership (the Magpies were knocked out of the play-offs in the final). For his efforts, Masters was voted Coach-of-the-Year. He steered Wests to the semi-finals again in the following two years.

After a disappointing 1981 season, when Wests failed to make the play-offs, Masters switched to St George. In 1985, the year he won his second Coach-of-the-Year accolade, he looked likely to achieve the ultimate success, with a Sydney Premiership. The Dragons were Minor Premiers in first-grade and reached the grand-final in all three grades. However while the lower grades won, Masters' first-grade outfit was beaten 7–6 by Canterbury-Bankstown. Eventually, Masters quit to pursue a career in sporting journalism.

Roy Masters

HAROLD MATTHEWS

Harold Matthews was one of the best known of Australia's national Rugby League secretaries. Although playing second-fiddle to the presidents with whom he served, Matthews had a tremendous influence on the game throughout the world.

Matthews never played a game of Rugby League. He began his administrative career in junior football in the Balmain area of Sydney and served for 21 years as the Balmain district club's secretary before becoming secretary to both the NSW and Australian Rugby Leagues in 1951. He retired because of ill health in 1967 and died four years later. A junior competition for Under-14 representative sides was later named in his honour.

COL MAXWELL

One Test for Australia (1948). Also played 11 minor games on one Kangaroo tour (1948–49).

Col Maxwell will be remembered in the history of Rugby League as an unwilling participant in one of the most controversial incidents in the game. As the 1948–49 Kangaroo side was being chosen a dejected Maxwell was on a train from Sydney to Newcastle. A big-hearted centre, whose form had so deteriorated after his one match for New South Wales earlier in the season that his club, Western Suburbs, had dropped him to reserve-grade, was going home to the industrial city to spend a few days with his family. When he arrived at Newcastle Railway Station a group of friends and family gave him the stunning news. Not only was he in the Kangaroo squad—he was captain. The selectors had dropped Len Smith, the captain-coach of the Australian side which had just beaten New Zealand in a Test. All the other 12 players had made the Kangaroo side. Maxwell proved to be a popular captain, but injury and illness limited his Test appearances to one lone match on tour. In retrospect, he should not have even played in that one, because he was not fully fit.

LES MEAD

One Test for Australia (1933). Also played 14 minor games on one Kangaroo tour (1933–34).

Les Mead had the misfortune to be playing football at the same time as Viv Thicknesse, one of the best halfbacks to turn out in the period during the two World Wars. As a result, Mead managed only one Test appearance, even though he was recognised for his brilliant combination with Western Suburbs club-mate Vic Hey (arguably one of the two greatest five-eighths Australia has known—the other being Wally Lewis). The rest of the time Mead played second-fiddle to Thicknesse.

An inspiring captain, Mead skippered Wests to its 1934 Sydney Premiership success (he was also a member of the 1930 side which triumphed) and in 1933 was leader of the NSW side. Mead was also a useful goalkicker. In 1932, a low-scoring year all round, he scored 107 points (10 tries and 37 goals), more than any other player in the Sydney competition.

MAL MENINGA

Thirty-four Tests for Australia (1982–91). Also played in the Bicentennial international against the Rest-of-the-World (1988), for Oceania against Europe (1984) and 28 minor games for Australia on three Kangaroo tours (1982, 1986 and 1990), two New Zealand tours (1985 and 1989) and one Papua New Guinea tour (1991).

Twice Mal Meninga suffered awful broken arms which would have ended the career of a lesser man. The tough, big-hearted centre fought back on both occasions to not only resume playing, but to make it back to the international ranks. Indeed, not only did Meninga regain his Test spot, he ended up, in 1990, winning the Adidas Golden Boot award as the finest player in the world. Later that year he achieved the ultimate by captaining Australia first in the domestic Tests and then on the triumphant Kangaroo tour of Britain and France.

It would have been a shame had the injuries robbed the fans of the Meninga brilliance. He showed just how good he was soon after forcing his way into the Test side in 1982, breaking up the fine centre combination of Mick Cronin and Steve Rogers. On the Kangaroo tour that year, Meninga set a host of records, including:

• Totals of 21 goals and 48 points in the three Tests against Britain, which were Ashes records in that country.

• The best tally by any player in an Ashes Test debut, 19 points in the First Test, at Hull.

• An average of 12.8 points per tour match, beating the previous Kangaroo best of Noel Pidding (in 1952–53) by two and a half points.

Kangaroo captain Mal Meninga is brought to a halt by two Great Britain defenders during a 1990 Ashes Test

When it came to kicking for goal on his later tours, Meninga played second fiddle for much of the time to Michael O'Connor and Greg Alexander.

However, he is one of only two players who have scored 500 points or more in all games in the green and gold (41 tries and 177 goals for 500 points). The other is Graeme Langlands (507). In Tests Meninga has notched a record 220 points (15 tries and 85 goals). By 1992, Meninga had played 34 Tests (13 against New Zealand, 11 versus Great Britain, five against France and five against Papua New Guinea), second only to Reg Gasnier's 36. In State-of-Origin, Meninga was the top-scorer in interstate clashes with 141 points (5 tries and 61 goals).

In club matches, Meninga's powerhouse displays were all important in Canberra's push to the top in the late 1980s. In 1987, he badly broke his arm after colliding with a goalpost in the first round match against Manly-Warringah. But he made a dramatic return in the preliminary final to inspire the Green Machine to a 32–24 success over Eastern Suburbs—and he was far from disgraced in the grand final won by Manly. The following year Canberra were without Meninga in the play-offs after he once again fractured his arm, this time in the Bicentennial international against the Rest-of-the-World. And the Raiders foundered in the minor semi-final.

In 1989, coach Tim Sheens appointed Meninga captain. It was a master stroke, copied 12 months later by the Test selectors. Meninga led by example and Canberra waltzed away with their first Sydney Premiership, beating Balmain 19–14 in the grand final. Meninga was even more dominant in 1990. In a home match against Eastern Suburbs, he scored 38 points (five tries and nine goals). Only one other player has scored more points in a single match in the history of the Premiership—Dave Brown, who notched 45 in 1935. In the final, against the Brisbane Broncos, Meninga scored 18 points to inspire Canberra to secure another grand final appearance. And once there, he led the Raiders to a second Premiership.

Meninga and the Raiders reached their third straight grand final in 1991. But the effort needed in a series of seven 'sudden-death' matches took its toll and Penrith triumphed. Canberra had been plagued by financial troubles with players forced to take a pay cut. And it was Meninga's rejection of some mammoth offers from British clubs to stay with the Raiders for 1992 which prompted team-mates to also reject big baits from elsewhere.

The English clubs had always been keen to secure Meninga's services. Once he made the trip north, to play for St Helens during the 1984–85 season, and scored 28 tries in just 31 matches.

DALLY MESSENGER

Seven Tests for Australia (1908–1910) and three Tests for New Zealand (1908). Also played for Australia in two internationals (1910) which for years were regarded as Tests and 29 minor games on one Kangaroo tour (1908–09).

At the Sydney headquarters of the Australian Rugby League is a huge photograph of Dally Messenger—but the plaque underneath does not identify him by name—only as 'The Master'. That is what Messenger was. Nearly every expert agrees that this goal-kicking centre was probably the greatest player the game has known.

Dally Messenger—the man they called 'The Master'

Messenger, almost single-handed, ensured the success of Rugby League in Australia when it broke away from the amateur ranks in 1907. He was already a Rugby Union great, a star of the NSW amateur side which scored a shock win over the 1906 New Zealand All Blacks, on their way home from a triumphant tour of Britain in which they lost only one of 59 matches. He was also in the Australian Rugby Union Test side which played the 1907 All Blacks. A few months after that series, when A H Baskerville took his 'All Golds' New Zealand Rugby League team to Sydney, en route to England, it was largely the decision by Messenger to turn professional that drew the crowds to watch.

Messenger so impressed Baskerville that he took the Australian with his squad to England, where local Rugby League and Soccer clubs fought for his services. Both Manchester United and Tottenham Hotspurs Soccer clubs offered him a then-staggering £1500 to join their ranks. He finished the tour having scored 146 points—an incredible 101 more than the next most successful tourist.

Having turned a deaf ear to all the British offers and returning to Australia, Dally M set about enthralling the home crowds in the first year of club Rugby League. His form was so good that he was soon back in England on a second tour—this time as captain of the Australian Test team. In one match on that first Kangaroo tour (against Hull), Messenger kicked a penalty goal from 73 metres out—recognised by the Guinness Book of Records as the longest successful kick in the game's history. Messenger had one more clash with the British, when he led the Australians at home in the 1910 series.

On the local front, Messenger repeated his international experience in 1911, by accepting, on one occasion, an invitation to travel north and play for Queensland, even though he was a New South Welshman, against New Zealand.

Dally M was also a great club man, the backbone of fine Eastern Suburbs sides which won the Sydney Premiership in 1911, 1912 and 1913. In 1911, he amassed 270 points (18 tries and 108 goals) in club and representative matches before being chosen to go to Britain with the second Kangaroo side. Unfortunately, for business and personal reasons he was unable to make the tour. After Easts won their third straight Premiership, in 1913, they won the Royal Agricultural Society Shield outright. To thank him for his role in the victories, the Eastern Suburbs club presented the Shield to Messenger.

Dally Messenger was christened Herbert Henry—but he was always known as Dally. He was given his nickname because of the Premier of New South Wales, William Bede Dalley. One day when the champion of the future was no more than a podgy toddler a neighbour remarked: 'Doesn't he look like Dalley?' With a slight change in spelling, the name stuck. Ironically, few modern New South Welshmen know who William Bede Dalley was, but they all know Dally Messenger.

METROPOLITAN CUP see *Second Division*

METROPOLITAN LEAGUE see *Second Division*

MIDWEEK CUP

Many times Sydney's Rugby League administrators tried to drum up enthusiasm for knock-out competitions they hoped might one day rival Britain's Challenge Cup in prestige. There was the City Cup, and then the State Cup—but Premiership-conscious clubs often fielded second-string sides. Fans, too, showed little interest and stayed at home.

All this changed in 1974. A jeans manufacturer combined with Sydney television station, Channel 10, to sponsor an exciting new knockout competition, the Amco Cup, and it was an immediate success. That first season, entry was confined to the Sydney clubs and the NSW country areas but, in later years, invitations went out to top Brisbane sides, some Queensland country teams and representative sides from New Zealand

and Papua-New Guinea. The first year produced a fairy-tale finish as Cinderella side Western Division, coached by former Test winger Johnny King, scored a shock win over another lowly-rated team, Penrith. Twelve months later all went according to the form book with the star-studded Eastern Suburbs side taking out the Cup and going on to win the Sydney Premiership.

When the sponsors of the Amco Cup decided to quit Rugby League in 1980, Sydney brewers Tooth and Co, who already provided financial backing for the Australian Test teams and other representative sides, were quick to step into the breach. At the start of 1984, another change of sponsors saw the Cup renamed yet again to the National Panasonic Cup (later just the Panasonic Cup). The Cup was scrapped after the Brisbane Broncos won an exciting 1989 final over lowly-rated Illawarra. Instead, the Rugby League authorities decided on a new televised pre-season knockout series.

Results of Finals in the Midweek Cup

AMCO CUP

Year	Winner	Score	Runner-up	Score
1974	Western Division	6	Penrith	2
1975	Eastern Suburbs	17	Parramatta	7
1976	Balmain	21	North Sydney	7
1977	Western Suburbs	6	Eastern Suburbs	5
1978	Eastern Suburbs	16	St George	4
1979	Cronulla-Sutherland	22	Brisbane	5

TOOTH CUP

Year	Winner	Score	Runner-up	Score
1980	Parramatta	8	Balmain	5
1981	South Sydney	10	Cronulla-Sutherland	2

KB CUP

Year	Winner	Score	Runner-up	Score
1982	Manly-Warringah	23	Newtown	8
1983	Manly-Warringah	26	Cronulla-Sutherland	6

NATIONAL PANASONIC CUP

Year	Winner	Score	Runner-up	Score
1984	Brisbane	12	Eastern Suburbs	11
1985	Balmain	14	Cronulla-Sutherland	12
1986	Parramatta	32	Balmain	16
1987	Balmain	14	Penrith	12

PANASONIC CUP

Year	Winner	Score	Runner-up	Score
1988	St George	16	Balmain	8
1989	Brisbane	22	Illawarra	20

PLAYER-OF-THE-SERIES

1976	John Gray (North Sydney)
1977	Graeme O'Grady (Western Suburbs)
1978	Kevin Hastings (Eastern Suburbs)
1979	Kurt Sorensen (Cronulla-Sutherland)
1980	Peter Sterling (Parramatta)
1981	Steve Rogers (Cronulla-Sutherland)
1982	Mike Eden (Manly-Warringah)
1983	Ian Schubert (Manly-Warringah)
1984	Wally Lewis (Brisbane)
1985	Scott Gale (Balmain)
1986	Ray Price (Parramatta)
1987	Ben Elias (Balmain)
1988	Peter Gill (St George)
1989	Terry Matterson (Brisbane)

GENE MILES

Fourteen Tests for Australia (1983–1987). Also played in Bicentennial international against the Rest-of-the-World (1988), one

minor international (1982), for Oceania against Europe (1984) and 19 minor games on two Kangaroo tours (1982 and 1986).

A block-busting footballer, Gene Miles struck fear into the heart of many an opponent during the 1980s. Miles, weighing 102kg (16 stone) and 1.85m (6ft 1in) tall, took a lot of stopping. Miles moved from Townsville in the north of Queensland in 1980 to play centre for Wynnum-Manly in the Brisbane competition. He soon made his mark, representing Queensland in his first State-of-Origin match the following season.

The big centre was a member of the 1982 Kangaroo side, nicknamed 'The Invincibles'. Although he turned out in an international against Wales, he failed to break into the Test lineup. That honour came the following year, at Brisbane's Lang Park in the second of two matches in a home-and-away series against New Zealand. For the next three years he was a Test regular, playing in all matches against the touring 1984 Lions and the New Zealand Kiwis the following year. With the 1986 Kangaroos, he appeared in all six Test matches, against Papua-New Guinea, Britain and France.

After the home Test against New Zealand in 1987, Miles was switched to the forwards. He soon adapted to become one of his country's finest second-rowers—making a comeback to the Australian side in 1988, for its Bicentennial international against the Rest-of-the-World. Miles was chosen to tour New Zealand with the Australian side in 1989 but was forced out of the team with a broken hand. The following year he quit representative football, even though he was regarded as the best second-rower in the world. He wanted to concentrate on his new job as captain of the Brisbane Broncos, in their third season in the Sydney Premiership competition. Miles helped steer the Broncos into the semi-finals for the first time and was rewarded for his efforts by being chosen as captain-of-the-year in the 1990 Dally M Awards.

Miles wound up his time in Broncos' colours with a testimonial year in 1991 before accepting a big offer to finish his career in England, with the Wigan club.

GAVIN MILLER

One Test for Australia (1988). Also played for Australia in the 1988 World Cup Final and the Bicentennial international against the Rest-of-the-World (1988) and for the Rest-of-the-World against Great Britain (1988).

For many years Sydney football chiefs did not realise the potential of forward Gavin Miller. After coming from the southern NSW country town of Goulburn in 1977, he played for three different clubs—Western Suburbs, Eastern Suburbs and Cronulla-Sutherland—with little success, before trying his luck in England in 1984, with Hull Kingston Rovers. Such was his form with Hull KR that, in 1986, he was named Player-of-the-Year in the English Championship.

Back in Sydney with Cronulla, Miller finally showed the Australian fans his true colours. When the Great Britain side toured in 1988 he made it to the top. He was chosen for the Presidents' XIII which beat the tourists before finally being called into the Test side for the World Cup qualifier against Papua-New Guinea. In the next international, the Bicentennial match against the Rest-of-the-World, Miller was named Man-of-the-Match. He was perhaps unlucky not to have been similarly honoured in the World Cup Final against New Zealand.

The year 1989 was Miller's finest—but he also experienced one of his greatest disappointments. Miller was captain of New South Wales in the State-of-Origin series and won every conceivable individual award—the Rothmans Medal, the Dally M Award, Rugby League Week's Player-of-the-Year and the NSW Rugby League Writers' Association Player-of-the-Season. However, inexplicably, Miller was overlooked for the Australian tour of New Zealand and the Trans-Tasman Test series against the Kiwis. He was never to be recalled to the Test side.

HORRIE MILLER

Horrie Miller was one of the longest serving secretaries on the NSW Rugby League. The Eastern Suburbs winger was appointed to the post in a 'palace coup' in 1909, which saw the three pioneer office-bearers, president Harry Hoyle, secretary James J Giltinan and treasurer Victor Trumper, overthrown. Miller was secretary, on and off until March 1946, when he was dismissed after an official inquiry 'into administrative matters'. There was no reason given for his sacking. Miller is also attributed as having coined, in the 1920s, the phrase 'The Greatest Game of All' to describe Rugby League. The expression was revived in Sydney in the 1950s by *Rugby League News*, the official NSW program, and in Brisbane by commentator George Lovejoy.

IAN MOIR

Eight Tests for Australia (1956–1959). Also played four matches in two World Cups (1954 and 1957), for Australia against the Rest-of-the-World (1957) and 14 minor games on one Kangaroo tour (1956–57).

Ian Moir was one of several great post-World War II wingers to play for Australia. A product of the tough Wollongong competition, the fast and elusive Moir reached the top while playing for South Sydney, where he achieved a remarkable attacking combination with fullback Clive Churchill. Moir entered the international arena during the inaugural World Cup competition in France, in 1954, with a match against Great Britain, at Lyon. He was later to play Tests against every Rugby League nation (four against New Zealand, three versus Britain and one against France).

The pinnacle of his career was in the 1957 World Cup series, won by Australia, soon after he had returned from his only Kangaroo tour. On that visit (1956–57), Moir had topped the Australian tryscoring with 13 from 16 matches.

Moir was also a major force in club football. He starred in three South Sydney Premiership-winning sides (1953, 1954 and 1955). His greatest success was in 1953, when he touched down for three tries in Souths' 31–12 win over St George in the grand final. That season he had topped Souths' scoring during the year with 23 tries. Moir finished his Sydney club career with Western Suburbs, bowing out after a disappointing season in 1960, during which he managed only one try in 14 matches.

JOHN MONIE

John Monie is the only coach to have steered sides to success in the biggest competitions in Rugby League on both sides of the world.

He had a good run with Parramatta in the Sydney Premiership before steering super-team Wigan to several English victories.

Monie had nine seasons with Parramatta, six with the first grade squad. He joined the Eels in 1981 as reserve grade coach (under the great Jack Gibson) and took his side to the grand final in that first season and the semi-finals a year later. Monie took over the senior side from Gibson in 1984 and came within a whisker of carrying off the J J Giltinan Shield. The Eels were beaten 6–4 by Canterbury-Bankstown in a gripping grand final.

Parramatta reached the final in 1985, before winning the Premiership the following year. Monie presided over a side weakened by the retirement of several stars such as Mick Cronin and Ray Price with moderate success before accepting the job with Wigan in 1989.

In his first season in Britain (1989–90) Monie steered the Riversiders to victory in the Challenge Cup, the Championship and the Regal Trophy as well as the semi-finals of the Premiership and the Lancashire Cup. For his efforts he was voted Coach-of-the-Year.

And he was at the helm when Wigan won the Championship-Challenge Cup double 12 months later. Monie got particular satisfaction when his club beat reigning Sydney Premiers Penrith 21–4 in the 1991 World Club Challenge at the start of the next British season.

RAY MORRIS

Ray Morris is Rugby League's most tragic player. The popular three-quarter from Sydney's University club was chosen in the 1933–34 Kangaroo side. He was never to wear the green and gold for Australia. He died from an ear infection in Malta en route to England. It is not certain just what caused the illness. It is suggested that he damaged an eardrum while boxing on the ship, the eardrum becoming infected while swimming at Colombo. Morris was so sick by the time the ship reached Malta that his team-mates had to sail on without him. He died two days later.

Ray Morris

ROD MORRIS

Fourteen Tests for Australia (1978–1982). Also played 23 minor games on two Kangaroo tours (1978 and 1982) and one World Championship tour of New Zealand (1977).

The Test selectors never really took Rod Morris seriously when he was playing in Brisbane. The Brisbane prop-forward turned in consistently good displays for his Brisbane club, Eastern Suburbs, and for the Queensland State side. However, the men who chose Australia's teams turned a blind eye, except for the time they included him in the 1977 World Championship squad which went to New Zealand. Even then, he played in only one minor match, against Auckland.

It was only when Morris moved south to Sydney to join Balmain that they really sat up and took notice. In his first season with the Tigers, Morris made his Test debut, against the touring New Zealand Kiwis, and was one of the first chosen for the 1978 Kangaroo tour of Britain and France. After playing all of the Tests in the next two series (against the British Lions in Australia and against New Zealand in Auckland), Morris decided to call it a day. He was eventually persuaded by the Balmain officials to play one more season. A late start to his playing year didn't help his chances of retaining his Test spot, but he forced his way into the Test lineup for the final clash with the touring Frenchmen.

Morris retired again—but once more he was persuaded to pull on the boots again mid-season, this time for the Brisbane club, Wynnum-Manly. It was to be his last 'Melba'. His form was such that he won a spot in the 1982 Kangaroos squad. He played 12 matches on tour, but couldn't make it back into the Test side and so retired for good.

STEVE MORRIS

Two Tests for Australia (1978).

Steve Morris will almost certainly go into the history books as the last player to gain selection in an Australian Test team while playing with a country club side. Since his selection in 1978, virtually every talented footballer has been snared at an early age to play in the Sydney Premiership. The chances of a star slipping through the nets cast by the Sydney talent scouts in the future is unlikely.

'Slippery' Morris was discovered by former English Test great Tommy Bishop. The Englishman was coach of the Southern Division side in the 1978 NSW Country Championships and snapped up the services of halfback Morris, who was working the scrums for the Dapto side in the Wollongong competition. Morris went on to represent Country and New South Wales that season before being chosen for the First Test against the touring New Zealand squad. He lost his spot in the Second Test to Queenslander Greg Oliphant, but came on as a replacement in that match. Morris never made the Test side again.

The following year he was lured to St George and in the same season helped the Dragons to a 17–13 grand final win over Canterbury-Bankstown. St George coach Roy Masters later switched him to the wing, where he was also a great success. Seven times in nine seasons (with St George and Eastern Suburbs), Morris figured among the top five Premiership tryscorers, with a season best of 19 touchdowns in 1983.

STEVE MORTIMER

Eight Tests for Australia (1981-1984). Also played for Oceania against Europe (1984) and nine minor games on one Kangaroo tour (1982).

A poor game for New South Wales in 1977 almost spelled the end to Steve Mortimer's Test hopes. It had been his chance to prove himself as the natural successor to the great Tommy Raudonikis as Australia's Test half. He blew his chance in a match against Queensland, and Raudonikis remained at the helm. However Mortimer never gave up. Four years later, when the Frenchmen visited Australia (and Raudonikis was languishing in the Newtown reserve grade side) Mortimer was given a second chance. He grabbed it with both hands to establish himself as Australia's top half.

He was again Australia's halfback against the New Zealand Kiwis in 1982 and in the inaugural Test against Papua-New Guinea, at the start of the 1982 Kangaroo tour. However he lost his spot for the Tests against Britain and France to Parramatta's Peter Sterling. When Sterling was injured, Mortimer was back in the green and gold for the second of two Tests against New Zealand the following year and for the final two clashes against the 1984 touring Great Britain team.

On the club scene, Mortimer was a vital cog in the Canterbury-Bankstown machine of the 1980s which won Sydney Premierships in 1984, 1985 and 1988. Indeed, all told, Mortimer played in six Sydney grand finals. With him in those balmy days were his two brothers, centres Chris and Peter Mortimer. Chris was a member of the 1986 Kangaroo squad, playing one Test, against Papua New Guinea. Injury forced the brilliant Steve Mortimer out of the game at the end of the 1988 season.

Steve Mortimer in the 1984 semi-final against Parramatta

REX MOSSOP

Nine Tests for Australia (1958–1960). Also played three matches in one World Cup (1960, one minor international (1960) and 22 minor games on one Kangaroo tour (1959–60) and one World Cup tour of Britain and France (1960).

Rex Mossop represented Australia in both codes of Rugby and later made a name for himself as one of his country's best-known television personalities.

In the amateur code, he played in five internationals, against New Zealand (1949 and 1951) and the touring British Lions (1950). When he turned professional, although over 30 years old, Mossop forced his way into the Test sides again. In 1958, he played all three Tests against the touring British side. The following year, he was chosen to tour with the Kangaroos, and tackled both Britain and France. Mossop also played against the Frenchmen at home in 1960, and went back to Britain at the end of the year for the World Cup. He played in all the Cup matches and, after the series, captained Australia in an international against France, at Toulouse.

Having retired from the field, Mossop began a long career in Sydney television, covering the top matches for, first, the Seven and, later, the Ten Network. He was the butt of many jokes for his excessive tautology during the football telecasts but this deterred neither Mossop nor the fans.

BARRY MUIR

Twenty-two Tests for Australia (1959–63). Also played three matches in one World Cup (1960), one minor international (1960), and 23 minor games on two Kangaroo tours (1959–60 and 1963–64) and one New Zealand tour (1961) and for the Rest-of-the-World against Britain (1960).

Barry Muir was a fiery, temperamental halfback. He was involved with clashes with referees on both sides of the world. However one of those who repeatedly criticized him, England's Eric 'Sergeant Major' Clay, nevertheless described him as one of the finest Australian players he had seen.

Muir first gained representative selection in 1951 in the Queensland schoolboys' side. He was 11 years old. It was an indication of greater things to come. Seven years later, Muir forced his way into the Brisbane side and next year into the Australian team, at the expense of the great Keith Holman. He continued as Australia's number one half until 1964, visiting Britain and France (both three times), New Zealand and Italy. He also played a Test in Australia against South Africa, thereby having the distinction of having played against five nations.

After he retired as a player, Muir took up coaching. He achieved a place in Australian sporting folk-lore when, as coach of the Queensland side in the interstate clashes with New South Wales, he called the southerners 'cockroaches'. It was a tag which stuck. Decades later the New South Welshmen are still always called cockroaches by their northern cousins— even away from the sporting arena. Muir had fair success with Queensland, with the Maroons scoring a rare win in 1975 (and just missing out on that year's series, when beaten by one point in the third and deciding clash). In a remarkable rags-to-riches story, Muir took Brisbane's Redcliffe side from second-last in 1972 to the grand final 12 months later.

NOEL MULLIGAN

Ten Tests for Australia (1946–51). Also played 21 minor games on one Kangaroo tour (1948–49) and one New Zealand tour (1949).

Noel Mulligan was one of the most versatile forwards in Australian football history. He was capable of playing in any position in the pack, although he was at his brilliant best at either lock or second-row.

Mulligan turned out for the Sydney clubs Newtown and St George, as well as Bowral in the NSW southern highlands, during the immediate post-World War II years. He made his Test debut against the touring 1946 British Lions and his fierce, low tackling and speed in attack provided many headaches for the tourists. The fine forward made two overseas tours— with the 1948–49 Kangaroos to Britain and France and to New Zealand in 1949. A measure of Mulligan's toughness can be gauged by the fact that he played through the final Test on the Kangaroo tour with a broken right leg. With no replacements allowed in those days, he refused to quit and leave his side one man short.

MARK MURRAY

Six Tests for Australia (1982–85). Also played in one minor international (1982) and 11 minor games on one Kangaroo tour (1982) and one New Zealand tour (1985).

Mark Murray can thank the State-of-Origin concept for his chance to play for Australia. The clever halfback, nicknamed 'Muppet', made his debut for Queensland in 1982—the first year the interstate series was based completely on where footballers started their careers and not where they lived at the time. Murray basked in the glory of Queensland's 2–1 victory. His consistent play was enough to earn him a spot on the Kangaroo tour of Papua New Guinea, Britain and France. Murray made his Test debut as a replacement in the Papua Test at Port Moresby and played in an international against Wales. However for the rest of the tour, Murray had to play in the shadow of the fine pair of Peter Sterling and Steve Mortimer.

The Queenslander played one game against New Zealand in 1983, two Tests in the series against the touring 1984 British Lions and the same number against New Zealand the following year. He was dropped, with several other Maroons, in controversial circumstances for the final clash with the Kiwis and was never to play Tests again. An eye injury, sustained off the field, brought an end to his representative career—but not before he had played 14 of the first 17 State-of-Origin matches (the last in 1986).

He later turned his hand to coaching. Graham Lowe wanted him as his assistant for the State-of-Origin clashes in 1991. Instead, Murray accepted the post of coach of Sydney's Eastern Suburbs under the management of super-coach Jack Gibson.

N

HERB NARVO

Four Tests for Australia (1937–38). Also played 18 minor games on one Kangaroo tour (1937–38).

Herb Narvo was recognised as one of the greatest forwards of all time—yet he probably would never have played for Australia if another champion had not been injured.

Narvo, a tough second-rower from Newcastle, joined Newtown in 1937. Critics threw up their hands in amazement when, at the end of that season, he was not among the 28 chosen to make the Kangaroo tour of Britain and France. A disappointed Narvo then considered accepting a lucrative offer to play for Huddersfield in the English Championship. The English club had approached Narvo on the recommendation of British players, impressed by his display for the Newcastle side which beat the 1936 Lions. However before Narvo could make up his mind, the news arrived that Kangaroo forward Joe Pearce had broken his leg while playing for the Australians in New Zealand en route to England. Narvo was named as his replacement and proved to be one of the heroes of that tour, playing in four of the five Tests.

He continued in Sydney football until 1949. Most of his time was spent with Newtown (for which he scored a try in the grand final when the Bluebags won the 1943 Premiership). For three years Narvo turned out as captain-coach for St George and in his first year at the helm (1946), the Dragons reached the Premiership grand final and won the Club Championship.

Narvo was also a fine boxer, who won the Australian heavyweight championship in only his fourth professional fight—knocking out the reigning champion in just 23 seconds. It was one of the fastest championship successes in history.

NATIONAL PANASONIC CUP see *Midweek Cup*

WEBBY NEILL

Played nine minor games for Australia on one Kangaroo tour (1911–12).

Webby Neill, a top footballer and later a fine referee, played his way into the record books during the first three years of Rugby League in Australia. In those years he had the unique distinction of winning Sydney Premiership medals—with two different clubs.

The classy fullback was a member of the South Sydney squads which won in 1908 and 1909. The next year, after swapping clubs, he notched the hat-trick with Newtown. Souths and Newtown had drawn 4–all in the final but Newtown took the title because it had won the Minor Premiership with 23 points to Souths' 22. Neill was selected as Australia's top fullback in the 1911–12 Kangaroo squad which toured Britain, but he lost his spot on tour to the legendary Howard Hallett, one of the greatest custodians the game has known.

After he finished as a player, Neill went on to become a respected referee. He was the centre of an incident during his only Test, the first clash of the 1932 Ashes series between Australia and Britain. Australia won the Test 8–6—but it could have been a different result. Britain's fullback Jim Sullivan had a goal disallowed after Neill noticed team-mate Martin Hodgson standing offside waiting for the kick to be taken.

NEWCASTLE

Newcastle was one of the original sides which kicked off the Sydney Premiership in 1908—but after only two seasons (during which it finished fifth and equal third) it quit to conduct its own competition. Some eight decades later it returned to the fold and soon established itself as one of the toughest sides in the Premiership.

Newcastle played two matches against A H Baskerville's New Zealand All Golds in 1908 and since then has played against almost every touring side to come to Australia, winning half of the matches since World War II (including one of only three defeats of the legendary 1962 British Lions). As a Division in the NSW Country Rugby League setup, Newcastle won eight Country Championships in the 26 years it competed. Over the years the Newcastle area was home to some of Australia's finest footballers, including 'The Little Master' Clive Churchill, wingers Johnny Graves and Brian Carlson, the great centre tactician Ross McKinnon, classy halfback Keith Froome, and forward greats Wally Prigg and Herb Narvo.

One of Newcastle's best seasons was 1964. It won its first Country Championship and followed that up with an upset success in the State Cup, beating three of the four semi-finalists from the Sydney Premiership competition in the process.

The return to the Sydney competition was not an easy one. The first time it was suggested, in the late 1970s, all 36 Newcastle delegates voted against the move, but gradually they were all won over. In April 1987, Newcastle were invited to join the Premiership fight—and accepted. Former international utility back Allan McMahon was appointed coach and three top New Zealanders Sam Stewart, Tony Kemp and James Goulding were signed up for the first season. Newcastle finished on top of only two sides in that first year (including fellow-newcomers, Gold Coast), but the huge crowds showed what support the Knights had. A crowd of 30 220—the highest away from the Sydney Cricket Ground or Sydney Sports Ground in 30 years—watched Newcastle play Brisbane.

The gradual push to the top began in 1989, when Newcastle moved up to seventh place, helped by the arrival of ex-Eastern Suburbs fullback Gary Wurth and clever five-eighth Michael Hagan. That year Stewart, Kemp and Goulding all flew home to New Zealand to play Tests for the Kiwis against the touring Australian side. Young prop Mark Sargent shared the Rothmans Medal, with Cronulla's Gavin Miller, as the best and fairest player in the Sydney Premiership. Newcastle had an unusual record in 1989. The Knights won and lost the same number of games—11. They also scored the same number of points as they had scored against them—281.

In 1990, Newcastle went within an ace of reaching the semi-finals for the first time. A controversial win over Balmain in the final match of the season saw them finish in equal fifth place. Balmain had its revenge however, by winning the midweek play-off for the last semi-final spot, at Parramatta Stadium. The Balmain game which got the Knights to the play-off drew a new record crowd of 32 217 to the Newcastle International Sports Ground. The Knights also drew 30 054 fans to their home game against Penrith and were involved in two other 20 000 plus crowds (versus Parramatta and Brisbane). Sargent made the Kangaroo squad to tour Britain and France at the end of that season, and winger Ashley Gordon's 130 points put him among the elite pointscorers. His 15 tries was second only to the 17 by Canberra's Mal Meninga.

Another good season seemed in store for the Knights in 1991 as they turned in some good early season performances. But a mid-season slump saw them drop out of contention. Dissension in the club and an alleged player revolt forced an early retirement of coach McMahon. The one bright spot was the selection of 28-year-old second-rower Mike McLean in the successful Queensland State-of-Origin side. McLean had joined Newcastle at the start of 1991 after five lean seasons at Eastern Suburbs.

NEWCASTLE

Founded: 1987
Entered Sydney Premiership competition: 1988
Home ground: Newcastle International Sports Stadium: (Record crowd—32 217)
Colours: Red and blue
Nickname: The Knights
Honours: Jersey Flegg Trophy—1991
Most games in a career: 64 by Michael Hagan
Most points in a career: 210 by Ashley Gordon
Most tries in a career: 24 by Ashley Gordon
Most points in a season: 130 by Ashley Gordon, 1990
Most tries in a season: 15 by Ashley Gordon, 1990
Rothmans Medal winner: Mark Sargent (1989)

Newcastle Against International Sides

Year		Opponents		Result	For	Against
1908	___	New Zealand	___	Lost	6	53
1908	___	New Zealand	___	Lost	8	34
1909	___	New Zealand	___	Lost	3	6
1910	___	Great Britain	___	Lost	8	24
1911	___	New Zealand	___	Lost	20	21
1912	___	New Zealand	___	Lost	4	20

Continued

Newcastle Against International Sides *continued*

Year	Opponents	Result	For	Against
1919	New Zealand	Lost	8	11
1920	Great Britain	Lost	10	17
1920	Great Britain	Lost	3	24
1921	New Zealand	Lost	14	27
1924	Great Britain	Lost	18	43
1925	New Zealand	Lost	11	29
1928	Great Britain	Lost	17	19
1930	New Zealand	Lost	22	25
1932	Great Britain	Lost	15	22
1936	Great Britain	Won	21	16
1938	New Zealand	Lost	19	30
1946	Great Britain	Won	18	13
1948	New Zealand	Lost	9	10
1950	Great Britain	Lost	10	21
1951	France	Lost	8	12
1952	New Zealand	Won	9	7
1953	American Allstars	Lost	10	19
1954	Great Britain	Won	11	10
1955	France	Won	17	15
1956	New Zealand	Won	20	5
1958	Great Britain	Lost	16	35
1959	New Zealand	Lost	6	25
1960	France	Lost	10	14
1962	Great Britain	Won	23	18
1963	New Zealand	Lost	6	24
1963	South Africa	Won	27	17
1964	France	Won	16	14
1966	Great Britain	Lost	2	5
1967	New Zealand	Won	14	7
1970	Great Britain	Lost	16	49
1977	France	Won	19	12
1978	New Zealand	Won	19	12
1979	Great Britain	Lost	12	25
1984	Great Britain	Lost	18	28
1986	New Zealand	Lost	17	22
1988	Great Britain	Lost	12	28

EDGAR NEWHAM

Two Tests for Australia (1946).

World War II cost Edgar 'Stumpy' Newham a long Test career. The long-striding Canterbury-Bankstown winger had only just arrived on the scene when hostilities broke out, and by the time he got his chance to wear the green and gold after the War (against the touring 1946 British Lions) he was 32 and nearing the end of his career.

Newham grew up in the country. Although a sensation for Cowra, in the central west, he had to trial for The Berries (as the Canterbury players were then nicknamed) before getting a spot in their first grade side. In his first season at Belmore, Newham figured in the Canterbury side which won the Premiership by beating Eastern Suburbs 19-6 in the final. He was in the Premiership-winning team again four years later (when Canterbury beat St George 11-9 in the grand final). That year Canterbury and Balmain both finished on 20 points at the top of the table—and in a midweek play-off for the Minor Premiership, Newham scored five tries to help Canterbury to a 26–20 victory. The five touch-downs are still a record for the club.

Newham was a paratrooper with the RAAF during the War. He returned to his home town of Cowra in 1946—and gained selection in the Test side even though he had missed selection in the Country lineup. He played in the first two Tests but a serious hip injury in the second encounter put him out of contention for the final Test and any future international football. Newham returned to Canterbury in 1948 for the last of his 79 first-grade matches—but was forced into retirement midway through the season with a recurrance of a shoulder injury suffered while in the RAAF.

NEW SOUTH WALES PLAYER-OF-THE-YEAR see either *EE Christensen* or *Rothmans Medal*

NEW SOUTH WALES TOURING SIDES

The first full Australian team to visit New Zealand crossed the Tasman in 1919, but by that time, two NSW sides had made visits. As most of the top players came from New South Wales, those State sides which visited New Zealand were virtually Test teams. On both the first two tours, the New South Welshmen met Kiwi Test squads—winning every encounter. A third such tour took place in 1922, but New South Wales has not sent a team since, although the capital, Sydney, did send a squad in 1976.

New South Wales to New Zealand
1912

New South Wales, in 1912, became the first Australian representative side to cross the Tasman. The combination was a brilliant one, built around such all-time greats as the Farnsworth brothers, Howard Hallett, 'Chook' Fraser, 'Pony' Halloway and Frank Burge. It lost only two matches, and it outclassed a home team 18–10 in what was really an unofficial Test.

Record in New Zealand

Played 10, Won 8, Lost 2, Points for 281, Points against 124

Match Results

Opponents	Venue	For	Against
Canterbury	Christchurch	5	28
Wellington	Wellington	45	13
Taranaki	Eltham	24	0
Auckland	Auckland	3	10
Rotorua	Rotorua	39	13
New Zealand	Auckland	18	10
Hawke's Bay	Napier	42	9
Canterbury	Christchurch	28	15
Wanganui	Wanganui	52	24
Auckland	Auckland	25	2

Team members: PA McCue (c), V Farnsworth, H Hallett, C Fraser, W Farnsworth, D Frawley, R Norman, A Broomham, T Gleeson, A Halloway, S Deane, D Garlick, D McGregor, H Thompson, JW Davis, WA Cann, F Burge, G Cummins, C McMurtrie, R Williams, W Haddock, C Sullivan, E Courtney, A Curran

1913

The NSW side which toured New Zealand in 1913 finished with a record unmatched by any other team which has crossed the Tasman before or since. The visitors were unbeaten in 11 games, running up huge scores in many of them. Their meeting with the New Zealand Test squad, at Wellington, seemed hardly more than a training run—the locals being overwhelmed 58–19.

Record in New Zealand

Played 11, won 11, Points for 427, Points against 110

Match Results

Opponents	Venue	*For*	*Against*
Canterbury	Christchurch	45	5
Auckland	Auckland	27	2
Waikato	Huntly	20	14
Wanganui	Wanganui	44	9
Hawke's Bay	Napier	31	12
Nelson	Nelson	66	2
Taranaki	Hawere	16	5
Rotorua	Rotorua	53	5
New Zealand	Auckland	33	19
Wellington	Wellington	34	18
New Zealand	Wellington	58	19

Team members: PA McCue (c), H Hallett, G Challis, H Horder, W Collins, S Deane, D Frawley, R Algie, H Thompson, H Naylor, L Cubitt, E Coyne, A Johnston, L O'Malley, JT Barnett, E Courtney, C Sullivan, WA Cann, W Haddock, R Craig, J Murray, WO Foord, A Curran

1922

The State team which went to New Zealand in 1922 must rank as one of the finest touring combinations anywhere, ever. Three of the all-time greats—Frank Burge, Jimmy Craig and Harold Horder—were the stars of a squad which won all six matches, some by big margins. A highlight of the tour was a match in Auckland in which the New South Welshmen who figured in the 1921–22 Kangaroo tour of Britain (bolstered by Auckland's Bert Laing, also a Kangaroo tourist) thrashed a combined side consisting of Auckland stars and other members of the NSW side.

Record in New Zealand

Played 6, won 6, Points for 233, Points against 92

Exhibition Match Result

Kangaroos 65 Combined XIII 27 (Auckland)

Other Matches

Opponents	Venue	*For*	*Against*
Auckland	Auckland	40	25
Auckland Province	Auckland	21	20
Bay of Plenty	Rotorua	29	5
Waikato	Huntly	17	12
King Country XIII	Taumarunui	87	16
Hawke's Bay/Auckland	Napier	39	14

Team members: W Benson, F Burge, H Caples, G Carstairs, J Craig (c), R Dunworth, W Gillespie, B Gray, H Horder, W Ives, A Johnston, E Lapham, R Latta, S Manstead, A O'Connor, C Prentice, N Proctor, J Robinson, F Rule, J Toohey, C Tye, R Vest

NEWTOWN

According to minutes taken at a meeting at Newtown Town Hall in early 1908, the team of the same name was the first Rugby League club officially formed in Australia. The minutes claim it came into existence on January 8, 1908, at a meeting convened by prominent Sydney sportsman James J Giltinan and Parliamentarian Henry Hoyle, two of the men instrumental in staging the first League matches in Australia, the previous year. However newspaper reports of the day suggest the meeting may have actually taken place a week later, after the Glebe club was formed. At the very least, Newtown received receipt No. 1 from the NSW Rugby League for its affiliation fees.

A little over three months after the January meeting, on 20 April 1908, a Newtown side ran onto the field at Wentworth Park for the first club game in Australia, against Eastern Suburbs. The Bluebags (later known as the Jets) continued in the Sydney Premiership competition until financial difficulties in the early 1980s forced the authorities to drop them.

The club's first Premiership, in 1910, was perhaps to be expected. Newtown had seven players from that side in the Kangaroo squad which toured Britain the following year. They were fullback Webby Neill, winger 'Boxer' Russell, the brothers Bill and Viv Farnsworth and forwards Bill Noble (who was also Newtown's secretary and delegate to the NSW Rugby League), Paddy McCue (who was NSW captain) and Joe Murray. Jack 'Towser' Barnett, who played against the touring 1910 British Lions, was another in Newtown's Premiership-winning side.

Russell, a star of the 1908 Wallabies Rugby Union team, went on to become a great coach and was at the helm when Newtown notched its second Premiership, in 1933. Another all-time great led the side onto the field for the club's third title. Frank 'Bumper' Farrell was captain of the successful 1943 combination in which he was partnered in the forwards by another champion, Herb Narvo. Narvo excelled in another sport, too, laying claim to the Australian heavyweight boxing title.

In the early 1950s, Newtown made a valiant effort to wrest the Premiership from the fine South Sydney line–up and was runner-up in 1954 and 1955. Test player Col Geelan was captain-coach of Newtown when it went down 23–15 in the 1954 finale. The side included past or future internationals, fullback Gordon Clifford, centre Dick Poole, five-eighth Tony Brown, lock/five-eighth Brian Clay and second-rower Henry Holloway. Poole was captain-coach a year later when Newtown went even closer, missing out by just one point. Poole also led his country's World Cup side to success in the 1957 series. Holloway was to make a name for himself as a coach in Brisbane. Clifford is remembered as the man who finally displaced 'The Little Master' Clive Churchill as Australia's Test fullback—and Brown and Clay were two of the finest stand-offs of their era.

Newtown's only real Premiership showings after that came as 'battlers' in 1973 and 1981. In the former season, the highly-respected coach Jack Gibson took the newly renamed Jets from being a team of nobodies to the Premiership semi-finals. Newtown also won the Pre-Season competition that year. Eight years later, Warren Ryan coached the Jets, who had started the season as 250–1 outsiders, into the grand final. Fifteen minutes from the end of the match, Newtown led 11–7 against Parramatta (which had beaten the Jets 33–9 and 27–5 in their home-and-away clashes that year). However the Eels found something extra in the final minutes to run out winners 20–11 and shatter the Jets' dreams. Among the stars that year were internationals Tom Raudonikis at half and utility back Phil Sigsworth. Slippery winger John Ferguson was to go on to wear the green and gold.

Financial difficulties about that time forced Newtown to seek an amalgamation with Campbelltown, to the south-west of Sydney. During 1983, Newtown played several games at Campbelltown, in preparation for its complete move the following season. However when Newtown was unable to sell its Leagues Club in Sydney, to provide finance to start afresh, the NSW Rugby League dropped it from the Premiership competition. This left the way open for Western Suburbs to make a successful move to

Campbelltown and avoid following Newtown into the wilderness. Eventually, the Leagues Club was sold and Newtown began once again, entering the Metropolitan Cup (the virtual Second Division) in 1991.

All told, Newtown won the Sydney Premiership in 1910, 1933 and 1943 (it was runner-up in 1913, 1914, 1929, 1944, 1954, 1955 and 1981), the Pre-Season Competition in 1973, the Club Championship in 1973, the City Cup in 1937, 1941, 1942 and 1945, the State Championship in 1941 and 1945, the Endeavour Cup in 1970 and the League Cup in 1921, 1924 and 1925.

FIRST EVER 1–0 WIN
The twelfth of May 1973 was a day for the record books—the first time in a major competition match anywhere in the world that a side won 1–0. A field goal by Newtown's Ken Wilson gave his club the narrow success over St George at the Sydney Cricket Ground. Until then, the smallest winning margin in any match had been 2–0. However the 1971 season had seen the introduction of new scoring rules, under which the value of a field goal was reduced from two points to one. All other goals remained at two points.

NEW ZEALAND

Rugby League made its first appearance in New Zealand in 1907 when a group of players was gathered together to choose a team to tour Australia and Great Britain—but it really had its beginnings two years earlier when the Rugby Union All Blacks visited Britain.

The All Blacks included in their number the champion winger George Smith. While on tour, Smith talked with officials of the breakaway Northern Rugby Union and was converted to the professional game. Back home, he persuaded another top player, Albert Baskerville, to get together a squad to go to England. Feeling in Union-conscious New Zealand was very much against the new code and the pair had to try to make their arrangements in secret. The secret was not kept well enough, for jeering crowds turned out to give the New Zealand side (nicknamed the 'All Golds' because of the professional nature of the players) an unpleasant farewell.

The public reaction in Sydney, the first stopover, was somewhat similar—at least until the visitors played the first of three games against a star-studded NSW side. The standard of play ensured the success of the new code in Australia. The 'All Golds' won all three games against New South Wales—12–8, 19–5 and 5–3. Their successes did not end there however. They beat Great Britain two Tests to one in the first-ever international series and then, on their way home, added Australia's scalp to their belt, once again by two Tests to one.

Players who caught the eyes of British talent scouts on that inaugural tour returned to play for English clubs. These included Smith (who signed with Oldham), centre Edgar Wrigley and forward William Trevarthan (Huddersfield) and centre Lance Todd (Wigan). Todd is remembered today by the trophy awarded to the Man-of-the-Match in each year's Challenge Cup Final at Wembley.

The Kiwis' second tour of Britain, in 1926–27, wasn't so succesful. They lost more than half their 34 games, including all three Tests—and some

These are early Australian stars who were selected to play (and officials) in the first matches in the southern hemisphere against the 1907 New Zealand All Golds touring side. *Back row:* C Hedley, G Brackenreg, A Hennessy, W Farnsworth, E Courtney, G Boss, A Dobbs; *Third row:* H Hoyle, R Graves, P Moir, H Hamill, H Glanville, S Pearce, A Burdon, H Gleeve; *Seated:* J Stuntz, WA Cann, E Fry, JJ Giltinan, H Messenger, H Brackenreg, R Marble; *Front row:* L d'Alpuget, F Cheadle, A Rosenfeld, J Hickey of the players went on strike. On return to New Zealand, seven were suspended for life for their part in the protest. The 1926–27 failure was not unique. The first tour success was not to be repeated for more than 60 years. Six tours saw only two successes in 18 Tests.

All this changed in 1971–72. The Kiwis, fresh from an upset win over Australia, downed Britain by two Tests to one and followed up with a two Tests won, one drawn, ascendancy over France. Just as on the first tour, many of the 1971–72 Kiwis impressed local clubs. This time however, offers made to the visitors were not lucrative enough. Wigan tried to persuade young centre Bernie Lowther and goal-kicking prop Henry Tatana to join its ranks, but Sydney club Canterbury-Bankstown won the bidding war for their services at the start of the 1972 season. Lowther and Tatana were not the first Kiwis to join Australian clubs. In the 1960s New Zealand authorities allowed their amateur Rugby League stars to reap the financial rewards of Australian football—as long as they had given sufficient Test service to their homeland. Mel Cooke, Ron Ackland, Jock Butterfield, Oscar Danielson—the list of New Zealanders who crossed the Tasman lengthened.

In the 1980s the trickle of players to Australia and Great Britain became a torrent. The Sorensen brothers, Dane and Kurt, Kiwi captains Mark Graham, Hugh McGahan and Dean Bell and a host of Test stars including Clayton Friend, Oscar Filipaina, Graham West, James Leuluai, Dane O'Hara, Fred Ah Kuoi, Joe Ropati, Gary Freeman, Darrell Williams, Brent Todd and Sam Stewart all tried their luck in the world's two major competitions.

New Zealand has had an enviable record in home internationals, especially at Auckland's famous Carlaw Park, where muddy conditions led to the downfall of many touring sides. Great Britain had beaten Australia in 1924, but, once across the Tasman, fell victim to New Zealand. The same thing happened in 1946, 1958 and 1962. France has visited New Zealand six times, losing five series and sharing one.

Australia won the series on each of its first two tours of the Shaky Isles (1919 and 1935)—but after World War II it was a different kettle of fish. Australia was beaten in 1953 and 1971 and only shared the series in 1949, 1961, 1965 and 1969. It was only in the 1980s that it began to exert some semblance of superiority. Under coach Graham Lowe, later to join Wigan and Manly-Warringah, New Zealand pulled off some shock victories against the almost invincible Aussies.

NEW ZEALAND V AUSTRALIA
Test Matches

1908

First Test
At RAS Showground, Sydney, Saturday, 9 May 1908
NEW ZEALAND 11 (J Wynyard 2, Baskerville tries, Turtill goal) d AUSTRALIA 10 (Lutge, Rosenfeld tries, Messenger 2 goals)
Australia: C Hedley, F Cheadle, J Devereux, H Messenger, J Rosewell, D McLean, A Rosenfeld, M Dore, R Graves, D Lutge, R Tubman, L O'Malley, A Hennessy
New Zealand: H Turtill, W Wynyard, J Barber, H Rowe, A Baskerville, W Tyler, J Wynyard, D Gilchrist, C Pearce, W Mackrell, W Trevarthan, C Byrne, H Wright

Second Test
At Brisbane Exhibition Ground, Saturday, 30 May 1908
NEW ZEALAND 24 (Rowe 2, J Wynyard, Cross tries, Wrigley 6 goals) d AUSTRALIA 12 (Hardcastle, Lutge tries, Messenger 3 goals)

Australia: E Baird, G Watson, H Messenger, J Devereux, F Cheadle, M Dore, A Rosenfeld, D Lutge, J Davis, R Graves, A Hennessy, S Pearce, W Hardcastle
New Zealand: E Tyne, H Rowe, W Wynyard, J Barber, W Tyler, E Wrigley, J Wynyard, A Lile, W Johnston, T Cross, W Trevarthan, C Pearce, C Byrne

Third Test

At RAS Showground, Sydney, Saturday, 6 June 1908
AUSTRALIA 14 (Messenger, Anderson, Graves, Jones tries, Messenger goal) d NEW ZEALAND 9 (J Wynyard try, Wrigley 3 goals)
Australia: C Hedley, J Devereux, F Cheadle, T Anderson, H Messenger, A Halloway, A Rosenfeld, D Lutge, R Graves, L Jones, W Cann, S Pearce, W Hardcastle
New Zealand: E Tyne, H Rowe, J Barber, W Wynyard, W Tyler, E Wrigley, J Wynyard, A Lile, W Johnston, C Pearce, W Trevarthan, T Cross, D Gilchrist

1909

First Test

At RAS Showground, Sydney, Saturday, 12 June 1909
NEW ZEALAND 19 (King 3, Byrne, McDonald tries, House 2 goals) d AUSTRALIA 11 (Davis, Bolewski tries, penalty try, Davis goal)
Australia: F Woolley, F Cheadle, M Bolewski, A Conlon, D Frawley, A Butler, A Halloway, J Davis, L O'Malley, W Noble, R Graves, W Cann, M Frawley
New Zealand: A House, G Hooker, H Rowe, E Buckland, R McDonald, A Carlaw, J Barber, A Lile, J Spencer, W Trevarthan, C Byrne, C Sullivan, B King

Second Test

At Brisbane Exhibition Ground, Saturday, 26 June 1909
AUSTRALIA 10 (Woodhead 2 tries, Brackenreg 2 goals) d NEW ZEALAND 5 (Rowe try & goal)
Australia: D McGregor, G Duffin, C Woodhead, A Broomham, W Heidke, H Dickens, M Dore, H Nicholson, V Anderson, L O'Malley, H Brackenreg, E Courtney, W Noble
New Zealand: A House, E Buckland, H Rowe, G Hooker, A Carlaw, R McDonald, J Barber, A Lile, W Trevarthan, J Spencer, C Byrne, H Knight, B King

Third Test

At RAS Showground, Sydney, Saturday, 3 July 1909
AUSTRALIA 25 (Woodhead 2, Conlon, Courtney, Broomham tries, Brackenreg 5 goals) d NEW ZEALAND 5 (Penalty try, Byrne goal)
Australia: F Wooley, F Cheadle, C Woodhead, A Conlon, A Broomham, J Levison, A Halloway, E Courtney, R Graves, H Brackenreg, W Cann, S Pearce, W Noble
New Zealand: G Spencer, E Buckland, T Houghton, H Rowe, R McDonald, A House, J Barber, A Lile, J Spencer, B King, C Byrne, W Trevarthan, H Knight

1919

First Test

At Wellington, Saturday, 23 August 1919
Crowd: 8000
AUSTRALIA 44 (Horder 2, Cubitt 2, Robinson, Burge, Johnston, Ryan, Watkins, Gilbert tries, Oxford 6, Burge goals) d NEW ZEALAND 21 (Ifwerson 2, Lang tries, Dufty 6 goals)
Australia: T Sweeney, H Horder, H Gilbert, L Cubitt, J Robinson, A Johnston, A Halloway, C Prentice, C O'Donnell, F Ryan, F Burge, A Oxford, J Watkins
New Zealand: C Dufty, G Iles, K Ifwerson, G Bradley, A.Morris, J Lang, H Neal, S Walters, S Lowry, W Williams, H Avery, W King, J Scott

Second Test

At Christchurch, Saturday, 30 August 1919
Crowd: 7200
NEW ZEALAND 26 (Walters 3, Williams, Iles, Avery tries, Ifwerson 3, Dufty goals) d AUSTRALIA 10 (Horder 2 tries & 2 goals)
Australia: T Sweeney, H Horder, L Cubitt, W Paten, J Robinson, A Johnston, A Halloway, C O'Donnell, C Prentice, F Ryan, F Burge, A Oxford, J Watkins. Replacement: C Thorogood
New Zealand: C Dufty, G Iles, K Ifwerson, G Bradley, J Sanders, A Morris, J Pollock, F Helander, S Lowry, W Williams, S Walters, H Avery, J Scott

Third Test

At Auckland, Saturday, 6 September 1919
Crowd: 24 300
AUSTRALIA 34 (Horder 2, Cubitt 2, Robinson 2, Burge, Johnston tries, Horder 5 goals) d NEW ZEALAND 23 (McGregor 2, Avery, Dufty, Walters tries, Ifwerson 3, Bradley goals)
Australia: C Fraser, J Robinson, L Cubitt, C Thorogood, H Horder, A Johnston, A Halloway, W Schultz, C O'Donnell, F Ryan, F Burge, R Townsend, J Watkins. Replacement: D Thompson
New Zealand: C Dufty, G Iles, W Davidson, K Ifwerson, A McGregor, G Bradley, W Walsh, T Haddon, S Lowry, W Williams, S Walters, H Avery, J Scott

Fourth Test
At Auckland, Saturday, 13 September 1919
Crowd: 15 000
AUSTRALIA 32 (Horder 3, Vest 2, Burge 2, Cubitt tries, Burge 3, Horder goals) d NEW ZEALAND 2 (Ifwerson goal)
Australia: C Fraser, H Horder, R Norman, L Cubitt, R Vest, A Johnston, D Thompson, W Schultz, C O'Donnell, F Burge, A Oxford, R Townsend, J Watkins
New Zealand: C Dufty, A McGregor, K Ifwerson, G Bradley, G Iles, J Lang, I Stewart, S Walters, W Somers, W Williams, T Haddon, H Avery, N Bass

1935

First Test
At Carlaw Park, Auckland, Saturday, 28 September 1935
NEW ZEALAND 22 (Brown 3, Glynn, Hutt, Kay tries, Satherley 2 goals) d AUSTRALIA 14 (Brown, Goodwin tries, Brown 4 goals)
Australia: L Ward, S Goodwin, W Mahon, D Brown (c), R Hines, E Norman, V Thicknesse, W Prigg, S Pearce, J Gibbs, R Stehr, P Fairall, F Curran
New Zealand: A Cooke, L Brown, E Mincham, G Tittleton, C Kay, S Prentice, R Powell, J Calder, L Hutt, J Laird, W Glynn, C Satherley, J Anderson

Second Test
At Carlaw Park, Auckland, Wednesday, 2 October 1935
AUSTRALIA 29 (Brown 2, Hines 2, Fairall 2, Stehr tries, Brown 4 goals) d NEW ZEALAND 8 (Hunt, Satherley tries, Satherley goal)
Australia: L Ward, R Hines, D Brown (c), R McKinnon, S Goodwin, E Norman, V Thicknesse, W Prigg, S Pearce, E Lewis, R Stehr, P Fairall, F Curran
New Zealand: A Cooke, L Brown, C Hunt, E Mincham, H Lilburne, C Kay, R Powell, J Calder, R Ward, J Laird, W Glynn, C Satherley, L Hutt

Third Test
At Carlaw Park, Auckland, Friday, 4 October 1935
AUSTRALIA 31 (McKinnon 2, Brown, Curran, Goodwin, Hines, Norman tries, Brown 5 goals) d NEW ZEALAND 8 (Riley 2 tries, Satherley goal)
Australia: L Ward, R Hines, R McKinnon, D Brown (c), S Goodwin, E Norman, V Thicknesse, W Prigg, S Pearce, E Lewis, R Stehr, P Fairall, F Curran
New Zealand: C Hunt, L Brown, C Kay, E Mitchell, B Riley, S Prentice, E Fletcher, J Calder, L Hutt, J Laird, R Lawless, C Satherley, H Tetley

1937

First Test
At Carlaw Park, Auckland, Saturday, 7 August 1937
Crowd: 12 000
AUSTRALIA 12 (Hazelton 2, Stehr, McLean tries) d NEW ZEALAND 8 (Bickerton, Davison tries, Davison goal)
Australia: L Ward, D McLean, J Beaton, R McKinnon, C Hazelton, E Norman, P Williams, W Prigg (c), E Lewis, S Pearce, R Stehr, F Nolan, J Gibbs
New Zealand: S Watene, C Davison, B Riley, R Chase, W Tittleton, N Bickerton, F Halloran, E McLeod, J Broderick, H Tetley, J Cootes, W Glynn, A Gault

Second Test
At Carlaw Park, Auckland, Saturday, 14 August 1937
NEW ZEALAND 16 (Davison 2, Bickerton, Satherley tries, Nepia 2 goals) d AUSTRALIA 15 (McLean 2, Nolan tries, Williams 2, Beaton goals)
Australia: L Ward, D McLean, J Beaton, R McKinnon, L Dawson, E Norman, P Williams, W Prigg (c), E Lewis, S Pearce, R Stehr, F Nolan, J Gibbs
New Zealand: G Nepia, C Davison, C Kay, W Tittleton, R Chase, N Bickerton, F Halloran, H Tetley, J Broderick, J Cootes, A Gault, B Satherley, W Glynn

1948

First Test
At Sydney Cricket Ground, Saturday, 29 May 1948
Crowd: 55 866
NEW ZEALAND 21 (Redmond 2, McBride tries, Clarke 6 goals) d AUSTRALIA 19 (Rayner try, Graves 5, Froome 3 goals)
Australia: N Pidding, P McMahon, L Smith (c), L Pegg, J Graves, W O'Connell, K Froome, W Tyquin, F de Belin, J Rayner, F Farrell, K Schubert, E Brosnan
New Zealand: W Clarke, J Forrest, M Robertson, A Wiles, D Redmond, A Graham, D Barchard, T Hardwick, C Humdell, C McBride, A Hambleton, P Smith (c), J Newton
Referee: T McMahon (Australia)

Second Test
At Brisbane Cricket Ground, Saturday, 12 June 1948
Crowd: 23 013
AUSTRALIA 13 (Tyquin, Pegg, McMahon tries, Froome 2 goals) d NEW ZEALAND 4 (Clarke 2 goals)
Australia: C Churchill, P McMahon, L Smith (c), L Pegg, J Graves, W O'Connell, K Froome, W Tyquin, F de Belin, D Hall, J Holland, K Schubert, N Hand
New Zealand: W Clarke, J Forrest, A Graham, M Robertson, D Redmond, R Cunningham, D Barchard, T Hardwick, C McBride, C Humdell, A Hambleton, P Smith (c), J Newton
Referee: S Chambers (Australia)

1949

First Test
At Basin Reserve, Wellington, Saturday, 17 September 1949
Crowd: 7737
NEW ZEALAND 26 (McBride 2, Graham 2, Baxter, Clarke tries, Clarke 4 goals) d AUSTRALIA 21 (Graves 2, McMahon, McCoy, O'Connell tries, Johnston 3 goals)
Australia: C Churchill, J Graves, M McCoy, I Johnston, P McMahon, W O'Connell, K Froome (c), L Cowie, F de Belin, J Rayner, N Mulligan, K Schubert, J Holland
New Zealand: W Clarke, D Redmond, M Robertson, T Baxter, W McKenzie, A Graham, J Russell-Greene, T Hardwick, C McBride, C Humdell, J Newton, R Aynsley, P Smith (c)
Referee: R Avery (New Zealand)

Second Test
At Carlaw Park, Auckland, Saturday, 8 October 1949
Crowd: 12 361
AUSTRALIA 13 (Froome, Mulligan, McCoy tries, Froome, McCoy goals) d NEW ZEALAND 10 (McKenzie, Baxter tries, Clarke 2 goals)
Australia: C Churchill, R Roberts, J Hawke, M McCoy, P McMahon, W O'Connell, K Froome (c), L Cowie, J Rayner, N Mulligan, J Holland, K Schubert, R Bull
New Zealand: W Clarke, W McKenzie, T Baxter, M Robertson, D Redmond, L Jordan, J Russell-Greene, T Hardwick, C McBride, J Newton, P Smith (c), G Davidson, R Westerley
Referee: R Avery (New Zealand)

1952

First Test
At Sydney Cricket Ground, Monday, 9 June 1952
Crowd: 56 376
AUSTRALIA 25 (Flannery 2, Pidding 2, Paul tries, Pidding 5 goals) d NEW ZEALAND 13 (Edwards, Baxter, Atkinson tries, White 2 goals)
Australia: C Churchill (c), N Pidding, N Hazzard, R Duncan, D Flannery, C Geelan, K Holman, A Paul, B Davies, F Ashton, C Gill, K Schubert, J Rooney
New Zealand: D White, J Edwards, R McKay, T Baxter, W McKenzie, C Eastlake, J Haig, T Hardwick (c), F Mulcare, A Atkinson, W McLennan, G Davidson, L Blanchard
Referee: G Bishop (Australia)

Second Test
At Brisbane Cricket Ground, Saturday, 28 June 1952
Crowd: 29 243
NEW ZEALAND 49 (Atkinson 2, McKay 2, Baxter, Mulcare, Eastlake, Davidson, Edwards tries, White 11 goals) d AUSTRALIA 25 (Geelan 3, Ashton, Holman tries, Pidding 5 goals)
Australia: C Churchill (c), D Flannery, N Hazzard, G Willoughby, N Pidding, C Geelan, K Holman, A Paul, F Ashton, B Davies, C Gill, K Schubert, K Hansen
New Zealand: D White, C Eastlake, R McKay, T Baxter, J Edwards, G Menzies, J Haig, T Hardwick (c), A Atkinson, F Mulcare, L Blanchard, G Davidson, W McLennan
Referee: G Bishop (Australia)

Third Test
At Sydney Cricket Ground, Wednesday, 2 July 1952
Crowd: 44 916
NEW ZEALAND 19 (Mulcare, McKay, Eastlake tries, White 5 goals) d AUSTRALIA 9 (Hazzard try, Churchill 3 goals)
Australia: C Churchill (c), D McGovern, R Duncan, N Hazzard, J Lumsden, C Geelan, C Donohoe, H Crocker, A Paul, T Tyrrell, C Gill, K Schubert, J Rooney
New Zealand: D White, C Eastlake, T Baxter, R McKay, J Edwards, G Menzies, J Haig, T Hardwick (c), A Atkinson, F Mulcare, W mcLennan, G Davidson, L Blanchard
Referee: G Bishop (Australia)

1953

First Test
At Addington Showground, Christchurch, Saturday, 27 June 1953
Crowd: 5509
NEW ZEALAND 25 (McKay 2, White, Edwards, Davidson tries, White 4, Bond goals) d AUSTRALIA 5 (Ashton try, Pidding goal)
Australia: C Churchill (c), B Carlson, H Wells, K McCaffery, N Pidding, R Banks, K Holman, H Crocker, F Ashton, B Davies, C Gill, K Kearney, R Bull
New Zealand: D White, J Edwards, R McKay, T Baxter, B Hough, W Sorensen, J Haig (c), A Atkinson, F Mulcare, R Neilson, W McLennan, G Davidson, J Bond
Referee: W Wilkinson (New Zealand)

Second Test
At Basin Reserve, Wellington, Saturday, 4 July 1953
Crowd: 5394
NEW ZEALAND 12 (McKay, Neilson tries, White 3 goals) d AUSTRALIA 11 (McCaffery 2, Carlson tries, Pidding goal)
Australia: C Churchill (c), N Pidding, K McCaffery, H Wells, B Carlson, R Banks, G Hawick, L Cowie, H Crocker, B Davies, C Gill, K Kearney, R Bull
New Zealand: D White, C Paskell, R McKay, T Baxter, J Edwards, W Sorensen, J Haig (c), A Atkinson, F Mulcare, R Neilson, J Bond, G Davidson, W McLennan
Referee: W Wilkinson (New Zealand)

Third Test
At Carlaw Park, Auckland, Saturday, 18 July 1953
Crowd: 16 033
AUSTRALIA 18 (Wells 2, Banks, Pidding tries, Pidding 3 goals) d NEW ZEALAND 16 (Edwards, White, Neilson, Mulcare tries, White 2 goals)
Australia: C Churchill (c), D McGovern, H Wells, K McCaffery, N Pidding, R Banks, G Hawick, H Crocker, B Drew, B Davies, C Gill. K Kearney, R Bull
New Zealand: D White, J Edwards, T Baxter, R McKay, V Bakalich, C Eastlake, J Haig (c), A Atkinson, F Mulcare, R Neilson, W McLennan, G Davidson, J Bond
Referee: R Avery (New Zealand)

1956

First Test
At Sydney Cricket Ground, Saturday, 9 June 1956
Crowd: 46 766
AUSTRALIA 12 (Adams 2, Poole, Moir tries) d NEW ZEALAND 9 (Belsham, Bakalich, Sorensen tries)
Australia: K McCrohon, D Adams, A Watson, R Poole, I Moir, C Connell, K Holman, I Doyle, T Tyquin, K O'Shea, R Bull, K Kearney (c), B Davies
New Zealand: D White, V Bakalich, T Baxter (c), W Sorensen, C Eastlake, G. Menzies, S Belsham, F Mulcare, C Johnson, C Riddell, D McRae, J Butterfield, H Maxwell
Referee: J Casey (Australia)

Second Test
At Brisbane Cricket Ground, Saturday, 23 June 1956
Crowd: 28 361
AUSTRALIA 8 (Poole, Watson tries, Clifford goal) d NEW ZEALAND 2 (White goal)
Australia: G Clifford, D Adams, R Poole, A Watson, D McGovern, C Connell, K Holman, I Doyle, T Tyquin, K O'Shea, B Davies, K Kearney (c), R Bull
New Zealand: D White, V Bakalich, C Eastlake, W Sorensen, T Hadfield, G Menzies, S Belsham, F Mulcare, H Maxwell, C Johnson, J Riddell, J Butterfield, D McRae
Referee: D Lawler (Australia)

Third Test
At Sydney Cricket Ground, Saturday, 30 June 1956
Crowd: 46 735
AUSTRALIA 31 (Adams 3, Watson 2, Holman, Henry tries, Pope 5 goals) d NEW ZEALAND 14 (Bakalich, Johnson tries, White 4 goals)
Australia: N Pope, D Adams, R Poole, A Watson, D McGovern, D Henry, K Holman, I Doyle, T Tyquin, K O'Shea, R Bull, K Kearney (c), B Davies
New Zealand: D White, V Bakalich, T Baxter (c), W Sorensen, C Eastlake, G Menzies, S Belsham, F Mulcare, C Johnson, J Riddell, D McRae, J Buttterfield, H Maxwell
Referee: D Lawler (Australia)

1959

First Test
At Sydney Cricket Ground, Saturday, 13 June 1959
Crowd: 38 613

AUSTRALIA 9 (Beattie try, Carlson 3 goals) d NEW ZEALAND 8 (Maxwell, Eastlake tries, Eastlake goal)
Australia: B Carlson (c), I Moir, H Wells, R Gasnier, T McDonald, A Brown, B Muir, J Raper, N Provan, J Paterson, D Beattie, N Kelly, W Wilson
New Zealand: G Phillips, R Griffiths, C Eastlake, G Turner, N Denton, G Menzies, K Roberts, R Percy, R Ackland, T Kilkelly, C Johnson (c), J Butterfield, H Maxwell
Referee: D Lawler (Australia)

Second Test
Brisbane Exhibition Ground, Saturday, 27 June 1959
Crowd: 30 994
AUSTRALIA 38 (Gasnier 3, Moir 3, Wells, Raper tries, Barnes 7 goals) d NEW ZEALAND 10 (Campbell, Ratima tries, Percy 2 goals)
Australia: K Barnes (c), I Moir, R Gasnier, H Wells, E Lumsden, A Brown, B Muir, J Raper, N Provan, J Paterson, D Beattie, N Kelly, W Wilson
New Zealand: G Phillips, N Denton, B Campbell, C Eastlake, R Griffiths, G Menzies, K Roberts, R Percy, R Ackland, T Kilkelly, C Johnson (c), J Butterfield, J Ratima
Referee: D Lawler (Australia)

Third Test
At Sydney Cricket Ground, Saturday, 4 July 1959
Crowd: 31 629
NEW ZEALAND 28 (Denton 2, Johnson, Cooke, Griffiths, Butterfield tries, Eastlake 5 goals) d AUSTRALIA 12 (Gasnier 2 tries, Barnes 3 goals)
Australia: K Barnes (c), I Moir, R Gasnier, H Wells, E Lumsden, A Brown, B Muir, J Raper, N Provan, J Paterson, W Wilson, N Kelly, D Beattie
New Zealand: G Phillips, R Griffiths, C Eastlake, G Turner, N Denton, G Menzies, K Roberts, M Cooke, R Ackland, T Kilkelly, C Johnson (c), J Butterfield, J Ratima
Referee: D Lawler (Australia)

1961

First Test
At Carlaw Park, Auckland, Saturday, 1 July 1961
Crowd: 11 485
NEW ZEALAND 12 (Emery, Farrar tries, R Cooke 2 goals, Phillips field goal) d AUSTRALIA 10 (Parish, Irvine tries, Parish 2 goals)
Australia: D Parish, K Irvine, R Gasnier, B Carlson (c), E Lumsden, A Summons, B Muir, J Sinclair, R Lynch, J Paterson, R Crowe, I Walsh, E Rasmussen.
New Zealand: G Phillips, B Reidy, G Turner, T Hadfield, R Cooke, G Menzies, G Farrar, M Cooke, R Ackland (c), D Hammond, H Emery, J Butterfield, J Paterson
Referee: R Avery (New Zealand)

Second Test
At Carlaw Park, Auckland, Saturday, 8 July 1961
Crowd: 12 424
AUSTRALIA 10 (Gasnier, Summons tries, Parish 2 goals) d NEW ZEALAND 8 (R Cooke 3, Phillips goals)
Australia: F Drake, K Irvine, D Parish, R Gasnier, E Lumsden, A Summons, B Muir (c), R Lynch, J Paterson, E Rassmussen, D Beattie, I Walsh, R Crowe
New Zealand: G Phillips, B Reidy, G Turner, T Hadfield, R Cooke, G Menzies, W Snowden, M Cooke, R Ackland (c), D Hammond, H Emery, T Reid, J Paterson
Referee: R Avery (New Zealand)

1963

First Test
At Sydney Cricket Ground, Saturday, 8 June 1963
Crowd: 48 300
AUSTRALIA 7 (Gasnier try, Hagan 2 goals) d NEW ZEALAND 3 (Denton try)
Australia: K Thornett, K Irvine, R Gasnier, G Langlands, R Hagan, E Harrison, B Muir, J Raper, P Provan, K Day, P Gallagher, I Walsh, W Wilson (c)
New Zealand: G Phillips, N Denton, R Bailey, G Kennedy, B Reidy, J Bond, W Snowden, M Cooke (c), R Ackland, D Hammond, H Emery, G Blackler, B Lee
Referee: J Bradley (Australia)

Second Test
At Lang Park, Brisbane, Saturday, 22 June 1963
Crowd: 30 748
NEW ZEALAND 16 (Reidy 3, McCracken tries, Fagan 2 goals) d AUSTRALIA 13 (Raper, Cleary, Gasnier tries, Langlands 2 goals)
Australia: K Thornett, K Irvine, R Gasnier. G Langlands, M Cleary, E Harrison, B Muir, J Raper, B Hambly, K Day, W Wilson (c), I Walsh, P Gallagher
New Zealand: J Fagan, K McCracken, R Bailey, G Kennedy, B Reidy, J Bond, W Snowden, M Cooke (c), R Ackland, B Lee, H Emery, J Butterfield, S Edwards
Referee: J Bradley (Australia)

Third Test
At Sydney Cricket Ground, Saturday, 29 June 1963
Crowd: 46 567
AUSTRALIA 14 (Thornett, Langlands, Kelly, Irvine tries, Irvine goal) d NEW ZEALAND 0
Australia: K Thornett, E Lumsden, R Gasnier, G Langlands, K Irvine, E Harrison, A Summons (c), J Raper, K Day, B Hambly, P Gallagher, I Walsh, N Kelly
New Zealand: J Fagan, K McCracken, R Bailey, G Kennedy, B Reidy, J Bond, W Snowden, M Cooke (c), R Ackland, B Lee, H Emery, J Butterfield, S Edwards
Referee: J Bradley (Australia)

1965

First Test
At Carlaw Park, Auckland, Saturday, 19 June 1965
Crowd: 13 295
AUSTRALIA 13 (Irvine 2, Weier tries, Johns 2 goals) d NEW ZEALAND 8 (Fagan 2, Kennedy 2 goals)
Australia: L Johns, M Cleary, R Gasnier, G Langlands, K Irvine, J Lisle, W Smith, B Hambly, J Morgan, M Veivers, L Weier, I Walsh (c), P Quinn
New Zealand: J Fagan, R Christian, R Bailey, P Schultz, B Langton, D Ellwood, W Snowden (c), R Sinel, D Hammond, E Moore, H Emery, C O'Neil, R Schofield. Replacement: G Kennedy (for Fagan)
Referee: J Percival (New Zealand)

Second Test
At Carlaw Park, Auckland, Saturday, 26 June 1965
Crowd: 11 383
NEW ZEALAND 7 (Bailey try, Fagan 2 goals) d AUSTRALIA 5 (Irvine try, Johns goal)
Australia: L Johns, M Cleary, R Gasnier, G Langlands, K Irvine, J Lisle, W Smith, B Hambly, M Vievers, J Morgan, P Quinn, I Walsh (c), L Weier
New Zealand: J Fagan, R Christian, R Bailey, G Kennedy, B Langton, P Schultz, W Snowden (c), R Sinel, D Hammond, K Dixon, E Moore, C O'Neil, S Edwards
Referee: J Percival (New Zealand)

1967

First Test
At Sydney Cricket Ground, Saturday, 10 June 1967
Crowd: 33 416
AUSTRALIA 22 (Hanigan 2, Irvine, Gleeson, Gasnier, Langlands tries, Langlands 2 goals) d NEW ZEALAND 13 (Christian, Danielson, Dixon tries, Tait 2 goals)
Australia: G Langlands, K Irvine, R Gasnier (c), J Greaves, L Hanigan, J Gleeson, W Smith, J Raper, D Tutty, A Thomson, P Gallagher, B Fitzsimmons, N Kelly
New Zealand: R Tait, R Christian, R Bailey, W White, E Baker, D Ellwood, R Irvine, B Castle (c), R Sinel, K Dixon, H Tatana, C O'Neil, O Danielson
Referee: C Pearce (Australia)

Second Test
At Lang Park, Brisbane, Saturday, 1 July 1967
Crowd: 30 122
AUSTRALIA 35 (McDonald 2, Irvine 2, Langlands, Raper, Hanigan tries, McDonald 6, Langlands goal) d NEW ZEALAND 22 (Sinel, Tait, Irvine, Baker tries, Tait 5 goals)
Australia: G Langlands, K Irvine, R Gasnier (c), J McDonald, L Hanigan, J Gleeson, W Smith, J Raper, A Thomson, R Lynch, P Gallagher, A Buman, N Kelly
New Zealand: R Tait, E Baker, R Bailey (c), R Christian, W Southorn, R Irvine, P Schultz, R Sinel, K Dixon, A Kriletich, O Danielson, C O'Neil, R Orchard
Referee: C Pearce (Australia)

Third Test
At Sydney Cricket Ground, Saturday, 8 July 1967
Crowd: 27 530
AUSTRALIA 13 (McDonald 2, K Irvine tries, McDonald 2 goals) d NEW ZEALAND 9 (Tait try & 3 goals)
Australia: G Langlands, K Irvine, R Gasnier (c), J McDonald, J King, J Gleeson, W Smith, J Raper, R Lynch, G Connell, N Kelly, A Buman, P Gallagher
New Zealand: D Ellwood, R Christian, L Mills, R Bailey (c), E Baker, R Tait, R Irvine, R Sinel, A Kriletich, K Dixon, R Orchard, C O'Neil, G Smith
Referee: C Pearce (Australia)

1969

First Test
At Carlaw Park, Auckland, Sunday, 1 June 1969
Crowd: 13 459
AUSTRALIA 20 (Coote 2, Pittard, Cootes tries, Johns 4 goals) d NEW ZEALAND 10 (Ladner 5 goals)

Australia: L Johns, J Cootes, G Langlands, J McDonald, R Honan, D Pittard, D Ward, R Coote, R McCarthy, R Costello, J Sattler (c), E Walters, J Wittenberg
New Zealand: D Ladner, D Keys, R Wilson, S Rolleston, M Brereton, T Patrick, G Cooksley, R Walker, A Kriletich, J Hibbs, W Noonan, C O'Neil (c), O Danielson
Referee: J Percival (New Zealand)

Second Test
At Carlaw Park, Auckland, Saturday, 7 June 1969
Crowd: 9 848
NEW ZEALAND 18 (Noonan, Orchard tries, Ladner 5 goals & field goal) d AUSTRALIA 14 (Coote, McCarthy tries, Johns 4 goals)
Australia: L Johns, R Honan, G Langlands, J McDonald, J Cootes, D Pittard, D Ward, R Coote, C Weiss, R McCarthy, J Wittenberg, E Walters, J Sattler (c)
New Zealand: D Ladner, P Orchard, M Brereton, B Clark, R Christian, G Woodard, G Cooksley, A Kriletich, W Noonan, B Deacon, D Gailey, C O'Neil (c), O Danielson
Referee: J Percival (New Zealand)

1971

Test
At Carlaw Park, Auckland, Saturday, 26 June 1971
Crowd: 13 917
NEW ZEALAND 24 (Whittaker 2, Orchard, Brereton tries, Tatana 6 goals) d AUSTRALIA 3 (Campbell try)
Australia: G Langlands (c), R Branighan, R Fulton, P Sait, L Williamson, A Branson, R Grant, K Campbell, R McCarthy, R Costello, R O'Reilly, B Fitzsimmons, J Sattler
New Zealand: M McClennan, J Whittaker, B Lowther, R Christian (c), M Brereton, G Woollard, K Stirling, E Heatley, G Smith, A Kriletich, H Tatana, C O'Neil, R Orchard
Referee: J Percival (New Zealand)

1972

First Test
At Sydney Cricket Ground, Saturday, 8 July 1972
Crowd: 29 714
AUSTRALIA 36 (Ambrum 2, Sullivan 2, McCarthy 2, Starling, Fulton tries, Langlands 6 goals) d NEW ZEALAND 11 (Whittaker try, R Orchard 4 goals)
Australia: G Langlands (c), M Harris, G Starling, R Fulton, G Ambrum, T Pickup, T Raudonikis, G Sullivan, J Elford, R McCarthy, R O'Reilly, E Walters, A Beetson
New Zealand: J Whittaker, P Orchard, R Christian (c), D Williams, M Brereton, D Sorensen, K Stirling, A Kriletich, J Greengrass, M Eade, R Orchard, J Fisher, D Gailey. Replacement: J O'Sullivan (for Sorensen)
Referee: K Holman (Australia)

Second Test
At Lang Park, Brisbane, Saturday, 15 July 1972
Crowd: 29 847
AUSTRALIA 31 (Elford 2, Fulton 2, Starling 2, Raudonikis tries, Stewart 5 goals) d NEW ZEALAND 7 (Eade try, Collicoat 2 goals)
Australia: G Langlands (c), W Stewart, G Starling, R Fulton, G Ambrum, T Pickup, T Raudonikis, G Sullivan, J Elford, R McCarthy, R O'Reilly, E Walters, A Beetson. Replacements: J Murphy (for McCarthy) and E Goodwin (for Ambrum)
New Zealand: W Collicoat, P Orchard, R Christian (c), J O'Sullivan, M Brereton, D Williams, S Dowsett, A Kriletich, J Greengrass, M Eade, D Gailey, J Fisher, R Paul. Replacement: R Bolton (for Kriletich)
Referee: K Holman (Australia)

1978

First Test
At Sydney Cricket Ground, Saturday, 24 June 1978
Crowd: 16 577
AUSTRALIA 24 (Rogers, Peponis, Fahey, Boustead tries, Cronin 6 goals) d NEW ZEALAND 2 (Jordan goal)
Australia: G Eadie, T Fahey, M Cronin, S Rogers, K Boustead, R Fulton, S Morris, R Price, R Reddy, G Pierce (c), I Thomson, G Peponis, G Olling. Replacement: G Oliphant
New Zealand: C Jordan, F Ah Kuoi, O Filipaina, D Williams, D O'Hara, J Smith, K Stirling (c), M Eade, A Coll, R Baxendale, L Proctor, G Taylor, A Rushton. Replacement: G Prohm
Referee: E Ward (Australia)

Second Test
At Lang Park, Brisbane, Saturday, 15 July 1978
Crowd: 14 000
AUSTRALIA 38 (Glover 2, Price 2, Boustead 2, Reddy, Rogers tries, Cronin 7 goals) d NEW ZEALAND 7 (O'Hara try, Jordan 2 goals)

Continued

1978 Second Test *continued*
Australia: J Dorahy, K Boustead, M Cronin, S Rogers, N Glover, R Fulton (c), G Oliphant, R Price, R Reddy, G Platz, G Olling, J Lang, J Donnelly. Replacement: J Donnelly
New Zealand: C Jordan, S Varley, O Filipaina, D Williams, D O'Hara, J Smith, K Stirling (c), M Graham, A Coll, G Prohm, L Proctor, A Rushton, I Bell
Referee: E Ward (Australia)

Third Test
At Sydney Cricket Ground, Saturday, 22 July 1978
Crowd: 6541
AUSTRALIA 33 (Fulton 2, Dorahy, Boustead tries, Cronin 9 goals) d NEW ZEALAND 16 (Jordan, O'Hara tries, Jordan 5 goals)
Australia: J Dorahy, N Glover, M Cronin, S Rogers, K Boustead, R Fulton (c), T Raudonikis, R Price, R Reddy, G Pierce, C Young, M Krilich, R Morris
New Zealand: C Jordan, F Ah kuoi, O Filipaina, D Williams, D O'Hara, J Smith, K Stirling (c), M Graham, A Coll, G Prohm, L Proctor, A Rushton, I Bell
Referee: G Cook (Australia)

1980

First Test
At Carlaw Park, Auckland, Sunday, 1 June 1980
Crowd: 12 321
AUSTRALIA 27 (Thompson 2, Young, Boustead, Reddy tries, Cronin 6 goals) d NEW ZEALAND 6 (O'Donnell 3 goals)
Australia: G Dowling, G Quinn, M Cronin, G Brentnall, C Anderson, A Thompson, T Raudonikis, R Price, L Boyd, R Reddy, C Young, G Peponis (c), R Morris
New Zealand: M O'Donnell, K Fisher, O Filipaina, J Leuluai, D O'Hara (c), G Smith, S Varley, M Graham, B Edkins, K Tamati, P Teariki, H Tamati, M Broadhurst
Referee: K Steel (New Zealand)

Second Test
At Carlaw Park, Auckland, Sunday, 15 June 1980
Crowd: 9706
AUSTRALIA 15 (Cronin, Reddy, Boyd tries, Cronin 3 goals) d NEW ZEALAND 6 (O'Donnell 3 goals)
Australia: G Dowling, G Quinn, M Cronin, G Brentnall, C Anderson, A Thompson, T Raudonikis, R Price, R Reddy, L Boyd, R Morris, C Young, G Peponis (c), C Young
New Zealand: M O'Donnell, K Fisher, O Filipaina, J Leuluai, D O'Hara, D Williams, G Smith, M Graham, B Edkins, A Coll, K Tamati, H Tamati, M Broadhurst
Referee: J Percival (New Zealand)

1982

First Test
At Lang Park, Brisbane, Saturday, 3 July 1982
Crowd: 14 000
AUSTRALIA 11 (Muggleton try, Cronin 4 goals) d NEW ZEALAND 8 (Smith 4 goals)
Australia: G Brentnall, J Ribot, M Cronin, S Rogers, K Boustead, W Lewis, S Mortimer, P Vautin, L Boyd, R Hancock, R Morris, M Krilich (c), C Young. Replacement: J Muggleton
New Zealand: G Kemble, G Prohm, J,Leuluai, O Filipaina, D O'Hara, F Ah Kuoi, G Smith, M Graham (c), B Gall, G West, M Broadhurst, H Tamati, K Tamati. Replacement: J Whittaker
Referee: F Lindop (Great Britain)

Second Test
At Sydney Cricket Ground, Saturday, 17 July 1982
Crowd: 16 775
AUSTRALIA 20 (Brentnall, Boustead, Lewis, Price tries, Cronin 4 goals) d NEW ZEALAND 2 (Smith goal)
Australia: G Brentnall, J Ribot, M Cronin, M Meninga, K Boustead, W Lewis, S Mortimer, R Price, L Boyd, J Muggleton, R Hancock, M Krilich (c), C Young. Replacements: S Rogers and S Morris
New Zealand: G Kemble, G Prohm, O Filipaina, J Leuluai, D O'Hara, F Ah Kuoi, G Smith, M Graham (c), B Gall, G West, M Broadhurst, H Tamati, K Tamati. Replacements: J Whittaker and H McGahan
Referee: F Lindop (Great Britain)

1983

First Test
At Carlaw Park, Auckland, Sunday, 12 June 1983
Crowd: 18 000
AUSTRALIA 16 (Grothe, Rogers tries, Meninga 4 goals) d NEW ZEALAND 4 (Leuluai try)
Australia: G Brentnall, K Boustead, M Meninga, S Rogers, E Grothe, W Lewis, P Sterling, P Vautin, P McCabe, W Fullerton Smith, G Gerard, M Krilich (c), D Brown. Replacements: M Murray (for Brentnall) and P Jarvis (for McCabe)

New Zealand: G Kemble, J Ropati, R O'Regan, J Leuluai, D Bell, F Ah Kuoi, G Smith, G Prohm, K Sorensen, M Graham (c), D Sorensen, H Tamati, M Broadhurst. Replacements: S Varley (for Kemble) and G West (for Graham)
Referee: R Whitfield (Great Britain)

Second Test
At Lang Park, Brisbane, Saturday, 9 July 1983
Crowd: 15 000
NEW ZEALAND 19 (West, Leuluai, Ropati tries, Wright 3 goals & field goal) d AUSTRALIA 12 (Grothe, Ella tries, Meninga 2 goals)
Australia: C Scott, K Boustead, M Meninga, G Miles, E Grothe, W Lewis, S Mortimer, R Price, P Vautin, W Fullerton Smith, D Brown, M Krilich (c), B Tessmann. Replacements: S Ella (for Mortimer) and R Brown (for Tessmann).
New Zealand: N Wright, J Ropati, J Leuluai, F Ah Kuoi, D Bell, G Smith, S Varley, G Prohm, K Sorensen, G West (c), D Sorensen, H Tamati, M Broadhurst. Replacements: R O'Regan (for Varley) and I Bell (for Tamati)
Referee: R Whitfield (Great Britain)

1985

First Test
At Lang Park, Brisbane, Tuesday, 18 June 1985
Crowd: 22 000
AUSTRALIA 26 (Ribot 2, Close, Cleal, Roach tries, Meninga 2, Ribot goals) d NEW ZEALAND 20 (McGahan, Filipaina, Bell tries, Filipaina 4 goals)
Australia: G Jack, J Ribot, C Close, M Meninga, J Ferguson, W Lewis (c), M Murray, W Pearce, P Wynn, N Cleal, S Roach, G Conescu, G Dowling. Replacement: P Tunks (for Cleal)
New Zealand: G Kemble, D Bell, G Prohm, J Leuluai, D O'Hara, O Filipaina, C Friend, H McGahan, M Graham (c), K Sorensen, O Wright, H Tamati, K Tamati. Replacements: R Cowan (for Graham) and M Elia (for Prohm)
Referee: J Rascagnares (France)

Second Test
At Carlaw Park, Auckland, Sunday, 30 June 1985
Crowd: 19 132
AUSTRALIA 10 (Ribot try, Meninga 2, Ribot goals) d NEW ZEALAND 6 (Leuluai try, Filipaina goal)
Australia: G Jack, J Ribot, C Close, M Meninga, J Ferguson, W Lewis (c), M Murray, W Pearce, P Wynn, P Vautin, S Roach, G Conescu, G Dowling. Replacements; N Cleal (for Wynn) and S Ella (for Meninga)
New Zealand: G Kemble, D Bell, G Prohm, J Leuluai, D O'Hara, O Filipaina, C Friend, H McGahan, M Graham (c), K Sorensen, K Tamati, H Tamati, O Wright. Replacements: J Ropati (for Bell) and R Cowan (for Wright)
Referee: J Rascagnares (France)

Third Test
At Carlaw Park, Auckland, Sunday, 7 July 1985
Crowd: 15 327
NEW ZEALAND 18 (Friend 2, Leuluai tries, Filipaina 3 goals) d AUSTRALIA 0
Australia: G Jack, J Ribot, C Close, M Meninga, S Ella, J Ferguson, W Lewis (c), D Hasler, W Pearce, P Wynn, P Vautin, S Roach, B Elias, P Tunks. Replacements: C Close (for Ferguson) and G Dowling
New Zealand: G Kemble, D Bell, G Prohm, J Leuluai, D O'Hara, O Filipaina, C Friend, H McGahan, K Sorensen, M Graham (c), K Tamati, H Tamati, O Wright. Replacements: J Ropati and R Cowan
Referee: J Rascagnares (France)

1986

First Test
At Carlaw Park, Auckland, Sunday, 6 July 1986
Crowd: 14 566
AUSTRALIA 22 (Kenny 2, Shearer, Folkes tries, O'Connor 3 goals) d NEW ZEALAND 8 (Bell try, Filipaina 2 goals)
Australia: G Jack, D Shearer, B Kenny, G Miles, M O'Connor, W Lewis (c), P Sterling, W Pearce, N Cleal, S Folkes, P Tunks, R Simmons, S Roach. Replacements: T Lamb (for Shearer) and B Niebling (for Tunks)
New Zealand: D Williams, J Ropati, D Bell, J Leuluai, D O'Hara, O Filipaina, S Cooper, G Prohm, H McGahan, M Graham (c), K Sorensen, W Wallace, O Wright. Replacements: R O'Regan (for Leuluai) and M Elia (for Wallace)
Referee: R Whitfield (Great Britain)

Second Test
At Sydney Cricket Ground, Saturday, 19 July 1986
Crowd: 34 302
AUSTRALIA 29 (Miles, Jack, Lewis, Kenny, Pearce tries, O'Connor 4 goals, Sterling field goal) d NEW ZEALAND 12 (Filipaina, O'Hara tries, Filipaina 2 goals)
Australia: G Jack, L Kiss, G Miles, B Kenny, M O'Connor, W Lewis (c), P Sterling, W Pearce, N Cleal, S Folkes, P Tunks, R Simmons, S Roach. Replacement: B Niebling (for Tunks)

Continued

1986 Second Test *continued*
New Zealand: G Kemble, D Bell, J Ropati, M Elia, D O'Hara, O Filipaina, G Freeman, G Prohm, H McGahan, M Graham (c), K Sorensen, B Harvey, O Wright. Replacements: S Cooper (for Ropati)
Referee: R Whitfield (Great Britain)

Third Test
At Lang Park, Brisbane, Tuesday, 29 July 1986
Crowd: 22 811
AUSTRALIA 32 (Kenny 2, Sterling, Lewis, Miles, O'Connor tries, O'Connor 4 goals) d NEW ZEALAND 12 (Williams 2 tries, Filipaina 2 goals)
Australia: G Jack, L Kiss, G Miles, B Kenny, M O'Connor, W Lewis (c), P Sterling, W Pearce, S Folkes, N Cleal, P Tunks, R Simmons, S Roach. Replacements: B Niebling (for Folkes) and T Lamb (for Pearce)
New Zealand: G Kemble, D Williams, J Ropati, G Prohm, D O'Hara, O Filipaina, G Freeman, R O'Regan, M Graham (c), H McGahan, K Sorensen, B Harvey, B Todd. Replacements: O Wright (for Todd) and S Cooper (for O'Hara)
Referee: R Whitfield (Great Britain)

1987

Test
At Lang Park, Brisbane, Tuesday, 21 July 1987
Crowd: 16 500
NEW ZEALAND 13 (Taylor, Mercer tries, Iro 2 goals, Cooper field goal) d AUSTRALIA 6 (Sterling try, O'Connor goal)
Australia: G Jack, M O'Connor, B Kenny, G Miles, D Shearer, W Lewis (c), P Sterling, R Lindner, W Pearce, B Niebling, G Dowling, R Simmons, P Tunks. Replacements: B Johnston (for Kenny) and L Davidson (for Dowling).
New Zealand: D Williams, M Elia, D Bell, K Iro, G Mercer, S Cooper, C Friend, H McGahan (c), M Horo, S Stewart, A Shelford, W Wallace, R Taylor. Replacements: G Freeman (for Cooper) and D Lonergan (for Taylor)
Referee: N Kesha (New Zealand)

1989

First Test
At Queen Elizabeth II Stadium, Christchurch, Sunday, 10 July 1989
Crowd: 15 000
AUSTRALIA 26 (Currie, Lewis, Walters, Sironen tries, Meninga 5 goals) d NEW ZEALAND 6 (Elia try, K Iro goal)
Australia: G Belcher, D Shearer, M Meninga, T Currie, M Hancock, W Lewis (c), G Alexander, P Vautin, B Clyde, P Sironen, S Roach, K Walters, S Backo. Replacements: M O'Connor (for Meninga) and B McGuire (for Roach)
New Zealand: D Williams, T Iro, K Iro, T Kemp, M Elia, S Cooper, C Friend, B Tuuta, S Stewart, H McGahan (c), J Goulding, B Harvey, B Todd. Replacement: G Freeman (for Friend)
Referee: R Tennant (Great Britain)

Second Test
At Rotorua International Showground, Sunday, 16 July 1989
Crowd: 26 000
AUSTRALIA 8 (Hancock try, Meninga 2 goals) d NEW ZEALAND 0
Australia: G Belcher, D Shearer, M Meninga, T Currie, M Hancock, W Lewis (c), G Alexander, P Vautin, B Clyde, P Sironen, S Roach, K Walters, S Backo. Replacement: D Hasler (for Alexander)
New Zealand: D Williams, T Iro, T Kemp, K Iro, G Mercer, S Cooper, G Freeman, B Tuuta, S Stewart, H McGahan (c), J Goulding, D Mann, B Todd. Replacements: P Bancroft (for Cooper) and M Horo (for Tuuta)
Referee: R Tennant (Great Britain)

Third Test
At Mt Smart Stadium, Auckland, Sunday, 23 July 1989
Crowd: 15 000
AUSTRALIA 22 (Meninga, O'Connor, Shearer, Currie, Clyde tries, O'Connor 2, Meninga goals) d NEW ZEALAND 14 (Elia, Mercer tries, Shelford 3 goals)
Australia: G Belcher, M Hancock, D Shearer, T Currie, M O'Connor, W Lewis (c), D Hasler, B Clyde, P Vautin, M Meninga, S Roach, K Walters, S Backo. Replacement: B McGuire (for Backo)
New Zealand: D Williams, G Mercer, K Iro, T Kemp, M Elia, K Shelford, G Freeman, H McGahan (c), M Horo, S Stewart, B Todd, D Mann, J Goulding. Replacements: B Tuuta (for Horo) and K Sherlock (for Kemp)
Referee: R Tennant (Great Britain)

1990

Test
At Athletic Park, Wellington, Sunday, 19 August 1990
Crowd: 25 000

AUSTRALIA 24 (Langer, McGaw, Hancock, Mackay tries, Meninga 4 goals) d NEW ZEALAND 6 (Panapa try, Ridge goal)
Australia: G Belcher, M Hancock, M Meninga (c), M McGaw, D Shearer, L Daley, A Langer, R Lindner, P Sironen, I Roberts, S Roach, K Walters, M Bella. Replacements: A Ettingshausen (for Belcher), G Lazarus (for Roach), B Mackay (for Lindner) and D Hasler (for Langer)
New Zealand: M Ridge, M Edwards, D Watson, D Williams, S Panapa, K Shelford, G Freeman, H McGahan (c), D Lonergan, T Nikau, P Brown, D Mann, B Todd
Referee: R Whitfield (Great Britain)

1991

First Test
At Olympic Park, Melbourne, Wednesday, July 3, 1991.
Crowd: 26 900 (Ground record)
NEW ZEALAND 24 (McCracken, Blackmore, Friend, Nikau tries, Botica 4 goals) d AUSTRALIA 8 (Walters try, Meninga 2 goals)
Australia: P Hauff, A Ettingshausen, M Meninga (c), C Johns, D Shearer, W Lewis, A Langer, B Clyde, R Lindner, I Roberts, S Roach, S Walters, M Bella, Interchange: D Gillespie (for Roach), Roach (for Gillespie), J Cartwright (for Lindner)
New Zealand: F Botica, J Williams, J McCracken, D Watson, R Blackmore, T Kemp, G Freeman (c), T Nikau, D Lonergan, E Koloto, B Todd, D Mann, P Brown. Interchange: C Friend (for Kemp), G Mann (for Lonergan), G Mercer (for Koloto) and M Patton (for Williams)
Referee: J Holdsworth (Great Britain)

Second Test
At Sydney Football Stadium, Wednesday, July 24, 1991.
Crowd: 34 911
AUSTRALIA 44 (Daley 2, Geyer, Clyde, Wishart, Gillespie, Carne, Hasler tries, Meninga 6 goals) d NEW ZEALAND 0.
Australia: A Ettingshausen, W Carne, M Meninga (c), L Daley, R Wishart, P Jackson, A Langer, B Clyde, D Gillespie, M Geyer, C Salvatori, S Walters, M Bella. Interchange: C Johns (for Wishart), I Roberts (for Bella), J Cartwright (for Geyer) and D Hasler (for Gillespie)
New Zealand: F Botica, J Williams, J McCracken, K Iro, R Blackmore, D Watson, G Freeman (c), T Nikau, D Lonergan, E Koloto, B Todd, D Mann, P Brown. Interchange: C Friend (for Koloto), G Mann (for Brown), G Mercer (for Lonergan) and M Patton (for Todd)
Referee: J Holdsworth (Great Britain)

Third Test
At Lang Park, Brisbane, Wednesday, July 31, 1991.
Crowd: 29 139
AUSTRALIA 40 (Carne, Meninga, Walters, Wishart, Clyde, Ettingshausen, Daley tries, Meninga 6 goals) d NEW ZEALAND 12 (McCracken, Blackmore tries, Botica 2 goals)
Australia: A Ettingshausen, W Carne, M Meninga (c), L Daley, R Wishart, P Jackson, A Langer, B Clyde, D Gillespie, M Geyer, C Salvatori, S Walters, M Bella. Interchange: C Johns (for Jackson), I Roberts (for Bella), J Cartwright (for Gillespie) and D Hasler (for Clyde)
New Zealand: F Botica, D Watson, J McCracken, K Iro, R Blackmore, G Freeman (c), C Friend, T Nikau, G Mann, B Todd, D Mann, P Brown. Interchange: E Koloto (for Mercer), E Faimolo (for Brown), J Williams (for McCracken) and M Patton (for G Mann)
Referee: J Holdsworth (Great Britain)

Leading Pointscorers in Australia v New Zealand Tests
(As of 1 January 1992)

	T	G	Pts
Mick Cronin (Aust)	1	39	81
Des White (NZ)	2	29	64
Mal Meninga (Aust)	2	35	78
Harold Horder (Aust)	9	8	43
Noel Pidding (Aust)	3	15	39
Dave Brown (Aust)	4	13	38
Olsen Filipaina (NZ)	2	14	36
Michael O'Connor (Aust)	2	13	34
WS Clarke (NZ)	1	14	31
Graeme Langlands (Aust)	3	11	31
Ken Irvine (Aust)	9	1	29
John McDonald (Aust)	4	8	28
Reg Gasnier (Aust)	9	—	27
Roger Tait (NZ)	2	10	26
Cyril Eastlake (NZ)	3	6	24
Frank Burge (Aust)	5	4	23
Les Johns (Aust)	—	11	22
Don Ladner (NZ)	—	11	22
Brett Kenny (Aust)	5	—	20
Keith Barnes (Aust)	—	10	20

Australia-New Zealand Test Records

Biggest win: 44 points, Australia 44 d New Zealand 0, First Test, at Melbourne, 1991 (Biggest New Zealand win: 24 points, New Zealand 49 d Australia 25, Second Test, at Brisbane, 1952)
Biggest crowd: 56 866, First Test, at Sydney Cricket Ground, 1952
Smallest crowd: 5394, Second Test, at Addington Showground, Christchurch, 1953
Most points in a match: 22 by Des White (NZ) (11 goals), Second Test, at Brisbane, 1952. (Most for Australia: 18 by John McDonald, 2 tries and 6 goals, Second Test, at Brisbane, 1967; and 18 by Mick Cronin, 9 goals, Third Test, at Sydney, 1978
Most tries in a match: 3 by Harold Horder (1919), Col Geelan (1952), Don Adams (1956) and Ian Moir (1959) for Australia and Brian Reidy (1963) and S Walters (1919) for New Zealand
Most goals in a match: (See *Most Points*)
Most Tests: 15 by Wally Lewis (Aust). (Most for New Zealand: 13 by Olsen Filipaina)

NEW ZEALAND V AUSTRALIA
World Cup and Championship Matches

1954

At Marseille, Sunday, 7 November 1954
Crowd: 20 000
AUSTRALIA 34 (Watson 3, Hawick, Bull, Kearney, O'Shea, Diversi tries, Pidding 5 goals) d NEW ZEALAND 15 (Ericsen try, McKay 6 goals)
Australia: C Churchill (c), N Pidding, H Wells, A Watson, D Flannery, R Banks, G Hawick, P Diversi, K O'Shea, H Crocker, B Davies, K Kearney, R Bull
New Zealand: N Denton, J Edwards, C Eastlake (c), R McKay, J Austin, W Sorensen, L Ericsen, A Atkinson, J Yates, J Butterfield, W mcLennan, L Blanchard, C Johnson
Referee: R Guidicelli (France)

1957

At Brisbane Cricket Ground, Saturday, 15 June 1957
Crowd: 29 636
AUSTRALIA 25 (Provan, Carlson, O'Shea, Moir, Wells tries, Barnes 5 goals) d NEW ZEALAND 5 (Johnson try, Sorensen goal)
Australia: K Barnes, I Moir, H Wells, R Poole (c), B Carlson, G Hawick, K Holman, B Clay, N Provan, K O'Shea, B Davies, K Kearney, W Marsh
New Zealand: P Creedy, V Bakalich, W Sorensen, R Ackland, T Hadfield, G Menzies, S Belsham, R Percy, J Yates, C Johnson (c), H Maxwell, J Butterfield, W McLennan
Referee: V Belsham (New Zealand)

1960

At Headingley, Leeds, Saturday, 1 October 1960
Crowd: 10 773
AUSTRALIA 21 (Carlson 3, Gasnier, Wells tries, Carlson 3 goals) d NEW ZEALAND 15 (Hadfield, Turner, Menzies tries, Eastlake 3 goals)
Australia: K Barnes (c), B Carlson, H Wells, R Gasnier, K Irvine, A Brown, B Muir, J Raper, B Hambly, R Mossop, D Beattie, N Kelly, G Parcell
New Zealand: G Phillips, T Hadfield, G Turner, C Eastlake, N Denton, G Menzies, K Roberts, M Cooke, R Ackland, L Olliff, C Johnson (c), J Butterfield, H Maxwell
Referee: E Clay (Great Britain)

1968

At Lang Park, Brisbane, Saturday, 1 June 1968
Crowd: 23 608
AUSTRALIA 31 (King 2, Rhodes, Coote, Jones tries, Simms 6 goals & 2 field goals) d NEW ZEALAND 12 (Dunn, Schultz tries, Wiggs 3 goals)
Australia: E Simms, J Rhodes, J Greaves, G Langlands, J King, A Branson, W Smith, J Raper (c), R Coote, R Thornett, E Rasmussen, F Jones, J Wittenberg. Replacement: R Fulton (for Branson)
New Zealand: D Ellwood, R Mincham, S Dunn, P Schultz, E Wiggs, J Bond (c), G Clark, A Kriletich, K Dixon, B Lee, H Tatana, C O'Neil, G Smith. Replacement: R Tait (for Bond)
Referee: J Percival (New Zealand)

1970

At Central Park, Wigan, Wednesday, 21 October 1970
Crowd: 9805

AUSTRALIA 47 (Cootes 2, Branighan, Fulton, Smith, McCarthy, Coote, Turner, Simms tries, Simms 9 goals & field goal) d NEW ZEALAND 11 (Smith try, Ladner goal & 3 field goals)
Australia: E Simms, R Branighan, J Cootes, R Fulton, L Williamson, D Pittard, W Smith, R Coote (c), P Sait, R McCarthy, R O'Reilly, E Walters, J O'Neill. Replacement: R Turner (for Coote)
New Zealand: D Ladner, R McGuinn, R Christian (c), B Lowther, M Brereton, G Woollard, G Cooksley, A Kriletich, E Heatley, W Deacon, D Gailey, C O'Neil, G Smith
Referee: W Thompson (Great Britain)

1972

At Parc de Princes, Paris, Wednesday, 1 November 1972
Crowd: 8000
AUSTRALIA 9 (Ward, Fulton tries, Branighan goal, Fulton field goal) d NEW ZEALAND 5 (Whittaker try, Wilson goal)
Australia: G Langlands (c), J Grant, R Branighan, G Starling, S Knight, R Fulton, D Ward, P Sait, J Elford, G Sullivan, R O'Reilly, E Walters, J O'Neill. Replacement: G Stevens (for Sait)
New Zealand: J Wilson, P Orchard, M Brereton, R Christian (c), J Whittaker, D Williams, B Tracey, P Gurnick, R Paul, M Eade, D Gailey, W Burgoyne, D Mann. Replacement: R Walker (for Paul)
Referee: M Naughton (Great Britain)

1975

At Lang Park, Brisbane, Sunday, 1 June 1975
Crowd: 10 000
AUSTRALIA 36 (Cronin 2, Langlands 2, Fulton, Platz, Randall, Branighan tries, Cronin 6 goals) d NEW ZEALAND 8 (Stirling, Whittaker tries, Collicoat goal)
Australia: G Langlands (c), C Anderson, R Fulton, M Cronin, T Fahey, T Pickup, R Strudwick, R Coote, L Platz, G Stevens, D Wright, J Lang, T Randall. Replacements: P Sait (for Wright) and R Branighan (for Fahey)
New Zealand: W Collicoat, M Brereton, J O'Sullivan, J Whittaker, P Orchard, D Williams, K Stirling (c), M Eade, R Baxendale, A Coll, G West, T Conroy, J Hibbs
Referee: F Escande (France)

At Carlaw Park, Auckland, Saturday, 27 September 1975
Crowd: 18 000
AUSTRALIA 24 (Quayle, Higgs, Cronin, Schubert tries, Cronin 6 goals0 d NEW ZEALAND 8 (Collicoat 4 goals)
Australia: G Eadie, J Rhodes, M Cronin, J Brass (c), I Schubert, J Peard, J Mayes, J Quayle, R Higgs, L Platz, I Mackay, G Piggins, G Veivers. Replacements: T Raudonikis (for Eadie) and D Fitzgerald (for Platz)
New Zealand: W Collicoat, P Orchard, J Matete, D Williams, F Ah Kuoi, R Jarvis, K Stirling (c), M Eade, R Baxendale, A Coll, D Sorensen, T Conroy, J Greengrass. Replacement: K Sorensen (for Coll)
Referee: F Lindop (Great Britain)

1977

At Carlaw Park, Auckland, Sunday, 29 May 1977
Crowd: 18 000
AUSTRALIA 27 (McMahon 2, Thomas, Harris, Peard tries, Cronin 6 goals) d NEW ZEALAND 12 (Smith, Rushton tries, Collicoat 3 goals)
Australia: G Eadie, M Harris, M Cronin, M Thomas, A McMahon, J Peard, T Raudonikis, G Pierce, R Higgs, T Randall, G Veivers (c), N Geiger, D Fitzgerald. Replacements: S Crear and R Reddy
New Zealand: W Collicoat, D O'Hara, O Filipaina, C Jordan, K Fisher, D Williams, J Smith, Whetu Henry, K Sorensen, A Coll (c), D Sorensen, A Rushton, Whare Henry. Replacements: J Whittaker and R Baxendale
Referee: W Thompson (Great Britain)

1988

For home-and-away qualifying games see *Third Test, at Auckland, 1985* (New Zealand 18 d Australia 0) and Third Test, at Brisbane, 1986 (Australia 32 d New Zealand 12)
Final
At Eden Park, Auckland, Sunday, 9 October 1988
Crowd: 46 000
AUSTRALIA 25 (Langer 2, Miller, Shearer tries, O'Connor 4 goals, Elias field goal) d NEW ZEALAND 12 (T Iro, K Iro tries, Brown 2 goals)
Australia: G Jack, D Shearer, A Farrar, M McGaw, M O'Connor, W Lewis (c), A Langer, W Pearce, G miller, P Sironen, S Roach, B Elias, P Dunn. Replacements: T Lamb (for Lewis) and D Gillespie (for Roach)
New Zealand: G Mercer, T Iro, K Iro, D Bell (c), M Elia, G Freeman, C Friend, M Horo, M Graham, K Sorensen, P Brown, W Wallace, A Shelford. Replacements: S Copper (for Mercer) and S Stewart (for Shelford)
Referee: G Ainui (Papua-New Guinea)

Most Test and World Series Appearances for New Zealand

	Tests	World Series games	Total
Dane O'Hara	35	1	36
Jock Butterfield	28	8	36
Cliff Johnson	25	9	34
Hugh McGahan	32	—	32
Roy Christian	26	6	32
Dennis Williams	18	14	32
Tony Coll	17	13	30
Roger Bailey	29	—	29
Tom Baxter	29	—	29
James Leuluai	29	—	29
Olsen Filipaina	26	3	29
Mark Graham	26	3	29

Most Points for New Zealand in Test and World Series Matches

	Appearances	Tries	Goals	Points
Des White	21	2	63	132
Olsen Filipaina	29	6	44	108
Jack Fagan	18	1	46	95
Don Ladner	8	—	38	76
WS Clarke	11	1	34	71
Warren Collicoat	16	—	35	70
Hugh McGahan	32	16	—	62
Cyril Eastlake	28	6	21	60
George Smith	14	1	24	51

A GALLERY OF NEW ZEALAND GREATS

Ron Ackland

One of the few New Zealanders to represent his country as both a back and a forward was Ron Ackland. He played international football for 10 years, during which time he appeared in two World Cups and seven Test series (19 matches). Ackland started out as a centre, in which position he first represented New Zealand (against Great Britain, in 1954). It was not until 1959 that he switched to the forwards—doing so because he unselfishly felt he was too slow for the backline. He became a regular in the New Zealand pack and proved himself one of the world's most intelligent forwards. Ackland made a big impact on Australian fans. He toured twice (in 1956, as a centre, and in 1959, as a second-rower). He also took part in the 1957 and 1960 World Cups. In 1961 he captained the Kiwis in both Tests against Australia.

Fred Ah Kuoi see alphabetical entry

Opai Asher see alphabetical entry

Alister Atkinson

A speedy lock-forward, Alister Atkinson played international football for just five years in the 1950s, but still ended his career with 71 games for his country, including 24 Test and World Cup appearances. All but one of the 24 were consecutive—a record for a New Zealander. Atkinson made four overseas tours—one to Australia (1952), two to Britain and France (1951–52 and 1955–56) and another to France (1954) for the inaugural World Cup. He later served in several major administrative posts in the NZ Rugby League.

AH Baskerville see alphabetical entry

Dean Bell see alphabetical entry

Jock Butterfield see alphabetical entry

Roy Christian

Roy Christian was the first New Zealand Rugby League player to be awarded the MBE for his services to sport. A descendant of Fletcher Christian of Mutiny On The Bounty fame, he was honoured in 1971 while captain of the Kiwi side. A winger, who moved to the centres, Christian first tasted international football when he toured Australia with New Zealand's Under-21 side in 1962. The following year he played his first senior international game for Auckland against the touring South African side. His Test debut was in 1965, against Australia, and from then on he was a regular in the Kiwi lineup (except for 1968, when a badly torn hamstring kept him out of the World Cup squad). Christian played 70 international matches including 26 Tests and World Cup games (eight against Australia, 12 versus Great Britain and six against France). Christian was elevated to the New Zealand captaincy in 1970, and led his country in two World Cups (1970 and 1972) and in Tests against every major Rugby League nation. He had a unique record for a top-level player. He began with the Otahuhu Leopards when he was just five years old and stayed with the club for more than a quarter of a century.

Roy Christian, a descendant of Fletcher Christian of mutiny on the *Bounty* fame, who captained New Zealand in the late 1960s and early 1970s

Craddock Dufty

Few fullbacks could equal Craddock Dufty's achievements. The Auckland star first appeared for the Kiwis at the age of 19, against the touring Australians in 1919, and held his Test spot for the next 11 years. Unfortunately, lack of regular international competition meant he only played 14 Tests—four on two tours of Australia (1925 and 1930) and one to Britain (1926–27). Dufty was a household name. Such was his prowess that the saying 'Give it to Dufty' was born—and remembered seven decades later. A powerful kicker, he humbled other top-class fullbacks. One performance, in particular, stands out. In the First Test against Britain, at Auckland's Carlaw Park in 1924, he completely outplayed Jim Sullivan, then regarded as the greatest custodian the world had known.

Cyril Eastlake

Few Rugby League players have been as versatile as Cyril Eastlake. In a country known for talented utility players, Eastlake, a five-eighth-cum-centre-cum-winger-cum-fullback, knew no peer. In the 1950s and early 1960s, he played 79 matches for New Zealand, including 28 games officially regarded in his home country as having Test status (12 against Australia, eight against Britain, seven versus France and one against a British Empire XIII). In doing so he notched 257 points (31 tries and 82 goals) of which 60 (six tries and 21 goals) came in 'Tests'. He toured Britain and France in 1951–52, made three tours of Australia (1952, 1956 and 1959) and turned out in the 1954 and 1957 World Cups (he was captain in the former series).

Jack Fagan

Only Des White has scored more points for New Zealand than Auckland fullback Jack Fagan. In 53 international games, Fagan scored 289 points (two tries and 140 goals). This tally included 95 points (one try and 46 goals) in his 18 Tests. The points tally is even more remarkable considering Fagan's international career was limited to the years 1961 to 1965. He had to quit the game the following year because of a badly broken arm. Fagan made three overseas tours—two to England and France (1961 and 1965) and one to Australia (1963).

Olsen Filipaina see alphabetical entry

Gary Freeman see alphabetical entry

Mark Graham see alphabetical entry

Tom Hadfield

It became apparent that winger Tom Hadfield was destined to play for New Zealand when, at the age of 15, he was a national schoolboy representative. Not only did he make the Test scene, but he went on to become his country's leading try-scorer—with 15 touchdowns in 17 Tests. It was a record which stood for almost 30 years, until Hugh McGahan scored his 16th Test try in 1989. Hadfield represented Auckland for the first time in 1955 and toured Australia with the Kiwis 12 months later. He made his last international appearance in 1961. It was a great final year, for Hadfield was centre in the sides which held Australia to a drawn series, and also turned out for Auckland which beat the tourists 13–8.

Travers Hardwick

Not only was he one of the most brilliant locks New Zealand has known, but Trav Hardwick became a successful coach of New Zealand sides. He initially played first grade football, for Ponsonby in the Auckland competition, in 1944, and within two years had made his Test debut against the touring British Lions. Hardwick starred on the 1947 Kiwi tour of Britain and France and against Australia the following season. He reached his peak in the early 1950s. Critics agree that the finest of his 14 Tests was in 1951 when he made his only home appearance against France. Hardwick switched to halfback when Jim Haig was injured and turned in a blinder. In 1952, he capped a fine career by leading the Kiwis on their trip to Australia. The New Zealanders took home the Trans-Tasman Trophy. After retiring, Hardwick coached the Maori side which toured Australia in 1956 and, from 1957 to 1960, guided the Test teams. During that period New Zealand beat France and went down narrowly to Australia. Hardwick was also a Test selector from 1971 to 1975.

Kevin Iro see alphabetical entry

Cliff Johnson

Cliff Johnson was one of the most capped players in New Zealand Rugby League history. The big Auckland forward had played a record 33 Test and World Cup matches when he quit the international scene in 1960. It's a figure since topped by only two other players. He was captain of the Kiwis in 14 of those internationals (1957–60). He also skippered the Rest-of-the-World in an international against 1960 World Cup winners, Britain, and was a member of the Rest which played Australia after it won the 1957 Cup. Johnson also played in 36 minor games on two tours of Australia (1956 and 1959) and one tour of Britain and France (1951–52). Johnson would still have had all records but for missing the 1955–56 northern hemisphere tour because of business commitments. A big man, 1.83m (6ft) tall and weighing 100kg (15 stone 10 lb), Johnson was equally at home in either the second-row or at prop. His shrewd tactical brain was the equal of any of his era.

James Leuluai

One of the first of the modern Kiwis to put their talents to the test in British club football, James Leuluai was also one of the most successful. He joined Hull a year after touring Britain and France with the 1980 New

Zealand side and two years after making his Test debut against the 1979 British Lions. He went on to play in two Challenge Cup Finals at Wembley (and a replayed Final at Headingley, Leeds). Leuluai was on the winning side in 1982 (when Hull beat Widnes 18–9 in the replay), but had to be content with losers' medals in 1983 (beaten by Featherstone Rovers) and 1985 (going down to Wigan). The great centre had tremendous acceleration, an uncanny ability to find gaps in the defence and was a tough cover-defender. Many critics rate him as New Zealand's best ever centre. His 29 Tests between 1979 and 1986 put him among the 10 most-capped New Zealanders in history. In those matches he scored 14 tries—just two less than the record number by Hugh McGahan. Leuluai also played in 24 minor games for New Zealand on one tour of Australia and Papua New Guinea (1982) and two tours of Great Britain and France (1980 and 1985). In 1984, he scored tries in eight consecutive club games—a record for Hull. The crack centre also played with Leigh, Wakefield Trinity and Doncaster and, in the 1989–90 season, scored his 100th English try.

Graham Lowe see alphabetical entry

Jarrod McCracken see alphabetical entry

Hugh McGahan see alphabetical entry

George Menzies

Hardly any five-eighth could match George Menzies during the 1950s. He ruled the roost in a period which saw some notable opposition—including David Bolton (Britain), Jacques Merquey (France) and Brian Clay (Australia). Menzies was an expert in getting the New Zealand backline moving, and was also one of the great exponents of the dummy pass. Weighing just under 73kg (11 stone 7lbs), he was often plagued by injuries. However he still managed to play 69 games, including 28 Test and World Cup matches, for New Zealand. He made eight overseas trips—to three World Cup contests and with the Kiwi tourists to Australia (three times) and the Northern Hemisphere (twice). After he retired as a player, Menzies excelled as a coach of the New Zealand West Coast side and the Test line-up.

Cec Mountford

Some gifted players also have the knack of imparting their knowledge to youngsters following in their footsteps. Five-eighth Cec Mountford was one of those players. His name was a household word in Britain where, in two decades of club football, he won almost every honour he could hope for—then repeated these successes as a coach. Mountford left his home town of Blackball in New Zealand in 1946 to join the English club Wigan. He was to figure in two successful Challenge Cup campaigns (1948 and 1951) and two Championship-winning sides (1947 and 1950) while at Central Park. In the latter Cup and Championship wins he was Wigan's skipper. Mountford later coached Warrington to victory in seven major competitions, including the 1954 Cup-Championship double. In 1961, he returned to New Zealand where he was national coach and a top official for many years.

George Nepia

New Zealanders regard George Nepia as the greatest Rugby fullback of all time. The tough Maori was a Rugby Union legend when financial difficulties during the Depression persuaded him to join the London club Streatham and Mitcham. He received a £500 signing-on fee—a King's ransom in those days. Nepia was a country boy, having learned his football on the paddocks of Hawke's Bay. One of his tutors at agriculture college was an American who laid the groundwork for two of Nepia's greatest footballing skills, the torpedo kick for touch (based on the concept of an American gridiron pass) and the crash tackle (another feature of gridiron). He played just one international—a 1937 match against the Australian Kangaroos en route to Britain.

Dane O'Hara

Winger Dane O'Hara shares the record for the most number of Test and World Series games played by a New Zealander. Between 1977 and 1986, he played 35 Tests (14 v Australia; 12 v Great Britain; 6 v France and 3 v Papua New Guinea) and one World Championship game. It was in this game, against Australia in 1977, that the 23–year-old O'Hara made his international debut. His 14 tries in these major matches is only two less than the New Zealand record set by Hugh McGahan. O'Hara spent most of his best years in Britain with the Hull club. Three times he made a Wembley Cup Final appearance (1982, 1983 and 1985) but he was never on the winning side. In 1982, Hull drew with Widnes, but O'Hara missed the replay, which his side won.

Colin O'Neil

The football world has known few hookers who could strike as fast as Colin O'Neil. Rarely was he outhooked during his international career in the late 1960s, at a time when hooking was still a specialist art. Explained Lory Blanchard, Kiwi coach during this period: 'When O'Neil was hooker, the backs used to take winning scrums for granted'. O'Neil began in top-class football in 1961, at the age of 19, but had to wait until veteran Jock Butterfield went to Australia to play for Manly-Warringah before he could take over as Test rake. O'Neil made his Test debut, against Australia in 1985, and 40 internationals later (of which 21 were Test or World Cup appearances) wound up his career against the same country, in 1971. Business commitments forced an early retirement. The highlight of his career came in 1969 when he led underdogs New Zealand to an 18–14 win over Australia. That season he was named New Zealand Player-of-the-Year.

Phil Orchard

Phil Orchard is the most prolific international try-scorer in New Zealand history. The Bay of Plenty winger scored 40 tries in Test, World Series and tour games for the Kiwis. His 15 tries in full internationals is second only to Hugh McGahan's 16 and the total he scored on the 1971 tour of Britain and France (27) is likely to remain a record forever, in these days of shorter tours. Orchard made his Test debut against Australia in 1969. He bowed out of the international scene after the 1975 World Championships, having played 10 Tests and 11 World Series matches.

George Smith

A champion winger, George Smith toured Great Britain with the 1905 All Blacks Rugby Union side. He saw his first game of League there and, back home, helped launch the new code in New Zealand. In 1907, he and AH Baskerville organised the first overseas League tour. Smith was vice-captain of the All Golds who toured Australia and Britain. He went back to England to join the Oldham club and figured in one Challenge Cup (1912) and three Championship (1909, 1910 and 1911) finals. Some of his team-mates were the Australians Sid Deane and George Anlezark and British great Jim Lomas. The second and third Championship clashes were won by Oldham—and, in the Cup Final appearance against Dewsbury, Smith turned out in the forwards, a far cry from his heady days on the wing.

Bill Sorensen

A tough centre-cum-five-eighth, Bill Sorensen was one of the mainstays of the New Zealand side in the 1960s. The Auckland star first appeared in his country's colours on the 1951 Kiwi tour of Britain and France. He made another four overseas trips—to two World Cups, a tour of Australia and another visit to the Northern Hemisphere. The 1955–56 tour of Britain and France proved just how tough Sorensen was. He played in 33 of the 37 games. All told, Sorensen played 14 Tests (five against each of Australia and Great Britain and four versus France), seven World Cup matches and one game for the Rest-of-the-World against the 1957 World Cup winners, Australia, which was regarded by New Zealand authorities as a full international. He played another 50 minor games while on tour. Sorensen scored 25 tries while wearing New Zealand colours.

Dane Sorensen see alphabetical entry

Kurt Sorensen see alphabetical entry

Lance Todd

Several of the New Zealanders who toured Britain with A H Baskerville's first team, in 1907, returned to play club football in England. Arguably the best of these was centre Lance Todd. He signed with Wigan in 1908

Lance Todd, the New Zealander who established himself as one of the greats of English club football

and, in the next five seasons, appeared in one Challenge Cup and four Championship finals. Todd became even better known as a BBC Rugby League commentator. He was killed in a car accident while returning home from a match at Oldham in 1942. Four years later, a trophy was established in his memory. The Lance Todd Trophy is awarded to the Man-of-the-Match in each year's Wembley Cup Final (for list of winners, see under Great Britain alphabetical entry).

Des White

The most prolific pointscorer in New Zealand international football was Des White. In a six-year stint on the international scene, the Auckland fullback notched a record 467 points (seven tries and 223 goals) in 61 games for his country, including 132 (two tries and 63 goals) in his 21 Test appearances. White made his Test debut in 1950 and achieved his greatest success two years later, on the first of two tours of Australia (the other was in 1956). He scored 107 points, to become the first and only Kiwi to top the century on such a tour. In the three Tests he booted 18 goals to equal the record set by French genius Puig Aubert 12 months before—and in the Second Test, in Brisbane, White landed 11 goals from 15 attempts—a world record which still stands.

Dennis Williams

Dennis Williams was destined to rewrite the New Zealand record books. In 1971, a day after his 18th birthday, he scored a dazzling try the first time he handled the ball in a Test—sparking the Kiwis from an eight-point deficit to victory over Britain, at Salford. The centre/five-eighth was to go on to play in 32 Test and World Series matches, including a record 29 in succession. He played against Australia 11 times, Great Britain and

431

France eight times each, England and Wales each twice and Papua New Guinea once. His last Test appearance was against the touring French side in 1981. When he retired only the great Jock Butterfield had played more full internationals for New Zealand.

NICKNAMES

It has become a tradition in Rugby League for footballers to give nicknames to team-mates. Almost from the day a new player joins a club, a nickname will be bestowed. Some are very clever, others quite crude. Many, like the nickname given to the 1930s footballer Edwin Brown would not be acceptable today. He was called 'Nigger'. Strangely enough it wasn't because of the colour of his skin—it was because Brown was always snappily dressed with highly polished brown shoes. The colour of the boot polish used on his shoes was 'Nigger Brown'.

Some of the Better-known Nicknames of those in the Football World

Abdul	Ian Walsh
Albert	Craig Young
Alf	Allan Langer
(The) Arrow	Tommy Ryan
(The) Axe	Trevor Gillmeister
Baa-Baa	Terry Lamb
Babe	Eddie Collins
Bandy	Don Adams
(The) Bear	Bob O'Reilly
Bert	Brett Kenny
Biscuits	Frank Stanton
Blocker	Steve Roach
Boller	Arthur Francis
Boxer	Charlie Russell
Bozo	Bob Fulton
Brandy	Greg Alexander
Bumper	Frank Farrell
Cement	David Gillespie
Changa	Graeme Langlands, Bill Schultz
Chow	John Hayes
Chic	Les Cowie
Chicka	John Ferguson, Brian Moore
Chicken George	Mal Meninga
Chimpy	Joe Busch
Chook	Charles Fraser, Johnny Raper
Chunky	Frank Burge
(The) Crow	Mick Cronin
Crusher	Noel Cleal
Dallas	John Donnelly
Dealer	Harry Wells
ET	Andrew Ettingshausen
Fatty	Paul Vautin
Firpo	Fred Neumann
Fletcher	Roy Christian
Golden Boot	Keith Barnes
(The) Grasshopper	Barry Gomersall
Guru	Eric Grothe
Hollywood	Greg Hartley
Horse	Bryan Niebling
Hoss	John Cartwright
Jersey	Harry Flegg, Larry O'Malley
Jethro	Geoff Gerard
Junior	Wayne Pearce
Killer	Ken Kearney
King Wally	Wally Lewis
Knocker	Steve Norton

Some of the Better-known Nicknames of those in the Football World

(The) Little Maestro	Roger Millward
(The) Little Master	Clive Churchill
Mongo	Ken Irvine
(The) Master	Dally Messenger
(The) Mayor of Parramatta	Ken Thornett
(The) Moose	Rex Mossop
Mr Perpetual Motion	Ray Price
Muppet	Mark Murray
Nigger	Edwin Brown
Pony- Arthur Halloway	
Poppa	Brian Clay
Punchy	Gordon Clifford
Puff the Magic Dragon	Reg Gasnier
Rambo	Ron Gibbs
Rocket	Rod Reddy
Rowdy	Dale Shearer
(The) Sergeant Major	Eric Clay
Skinny	Frank McMillan
Slippery	Steve Morris
Sludge	Steve Rogers
Smacker	Alf Blair
Snowy	Arthur Justice
Sparkles	Mark McGaw
Sticks	Norm Provan
Stumpy	Edgar Newham
(The) Toowoomba Ghost	Eric Harris
Towser	Jack Barnett
Wacka	Johnny Graves
Whip	Reg Latta
Whiz	Steve Martin
(The) Wild Bull of the Pampas	Vince Karalius
Wombat	Graham Eadie
Yappy	Keith Holman
Zip Zip	Steve Ella
Zorba	Peter Peters

BRYAN NIEBLING

Thirteen Tests for Australia (1984–87). Also played five minor games on one Kangaroo tour (1986).

Second-rower Bryan Niebling showed his potential on Queensland's trail-blazing tour of Britain in 1983. Affectionately known to team-mates as - 'Horse', Niebling galloped through the British defences with his powerful, long-striding runs. The following year, the star from the Brisbane club Redcliffe made his Test debut against the touring British Lions. He was to go on to play a total of 13 Tests in just three years, highlighted by the unbeaten run with the Kangaroos through Britain and France in 1986.

After playing against New Zealand in 1987, Niebling was one of several locals to join the Brisbane Broncos for their first season in the Sydney Premiership. He was plagued by injuries and a loss of form, and in 1989 accepted an offer to play with English Second Division club Hull Kingston Rovers. He was an instant success and helped the club gain promotion for the 1990–91 season.

NISSAN SEVENS

Sevens football has for many years been a feature of Rugby Union, where the Hong Kong Sevens draws top-flight teams from around the world. It caught on in the early 1980s in British Rugby League circles before Australia finally took the plunge in 1988, with a seven-a-side competition introduced as a curtain-raiser to the Premiership.

South Sydney won that first Nissan Sevens, thanks largely to a sensational display by Phil Blake, who scored 62 points in Souths' three 14–minute games, including an incredible 26 in the semi-final, in which the Rabbitohs beat Penrith 46–20. The popularity of the one-day tournament skyrocketed. And, in 1991, some 29 293 fans jammed Parramatta Stadium to see the 16 sides battle it out. It was a ground record, 2050 more than the previous best.

In 1992, the NSWRL decided to expand the competition and invited teams from overseas, including the winners of the 1991 World Club Challenge, Wigan, the fledgling Soviet Union, and Rugby Union strongholds South Africa and Western Samoa.

Winners of the Nissan Sevens

1988	———	South Sydney
1989	———	Balmain
1990	———	Manly-Warringah
1991	———	Newcastle

Sevens Records

Most points in a match: 26 by Phil Blake (South Sydney) v Penrith, 1988 (3 tries & 7 goals)
Most tries in a match: 4 by Mark Ross (Gold Coast) v Cronulla–Sutherland, 1988
Most points in a tournament: 62 by Phil Blake (South Sydney), 1988 (8 tries & 15 goals)
Most tries in a tournament: 8 by Phil Blake (South Sydney), 1988

ERNIE NORMAN

Twelve Tests for Australia (1932–37). Also played 21 minor games on one Kangaroo tour (1937–38) and one New Zealand tour (1935).

Ernie Norman

Injury cost Ernie Norman dearly. The 21–year-old was unquestionably the best five-eighth in Australia when it came time for the 1933–34 Kangaroo side to tour Britain. However, badly torn ligaments which had earlier ruled him out of interstate clashes, forced him to withdraw from the Kangaroo squad. Norman was given his chance to visit England four years later and was one of the stars of the Kangaroo side, playing in 21 of the 25 matches.

He also visited New Zealand twice, once with his club side Eastern Suburbs (in 1931) and again with the Australian team (in 1935). He also turned out in 12 Tests in five different series (seven Tests versus Great Britain and five against the Kiwis).

With Easts, he appeared in three different Premiership-winning sides (1935, 1936 and 1937), scoring a try in Easts 32–12 success over Balmain to win the second of those titles.

NORTH ISLAND (NEW ZEALAND) TOUR OF QUEENSLAND—

New Zealand's North Island made a short tour of Queensland in 1968. The side, led by Kiwi skipper Bruce Castle, was a good one with most tourists being either past or future Test or World Series players.

Record in Queensland

Played 4, Won 3, Lost 1, Points for 93, Points against 56

Match results

Opponents	Venue (Attendance)	For	Against
Ipswich	Ipswich (750)	36	11
Wide Bay	Maryborough (1035)	20	16
Central Queensland	Rockhampton (2216)	20	21
South Queensland	Brisbane (2212)	17	8

Individual Records

	Matches	Tries	Goals	Points
H Tatana	4	3	15	39
R Mincham	4	5	—	15
W White	3	5	—	15
E Baker	4	3	—	9
B Castle (c)	3	2	—	6
E Wiggs	2	—	3	6
R Sinel	3	1	—	3

Also toured: D Ellwood (3 matches), R Tait (4), E Carson (4), A Kriletich (4), E Moore (3), L Morgan (3), D Parkinson (4), P Schultz (3), V Yates (3), G Woollard (1)

NORTH SYDNEY—————————————————————

North Sydney fans have had to put up with a lot of ribbing over the years. Indeed, in the 1980s, the club's continual poor performances spawned a series of unkind jokes such as 'Did you hear about the Irish burglar? He broke into Norths' trophy room!'. But unfortunately Norths has a pretty ordinary record in the Sydney Premiership competition. It was one of the founder clubs, back in 1908, but more than eight decades later North Sydney had won only two titles (in 1921 and 1922). The side which took out those two Premierships is, however, regarded by critics as one of the best club combinations ever.

Duncan Thompson, the halfback, was the brains behind the side. Outside him were five-eighth Dallas Hodgins (considered unlucky not to have been chosen for the 1921–22 Kangaroo side which toured Britain), international centres Frank Rule and Herman Peters and the immortal wingers Harold Horder and Cec Blinkhorn. All four of the three-quarters were chosen for the 1921–22 tour and Horder and Blinkhorn topped the Kangaroo pointscoring. Horder headed the list with 127 points, from 35 tries and 11 goals. Blinkhorn was second with 117 points from 39 tries (still a

Kangaroo touchdown record). Incidentally, Thompson made it a great visit for the Norths lads by finishing fourth in the overall scoring, with 107 points (three tries and 49 goals).

Horder and Blinkhorn were no less prolific with North Sydney. In 1922, they scored 37 tries between them—a record for a pair of club wingers. Next year, Horder scored 17 tries and 50 goals in Norths' 17 games while Blinkhorn went over for 20 tries. Norths had another great winger in the late 1950s and 1960s, Ken Irvine. He came through Norths' junior ranks and went on to break club and international records. Irvine was the greatest try-scorer Australian football has known. When he finished representative football he was only four short of becoming the first man to score a century of tries for Australia in all matches. He scored more in Tests than any other footballer (31)—and he led the try-scoring lists against each of his era's other League playing nations: 12 against Britain (in only nine matches), nine against New Zealand, six against France and four against South Africa. Irvine's final club tally of 169 is a Norths' record.

The club can be considered unlucky not to have had at least one other Premiership to its credit. In 1943, Norths had a fine lineup and was favourite for the title. Just before the end of the season however, two key players, fullback Neville Butler and lock Harry Taylor, went off to fight in World War II. Butler was killed in action. Norths, captained by Frank Hyde, who later became a top radio commentator, sorely missed the stars and Newtown, which had failed to win any of its five earlier clashes with Norths that year, managed to carry off the grand final 34–7.

Norths fans got a short burst of adrenalin in the mid-1960s. After five years with Wigan, the fine South African fullback, Fred Griffiths, accepted a lucrative offer to become Norths' captain-coach. He was an instant success. In 1963, he took Norths from last to fifth, the following year to the semi-finals for the first time in 10 years and in 1965 to the preliminary final.

After facing severe financial crises in the early 1980s, Norths eventually took on a new lease of life. The famous North Sydney Oval was upgraded, without losing the traditional architectural style of the early 20th Century— and as the nineties dawned a new administration took over, led by the head of the ABC and former chief of the NSW Railways, David Hill. With ex-Kangaroo Steve Martin as coach, several young stars emerged from within the Norths' ranks including five-eighth Jason Martin (Rookie-of-the-Year in the 1990 Dally M Awards) and second-rower David Fairleigh. With the help of the first Players' Draft, the ranks were bolstered by several experienced players, centre Peter Jackson, hooker Mario Fenech and utility back Phil Blake, for the 1991 season.

And it all paid off. From a side which had been the butt of jokes from fans of opposing sides. Norths emerged as Premiership contenders. Jackson regained his Test spot, while Fairleigh and lock Greg Larson represented in the State-of-Origin series, too. And the Bears finished third on the competition table, their first taste of semi-final football in almost a decade. Another find of 1991 was former New Zealand Rugby Union winger Daryl Halligan, who topped the season's pointscoring charts with 196 points (13 tries and 72 goals).

NORTH SYDNEY

Founded: 1908
Entered Sydney Premiership competition: 1908
Home ground: North Sydney Oval (Record crowd—22 037)
Colours: Black and red
Nickname: The Bears
Honours:
  Sydney Premiership—Winners, 1921, 1922; Runners-up, 1943
  City Cup—1920, 1922
  Reserve-grade Premiership—1940, 1942, 1955, 1959, 1989, 1991
  League Cup—1914
  Third-grade Premiership—1937, 1945, 1946, 1959
  President's Cup—1918, 1933
Most games in a career: 210 by Norm Strong
Most points in a career: 681 by Alan Arkey
Most tries in a career: 169 by Ken Irvine
Most points in a season: 196 by Daryl Halligan, in 1991
Most tries in a season: 20 by Cec Blinkhorn, in 1922
Rothmans Medal winners: Nil
Sun-Herald Best-and-Fairest Player: Jim Gillon (1952), Brian Carlson (1961)

O

OCEANIA

Australia, New Zealand and Papua New Guinea combined to form an Oceania team for a one-off match in 1984 against Europe (Britain and France) to celebrate the 50th anniversary of the start of Rugby League in France. The Oceania team played in a royal blue jumper sporting a yellow Southern Cross and was coached by Kiwi mentor Graham Lowe. Europe was in the hands of French coaching chief Louis Bonnery. One of the Australians chosen, Craig Young, missed out on the match because he found out his passport was out of date the day before he was due to leave for Paris. His place was taken by Brad Tessmann. Oceania, with six Australians, won easily 54–4 before a disappointing crowd of about 2000, running in 11 tries to one.

At Stade de la Cipalle Velodrome, Paris, Saturday, 14 April 1984
Crowd: 2000
OCEANIA 54 (Tessmann 2, Miles 2, McGahan 2, Alfield, Mortimer, Boustead, Graham, Togila tries, Meninga, H Tamati,Boustead, Togila, K Tamati goals) d EUROPE 4 (Hanley try)
Oceania: Robin Alfeld (NZ), Kerry Boustead (Aust), Mal Meninga (Aust), Gene Miles (Aust), Dean Bell (NZ), Wally Lewis (Aust) (c), Steve Mortimer (Aust), Ray Price (Aust), Mark Graham (NZ), Wayne Pearce (Aust), Brad Tessmann (Aust), Howie Tamati (NZ), Kevin Tamati (NZ). Replacements: Shane Varley (NZ), Hugh McGahan (NZ), David Noifa (PNG) and Ekon Togila (PNG)
Europe: Patrick Wosniack (Fr), Patrick Solal (Fr), Phillippe Fourquet (Fr), Ellery Hanley (GB), Des Drummond (GB), Andre Perez (Fr), Ray Ashton (GB), Joel Roosebrouck (Fr) (c), Guy Lafforge (Fr), Mick Worrall (GB), Dominique Baloup (Fr), Thierry Bernabe (Fr), Max Chantal (Fr). Replacements: Des Foy (GB), Steve Fenwick (GB) and Patrick Trinque (Fr). Tommy David (GB) was chosen as a replacement but was injured in training
Referee: Julien Rascagnares (France)

MARTIN OFFIAH

Twenty Tests for Great Britain (1988–1991). Also played for Great Britain against the Rest-of-the-World (1988) and 10 minor games for on one tour of Australasia and Papua New Guinea (1988) and one New Zealand tour (1990).

There has been no more exciting a player in the modern era than winger Martin Offiah. A 21-year old London-born speedster of Nigerian parents, he burst upon the scene during the 1987–88 season, scoring 44 tries for

Widnes. It was the best by anyone in the Championship. He was top-scorer the next three seasons, too, with 60, 45 and 49 apiece.

Offiah was a sensation on the 1988 Lions tour of Australasia, scoring 19 tries in his 13 tour appearances. By 1992, he had made another three trips down under. The first, in 1989, was to play for Eastern Suburbs in the Sydney Premiership competition. In what was a disappointing season for the Roosters, Offiah topped the club try-scoring lists, with nine touchdowns in his 13 matches. Offiah was back in the Southern Hemisphere a year later with the Lions. He joined them after the Papua New Guinea leg of the tour, when he had recovered from an injury, and played in the three New Zealand Tests. And he was in the British lineup which gave the Kangaroos a real shock later that year.

His most recent visit was in 1991. For a while he appeared to have priced himself out of the Sydney club market. But finally, St George signed him for half the season. He was an instant success, scoring in each of his first eight matches, including three tries against his old club, Easts. He finished the Premiership year with 11 tries. Before joining the Saints, Offiah had run rampant against France. In his 20th Test, at Headingley, he went over for five tries.

But as the 1991–92 British season began, Offiah was in conflict with his club, Widnes and, in a bitter war of words, even threatened to leave Rugby League altogether to pursue a career in American Football.

WALLY O'CONNELL

Ten Tests for Australia (1948–51). Also played 19 minor games on one Kangaroo tour (1948–49) and one New Zealand tour (1949).

When the great Pat Devery was lured to Britain just after World War II, there was another fine young player waiting to step into his shoes—Eastern Suburbs five-eighth Wally O'Connell. The short, chunky stand-off lost nothing by comparison with Devery. O'Connell was sharp in attack and a master of the blindside play. He had starred in the Easts' side which had carried off the 1945 Sydney Premiership, beating Balmain 22–18 in the final.

O'Connell made his Test debut against the touring New Zealanders in 1948 and in the next three years represented his country against all Rugby League nations (four times against the Kiwis and three times each against France and Great Britain). He was later to play in Wollongong before returning to Sydney as captain-coach of Manly-Warringah, which he took to its first grand final since entering the competition. However that 1951 side, with an injured O'Connell watching from the sideline, was humbled 42–14 by a great South Sydney combination.

MICHAEL O'CONNOR

Sixteen Tests for Australia (1986–1989). Also played in 1988 World Cup final, for the Rest-of-the-World against Great Britain (1988) and 15 minor games on one Kangaroo tour (1986) and two New Zealand tours (1985 and 1989).

In a period of just 10 weeks in late 1986, Michael O'Connor virtually rewrote the Rugby League Test record books, notching point-scoring records against

Michael O'Connor

two of the major nations and equalling the top figure against a third. O'Connor, a member of the Kangaroo touring squad, scored a record 22 points (two tries and seven goals) against Papua-New Guinea and 22 points (three tries and five goals) against Great Britain. And his 20 points (three tries and four goals) equalled the previous best against France. In eight Test matches during 1986, O'Connor scored an incredible 116 points (at an average of 14 a match). The other nation involved was New Zealand.

The pointscoring wizard was a champion Rugby Union three-quarter before top Sydney club St George lured him into the professional game. He was a schoolboy star while playing for Phillip College in the ACT. He topped the pointscoring for the Australian schoolboys side, nicknamed 'The Invincibles', which toured Britain, Europe and Japan in 1977–78, scoring 78 points in 12 matches. He was also top pointscorer on the four-match tour of New Zealand two years later. He made his Rugby Union Test debut in 1979 as an 18–year-old. In the next three years as a lilywhite, he was capped 13 times (against Argentina, Fiji, New Zealand, France, England, Ireland, Wales and Scotland).

O'Connor took a couple of years to hit the top in League (playing only 21 games in the first two years and scoring 76 points for St George). However once he made it into the representative sides in 1985 there was no stopping him. He was chosen in the Australian team to tour New Zealand later that year (scoring a try in his first game in the green and gold and nine goals in the last match of the tour). Just before the 1986 Kangaroo tourists flew out for Britain, O'Connor accepted a huge offer to switch clubs, to Manly-Warringah. Manly would probably have had to pay much more if it had waited until after the tour. As well as the Test records, O'Connor topped the tour listings with 170 points in 13 matches. His tally for 1986 was 380 points (210 for Australia, 24 for New South Wales, 18 for City and 128 for St George). In 1988, O'Connor set even more pointscoring records. He scored a world-record 30 Test points in an international against Papua-New Guinea, at Wagga Wagga. His four tries and seven goals helped Australia to a record 70–8 victory.

O'Connor toured New Zealand again in 1989, but an injury late in the 1990 season, aggravated during the final five Premiership play-offs, cost him a certain second Kangaroo tour.

LARRY 'JERSEY' O'MALLEY

Five Tests for Australia (1908–09). Also played 31 minor games on one Kangaroo tour (1908–09).

Rugged Eastern Suburbs forward Jersey O'Malley was one of the pioneer stars of Australian Rugby League. He was a member of the Easts side which played in the very first club match, when it beat Newtown 32–16 on 20 April 1908. At the end of that season he was one of the first chosen in the first Kangaroo side to tour Britain. O'Malley was a tower of strength on that visit, playing in 34 of the 46 matches—more than any of his team-mates. Indeed, eight decades later, it stands as a record for a Kangaroo tourist and will never be beaten, as tours are now restricted to about 15 games.

The tough forward was twice sent from the field by referees on that pioneering visit, both times at Wigan—first against Lancashire and later against the club itself. On the first occasion he was exonerated, a victim of mistaken identity—but he received a one-match suspension for the second dismissal. Back in Sydney, O'Malley was a member of the Easts' sides which won three straight Premierships in 1911, 1912 and 1913.

JOHN O'NEILL

Two Tests for Australia (1973–74). Also played seven matches in two World Cups (1970 and 1972), one match in one World Championship (1975) and five minor games on one Kangaroo tour (1973).

The Australian record crowd of 78 056 which watched the 1965 Sydney Premiership grand final were not just watching the great St George machine grind to yet another in its unprecedented successes. They were also witnessing the birth of a great pack of South Sydney forwards. One of them was 21–year-old prop John O'Neill. However it was to be five years before the Australian selectors realised just what a great player he was. O'Neill had to wait until the end of the 1970 season before he was considered good enough to wear the green and gold for his country. Even then, it was only an outstanding display in Souths' 23–12 demolition job on Manly-Warringah in that year's grand final that won him the spot in the World Cup squad. He grabbed his opportunity with both hands. He was one of the stars of the team which won the Cup, playing through all but five minutes of the final against Britain with a gash in his ankle so deep that it was almost to the bone.

O'Neill was also one of the mainstays of the Australian line–up in the unlucky defence of the Cup in France two years later. He was laid low by injury during the 1973 Kangaroo tour of Britain and France, playing in only six matches, including one Test against the Frenchmen. A lone Test against the touring 1974 British Lions and a game against Wales in the World Championship the following year rounded off O'Neill's international career.

For Souths, he was a tower of strength, especially in the Rabbitohs' Premiership-winning sides of 1967, 1968, 1970 and 1971. A year after the last Souths' success, O'Neill switched to Manly-Warringah where he helped in the Sea Eagles Premiership wins of 1972 and 1973, to bring his record to six Premierships in seven years.

BOB O'REILLY

Nine Tests for Australia (1971-74). Also played seven matches in two World Cups (1970 and 1972), one minor international (1970) and 11 minor games on one Kangaroo tour (1973) and one New Zealand tour (1971).

They called Bob O'Reilly 'The Bear'. It was an apt name for a man who, in his prime, was the best front-row forward in the world. His bear-like rushes left many an opponent bruised and battered.

Bob O'Reilly

O'Reilly showed early promise at the age of 16, when he was dux of the NSW Coaching School of 1966. He made Parramatta's first-grade side a year later. It was the start of what, at the time, was the most successful career in the history of Sydney club football. In 1982, O'Reilly played his 300th grade game. Only weeks before he had eclipsed the first-grade record of St George great Norm Provan (265). Most of O'Reilly's matches had been in the Parramatta colours, but 34 games were with Penrith and another 38 with Eastern Suburbs.

The top prop made his first international appearance in the 1970 World Cup Series in England. He later played nine Tests (five against Britain, three against New Zealand and one versus France). The highlight of his international career was the 1973 Kangaroo tour of Britain and France when he played a major role in Australia's comeback to win the Ashes series. However nothing was as satisfying as Parramatta's 1981 Premiership success. O'Reilly, who had twice tasted grand final defeat in his 15 years of club football, wept openly after the Eels beat Newtown 20–11 to take out the Sydney title.

KEL O'SHEA

Fifteen Tests for Australia (1954–58). Also played five matches in two World Cups (1954 and 1957), one international against the Rest-of-the-World (1957) and eight minor games on one Kangaroo tour (1956–57).

Kel O'Shea figured with Norm Provan as one of the greatest second-row combinations in the history of the game. Tall and rangy, like his partner, O'Shea was a rugged attacker and a fine cover-defender. For a man so large, he was also fast. He first made his mark in Queensland (with Ayr Colts), from where he was called into the Australian line–up to team with Provan against the 1954 British Lions touring side. Over the following four years they played together against every major Rugby League nation. All told, O'Shea played 15 Tests (nine against Great Britain and three each against New Zealand and France).

After missing the 1955 Tests against the touring Frenchmen through injury, O'Shea moved south to join Sydney's Western Suburbs club, which spent big money for established stars to bolster a side languishing at the bottom of the competition table. The Wests' team was nicknamed 'The Millionaires' because of the money spent. O'Shea proved to be a good buy and had many memorable clashes with Provan, who captained Wests' arch-rival, St George. O'Shea played in two grand finals (1958 and 1960), but on both occasions the mighty St George machine triumphed over his club.

OTHER NATIONALITIES

Other Nationalities was the name given to the sides of Australians, New Zealanders and South Africans who played in the International Championship (against England, Wales and France) between 1949 and 1955. Those in the Other Nationalities sides were all attached to English clubs. Australians who starred included Trevor Allan, Harry Bath, Brian Bevan, Arthur Clues, Lionel Cooper, Pat Devery and Tony Paskins. Other

Nationalities won the International Championship twice (in 1953 and 1955), and it won 14 of the 24 games it played.

In Australia, an Other Nationalities side was gathered for a once-only match against Sydney Colts, as a curtain-raiser to the Third Test between Australia and the 1964 French touring side. It had been hoped that the clash would bolster the attendance, hit by the Frenchmen's poor form. The Other Nationalities side included two of the French tourists, who had not managed to make the Test XIII. The Colts won the match 25–16. The Other Nationalities line–up was: Fred Griffiths (captain-coach, from South Africa), Mike Jackson (England), Derek Hallas (England), Fred Pickup (England), Col Greenwood (South Africa), Lewis Jones (Wales), Ivor Lingard (England), Roger Pearman (England), Dick Huddart (England), Michel Bardes (France), Nat Silcock (England), Jock Butterfield (New Zealand), Jean Pano (France). Replacement: Frank Halliwell (England).

ARTHUR OXFORD

Five Tests for Australia (1919–24). Also played one minor match on one New Zealand tour (1919).

Arthur Oxford played in only a handful of Test matches for Australia, but the tough forward was a much better footballer than this would indicate. Oxford was equally at home in the front or second-row. He played 203 first-grade games in the Sydney Premiership competition (118 for Eastern Suburbs and 85 for South Sydney) in the decade after World War I, and was a member of Easts' Premiership-winning side in 1923. He was a superb goalkicker and indeed, Harold Horder, one of the most prolific scorers of all time, used to play second-fiddle to Oxford when the pair turned out together for New South Wales.

On the 1919 tour of New Zealand, Arthur Oxford scored with 23 successive kicks for goal. This record stood for 59 years until bettered by Mick Cronin in the First Test against New Zealand in 1978—but Cronin's final tally of 26 without a miss included kicks taken in Sydney club matches. Oxford, in the latter of two Tests against Great Britain, played a major role in a face-saving Australian Third Test victory which prevented Britain making a clean-sweep of the 1924 Ashes series. Australia had been hanging on grimly to a three-point lead when, near the end of the match, its backline swept downfield. Winger Cec Aynsley was trapped and decided to short-kick over the opposition. Oxford burst through from an almost impossible position to gather and score—putting the match beyond any doubt.

P

PACIFIC CUP

The Pacific Cup was introduced in 1975 to provide international competition for the poor relations of Rugby League in the southern hemisphere. It was the brainchild of Keith Gittoes, then the assistant secretary of the NSW Rugby League. Papua New Guinea had been elected to the International Board of Rugby League the previous year—but it was not yet powerful enough to take on the four established countries. It's capital, Port Moresby was chosen as the venue for the inaugural contest. The others invited were the New Zealand Maoris and three of the weaker representative sides of Australia—Western Australia, Victoria and the Northern Territory. The Northern Territory had to drop out. A massive cyclone had devastated its capital, Darwin, the previous Christmas and halted all League. A capacity crowd of 14 000 saw the Maoris beat the local side in the final to become the first winners of the Pacific Cup.

The second contest was held in New Zealand at the end of the 1977 season. The Maoris again proved to be the best side, beating Western Australia in the final. The surprise of the tournament was the first-round defeat of Papua New Guinea by Western Australia. Only a few months before, Papua New Guinea had downed the French World Championship side in Port Moresby.

The competition went into limbo after 1977, but it was revived 11 years later, in Western Samoa. Once again the Maoris proved victorious. Former New Zealand Test star Olsen Filipaina played for Western Samoa and ex-St George forward John Fifita for Tonga.

A team of Australian Aborigines and Torres Strait Islanders joined the fray for the 1990 Cup, in Tonga. The side consisted mainly of young players, but was bolstered by three stars from the Sydney Premiership competition, Ron Gibbs (Gold Coast), Ricky Walford (St George) and Graham Lyons (South Sydney).

1975 Port Moresby, Papua New Guinea

Results

Western Australia	23	Victoria	21
New Zealand Maoris	41	Papua New Guinea	15
Papua New Guinea	15	Western Australia	13
New Zealand Maoris	61	Victoria	3
Papua New Guinea	38	Victoria	0
New Zealand Maoris	38	Western Australia	15

Final

New Zealand Maoris	38	Papua New Guinea	13

1977, New Zealand

Venue	Results			
Huntly	New Zealand Maoris	27	Northern Territory	10
Huntly	Western Australia	33	Papua New Guinea	19
Rotorua	Victoria	14	Western Australia	10
Rotorua	New Zealand Maoris	25	Papua New Guinea	17
Tokoroa	Papua New Guinea	25	Northern Territory	14
Tokoroa	New Zealand Maoris	78	Victoria	0
Huntly	Papua New Guinea	42	Victoria	12
Huntly	Western Australia	23	Northern Territory	16
Auckland	Northern Territory	33	Victoria	29
Auckland	New Zealand Maoris	28	Western Australia	4

Final

Auckland	New Zealand Maoris	35	Western Australia	12

1988, Apia, Western Samoa

Results

Cook Islands	19	Tokelau	10
Western Samoa	52	Cook Islands	16
Western Samoa	40	Tokelau	18
New Zealand Maoris	42	American Samoa	10
Tonga	38	American Samoa	14
New Zealand Maoris	42	Tonga	16

Semi-Finals

New Zealand Maoris	70	Cook Islands	20
Western Samoa	40	Tonga	30

Final

New Zealand Maoris	19	Western Samoa	16

1990, Nuku'alofa, Tonga

Preliminary Round points:

Group A—New Zealand Maoris, 6; Australian Aborigines, 4; Papua New Guinea, 2, Friendly Islands, 0
Group B—Western Samoa, 6, Tonga, 4; Tokelau, 2; Niue, 0

Semi-finals

Western Samoa	26	Australian Aborigines	16
New Zealand Maoris	32	Tonga	10

Final

Western Samoa	26	New Zealand Maoris	18

PANASONIC CUP see *Midweek Cup*

PAPUA NEW GUINEA

Rugby League in Papua New Guinea has progressed rapidly since its almost insignificant start in 1949. In July that year, the first competition kicked off with just two teams. One was drawn from public servants working in the capital, Port Moresby, for the Australian Department of Works, the other from banks, other business houses and an oil exploration company. The sides met each other six times in that first season. Later a flourishing competition developed with sides such as Brothers, Tigers, Hawks, Wests, Easts, Defence, DCA, Paga, Magani and Tarangau, taking part. Teams also sprang up in other areas.

In 1974, Papua New Guinea was admitted as the fifth country in the International Rugby League. It played its first international in 1975, when the English World Championship side stopped over in Port Moresby. England won easily, 40–12. Two years later, in its next international, Papua New Guinea fared much better, with a 37–6 win over France. Papua New Guinea made its first full tour of another Rugby League nation in 1979. It played matches in France and England and took part in its first Test matches, going down 15–9 and 16–2 to France.

Papua New Guinea knew it had arrived on the international scene when it drew the 1981 Test against the touring Frenchmen. Then in 1986 it scored its first win, beating New Zealand 24–22 at Port Moresby. In 1990, the locals were over the moon when the Test side beat Great Britain 20–18 at Goroka—but there were setbacks, too.

In 1988, Australia ran up a world record Test score when beating Papua New Guinea 70–8 at Wagga Wagga—and Queensland scored the biggest win in the history of Rugby League representative games in 1983 when it beat a President's XIII containing eight Papua New Guinea Test players 106–3 at Port Moresby. The previous biggest was Great Britain's 101–0 thrashing of South Australia in 1914. The Queensland score would almost certainly have been bigger had officials not called a halt to the Port Moresby match 12 minutes early, to save the locals further embarrassment.

As the 1990s dawned, Papua New Guinea was planning for an improvement in international form by the introduction of a strong local representative competition involving the Port Moresby Vipers, Mt Hagen Eagles, Lae Bombers, Goroka Lahanis and Kundiawa Warriors. (See also *Kumuls*)

GALLERY OF PNG GREATS

Dairi Kovae

Utility back Dairi Kovae was one of the most spectacular of Papua New Guinea's players when the young country began a major assault on the international scene in the 1980s. He was equally at home at fullback, centre or on the wing, where he was chosen as the Kumuls' only representative in the 1988 Bicentennial international between Australia and the Rest-of-the-World. He made his Test debut in 1986 and, by 1991, had appeared in nine Tests (four against New Zealand, two each against Australia and Britain and one versus France), and was his nation's leading try-scorer with five. He had a short Australian spell with North Sydney.

Bal Numapo

The most capped player in Papua New Guinea, Kundiawa three-quarter Bal Numapo is also its top Test scorer with 51 points from four tries, 17 goals and one field goal in his 14 internationals (six against New Zealand, five versus Great Britain, two against Australia and one against France).

Numapo was also a member of the Rest-of-the-World side which took on Great Britain at Headingley, Leeds, in 1988. He made his Test debut on the tour of Britain in 1984 and in 1987, 1988 and 1990 captained his country. Numapo spent one season in Sydney with Canterbury-Bankstown (1989) but failed to play first-grade.

AUSTRALIA V PAPUA NEW GUINEA

Test Matches

1982
At Lloyd Robson Oval, Port Moresby, Saturday, 25 September 1982.
Crowd: 15 000
AUSTRALIA 38 (Ribot 4, Brentnall 2, Meninga, Rogers, Boustead, Kenny tries, Meninga 4 goals) d PAPUA NEW GUINEA 2 (Kungas Kuveu goal)
Australia: G Brentnall, J Ribot, M Meninga, S Rogers, K Boustead, B Kenny, S Mortimer, R Price, J Muggleton, R Reddy, C Young, M Krilich (c), R Hancock. Replacements: M Murray and R Brown
Papua New Guinea: K Kuveu, A Rero, I Segeyaro, J Yip, D Timi, J Joseph, A Kababas, R Loitivi, L Tete, A Taumako, J Tep, O Asotau, T Gau, Replacements: F Matmillo and E Togili

1986
At Lloyd Robson Oval, Port Moresby, Saturday, 4 October 1986
Crowd: 17 000
AUSTRALIA 62 (Kiss 2, O'Connor 2, Cleal 2, Mortimer, Jack, Lindner, Roach, Hasler, Lewis tries, O'Connor 7 goals) d PAPUA NEW GUINEA 12 (Numapo 2 tries, Kovae 2 goals)
Australia: G Jack, M O'Connor, G Miles, C Mortimer, L Kiss, W Lewis (c), D Hasler, R Lindner, N Cleal, P Dunn, B Niebling, R Simmons, S Roach. Replacements: M Meninga and P Sironen
Papua New Guinea: D Kovae, J Katsir, L Atoi, B Numapo, M Kerekere, D Haili, T Kila (c), A Taumaku, B Waketsi, B Ako, A Lumutopa, R Heni, J Tep. Replacements: K Saea and N Andy
Referee: N Kesha (New Zealand)

1988
At Eric Weissel Oval, Wagga Wagga, Wednesday, 20 July 1988
Crowd: 11 685
AUSTRALIA 70 (O'Connor 4, Langer 2, Meninga 2, Jack, Lewis, Currie, Fullerton Smith, Miller, Conescu tries, O'Connor 7 goals) d PAPUA NEW GUINEA 8 (Morea try, Numapo 2 goals)
Australia: G Jack, M O'Connor, M Meninga, P Jackson, T Currie, W Lewis (c), A Langer, W Pearce, G Miller, W Fullerton Smith, P Daley, G Conescu, P Dunn. Replacements: D Hasler (for Lewis) and P Vautin (for Fullerton Smith)
Papua New Guinea: I Wanega, A Krewanty, D Kovae, B Numapo (c), M Morea, L Atoi, D Haili, J Gispe, T Evai, M Kombra, D Ben-Moide, M Matmillo, T Rombuk. Replacements: A Kuno (for Kombra) and S Karara (for Gispe)
Referee: N Kesha (New Zealand)

1991

First Test
At Danny Leahy Oval, Goroka, Sunday, October 6, 1991.
Crowd: 13 000
AUSTRALIA 58 (Wishart 3, Carne 3, Fittler 2, Ettingshausen 2, Lyons, Roberts tries, Belcher 5 goals) d PAPUA NEW GUINEA 2 (Wanega goal).
Australia: G Belcher, R Wishart, A Ettingshausen, M Meninga (c), W Carne, C Lyons, G Toovey, B Fittler, I Roberts, B Clyde, G Lazarus, Kerrod Walters, M Bella. Replacements: C Johns (for Ettingshausen), Kevin Walters (for Toovey), G Coyne (for Bella) and S Gourley (for Lazarus).
Papua New Guinea: I Wanega, L Palangat, C Itan, R Wagambie, K Sinemau, S Haru (c), S Karara, J Gispe, T Daki, M Tiri, D Ben Moide, D Moi, J Unagi. Replacements: J Kourou (for Wagambie), N Lapan (for Unagi), J Naipao (for Wanega) and K Paglipari (for Ben Moide).
Referee: D Hale (New Zealand)

Second Test
At Loyd Robson Oval, Port Moresby, Sunday, October 13, 1991.
Crowd: 14 500
AUSTRALIA 40 (Carne 3, Belcher, Ettingshausen, Jackson, Meninga, Wishart, Clyde tries, Meninga 2 goals) d PAPUA NEW GUINEA 6 (Haru try, Boge goal)
Australia: G Belcher, R Wishart, A Ettingshausen, M Meninga (c), W Carne, P Jackson, G Toovey, B Fittler, I Roberts, B Clyde, G Lazarus, Kerrod Walters, M Bella. Replacements: C Johns (for Wishart), C Lyons (for Jackson), Kevin Walters (for Kerrod Walters) and G Coyne (for Bella).
Papua New Guinea: P Boge, L Palangat, K Sinemau, R Wagambie, J Kouoru, S Haru (c), S Karara, J Gispe, K Paglipari, T Daki, J Naipao, D Moi, J Unagi. Replacements: N Kera (for Moi), N Lapan (for Daki), J Uradok (for Palangat) and L Hoffman (for Gispe).
Referee: D Hale (New Zealand)

DON PARISH

Three Tests for Australia (1961–62). Also played 17 minor games on one Kangaroo tour (1959–60) and one New Zealand tour (1961).

Don Parish made only three Test appearances, largely because he had the misfortune to be playing at the same time as several other accomplished stars. A utility back, he had to compete for Australian guernseys as a winger with players such as Eddie Lumsden, Ken Irvine, Brian Carlson and Peter Dimond and as a fullback with Keith Barnes. Parish made two international tours—to England and France with the 1959–60 Kangaroos and to New Zealand in 1961. On the latter trip, he was leading scorer with 58 points (four tries and 23 goals) in seven matches. In 1962 Parish appeared in the home series against Britain.

He was also a successful coach. While still playing, he steered Wollongong Western Suburbs to two Illawarra Premierships, in the days before the Steelers tried their luck in the Sydney competition. After he hung up his boots, he coached the Illawarra representative side to victory in the NSW Country Championships. Parish also had spells with two Sydney clubs. He lifted Western Suburbs (his old Sydney club) from wooden-spooners to the preliminary final in 1974 and won the Coach-of-the-Year award. However he failed to perform similar miracles with Penrith, who remained firmly near the foot of the Premiership table.

PARRAMATTA

It took years of pressure to persuade the Rugby League hierarchy that Parramatta was worthy of a place in the Sydney Premiership competition. Parramatta had a strong junior League when, in 1936, a group of supporters banded together and approached the NSW Rugby League to ask that their district be allowed to contend for the major title. Western Suburbs would have lost a lot of its territory if Parramatta had been given the go-ahead—and out Parramatta way were some fine up-and-coming youngsters who would be lost by Wests. Even so, the Magpies supported Parramatta in its application. Unfortunately for the fans out west, the other clubs did not and the application was dismissed. World War II came and went before the club got the green light. Parramatta and Manly-Warringah were promoted together in 1947.

Then the long, uphill battle really started. For many years, Parramatta suffered at the hands of the longer-established clubs. Mammoth defeats were regular fare for Parramatta during the first 15 years. The worst was a 61–4 drubbing by the great St George combination at Cumberland Oval in 1959. However everything began to change in the early 1960s. Parramatta adopted a policy of buying stars to help the local products. Among the big names lured to Parramatta were Ron Boden, Brian Hambly, Bob Bugden and Ron Lynch—all internationals. The most important signings of all though, were the brothers Thornett—Ken, the fullback who had set the English club scene alight and who was later dubbed 'The Mayor of Parramatta', and second-rower Dick, who had tamed the finest international forwards the Rugby Union code could throw up. Both went on to represent Australia in Rugby League Tests. The most important factor was their ability, in 1962, to help lift Parramatta to the semi-finals for the first time in the club's history. Regrettably, it was to be a brief period of glory. The club soon drifted back among the also-rans of the competition.

Parramatta had a succession of good coaches, including the former Australian captains Ken Kearney and Ian Walsh and the cunning Englishman David Bolton. However, it was not until Norm Provan, who had coached St George to several of its world record string of Premierships, took over in 1975, that the Eels returned to near the top again. Provan guided the Eels to success in the pre-season competition and a semi-final berth. Terry Fearnley took over the reins the following year and the top form continued.

A Parramatta line-up inspired by Test stars Ray Higgs and John Peard reached the grand final for the first time in 1976, but, as every player knows, a grand final is usually won by the team with most big match experience. A nervous Parramatta side bombed at least two tries, allowing Manly-Warringah to snatch a 13–10 victory.

In the next year's competition, Parramatta was strengthened by the signing of goal-kicking Test centre Mick Cronin. The Eels seemed unbeatable when they raced to a convincing win in the Minor Premiership—but again they failed when it came to the grand final. The Eels trailed 0–9 at half-time against St George. They rallied in the second half to draw level near full-time. An extra 20 minutes failed to break the deadlock and, for the first time, the grand final had to be replayed. In the replay, Parramatta was outgunned 22–0. The Eels had let slip another opportunity.

In 1978, Parramatta was beaten in the semi-finals by Manly-Warringah, which forced its way through from the bottom half of the play-off draw to win the Premiership, and in 1979, Canterbury-Bankstown upset the more-fancied Eels in the final. In 1980, Parramatta was coached by its former star player John Peard, but failed to reach the semi-finals. The Eels however won the Club Championship for the fifth successive year. That 1980 success was unique in so far as it was the first time a club which missed the first-grade semi-finals had carried off the Club Championship.

In the never-say-die quest for a Premiership, Parramatta signed up the great coach Jack Gibson. The move paid off handsomely. In the first season under Gibson, Parramatta won the first-grade title for the first time. Gibson repeated the dose in 1982, steering the Eels to a 21–8 grand final win over arch-rivals Manly-Warringah. Parramatta also stretched its Club Championship run to a record seventh straight season. In addition six Parramatta players made the Kangaroo side that year—winger Eric Grothe, utility back Steve Ella, halfback Peter Sterling, five-eighth Brett Kenny, lock Ray Price and second-rower John Muggleton.

By this time centre Mick Cronin had bowed out of Test football after snaring almost every record possible. When he retired four years later, Cronin was the greatest pointscorer in the history of the Sydney Premiership (with 1971 points). As well, he scored the most in a Sydney season (282 in 1982), the most in a calendar year (547 from 52 games in 1978), the most points by a player from any country in World Series clashes (108), the most in the world in Tests (201), the most points in a Test series (54 against Great Britain in 1979) and the most successive successful kicks for goal in top-class Rugby League (26 in 1978).

Parramatta made it three Premierships in a row in 1983 before Gibson announced he was quitting. That year the club made history when it provided the entire NSW backline for the second State-of-Origin match against Queensland. The Eels also provided two other representatives—lock and captain Ray Price and reserve forward Stan Jurd. The Parramatta backline which played for New South Wales was wingers Eric Grothe and Neil Hunt, centres Mick Cronin and Steve Ella, and halves Brett Kenny and Peter Sterling. The selectors also had Parramatta's David Liddiard on standby as the shadow fullback.

In 1984, with new coach John Monie, Parramatta went within a whisker of making it four in a row. The Eels were beaten 6–4 by Canterbury-Bankstown in a gripping grand final—and Cronin missed what, for him, should have been a relatively easy shot at penalty goal, in the dying minutes of play—a goal which would have forced the match into extra time. Canterbury also eliminated Parramatta the following year, this time in the preliminary final, before going on to win the Premiership. The Eels had their revenge a year later however, in the only grand final in which a try has not been scored. Parramatta won the dour struggle 4–2. It was a fitting result as the match brought down the curtain on the career of two of the greatest of Parramatta's players—Mick Cronin and Ray Price. Both had been rewarded with success in the Rothmans Medal, awarded annually to the finest player in the Sydney Premiership competition. Cronin is the only player to have won it in successive years (1977 and 1978), while Price won it in 1979.

It is perhaps fitting that another star of that era, Peter Sterling has also won it twice (a feat shared by just one other player, South Sydney's Denis Pittard). Sterling won the Medal in 1987 and again in 1990. The Sterling performance is remarkable, considering Parramatta failed to make the semi-finals in either of those years (finishing seventh in 1987 and eighth in 1990).

The 1990 season was the first in which Cronin had control as coach of the Eels, trying to guide a crop of youngsters, most of whom were under the age of 22.

The Eels finished just three points out of the semi-finals that year. But in 1991, after a disastrous start in which an injury to Sterling put him out for the season, Parramatta struggled to extricate itself from the foot of the table, finishing ahead of only the Gold Coast.

PARRAMATTA
Founded: 1946
Entered Sydney Premiership competition: 1947
Colours: Blue and gold
Home ground: Parramatta Stadium (Record Parramatta club crowd—27 243)
Nickname: The Eels
Honours:
  Sydney Premiership—Winners, 1981, 1982, 1983, 1986; Runners-up, 1976, 1977, 1984
  Midweek Cup—1980, 1986
  Flowers Memorial Pennant (Club Championship)—1976, 1977, 1978, 1979, 1980, 1981, 1982, 1986
  Pre-Season Competition—1975
  Reserve Grade Premiership—1975, 1977, 1979
  Third Grade Premiership—1964, 1982, 1984
  Under-23 Premiership—1979, 1980
  President's Cup—1975, 1988
  Flegg Memorial Trophy—1970, 1985
  SG Ball Cup—1966, 1967, 1968, 1973, 1983, 1985
Most first grade games: 258 by Ray Price
Most points in a career: 1971 by Mick Cronin

Most tries in a career: 96 by Brett Kenny
Most points in a season: 282 by Mick Cronin, in 1978
Most tries in a season: 23 by Steve Ella, in 1982
Rothmans Medal winners: Ray Higgs (1976), Mick Cronin (1977 and 1978), Ray Price (1979), Peter Sterling (1987 and 1990)
NSW Player-of-the-Year: Ken Thornett (1965), Mick Cronin (1977)
Dally M Award winners: Ray Price (1982), Peter Sterling (1986 and 1987)
Rugby League Week Player-of-the-Year: Ray Higgs (1976), Mick Cronin (1977), Geoff Gerard (1978), Peter Sterling (1984, 1986 and 1987)
Sun Herald Best-and-Fairest Player: Ken Thornett (1965), Ron Lynch (1966)
Coach-of-the-Year: Ian Walsh (1971), Terry Fearnley (1976), Jack Gibson (1982)

TONY PASKINS

Tony Paskins never played a Test match for Australia, but his performances both in his own country, and in Britain, rank him as one of the best players of the 1950s and 1960s. He was a Rugby Union player in Sydney when spotted by Gus Risman, the captain of the 1946 touring British side. After the tour, Risman persuaded Workington Town to snap up Paskins' services for the following British season. The Sydney player turned out for the Cumbrian club for seven seasons during which he excelled for Other Nationalities in the four-cornered International Championship, which also involved England, Wales and France.

Paskins returned home in 1955 to captain Eastern Suburbs, before going on to coach the country club Oberon. It was while there that he made his greatest impact on Australian football, leading the Country Firsts representative sides to two successive upset victories over City Firsts (in 1961 and 1962). Paskins captained New South Wales against the touring 1962 British Lions but was overlooked when the Test sides were chosen. He had a further spell in Sydney football, coaching Manly-Warringah, before returning to the country where he continued playing until the age of 43.

ARTHUR PATTON

Arthur Patton was one of the toughest Australian wingers of all time. He played 15 seasons of top-flight Rugby League—even two broken legs could not stop him from continuing to the fray. Respected Sydney journalist Tom Goodman rated Patton as the fastest runner with the ball seen in Sydney football. An indication of his speed was his performance in the 1937 Stawell Gift footrace, the country's premier professional sprint. He was beaten into third place in the final, just 20 cm (9 in) behind two athletes to whom he gave starts of more than a metre.

Patton was robbed of a Test career by World War II Several times he topped 50 tries in a season. In 135 games for Balmain he notched 119 tries, becoming the first man in Sydney Rugby League to score a century of tries for a single club. His final appearance on the football field was for Balmain, against St George, in the 1948 Sydney Premiership final. It was an heroic performance. Patton broke a leg early in the first half when tackled 10 metres from the tryline after a 60–metre dash. Replacements were not allowed in those days and Patton refused to leave his team-mates despite their urging to go to the dressing room. He played the rest of the match in great pain, with his injured leg heavily strapped so he could stay on his feet. His courage was rewarded when Balmain scraped home winners 13–12.

COL PEARCE

Col Pearce was one of Australia's best-known referees and later became a respected media critic and commentator. As a referee he was without peer throughout the 1960s, with his international career stretching from 1960 to 1968. During his 24 years as a professional adjudicator, Pearce controlled nine Tests (one Australia-France in 1960, three Australia-France in 1964, two Australia-Britain in 1966 and three Australia-New Zealand in 1967), three World Cup clashes (in 1968), 11 New South Wales v Queensland matches, six Great Britain-New South Wales games and more than 400 club matches. His five straight Sydney Premiership grand finals (between 1964 and 1968) is the second most by any referee.

Turning to the media, Pearce wrote for the *Sun-Herald* newspaper, appeared on television sporting shows on the Seven Network and called matches for radio station 2UE.

JOE PEARCE

Thirteen Tests for Australia (1932–36). Also played 23 minor games on two Kangaroo tours (1933–34 and 1937–38) and one New Zealand tour (1935).

Sid 'Joe' Pearce, like his father, the hooker Sandy Pearce, became one of Rugby League's all-time greats. During the 1930s, he was unmatched as a second-row forward—in which position he introduced a revolutionary style of ball-carrying play. Joe Pearce began his Sydney football as a fullback with Eastern Suburbs' lower grade sides. It was not until he switched to the forwards did he really make his mark.

He played his first Test against the touring British side in 1932 and went on to appear in 13 Tests (eight against Britain and five against New Zealand). He made two tours of Britain and one of New Zealand. The last of these, with the 1937–38 Kangaroos, was disastrous for Pearce. The Kangaroos stopped off in New Zealand and Joe broke a leg when he crashed into the great Maori fullback George Nepia in one of the matches there. The Australian Board of Control (the forerunner of the Australian Rugby League) allowed him to travel on to Britain with his team-mates although it was obvious he would not be able to play again on the tour. The injury spelled an end to Joe Pearce's international career—just as a broken leg on a Kangaroo tour had ended his father's footballing days. However, it did not stop him from playing altogether and he was still being selected in NSW representative sides as late as 1941.

SANDY PEARCE

Fourteen Tests for Australia (1908–21). Also played 49 minor games on two Kangaroo tours (1908–09 and 1921–22).

Sid 'Sandy' Pearce, one of Australia's greatest hookers, was known to his contemporaries as 'The Gentle Giant'. He played the game hard but was never dirty. As a scrummager, he knew no equal. Pearce came from a sporting family which provided great rowers, swimmers and Rugby League players. They included Bobby Pearce, regarded by most experts as the greatest sculler the world has ever known.

Sandy Pearce was one of the pioneers who played the first Rugby League games in Australia, in 1907, turning out for New South Wales against A H Baskerville's touring New Zealanders. He played a full Test series against the tourists when they returned to Australia on their way home from the British part of their trail-blazing trip. Pearce also made two Kangaroo tours of Britain. He went with the first side, in 1908–09, was unavailable for the second Kangaroo visit three years later, but made the 1921–22 side, by which time he was 38 years old. The Sydney star suffered a broken leg in the match against Dewsbury on that last visit. The injury brought his splendid career to an end. Such was his popularity though, that as he lay in hospital with a leg in plaster, hundreds of English fans went to visit him, many of them taking expensive presents.

After his playing days were over, Sandy Pearce turned to coaching the Sydney University side—an enthusiastic group of youngsters who often found the going tough against the seasoned professionals of the Sydney Premiership competition. Pearce died suddenly in November 1930, nine years after his last Kangaroo tour, of what was described as a strained heart. He was just 47.

WAYNE PEARCE

Eighteen Tests for Australia (1982–88). Also played in 1988 World Cup final, the Bicentenary international against the Rest-of-the-World (1988), for Oceania against Europe (1984) and 10 minor games on one Kangaroo tour (1982) and one New Zealand tour (1985).

It is doubtful whether there was ever a fitter Rugby League footballer than Wayne 'Junior' Pearce. A non-drinker and no-smoker, he epitomised all that was good about the sport. Ironically it was an injury, albeit to his eye, which nearly brought about an end to his career before it had really got off the ground. It was in 1981 and doctors warned that if he continued playing the game he loved he could lose the sight in the eye. Pearce gambled on an operation curing the problem. Twelve months later he was rewarded with a new lease of life which won him a spot in the 1982 Kangaroos touring side.

He was chosen as understudy lock to the brilliant Ray Price—his boyhood hero. Such was Pearce's form in the early matches against English club sides however, that he was switched to the second-row to give him a chance to make the side for the Test matches against Great Britain. This was the start of a brilliant international career. Before he quit the Test scene at the end of 1988 he had played 18 Tests (eight against Britain, seven versus New Zealand, two against France and one against Papua New Guinea).

It looked like Pearce's time in the international arena was over even before that. He was dropped from the Australian side for the historic 100th Anglo-Australian Test at the Sydney Football Stadium in 1988. However he forced his way back for all the other internationals that year—bowing out after Australia's World Cup victory over New Zealand. Pearce would have played many more internationals but for missing the 1986 Kangaroo

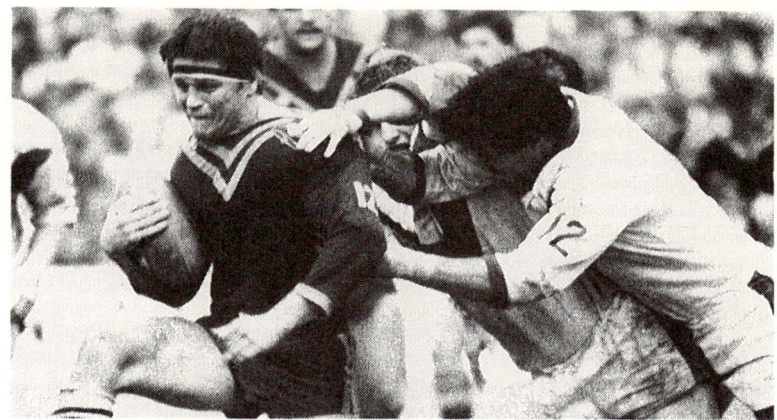

Wayne Pearce in action against Great Britain in 1984

tour because of an awful leg injury. He was still a worthy Test player when he quit representative football.

He had two more seasons with Balmain before finally retiring at the end of the 1990 season, calling it a day after 187 first-grade games (7 short of Keith Barnes' club record). Tiger fans were hoping for a fairytale finish to Junior's illustrious career. It was not to be. Balmain scraped into the semi-finals after beating Newcastle in a playoff for fifth spot, but then were eliminated by Manly-Warringah in the minor qualifying semi-final.

JOHN PEARD

Played eight matches for Australia in two World Championships (1975 and 1977).

John Peard

John Peard is the man generally recognised as having perfected the 'bomb' (once known as the up-and-under) as a try-scoring weapon of the 1970s and 1980s. The St George, Parramatta and Eastern Suburbs five-eighth helped his sides to many wins with high, accurate kicks which fell just behind the try-line. Explained Peard: 'The bomb had modest beginnings, but, when Parramatta coach Terry Fearnley ordered me to develop it to the full, it certainly exploded'.

Peard starred in Easts' Premiership-winning sides in 1974 and 1975. He made his international debut in the second half of the 1975 World Championships, with matches in New Zealand, Wales, France and England, and two years later he played in the next World Series. By then he had switched to the Parramatta club.

A bad groin injury, which affected his performance in the famous 1977 tied grand final, eventually forced Peard to end his playing career. He continued as a coach, with the highlight in 1988, when he coached the NSW State-of-Origin side. Peard also achieved a great measure of success as a radio and television commentator, offering expert advice during major matches.

PENRITH

Penrith's first couple of decades in the Premiership race were hardly inspiring. However the fans who never gave up hope were rewarded as the 1990s dawned and the Panthers finally shrugged off their image as the 'Chocolate Soldiers' of the major League, with a dramatic push into the 1990 grand final. Penrith moved up from the Second Division in 1967 (with Cronulla-Sutherland) and for the first 18 seasons never finished higher than seventh. In 1985 the change began with the first semi-final appearance, culminating in the trip to the grand final five years later. Penrith stalwarts point to the history of the two previous clubs to join the Sydney big time— Manly-Warringah took 26 years to win its first Premiership and Parramatta 34 years.

Penrith had its Rugby League origins as far back as 1927 when it was a junior club. With a burgeoning nursery of talent, the club gradually forced its way up. It was one of the top Second Division clubs in the 1960s and, in 1966, managed to toss the formidable Wentworthville combination to win the Second Division crown. It was a good year to succeed—for that was when the NSW Rugby League chiefs were deciding which new clubs would join the 10 established Premiership sides.

Penrith had a couple of early tastes of success in the big league. In 1968, just 12 months after joining the elite, the Panthers surprised by winning the Wills Cup (the pre-season competition). In 1974 they managed to fight their way through to the first final of the Amco Cup (the televised midweek knockout tournament)—once there though, they went down to Western Division, 6–2.

In an effort to find an answer to the tricky Premiership question the Panthers cast their net wide. They signed two South African Rugby Union stars in 1973, but the illustrious imports did not make the grade. Some stars from England did. British Test men Mike Stephenson, Bill Ashurst and David Topliss all turned out with Penrith.

Ashurst came from Wigan with a reputation as big as his huge frame and he sporadically lived up to it. He turned in some devastating performances for Penrith but, suddenly, in 1977, quit Australia without notifying the Panther officials. Eventually, after some bitter wrangling, he was cleared to play football again in Britain. Mike Stephenson was a great buy. He came to Australian 1973, on a $39 000 transfer fee—a tidy sum in those days. He gave yeoman service to Penrith until injury forced him to retire in 1978.

The real start of a surge to the top came with coach Tim Sheens. He took over in 1984 and guided the Panthers from 11th to within a point of the semi-finals. 'We will make the semis next year,' he predicted at the end of that season. They did, even though they were eliminated 38–6 by Parramatta. They were fired by a young Greg Alexander whose 194 points broke the club record. Alexander was to make a name internationally over the coming years. Veteran Geoff Gerard, the 1978 Kangaroo, joined the Panthers from Manly. Two other future Test players also turned out for Penrith that year—hooker Royce Simmons and second-rower John Cartwright.

Another two destined to wear the green and gold appeared 12 months later in the lower grades—Mark Geyer and Mark Carroll (although Carroll slipped through the Penrith net and ended up at South Sydney). Sheens left in 1988 to take over at Canberra (where he scored two Premierships in his first three years). That season the Panthers were poised to take the Minor Premiership, but after losing their last three games they missed the semis.

In 1989, Penrith finished second on the points table after the preliminary rounds—but crashed out with successive defeats in the playoffs to Premiers Canberra (31–10) and Balmain (24–12).

For 1990, the Panthers turned to a former Panther player, Phil Gould— unwanted by Canterbury-Bankstown despite considerable success with the Bulldogs. Gould lit a fire in the bellies of his players. Penrith finished third on the table, just two points behind Minor Premiers, Canberra. The Panthers accounted for Brisbane 26–16 and Canberra 30–12 to reach the grand final. Spirit was high, but when it came to the season's finale, Canberra's experience provided the difference. After leading 12–0, the Raiders finally triumphed 18–14 to snare back-to-back Premierships. Penrith were rewarded however with four spots in the Kangaroo squad to tour Britain and France—Alexander, Cartwright, Geyer and 18–year-old centre Brad Fittler.

It was to be a different story the following year. Except for a couple of weeks, Penrith led the table from the very first round, losing only four of the preliminary rounds. The Minor Premiership victory, by six points, was one of the most decisive in decades. The Panthers came up against Canberra in the grand final again, but this time the result was reversed. In its 25th year in the competition, Penrith won its first Premiership, beating the Raiders 19–12. The win provided a fairytale finish to the career of Penrith's international hooker Royce Simmons. In the last of his 259 matches—a new record for Penrith (including 233 in first-grade)—he scored two of Penrith's three tries, which was no mean feat for a player who was lucky to score that many in a couple of seasons. It was a fitting finish to the season for the other Panther internationals, skipper Alexander, Geyer, Cartwright and Fittler.

No sooner had the euphoria dissipated than Penrith was off to England to play Wigan in the World Club Challenge. But the Panthers were without Fittler (who was with the Australian side in Papua New Guinea), Geyer (thanks to a passport mixup) and several other young stars (who for personal reasons declined the trip). Although jet-lagged and with no proper training runs, Penrith held the star-studded Wigan lineup for most of the match, but finally went down 21–4.

PENRITH
Founded: 1927
Entered Sydney Premiership competition: 1967
Home ground: Penrith Park (Record crowd—21 956)
Colours: Black, white, green, yellow and red (formerly brown and white)
Nickname: The Panthers
Honours:
    Sydney Premiership—Winners, 1991; Runners-up: 1990
    Pre-Season competition 1968
    Second Division Premiership—1966
    Under-23 Premiership—1978
    Flegg Memorial Trophy—1977
    SG Ball Cup—1977, 1981
Most games in a career: 233 by Royce Simmons
Most points in a career: 883 by Greg Alexander
Most tries in a career: 83 by Greg Alexander
Most points in a season: 196 by Greg Alexander, in 1985
Most tries in a season: 16 by Graham Mackay, in 1991
Rothmans Medal winners: Nil
Dally M Awards: Greg Alexander (1985)

PENRITH TOUR OF FRANCE

Soon after being beaten by Balmain for the fifth semi-final spot in the 1988 Sydney Premiership, the Panthers made a four-match tour of France—the first ever by an Australian club. Although beaten by a representative side from the Aude district, the Panthers thrashed the French champions Le Pontet and overcame a virtual French Test XIII

Record in France

Played 4, Won 3, Lost 1, Points for 88, Points against 38

Match Results

Opponents	Venue	For	Against
Midi-Pyrenees Selection	Toulouse	16	6
L'Aude Selection	Carcassonne	9	12
Le Pontet	Le Pontet	40	4
French Selection	Perpignan	23	16

GEORGE PEPONIS

Eight Tests for Australia (1978–80). Also played seven minor games on one Kangaroo tour (1978) and one New Zealand tour (1980).

In the 1940s, Canterbury-Bankstown had in its ranks the man they called 'The Prince of Hookers', Roy Kirkaldy. He set a standard not equalled there for 35 years. The man who did that was George Peponis. A doctor of Greek descent, Peponis not only played Test football but also joined a long line of great hookers who have captained their country.

Peponis began his football in the Canterbury junior ranks, representing the district in the SG Ball, Jersey Flegg and President's Cups. He made his grade debut in 1972. He was called into the Test side for the First Test against New Zealand in 1978 but a subsequent suspension and good form by Manly-Warringah's Max Krilich kept Peponis out of the Test arena

George Peponis with the JJ Giltinan Shield after Canterbury won the 1980 Grand Final

until the decider against Britain, in England, that year. When Bob Fulton bowed out of international football at the end of the Kangaroo tour, Peponis stepped into the role of captain for the record-shattering Ashes win in Australia in 1979.

Peponis also played a major role in the revival of Canterbury in the Sydney Premiership when, against all odds, the Bulldogs fought their way through to the 1979 grand final and the following year took out the Premiership itself.

PETER PETERS

Peter Peters, nicknamed Zorba because of his Greek heritage, was one of Sydney's top footballers during the 1970s. He was a rugged second-row forward for Manly-Warringah and was a member of the Sea Eagles side which won the violent 1973 grand final against Cronulla-Sutherland.

Peters would stand for no nonsense on the field. He also refused to give an inch in his later career on television and radio and in football magazines. He had spells on both Channel 9 and 10, but it was with Sydney radio station 2GB that he really made his mark. The station's sports director Richard Fisk, in a bold gamble, teamed Peters with controversial referee Greg 'Hollywood' Hartley, who had no radio experience at all. The move was an outstanding success. Hollywood and Zorba topped the ratings for several seasons. Their raucous calls earned them the title of 'The Decibel Duo'. When they called Test matches from the public stands in Britain and New Zealand, the local fans could not believe their ears. At the end of 1990, Peters became the highest paid sporting caller in Australia when he switched to rival station 2KY, taking Hartley and several of his support team with him.

NOEL PIDDING

Sixteen Tests for Australia (1948–54). Also played three World Cup matches (1954) and 23 minor games on one Kangaroo tour (1952–53) and one New Zealand tour (1953).

'Rugby League's Bradman'—that's what a British sporting publication called Noel Pidding when he was on tour with the 1952–53 Kangaroos. At the very least, post-World War II football has known few pointscorers to rival him. In one Sydney club match, for St George against Eastern Suburbs, he notched 10 points in just two minutes. Pidding, from the NSW coalfields town of Maitland, seemed destined for a great future as Australia's fullback when chosen for the First Test against New Zealand in 1948. But 'The Little Master', Clive Churchill, also appeared on the scene that year and took over. It was not until Pidding switched to the wing, the following year, that he regained a berth in the Test team.

Pidding played in eight Test series, against each of the other Rugby League nations, and scored 124 points. He made two full overseas tours, to Britain and France with the 1952–53 Kangaroos and to New Zealand in 1953. He also went to France for the inaugural World Cup in 1954. The Kangaroo trip was the highlight of his career. He easily led the scoring lists with 228 points. Only the great Dave Brown, on the 1933–34 visit, has topped this (with 285)—but Brown played in 10 more matches on his tour than did Pidding. Brown's average per match (8.9 points) was well below Pidding's (10.4).

GREG PIERCE

Three Tests for Australia (1973–78). Also played five matches in two World Championships (1975 and 1977), one minor international (1978) and 14 minor games on two Kangaroo tours (1973 and 1978) and two World Championship tours (1975 and 1977).

Greg Pierce

In the mid-1970s, Australian Test selector Arthur Folwell watched his grandson playing for the Cronulla-Sutherland Under-16 side. Folwell turned to a companion and said: 'He's going to play for Australia one day'. Not only did Greg Pierce play for Australia, he captained his country in Test and World Championship matches.

Forty years after his grandfather toured Britain, Pierce made the trip there for his first taste of international football. He toured again with the successful 1975 Australian World Championship side, captained Australia in its World Championship match in New Zealand in 1977 and went back to Britain as vice-captain of the 1978 Kangaroos. The last visit was unfortunate for Pierce. In the match against Wales, early on the tour, he suffered an awful injury to a knee, was carried off on a stretcher and missed the rest of the tour games. Indeed, he was not back to peak fitness for another 18 months, but showed his mettle by returning to captain the Sharks in the Sydney Premiership.

After he retired as a player in 1980, Pierce had a spell as coach of Cronulla, with moderate success.

DENIS PITTARD

Two Tests for Australia (1969). Also played three games in one World Cup (1970), one minor international (1970) and three minor games on one New Zealand tour (1969) and one World Cup tour (1970).

Five-eighth Denis Pittard is one of a select few players to have won the prestige Rothmans Medal twice. The only others to have achieved this honour are the Parramatta pair Mick Cronin and Peter Sterling. Pittard won the Rothmans in its second year, 1969, and repeated the effort two years later. At the time, he was playing with South Sydney, having switched from Western Suburbs in 1968, when Souths needed a replacement for the great Jim Lisle.

The classy Pittard had only a brief period in the international limelight. He made his Test debut on the 1969 tour of New Zealand. He was also a member of the successful Australian World Cup squad the following year. However after the classy Bob Fulton was switched from centre to five-eighth for the Cup final, it was the end of Pittard's international days. Pittard played in three Premiership-winning sides at Souths (1968, 1970 and 1971), forming a great scrum-base combination with Test half Bob Grant.

DICK POOLE

Ten Tests for Australia (1956–57). Also played three World Cup matches (1957), for Australia against the Rest-of-the-World (1957) and 11 minor games on one Kangaroo tour (1956–57).

Asthma, suffered since childhood, curtailed Dick Poole's career. Despite this, he can boast an enviable record both as a captain and coach of top sides. Poole turned out for Newtown in the Sydney Premiership competition for 10 seasons (1949–58) and later for Western Suburbs (for two and a half years). For the last four years of his spell with Newtown,

Dick Poole on the attack for Newtown in a 1954 game against Eastern Suburbs

he was captain-coach. He helped the club through to the grand final in 1955, where his boys lost by just one point.

The tough centre figured prominently in the international sphere, as a vital cog in the Test backline in matches against the three other League nations and as captain-coach of the unbeaten 1957 World Cup team. Poole retired as a player in 1961 but coached Newtown again for three seasons in the late 1960s.

NORM POPE

One Test for Australia (1956).

Norm Pope played only one Test for Australia. He turned out as fullback in the Third Test against New Zealand in 1956, kicking five goals in Australia's 31–14 success. Although it was his one taste of international glory, many critics thought he was unlucky not to have gained selection in the Kangaroo squad which toured Britain and France later that year. However Pope will still be remembered as one of the finest goalkickers in the history of Australian Rugby League. Playing for Valleys in the Brisbane Premiership he topped the 200–point mark four times. In 1953 he scored an incredible 330 points (10 tries and 150 goals). Two years later, when Valleys swept the competition, unbeaten, he scored 245. The next season it was 224 and in 1957 he notched 297 points. That last year, Valleys also won the 'Premiership.

PREMIERSHIP see *Sydney Premiership, Brisbane Premiership*

PRE-SEASON COMPETITION

In the early 1960s a full-scale pre-season competition was introduced to provide an incentive for the clubs to play serious football and for the fans to pay money to watch in the weeks before the Premiership began. The idea was an instant success with crowds of more than 15 000 turning up to watch the matches. However in the early 1980s, when the number of teams in the Premiership was increased to 14, with four extra competition rounds, it was decided to scrap the season preview. In 1990, Channel 10 introduced a new pre-season knockout (see Channel 10 Challenge Cup).

Pre-season Competition Winners

1963	_____	St George
1964	_____	St George
1965	_____	St George
1966	_____	South Sydney
1967	_____	Balmain
1968	_____	Penrith
1969	_____	South Sydney
1970	_____	Canterbury-Bankstown
1971	_____	St George
1972	_____	South Sydney
1973	_____	Newtown
1974	_____	Eastern Suburbs
1975	_____	Parramatta
1976	_____	Balmain
1977	_____	Eastern Suburbs
1978	_____	South Sydney
1979	_____	Eastern Suburbs
1980	_____	Manly-Warringah

PRESIDENT'S CUP

The President's Cup is the competition for Under-21 players conducted in conjunction with the Premiership. Until 1988, the teams took part in a short mid-season competition and were chosen from the junior ranks. The best of them would then, inevitably, be drafted into the lower grades of the district club for the remainder of the season. In 1988, the Under-23 competition was scrapped and replaced by the President's Cup.

Winners of the President's Cup

1910	_____	Eastern Suburbs	1935	_____	St George
1911	_____	Eastern Suburbs	1936	_____	South Sydney
1912	_____	Balmain	1937	_____	Northern Suburbs
1913	_____	Eastern Suburbs	1938	_____	Eastern Suburbs
1914	_____	Balmain	1939	_____	Balmain
1915	_____	Eastern Suburbs	1940	_____	Balmain
1918	_____	North Sydney	1941	_____	St George
1919	_____	Newtown	1942	_____	South Sydney
1920	_____	Eastern Suburbs	1943	_____	South Sydney
1921	_____	Newtown	1944	_____	Newtown
1922	_____	Eastern Suburbs	1945	_____	Western Suburbs
1923	_____	Eastern Suburbs	1946	_____	Manly-Warringah
1924	_____	Eastern Suburbs	1947	_____	Western Suburbs
1925	_____	Western Suburbs	1948	_____	Eastern Suburbs
1926	_____	Balmain	1949	_____	Eastern Suburbs
1927	_____	Eastern Suburbs	1950	_____	Newtown
1928	_____	Newtown	1951	_____	South Sydney
1929	_____	Balmain	1952	_____	Balmain
1930	_____	Balmain	1953	_____	South Sydney
1931	_____	Canterbury-Bankstown	1954	_____	Balmain
1932	_____	Balmain	1955	_____	Eastern Suburbs
1933	_____	North Sydney	1956	_____	Newtown
1934	_____	Southern Districts	1957	_____	St George

Continued

Winners of the President's Cup *continued*

1958	_____	Western Suburbs
1959	_____	Balmain
1960	_____	South Sydney
1961	_____	South Sydney
1962	_____	South Sydney
1963	_____	South Sydney
1964	_____	South Sydney
1965	_____	South Sydney
1966	_____	Balmain
1967	_____	Balmain
1968	_____	South Sydney
1969	_____	South Sydney
1970	_____	Manly-Warringah
1971	_____	South Sydney
1972	_____	South Sydney

1973	_____	Balmain
1974	_____	South Sydney
1975	_____	Parramatta
1976	_____	Canterbury-Bankstown
1977	_____	South Sydney
1978	_____	Eastern Suburbs
1979	_____	Parramatta
1980	_____	South Sydney
1981	_____	St George
1982	_____	South Sydney
1983	_____	South Sydney
1984	_____	Illawarra
1985	_____	Penrith
1986	_____	Penrith
1987	_____	Eastern Suburbs

(For winners since 1987, see *Sydney Premiership* entry)

PRESIDENT'S XIII

Occasionally players on the fringe of Test selection have been rewarded with a game for the President's XIII. The first time the Australian Rugby League decided to chose such a team was in 1985 when a match was arranged against the Papua New Guinea Test side as part of that country's celebration of 10 years of independence. The President's XIII was chosen from teams not involved in either the Sydney or Brisbane Premiership semi-finals. The Australian youngsters were captained by veteran winger John Ribot in his farewell match. Ribot had a fitting finale to his career, scoring a try and kicking seven goals for a personal tally of 18 points. Among the future Test stars in the side were Dale Shearer and Andrew Ettingshausen. Papua New Guinea were outplayed 62–14.

Three years later a President's XIII played the touring British Lions under lights at Queanbeyan. Captain was South Sydney hooker Mario Fenech, who had played in the previous side in Port Moresby. Britain was beaten 24–12 but showed a fighting spirit when it looked as if the Aussie Test hopefuls might walk all over them after racing to a 10–0 lead after only 12 minutes. Best on the night was Eastern Suburbs forward David Trewhella.

How the President's XIII have Fared

1985
At Lloyd Robson Oval, Port Moresby, September, 1985
Crowd: 12 000
PRESIDENT'S XIII 62 (D Shearer 2, C O'Sullivan 2, A Ettingshausen 2, J Ribot, D Carney, G Rix, D Hatch, M Fenech tries, J Ribot 7, D Carney 2 goals) d PAPUA-NEW GUINEA 14 (D Noifa, M Kerekere tries, B Numapo 3 goals)

1988
At Seiffert Oval, Queanbeyan, 5 July 1988
Crowd: 6037
PRESIDENT'S XIII 24 (M Meninga, G Bradley, G Alexander, S O'Brien, G Lazarus tries, M Meninga 2 goals) d GREAT BRITAIN 16 (P Ford 2, M Gregory tries, P Loughlin 2 goals)

RAY PRICE

Twenty-two Tests for Australia (1978–84). Also played for Oceania against Europe (1984) and 16 minor games on two Kangaroo tours (1978 and 1982) and one New Zealand tour (1980).

They called Ray Price 'Mr Perpetual Motion'. It was a good description. Whether in cover-defence or backing up a team-mate with the ball, Price missed not a moment's action on the field.

A Rugby Union international (with eight caps in two years, against New Zealand, England, Japan and the American Eagles), Price swapped codes to join Parramatta in 1976. He was an 'overnight sensation' in club football. However, the representative selectors were sanguine about him until the 1978 series against the New Zealand Kiwis. Such was his form that year, that the Test panel switched captain Greg Pierce from the lock spot into the second-row to give Price a chance in the Test arena. He was a regular fixture from then on. Price was one of the stars of the 1978 Kangaroo side which toured Britain and France and tied his British opponents in knots in a return Ashes series on home soil the following year.

Ray Price

His displays in 1979 won him the Harry Sunderland Medal as Man-of-the-Series, and in club games that season he played so well that his taking of the Rothmans Medal as the year's best-and-fairest was a foregone conclusion. Price also won the Dally M Award as Player-of-the-Year. He was to win a second Dally M in 1982. Price toured New Zealand in 1980 and made a second Kangaroo tour in 1982 as part of the team dubbed 'The Invincibles'—the first to go through a tour unbeaten. He retired from representative football after the 1984 Ashes series in Australia.

He and fellow international and Parramatta team-mate Mick Cronin hung up their boots after the Eels' grand final success in 1986. By that time, Price had played a club record 258 games for Parramatta. During his decade with the Eels, Price was involved in four Premiership-winning sides (1981, 1982, 1983 and 1986).

WALLY PRIGG

Nineteen Tests for Australia (1929–38). Also played 70 minor games on three Kangaroo tours (1929–30, 1933–34 and 1937–38) and one New Zealand tour (1935).

Wally Prigg was without peer as a lock-forward during the 1930s . He was one of the fastest forwards in Rugby League and an expert at sending team-mates through the smallest of openings.

Prigg made his international debut in 1929, in the Second Test of the Kangaroo tour of Great Britain. He was to be the number one choice as Australia's lock for the next decade, missing only two Tests (the last two of the 1932 series against Britain) through injury. For some time he had the added responsibility of captaincy, including Australia's first Test clash with France, at Paris in 1938. The Newcastle star is one of a select few to have made more than two Kangaroo tours, and his 19 Test appearances (12 against Britain, five versus New Zealand and two against France) was a record at the time. It was only bettered in the years after World War II, when international tours became more regular. (Prigg's 19 Tests stretched over 10 years, while the current record-holder, Reg Gasnier, was able to notch his 36 in one season less).

NORM PROVAN

Fourteen Tests for Australia (1954–60). Also played four matches in two World Cups (1954 and 1957), for Australia against the Rest-of-the-World (1957) and 12 minor games on one Kangaroo tour (1956–57).

Norm Provan established a reputation in the 1950s as one of the greatest second-rowers of his era—and then in the 1960s, the twilight years of his career, he carved out a new name as a top captain-coach.

Provan entered the St George lineup in 1951 and soon made an impact as a tough, thinking forward. In 1953, he played his first representative game and, a year later, appeared in his first Test match (against Britain). He was to be a Test regular for the next five years.

'Sticks', as Provan was known, figured in the first World Cup series, in France, in 1954. Two years later he was back in the Northern Hemisphere with the Kangaroos side. He was also a member of the Australian side which humiliated the opposition to win the 1957 World Cup on home territory. At the start of the 1962 season, Provan took over as captain-coach of the great St George club combination and, before retiring in 1966, steered the Dragons to four of their record 11 straight Premiership successes. Provan played in 10 successive Premiership-winning sides, a feat no player, St George or otherwise, has equalled at top level.

In the 1970s, Provan had two spells as a non-playing coach of Sydney club sides. He was at the helm of Parramatta in 1975 and guided the Eels to success in the pre-season competition and to a semi-final berth. In 1978 and 1979 he coached Cronulla-Sutherland. During the first season, Provan steered the Sharks into the grand final of the Premiership. They drew that match, but lost the replay to Manly-Warringah. Next year, Cronulla won the rich Amco Cup midweek competition and finished third in the Premiership.

Norm Provan and his brother Peter hold a unique record in the Sydney Premiership. They are the only brothers to have captained different clubs to Premiership success—Norm with St George from 1962 to 1966 and Peter with Balmain in 1969.

BERNIE PURCELL

One Test for Australia (1950). Also played seven minor games on one Kangaroo tour (1956–57).

Bernie Purcell made his mark in various spheres of Rugby League—first as a forward, then as a coach and later as a newspaper columnist covering the game he played so well.

Second-rower Purcell is the only forward to have scored more than 1000 points in a first-grade career in Sydney football. In 168 games for South Sydney, between 1949 and 1960, Purcell notched 1120 points (from 36 tries and 506 goals), helping the Rabbitohs to four Premierships. He missed out on a fifth when he went to the country for two years to coach Cootamundra. Purcell played only one Test (the third and deciding clash with Britain in 1950, when Australia won the Ashes for the first time in three decades). However he made a Kangaroo tour of Britain and France in 1956, a visit on which injury restricted him to just seven games. After his retirement as a player, Purcell coached Souths for three seasons before turning his talents to writing for the Sydney *Daily Mirror* newspaper.

Q

JOHN QUAYLE

Played two matches for Australia in one World Championship (1975). Also played two minor games on one World Championship tour (1975).

John Quayle was a fine lock forward who played for Australia in the 1975 World Championships—but perhaps he will be best remembered as an administrator.

Quayle began his first-grade football career with Eastern Suburbs, but it was not until he switched to Parramatta, in 1973, that he made a name for himself. That year he was in the New South Wales State side and was considered unlucky not to have toured Britain and France with the Kangaroos. He gained his chance to wear the green and gold two years later when Parramatta, under coach Norm Provan, made the semi-finals after two midweek playoffs for the fifth spot. Although beaten by Manly-Warringah in the semis, Quayle and fellow-Eels, Ray Higgs, Denis Fitzgerald and Jim Porter impressed the selectors, who chose them for the World Championship squad for the away games in New Zealand, Britain and France. Quayle turned out in the games against the Kiwis and Wales.

Quayle quit the football field after the 1976 season and turned his talents to administration, first with Eastern Suburbs and then later as general-manager of the NSW Rugby League. He was at the helm for the introduction of such innovations as the salary cap and the ill-fated players' draft, the axing of Newtown and the attempted axing of Western Suburbs from the Sydney Premiership, and the inclusion of the Brisbane, Newcastle and Gold Coast sides.

QUEENSLAND

It cost just five pence (four cents) to start Rugby League in Queensland—a penny stamp on each of five letters sent out by SB (Siney) Boland, inviting interested parties to join him at the inaugural meeting in 1907. The tiny outlay is somewhat symbolic for Queensland has almost always been the poor relation of Australian football. There has very often been less money to pay the players than in New South Wales and officials could never aspire to the top positions in the League hierarchy. Often the northerners can quite justifiably point out they have been badly treated when it came to the selection of Australian sides.

Since the first interstate clash, in 1908, Queensland teams struggled to challenge the supremacy of New South Wales—and it was only the introduction of the State-of-Origin system for interstate matches in the 1980s that corrected the imbalance. There had been other unsuccessful methods tried by the Queenslanders. Rules were introduced in the 1960s to prevent the poaching of the State's best players, but the authorities found that Test players of the calibre of John Wittenberg, who wanted to join St George, were willing to sit out a season on the sidelines to take advantage of the rewards of southern football.

Queensland's major competition, the Brisbane Premiership, was the brainchild of officials in the 1920s. Before then, Rugby League in the State had been restricted to a competition between clubs from Brisbane and the neighbouring city of Ipswich, and small competitions elsewhere. A split developed between the Brisbane and Queensland Rugby League bodies in 1920. The six Brisbane clubs noted that they each paid the same affiliation fee as did Toowoomba and Ipswich, but had only one vote between them. The other two centres ran their own affairs while the Queensland Rugby League had the final say as far as Brisbane was concerned. The dispute took two years to settle but, when the fighting died down, Brisbane had won the right to its own club competition.

In 1922, the first all-Brisbane Premiership took place with six teams: Brothers, Carlton, Coorparoo, Fortitude Valley, University and Western Suburbs—and over the years it prospered. Unfortunately, when Brisbane joined the Sydney competition in 1988, the local competition took a back seat. Not so, the State-of-Origin matches between Queensland and New South Wales, in which players turn out for the State in which they played their first senior football. Queensland, able to draw on all the stars who had defected south, soon established its superiority. By the 1990s these three clashes every year had achieved a status rivalling the Test matches between Australia and Great Britain.

In 1982, a Queensland-wide competition, the Winfield State League, was introduced to give country players a taste of top-class football. It took until 1989 for a country side (in this case, Central Queensland) to reach the final. Then, two years later, it was an all-country final with North Queensland, coached by former Test star Kerry Boustead, beating Central Queensland 44–30.

QUEENSLAND TO NEW ZEALAND

1925

Many New Zealand critics regard the Queensland side which toured the Shaky Isles in 1925 as the greatest Rugby League team to visit that country— and that includes all the Test sides from Australia, Great Britain, France and South Africa. The Queensland side included such great names as Jimmy Craig, Tommy Gorman, Vic Armbruster, Herb Steinhort, Norm Potter,

Cec Aynsley, Jim Bennett and 'Nigger' Brown. They played two games against the full New Zealand Test side, losing one by a mere point and winning the other convincingly. In the former match Aynsley scored four tries. On the whole tour he touched down for a remarkable 34 tries. The Queensland side was the first international touring team managed by the famous Harry Sunderland.

Record in New Zealand

Played 11, Won 9, Lost 1, Drawn 1, Points for 518, Points against 186

Match Results

Opponents	For	Against
New Zealand	24	25
Auckland	18	18
South Auckland	57	24
New Zealand	35	14
New Zealand XIII	44	20
West Coast	27	10
Canterbury	57	15
Combined South Canterbury	81	34
Otago	63	2
Canterbury	58	10
Auckland Province	54	14

Individual records

	Tries	Goals	Points
J Craig	2	60	126
C Aynsley	34	11	124
W Spencer	19	1	59
H Steinohrt	7	1	23
G Crouch	7	—	21
N Potter (c)	7	—	21
G Moores	6	1	20
V Armbruster	6	1	20
W Paten	5	—	15
J Purcell	4	—	12
T Gorman	4	—	12
J Bennett	3	1	11
J McBrien	3	—	9
P Parcells	2	1	8
C Connell	2	1	8
E Frauenfelder	2	—	6
H Leibke	2	—	6
A Henderson	2	—	6
A Edwards	1	1	5
C Thompson	1	—	3
J O'Mara	1	—	3
H Parry	1	—	3
E Brown	—	—	—

1972

Queensland's representative side made a quick visit to New Zealand in 1972, as a lead-up to its annual clashes with New South Wales. Queensland won all three matches, including a one-point victory over the powerful Auckland combination. The Bananabenders also beat NSW country side Monaro, 37–12, on return to Australia.

Record in New Zealand

Played 3, Won 3, Points for 65, Points against 31

Match Results

Opponents	Venue	For	Against
Wellington	Wellington	26	3
Canterbury	Christchurch	21	11
Auckland	Auckland	18	17

Individual point-scorers

	Tries	Goals	Points
W Stewart	2	6	18
G Tucker	3	4	17
J Grant	3	—	9
J Lang	2	—	6
C Weiss (c)	2	—	6
M Peut	1	—	3
R Twist	1	—	3
P Hall	1	—	3

Also toured: D Roderick, W Orr, G Pearson, W Bennett, A Connell, R McCarron, M Seary, J Murphy, P Braithwaite, G Dobrich, L Hutchinson, S Crear

1990

A Queensland Residents' side, as distinct from a State-of-Origin team, made a short tour of New Zealand at the end of the 1990 season. Coached by the former great halfback Tom Raudonikis, Queensland ran up a cricket score in its first match, but was then held to a draw by the Wellington provincial side, which, earlier in the year, had beaten the touring British Lions. It finished with a comfortable victory over Canterbury, which had also downed Great Britain.

Record in New Zealand

Played 3, Won 2, Drawn 1, Points for 126, Points against 32

Match Results

Opponents	Venue (Attendance)	For	Against
Manawtu	Palmerston North (100)	76	2
Wellington	Wellington (900)	18	18
Canterbury	Christchurch (800)	32	12

Individual point-scorers

	Tries	Goals	Points
B Norton	1	15	34
D Bourke	5	—	20
K Robertson	3	—	12
P Hamilton	3	—	12
B Holmes	3	—	12
T Catton	2	—	8
S Day	1	—	4
D Dixon	1	—	4
M Kings	1	—	4
I McKenzie	1	—	4
R Pearce	1	—	4
T Schodel	1	—	4
C Spark	1	—	4

Also toured: K Langer (c), P Coyne, F Rolls, S Rubesaame

QUEENSLAND TO PAPUA NEW GUINEA————————————

1983

Queensland made a lightning tour of Papua New Guinea as part of its preparation for the 1983 State-of-Origin series. In one of the two games on the tour it set a world record for a representative match, beating the President's XIII by 106–3. It ran in 20 tries against a side which contained eight Papua New Guinea Test players. The score would have been even more devastating had not officials called the match off 12 minutes early to save the locals from further embarrassment.

Record in Papua New Guinea

Played 2, Won 2, Points for 140, Points against 19

Match Results

Opponents	Venue (Attendance)	For	Against
Highlands Zone	Mt Hagen (8000)	34	16
President's XIII	Port Moresby (12 000)	106	3

Individual point-scorers

	Tries	Goals	Points
M Meninga	3	8	28
B Tessmann	5	—	20
C Scott	2	6	20
T Butler	4	—	16
W Challis	2	—	8
C Heugh	2	—	8
W Fullerton Smith	2	—	8
S Stacey	2	—	8
G Miles	2	—	8
R Poulsen	1	—	4
P Bartier	1	—	4
B Niebling	1	—	4
W Lewis (c)	—	2	4

Also toured: M Murray, G Conescu, M Bella and J Kilroy

QUEENSLAND TO GREAT BRITAIN————————————

1983

In a bold experiment, Queensland made a short tour of Great Britain at the end of the 1983 Australian season. The team, only a couple of days off the plane, was flat in its first match and went down narrowly to Hull Kingston Rovers in a fiery game. The winning try was to be the only one scored against Queensland on the tour. The Maroons were in top form to thrash Wigan and Leeds in their other two games. Star of the side was captain Wally Lewis, who was named Man-of-the-Match twice.

Record in Great Britain

Played 3, Won 2, Lost 1, Points for 104, Points against 12

Match Results

Opponents	Venue (Attendance)	For	Against
Hull Kingston Rovers	Hull (6383)	6	8
Wigan	Wigan (9749)	40	2
Leeds	Leeds (5647)	58	2

Individual point-scorers

	Tries	Goals	Points
S McNally	—	11	22
W Lewis (c)	3	1	14
G Miles	3	—	12
W Lindenberg	2	—	8
M Brennan	2	—	8
B French	2	—	8
C Scott	2	—	8
J Kilroy	2	—	8
C Phelan	1	—	4
C Heugh	1	—	4
W Fullerton Smith	1	—	4
G Dowling	1	—	4

Also toured: B Tessman, M Murray, L Brigginshaw, P Khan, S Stacey, B Niebling, G Jones, T Paterson, S Bernardin

QUEENSLAND TO FRANCE

1989

A Queensland Residents' side toured France in 1989. The tour was devalued however, by demands that the tourists must sign to play in the domestic competitions the following year and not join the Sydney Premiership, before they were allowed in the team. As a result several players opted to stay at home. The Maroons were untroubled in any of the four matches.

Record in France

Played 4, Won 4, Points for 126, Points against 22

Match Results

Opponents	Venue (Attendance)	For	Against
Aquitaine-Midi Pyrenees	Villeneuve (2000)	42	8
L'Aude Selection	Carcassonne (1100)	32	4
Rousillon	St Esteve (2500)	22	10
Cote d'Azur	Carpentras (1000)	30	0

Individual point-scorers

	Tries	Goals	Points
G Harvey	2	16	40
S Buckley	6	—	24
R Ovens	3	—	12
T Cook	3	—	12
S Parcell	—	5	10
M Kings	2	—	8
B Holmes (c)	1	—	4
C Spark	1	—	4
R Pearce	1	—	4
B Johnson	1	—	4
C Hastings	1	—	4

Also toured: D Bourke, K Cook, K Robertson, K Langer, S Rubesaame, D Wolens, F Rolls, T Catton, S Bella, S Smith

QUEENSLAND STATE LEAGUE

In a bold move, in 1981, the Queensland Rugby League decided to introduce a statewide competition. The first Queensland State League began the following year. All eight Brisbane clubs were involved, as well as the Gold Coast, North Queensland, Toowoomba, Wide Bay, Ipswich and Central Queensland.

The State League replaced the first round of the Brisbane Premiership with the semi-finals and final being held in May. The Brisbane clubs then switched back to their own Premiership competition for the remainder of the season. However, in 1991, the format was changed. The Brisbane clubs were combined into two teams, Brisbane Metros and Brisbane Capitols. And the Northern Territory was invited to enter a team for the four week competition. For the first time two country sides fought out the final, North Queensland beating Central Queensland 44–30.

The most successful of all players in the State League has been former Australian captain Wally Lewis. He was with Valleys which won in 1983 and then switched to Wynnum-Manly which took out the title in the next four years.

STATE LEAGUE FINALISTS

Year	Winner	Runner-up
1982	Easts	Redcliffe
1983	Valleys	Easts
1984	Wynnum-Manly	Souths
1985	Wynnum-Manly	Brothers
1986	Wynnum-Manly	Redcliffe
1987	Wynnum-Manly	Redcliffe
1988	Seagulls-Diehards	Easts
1989	Easts	Central Queensland
1990	Valleys	Easts
1991	North Queensland	Central Queensland

PAUL QUINN

Seven Tests for Australia (1963–65). Also played 20 minor games on one Kangaroo tour (1963–64) and one New Zealand tour (1965).

Paul Quinn was the first Test player from the NSW south coast town of Gerringong, but he was later to be upstaged by another young man from the same town—the great Mick Cronin.

Quinn, a hard-working prop, first gained attention in 1962 with solid games for Country Seconds and for Southern Division against the touring British Lions. A year later he was even more dominant, playing for Country Firsts and New South Wales (against the touring New Zealand side). He was reserve for the Third Test against the Kiwis before making his Test debut against the visiting South African side. A good performance sealed a spot in the Kangaroo squad to tour Britain and France, where he played another three Tests. Quinn moved to Sydney in 1964 to join Newtown. He played against France that year and was one of the stars of the Australian team which toured New Zealand in 1965. This was the end of his representative career, but he continued to give sterling service as captain of the Newtown Bluebags.

R

Played eleven matches for Australia two World Championships (1975 and 1977). Also played five minor games on one Kangaroo tour (1973)

Second-row forward Terry Randall was regarded as the 'iron man' of the Australian forward pack during the 1970s. He was 1.83m (6 ft) tall, weighed 93kg (14½ stone), and was one of the most punishing tacklers the game has known.

He began his career in 1969 as a centre with Manly-Warringah, but three years later Manly coach Ron Willey switched him to the forwards. It was a shrewd move. That year Randall played a major role in helping the Sea Eagles to their first Sydney Premiership. The following season, Manly won again and Randall was one of four players from the club to make the Kangaroo side to tour Britain and France. It was a wretched tour as far as Randall was concerned. He injured an ankle in the first match of the tour (against Salford) and later broke his right hand (against Leigh). As a result, he played only five games on tour.

He was to shine in years to come however. During the 1975 World Championship series, he played in seven of Australia's eight games and two years later he appeared in all four Championship matches. Australia was triumphant in both series. Randall's 11 World Series appearances is third only to Bob Fulton's 15 and Arthur Beetson's 14. In 1978, the year he was again one of Manly's stars in the surge to another Premiership success, Randall made himself unavailable for the Kangaroo tour for personal reasons, but he continued as a force in Premiership matches for several seasons.

JOHNNY RAPER

Thirty-three Tests for Australia (1959–68). Also played six matches in two World Cups (1960 and 1968) and 35 minor games on three Kangaroo tours (1959–60, 1963–64 and 1967–68).

Many experts have labelled Johnny Raper the greatest Rugby League forward of all time. At the very least, he stands out as one of the post-World War II greats of the game. He was a dominant force for more than a decade—and most lock-forwards who came later (including his immediate successor in the Test arena, Ron Coote) modelled their play on his combination of tough cover defence and enterprising attack.

Raper began his first-grade career with the Newtown club in 1957, when he was just 16 years old. He made his mark within 12 months, representing twice against the touring British side, for Sydney and for Sydney Colts. After the latter match, the great English lock Vince Karalius gave him his Great Britain jumper with the words: 'You'll earn many Aussie ones in the years to come'. How prophetic! Raper was to play 39 internationals (33 Tests and six World Cup games). Only his contemporaries, Graeme Langlands and Reg Gasnier, have worn the green and gold in major matches on more occasions.

Johnny Raper

In 1959, 'Chook', as he was affectionately known, changed clubs and joined the superb St George outfit. At the end of that year, he was chosen for the Kangaroo side to tour Britain, France and Italy. St George provided the two locks in that side (the other was Brian Clay) and Raper was to play his first Test match at five-eighth. He remained an automatic choice for the Australian side until he retired in 1968. Raper played five series against Great Britain, five against France, three against New Zealand and one against South Africa. He missed two tours of New Zealand because of last-minute injuries. Raper's 13 Tests against France is a record for his country (and, in these days of France's limited participation in Test football, is likely to remain so forever).

Raper won two NSW Player-of-the-Year awards (in 1960 and 1964)—and he had another great year in 1968. The year before, he had toured Britain and France as Kangaroo vice-captain (to St George club-mate Reg Gasnier). When Gasnier was badly injured on tour, Raper took over as skipper. In 1968, Raper was named as captain of the Australian World Cup side. It was a fitting finale to his international career. The Australians were untroubled to win the Cup, trouncing France 20–2 in the final.

With St George, Raper figured in eight straight Premiership-winning sides (1959 to 1966), playing centre in the first success and lock in the others. After he finished as a player, with five seasons in the Newcastle competition, Raper tried his hand at coaching. Spells at Cronulla-Sutherland (1975 and 1976) and Newtown (1978) failed however to produce any real success. He was later to serve with distinction as an Australian Test selector.

ELTON RASMUSSEN

Fifteen Tests for Australia (1959–1967). Also played two matches in two World Cups (1960 and 1968) and 35 minor games on two Kangaroo tours (1959–60 and 1967–68), one New Zealand tour (1961) and one World Cup tour (1960).

Elton Rasmussen was the quiet achiever of Australian Rugby League in the 1960s. While others had their names in the headlines, Rasmussen went about his work with a minimum of fuss—but the big Toowoomba forward was well-respected by opponents both at club and international level.

Rasmussen forced his way into the Queensland pack as a 21–year-old, in 1959. His play helped Queensland to an historic three-one win in the annual series against New South Wales and, at the end of that year, he was one of five Queensland forwards chosen in the Kangaroo side to tour Britain and France. For the next three years Rasmussen was a Test regular, making it back to Britain for the World Cup 12 months later and then to New Zealand in 1961. After the 1962 series against the touring British Lions, by which time he had moved south to join the mighty St George club, he slipped out of favour. He returned with a vengeance in 1967, and played all Tests on his second Kangaroo tour. Rasmussen wound up his international career in the 1968 World Cup, played in Australasia. The tough forward played in five of St George's Premiership-winning sides (1962–1966).

TOM RAUDONIKIS

Twenty Tests for Australia (1971–80). Also played nine matches in one World Cup (1972) and two World Championships (1975 and 1977), one minor international (1975) and 23 minor games on two Kangaroo tours (1973 and 1978), one New Zealand tour (1980) and two World Championship tours (1975 and 1977).

Sydney's Western Suburbs club has boasted a long list of top halfbacks. One was Arthur Summons, who captained Australia and was instrumental in persuading Wests to sign up another who was destined to captain his country, Tom Raudonikis. Summons finished his career in the southern NSW town of Wagga Wagga. And it was there that he discovered Raudonikis. Raudonikis' class was such that, even though Wests were languishing near the bottom of the Sydney Premiership ladder when he joined, he still managed to catch the eye of the representative selectors. He made his Test debut in 1971, against New Zealand, and became a regular in the Australian sides.

The highlight of his career came on the 1973 Kangaroo tour. Both captain Graeme Langlands and vice-captain Bob McCarthy were injured, and so, in the Third, and deciding, Test the mantle of leadership fell on Raudonikis. He responded to the challenge and led the Kangaroos to a 15–5 victory.

He was also an inspiration in club football. His play was a vital factor in Western Suburbs' rise, in the 1970s, from being also-rans to Premiership contenders. In 1980, he surprised everyone by switching to Newtown, where he helped provide a new spirit among the Jets. A year later they made it to the grand final, despite being written off by the critics as no-hopers.

Tom Raudonikis

Later, as a non-playing coach, Raudonikis inspired Brisbane newcomers Ipswich to some fine performances. While at Ipswich, he was able to unearth yet another of Australia's great halfbacks, Allan Langer. In 1987, he steered Ipswich to its first Brisbane grand final, where Raudonikis' charges went down courageously to Seagulls-Diehards 17–14. Raudonikis was also coach of the Queensland Residents' sides which beat the touring 1990 Frenchmen and then made a successful tour of New Zealand. That same year he shocked everyone by coaching the unfancied Norths to the grand final of the Brisbane Premiership, where they went down by just one point to the high-flying Valleys combination.

BILL RAYNER

Two Tests for Australia (1960). Also played one minor international (1960) and for the Rest-of-the-World against Great Britain (1960).

Out at Parramatta's home ground, Cumberland Oval, in the 1950s and 1960s, there was no dispute about which hooker held pride of place in the minds of the fans. Their hero was Bill Rayner. Rayner played only two Test matches for Australia, but he was playing at the same time as two of the greatest hookers in Australian football history, Ian Walsh and Noel Kelly.

Rayner, a tough, rugged rake, set a record of 203 first grade games for Parramatta, including a remarkable 159 straight. He joined the club from Yass, in southern New South Wales, from where he had been selected to play for Monaro against Great Britain in 1954 and for Southern Division against France a year later. Rayner's two Tests were against the 1960 touring Frenchmen. Later that year he was reserve hooker for the Australian side which competed in the World Cup, in England. He did not turn out in the World Cup proper, but was hooker for the Rest-of-the-World side which played the Cup-winners, Great Britain, at the end of the competition. He also played for Australia in an international against France, at Toulouse, after the World Series.

JACK RAYNER

Five Tests for Australia (1948–49). Also played 27 minor games on one Kangaroo tour (1948–49) and one New Zealand tour (1949).

Jack Rayner was a fine representative player, with Tests against New Zealand and Great Britain to his credit. But he is probably best remembered however for his impact on the Sydney club scene. He was at the helm to guide South Sydney to five Premierships in six seasons, during the early 1950s.

The tall second-rower made his Test debut against the New Zealand tourists in 1948. In the next 12 months, he toured each of the major Rugby League nations, to Britain and France with the 1948–49 Kangaroo squad (his 24 games exceeding the number played by each of his 25 team-mates) and across the Tasman to New Zealand, in 1949.

South Sydney officials recognised the leadership qualities of this tough policeman and gave him the job as the club's captain-coach, with the task of turning a bunch of raw youngsters into a team capable of winning the Premiership. Rayner rose to the occasion, and transformed them into world-beaters. The only time Souths failed to win the Premiership in the years from 1950 to 1955 was when the Rabbitohs had to do without their Kangaroo stars for half the 1952 season.

Some of Rayner's youngsters turned out to be real champions, including the man they called -'The Little Master', Clive Churchill, one of Australia's finest locks, Chic Cowie, and the high-scoring wingers Johnny Graves and Ian Moir. Rayner narrowly missed one major record for Souths. When he retired in 1956, he had played 195 first-grade games, just one short of the club record set a quarter of a century earlier by Benny Wearing.

RECORDS see *World Records*

ROD REDDY

Sixteen Tests for Australia (1978–82). Also played one match in one World Championship (1977), two minor internationals (1978 and 1982) and 19 minor games on two Kangaroo tours (1978 and 1982) and one World Championship tour (1977).

Rod Reddy, 'The Rockhampton Rocket', was one of the great Australian forwards of the late 1970s and early 1980s. A brilliant, running second-row forward who made his name with St George, Reddy was a vital cog in the Dragons' Premiership successes of 1977 and 1979, as well as Australia's Test victories against New Zealand and Britain.

Cartilage problems probably cost him a place in the Australian side for at least two seasons before he finally made his international debut during the 1977 World Championships. The following year Reddy was one of the stars against the touring New Zealand Kiwis, sharing the Man-of-the-Match award in the Second Test. On the subsequent Kangaroo tour of Britain and France, 'Rocket' Reddy starred early but missed half the

Rod Reddy

Tests through injury. He was back with a vengeance in Australia's Ashes whitewash of Britain in 1979—and he played a major role in Australia's defeat of New Zealand the following year, scoring a try in both Test encounters. In the next two years Reddy had wretched seasons, plagued by one injury after another. The Australian selectors dropped a bombshell by including him in the 1982 Kangaroo side, even though he had played only 10 first-grade games for St George during the Premiership competition that year. Reddy justified the selectors' faith with great games on each of the Tests on tour.

After playing 204 first-grade games for St George, Reddy eventually returned to his native Queensland, and in 1987, he finished with football in Australia in a blaze of glory, as captain-coach of the Townsville side which won the prestige Foley Shield—beating traditional rivals Cairns 30–26 in the final. He then went to England to take over as coach of the ailing Barrow side. His efforts succeeded when Barrow was elevated to the First Division of the English Championship race in 1989. When the club had a dismal first season, winning only one match, Reddy was asked to leave, but others recognised his talents, and Reddy was asked to return to St George as its assistant coach in 1991.

REFEREES

The least loved man on the Rugby League field is usually the referee. Whatever decision he makes will upset the fans of one side, but without him there would be no order on the football field. Criticism of referees has increased since the advent of television. The referees must make decisions in a split second on the field of play, while television can replay the events leading to each ruling over and over again, in slow motion and stop-frame.

Some of Australia's most famous referees have been George Bishop, the two Tom McMahons, Webby Neill, Darcy Lawler, Col Pearce, Keith Holman, Greg Hartley and Barry Gomersall. Much of the criticism of referees in Australia has been stifled in recent years by a directive of the League hierarchy, which has seen players, coaches and officials fined up to $10 000 for public complaints.

Some of the Top Non-Australian Referees

Graham Ainui: New Guinea policeman Graham Ainui was the first man from his country to make a name for himself as an international referee. He initially gained attention as a touch judge for the first international played by Papua New Guinea (against France, in 1977). Experience gained in Australian matches while based in Canberra, training with the Federal Police, set him on a path to the top. In 1984 he was the first non-Australian referee to control a Port Moresby grand final. In 1988, Ainui was the man-in-the-middle when Australia took on the Rest-of-the-World in the Bicentenary international at the Sydney Football Stadium. His performance was such that he was an automatic choice as the neutral referee in the World Cup final between Australia and New Zealand a few months later—and he was in charge again when France and Australia played their World

Cup qualifying Test in 1990 and for the France-New Zealand Tests a year later.

Rev Frank Chambers: A Huddersfield star, Frank Chambers played for his club's senior side when only 16 and for Yorkshire before he had turned 21. It is as a referee however that Chambers is best remembered. He controlled, among other matches, games involving the Kangaroo sides, the 1928 English Championship and the 1924 Challenge Cup finals. He was respected for his fairness and authority. Chambers was the first whistle-man to receive an OBE for his services to sport.

Eric Clay: They nicknamed Eric Clay 'The Sergeant Major' because of his tough, no-nonsense approach. Clay became one of the game's most controversial middle men. He began refereeing in 1947 and continued until a 50–years-of-age limit forced him to retire in 1972. For the last 13 years of his career, Clay regularly controlled international matches. It was in these matches that he often came in for criticism from supporters of French and Australasian teams. In one famous incident, after the Third Test in the 1963 Ashes series, Australian manager Jack Lynch accused Clay of blatantly favouring the Englishmen—but Clay was unperturbed about this and other attacks. He explained: 'Criticism never worried me. One can't expect to please everybody and my conscience was always clear'.

Jack Percival: Referees are always subject to criticism, but New Zealander Jack Percival seemed to have more than his fair share. British international sides were particularly upset by him. During the 1968 World Cup, he irked the British by repeatedly awarding second penalties when they failed quickly to retire the required 10 yards (11 metres). This earned him the nickname in the Australian Press of 'Ten-Yard Jack'. Percival's refereeing of the first NZ-Britain Test in 1974 so annoyed the beaten British that they swore they would refuse to play under his control again. Of course, they did. Percival ran over 20 Tests, World Cup and World Championship matches in a career spanning more than two decades. He had the 1968 World Cup final, in Sydney, and went to Britain and France to referee matches during the 1975 World Championship.

Fred Lindop: Wakefield's Fred Lindop was the first British referee to officiate at international level in Australasia, being flown out to control the New Zealand versus Australia clash at Auckland in the 1975 World Championships. He was to referee a further match on his home territory (Wales v France) before controlling the England-Australia 'grudge match' after the Championships were over. It wasn't his first taste of international football. He had gained prominence when he refereed all three Tests on the 1967 Kangaroo tour of Britain. His career included appointments to all styles of major matches, as well as the 1970 World Cup final, one of the most brutal matches in Rugby League history (see *Famous Matches* entry). He became one of only two referees to officiate in three World Series when he controlled the World Cup qualifying Test between Australia and France in 1986. He later became Britain's Director of Refereeing.

Julien Rascagnares: French referees have so often earned the ire of touring Australian sides because of their blatant bias. Not so Julien Rascagnares, who, in 1982, became the first Frenchman to referee a Great Britain-Australia Test. Such was his performance in the first encounter that both sides had no hesitation in asking him to control the other two. He was later asked to go to Australia to referee club and representative games in 1983 and the 1984 Anglo-Australian Test series. He was in charge again for the 1985 New Zealand-Australia clashes on both sides of the Tasman and made it a third Ashes series in 1986. His six Anglo-Australian matches is second only to the eight by the great Australian referees Tom McMahon Snr and Darcy Lawler.

Frank Renton: In a career spanning more than 40 years, Britain's Frank Renton controlled more than 1500 matches. He began refereeing at the age of 23 and was still active on the field at 65. He was in charge of three Challenge Cup finals, in 1900, 1907 and 1921. The 1907 match was the first played between 13-a-side teams. Renton also had control of the first international between Australia and England, in 1908. His only Ashes Test was the second encounter of the 1911–12 series.

Claude Teisseire: Only occasionally do great Rugby League players turn their talents to refereeing—and make it to the top. One such player was Frenchman Claude Teisseire, who played 17 Tests and World Cup matches between 1952 and 1961. He played four Tests against Australia, during the 1952–53 and 1955 series, and two World Cup matches, in 1954 and 1957. As a referee, he renewed his acquaintance with the Australians just once, controlling the international at Perpignan after the 1970 World Cup.

Billy Thompson: A former Huddersfield Soccer player, Billy Thompson swapped codes and became one of Britain's most famous referees, controlling a host of Tests, Challenge Cup finals and World Series matches during his career. He is one of only two referees to have officiated in three World Series, controlling three 1970 World Cup matches in England, two 1975 World Championship games in France and three 1977 World Championship clashes in Australasia. Thompson was the referee in the final of the 1977 Championship, between Great Britain and Australia. There was supposed to be a neutral referee, but Australia was so impressed with Thompson that they asked him to take charge.

A Queensland country referee, Kevin Hauff, created history in 1990 when he sent all 26 players to the sin-bin for 10 minutes. Hauff was in charge of a match between Barcaldine and Blackall in the central-west of the State. He had just sin-binned two players when their team-mates started an all-in brawl, so Hauff ordered each side to go behind their own tryline and think about whether they wanted to play football or fight. The cooling off period worked—except in the case of one Baracaldine player, who was sent off later in the match for throwing a punch.

MAL REILLY

Six Tests for Great Britain (1970). Also played three matches for Britain in one World Cup (1970) and one international for England (1977).

Mal Reilly was one of the greatest of a long list of fine British players who tried their luck in the Sydney Premiership competition. His four-year spell with Manly-Warringah in the early 1970s cost him a long Test career, but he was later to make up for that by coaching Great Britain to its greatest successes in two decades.

Reilly, a lock forward with few equals, burst upon the scene for Castleford in the late 1960s. In only his second season he won the Lance Todd Trophy as Man-of-the-Match in the 1969 Wembley Challenge Cup final, in which Castleford beat Salford 11–6. A year later he helped his side beat Wigan 7–2, before heading south with the British Lions, who took the Ashes back to Britain. Another great display in the 1970 World Cup in England ensured that Manly would open its cheque book wide.

The Sea Eagles paid a record (for an overseas player) $30 000 transfer fee to ensure Reilly was playing in the maroon and white. The contract sadly prevented Reilly from turning out for Britain for the next four years. Reilly played an important role in Manly's surge to its first two Premierships (in 1972 and 1973). His creative skills gave Manly's fine backs, which included international stars such as Bob Fulton, Ken Irvine, Ray Branighan, Dennis Ward and Graham Eadie, a chance to run riot. Reilly returned to Britain after his Manly stint. Despite a bad knee, he still managed to perform well as captain-coach of Castleford (and made a brief one-match return to the international arena in 1977).

As a non-playing coach he was sensational. He took over the British Test side in 1988. In the 100th Ashes Test, at the Sydney Football Stadium, he almost orchestrated a boil-over and in the Third Test, Reilly's side ended a 15–match Australian winning streak, then two years later, Britain triumphed in its first Test win against Australia on home soil since 1978.

REST-OF-THE-WORLD

When the World Cup was instigated in 1954, the winner was decided by either of two methods. If, after each of the countries had played each other, there was a clear leader on the points table, that nation was declared the winner. If not, the top two sides played off in a final. When there was no final, the winner played a side chosen from the other three squads— the Rest-of-the-World. After Australia beat the Rest-of-the-World in 1957 and Britain repeated the dose three years later, it was decided to change the rules to have a final every time the World Cup was decided.

There have been two other Rest-of-the-World teams chosen—both in 1988. The first played Australia in an international, at the Sydney Football Stadium, to commemorate Australia's Bicentenary. The second played Great Britain, at Headingley, to celebrate the opening of Britain's Rugby League Hall-of-Fame. In both cases the Rest-of-the-World was beaten.

1957

At Sydney Cricket Ground, Saturday, 29 June 1957
Crowd: 30 675
AUSTRALIA 20 (Provan, Moir, Poole, Ritchie tries, Carlson 3 goals & field goal) d REST-OF-THE-WORLD 11 (Benausse, Ashton, Merquey tries, Sorensen goal)
Australia: B Carlson, R Ritchie, R Poole (c), H Wells, I Moir, G Hawick, K McCaffery, B Clay, N Provan, K O'Shea, B Davies, K Kearney, W Marsh
Rest-of-the-World: L Jones (GB), M Voron (Fr), J Merquey (Fr) (c), W Sorensen (NZ), E Ashton (GB), G Benausse (Fr), S Belsham (NZ), J Whiteley (GB), J Riddell (NZ), G Gunney (GB), H Maxwell (NZ), A Apelian (Fr), C Johnson (NZ)
Referee: V Belsham (New Zealand)

1960

At Odsal Stadium, Bradford, Monday, 10 October 1960
Crowd: 3908
GREAT BRITAIN 33 (Ashton 2, Murphy 2, Myler 2, Davies, Shaw, Sullivan tries, Rhodes 3 goals) d REST-OF-THE-WORLD 27 (Menzies 3, Gruppi 2, Gourbal, Hadfield tries, Mantoulan 2, Eastlake goals)
Great Britain: A Rhodes, J Challinor, E Ashton (c), A Davies, M Sullivan, F Myler, A Murphy, V Karalius, B Shaw, D Turner, J Wilkinson, J Shaw, B McTigue
Rest-of-the-World: C Eastlake (NZ), T Hadfield (NZ), R Boden (Aust), C Mantoulan (Fr), R Gruppi (Fr), G Menzies (NZ), B Muir (Aust), Y Gourbal (Fr), B Hambly (Aust), R Eramouspe (Fr), D Beattie (Aust), W Rayner (Aust), C Johnson (NZ) (c)
Referee: E Martung (France)

1988

At Sydney Football Stadium, Wednesday, 27 July 1988
Crowd: 15 301.
AUSTRALIA 22 (McGaw 2, Lewis, Ettingshausen tries, Meninga 3 goals) d REST-OF-THE-WORLD 10 (Iro, M Gregory tries, Mercer goal)
Australia: G Jack, A Ettingshausen, M Meninga, M McGaw, A McIndoe, W Lewis (c), A Langer, W Pearce, G Miles, G Miller, S Backo, G Conescu, S Roach. Replacements: D Hasler (for Meninga) and W Fullerton Smith (for Miller)
Rest-of-the-World: G Mercer (NZ), H Gill (GB), K Iro (NZ), D Bell (NZ), D Kovae (PNG), S Cooper (NZ), A Gregory (GB), E Hanley (GB), M Gregory (GB), M Graham (NZ) (c), A Shelford (NZ), W Wallace (NZ), K Ward (GB). Replacements: J P Pougeau (Fr) (for Kovea) and S Stewart (NZ) (for M Gregory)
Referee: G Ainui (Papua-New Guinea)

At Headingley, Leeds, Saturday, 29 October 1988
Crowd: 12 409
GREAT BRITAIN 30 (Schofield, Offiah, Hanley, Stephenson, Edwards tries, Stephenson 5 goals) d REST-OF-THE-WORLD 28 (O'Connor, Graham, Cleal, Brown, Ratier tries, O'Connor 4 goals)
Great Britain: P Loughlin, D Plange, G Schofield, D Stephenson, M Offiah, S Edwards, A Gregory, E Hanley (c), A Platt, M Gregory, H Waddell, K Beardmore, K Ward. Replacements: D Hulme and R Powell
Rest-of-the-World: D Shearer (Aust), A Krewanty (PNG), B Numapo (PNG), M O'Connor (Aust), H Ratier (Fr), S Ella (Aust), A Langer (Aust), G Miller (Aust), N Cleal (Aust), M Graham (NZ) (c), S Backo (Aust), T Valero (Fr), K Sorensen (NZ). Replacements: C Lyons (Aust) and P Brown (NZ)
Referee: J Holdsworth (Great Britain)

JOHN RHODES

Played 10 matches for Australia in one World Cup (1968) and one World Championship (1975). Also played one international (1975) and two minor games on one World Championship tour (1975). Persistent injuries cost winger-cum-centre John Rhodes what critics had predicted would be a great international career. At the end of the 1968 World Cup, the respected *Sydney Morning Herald* noted, 'Australia can look to a long representative life from its two 20–year-olds, Bobby Fulton and John Rhodes'.

In Fulton's case it was—but the Canterbury winger Rhodes had to wait another seven years before he made it back to the international arena. Rhodes played all four matches for Australia in its 1968 World Cup success.

In his comeback at 28, by which time he was playing for Wynnum-Manly in the Brisbane competition, he turned out in six of the eight World Championship matches. He was also one of the fine performers in the Australian side which beat England in a 'grudge match' after the Championship success. He showed the locals what a top three-quarter he was with three dazzling tries in a tour match against Salford.

JOHN RIBOT

Nine Tests for Australia (1981–85). Also played 16 minor games on one Kangaroo tour (1982) and one New Zealand tour (1985).

Critics were amazed in 1980 when Roy Masters, coach of Sydney's Western Suburbs club, switched lock-forward John Ribot to the wing. Ribot had played in the Queensland representative pack in 1977 (scoring two tries against Great Britain) and was reserve forward for New South Wales the following year. Masters' move was based on sound reasoning however. Although Ribot was big, 1.85m (6 ft 1 in) tall and weighing 92kg (14 st 7 lb), he was also one of the fastest men in Rugby League. Ribot made a dramatic rise to the top in his new spot on the wing. He scored at least one try in almost every club game and in 1981 achieved what he had never been able to do as a forward—win a spot in the Australian Test side, for the series against the touring Frenchmen.

In 1982, despite a legal furore, Ribot switched to Manly-Warringah and continued his great form. At the end of the year he was chosen for the Kangaroo tour. He was a sensation, especially in France, the land of his forefathers (His full name was John Ribot de Bressac). His 25 tries was the best by any of the tourists, and only the prolific Mal Meninga beat him in the pointscoring lists. Against Roanne, Ribot scored three tries and kicked 10 goals from 14 attempts for 29 points. He also notched another four touchdowns against Roanne and three against the most famous of all the French clubs, XIII Catalan.

Winger John Ribot makes a break for his third Sydney club side, Manly-Warringah

After a couple of years in the wilderness, Ribot was recalled to the Australian team for a 1985 Brisbane Test against New Zealand and later, as a last-minute replacement for injured Parramatta winger Eric Grothe, for the team to tour the Shaky Isles. He quickly made his presence felt, scoring two tries at Lang Park in Australia's 26–20 victory. Then, at Auckland's Carlaw Park, he scored 90 seconds from the final whistle to help Australia snatch a 10–6 victory and seal the series. The tour was a dramatic finale to Ribot's playing career. He retired at the end of 1985, but continued as an official, first with the Queensland Rugby League and then as general manager of the Brisbane Broncos in their first years in the Sydney Premiership.

BILL RICHARDS

Four Tests for Australia (1920–1922). Also played 14 minor games on one Kangaroo tour (1921–22).

Brisbane forward Bill Richards earned a place in Rugby League annals in the Third Test against Great Britain in 1920—but it was an unwanted distinction. Richards became the first Australian to be sent off in a Test match, when referee Tom McMahon dismissed him for allegedly tripping the Leeds winger Squire Stockwell. Most commentators felt Richards had been unfairly treated, as he was universally regarded as a very honest performer who always played by the rules.

The toiler from Brisbane Western Suburbs was equally at home at either lock or in the second row. He played all three Tests in the 1920 series and was one of the first chosen for the 1921–22 Kangaroo tour. His international career came to an end in Britain, in the Third Test, at Salford. Ironically, Richards was one of three Kangaroo players sent off in a brawling match against Rochdale Hornets (the others were Mick Prentice and Rickety Johnston), and received a one-match suspension from the British authorities.

ALAN RIDLEY

Five Tests for Australia (1933–36). Also played 32 minor games on two Kangaroo tours (1929–30 and 1933–34).

Alan Ridley

Alan Ridley was big and fast. There were few opposing wingers who could match either his strength or speed. Ridley was playing in Queanbeyan in southern New South Wales when he was selected in the 1929–30 Kangaroo side. Because of an injured knee, he played only seven games on that tour, but scored 11 tries, showing what a force he would have been had he remained fit. Five of the tries were in the match against Castleford— two of them 80–metre dashes. A local critic wrote before the injury: 'He will probably return to Australia as great, if not greater, than Cec Blinkhorn was'. Blinkhorn at the time was regarded as the ultimate winger. So it was no mean praise.

Ridley's second Kangaroo tour was more satisfying. He finished with a personal tally of 25 tries and was second only to the great Dave Brown on the pointscoring table. Newspapers in Yorkshire dubbed him 'Ridley the Roamer' because of his penchant for roaming across towards the opposite wing in search of the ball and providing the overlap in backline moves. Against Leeds he scored a sensational try, sprinting 80 metres along the sideline after an intercept. The Leeds fullback had him hemmed in within a metre of touch, but a Ridley dummy completely fooled him. 'Ridley's try was the gem of the whole tour,' wrote one English journalist.

On the club scene, the big winger played an important role with Western Suburbs, after he moved to Sydney in 1931. He starred in the Magpies' side which took out the 1934 Premiership, scoring two of Wests' three tries in its 15–12 success over the star-studded Easts combination in the final.

STEVE ROACH

Nineteen Tests for Australia (1985–91). Also played in the 1988 World Cup Final, the Bicentennial international against the Rest-of-the-World (1988) and 18 minor games on two Kangaroo tours (1986 and 1990), two New Zealand tours (1985 and 1989) and one Papua New Guinea tour (1991).

Steve 'Blocker' Roach was one of the biggest and toughest of the forwards of the modern Rugby League era. Standing 1.80m (5ft 11in) tall and weighing 105kg (16st 7lb), he would regularly break even the tightest defence with his bullocking runs from the rucks.

He played his early football with Illawarra Western Suburbs in the Wollongong competition before transferring to the Balmain junior ranks. He made it to the senior lineup in 1982, as a raw front-rower. It wasn't long before Roach made his mark, being called into the NSW State-of-Origin side in 1984. A year later he made his Test debut, scoring a try in his first international, against New Zealand at Brisbane's Lang Park, before touring the Shaky Isles, where he played another two Tests. After three more clashes against the Kiwis the following year, Roach was one of the first chosen for the 1986 Kangaroo touring side. However after playing against Papua New Guinea and in the First Test against Britain, he was sidelined with a badly dislocated shoulder, suffered in a match against St Helens, and was forced to miss the remaining internationals.

The big prop also missed most of the following season with an awful knee injury. He bounced back in 1988 to regain his international spot

Kangaroo prop Steve Roach in a typical burst against Leeds

for the Bicentennial clash with the Rest-of-the-World and the successful World Cup final. In 1989, Roach was surprisingly overlooked for the State-of-Origin matches. When he was chosen for the tour of New Zealand however he showed the folly of the NSW selectors with performances which won him the Man-of-the-Series award.

Despite missing matches through injury and suspension in the run-up to the 1990 Tests against the Frenchmen (at Parkes) and the Kiwis (at Wellington), Roach was again chosen on reputation—and in both cases turned in sterling performances. He toured Britain and France with the 1990 Kangaroos and played in all five Tests. He was sinbinned in two of them—the Third Test against Britain and the Second Test versus France.

When New Zealand scored a shock win over Australia in the First Test of the 1991 series, Roach was one of the locals made a scapegoat and dropped for the remaining two clashes. There was little comment when he was not chosen in the Australian side to tour Papua New Guinea at the end of that season. But when Easts' prop Craig Salvatori was injured in the first game, Roach was flown up as a replacement. Sadly, in his first match, he suffered a broken ankle which put paid to his attempt to regain his Test spot.

IAN ROBERTS

Six Tests for Australia (1990–91). Also played two minor games on one Papua New Guinea tour (1991).

Ian Roberts had just turned 20 when, in 1985, he was drafted into South Sydney's reserve grade side after the mid-season President's Cup under-21 competition. The Rabbitohs were so impressed with the tall front-rower that they signed him up for three years. Their confidence was justified. But for a three-season battle with a chronic groin injury, he would have been a certain Test selection within a couple of years of his senior debut.

He made the City Seconds side in his first season with the firsts (1986). Two years later he starred for City Origin before being selected in the NSW State-of-Origin side. But injury forced his withdrawal. He played only 10 games that year and seven the next.

But such was his potential impact on the game that Manly-Warringah offered him a huge signing on fee to switch clubs. In 1990, he battled back from the injury to play for City Origin and NSW before being selected in the one-off Test against New Zealand. Sadly, the groin-tear flared again in the semi-finals and Roberts missed out on certain selection in the Kangaroos side to tour Britain and France.

He was back at full throttle in 1991, playing all three Tests against the touring New Zealanders (albeit the last two as a replacement) before being chosen for the Australian side to tour Papua New Guinea.

RON ROBERTS

Two Tests for Australia (1949–50). Also played in five minor games on one New Zealand tour (1949).

One try sealed a place in Rugby League folklore for St George winger Ron Roberts. It was a try which the respected football magazine *Rugby League Week* listed as the greatest single moment in the history of the game in Australia.

Roberts, a tall, burly winger was notorious for his bad handling. He held the one pass which mattered however—and scored the try which gave Australia the Ashes which had been firmly in Britain's hands for 30 years. It was in the Third Test of the 1950 series. The tourists had won the First Test at the Sydney Cricket Ground, but Australia had equalised in Brisbane. The decider was held on a quagmire at the SCG Some 14 minutes from the end, in pouring rain, the two sides were locked 2–all. From a play-the-ball Australia executed a backline movement which saw an overlap. Centre Keith Middleton fired the greasy ball to an unmarked Roberts, who caught it perfectly and sailed in for the only try of the match. A few moments later he dropped another pass with the line wide open. It did not matter. Australia had won the match and regained the Ashes after so long a drought. Roberts played only one other Test—on the tour of New Zealand the previous year. But he will always be remembered for his 1950 try.

On the club scene, he was a real match-winner and scored two tries in St George's 19–12 victory over South Sydney in the 1949 Sydney Premiership grand final.

LATCHEM ROBINSON

Norman 'Latchem' Robinson was a fine Rugby League player—but he was better known as a coach and administrator. He had a spectacular rise to prominence as a player. After only one match as Balmain's first-grade halfback he was chosen, in 1923, to tour Queensland with the NSW side. He was to remain his State's half for three seasons, but at that time, two of the all-time great halfbacks, Jimmy Craig and Duncan Thompson, were playing. Robinson therefore never made the Test side.

Robinson coached his old club to great success after he hung up his boots. He was the Tigers' mentor from 1944 to 1947, during which time they won three Sydney Premierships and were runners-up the other year. He also had a period as coach in the 1950s and took Balmain to the 1956 grand final. He managed the 1952–53 Kangaroos and the 1957 Australian World Cup squad. Critics agree that Robinson's shrewd football brain played a major part in the 1957 success.

For a while, Robinson was also a Test selector. He was one of the five involved in one of the greatest selection shocks in the history of the game—the omission from the 1948–49 Kangaroo touring side of Len Smith, who only weeks before had been Australia's captain-coach in the Tests against New Zealand. Robinson died in 1980 shortly before a stand named in his honour was opened at Balmain's home ground, Leichhardt Oval.

STEVE ROGERS

Twenty-one Tests for Australia (1978–83). Also played three matches in one World Championship (1975) and 30 minor games on three Kangaroo tours (1973, 1978 and 1982) and two World Championship tours (1975 and 1977).

Steve Rogers was one of Rugby League's outstanding players of the late 1970s and early 1980s. An exciting centre, his play was characterised by dazzling acceleration and an elusive swerve. He first appeared in Sydney first grade football, for Cronulla-Sutherland, in 1973. That same year, thanks to the form he showed in Cronulla's drive to the grand final, the 18–year-old was chosen as the baby of the Kangaroo side to tour Britain and France. Rogers did not make the Test side, but had a good tour, brought to a premature end when he suffered a broken jaw in the match against Les Espoirs (French Hopefuls) at Bordeaux.

In 1975, Rogers was one of the stars of the Australian side which won the World Championship. He was also one of the first chosen in the Australian squad for the 1977 World Championship, but injured in a warm-up match against New Zealand's South Island (a game in which he scored four tries), he missed the entire series.

Strange as it may seem, Rogers only made his Test debut in 1978— against the touring New Zealand Kiwis. He played Tests against Britain and France on the 1978 Kangaroo tour and against the touring British Lions in 1979 and the Frenchmen two years later. Selectors dropped a bombshell by dropping Rogers from the Australian side for the Second Test against the 1982 Kiwis. He was given a reprieve however when his replacement, Queensland's Mal Meninga, was injured early in the game. Rogers was a real force on the Kangaroo tour at the end of the year, playing against Papua New Guinea, Britain and France.

Upon his return to Australia, Rogers switched clubs to St George, becoming the highest paid footballer in the Sydney competition. He was to play only one more Test, against the 1983 New Zealand side. After an injury-plagued two seasons with the Dragons, 'Sludge', as Rogers was affectionately known, returned to the Sharks. However in the first match of the 1985 season he broke his jaw. Rogers made his return to the game at the start of the 1985–86 English season, with Widnes—but after only

13 minutes on the field he broke a leg. It was a sad finale to a great career.

ALBERT ROSENFELD

Four Tests for Australia (1908). Also played 13 minor games on one Kangaroo tour (1908–09).

The Rugby League world has never known a scoring machine the equal of Albert Rosenfeld. His records, set in the early years of the code, remain intact almost eight decades later. Rosenfeld was one of the pioneers of the game in Australia, but it was in England that he became a living legend. His early representative appearances were at five-eighth. He played in that position in the very first League match played in Australia (New South Wales versus New Zealand on August 17, 1907) and in the first Test series (also against New Zealand, in 1908).

He joined the Huddersfield club in England as a winger-cum-centre after starring on the first Kangaroo tour of Britain, in 1908–09. He was lucky to have even been in the touring side, being one of three players added to the squad after a public outcry concerning their original omission. With Huddersfield, Rosenfeld became the first player to top 400 tries in a career. He notched a record 78 tries in the 1911–12 season, and improved on it with 80 two seasons later (he scored a 'meagre' 56 in the season between). Rosenfeld was also one of the stars of the world record scoring match when, in 1914, Huddersfield downed Swinton Park 119–2 in a Challenge Cup match.

Albert Rosenfeld

Rosenfeld played in 14 major finals with Huddersfield and was only in the beaten side three times. They included Challenge Cup victories in 1913 and 1915 and English Championship wins in 1912, 1913 and 1915. Sadly, in the one Championship final in which he captained Huddersfield,

1920, his side went down narrowly 3–2 to Hull. Rosenfeld's record would have been even more impressive except he played no football for more than three years while on active service during World War I—a period when his career was at its zenith.

HOW ROSENFELD SCORED HIS TRIES AT HUDDERSFIELD

Season	Tries
1909–10	24
1910–11	42
1911–12	78
1912–13	56
1913–14	80
1914–15	55
1915–16	15
1919–20	31
1920–21	9
1921–22	5
1922–23	6
TOTAL	401

ROYAL AGRICULTURAL SOCIETY SHIELD

The Royal Agricultural Society Shield was the first major trophy in Australian Rugby Leage. Donated by the trustees of the Sydney Showground where the first matches were played in 1907, it was awarded to the winning club in the Sydney Premiership. When Eastern Suburbs won in three successive years just before World War I, it won the trophy outright. Easts gave the shield to Dally Messenger, who captained the side in each of its three Premiership successes.

The ownership of the shield was the subject of a court battle between the NSW Rugby League and the great player's grandson, Dally Messenger III, in the early 1990s. The dispute was finally resolved when the League deferred to Messenger in 1991.

WINNERS OF THE RAS SHIELD

Year	Winner
1908	South Sydney
1909	South Sydney
1910	Newtown
1911	Eastern Suburbs
1912	Eastern Suburbs
1913	Eastern Suburbs

ROTHMANS MEDAL

The Rothmans Medal is awarded each year to the Best-and-Fairest Player in the Sydney Premiership competition. It is decided at the end of the second round on votes from referees which are cast after every match. If a player is sent from the field and convicted of an offence during the season he is ineligible for the award.

Only three players have won the medal twice. South Sydney five-eighth Denis Pittard scored in 1969 and 1971, Mick Cronin, Parramatta's goalkicking centre, won in 1977 and 1978, and his Parramatta team-mate, halfback Peter Sterling, won in 1987 and 1990. The record points tally in the voting is 32, by Cronin when winning his second medal. It was also the easiest win, as he was 11 points ahead of his nearest rival. Perhaps the unluckiest player was Eastern Suburbs lock-forward Ron Coote. In 1973, he missed out on the medal by just one point, and he was runner-up again the following year.

WINNERS OF THE ROTHMANS MEDAL

1968 _____ Terry Hughes (Cronulla-Sutherland)	1980 _____ Geoff Bugden (Newtown)
1969 _____ Denis Pittard (South Sydney)	1981 _____ Kevin Hastings (Eastern Suburbs)
1970 _____ Kevin Junee (Eastern Suburbs)	1982 _____ Greg Brentnall (Canterbury-Bankstown)
1971 _____ Denis Pittard (South Sydney)	1983 _____ Mike Eden (Eastern Suburbs)
1972 _____ Tom Raudonikis (Western Suburbs)	1984 _____ Terry Lamb (Canterbury-Bankstown)
1973 _____ Ken Maddison (Cronulla-Sutherland)	1985 _____ Wayne Pearce (Balmain)
1974 _____ Graham Eadie (Manly-Warringah)	1986 _____ Mal Cochrane (Manly-Warringah)
1975 _____ Steve Rogers (Cronulla-Sutherland)	1987 _____ Peter Sterling (Parramatta)
1976 _____ Ray Higgs (Parramatta)	1988 _____ Barry Russell (Cronulla-Sutherland)
1977 _____ Mick Cronin (Parramatta)	1989 _____ Gavin Miller (Cronulla-Sutherland)
1978 _____ Mick Cronin (Parramatta)	1990 _____ Peter Sterling (Parramatta)
1979 _____ Ray Price (Parramatta)	1991 _____ Ewan McGrady (Canterbury-Bankstown)

RUGBY LEAGUE WEEK PLAYER-OF-THE-YEAR

Each week the respected magazine *Rugby League Week* rates the performances of each of the Sydney Premiership first–grade players. The players are given a score out of 10 and the points tallied at the end of the season to choose the best player in the competition. Twelve times a player has scored 10 out of 10 for a match. Peter Sterling (Parramatta) is the only player to have twice achieved this distinction of playing the ultimate game—in 1986 and 1987.

WINNERS OF RUGBY LEAGUE WEEK'S PLAYER-OF-THE-YEAR AWARD

1970 _____	Tommy Bishop (Cronulla-Sutherland)
1971 _____	Bob Grant (South Sydney)
1972 _____	John Ballesty (Eastern Suburbs)
1973 _____	John Mayes (Manly-Warringah)
1974 _____	Arthur Beetson (Eastern Suburbs)
1975 _____	Bob Fulton (Manly-Warringah)
1976 _____	Ray Higgs (Parramatta)
1977 _____	Mick Cronin (Parramatta)
1978 _____	Geoff Gerard (Parramatta)
1979 _____	Ray Price (Parramatta)
1980 _____	Kevin Hastings (Eastern Suburbs)
1981 _____	Kevin Hastings (Eastern Suburbs)
1982 _____	Kevin Hastings (Eastern Suburbs)
1983 _____	Phil Sigsworth (Manly-Warringah)
1984 _____	Peter Sterling (Parramatta)
1985 _____	Ray Price (Parramatta)
1986 _____	Peter Sterling (Parramatta)
1987 _____	Peter Sterling (Parramatta)
1988 _____	Ben Elias (Balmain)
1989 _____	Gavin Miller (Cronulla-Sutherland)
1990 _____	Mal Meninga (Canberra)
1991 _____	Ewan McGrady (Canterbury-Bankstown)

CHARLIE 'BOXER' RUSSELL

Three Tests for Australia (1910–11). Also played 22 minor games on one Kangaroo tour (1911–12).

Boxer Russell was a champion three-quarter in both codes of Rugby. In the amateur game he played three Tests against the touring 1907 New Zealand All Blacks and the following year was one of the stars of the first Wallaby tour of Britain. He played in the only two Tests, scoring two of Australia's three tries in the 9–3 success over England, at Blackheath, and one of the two touchdowns when the tourists lost 9–6 to Wales, at

Cardiff. Russell's 24 tries on that tour still stands as a Wallaby record. He was also a member of the Australian side which won a gold medal at the 1908 London Olympics.

Back home, Russell was one of the Wallabies who accepted hefty cash offers to switch codes and play a series of games against the Kangaroos. Russell, himself, became a Kangaroo in 1911, playing in 24 of 36 games.

On the club scene, he was an important player in the Newtown side which won the club's first Premiership, in 1910. He went on to become a great non-playing coach and was at the helm when Newtown notched its second Premiership, in 1933.

KEVIN RYAN

Two Tests for Australia (1964). Also played four minor games on one Kangaroo tour (1963-64).

Kevin Ryan played just two Rugby League internationals for Australia, but his club career alone entitles him to a place among the greats of the game. He already had five Rugby Union internationals (three versus the New Zealand All Blacks and one each against England and the Maoris) and a Wallaby tour of the British Isles behind him when he joined the St George professionals in 1960. He appeared in all of the Saints' Premiership winning sides in the next seven years. When he left, in 1967, to become captain-coach of Canterbury-Bankstown, he was instrumental in bringing to an end the Dragons' record run of 11 successive titles. Canterbury downed St George 12-11 in the final that year, but lost to South Sydney in the grand final a week later.

Ryan had little luck on the Rugby League international scene. He was chosen for the 1963-64 Kangaroo squad to tour Britain and France, but tore a cartilage in the match against Hull before the First Test (only his fourth game in England) and missed the rest of the tour. Back home, the next year he played two Tests against the touring Frenchmen. After he retired, Ryan, a barrister, won a seat in the NSW Parliament. His legal expertise was brought into action in 1990 after he was elected leader of the Players' Association in order to head the fight against the introduction of the Players' Draft.

TOMMY RYAN

Four Tests for Australia (1952-53). Also played 16 minor games on one Kangaroo tour (1952-53).

Team-mates nicknamed burly winger Tommy Ryan 'The Arrow'. It was apt, for Ryan knew of no way to go for the tryline other than straight and fast. Ryan joined St George from his home town of Inverell in northern New South Wales as 20-year-old, in 1950. He soon made his mark as a bustling centre. In 1952, he broke into the representative ranks, with both City and New South Wales. He was such a success that it was a foregone conclusion that he would make the Kangaroo squad to tour Britain and France at the end of the year.

On tour, Ryan was switched to the wing, where he had played all his schoolboy football. He was an instant success, making his debut in the Third Test against Britain and playing all three internationals against France. In his debut against each country he went over for two fine tries. They were part of a tally of 24 he scored in his 16 tour matches—second only to Brian Carlson's 29. In 1956 and 1957, Ryan played in the first two of the St George sides which strung together a world record 11 straight Premierships. In the latter year, he broke the club try-scoring record with 26 touchdowns—a record which still stood more than three decades later.

WARREN RYAN

Among the many fine coaches of the modern era there were few who could match the record of Warren Ryan.

From the moment he took over as coach of the Western Suburbs Under-23 side in 1978, it was obvious he was destined to write his name in the record books. That first year, Wests were languishing with only two sides behind them at the half-way mark, but Ryan inspired the youngsters to a series of do-or-die efforts to steer them into the grand final.

His first senior side was Newtown. When he took over in 1979, the Jets record was three straight wooden spoons. There was only marginal improvement the first season but in 1980 they were challenging for a semi-final spot. In 1981, Ryan almost achieved the impossible, when Newtown, with only a couple of established stars and 500–1 outsiders in the competition, shocked everyone by reaching the grand final only to fall late in the match to the great Parramatta lineup.

In 1984, Ryan took over Canterbury's coaching, won Premierships in his first two years and reached the grand final the next. Sadly, internal bickering resulted in a poor season in 1987 and, disillusioned, Ryan switched to Balmain. The Tigers went close that first year. Forced into a midweek play-off with Penrith for the fifth and final semi-final spot, they then won a series of sudden-death matches. Balmain beat, in turn, Penrith, Manly-Warringah, Canberra and Cronulla to reach the grand final. But the run had taken its toll and Balmain was no match for Canterbury-Bankstown in the season's finale, going down 24–12.

Balmain were back in the grand final 12 months later. And after they led Canberra 12–2 at half-time another Ryan Premiership looked likely. But the Raiders fought back and a Canberra try 90 seconds from the final hooter equalled the score. At 14–all the two sides played an extra 10 minutes each way and Canberra snatched the game away from Balmain with a try and field goal.

Ryan had the Tigers in the semis again in 1990 but then accepted a real challenge—to pull Wests out of the mire. Several Canterbury stars queued up to play for their old boss and the new combination helped the Magpies into the semi-finals for the first time in almost a decade.

S

ST GEORGE

No football code, anywhere in the world, can boast a record to equal St George's 11 straight Sydney first grade Premiership victories. From 1956 to 1966, the Dragons ruled the roost. They had some close calls. Western Suburbs got to within three points of them in the 1962 grand final and five points a year later—but, by and large, there was little threat to St George's superiority during that era. Only South Sydney has won more Premierships than has St George, however the Dragons entered the Premiership race in 1921, while Souths was a foundation member, back in 1908.

Considering the success of St George, the opposition to its original bid to join the Premiership competition seems incredible. Several requests were turned down before the persistence of the St George officials paid off. The club's first match was against Glebe on St George's Day (April 23). It was a fine debut. Glebe managed to scrape home 4–3. The euphoria of the first performance soon wore off however, as the newcomers proved little match for the other established clubs. St George won only three of its 16 games that year (two of them at the expense of University, which had been admitted to the top competition only 12 months before). The second season was even more disappointing—just two wins, both against University.

The rot continued until 1927, when club officials boldly signed up the great forward Frank Burge as player-coach. Burge's fee for the season was then the biggest paid by any Australian club. The money was well spent. Burge took St George from the bottom of the table to the 1927 Premiership final, where a fine South Sydney combination had to produce its best form of the season to win 20–11. Burge remained as coach for another three seasons and each time St George made the semi-finals. In the last of those years, 1930, St George went within an ace of winning its first Premiership. Saints beat the Minor Premiers, Western Suburbs, 14–6 in the final. Under the system operating at that time however, the Minor Premiers had the right to challenge in a grand final if beaten in the playoffs. Wests turned the tables 27–2.

St George had to wait 20 years before it finally succeeded in the Premiership race, in 1941. Saints beat Eastern Suburbs 31–14 in the final. It reached the final again 12 months later, but Canterbury-Bankstown fullback Lin Johnson snatched a last-minute goal to steer the Berries to an 11–9 victory. The Saints' next success was in 1949. They owed much to a solid pack and a backline which included Noel Pidding, Doug McRitchie, Ron Roberts, Johnny Hawke and Matt McCoy, all who wore the green and gold for Australia at some stage during their careers.

St George reached the grand final in 1953, but found South Sydney too strong. When Souths' reign came to an end after the 1955 season, Saints were ready to take over. And how! Under a succession of top coaches— Norm Tipping, Ken Kearney, Norm Provan and Ian Walsh—the Dragons steamrolled their way to Premiership after Premiership. Their peak season was 1963. That year, St George won the Premiership in all three grades, the Club Championship and the Pre-season Competition—a feat never before accomplished. To cap it all, St George beat New Zealand 22–7. It was only the second time an Australian club had played a touring international side, and it was the first time one had beaten the tourists.

Twelve months earlier, St George had played Britain before a Sydney Cricket Ground crowd of 57 895, an amazing number for a midweek afternoon. The British turned in a powerhouse display to swamp the Dragons 33–5, after St George had led 5–0 early in the game.

St George broke many records during its stay at the top. In the 1963 grand final, 69 860 hardy fans braved the cold and the rain to watch the Saints down Western Suburbs 8–3 on a SCG quagmire. This figure was only 559 short of the then-record Australian attendance (and the biggest for a club game). The record was smashed two years later. Some 78 056 fans jammed the SCG to see the St George-South Sydney grand final. Many thousands more clambered over the walls once police ordered the gates closed, and were not included in the official attendance. This is a record which will never be beaten. All major Rugby League matches are now played at the Sydney Football Stadium which has a capacity of just under 42 000. During the decade-plus St George was at the head of the table, it boasted a host of fine players. These included five who were to captain Australia—hookers Ken Kearney and Ian Walsh, centres Reg Gasnier and Graeme Langlands and lock Johnny Raper.

The 1956–57 Kangaroo side contained four Saints players—Kearney (captain), centre Kevin O'Brien, and forwards Norm Provan and Bryan Orrock. Three years later the number had risen to seven—Gasnier, Raper, winger Eddie Lumsden, centre Johnny Riley, halfback Bob Bugden, lock Brian Clay and front-rower Billy Wilson. In 1963–64 five Dragons went on tour—Walsh, Gasnier, Langlands, Raper and prop Kevin Ryan. Indeed, when utility player Brad Mackay toured with the 1990 side, he maintained a unique St George tradition of supplying at least one player to every Kangaroo side (albeit, in 1986, Michael O'Connor had announced before the tour had got underway that he would quit the Dragons to join Manly for the 1987 season).

Ironically, Kevin Ryan, the hero of the last seven of St George's record run of Premierships, played a major role in the eventual downfall of St George. He transferred to Canterbury and was captain-coach of that side when it knocked St George out of the Premiership race the same year (1967) with a narrow win in the preliminary final. Although no longer Premiers, St George continued to be among the top sides. When they missed the semi-finals in 1974, everyone thought it was the end at last. However, 12 months later, they bounced back. Not only did they make the semis, but they downed glamour side Eastern Suburbs to reach the grand final. Unfortunately, it was a different matter in the deciding finale to the Premiership. Easts turned in an astounding display of power and finesse to thrash St George 38–0 in an unprecedented humiliation.

Gradually, the last of the St George stars from its golden era hung up their boots. Among the last to go were the immortals Graeme Langlands and Billy Smith. However, a new breed of stars soon emerged under the coaching of former St George hero Harry Bath. In 1977, these young players, affectionately known as 'Bath's Babes', shocked everyone—themselves included—by downing hot favourites Parramatta in the grand final replay (the original match had been drawn 9–all). The margin of victory, 22–0, was proof of their coming of age. Two years later, Bath again steered St George to a Premiership—this time beating Canterbury.

St George came within an ace of sweeping the honours in 1985. The Dragons were Minor Premiers in all three grades (winning the Club Championship). The two lower grades both won their respective grand finals, but the first–grade side was pipped 7–6 by Canterbury. St George had won all four previous encounters with the Bulldogs that year, but lost the one which counted. Coach Roy Masters received some consolation by being named Coach-of-the-Year.

In 1989, in an effort to drag the Saints out of a slump, which had seen them drop to 10th place in the competition, the hero of the 1977 and 1979 Premiership wins, Craig Young, was given the job of coaching the side he had skippered for most of the previous decade—but when little success was forthcoming he was unceremoniously dumped mid-season in 1990.

Former Illawarra coach Brian Smith was brought back from England, where he was in a successful season with Hull, to take over the reins. The Dragons finished just two points out of the final five in 1991. British Test player Martin Offiah added some excitement to the backline. And Scott Gourley, a former Rugby Union Test forward (and son of an old St George star of the 1960s, Robin Gourley) came of age and was rewarded with selection in the Australian side which toured Papua New Guinea.

ST GEORGE

Founded: 1921
Entered Sydney Premiership competition: 1921
Home ground: Kogarah Jubilee Oval (Record crowd—23 582)
Colours: Red and white
Nickname: The Dragons
Honours:
  Sydney Premiership—Winners, 1941, 1949, 1956, 1957, 1958, 1959 (unbeaten), 1960, 1961, 1962, 1963, 1964, 1965, 1966, 1977, 1979; Runners-up, 1927, 1930, 1933, 1937, 1942, 1946, 1953, 1971, 1975, 1985
  Flowers Memorial Pennant (Club Championship)—1940, 1942, 1946, 1949, 1951, 1955, 1956, 1957, 1958, 1959, 1962, 1963, 1964, 1965, 1966, 1971, 1984, 1985
    Midweek Cup—1988
    Pre-season Competition—1963, 1964, 1965, 1971
    City Cup—1944, 1959
    State Championship—1944
    Reserve-grade Premiership—1938, 1962, 1963, 1964, 1976, 1985
    Third-grade Premiership—1940, 1942, 1949, 1951, 1953, 1957, 1963, 1965, 1966, 1983

Under-23 Premiership—1972, 1974, 1985, 1987
President's Cup—1935, 1941, 1957, 1981
Flegg Memorial Trophy—1975
SG Ball Cup—1975
Most first-grade games: 256 by Norm Provan
Most points in a career: 1556 by Graeme Langlands
Most tries in a career: 143 by Johnny King
Most points in a season: 225 by Harry Bath, in 1958
Most tries in a season: 26 by Tommy Ryan, in 1957
Rothmans Medal winners: Nil
NSW Player-of-the-Year: Ken Kearney (1955), Norm Provan (1957), Reg Gasnier (1959, 1961 & 1964),
   Johnny Raper (1960 & 1964), Ian Walsh (1963), Billy Smith (1966), Graeme Langlands (1970)
Sun-Herald Best-and-Fairest Player: Norm Provan (1954), Johnny Raper (1960, 1963 & 1967), Billy Smith
   (1966), Graeme Langlands (1970)
Coach-of-the-Year: Harry Bath (1977), Roy Masters (1985)

St George hooker Chris Guider made history in 1985 when he played in all three Sydney Premiership grand finals. He was chosen as hooker for the Under-23 side which beat Parramatta 24–20. He also came on as a replacement in the reserve–grade against Canberra (won 22–16 by St George) and in the first–grade against Canterbury-Bankstown (which the Saints lost 7–6). The feat is unique in the annals of Rugby League.

ST HELENS

St Helens is one of Britain's most famous clubs. Founded in 1890, it was one of the original Rugby Union clubs to break away and form the new code in 1895. The Saints have traditionally provided some of the toughest opposition for touring sides from Australia and New Zealand. Since World War II, the Kangaroos have suffered six defeats at the hands of the Lancashire club.

St Helens, in 1976, became the first British club to make a tour of Australasia. It was a financial success, but the visitors disappointed by losing all three matches, including one against Sydney's Eastern Suburbs for the unofficial World Club Championship. Its second tour down under, in 1985, was not much better. The holder of the English Premiership Trophy won only one of its four matches, all of which were in New Zealand.

ST HELENS TOURS OF AUSTRALASIA

1976

Record in Australia
Played 2, Lost 2, points for 17, Points against 46

Record in New Zealand
Played 1, Lost 1, Points for 13, Points against 20

Match results

Opponents	Venue (Attendance)	For	Against
Queensland	Brisbane (11 000)	15	21
Eastern Suburbs	Sydney (26 856)	2	25
Auckland	Auckland (11 500)	13	20

1985

Record in New Zealand
Played 4, Won 1, Lost 3, Points for 100, Points against 102

Match Results

Opponents	Venue	For	Against
Canterbury	Christchurch	24	30
Waikato	Huntly	24	34
Manukau	Auckland	10	26
Northern Districts	Whangerei	42	12

PAUL SAIT

Seven tests for Australia (1971-74). Also played nine matches in two World Cups (1970 and 1972) and one World Championship (1975). Also played 10 minor games on one Kangaroo tour (1973) and one New Zealand tour (1971).

Paul Sait was one of the most versatile utility players Australia produced in the post-World War II era. He was equally at home in the centres or in the forwards, at lock or second-row.

Sait first achieved prominence at the end of the 1970 season, when the 22–year-old was chosen as a centre in the Australian World Cup squad for the series in England. However, he turned out as a second-rower in the three preliminary matches before switching to the backs for the Cup final, in which Australia downed Great Britain 12-7. It was also at centre that Sait played his first Test, on the 1971 tour of New Zealand. Sait had a great Kangaroo tour in 1973. He also appeared in two more World Series before bowing out of international football in 1975.

On the club scene, he was a vital player in the South Sydney sides which won the Sydney Premiership in 1970 and 1971. From his first days at Souths in 1969 until he retired in 1978, Sait appeared in 154 first–grade games for the Rabbitohs. He would have appeared in more but for missing much of 1977 through injury.

CRAIG SALVATORI

2 Tests for Australia (1991). Also played one minor game on one Papua New Guinea tour (1991)

When big Craig Salvatori was graded from the Dunbar Raiders in the Eastern Suburbs junior competition in 1985, there were high hopes that the 19-year-old would make it to the top.

He did—but it took several seasons in the lower grades and a couple in the senior ranks before he managed to catch the eye of the representative selectors. A new-found confidence under the guidance of the Easts management/coaching duo of Jack Gibson and Mark Murray suddenly skyrocketed him into the 1991 City Origin lineup, the side for the third State-of-Origin clash (albeit on the interchange bench) and then, finally, into the Test side.

The Test selectors wanted new blood after a humiliating defeat at the hands of New Zealand in the First Test of the 1991 series. And the 187 cm (6ft 2 in), 101 kg (15 st 13 lb) prop filled the bill. His bruising runs and torrid defence were instrumental in helping Australia win the final two encounters with the Kiwis.

Salvatori was one of the first chosen for the end-of-season tour of Papua New Guinea. But a serious knee injury in the first match, against Northern Zone, at Lae, forced him to quit and return home for surgery.

MARK SARGENT

Three Tests for Australia (1990). Also played six minor games on one Kangaroo tour (1990).

Tough prop Mark Sargent showed promise while playing with Canterbury-Bankstown in the late 1980s, but he had trouble cementing a first grade spot in a pack loaded with internationals. In 1989 therefore, he switched to Newcastle, the city where he had begun his football as a teenager (with Central Charlestown Juniors). The bold move paid off handsomely. That year he was chosen for the Country Origin side to play City. At the end of the year he was joint winner of the Rothmans Medal as the best-and-fairest player in the Sydney Premiership competition—no doubt helped by an incredible 514 tackles made in 21 matches (at an average of more than 24 a game).

His form was no less devastating in 1990, finishing close to the winner in the Rothmans Medal voting despite missing five matches with a damaged ankle. The selectors were impressed and chose the big forward in the 1990 Kangaroo squad to tour Britain and France. Sargent was one of the tour finds. He was chosen as a reserve for the last three Tests—and got a run in each game. His six tries on tour was the most by any of the Australian forwards.

JOHN SATTLER

Four Tests for Australia (1969–71). Also played 12 minor games on one Kangaroo tour (1967–68) and two New Zealand tours (1969 and 1971).

As a schoolboy, John Sattler detested Rugby League. He lost count of the number of times he was punished for skipping winter sports' afternoons. 'I hated Rugby League and flatly refused to play,' he admitted years later. It was only after he left school that Sattler changed his opinion. Luckily he did so, for he went on to become a Rugby League legend—one of the roughest, toughest footballers in the game's history. Sattler was a real Dr Jekyll and Mr Hyde. On the field he was recognised as one of the wildest men Rugby League has known, but after the match was over he was a quietly-spoken, hard-working, family man.

Sattler did not play a competition game of Rugby League until he was 16, when he was persuaded to turn out with a junior side at Kurri Kurri, in the coalfields area of the NSW Hunter Valley. As a lock-forward, he was one of the stars in the Newcastle representative side which beat the touring 1962 Great Britain side in a vicious match. South Sydney persuaded him to join its young side the following season. So began an illustrious career in big-time football. Sattler was to lead Souths to four Premierships, in 1967, 1968, 1970 and 1971.

No performance was more inspiring than that in the 1970 grand final win over Manly-Warringah. He played almost the entire game with his jaw smashed in three places after a rival caught him from behind. Twelve teeth were crushed in the incident. A lesser player would have quit, but Sattler remained on the field to inspire his side. 'While the injury was bad, I have only fond memories of that game,' Sattler later recalled.

South Sydney captain John Sattler is chaired from the field by team-mates after the Rabbitohs won the 1967 Grand Final

Sattler toured Great Britain and France with the 1967–68 Kangaroos, even though he had not yet played for New South Wales. He was captain of the Australian side which toured New Zealand in 1969, and he also skippered Australia in a Test against the touring 1970 Englishmen. He may well have been skipper of the victorious 1970 World Cup squad, but for the broken jaw which ruled him out of contention.

His career spanned 14 seasons, two in the Newcastle competition, nine with Souths and the final three in Brisbane. In that period, he achieved a record of being sent off 15 times. Suspensions cost him 30 weeks of play, a huge period in his era—yet his wife once described him as being 'as gentle as a lamb'.

GARRY SCHOFIELD

Thirty-two Tests for Great Britain (1984–91). Also played 14 minor games on two Lions tours of Australasia (1984 and 1988) and one tour of Papua New Guinea and New Zealand (1990.)

Garry Schofield was one of the world's top centres in the 1980s. However after six seasons in the three-quarters he was switched to five-eighth and became even more devastating—helping scheme several surprise British Test wins.

Schofield, nicknamed 'The Poacher', was a champion amateur footballer, captaining the British Under-19 'Young Lions' side on its 1983 tour of New Zealand. He made his first team debut for Hull the same year and was an instant sensation, topping the try-scoring lists in his first season with 38 (10 more than his nearest rival)—and he made his Test debut, in the second of two clashes against France, at Headingley.

Although only 18, Schofield was one of the stars of the Great Britain squad which toured Australasia and Papua New Guinea in 1984. He played in the first four Tests on tour, before being ruled out for the final three because of a hairline fracture of the leg. The Sydney scouts were impressed, and Schofield spent three seasons with Balmain (1985, 1986 and 1987) before returning with the 1988 British Lions touring side. In the meantime he had set a British Test record with four tries in a 1985 match against New Zealand and his 1987 move to Leeds had attracted a then world record $300 000 transfer fee.

Schofield was back in Australia in 1989, this time with Western Suburbs, and he toured Papua New Guinea and New Zealand in 1990. It was on this tour that Schofield switched to five-eighth with so much success that he was named Man-of-the-Series against the Kiwis. Then, in the First Test against the touring Australian Kangaroos, at Wembley Stadium, his outstanding performance helped steer the British to their first home Test win since 1978. In early 1991, he inspired Britain to its biggest ever win over France. Schofield's three tries in the 60–4 thrashing earned yet another Man-of-the-Match award. Later in the year, Schofield captained Britain when it throttled Papua New Guinea 56–4.

IAN SCHUBERT

Four matches for Australia in one World Championships (1975). Also played in one minor international (1982) and 25 minor games on two Kangaroo tours (1978 and 1982) and one World Championship tour (1975).

Few footballers have made such a spectacular debut in senior international football as Ian Schubert, a winger from Sydney's Eastern Suburbs club. Schubert, whose long blond hair was a hit with many fans, was a member of the sensational 1972 Australian schoolboys' side which toured Great Britain. He was still playing schoolboy football in 1974. A year later however, at the age of 19, he became one of the stars of the Australian senior side which played in the final matches of the World Championship in New Zealand, France and Britain. He played in the last four games and notched a hat-trick of tries in two of those matches.

Ian Schubert

The great coach, Roy Francis, who presented Schubert with his Man-of-the-Match award after the clash with Wales at Swansea, described him as the greatest Australian find in many years. Schubert never quite reached those dizzy heights again, although he was a member of the next two Kangaroo touring sides (1978 and 1980), and his 269 first grade games for Easts, Manly-Warringah and Western Suburbs was the third highest tally in the history of the Sydney Premiership.

KEVIN SCHUBERT

Nineteen Tests for Australia (1948–52). Also played 39 minor games on two Kangaroo tours (1948–49 and 1952–53) and one New Zealand tour (1949).

Kev Schubert was one of Australia's most successful hookers. In just four years, after World War II, he played in 19 Tests (eight against Britain, seven against New Zealand and four against France). He also made two Kangaroo tours and one to New Zealand.

Schubert made his Test debut against the visiting New Zealand Kiwis in 1948. He held the spot until Ken Kearney took over on the 1952–53 Kangaroo tour. Highlight of Schubert's international career was undoubtedly the 1950 series against Britain, when Australia regained the Ashes for the first time in 30 years. British captain Ernest Ward described Schubert's play in the series as outstanding. 'He was the complete hooker,' said Ward. Schubert's 29–19 success over the great Joe Egan in the Third (and deciding) Test scrums proved vital in Australia's narrow victory.

In club football, Schubert skippered Manly-Warringah in the 1951 Premiership grand final (as stand-in for injured captain-coach Wally O'Connell). The injury-hit Seagulls were no match for the great South Sydney combination however, going down 42–14.

BILL SCHULTZ

Seven Tests for Australia (1919–21). Also played 26 minor games on one Kangaroo tour (1921–22) and one New Zealand tour (1919).

In the late 1980s, Rugby League historian George Crawford was asked to choose the best composite teams from each of the Sydney Premiership clubs. When it came to the Balmain side, Crawford had no hesitation in naming Bill 'Changa' Schultz as one of the props (with Steve Roach) ahead of fine internationals such as Arthur Beetson, Bill Marsh, Rod Morris and Barry McTaggart.

Schultz was a tough campaigner who made his Test debut on the 1919 visit to New Zealand. He played against the touring British Lions in 1920 and locked horns with the British again on the 1921–22 Kangaroo tour. On this tour he played 24 games (only a handful of team-mates played more). He was sent off for punching in a brawling match against Hull Kingston Rovers, having retaliated after being given a bloody nose.

For Balmain, Schultz was a tower of strength, helping the Watersiders (as the players were then known) to five Premierships in six seasons (1915, 1916, 1917, 1919 and 1920) and a sixth four years later (1924).

SECOND DIVISION_____

The first attempts to get a Sydney Second Division competition off the ground took place in 1963. Nine teams on the fringe areas of the city and a tenth from Sydney University (coached by former World Cup captain Dick Poole) competed in what was called the Inter-District Competition. Kingsford, from the heart of the South Sydney area, won the grand final at Henson Park, beating Cronulla-Caringbah (the forerunner of the Premiership side Cronulla-Sutherland) 9–7.

From 1964 to 1973, the competition was actually called the Second Division. The outstanding club was Wentworthville which won eight of the 10 titles. Much of the credit for their success must go to captain-coach Lewis Jones, the Welsh footballing legend. Penrith won in 1966 and next year was chosen (with Cronulla) to move into the first division Premiership competition.

The Second Division competition was again renamed in 1974, as the Metropolitan League, only to be scrapped after 1976. However, the whole idea was rekindled in 1990 as the Metropolitan Cup with seven teams, Ryde-Eastwood, Wentworthville, Mt Pritchard, Hills District, Bankstown Greyhounds, Guildford and Wests Leagues. Ryde-Eastwood, which, ironically, had won four of the last five Premierships in the 1970s, won the title. In 1991, more teams were added, including the famous Newtown side, one of the original clubs when the Sydney Premiership was first formed back in 1908.

The Ryde-Eastwood stranglehold was broken that season. It was beaten 21–6 in the grand final by Guildford.

SYDNEY SECOND DIVISION PREMIERS

Inter-District Competition

1963	Kingsford

Second Division

1964	____	Wentworthville
1965	____	Wentworthville
1966	____	Penrith
1967	____	Wentworthville
1968	____	Wentworthville
1969	____	Wentworthville
1970	____	Wentworthville
1971	____	Wentworthville
1972	____	Ryde-Eastwood
1973	____	Wentworthville

Metropolitan League

1974	____	Ryde-Eastwood
1975	____	Ryde-Eastwood
1976	____	Ryde-Eastwood

Metropolitan Cup

1990	____	Ryde-Eastwood
1991	____	Guildford

SENT OFF_____

The strongest possible penalty a referee can impose on a player is to send him from the field. Players can be sent off for a variety of reasons, including kicking, punching, gouging, tripping and head-high tackles. A player sent off cannot be replaced, so his team-mates have to continue with a depleted side.

Once sent off, the player must face a judiciary hearing to decide whether the offence warrants a further penalty. In the 1980s, in an effort to stamp out foul play, Rugby League authorities began imposing stiff penalties. Although players in minor competitions have been suspended for life (for striking a referee), the longest penalty in the big League was handed out to Manly-Warringah forward Les Boyd—although, in his case, he wasn't sent off. In June 1983, in the State-of-Origin match against Queensland, Boyd hit opposition forward Darryl Brohmann with an elbow, badly smashing the Queenslander's jaw. Boyd was cited after the match and suspended for 12 months. Then, after only his fourth match following the ban, he was again cited—for gouging an opponent's eye. This time he was suspended for 15 months. Boyd also is the most recent Australian to be sent off in an Ashes Test—in the Second Test of the 1982 series, at Wigan.

These days there are fewer players sent off, because referees now have the option of sending those involved in minor or technical offences to the sin-bin for 10 minutes. By the 1990s, 36 players had been sent off in Test matches between Australia and Great Britain. Predictably, the rate of dismissals of British players by Australian referees was twice that of local stars—and the opposite was the case in England.

Only two players have been dismissed more than once in Ashes Tests—both of them tough prop-forwards. Australian Ray Stehr was sent off twice during the 1936 series. Britain's Cliff Watson received his marching orders in Tests in 1963 and 1966. The most in any one Test is three. In the Third Test, at the Sydney Cricket Ground, in 1962, British players Mick Sullivan and Derek Turner and Australia's Dud Beattie were sent from the field. In the third encounter of the next series, at Headingley, Leeds, in 1963, Watson went together with Australians Brian Hambly and Barry Muir.

PLAYERS SENT OFF IN ANGLO-AUSTRALIAN TESTS

For Australia	*For Great Britain*
Bill Richards (1920)	George Ruddick (1910)
Norm Potter (1924)	Frank Gallagher (1924)
Jim Bennett (1924)	Bill Horton (1928)
Ray Stehr (1936, 1936)	Nat Silcock (1936)
Arthur Clues (1946)	Jack Arkwright (1936)
Duncan Hall (1952)	Jack Kitching (1946)
Dud Beattie (1962)	Joe Egan (1946)
Brian Hambly (1963)	Ken Gee (1950)
Barry Muir (1963)	Tommy Bradshaw (1950)
Dennis Manteit (1967)	Mick Sullivan (1962)
Noel Kelly (1967)	Derek Turner (1962)
Arthur Beetson (1970)	Cliff Watson (1963, 1966)
Tom Raudonikis (1978)	Bill Ramsay (1966)
Les Boyd (1982)	Syd Hynes (1970)
	Brian Lockwood (1973)
	Steve Nash (1978)
	Trevor Skerrett (1979)
	Lee Crooks (1982)
	David Hobbs (1984)

SEVEN-A-SIDE FOOTBALL (SEVENS) see *Nissan Sevens*

BILL SHANKLAND_____

Four Tests for Australia (1929–30). Also played 19 minor games on one Kangaroo tour (1929–30).

Bill Shankland was one of Australia's finest and most versatile sportsmen, excelling in both Rugby League and golf. He twice finished high in the famous British Open Golf Championship (third in 1939 and fourth in 1948). Shankland's versatility was never more evident than on the football field. He began as a halfback, played Tests as a winger, and later turned out in major Cup and Championship ties for the English club Warrington, as a five-eighth, centre and fullback.

Shankland, from the north coast of New South Wales, began his Sydney career with Glebe in 1927. Two seasons later, after moving to Eastern Suburbs, he made his representative debut as halfback for New South Wales in the annual clashes against Queensland. He switched to the wing, where his strong, fast running and terrifying tackling quickly led him to even greater success.

Bill Shankland toured England with the 1929–30 Kangaroos and accepted an offer to play with the Lancashire club, Warrington

He went to Britain with the 1929–30 Kangaroos and was leading try-scorer in the four Tests. In his 23 tour games, Shankland scored 24 tries and kicked 16 goals for 104 points, the second highest by any of the Aussies. So impressed were the British that a host of clubs fought to persuade him to join their ranks. Warrington won that race, mainly because Shankland liked the golfing facilities there. He captained the club in two Wembley Challenge Cup finals (1933 and 1936) and played in two Championship finals (1935 and 1937). Cup and Championship medals eluded him however, as Warrington were beaten in all four clashes. Shankland was a member of the Warrington side which beat the 1937–38 Kangaroos 8–6.

DALE SHEARER

Sixteen Tests for Australia (1986–91). Also played 19 minor games for Australia on two Kangaroo tours (1986 and 1990) and one New Zealand tour (1989).

North Queenslander Dale Shearer was one of Rugby League's most versatile backs. He could play in virtually any position in the backline and, in representative football, turned out as a fullback, winger and centre.

As a 20–year-old, he was lured to the Sydney competition in 1985 by Manly-Warringah coach Bob Fulton and was an instant success. In his second year he made the Australian team for the First Test against New Zealand (scoring a try in his debut), but a groin injury forced him out of the remaining two clashes. Shearer was an automatic selection for the Kangaroo side to tour Britain and France at the end of that season, forcing his way back into the Test side for the second match against Britain, at Elland Road, Leeds. In the final encounter against France, at Toulouse, Shearer equalled the Australian Test try-scoring record, going over for four in his side's 52–0 victory. His 12 tries (from 13 matches) was the third best of the tourists.

The following season, Shearer scored a try for Queensland in each of the four State-of-Origin matches (including the one at Long Beach, California)—but he suffered the disappointment of being one of the Australians on the receiving end of a 13–6 defeat at the hands of the New Zealanders in the lone Test of the year. A crippling injury saw the classy back on the sidelines for most of 1988. But he made a return for the World Cup final against New Zealand in Auckland at the end of the season. And, the following year, he was one of the stars of Australia's 3–0 whitewash of the Kiwis.

On the club scene, he was a member of Manly's 1987 Premiership-winning side, but a bitter dispute saw him take the club to court in 1989 in an effort to win the right to return to Queensland. Although he lost the case, a compromise was eventually hammered out and Shearer linked up with the Brisbane Broncos in 1990. That year he played against the touring Frenchmen and in the one-off Test against New Zealand before making his second Kangaroo tour. Shearer played in all five Tests on tour, the first four on the wing and the last (the Second Test against France) in the centre.

An out-of-form Shearer was a surprise selection in the Australian team for the First Test of the 1991 series against New Zealand. But when the Kiwis scored a shock win, he was one of the home players to be dropped for the remaining two clashes. His form further deteriorated until near the end of the season he was dropped from the Broncos first-grade side.

TIM SHEENS

Tim Sheens played a record 258 games as a front-row forward for Penrith in 13 seasons between 1970 and 1982. But it was to be as a coach that he achieved real fame.

After one season in the country, as coach of Campbelltown City in the Group 6 competition, he was given the job of mentor of the Panthers, who had tried a number of coaches with little success. Sheens brought a new determination to Penrith and in 1985 the Panthers reached the semi-finals for the first time since entering the Premiership race in 1967. His dream of winning the crown was never fulfilled. A huge offer lured him to Canberra in 1988.

Success there was almost instantaneous. In 1988, Sheens steered the Raiders into the semi-finals. The following year, they became the first club to win the premiership from number four spot in the semi-final lineup. And to prove it was no fluke they won the title the following year, too.

In 1991, Canberra, plagued by crippling financial problems, looked down and out mid-way through the season. But seven straight wins at the end of the season, saw Sheens' side in the grand final once again. But the fairytale finish was not to be, Penrith winning the vital finale 19–12. Ironically, in that match, his old team-mate, international hooker Royce Simmons, played his 259th game to break Sheens' Penrith record.

Sheens was appointed coach of the NSW State-of-Origin side in 1991, but Queensland won the series 2–1.

ROYCE SIMMONS

Ten Tests for Australia (1986–87). Also played 5 minor games on one Kangaroo tour (1986).

Penrith star Royce Simmons was one of a handful of fine hookers who vied for the Australian Test spot in the late 1980s—and in a period of just over 12 months he appeared in 10 Tests.

Simmons, originally from Cowra in the central west of New South Wales, became the first player from the Penrith Panthers to wear the green and gold when he was chosen in the Australian side to play New Zealand in the First Test, at Auckland, in 1986. He was 26 years old. His form was such that he played the other two internationals when New Zealand toured Australia later that year, the one-off Test against Papua New Guinea in Port Moresby, and the five Tests on the Kangaroo tour of Britain and France. The euphoria was soon over. The following year, New Zealand scored a 13–6 victory in the lone Test at Brisbane's Lang Park. Simmons was never to play for his country again, thanks to the challenge of Queensland's Greg Conescu and Balmain's Ben Elias.

By the end of the 1989 season, Simmons had become the first Penrith player to top 200 first grade games for the Panthers. That year they finished second on the competition table, but bowed out with back-to-back losses in the semi-finals. A year later, Simmons skippered the Panthers in their first grand final—only to see the Canberra Raiders triumph.

Simmons retired after the 1991 season. And what a fairytale finish to his career it was. Penrith finally broke through to become Premiers with a 19–12 victory over Canberra in the grand final. And Simmons played a major role in the victory scoring two of Penrith's three tries—no mean feat for a player who was lucky to score that many in a couple of seasons. Many critics believed that Simmons, in the last of his 259 Premiership matches (a new record for Penrith, including 233 in first grade), was unlucky not to have been awarded the Clive Churchill Medal as the Man-of-the-Match.

ERIC SIMMS

Eight matches for Australia in two World Cups (1968 and 1970). Also played in one minor international (1970) and in two minor games on one World Cup tour (1970).

Eric Simms had only a brief spell in the Rugby League limelight, but few contemporaries will ever forget his performances. In his short international career, the South Sydney fullback set many goal-kicking records.

Simms became a regular in Souths' first grade side in 1966. Within a year-and-a-half, he found himself in Australia's 1968 World Cup squad. He had a sensational international debut. In the four matches needed for Australia to win the Cup, he kicked 25 goals (50 points). His average of 12.5 points per match remains a World Series record. Two years later, in his only other international appearances, he scored well again. That year he had been overlooked for all representative matches, but was a last-minute selection for the World Cup squad after captain Graeme Langlands withdrew because of injury. Simms showed the selectors had chosen the right replacement with 37 points in the four games—a major factor in Australia's success in the Cup contest.

On the club scene, Simms was also a prolific scorer. His career tally of 1843 is a South Sydney record. In 1969, he scored 265 points (one try, 112 goals and 19 field goals—then worth two points) to shatter the long-standing record set by Dave Brown in 1935. Ironically, that season proved a disappointment. Souths' run of successes was broken when Balmain beat the Rabbitohs in the grand final.

Simms had a penchant for kicking field goals. His best was five in one club game. Indeed, he kicked four field goals (and another three goals from place-kicks) in Souths' 1970 grand final success. These four proved to be the straw that broke the camel's back. The authorities, upset that so many games were being decided by accurate field goal shots by players such as Simms, soon after reduced their value to one point.

PAUL SIRONEN

Eleven Tests (1986–1990). Also played in 1988 World Cup final and 16 minor games on two Kangaroo tours (1986 and 1990) and one New Zealand tour (1989).

Big second-row forward Paul Sironen made a dramatic rise to Test football. In the pre-season trials at the start of 1986 he was in Balmain's reserve grade squad. By the end of the year, the 21–year-old had toured Papua New Guinea, Britain and France with the Kangaroos and had played in his first Test matches.

Sironen made the (Sydney) City Seconds side that first season, but it was his great form in the final five play-offs which won him a spot in the Kangaroo line-up and the honour of being named Rookie-of-the-Year in the Sydney Premiership. He played his first Test at Port Moresby, coming on as a replacement against Papua New Guinea. Although he did not play against Great Britain, his form was such that he was chosen for the First Test against France, at Perpignan. He missed the second encounter, at Carcassonne, because of an injured elbow.

The big forward was overlooked for the Tests in 1987 and 1988 but was back for the 1988 World Cup final against New Zealand, at Eden Park, Auckland. In 1989, he was Man-of-the-Match in the first two Tests on the tour of New Zealand. Again an injury—this time to his ankle—forced him out of the final clash. In 1990, Sironen played the one-off Tests against

Kangaroo second-rower Paul Sironen crashes over for a try against Leeds on the 1990 tour

France and New Zealand. He obviously enjoyed playing in the Shaky Isles, because in the latter Test, at Athletic Park, Wellington, he was again named Man-of-the-Match. This, and fine displays for Balmain saw him one of the first picked in the Kangaroo squad for his second tour of Britain and France, on which he played all five Tests. In the Third Test against Britain it was his crash-tackling of British captain Ellery Hanley which kept the great player uncharacteristically quiet. Sadly, at the peak of his career, Sironen missed most of 1991 season through injury.

BILLY SMITH

Eighteen Tests for Australia (1964–70). Also played eight matches in two World Cups (1968 and 1970), one minor international (1970) and 15 minor games on one Kangaroo tour (1967–68) and one New Zealand tour (1965).

Few halfbacks have had careers to equal that of Billy Smith. He was the backbone of both the Australian Test and St George club line-ups for many years.

Smith made his first-grade debut, as a centre, with the Dragons in 1963 and, after switching to half, played his first representative game 12 months later. During the next five years, he missed only one Test match in which Australia was involved, and this because he was sidelined through injury. Smith appeared in 18 Tests (seven against Britain, five against New Zealand and six against France). Twice he won the Harry Sunderland Medal as the best Australian player in a home series (in 1966, against Britain, and the following year, against New Zealand).

Smith was one of the stars of Australia's World Cup victories in 1968 and 1970 (he won the Man-of-the-Match award in the game against Britain in the latter series). Soon after the 1970 World Cup, Smith was dropped from the Test side, although many critics regarded him as superior to the halfbacks who replaced him. However, Smith continued to give St George good and continuous service for several years, playing a club record 296 games (including 234 in first-grade) before calling it a day. He was in Premiership-winning sides on four occasions (1963, 1964, 1965 and 1966). In 1966, he was named NSW Player-of-the-Year and also won the prestige Sun-Herald Best-and-Fairest Player award.

LEN SMITH
Two Tests for Australia (1948).

Every time selectors sit down to choose a Kangaroo side to tour Britain and France, the odds are that they will produce one or two shocks. The daddy of all these surprises came in 1948, when the panel failed to include the captain-coach of the national side which had just downed New Zealand in the second game of a two-Test series. He was Len Smith. The enormity of the selection bombshell can be gauged by the fact that Smith was named as NSW Player-of-the-Year for his 1948 performances before the Kangaroo side was selected. Outspoken Rugby League player-turned-commentator Ross McKinnon described the decision as 'one of the greatest injustices ever perpetrated against any man in any sport'.

Smith played only two Tests for Australia. But that selection shock ensures him a prominent place in Australian Rugby League history. Nevertheless, Smith was one of the finest centres ever produced and he holds the distinction of being Australia's first ever captain-coach. He was a member of the Rugby Union Wallabies who went to England in 1939, but found their tour called off, without a game being played, because of the outbreak of World War II. In 1942 he was chosen to captain the British Empire Rugby Union side in a game against Britain, in Egypt. That, too, was called off at the last moment because of the hostilities.

Smith was one of the stars of the Newtown side which won the Sydney League Premiership in 1943.

SORENSEN BROTHERS
DANE SORENSEN
Twelve Tests for New Zealand (1979–85). Also played six matches in two World Championships (1975 and 1977).

KURT SORENSEN
Twenty Tests for New Zealand (1983–89). Also played five matches in two World Championships (1975 and 1977) and in the 1988 World Cup final.

The Sorensens, Kurt and Dane, were the finest family combination to play for New Zealand. The pair also had great club careers—both of them in Sydney, and Kurt in Great Britain. In addition they were instrumental in getting changes to the international laws—forcing clubs to release overseas players for Test matches. Both had wanted to play for New Zealand in the early 1980s, but at the time, their club, Cronulla-Sutherland, refused to allow them to do so. The International Board stepped in, and the pair were able to resume their international careers in 1983—Dane's continuing until the 1985 Kiwi tour of Britain and France and Kurt's until the following tour in 1989.

Although Dane had played a minor game on the lightning 1972 tour of Australia, the Auckland brothers, both big strong forwards, made their debuts in major international competition during the 1975 World Championships, Dane in the front-row against France and Kurt, three matches later as a replacement against Australia. Both appeared in the next Championships, in 1977, before Dane accepted an offer to join Cronulla. A year later Kurt wanted to move to Sydney too, but was refused permission by the NZ Rugby League. He sat out a season to beat the transfer ban and joined his brother in the Cronulla pack in 1979.

The pair spent one unhappy year with Eastern Suburbs, in 1984, before returning to Cronulla. After one more season and a total of 116 first–grade games with the Sharks, Kurt headed off to Britain to join Widnes, while Dane played out his career with Cronulla, retiring in 1989 after a club record 216 first–grade appearances. Kurt was rewarded richly for his British sojourn. He captained Widnes to Championship and Premiership successes in both 1988 and 1989. In 1989 he was skipper when Widnes downed Canberra to win the World Club Championship.

SOUTH AFRICA

During the late 1950s and early 1960s an abortive attempt was made to get Rugby League started in South Africa. There was bitter opposition from Rugby Union officials who even went as far as telling schoolboys they would be declared professional if they played on a ground on which Rugby League players had trained.

The first games in South Africa were exhibitions by the British and French sides on their way home from the 1957 World Cup series in Australia. Five years later, on July 13, 1962, the first club matches were played.

South Africa made its first overseas tour the next year, to Australia and New Zealand. English clubs had promised to release for the tour top South Africa stars playing there, but most reneged on their agreement. The tourists, led by Dawie Ackermann, proved no match for Australia and were soundly beaten in two Tests. They won only two of their minor games. However they shocked with a 4–3 Test win over New Zealand on a mud-covered Carlaw Park field in Auckland. This was South Africa's brief moment of glory—as the game back home soon slipped into oblivion. There were new moves at the end of 1991 to get it going again and a side was invited to take part in the World Sevens in Sydney in early 1992.

A Gallery of Great South African Players

Dawie Ackermann

A former Springbok Rugby Union star who played Tests against Australia on the 1956 Springbok tour, lock-forward Dawie Ackermann was one of the figures who tried to get the game underway in South Africa. In 1963, he was chosen as captain of the one and only South African Rugby League side to make an overseas visit. The side was soundly trounced by Australia, but won the lone New Zealand Test. Ackermann dropped out of the game soon after he returned from that tour.

Fred Griffiths see alphabetical entry

Trevor Lake

Trevor Lake was one of the many top players to leave the amateur ranks in southern Africa during the 1960s and make a mark in Rugby League in England. Lake, a Rhodesian, joined the English club Wigan in 1962. In that first season, he scored 12 times in 17 matches. Next year his tally was 43—second only to international John Stopford. And in the 1964–65 season, Lake became the top try-scorer in England, with 40. He was still at his top when he decided to try his luck with St George in the Sydney competition. But injury and subsequent loss of form led to a disappointing stay with the Dragons. Lake was the business brains behind a new attempt to get league going in South Africa after the 1991 dismantling of Apartheid.

Louis Neumann

When Leeds lured Louis Neumann to Britain in 1961, he was one of the best Rugby Union players in South Africa. A tough second-rower or prop-forward, he soon established himself as one of the top players in the professional code. He moved to Australia in 1967 and played for Eastern Suburbs and Penrith before ending his career in the country.

Wilf Rosenberg

After a handsome offer from Leeds, Wilf Rosenberg quit Rugby Union in his native land and went to Britain where he thrilled fans with his speedy wing play. In 80 matches with Leeds, he went over for 72 tries. He was one of the club's mainstays in a period highlighted by the 1961 Challenge Cup Final victory over Warrington. Rosenberg later went to Hull where he scored 43 tries in 86 games.

Tom Van Vollenhoven

Of all the South African stars who appeared in English Rugby League, possibly the best was winger Tom Van Vollenhoven. He was a Union star when he signed with St Helens in 1957. He had toured Australia and New Zealand with the Springboks the previous year and had played in four Tests against the 1955 British Lions. He quickly adapted to Rugby League and topped the British try-scoring lists in each of his first three seasons. In doing so, he quickly eclipsed Alf Ellaby's St Helens try-scoring record (with 62 in the 1958–59 season). The speedster scored three tries in the Championship final against Hull in 1959.

South Africa's great winger Tom Van Vollenhoven touches down for a try in an English club game for St Helens

SOUTH AFRICA V AUSTRALIA
TEST MATCHES
1963

First Test
At Lang Park, Brisbane, Saturday, 20 July 1963
Crowd: 10 210
AUSTRALIA 34 (Langlands 2, Irvine, Gasnier, Lumsden, Harrison, Raper, Day tries, Johns 5 goals) d SOUTH AFRICA 6 (Smit 3 goals)
Australia: L Johns, K Irvine, G Langlands, R Gasnier, E Lumsden, E Harrison, A Summons (c), J Raper, K Day, R Thornett, P Gallagher, I Walsh, N Kelly
South Africa: G Smit, J Gaydon, A Skene, J Pieterse, B Erasmus, C Greenwood, M Gericke, V Jacobs, D Ackermann (c), M Vermaas, J Verwey, B Oberholzer, M Pelser
Referee: J Bradley (Australia)

Second Test
At Sydney Cricket Ground, Saturday, 27 July 1963
Crowd: 16 995
AUSTRALIA 54 (Langlands 2, K Thornett 2, Irvine 2, Harrison, Gasnier, Johns, Muir, Raper, Gallagher tries, Johns 9 goals) d SOUTH AFRICA 21 (Greenwood 2, Oberholzer, Gericke, Pieterse tries, Griffiths 3 goals)
Australia: L Johns, K Irvine, R Gasnier (c), K Thornett, G Langlands, E Harrison, B Muir, J Raper, K Day, R Thornett, P Quinn, N Kelly, P Gallagher
South Africa: G Smit, J Pieterse, F Griffiths, A Skene, B Erasmus, C Greenwood, M Gericke, D Ackermann (c), G Van Zyl, V Jacobs, W Vermaas, J Verwey, B Oberholzer. Replacement: H Bennett (for Verway)
Referee: J Bradley (Australia)

SOUTH AFRICA TO AUSTRALIA AND NEW ZEALAND
1963

Record in Australia
Played 9, Won 2, Lost 7, Points for 165, Points against 277

Test Match Results

| South Africa | 6 | Australia | 34 | (Brisbane, 10 210) |
| South Africa | 21 | Australia | 54 | (Sydney, 16 995) |

Other Matches

Opponents	Venue (Attendance)	For	Against
Northern Division	Tamworth (5750)	20	10
Monaro	Canberra (3500)	41	2
Sydney	Sydney (18 219)	5	49
Queensland	Brisbane (6752)	16	32
South Queensland	Brisbane (2187)	17	27
Newcastle	Newcastle (7634)	17	27
Parramatta	Sydney (5372)	18	39

Record in New Zealand
Played 4, Won 2, Lost 2, Points for 37, Points against 37

Test Match Result

South Africa	4	New Zealand	3	(Auckland)

Other Matches

Opponents	Venue	For	Against
Wellington	Wellington	21	12
South Island	Christchurch	8	12
Auckland	Auckland	4	10

Leading Point-scorers

	Matches	Tries	Goals	Points
G Smit	10	2	23	52
F Griffiths	5	2	17	40
J de Waal	6	6	—	18
J Pieterse	11	4	—	12
M Pelser	4	3	—	9
A Skene	7	3	—	9
C Greenwood	7	3	—	9
F Gericke	8	1	3	9

Also toured: D Ackermann (c), H Bennett, G Coetzer, B Erazmus, R Peacock, K Pelser, N Rens, B Oberholzer, O Odendaal, O Oosthuizan, G van Zyl, W Vermaas, J Verwey. Australians G Wilson (Newtown) and F Anderson (Canterbury-Bankstown) were seconded to the team for the New Zealand leg of the tour

SOUTH SYDNEY

South Sydney is the most successful club in the history of Australian Rugby league. In the eight decades of the code it has notched 20 Premierships and has been runner-up another 12 times.

The club was founded in 1908 and joined eight other teams in the inaugural Sydney competition. That year Souths began as they intended to continue, beating Eastern Suburbs 14–12 in the final to take out the Premiership. Twelve months later the Rabbitohs made it two in a row. Souths record was further enhanced by three periods when they reined supreme in Sydney football—in the 1920s, the early 1950s and the late 1960s and early 1970s.

In a remarkable 10–year period from 1923 to 1932 the Rabbitohs won the Premiership seven times and were runners-up twice. Only in 1930, when Western Suburbs won its first title, did Souths fail to finish in the top two. It was during these golden years that Benny Wearing turned out for Souths. Many critics regard Wearing as one of the top half-dozen wingers to ever play football in Australia. At the very least, he is remembered as the man who turned out in a then-record 196 games for South Sydney.

A quarter of a century later another South Sydney great went within one match of Wearing's record. In doing so, Jack Rayner led the Rabbitohs to another string of successes. Rayner had already toured Britain, France and New Zealand when he was appointed captain-coach of an inexperienced team of raw South Sydney youngsters. However he moulded those kids into a world-beating combination, which except for one year, won all the Sydney Premierships between 1950 and 1955—and the year Souths didn't win (1952) the club had to do without its Test stars for half a season, as they made their way to England on a Kangaroo tour. Some of Rayner's youngsters turned out to be real champions—Clive Churchill, the fullback they dubbed 'The Little Master', Chic Cowie, one of Australia's finest post-World War II locks, and Johnny Graves and Ian Moir, two brilliant try-scoring wingers.

Churchill, too, made a name for himself as a coach of the Rabbitohs. In the late 1960s he helped lift South Sydney out of the doldrums to become Premiers in 1967, 1968, 1970 and 1971. Once again a group of fine young players helped. In fact, the Souths' pack at the time provided most of the Australian forward line–up. One of them, Bob McCarthy, set a new record of 211 first-grade games for the Rabbitohs.

When South Sydney won the 1970 Premiership, the Rabbitohs almost fielded an international line-up. The team which beat Manly 23–12 was Eric Simms, Mike Cleary, Arthur Branighan, Paul Sait, Ray Branighan, Denis Pittard, Bob Grant, Ron Coote, Bob McCarthy, Gary Stevens, John O'Neill, Elwyn Walters and John Sattler (c). Only Arthur Branighan and Stevens had not played for Australia, but Stevens achieved that distinction two years later. To make it even more impressive, Bob Honan, who came on during the match as a replacement for the injured Sait, was also an international.

Unfortunately, in the early 1970s, the licenced club which helped provide the cash to pay Souths' stars ran into financial difficulties. The money dried up and other richer clubs were able to poach most of Souths' best players. The Rabbitohs were still able to field a respectable team, but it was to be more than a decade before they were able to challenge the top sides again.

They did so under the tutorship of an old Souths' international—former hooker George Piggins. Piggins took them to the Minor Premiership in 1989. However the young Rabbitohs faltered in the play-offs, going down first to Balmain (20–10) and then to the ultimate Premiers, Canberra (32–16). Once again, financial problems hit the grand old club as they plummeted in one season to wooden spooners. At the end of 1990, Piggins relinquished his coaching role to try to steer the licenced club out of troubled waters.

SOUTH SYDNEY

Founded: 1908
Entered Sydney premiership competition: 1908
Home ground: Sydney Football Stadium (Record crowd—20 685)
Colours: Green and red
Nickname: The Rabittohs
Honours:
  Sydney Premiership—Winners, 1908, 1909, 1914, 1918, 1925 (unbeaten), 1926, 1927, 1928, 1929, 1931, 1932, 1950, 1951, 1953, 1954, 1955, 1967, 1968, 1970, 1971; Runners-up, 1910, 1916, 1917, 1920, 1923, 1924, 1935, 1937, 1939, 1949, 1952, 1965, 1969
  Flowers Memorial Pennant (Club Championship)—1932, 1933, 1952, 1953, 1954, 1967, 1968, 1969
  Midweek Cup—1981
  City Cup—1912, 1919, 1924, 1925
  Reserve-grade Premiership—1913, 1914, 1917, 1923, 1924, 1925, 1926, 1927, 1929, 1931, 1932, 1934, 1943, 1945, 1952, 1953, 1956, 1966, 1968
  League Cup—1915, 1916, 1917, 1918, 1919, 1922
  Third-grade Premiership—1908, 1912, 1918, 1925, 1928, 1933, 1962, 1969

Under-23 Premiership—1981, 1986
President's Cup—1936, 1942, 1943, 1951, 1953, 1960, 1961, 1962, 1969
Flegg Memorial Trophy—1962, 1964, 1966, 1967, 1968, 1969, 1972, 1978
SG Ball Cup—1965, 1969, 1974, 1975, 1976
Most first grade games: 211 by Bob McCarthy
Most points in a career: 1843 by Eric Simms
Most tries in a career: 133 by Benny Wearing
Most points in a season: 265 by Eric Simms, in 1969
Most tries in a season: 29 by Les Brennan, in 1954
Rothmans Medal winner: Denis Pittard (1969 and 1971)
NSW Player-of-the-Year: Clive Churchill (1949, 1950 and 1952), Jack Rayner (1953), Ron Coote (1968 and 1969)
Rugby League Week Player-of-the-Year: Bob Grant (1971)
Sun-Herald Best-and-Fairest Player: Clive Churchill (1952), Fred Nelson (1958), Richie Powell (1964), Denis Pittard (1972 and 1973)
Coach-of-the-Year: George Piggins (1986)

SOVIET UNION

Rugby Union has been played behind the Iron Curtain for many years, but it was only with the move towards democracy in the Eastern Bloc countries that thoughts of possible conversion to League took place.

In 1990, sporting officials in Moscow decided it was time to embrace the professional code. In April that year three teams, the Moscow Magicians, Leningrad and Tiraspol, were sent to Britain for extensive coaching, after which they played matches against leading amateur sides. Australian Rod Reddy was one of the coaches seconded to help the Soviets. The majority of the players were Union converts and two of the Tiraspol side had just missed out on selection in the Soviet sprint team for the 1988 Seoul Olympics.

Back home, in late 1990, a tournament was staged in the Black Sea city of Tiraspol, with leading British referee Fred Lindop controlling the final match between Tiraspol and Moscow before a crowd of 5000. For further education Moscow visited the Toulouse area of France, while Tiraspol went to Paris.

The first national competition began in 1991 with eight professional teams, Moscow Magicians, Moscow Spartak, Moscow Bears, Red Arrows, Tiraspol, Lions of St Petersburg, Kazan and Stars of Asia. Moscow Magicians won the first Championship after being unbeaten in 14 matches (scoring 810 points to 152). In the Challenge Cup Final, played as a major promotion at Dnepropetrovsk, in Ukraine, in October 1991, the Championship runners-up Tiraspol beat Moscow Magicians 26–16. For 1992, there was a further rearrangement with Ukraine and Georgia, the latter one of the most powerful Rugby Union republics, joining the fray and each of seven republics holding their own Championship.

In October 1991, the Soviet Union went to France to play it's first Test match. France was too strong in the match at Lyon, running out the winner 26–6. But the visitors were not disgraced with lock forward Peter Sokolow being the star Soviet player.

DAN STAINS

Three appearances for Australia on one New Zealand tour (1989).

Dan Stains has been one of the quiet achievers of Rugby League. The tough forward had one of the best front-on tackling games seen in the modern era. He first made his impact on the representative scene in 1989 when called into the Queensland side for the third State-of-Origin clash with New South Wales, after Bob Lindner broke his leg in the second clash.

A fine game and another injury, this time to block-busting second-rower Gene Miles, saw him gain late selection in the Australian side to tour New Zealand. Although he did not play in a Test he gave notice of his great future with fine performances against the New Zealand President's XIII and Wellington. Stains would almost certainly have toured Britain and France with the 1990 Kangaroos but for injuries—a back problem after the second State-of-Origin and then a shoulder problem which required surgery.

FRANK STANMORE

Ten Tests for Australia (1950–53). Also played 21 minor games on one Kangaroo tour (1952–53) and one New Zealand tour (1949).

Frank Stanmore had a relatively brief period in the Test arena, but in that time, he established himself as one of Australia's best five-eighths of the post-World War II era.

Stanmore strode into the limelight in 1948 when he was five-eighth for both (Sydney) City Firsts and New South Wales. However, Wally O'Connell was preferred for the Tests against the touring New Zealand side and Stanmore also missed out on selection in the Kangaroo squad to tour Britain and France. He made the Australian team which crossed the Tasman the following year, but did not play in either of the two Tests against the Kiwis. He had to wait until the 1950 Ashes series against the British Lions to make his Test debut. He played in the series against France in 1951 and belatedly made a Kangaroo touring side the following year. On that tour, Stanmore set a remarkable record for his era. He captained the Australians in seven matches and the Kangaroos won all seven.

The fine stand-off struck up a great scrum-base partnership with Western Suburbs halfback Keith Holman. The two appeared in several Tests together and were vital cogs in a fine Wests machine. Stanmore was a member of the Wests side which won the Sydney Premiership in 1948, and the team which lost the grand final to South Sydney two years later. However he, like Holman, missed the Magpies' next success, in 1952, because he was en route to England with the Kangaroos.

FRANK STANTON

Played 18 minor games for Australia on one Kangaroo tour (1963–64).

Frank Stanton was a fine utility back whose good form with Manly-Warringah earned him a tour of Britain and France with the 1963–64 Kangaroos.

He did not play any of the Tests, and it is as a coach that he is best remembered. He took over as mentor of the Manly side in 1975 and in the next four seasons steered them to two Premierships (1976 and 1978). Stanton was appointed Australia's Test coach in 1978 and in the next five years was rewarded with whitewash wins over Great Britain (1979 and 1982), New Zealand (1978, 1980 and 1982) and France (1981 and 1982).

His 1982 Kangaroo side also won the first ever Test played against Papua New Guinea.

The 1982 combination was Australia's most successful, becoming the first touring side to remain unbeaten. This made up for the disappointment of Stanton's previous Kangaroo experience, in 1978. Those Kangaroos beat Britain two Tests to one, but were shocked by France, which beat them in their two Test clashes. That was the only blot on Stanton's international copybook.

GEOFF STARLING

Seven Tests for Australia (1972–73). Also played in four matches in one World Cup (1972) and 11 minor games on one Kangaroo tour (1973) and one New Zealand tour (1971).

When Geoff Starling was chosen to tour New Zealand with the 1971 Australian team, he became the youngest player ever to wear the green and gold for Australia. He was just 18 years and 178 days old when he played against the New Zealand Second XIII, in the first of his two games on that short tour. It had been a meteoric rise for the red-haired Balmain centre, for only 12 months earlier he had been captain of the club's team which took part in the Jersey Flegg Trophy under-18 competition.

Starling made his Test debut against the New Zealand Kiwis in 1972, played in the 1972 World Cup in France and was a member of the Kangaroo side which toured Britain and France in 1973. After the Australians' match against Yorkshire, the famous referee Fred Lindop said he would gladly pay to watch Starling play. In the First Test against France, at Perpignan, Starling showed his versatility by playing lock, after the forward pack had been decimated by injuries. The Kangaroo tour was his last sortie into the international arena. A severe illness brought about a premature end to his brilliant career in top-class football.

STATE CHAMPIONSHIP see *Extinct Competitions*

STATE CUP see *Extinct Competitions*

STATE-OF-ORIGIN MATCHES

For Australians, one of the major stepping-stones to international football has always been the annual New South Wales-Queensland clashes. Over the years many a dark-horse made the Australian Test line–up or touring side after just one or two top games for his State.

Until the 1980s, the teams were chosen according to where the footballers were playing at the time. From the very first clash in 1908 New South Wales was dominant, except for a brief period in the early 1920s. New South Wales had a dream run from 1962 to 1967 when, in 22 games, it won 21 times and drew on the other occasion. However the longest winning trot by New South Wales was from 1908 to 1921, when the southern State won the first 22 games ever played. Queensland then won eight straight—its longest sequence.

The biggest win by New South Wales was in 1957 when Queensland was crushed 69–5 in a midweek game at the Sydney Cricket Ground. Greg Hawick kicked a record 15 goals. Queensland's biggest victory was 38–0, at Brisbane, in 1926. Dally Messenger, the man they dubbed 'The Master', holds the points record with 32 in one game (four tries and 10 goals), at Sydney, in 1911. Clive Churchill, 'The Little Master', also claims a record— the 26 consecutive matches, from 1948 to 1955, for New South Wales. Graeme Langlands (NSW) played more games than anyone else—33 and winger Sid Goodwin (NSW) went over for a record bag of tries—six in a match on the King's Birthday weekend in 1939.

During the 1970s the clashes became so one-sided that the authorities, in 1980, decided to change the format. The first two games that year were the normal interstate matches, with players representing the State in which they were resident. New South Wales won both, stretching its record to 15 straight successes. The third game in 1980 was a State-of-Origin match at Brisbane's Lang Park. Seven stars who played in the Sydney Premiership competition—Kerry Boustead, Alan Smith, Greg Oliphant, Rod Reddy, Arthur Beetson, John Lang and Rod Morris—turned out for their native Queensland. With their help, the Queensland side won 20–10. The game drew a big crowd of 33 210.

The experiment was repeated in 1981, with Queensland reinforced by Sydney players such as Rod Morris, Paul Khan, Mitch Brennan and Paul McCabe. Again Queensland won, this time by 22–15. From then on it was decided to play all interstate clashes under the State-of-Origin format.

The first year (1983), Queensland won the series 2–1. New South Wales' first success came under the captaincy of Steve Mortimer, in 1985. The following year saw the first whitewash, with the Blues winning 3–0. Queensland's 3–0 success in 1988 (inspired by great performances by such stars as Wally Lewis, Sam Backo and Allan Langer) was the Maroons' first clean-sweep in 64 years. To show it was no fluke, Queensland won the 1989 series 3–0, too.

The 1990 series was controversial. New South Wales won a low-scoring first match 8–0 before a record Sydney Football Stadium crowd of 41 235. Then in the second clash at Melbourne's Olympic Park, in a bold move to introduce the 13-a-side game to Victoria, the scores were locked 6–all with a few minutes to play, when referee Greg McCallum penalised Queensland halfback Allan Langer for allegedly stealing the ball from the Blues' prop Glenn Lazarus. The two points from the goal put New South Wales in front. As the Queenslanders threw the ball around in a mad attempt to come back, NSW centre Brad Mackay scored an intercept try to seal the match. The Queenslanders, captain Wally Lewis in particular, were furious—but nothing could be done, the result was on the scoreboard. Queensland came back in the final match—but it was all too late.

Only two points separated the two States in the 1991 series, the closest on record. Queensland won the first clash, at Lang Park, 6–4, with a goal by centre Mal Meninga being the difference after both sides scored one try. New South Wales levelled the series with a 14–12 victory at the Sydney Football Stadium three weeks later, this time a goal by Michael O'Connor providing the difference. And in the decider, at Lang Park, Queensland triumphed, again thanks to a Meninga goal. This was the last Origin appearance for the great Wally Lewis, after a record 29 clashes and eight

Man-of-the-Match awards (also a record). He finished his speech as the winning captain with the words: 'This has been the greatest series ever. Thank you and goodbye.'

INTERSTATE MATCHES

Year	Venue	Result			
1908	Sydney	New South Wales	43	Queensland	0
1908	Sydney	New South Wales	37	Queensland	8
1908	Sydney	New South Wales	12	Queensland	3
1910	Brisbane	New South Wales	40	Queensland	21
1910	Brisbane	New South Wales	32	Queensland	18
1910	Brisbane	New South Wales	19	Queensland	3
1911	Sydney	New South Wales	65	Queensland	9
1911	Sydney	New South Wales	49	Queensland	0
1911	Sydney	New South Wales	32	Queensland	8
1912	Sydney	New South Wales	65	Queensland	9
1912	Sydney	New South Wales	32	Queensland	4
1913	Brisbane	New South Wales	27	Queensland	12
1913	Brisbane	New South Wales	21	Queensland	17
1915	Sydney	New South Wales	53	Queensland	9
1915	Sydney	New South Wales	39	Queensland	6
1919	Sydney	New South Wales	33	Queensland	18
1919	Sydney	New South Wales	12	Queensland	7
1919	Brisbane	New South Wales	24	Queensland	10
1919	Brisbane	New South Wales	13	Queensland	10
1920	Sydney	New South Wales	40	Queensland	18
1921	Sydney	New South Wales	37	Queensland	11
1921	Brisbane	New South Wales	34	Queensland	20
1922	Sydney	Queensland	25	New South Wales	9
1923	Sydney	Queensland	18	New South Wales	13
1923	Brisbane	Queensland	25	New South Wales	10
1924	Sydney	Queensland	22	New South Wales	20
1924	Sydney	Queensland	20	New South Wales	7
1924	Brisbane	Queensland	36	New South Wales	6
1925	Sydney	Queensland	23	New South Wales	15
1925	Sydney	Queensland	27	New South Wales	13
1925	Sydney	New South Wales	27	Queensland	16
1925	Brisbane	Queensland	26	New South Wales	8
1925	Brisbane	Queensland	23	New South Wales	18
1926	Sydney	New South Wales	30	Queensland	17
1926	Sydney	New South Wales	5	Queensland	3
1926	Newcastle	Queensland	26	New South Wales	11
1926	Brisbane	Queensland	38	New South Wales	0
1926	Brisbane	Queensland	37	New South Wales	19
1927	Sydney	New South Wales	14	Queensland	10
1927	Sydney	New South Wales	13	Queensland	11
1927	Brisbane	Queensland	11	New South Wales	7
1927	Brisbane	New South Wales	15	Queensland	11
1928	Sydney	Queensland	25	New South Wales	9
1928	Sydney	New South Wales	16	Queensland	7
1928	Brisbane	Queensland	28	New South Wales	17
1928	Brisbane	Queensland	21	New South Wales	10
1929	Sydney	New South Wales	21	Queensland	8
1929	Sydney	New South Wales	17	Queensland	8
1929	Sydney	New South Wales	12	Queensland	10
1929	Brisbane	New South Wales	16	Queensland	14
1929	Brisbane	New South Wales	11	Queensland	8
1930	Sydney	New South Wales	18	Queensland	11
1930	Sydney	Queensland	25	New South Wales	11
1930	Brisbane	New South Wales	15	Queensland	12
1931	Sydney	New South Wales	39	Queensland	17
1931	Sydney	Queensland	23	New South Wales	20
1931	Sydney	New South Wales	28	Queensland	6
1931	Brisbane	Queensland	15	New South Wales	8
1931	Brisbane	Queensland	4	New South Wales	3
1932	Sydney	Queensland	23	New South Wales	15
1932	Sydney	New South Wales	9	Queensland	9
1932	Brisbane	Queensland	19	New South Wales	9
1933	Sydney	New South Wales	24	Queensland	0
1933	Sydney	New South Wales	15	Queensland	13
1933	Sydney	New South Wales	17	Queensland	14
1933	Brisbane	Queensland	10	New South Wales	8
1934	Sydney	New South Wales	13	Queensland	0

Continued

INTERSTATE MATCHES *continued*

Year	Venue	Result				
1934	Sydney	New South Wales	42	Queensland	9
1934	Sydney	Queensland	14	New South Wales	10
1934	Brisbane	Queensland	25	New South Wales	25
1934	Brisbane	Queensland	22	New South Wales	20
1935	Sydney	New South Wales	33	Queensland	16
1935	Sydney	New South Wales	18	Queensland	14
1935	Sydney	New South Wales	51	Queensland	8
1935	Brisbane	Queensland	22	New South Wales	20
1935	Brisbane	New South Wales	23	Queensland	9
1936	Sydney	New South Wales	30	Queensland	13
1936	Sydney	New South Wales	24	Queensland	13
1936	Brisbane	New South Wales	16	Queensland	14
1937	Sydney	New South Wales	21	Queensland	9
1937	Sydney	New South Wales	31	Queensland	3
1937	Brisbane	New South Wales	16	Queensland	11
1938	Sydney	New South Wales	20	Queensland	19
1938	Sydney	New South Wales	44	Queensland	7
1938	Brisbane	Queensland	36	New South Wales	22
1939	Sydney	New South Wales	50	Queensland	15
1939	Sydney	New South Wales	54	Queensland	13
1939	Brisbane	Queensland	29	New South Wales	13
1939	Brisbane	Queensland	23	New South Wales	13
1940	Sydney	New South Wales	52	Queenslan	11
1940	Sydney	Queensland	19	New South Wales	16
1940	Brisbane	Queensland	45	New South Wales	8
1940	Brisbane	Queensland	23	New South Wales	15
1941	Sydney	New South Wales	18	Queensland	14
1941	Sydney	New South Wales	44	Queensland	10
1941	Brisbane	New South Wales	23	Queensland	16
1941	Brisbane	Queensland	27	New South Wales	21
1945	Sydney	New South Wales	37	Queensland	12
1945	Brisbane	New South Wales	30	Queensland	19
1946	Sydney	New South Wales	46	Queensland	10
1946	Sydney	New South Wales	24	Queensland	6
1946	Brisbane	New South Wales	30	Queensland	14
1947	Sydney	New South Wales	29	Queensland	15
1947	Sydney	Queensland	18	New South Wales	9
1947	Brisbane	New South Wales	22	Queensland	10
1947	Brisbane	New South Wales	13	Queensland	13
1948	Sydney	New South Wales	23	Queensland	9
1948	Sydney	Queensland	17	New South Wales	15
1948	Brisbane	New South Wales	9	Queensland	8
1948	Brisbane	New South Wales	22	Queensland	10
1949	Sydney	New South Wales	19	Queensland	3
1949	Sydney	New South Wales	33	Queensland	3
1949	Brisbane	New South Wales	44	Queensland	10
1949	Brisbane	New South Wales	33	Queensland	13
1950	Sydney	New South Wales	45	Queensland	12
1950	Sydney	New South Wales	9	Queensland	9
1950	Brisbane	New South Wales	25	Queensland	5
1951	Sydney	Queensland	29	New South Wales	18
1951	Sydney	New South Wales	31	Queensland	8
1951	Brisbane	Queensland	39	New South Wales	23
1952	Sydney	New South Wales	18	Queensland	17
1952	Sydney	New South Wales	27	Queensland	10
1952	Brisbane	New South Wales	38	Queensland	17
1953	Sydney	New South Wales	26	Queensland	15
1953	Sydney	New South Wales	27	Queensland	16
1953	Brisbane	Queensland	32	New South Wales	23
1953	Brisbane	Queensland	22	New South Wales	13
1954	Sydney	New South Wales	26	Queensland	23
1954	Sydney	New South Wales	18	Queensland	13
1954	Brisbane	New South Wales	46	Queensland	7
1954	Brisbane	New South Wales	26	Queensland	21
1955	Sydney	New South Wales	17	Queensland	15
1955	Sydney	Queensland	30	New South Wales	28
1955	Brisbane	New South Wales	25	Queensland	18
1955	Brisbane	Queensland	34	New South Wales	12
1956	Sydney	New South Wales	28	Queensland	26
1956	Sydney	Queensland	28	New South Wales	20
1956	Brisbane	New South Wales	26	Queensland	18
1956	Brisbane	New South Wales	23	Queensland	19
1957	Brisbane	New South Wales	49	Queensland	11
1957	Brisbane	New South Wales	29	Queensland	12
1957	Sydney	New South Wales	69	Queensland	5

▶

INTERSTATE MATCHES

Year	Venue	Result			
1957	Sydney	New South Wales	45	Queensland	12
1958	Sydney	New South Wales	25	Queensland	14
1958	Brisbane	New South Wales	29	Queensland	20
1958	Brisbane	New South Wales	23	Queensland	15
1959	Brisbane	Queensland	17	New South Wales	15
1959	Brisbane	New South Wales	24	Queensland	14
1959	Sydney	Queensland	23	New South Wales	11
1959	Sydney	Queensland	18	New South Wales	14
1960	Sydney	New South Wales	22	Queensland	21
1960	Sydney	Queensland	17	New South Wales	12
1960	Brisbane	Queensland	13	New South Wales	0
1961	Brisbane	New South Wales	33	Queensland	14
1961	Sydney	New South Wales	21	Queensland	20
1961	Sydney	New South Wales	18	Queensland	2
1961	Brisbane	Queensland	15	New South Wales	2
1962	Brisbane	Queensland	20	New South Wales	17
1962	Sydney	New South Wales	28	Queensland	8
1962	Sydney	New South Wales	19	Queensland	14
1962	Brisbane	New South Wales	25	Queensland	12
1963	Brisbane	Queensland	19	New South Wales	19
1963	Brisbane	New South Wales	20	Queensland	10
1963	Brisbane	New South Wales	53	Queensland	7
1963	Sydney	New South Wales	31	Queensland	5
1963	Sydney	New South Wales	13	Queensland	5
1964	Sydney	New South Wales	28	Queensland	12
1964	Sydney	New South Wales	41	Queensland	3
1964	Brisbane	New South Wales	31	Queensland	5
1964	Brisbane	New South Wales	22	Queensland	11
1965	Sydney	New South Wales	31	Queensland	7
1965	Sydney	New South Wales	22	Queensland	4
1965	Brisbane	New South Wales	30	Queensland	9
1965	Brisbane	New South Wales	22	Queensland	15
1966	Sydney	New South Wales	16	Queensland	6
1966	Sydney	New South Wales	28	Queensland	10
1966	Brisbane	New South Wales	28	Queensland	20
1966	Brisbane	New South Wales	27	Queensland	3
1967	Sydney	New South Wales	14	Queensland	8
1967	Sydney	New South Wales	28	Queensland	9
1967	Brisbane	Queensland	16	New South Wales	16
1967	Brisbane	Queensland	13	New South Wales	11
1968	Sydney	New South Wales	30	Queensland	7
1968	Brisbane	Queensland	15	New South Wales	8
1968	Brisbane	New South Wales	29	Queensland	11
1969	Brisbane	New South Wales	26	Queensland	0
1969	Brisbane	New South Wales	32	Queensland	13
1969	Sydney	New South Wales	33	Queensland	17
1969	Newcastle	New South Wales	22	Queensland	2
1970	Brisbane	Queensland	16	New South Wales	16
1970	Brisbane	New South Wales	22	Queensland	9
1970	Sydney	New South Wales	34	Queensland	8
1970	Newcastle	New South Wales	12	Queensland	3
1971	Brisbane	New South Wales	30	Queensland	2
1971	Sydney	New South Wales	17	Queensland	15
1972	Brisbane	New South Wales	29	Queensland	5
1972	Brisbane	New South Wales	27	Queensland	6
1972	Sydney	Queensland	11	New South Wales	10
1973	Sydney	New South Wales	26	Queensland	0
1973	Brisbane	New South Wales	16	Queensland	0
1973	Brisbane	New South Wales	10	Queensland	0
1974	Brisbane	New South Wales	13	Queensland	13
1974	Brisbane	Queensland	4	New South Wales	4
1974	Sydney	New South Wales	22	Queensland	13
1975	Brisbane	Queensland	14	New South Wales	8
1975	Brisbane	New South Wales	27	Queensland	18
1975	Sydney	New South Wales	9	Queensland	8
1976	Sydney	New South Wales	33	Queensland	9
1976	Brisbane	New South Wales	10	Queensland	5
1976	Brisbane	New South Wales	15	Queensland	13
1977	Brisbane	New South Wales	19	Queensland	3
1977	Brisbane	New South Wales	14	Queensland	13
1978	Brisbane	New South Wales	25	Queensland	19
1978	Brisbane	New South Wales	12	Queensland	11
1978	Sydney	New South Wales	28	Queensland	12
1979	Brisbane	New South Wales	30	Queensland	5

Continued

INTERSTATE MATCHES *continued*

Year	Venue	Result			
1979	Brisbane	New South Wales	31	Queensland	7
1979	Sydney	New South Wales	35	Queensland	20
1980	Brisbane	New South Wales	35	Queensland	3
1980	Sydney	New South Wales	17	Queensland	7
1981	Brisbane	New South Wales	10	Queensland	2
1981	Sydney	New South Wales	22	Queensland	9

STATE-OF-ORIGIN MATCHES

Year	Venue	Results				Attendance
1980	Brisbane	Queensland	20	New South Wales	10	33 210
1981	Brisbane	Queensland	22	New South Wales	15	25 613
1982	Brisbane	New South Wales	20	Queensland	16	27 326
1982	Brisbane	Queensland	11	New South Wales	7	19 435
1982	Sydney	Queensland	10	New South Wales	5	20 242
1983	Brisbane	Queensland	24	New South Wales	12	29 412
1983	Sydney	New South Wales	10	Queensland	6	21 620
1983	Brisbane	Queensland	43	New South Wales	22	26 084
1984	Brisbane	Queensland	29	New South Wales	12	33 662
1984	Sydney	Queensland	14	New South Wales	2	29 088
1984	Brisbane	New South Wales	22	Queensland	12	16 559
1985	Brisbane	New South Wales	18	Queensland	2	33 011
1985	Sydney	New South Wales	21	Queensland	14	39 068
1985	Brisbane	Queensland	20	New South Wales	6	18 825
1986	Brisbane	New South Wales	22	Queensland	16	33 000
1986	Sydney	New South Wales	24	Queensland	20	40 707
1986	Brisbane	New South Wales	18	Queensland	16	21 097
1987	Brisbane	New South Wales	20	Queensland	16	33 411
1987	Sydney	Queensland	12	New South Wales	6	42 048
1987	Brisbane	Queensland	10	New South Wales	8	33 000
1987	Long Beach, California	New South Wales	30	Queensland	18	12 349
1988	Sydney	Queensland	26	New South Wales	18	26 441
1988	Brisbane	Queensland	16	New South Wales	6	31 817
1988	Sydney	Queensland	38	New South Wales	22	16 910
1989	Brisbane	Queensland	36	New South Wales	6	32 000
1989	Sydney	Queensland	16	New South Wales	12	40 000
1989	Brisbane	Queensland	36	New South Wales	16	33 000
1990	Sydney	New South Wales	8	Queensland	0	41 235
1990	Melbourne	New South Wales	12	Queensland	6	25 800
1990	Brisbane	Queensland	14	New South Wales	10	33 000
1991	Brisbane	Queensland	6	New South Wales	4	31 500
1991	Sydney	New South Wales	14	Queensland	12	41 520
1991	Brisbane	Queensland	14	New South Wales	12	32 500

RAY STEHR

Eleven Tests for Australia (1933–37). Also played 44 minor games on two Kangaroo tours (1933–34 and 1937–38) and one New Zealand tour (1935).

Ray Stehr was a rebel. One of the finest front-row forwards the game has known, he gave no quarter on or off the field. Stehr played 117 representative games, including 11 Tests, and was sent off in dozens of these encounters (including twice in the three Tests when the British Lions toured Australia in 1936). Both as a player and later as a commentator, he had running verbal battles with referees, tour managers and officials. Some of his most vehement clashes were with Jersey Flegg, the chairman of the Board of Control (as the Australian Rugby League was then known). Stehr dubbed it the Board of No Control.

Stehr was in the headlines almost from the day he pulled on his first Eastern Suburbs jumper. After a few games in the reserve–grade side in 1928, Stehr was called into the top side for a match against Newcastle. He was only 15 years old, the youngest player ever to appear in a Sydney

Ray Stehr

first-grade Rugby League side. He had his Test baptism on the 1933–34 Kangaroo tour of Britain, the first of two visits to the northern hemisphere. He also toured New Zealand in 1935.

Stehr was known for his tight play in the loose, his great scrummaging and straight, hard running. He once summed up the style of play which characterised his career: 'I've found that the bruises help make a man out of you'.

HERB STEINOHRT

Nine Tests for Australia (1928–32). Also played 18 minor games on one Kangaroo tour (1929–30).

Herb Steinohrt made a name for himself as a player, then as a coach and finally as a selector of representative teams. A rugged forward, he could play in any position in the pack. When a team of experts sat down in 1982 to pick the finest Australian Rugby League team of all time, his name was on the short-list of 10 for the two front-row spots.

He first made his mark in the mid-1920s, as a member of the unmatched Toowoomba (Queensland) front-row, with Dan Dempsey and Jim Bennett. This powerful trio laid the foundation for Toowoomba's shock 23–20 win over the touring British side in 1924. They also played vital roles in Queensland's supremacy over New South Wales, in which the Maroons won 13 of the 16 games played between 1922 and 1926. As well, Steinohrt was a member of the Queensland side which went to New Zealand in 1925. This side is rated by many New Zealand critics as the finest touring combination ever to visit the Shaky Isles.

The big forward represented Australia in three series against Great Britain (1928, 1929–30 and 1932). On the last occasion he captained his country in the three Tests. Steinohrt retired as a player in 1938 and served as coach and selector for Queensland. He was also an Australian Test selector.

MIKE STEPHENSON

Two Tests for Great Britain (1971–72). Also played four matches in one World Cup (1972).

Hooker Mike Stephenson swapped what would have been a long international career in Britain for the chance of a new life in Australia. He never regretted the move.

Stephenson played two Tests (against New Zealand and France) before starring for Britain in its 1972 World Cup success. He scored three tries in the four Cup games—an unprecedented feat by a hooker. This, and a brilliant club display, in which he led Dewsbury to its one and only English Championship, during the 1972–73 season, attracted the attention of scouts from the Penrith club. His display in the Championship Final, in which he scored two tries and led Dewsbury to a 22–13 victory over Leeds, was particularly sensational. The performance won him the Harry Sunderland Memorial Trophy as the Man-of-the-Match.

Penrith had no hesitation in handing over what was then a hefty $40 000 transfer fee to secure Stephenson's services. The money was well-spent. Even though Penrith never reached any great heights, Stephenson gave sterling service in a young side, before a broken jaw in 1978 forced a premature retirement from the game. Ironically, the youngster who took over the captaincy from Stephenson, 20–year-old Phil Gould, was to go on to become coach of the first Panthers team to win the Premiership (in 1991).

Stephenson continued in the game. He collected Rugby League memorabillia and set up a travelling exhibition which toured Australian cities and country centres in the 1980s and 1990s.

PETER STERLING

Eighteen Tests for Australia (1982–88). Also played 12 minor games on two Kangaroo tours (1982 and 1986).

As a schoolboy, Peter Sterling showed the promise that would eventually make him a Test super-star—one of the finest halfbacks in the history of the game. In 1978, Sterling, then playing as a five-eighth, turned in a brilliant performance to steer Fairfield Patrician Brothers to a 19–3 victory over Padua in the final of the Amco Shield (the televised schools' championship). He was also named as the Shield's Player-of-the-Year. Such was Sterling's ability that he played a game for Parramatta's first-grade side that year, while still at school.

He was nursed along in the Eels' lower grade sides the following year. Then, in 1980, he really burst upon the scene, establishing himself as the club's number one halfback and winning the Tooth Cup super-star award. Sterling continued his great form in 1981, making the NSW State-of-Origin side and playing a major role in Parramatta's march towards its first Sydney Premiership. His form for Parramatta as it advanced to a second Premiership won him a spot in the 1982 Kangaroos touring squad. Once in Britain he relished the conditions and displaced Steve Mortimer from the Test halfback spot. Sterling was never to be challenged until he finally quit the representative scene after the 1988 series against the touring Great Britain side.

Peter Sterling in action for English club Hull in 1985

Sterling's finest year was undoubtedly 1987, when his play laid the foundations for success in all individual awards—the Adidas Golden Boot (as the best player in the world) and the Rothmans Medal (as the best in the Sydney Premiership), as well as Rugby League Week's Player-of-the-Year and the Dally M Award. Even though he had quit big football, his form continued to be outstanding. In 1990, he was a stand-out winner of his second Rothmans Medal. The respected English magazine *Open Rugby* also named him as the best halfback in the world in its annual ratings at the end of 1990, even though he wasn't playing Test football.

In club football, Sterling was a member of Parramatta's Premiership-winning sides of 1981, 1982, 1983 and 1986. In the northern hemisphere he narrowly missed out on similar success. He was a member of the Hull side which went down 28–24 to Wigan in the 1985 Challenge Cup Final at Wembley Stadium.

GARY STEVENS

Five Tests for Australia (1973–74). Also played six matches in one World Cup (1972) and one World Championship (1975), and five minor games on one Kangaroo tour (1973).

Gary Stevens was a consistent second-rower, who in pub discussions is often overlooked because of the deeds of some of his more illustrious South Sydney team-mates, including Ron Coote, John O'Neill and Bob McCarthy. In the space of three years Stevens played 11 Tests and World Series matches for his country and never once let his side down. He also earns a place in the annals of Rugby League as one of only two players who emulated their grandfathers by playing for Australia (the other is Greg Pierce). Gary's grandfather was Arthur Oxford, a goalkicking star of the early days of Australian Rugby league.

Stevens played 163 first-grade games for the Rabbitohs in 12 seasons, from 1965 to 1976. For the first five seasons, he had trouble cementing a first-grade spot in the star-studded pack, but all that changed in 1970 when Stevens was a vital cog in the Souths' side which won the Premiership. He was considered a trifle unlucky not to have made the World Cup squad at the end of that year (even though eight of his team-mates did).

It was to be another two years before he made his international debut, in the World Cup, in France. A Kangaroo tour followed in 1973 and he was a member of the Test side which retained the Ashes against the touring British Lions in 1974. Stevens bowed out of international football during the 1975 World Championships, playing the home games against New Zealand, Wales and England. He quit Souths a year later, but proved how well he was still playing by sharing the Souths' best-and-fairest award for that final season. Stevens finished his career with two seasons playing for the Canterbury-Bankstown Bulldogs (1977 and 1978).

RICKY STUART

Five Tests for Australia (1990). Also played four minor games on one Kangaroo tour (1990).

Halfback Ricky Stuart is one of the select group of players who have represented Australia in both codes of Rugby. As an amateur he made a tour of Argentina with the Wallabies in 1987. The fact that he had to play second fiddle to Australian skipper Nick Farr-Jones, one of the greatest Rugby Union halfbacks in the history of the game, made it easier for the Canberra hierarchy to persuade Stuart to join the professional ranks the following year.

Australian Test halfback Ricky Stuart in action during the 1990 Ashes series

Stuart made his first-grade debut in League in July 1988 and, after a hesitant start, soon established himself as one of the best on-field generals the game has known, shrugging off chronic ankle and chest injuries to get to the top. His attacking brilliance and tactical kicking were important factors in Canberra's surge to successive Premierships in 1989 and 1990. In the 1990 grand final he turned in a sensational display which earned him the Clive Churchill Medal as the Man-of-the-Match. It also cemented a spot for him in the Kangaroo squad to tour Britain and France.

The brilliant schemer had a disappointing game after being chosen out of position at five-eighth in the First Test, at London's Wembley Stadium. When switched back to his normal spot at half for the second encounter, in Manchester however, he starred, setting up the match-winning try with a 70–metre run from inside his own quarter in the dying seconds of the match. In the Third Test, in which Australia retained the Ashes, Stuart was particularly dominant—winning the Man-of-the-Match award. Carrying an injury into the game, he played only 18 minutes of the First Test against France, at Avignon, but was back, if somewhat subdued, for the final clash, at Perpignan.

A torn groin muscle cost him his Test spot in 1991, but he put off an operation and continued playing (albeit with pain-killing injections) to help Canberra through to its third straight grand final.

CON SULLIVAN

Five Tests for Australia (1910–1914). Also played two internationals (1910) which for many years were regarded as Tests and nine minor games for Australia on one Kangaroo tour (1911–12).

North Sydney's Con Sullivan was one of the finest forwards in the pioneer days of Rugby League in Australia. He played either prop or in the second-row. According to the 1911–12 Kangaroo manager John Quinlan, one of the keenest students of the game, 'for getting the backs moving from a ruck, Con Sullivan was unquestionably the greatest forward I have ever seen'.

Sullivan made his Test debut against the touring 1910 British Lions. He played in three of four 'internationals' against the tourists. All three were for years accepted as Test matches, but today only the first is still recognised as a Test appearance for Sullivan. The Norths forward toured Britain with the 1911–12 Kangaroos, playing one Test. He finished his international career with all three Tests against the 1914 Great Britain tourists, including the famous Rorke's Drift Test. In the meantime he had made two tours of New Zealand with NSW representative sides (in 1912 and 1913).

ARTHUR SUMMONS

Nine Tests for Australia (1961–64). Also played 18 minor games on one Kangaroo tour (1963–64) and one New Zealand tour (1961).

In a 10–year international career, Arthur Summons established himself as one of the all-time greats in both codes of Rugby. The clever halfback cum five-eighth played for Australia against most major Rugby Union nations. As a professional, he highlighted a nine-Test career (three each against Britain and New Zealand, two against France and one versus South Africa) by coaching the 1963 Kangaroos to the first all-Australian Ashes success in Britain (the previous side to win, in 1911–12, had contained New Zealand players).

Summons appeared in 10 Rugby Union internationals and made one Wallaby tour of the British Isles (1958–59) before swapping codes to join Sydney's Western Suburbs club at the start of the 1960 season. At first, he found it hard to adjust to the professional game and played only seven first grade games in his first year with Wests. However the following season he began to fire and made the Australian side which toured New Zealand. Then came his greatest triumphs.

In 1962, the all-conquering British team looked likely to become the first side to win three Tests on an Australian tour. Summons, chosen as captain for the final encounter, inspired the Australians with a stirring pre-match speech and then led them brilliantly on the field. To cap it all, he scored a length of the field try. Australia scraped home by one point to deny the visitors a clean sweep. Next year, Summons captained Australia against New Zealand and South Africa. At the end of the domestic season, he was chosen as captain-coach of the Kangaroos. He missed all three Tests in England because of injury, but his dressing-room pep-talks were a major motivating factor in the Australian success.

Arthur Summons

His farewell to the international scene as a player was on that tour, in the Third Test against France, in Paris. Summons later moved to the country to coach the Wagga Magpies. He made a brief return to international football as non-playing coach of the 1970 Australian Test sides which lost the Ashes series to Britain.

Arthur Summons may have captained Australia in just five Tests—against Great Britain (1962), New Zealand (1963), France (1963/64) and South Africa (1963). But all five Tests were won by Australia.

HARRY SUNDERLAND

No man did more to promote Rugby League at an international level than Harry Sunderland. Once secretary of the Queensland Rugby League, Sunderland managed three Australian teams on tours of Britain (1929–30, 1933–34 and 1937–38), took English teams to Australia and helped introduce the sport to France in the 1930s. He also made a vain attempt to establish the code in the United States. Convinced that the fans would take to the game if they saw the best, he organised two matches between the Australian and New Zealand teams on their way home from the 1954 World Cup in France. The experiment was, unfortunately, a failure. Sunderland died in England in 1960, aged 74 years. And two major awards were instituted in his memory.

Famous Australian Administrator Harry Sunderland, whose name is remembered in his country's most prestigious international award, the Harry Sunderland Medal

The Harry Sunderland Memorial Medal was originally for the best local player in each international series played in Australia, but for some inexplicable reason, since 1970 it has only been awarded in Anglo-Australian Test series.

The Harry Sunderland Memorial Trophy goes to the Man-of-the-Match in the English Premiership Final. Two Australians have won the Trophy since its inception in 1965—John Dorahy (Hull Kingston Rovers) in 1984 and Les Boyd (Warrington) two years later.

WINNERS OF THE HARRY SUNDERLAND MEDAL

Year	Opponents	Winner
1964	France	Johnny Raper (St George)
1966	Great Britain	Billy Smith (St George)
1967	New Zealand	Billy Smith (St George)
1970	Great Britain	Ron Coote (South Sydney)
1974	Great Britain	Ron Coote (Eastern Suburbs)
1979	Great Britain	Ray Price (Parramatta)
1984	Great Britain	Wayne Pearce (Balmain)
1988	Great Britain	Wally Lewis (Brisbane)

Winners of Harry Sunderland Trophy see *Great Britain* entry

SUSPENSIONS see *sent off*

SYDNEY CRICKET GROUND

The Sydney Cricket Ground is one of the most famous sporting arenas in the world. Naturally enough, considering its name, it was designed as a ground for cricket and to this day at least one cricket Test match is played there when international sides visit Australia. For many decades however, it was also the most important Rugby League ground in Australia.

The first League match played there was on 22 June 1911. Between then and 27 September 1987 (when Manly-Warringah beat Canberra to win the Sydney Premiership in the last League game on the famous ground) every major Rugby League game in New South Wales had the SCG as its venue—including Test matches, State-of-Origin clashes and Premiership finales.

Anglo-Australian Test matches at the SCG regularly drew crowds in excess of 60 000. The record Test crowd is 70 204, during the 1932 series—but this is not the largest SCG crowd ever. A New South Wales-Britain clash in 1950 drew 25 more people. For the 1965 Premiership grand final between St George and South Sydney, some 78 056 people were recorded as passing through the turnstiles. The crowd, in fact, was much larger because, after the 'House Full' signs were posted and the gates closed, many thousands scaled the walls to get inside.

SYDNEY FOOTBALL STADIUM

For decades Rugby League had to stage its major matches on a field designed not for football but for cricket—the Sydney Cricket Ground (see above). Then, in 1988, all that changed with the construction of the Sydney Football Stadium, adjacent to the SCG. It cost $62 million to build, much of it financed by membership passes. The ground holds more than 40 000—all seated—and features an electronic scoreboard and giant video replay screen.

The Stadium has been the home for the Eastern Suburbs and South Sydney clubs (and, for a while St George). Easts played St George in the first game on 4 March 1988. The first international was the 100th Test between Australia and Great Britain on 11 June 1988. Grand finals are now always sell-outs, with a record 41 815 watching the 1991 clash between Canberra and Penrith. The record club crowd is 24 275 who watched Souths and Parramatta, on 24 June 1989.

SYDNEY PREMIERSHIP

When people overseas think of Australian Rugby League, they invariably think of the Sydney Premiership competition. It was in Sydney that the professional code began, and over the years, it has been in Sydney that the bulk of the Rugby League talent has been centred. Today however, the title of the competition is a misnomer. Only nine of the 16 teams are based in the Sydney metropolitan area. Three (Western Suburbs, Penrith and Illawarra) are away to the west and south, another (Newcastle) is 150km to the north, Canberra is in the Australian Capital Territory, the Gold Coast is on the NSW-Queensland border and Brisbane is fair square in Queensland—and there have been discussions concerning possible teams from Perth and North Queensland.

The Sydney competition began in 1908, with nine teams—Balmain, Cumberland, Eastern Suburbs, Glebe, Newcastle, Newtown, North Sydney, South Sydney and Western Suburbs. The first Premiers were Souths. It was a significant win, for Souths have gone on to become the most successful club in Australian Rugby League history. In those early days the Premiership usually went to the side with the best record after two rounds of home and away games. This was to be changed to a system of semi-finals and finals, with the Minor Premiers (the club leading the competition after the home and away games) having the right of challenge if beaten in the play-offs. This eventually gave way to a top-four play–off leading to a grand final (with no challenge for the Minor Premiers) and, in turn, to a top-five play-off, with the grand final deciding the Premiership.

Down through the years, many glamour sides have ruled the roost in Sydney. The most famous are:
- Eastern Suburbs in the pre-World War I era.
- South Sydney in the 1920s.
- Eastern Suburbs in the late 1930s.
- South Sydney soon after World War II
- St George in the 1960s.
- Parramatta in the early 1980s.

Eastern Suburbs swept all before it to take out the Premierships in 1911, 1912 and 1913. The next three seasons saw the club successful in the City Cup. The 1913 combination was perhaps unique in the early history of the game. Every player had represented New South Wales and 10 had played for Australia. The 10 were Les Cubitt, Dan Frawley, 'Pony' Halloway, 'Dally' Messenger, Wally Messenger, Larry 'Jersey' O'Malley, 'Sandy' Pearce, Bob Tidyman, 'Bluey' Watkins and Robert Williams.

The first great South Sydney era began 10 years later. In the following decade, Souths won the Premiership seven times and was runner-up twice. Only once in this period—in 1930, when Western Suburbs won its first title—did Souths fail to finish either first or second. There were some great names in the Souths line–up during this period, and none was more exciting than winger Benny Wearing, who played a record 196 first grade games for the Rabbitohs. Others included Alf 'Smacker' Blair, who captained Souths in several of their Premiership wins, second-rower George Treweek and the brothers Alf and Frank O'Connor.

Few sides have been so superior to the others as Eastern Suburbs was in 1935, 1936 and 1937. The club lost only one first grade match in the first season and was unbeaten in the other two. These were the years of the great Dave Brown. A pointscoring phenomenon, Brown broke all records in 1935—scoring 38 tries and kicking 65 goals for a total of 244 points. All this in just 15 games—an average of more than 16 points per outing! Spurred on by Brown's scoring feats, Easts that year notched no fewer than 139 tries and 108 goals for a record 633 points.

However Eastern Suburbs was not a one-man team. Eight members of the side were selected for the 1937–38 Kangaroo tour of Britain. One of them, Fred Tottey, broke a leg in a pre-tour game and a second, Joe Pearce, suffered a similar injury in Auckland, New Zealand, en route to Britain. The other six—Jack Beaton, Harry Pierce, Ernie Norman, Ray Stehr, Ross McKinnon and Andy Norval—all appeared in Tests against Britain on tour.

Easts were unlucky not to have notched a couple of Premierships earlier in the 1930s. In the 1931 final, South Sydney scored a lucky last-minute try when referee Lal Deane accidentally got in the way of defender Dave Brown. The Souths try under the posts enabled the Rabbitohs to pip Easts 13–8. Three years later, a mistake after the final bell let Western Suburbs snatch a converted try—and the Premiership. One of Easts' players was in possession when the bell sounded. As soon as the ball went dead, Easts would be victors. However, a Wests player called for a pass, the confused Easts' man fell for the trick, and the resulting try gave Wests a 15–12 victory.

Souths came from the bottom of the table to rule the roost as the 1950s dawned. The Rabbitohs were wooden-spooners in 1945 and 1946 (winning just one match in the former season and losing all 14 games 12 months later). By 1949 however, they had reached the grand final and then won five of the next six Premierships. Under coach Jack Rayner a long list of Test stars emerged. These included fullback Clive Churchill, who was dubbed 'The Little Master', dynamic lock 'Chic' Cowie and fine three-quarters Harry Wells, Johnny Graves and Ian Moir.

The 1956 season heralded the most remarkable run of success experienced by a major football club in any code anywhere in the world. St George beat Balmain in the grand final that year. The Dragons were to go on to a record string of 11 successive Premierships—and even after the club was finally dethroned in 1967, it was to continue as a regular semi-finalist until 1974. The St George sides provided the nucleus of the Australian Test sides during this period, with five of the stars (Ken Kearney, Ian Walsh, Reg Gasnier, Johnny Raper and Graeme Langlands) going on to captain their country.

St George also had the honour of being the first Australian club side to play Britain. Some 57 895 people packed the Sydney Cricket Ground for the midweek game against the 1962 tourists. Unfortunately, it proved to be no real contest. The visitors ran out easy winners 33–5.

It is perhaps to be expected that St George and South Sydney, the two most successful Sydney clubs, would hold the record for the biggest attendance at a Rugby League match in Australia, surpassing even huge crowds drawn to some of the Anglo-Australian Test matches. Officially, the crowd at the 1965 grand final between Souths and the Saints was

78 056—but many thousand more scaled the walls of the Sydney Cricket Ground after the gates were closed and the 'House Full' signs raised. This figure will never be topped. All major matches are now at the Sydney Football Stadium where the capacity is just under 42 000.

In the 1970s, Sydney football took on a distinctly different look with the influx of British and New Zealand stars. One of the most successful of these newcomers was English halfback Tommy Bishop. He joined Cronulla-Sutherland as captain–coach and transformed a moderate side which had been languishing towards the bottom of the Premiership table, into a top-class combination which reached the grand final in 1973 and gave it a big shake. Overseas stars, including British Test men Malcolm Reilly and Phil Lowe, also played major roles in the 1970s success of Manly-Warringah. Another Englishman, Kevin Ward, was the hero in Manly's victory in the 1987 grand final, the last played at the Sydney Cricket Ground. Manly won its first title in 1972. Parramatta, who first joined the Premiership race with the Sea Eagles in 1947, had to wait another nine years for its first success.

Under the great coach Jack Gibson, the Eels then dominated for several years, winning in 1981, 1982, 1983 and 1986 and reaching the grand final in 1984. It's side was choc-full with talent. Nine of its 1981 grand final team had played for Australia or would do so in the immediate future— Mick Cronin, Steve Ella, Eric Grothe, Brett Kenny, Peter Sterling, Ray Price, John Muggleton, Ron Hilditch and Bob O'Reilly. Six of the Kangaroos which toured Britain and France the following year were from the Parramatta ranks.

When the final-five playoffs were introduced, the experts reckoned it was impossible for a team to come from either of the bottom two spots to win the Premiership. In 1988, Balmain almost did! The Tigers beat Penrith in a play-off for fifth spot and then, in turn beat Manly 19–6, Canberra 14–6 and Cronulla 9–2 before going down to Canterbury-Bankstown 24–12 in the grand final.

The following year, Canberra provided the fairytale finish to the season. The Raiders finished fourth, before beating Cronulla 31–10, Penrith 27–18 and Minor Premiers South Sydney 32–16 to progress into the grand final. There, they fought back to snatch a last-minute try to finish 14–all at full-time. The Raiders scored a try and a field goal in extra time to create history with 19–14 victory. They retained their title 12 months later, beating Penrith in the first grand final involving teams who were not based in the centre of Sydney.

The same two sides fought out the 1991 grand final but with a different result. The Penrith Panthers, celebrating their 25th anniversary in the competition, won 19–12 to take out their first Premiership.

SYDNEY PREMIERSHIP RECORDS
Most points in one season by a club: 633 by Eastern Suburbs, in 1935
Most points in one season by a player: 282 by Mick Cronin (Parramatta), in 1978
Most tries in one season: 38 by Dave Brown (Eastern Suburbs), in 1935
Most goals in one season: 131 by Eric Simms (South Sydney), in 1969
Most points in one match: 45 by Dave Brown (Eastern Suburbs), in 1935
Most tries in one match: 8 by Frank Burge (Glebe), in 1920

SYDNEY PREMIERSHIP WINNERS

Year	Premiers		Year	Premiers
1908	South Sydney		1950	South Sydney
1909	South Sydney		1951	South Sydney
1910	Newtown		1952	Western Suburbs
1911	Eastern Suburbs		1953	South Sydney
1912	Eastern Suburbs		1954	South Sydney
1913	Eastern Suburbs		1955	South Sydney
1914	South Sydney		1956	St George
1915	Balmain		1957	St George
1916	Balmain		1958	St George
1917	Balmain		1959	St George
1918	South Sydney		1960	St George
1919	Balmain		1961	St George
1920	Balmain		1962	St George
1921	North Sydney		1963	St George
1922	North Sydney		1964	St George
1923	Eastern Suburbs		1965	St George
1924	Balmain		1966	St George
1925	South Sydney		1967	South Sydney
1926	South Sydney		1968	South Sydney
1927	South Sydney		1969	Balmain
1928	South Sydney		1970	South Sydney
1929	South Sydney		1971	South Sydney
1930	Western Suburbs		1972	Manly-Warringah
1931	South Sydney		1973	Manly-Warringah
1932	South Sydney		1974	Eastern Suburbs
1933	Newtown		1975	Eastern Suburbs
1934	Western Suburbs		1976	Manly-Warringah
1935	Eastern Suburbs		1977	St George
1936	Eastern Suburbs		1978	Manly-Warringah
1937	Eastern Suburbs		1979	St George
1938	Canterbury-Bankstown		1980	Canterbury-Bankstown
1939	Balmain		1981	Parramatta
1940	Eastern Suburbs		1982	Parramatta
1941	St George		1983	Parramatta
1942	Canterbury-Bankstown		1984	Canterbury-Bankstown
1943	Newtown		1985	Canterbury-Bankstown
1944	Balmain		1986	Parramatta
1945	Eastern Suburbs		1987	Manly-Warringah
1946	Balmain		1988	Canterbury-Bankstown
1947	Balmain		1989	Canberra
1948	Western Suburbs		1990	Canberra
1949	St George		1991	Penrith

Lower Grade Premiership Winners

Reserve–Grade

Year	Premiers		Year	Premiers
1908	Eastern Suburbs		1935	Eastern Suburbs
1909	Eastern Suburbs		1936	Western Suburbs
1910	Eastern Suburbs		1937	Eastern Suburbs
1911	Eastern Suburbs		1938	St George
1912	Glebe		1939	Canterbury-Bankstown
1913	South Sydney		1940	North Sydney
1914	South Sydney		1941	Balmain
1915	Balmain		1942	North Sydney
1916	Balmain		1943	South Sydney
1917	South Sydney		1944	Balmain
1918	Glebe		1945	South Sydney
1919	Glebe		1946	Balmain
1920	Glebe		1947	Newtown
1921	Glebe		1948	Newtown
1922	Newtown		1949	Eastern Suburbs
1923	South Sydney		1950	Balmain
1924	South Sydney		1951	Newtown
1925	South Sydney		1952	South Sydney
1926	South Sydney		1953	South Sydney
1927	South Sydney		1954	Manly-Warringah
1928	Balmain		1955	North Sydney
1929	South Sydney		1956	South Sydney
1930	Balmain		1957	Balmain
1931	South Sydney		1958	Balmain
1932	South Sydney		1959	North Sydney
1933	Balmain		1960	Manly-Warringah
1934	South Sydney		1961	Western Suburbs

▶

Lower Grade Premiership Winners

Reserve–Grade

1962	St George	1977	Parramatta
1963	St George	1978	Balmain
1964	St George	1979	Canterbury-Bankstown
1965	Balmain	1980	Canterbury-Bankstown
1966	South Sydney	1981	Western Suburbs
1967	Balmain	1982	Balmain
1968	South Sydney	1983	South Sydney
1969	Manly-Warringah	1984	Balmain
1970	Newtown	1985	St George
1971	Canterbury-Bankstown	1986	Eastern Suburbs
1972	Canterbury-Bankstown	1987	Penrith
1973	Manly-Warringah	1988	Manly-Warringah
1974	Newtown	1989	North Sydney
1975	Parramatta	1990	Brisbane
1976	St George	1991	North Sydney

Third–Grade

(Under-23s from 1972 to 1981 and from 1985 to 1987. President's Cup from 1988)

1908	South Sydney	1950	Balmain
1909	South Sydney Federal	1951	St George
1910	Sydney	1952	Manly-Warringah
1911	Leichhardt	1953	St George
1912	South Sydney	1954	Balmain
1913	South Sydney Federal	1955	Balmain
1914	Eastern Suburbs	1956	Balmain
1915	Balmain	1957	St George
1916	Balmain	1958	Western Suburbs
1917	Eastern Suburbs	1959	North Sydney
1918	South Sydney	1960	Balmain
1919	Balmain	1961	Western Suburbs
1920	Newtown	1962	South Sydney
1921	Mascot	1963	St George
1922	Mascot	1964	Parramatta
1923	Kensington	1965	St George
1924	Eastern Suburbs	1966	St George
1925	South Sydney	1967	Western Suburbs
1926	Balmain	1968	Balmain
1927	Glebe	1969	South Sydney
1928	South Sydney	1970	Eastern Suburbs
1929	Eastern Suburbs	1971	Canterbury-Bankstown
1930	Eastern Suburbs	1972	St George
1931	Eastern Suburbs	1973	Balmain
1932	Eastern Suburbs	1974	St George
1933	South Sydney	1975	Cronulla-Sutherland
1934	Balmain	1976	Eastern Suburbs
1935	Newtown	1977	Western Suburbs
1936	Western Suburbs	1978	Penrith
1937	North Sydney	1979	Parramatta
1938	Western Suburbs	1980	Parramatta
1939	Western Suburbs	1981	South Sydney
1940	St George	1982	Parramatta
1941	Eastern Suburbs	1983	St George
1942	St George	1984	Parramatta
1943	Newtown	1985	St George
1944	Western Suburbs	1986	South Sydney
1945	North Sydney	1987	St George
1946	North Sydney	1988	Parramatta
1947	Eastern Suburbs	1989	South Sydney
1948	Balmain	1990	Canberra
1949	St George	1991	Canterbury–Bankstown

Only four times in the history of Sydney Rugby League has one club made a clean sweep of all three Premierships. Balmain did it in 1915 and 1916, South Sydney in 1925 and St George in 1963.

Post-War Grand Final Results

Year	Result				Attendance
1947	Balmain	13	Canterbury-Bankstown	9	29 292
1948	Western Suburbs	8	Balmain	5	29 122
1949	St George	19	South Sydney	12	56 534
1950	South Sydney	21	Western Suburbs	15	32 373

Continued

Post-War Grand Final Results *continued*

Year	Result					Attendance
1951	South Sydney	42	Manly-Warringah	14		28 505
1952	Western Suburbs	22	South Sydney	12		41 060
1953	South Sydney	31	St George	12		44 581
1954	South Sydney	23	Newtown	15		45 759
1955	South Sydney	12	Newtown	11		42 466
1956	St George	18	Balmain	12		61 987
1957	St George	31	Manly-Warringah	9		54 399
1958	St George	20	Western Suburbs	9		63 282
1959	St George	20	Manly-Warringah	0		49 457
1960	St George	31	Eastern Suburbs	6		53 156
1961	St George	22	Western Suburbs	0		61 196
1962	St George	9	Western Suburbs	6		44 184
1963	St George	8	Western Suburbs	3		69 860
1964	St George	11	Balmain	6		61 369
1965	St George	12	South Sydney	8		78 056
1966	St George	23	Balmain	4		61 129
1967	South Sydney	12	Canterbury-Bankstown	10		58 358
1968	South Sydney	13	Manly-Warringah	9		54 255
1969	Balmain	11	South Sydney	2		61 129
1970	South Sydney	23	Manly-Warringah	12		53 241
1971	South Sydney	16	St George	10		62 828
1972	Manly-Warringah	19	Eastern Suburbs	14		54 357
1973	Manly-Warringah	10	Cronulla-Sutherland	7		52 044
1974	Eastern Suburbs	19	Canterbury-Bankstown	4		57 214
1975	Eastern Suburbs	38	St George	0		63 047
1976	Manly-Warringah	13	Parramatta	10		57 343
1977	St George	9	Parramatta	9		65 959
1977 *	St George	22	Parramatta	0		48 828
1978	Manly-Warringah	11	Cronulla-Sutherland	11		51 510
1978 *	Manly-Warringah	16	Cronulla-Sutherland	0		33 552
1979	St George	17	Canterbury-Bankstown	13		50 991
1980	Canterbury-Bankstown	18	Eastern Suburbs	4		52 881
1981	Parramatta	20	Newtown	11		57 333
1982	Parramatta	21	Manly-Warringah	8		52 186
1983	Parramatta	18	Manly-Warringah	6		40 285
1984	Canterbury-Bankstown	6	Parramatta	4		47 076
1985	Canterbury-Bankstown	7	St George	6		44 569
1986	Parramatta	4	Canterbury-Bankstown	2		45 843
1987	Manly-Warringah	18	Canberra	8		50 201
1988	Canterbury-Bankstown	24	Balmain	12		40 000
1989	Canberra	19	Balmain	14		40 500
1990	Canberra	18	Penrith	14		41 535
1991	Penrith	19	Canberra	12		41 815

(Figures for 1950 and 1953 are for the final. No grand final was required)
* Replay

Sydney Grand Final Records

Teams:
Most consecutive successes—11 by St George, between 1956 and 1966
Biggest winning margin—38 by Eastern Suburbs, against St George in 1975
Most points—42 by South Sydney, against Manly-Warringah in 1951
Most tries—8 by South Sydney (1951) and Eastern Suburbs (1975)

Individuals:
Most successes—10 by Norm Provan (St George), between 1956 and 1965
Most points—16 by Harry Bath (St George), in 1957
Most tries—4 by Johnny Graves (South Sydney), in 1951
Most goals—8 by Harry Bath (St George), in 1957
Most field goals—4 by Eric Simms (South Sydney), in 1970
Most matches refereed—7 by Darcy Lawler (plus 1953 final when no grand final was required)

Biggest Wins in Sydney Premiership

St George 91 d Canterbury-Bankstown 6, in 1935
Eastern Suburbs 87 d Canterbury-Bankstown 7, in 1935
Manly-Warringah 70 d Penrith 7, in 1973
South Sydney 67 d Western Suburbs 0, in 1910
Canberra 66 d Eastern Suburbs 4, in 1990

Most Individual Points in a Sydney Premiership Match

45 Dave Brown (Eastern Suburbs) (5 tries & 15 goals) v Canterbury Bankstown, in 1935
38 Dave Brown (Eastern Suburbs) (6 tries & 10 goals) v Canterbury Bankstown, in 1935
38 Mal Meninga (Canberra) (5 tries & 9 goals) v Eastern Suburbs, in 1990
36 Les Griffen (St George) (2 tries & 15 goals) v Canterbury-Bankstown, in 1935
36 Jack Lindwall (St George) (6 tries & 9 goals) v Manly-Warringah, in 1947

Most Individual Tries in a Sydney Premiership Match

8 Frank Burge (Glebe) v University, in 1920
7 Rod O'Loan (Eastern Suburbs) v University, in 1935
6 Frank Burge (Glebe) v North Sydney, in 1916
6 Alan Ridley (Western Suburbs) v Newtown, in 1936
6 Jack Troy (Newtown) v Eastern Suburbs, in 1950
6 Dave Brown (Eastern Suburbs) v Canterbury-Bankstown, in 1935
6 Jack Lindwall (St George) v Manly-Warringah, in 1947

Recent Premiership Top-scorers—Season by Season

	Tries	Field goals	Goals	Points
1991				
Daryl Halligan (Norths)	13	—	72	196
Matthew Ridge (Manly)	6	2	79	184
Jason Taylor (Wests)	1	6	8	170
Mal Meninga (Canberra	13	—	57	166
Ricky Walford (St George)	9	—	55	146
Greg Alexander (Penrith)	9	3	50	139
1990				
Mal Meninga (Canberra)	17	—	72	212
Greg Alexander (Penrith)	13	—	59	170
Dale Shearer (Brisbane)	10	—	46	132
Ricky Walford (St George)	14	—	38	132
Ashley Gordon (Newcastle)	15	—	35	130
Terry Lamb (Canterbury)	6	—	47	118
1989				
Ricky Walford (Brisbane)	13	—	47	146
Andy Currier (Balmain)	10	—	53	146
Neil Baker (Penrith)	6	7	50	131
Alan Wilson (Cronulla)	11	1	40	125
Laurie Daley (Canberra)	16	—	27	118
Terry Matterson (Brisbane)	5	—	42	104
1988				
Gary Belcher (Canberra)	10	—	89	218
Michael O'Connor (Manly)	17	—	65	198
Terry Lamb (Canterbury)	9	5	68	177
Alan Wilson (Cronulla)	8	1	70	173
Ross Conlon (Balmain)	2	—	80	168
1987				
Ross Conlon (Balmain)	5	—	88	196
Terry Lamb (Canterbury)	16	1	57	179
Dean Carney (Illawarra)	7	2	64	158
Mal Cochrane (Manly)	5	—	59	138
Michael O'Connor (Manly)	11	—	39	122
Mark Ellison (Souths)	4	3	48	115
1986				
Terry Lamb (Canterbury)	12	10	76	210
Ross Conlon (Balmain)	4	—	90	196
Greg Alexander (Penrith)	11	1	69	183
Mal Cochrane (Manly)	4	—	78	172
Neil Baker (Souths)	5	20	64	168
Mal Meninga (Canberra)	3	1	65	143
1985				
Mick Cronin (Parramatta)	6	—	90	204
Greg Alexander (Penrith)	14	2	69	196
Ross Conlon (Balmain)	4	—	90	196
Dean Carney (Cronulla)	11	—	75	194
Michael O'Connor (St George)	6	1	80	187
Ron Giteau (Canberra)	3	1	77	167
1984				
Steve Gearin (St George)	7	—	81	190
Tony Armstrong (Canterbury)	9	—	75	186

Continued

Recent Premiership Top-scorers—Season by Season *continued*

	Tries	Field goals	Goals	Points
Neil Baker (Souths)	5	6	68	162
Ron Giteau (Canberra)	6	1	68	161
Mark Levy (Penrith)	2	—	67	142
Steve Hegarty (Manly)	4	1	56	129
1983				
Mike Eden (Easts)	12	2	103	256
Graham Eadie (Manly)	7	—	99	226
Mick Cronin (Parramatta)	4	—	105	226
Ross Conlon (Canterbury)	7	—	82	192
Steve Gearin (St George)	8	—	80	192
1982				
Mick Cronin (Parramatta)	11	—	123	279
Steve Rogers (Cronulla)	9	2	79	187
Tony Melrose(Souths)	8	4	79	186
Ron Giteau (Easts)	5	1	79	174
John Dorahy (Illawarra)	6	1	70	159
Mike Eden (Manly)	2	—	71	148
1981				
Steve Rogers (Cronulla)	14	—	76	194
Steve Gearin (Canterbury)	13	—	72	183
Mick Cronin (Parramatta)	6	—	78	174
Ron Giteau (Easts)	6	1	63	145
Mark Ross (Souths)	8	—	58	140
Ken Wilson (Newtown)	3	6	52	119
1980				
Steve Gearin (Canterbury)	14	—	89	220
Ken Wilson (Newtown)	5	2	90	197
Ron Giteau (Wests)	8	—	78	180
Mick Cronin (Parramatta)	6	—	79	176
Graham Eadie (Manly)	2	—	80	166
Wayne Miranda (Balmain)	1	—	78	159
1979				
Mick Cronin (Parramatta)	15	—	104	253
Steve Gearin (Canterbury)	12	—	104	244
George Grant (St George)	1	—	104	211
Graham Eadie (Manly)	6	1	68	155
John Dorahy (Illawarra)	6	1	66	151
Ken Wilson (Newtown)	3	2	63	137
1978				
Mick Cronin (Parramatta)	16	—	117	282
Peter Rowles (Wests)	8	3	94	215
Steve Gearin (Canterbury)	7	—	58	137
John Gray (Manly)	4	—	61	134
Barry Andrews (Cronulla)	5	—	59	133
Kevin Stevens (Easts)	3	—	59	127
Peter Schofield (Norths)	3	—	59	127

Top Try-scorers

1991

Alan McIndoe (Illawarra)	19
Graham Mackay (Penrith)	16
Steve Renouf (Brisbane)	15
Ewan McGrady (Canterbury)	14
Paul Martin (Canberra)	14

1990

Mal Meninga (Canberra)	17
Willy Carne (Brisbane)	15
Ashley Gordon (Newcastle)	15
Ricky Walford (St George)	14
Alan McIndoe (Penrith)	14

▶

Top Try-scorers

1989

Gary Belcher (Canberra)	17
Laurie Daley (Canberra)	16
Greg Alexander (Penrith)	15
Andrew Ettingshausen (Cronulla)	14
Ricky Walford (St George)	13

1988

John Ferguson (Canberra)	20
Andrew Ettingshausen (Cronulla)	17
Michael O'Connor (Manly)	17
Wally Lewis (Brisbane)	15
Ricky Walford (St George)	15

1987

Terry Lamb (Canterbury)	16
Matthew Corkery (Canberra)	14
Brian Johnston (St George)	13
Dale Shearer (Manly)	13
Steve Morris (Easts)	12

1986

Phil Blake (Manly)	13
Garry Schofield (Balmain)	13
Terry Fahey (Canberra)	12
Rod Pethybridge (Wests)	12
Steve O'Brien (Canterbury)	12

1985

Steve Linnane (St George)	16
Greg Alexander (Penrith)	14
Steve Ella (Parramatta)	14
John Davidson (Balmain)	12
Steve Morris (St George)	12
Eric Grothe (Parramatta)	12

1984

Terry Lamb (Canterbury)	17
Steve Morris (St George)	16
Steve Broughton (Wests)	12
Dean Carney (Cronulla)	12
Eric Grothe (Parramatta)	12
Steve Ella (Parramatta)	12

1983

Phil Blake (Manly)	27
Brett Kenny (Parramatta)	21
Neil Hunt (Parramatta)	20
Chris Anderson (Canterbury)	19
Steve Morris (St George)	19
Shane McKellar (Illawarra)	18

1982

Steve Ella (Parramatta)	21
John Ribot (Manly)	20
Steve Morris (St George)	17
Steve Broughton (Wests)	17
Eric Grothe (Parramatta)	16

1981

Terry Fahey (Easts)	15
Steve Rogers (Cronulla)	14
Steve Ella (Parramatta)	13
John Gibbs (Manly)	13
Steve Gearin (Canterbury)	13
Brett Kenny(Parramatta)	12

1980

John Ribot (Wests)	16
Wayne Wigham (Balmain)	16

Continued

Top Try-scorers *continued*

Neville Glover (Parramatta)	12
Marvin Hicks (Penrith)	12
Steve Morris (St George)	11
Tom Mooney (Manly)	11

1979

Mitch Brennan (St George)	16
Tom Mooney (Manly)	16
Mick Cronin (Parramatta)	15
Steve Morris (St George)	14
Larry Corowa (Balmain)	14

1978

Larry Corowa (Balmain)	24
Mick Cronin (Parramatta)	16
Mitch Brennan (St George)	14
Peter Craig (Norths)	14
Neville Glover (Parramatta)	13
John Ribot (Wests)	12

Top Goalkickers
(Field goals shown in brackets)

1991

Jason Taylor (Wests)	80 (6)
Matthew Ridge (Manly)	79 (2)
Daryl Halligan (Norths)	72 (-)
Mal Meninga (Canberra)	57 (-)
Ricky Walford (St George)	55 (-)
Greg Alexander (Penrith)	50 (3)

1990

Mal Meninga (Canberra)	72 (-)
Greg Alexander (Penrith)	59 (-)
Terry Lamb (Canterbury)	47 (-)
Rod Wishart (Illawarra)	46 (-)
Dale Shearer (Brisbane)	46 (-)
Matthew Ridge (Manly)	43 (-)

1989

Andy Currier (Balmain)	53 (-)
Neil Baker (Penrith)	50 (7)
Ricky Walford (St George)	47 (-)
Terry Matterson (Brisbane)	42 (-)
Mark Ellison (Souths)	40 (3)
Alan Wilson (Cronulla)	40 (1)

1988

Gary Belcher (Canberra)	89 (-)
Ross Conlon (Balmain)	80 (-)
Alan Wilson (Cronulla)	70 (1)
Terry Lamb (Canterbury)	68 (5)
Neil Baker (Penrith)	65 (7)
Michael O'Connor (Manly)	65 (-)

1987

Ross Conlon (Balmain)	88 (-)
Dean Carney (Illawarra)	64 (2)
Mal Cochrane (Manly)	59 (-)
Terry Lamb (Canterbury)	57 (1)
Mark Ellison (Souths)	48 (3)
John Muggleton (Parramatta)	45 (2)

1986

Ross Conlon (Balmain)	90 (-)
Mal Cochrane (Manly)	78 (-)
Terry Lamb (Canterbury)	76 (10)
Greg Alexander (Penrith)	69 (1)
Mal Meninga (Canberra)	65 (1)
Neil Baker (Souths)	64 (20)

Top Goalkickers
(Field goals shown in brackets)

1985

Ross Conlon (Balmain)	90 (-)
Mick Cronin (Parramatta)	90 (-)
Michael O'Connor (St George)	80 (1)
Ron Giteau (Canberra)	77 (1)
Greg Alexander (Penrith)	66 (2)

1984

Steve Gearin (St George)	81 (-)
Tony Armstrong (Cronulla)	75 (-)
Neil Baker (Souths)	68 (6)
Ron Giteau (Canberra)	68 (1)
Mark Levy (Parramatta)	67 (1)
Steve Hegarty (Manly)	56 (1)

1983

Mick Cronin (Parramatta)	105 (-)
Mike Eden (Easts)	103 (2)
Graham Eadie (Manly)	99 (-)
Ron Giteau (Canberra)	86 (1)
Ross Conlon (Canterbury)	82 (-)
Steve Gearin (St George)	80 (-)

1982

Mick Cronin (Parramatta)	123 (-)
Tony Melrose (Souths)	79 (4)
Steve Rogers (Cronulla)	79 (2)
Ron Giteau (Easts)	79 (1)
Mike Eden (Manly)	71 (-)
John Dorahy (Illawarra)	70 (-)

1981

Mick Cronin (Parramatta)	78 (-)
Steve Rogers (Cronulla)	76 (-)
Steve Gearin (Canterbury)	72 (-)
Ron Giteau (Easts)	63 (1)
Mark Ross (Souths)	58 (-)
Ken Wilson (Newtown)	52 (6)

1980

Ken Wilson (Newtown)	90 (2)
Steve Gearin (Canterbury)	89 (-)
Graham Eadie (Manly)	80 (-)
Ron Giteau (Wests)	78 (-)
Wayne Miranda (Balmain)	78 (-)
Graeme Wynn (St George)	65 (-)

1979

Mick Cronin (Parramatta)	104 (-)
George Grant (St George)	104 (-)
Steve Gearin (Canterbury)	104 (-)
Graham Eadie (Manly)	68 (1)
John Dorahy (Wests)	66 (1)
Rod Henniker (Norths)	65 (-)

1978

Mick Cronin (Parramatta)	117 (-)
Peter Rowles (Wests)	94 (3)
John Gray (Manly)	61 (-)
Barry Andrews (Cronulla)	59 (-)
Kevin Stevens (Easts)	59 (-)
Peter Schofield (Norths)	59 (-)

British Players Who Have Appeared in Sydney Premiership Grand Finals

On the winning side: Dick Huddart (St George, 1966), David Bolton (Balmain, 1969), Malcolm Reilly (Manly-Warringah, 1972 and 1973), Gary Stephens (Manly-Warringah, 1976), Steve Norton (Manly-Warringah, 1976), Phil Lowe (Manly-Warringah, 1976), Kevin Ward (Manly-Warringah, 1987)
On the losing side: David Bolton (Balmain, 1966), Merv Hicks (Canterbury-Bankstown, 1967), Ken Batty (St George, 1971), Tommy Bishop (Cronulla-Sutherland, 1973), Cliff Watson (Cronulla-Sutherland, 1973), Bob Wear (Cronulla-Sutherland, 1973), Brian Lockwood (Canterbury-Bankstown, 1974), Ellery Hanley (Balmain, 1988).

SYDNEY CLUBS AGAINST TOURING INTERNATIONAL SIDES

For years, Sydney clubs lobbied to be given the chance to play against touring international sides, just as their counterparts in Britain did. There was a suggestion that the top club combinations would provide tougher opposition than some of the representative sides. Eventually, in 1962, the authorities relented and scheduled a match between the great St George side and the touring British Lions. A weekday record crowd of 57 895 turned up at the Sydney Cricket Ground for the battle, four days after the Third Test. St George scored first, then the British juggernaut flattened the Dragons, finally posting a 33–5 victory. Future club sides fared much better. Indeed, in 1988, just before the First Test, Manly-Warringah whitewashed Britain 30–0 at Brookvale Oval under lights.

Year	Result				Attendance
1962	St George	5	Great Britain	33	57 895
1963	St George	22	New Zealand	7	19 160
1963	Parramatta	39	South Africa	18	5372
1966	Balmain	9	Great Britain	8	22 369
1968	Western Suburbs	10	France	11	8000
1984	North Sydney	8	Great Britain	14	4067
1988	Manly-Warringah	30	Great Britain	0	11 131

SYDNEY TOUR OF NEW ZEALAND

A young Sydney side, selected from the teams which did not make the final three in the Premiership playoffs, made a short tour of New Zealand at the end of the 1976 season. The tour was a disappointment—with only a few players, including Test halfback Tom Raudonikis and Balmain lock Neil Pringle, showing top form. Of the five games played, Sydney won only two (admittedly by big margins). In the only two major clashes (against New Zealand and Auckland) the tourists were thoroughly outplayed.

Record in New Zealand

Played 5, Won 2, Lost 3, Points for 124, Points against 64

Match Results

Opponents	Venue (Attendance)	For	Against
Waikato	Huntly (1300)	41	3
New Zealand XIII	Auckland (4000)	5	18
North Island	Hastings (1000)	54	8
South Island	Christchurch (3000)	17	18
Auckland	Auckland (8500)	7	17

Individual Records

	Matches	Tries	Goals	Points
G Cox	5	2	13	32
D Moseley	2	—	6	12
M Raftery	3	4	—	12
E Goodwin	5	4	—	12
D Grant	4	4	—	12
N Pringle	5	3	—	9
G West	2	2	—	6
T Fahey	5	2	—	6
P Hayward	3	2	—	6
A McMahon	4	1	—	3
A Mountier	3	1	—	3
S Edge	2	1	—	3
T Raudonikis (c)	4	1	—	3
W Annabel	5	1	—	3

▶

Individual Records

	Matches	Tries	Goals	Points
J Dorahy	2	—	—	—
L Mara	5	—	—	—
J King	1	—	—	—
S Lavers	3	—	—	—
B Walker	2	—	—	—
G Boatswain	4	—	—	—
J Donnelly	3	—	—	—
P Charlton	2	—	—	—

T

TEST MATCHES

The climax of any Rugby League player's career is the moment he runs onto the field for his first international match. For Australians there are plenty of opportunities to achieve this honour—since World War II hardly a year has gone by without a Test, World Cup, World Championship or major tour.

The first Test series took place in 1907 when AH Baskerville took the New Zealand All Golds to Britain and stopped off in Australia on the way there and, again, on the way home. Since then, there have been more than 300 Tests involving Australia, France, New Zealand, Papua-New Guinea and South Africa. Of these, only Anglo-Australian series have consistently drawn large crowds. These Tests bring out feelings of patriotism almost unknown in other clashes. There are many stories of players carrying on with crippling injuries simply because they were playing for their country.

For many years Britain had a virtual mortgage on these series. The very early series were shared, but, after the 1920 victory, Australia had to wait three decades (during which there were 10 series) for its next win - a dramatic two Tests to one success in 1950. Britain ruled the roost in the late 1950s and 1960s. Since then, Great Britain has managed to win only six of the 30 Tests played. Australia's winning streak of 15 games since 1978 was only broken in the final Test of the 1988 series, at the Sydney Football Stadium.

Australia v Great Britain

Year	Venue	Results				Attendance
1908	Park Royal	Australia	22	Great Britain	22	2000
1909	Newcastle	Great Britain	15	Australia	5	22 000
1909	Birmingham	Great Britain	6	Australia	5	9000
1910	Sydney	Great Britain	27	Australia	20	42 000
1910	Brisbane	Great Britain	22	Australia	17	18 000
1910*	Sydney	Australasia	13	Great Britain	13	50 000
1910*	Sydney	Australasia	32	Great Britain	15	50 000
1911	Newcastle	Australasia	19	Great Britain	10	5317
1911	Edinburgh	Australasia	11	Great Britain	11	8000
1912	Birmingham	Australasia	33	Great Britain	8	4000
1914	Sydney	Great Britain	23	Australia	5	40 000

►

Australia v Great Britain

Year	Venue	Results				Attendance
1914	Sydney	Australia	12	Great Britain	7	38 000
1914	Sydney	Great Britain	14	Australia	6	34 420
1920	Brisbane	Australia	8	Great Britain	4	28 000
1920	Sydney	Australia	21	Great Britain	8	40 000
1920	Sydney	Great Britain	23	Australia	13	32 000
1921	Leeds	Great Britain	6	Australasia	5	31 700
1921	Hull	Australasia	16	Great Britain	2	21 504
1922	Salford	Great Britain	6	Australasia	0	22 000
1924	Sydney	Great Britain	22	Australia	3	50 005
1924	Sydney	Great Britain	5	Australia	3	33 842
1924	Brisbane	Australia	21	Great Britain	11	39 000
1928	Brisbane	Great Britain	15	Australia	12	39 300
1928	Sydney	Great Britain	8	Australia	0	44 548
1928	Sydney	Australia	21	Great Britain	14	37 000
1929	Hull	Australia	31	Great Britain	8	20 000
1929	Leeds	Great Britain	9	Australia	3	31 402
1930	Swinton	Great Britain	0	Australia	0	33 809
1930	Rochdale	Great Britain	3	Australia	0	16 743
1932	Sydney	Great Britain	8	Australia	6	70 204
1932	Brisbane	Australia	15	Great Britain	6	26 574
1932	Sydney	Great Britain	18	Australia	13	50 053
1933	Manchester	Great Britain	4	Australia	0	33 000
1933	Leeds	Great Britain	7	Australia	5	29 688
1933	Swinton	Great Britain	19	Australia	16	10 990
1936	Sydney	Australia	24	Great Britain	8	63 920
1936	Brisbane	Great Britain	12	Australia	7	29 486
1936	Sydney	Great Britain	12	Australia	7	53 546
1937	Leeds	Great Britain	5	Australia	4	31 949
1937	Swinton	Australia	13	Great Britain	3	31 724
1937	Huddersfield	Australia	13	Great Britain	3	9403
1946	Sydney	Australia	8	Great Britain	8	64 526
1946	Brisbane	Great Britain	14	Australia	5	40 500
1946	Sydney	Great Britain	20	Australia	7	35 294
1948	Leeds	Great Britain	23	Australia	21	36 354
1948	Swinton	Great Britain	16	Australia	7	43 500
1949	Bradford	Great Britain	23	Australia	9	36 294
1950	Sydney	Great Britain	6	Australia	4	47 215
1950	Brisbane	Australia	15	Great Britain	3	35 000
1950	Sydney	Australia	5	Great Britain	2	47 178
1952	Leeds	Great Britain	19	Australia	6	34 305
1952	Swinton	Great Britain	21	Australia	5	32 421
1952	Bradford	Australia	27	Great Britain	7	30 509
1954	Sydney	Australia	37	Great Britain	12	65 885
1954	Brisbane	Great Britain	38	Australia	21	46 355
1954	Sydney	Australia	20	Great Britain	16	67 577
1956	Wigan	Great Britain	21	Australia	10	22 473
1956	Bradford	Australia	22	Great Britain	9	23 334
1956	Swinton	Great Britain	19	Australia	0	13 515
1958	Sydney	Australia	25	Great Britain	8	68 777
1958	Brisbane	Great Britain	25	Australia	18	33 563
1958	Sydney	Great Britain	40	Australia	17	68 720
1959	Swinton	Australia	22	Great Britain	14	34 964
1959	Leeds	Great Britain	11	Australia	10	30 301
1959	Wigan	Great Britain	18	Australia	12	26 089
1962	Sydney	Great Britain	31	Australia	12	70 174
1962	Brisbane	Great Britain	17	Australia	10	34 766
1962	Sydney	Australia	18	Great Britain	17	42 104
1963	Wembley	Australia	28	Great Britain	2	13 946
1963	Swinton	Australia	50	Great Britain	12	30 843
1963	Leeds	Great Britain	16	Australia	5	20 497
1966	Sydney	Great Britain	17	Australia	13	57 962
1966	Brisbane	Australia	6	Great Britain	4	45 057
1966	Sydney	Australia	19	Great Britain	14	63 503
1967	Leeds	Great Britain	16	Australia	11	22 293
1967	White City	Australia	17	Great Britain	11	17 445
1967	Swinton	Australia	11	Great Britain	3	13 515
1970	Brisbane	Australia	37	Great Britain	15	42 807
1970	Sydney	Great Britain	28	Australia	7	60 962
1970	Sydney	Great Britain	21	Australia	17	61 258
1973	Wembley	Australia	21	Great Britain	12	9875
1973	Leeds	Australia	14	Great Britain	6	16 674
1973	Warrington	Australia	15	Great Britain	5	10 019
1974	Brisbane	Australia	12	Great Britain	6	30 280
1974	Sydney	Great Britain	16	Australia	11	48 006

Continued

549

Australia v Great Britain *continued*

Year	Venue	Results				Attendance
1974	Sydney	Australia	22	Great Britain	18	55 505
1978	Wigan	Australia	15	Great Britain	9	17 644
1978	Bradford	Great Britain	18	Australia	14	26 761
1978	Leeds	Australia	23	Great Britain	6	30 604
1979	Brisbane	Australia	35	Great Britain	0	23 051
1979	Sydney	Australia	24	Great Britain	16	28 857
1979	Sydney	Australia	28	Great Britain	2	16 844
1982	Hull	Australia	40	Great Britain	4	26 771
1982	Wigan	Australia	27	Great Britain	6	23 126
1982	Leeds	Australia	32	Great Britain	8	17 328
1984	Sydney	Australia	25	Great Britain	8	30 190
1984	Brisbane	Australia	18	Great Britain	6	31 000
1984	Sydney	Australia	20	Great Britain	7	18 756
1986	Manchester	Australia	38	Great Britain	16	50 583
1986	Leeds	Australia	34	Great Britain	4	30 808
1986	Wigan	Australia	24	Great Britain	15	20 169
1988	Sydney	Australia	17	Great Britain	6	24 202
1988	Brisbane	Australia	34	Great Britain	14	27 103
1988	Sydney	Great Britain	26	Australia	12	15 994
1990	Wembley	Great Britain	19	Australia	12	52 569
1990	Manchester	Australia	14	Great Britain	10	46 615
1990	Leeds	Australia	14	Great Britain	0	32 500

* Matches for many years regarded as Tests

Australia v New Zealand

Year	Venue	Results				Attendance
1908	Sydney	New Zealand	11	Australia	10	
1908	Brisbane	New Zealand	24	Australia	12	
1908	Sydney	Australia	14	New Zealand	9	
1909	Sydney	New Zealand	19	Australia	11	
1909	Brisbane	Australia	10	New Zealand	5	
1909	Sydney	Australia	25	New Zealand	5	
1919	Wellington	Australia	44	New Zealand	21	8000
1919	Christchurch	New Zealand	26	Australia	10	7200
1919	Auckland	Australia	34	New Zealand	23	24 300
1919	Auckland	Australia	32	New Zealand	2	15 000
1935	Auckland	New Zealand	22	Australia	14	
1935	Auckland	Australia	29	New Zealand	8	
1935	Auckland	Australia	31	New Zealand	8	
1937	Auckland	Australia	12	New Zealand	8	12 000
1937	Auckland	New Zealand	16	Australia	15	
1948	Sydney	New Zealand	21	Australia	19	55 866
1948	Brisbane	Australia	13	New Zealand	4	23 013
1949	Wellington	New Zealand	26	Australia	21	7737
1949	Auckland	Australia	13	New Zealand	10	12 361
1952	Sydney	Australia	25	New Zealand	13	56 326
1952	Brisbane	New Zealand	49	Australia	25	29 245
1952	Sydney	New Zealand	19	Australia	9	44 916
1953	Christchurch	New Zealand	25	Australia	5	5509
1953	Wellington	New Zealand	12	Australia	11	5394
1953	Auckland	Australia	18	New Zealand	16	16 033
1956	Sydney	Australia	12	New Zealand	9	46 766
1956	Brisbane	Australia	8	New Zealand	2	28 361
1956	Sydney	Australia	31	New Zealand	14	46 735
1959	Sydney	Australia	9	New Zealand	8	28 766
1959	Brisbane	Australia	38	New Zealand	10	30 994
1959	Sydney	New Zealand	28	Australia	12	31 629
1961	Auckland	New Zealand	12	Australia	10	11 485
1961	Auckland	Australia	10	New Zealand	8	12 424
1963	Sydney	Australia	7	New Zealand	3	48 330
1963	Brisbane	Australia	16	New Zealand	13	30 748
1963	Sydney	Australia	14	New Zealand	0	46 567
1965	Auckland	Australia	13	New Zealand	8	13 295
1965	Auckland	New Zealand	7	Australia	5	11 383
1967	Sydney	Australia	22	New Zealand	13	33 416
1967	Brisbane	Australia	35	New Zealand	22	30 122
1967	Sydney	Australia	13	New Zealand	9	27 530
1969	Auckland	Australia	20	New Zealand	10	13 459
1969	Auckland	New Zealand	18	Australia	14	9848
1971	Auckland	New Zealand	24	Australia	3	13 917
1972	Sydney	Australia	36	New Zealand	11	29 714
1972	Brisbane	Australia	31	New Zealand	7	24 000

▶

Australia v New Zealand

Year	Venue	Results				Attendance
1978	Sydney	Australia	24	New Zealand	2	16 577
1978	Brisbane	Australia	38	New Zealand	7	14 000
1978	Sydney	Australia	33	New Zealand	16	6541
1980	Auckland	Australia	27	New Zealand	6	12 321
1980	Auckland	Australia	15	New Zealand	6	9706
1982	Brisbane	Australia	11	New Zealand	8	14 000
1982	Sydney	Australia	20	New Zealand	2	16 755
1983	Auckland	Australia	16	New Zealand	4	18 000
1983	Brisbane	New Zealand	19	Australia	12	15 000
1985	Brisbane	Australia	26	New Zealand	20	23 000
1985	Auckland	Australia	10	New Zealand	6	19 132
1985	Auckland	New Zealand	18	Australia	0	15 327
1986	Auckland	Australia	22	New Zealand	8	14 566
1986	Sydney	Australia	29	New Zealand	12	34 302
1986	Brisbane	Australia	32	New Zealand	12	22 811
1987	Brisbane	New Zealand	13	Australia	6	16 500
1989	Christchurch	Australia	26	New Zealand	6	17 000
1989	Rotorua	Australia	8	New Zealand	0	26 000
1989	Auckland	Australia	22	New Zealand	14	15 000
1990	Wellington	Australia	24	New Zealand	6	25 000
1991	Melbourne	New Zealand	24	Australia	8	26 900
1991	Sydney	Australia	44	New Zealand	0	34 911
1991	Brisbane	Australia	40	New Zealand	12	33 000

Australia v France

Year	Venue	Results				Attendance
1938	Paris	Australia	35	France	6	—
1938	Marseille	Australia	16	France	11	24 000
1949	Marseille	Australia	29	France	10	15 796
1949	Bordeaux	Australia	10	France	0	17 365
1951	Sydney	France	26	Australia	15	60 160
1951	Brisbane	Australia	23	France	11	35 000
1951	Sydney	France	35	Australia	14	67 009
1952	Paris	Australia	16	France	12	18 327
1952	Bordeaux	France	5	Australia	0	23 419
1953	Lyon	France	13	Australia	5	17 454
1955	Sydney	Australia	20	France	8	67 748
1955	Brisbane	France	29	Australia	28	45 745
1955	Sydney	France	8	Australia	5	62 458
1956	Paris	Australia	15	France	8	10 789
1956	Bordeaux	Australia	10	France	6	11 379
1957	Lyon	Australia	25	France	21	5743
1959	Paris	Australia	20	France	19	9864
1959	Bordeaux	Australia	17	France	2	8848
1960	Roanne	Australia	16	France	8	3437
1960	Sydney	Australia	8	France	8	49 868
1960	Brisbane	Australia	56	France	6	32 644
1960	Sydney	France	7	Australia	5	29 127
1963	Bordeaux	France	8	Australia	5	4261
1963	Toulouse	Australia	21	France	9	6932
1964	Paris	Australia	16	France	8	5979
1964	Sydney	Australia	20	France	6	20 270
1964	Brisbane	Australia	27	France	2	20 076
1964	Sydney	Australia	35	France	9	16 731
1967	Marseille	Australia	7	France	7	5193
1967	Carcassonne	France	10	Australia	3	4193
1967	Toulouse	France	16	Australia	13	5000
1973	Perpignan	Australia	21	France	11	7630
1973	Toulouse	Australia	14	France	3	7060
1978	Carcassonne	France	13	Australia	10	7000
1978	Toulouse	France	11	Australia	10	6500
1981	Sydney	Australia	43	France	3	16 277
1981	Brisbane	Australia	17	France	2	14 000
1982	Avignon	Australia	15	France	4	6000
1982	Narbonne	Australia	23	France	9	5000
1986	Perpignan	Australia	44	France	2	6000
1986	Carcassonne	Australia	52	France	0	3000
1990	Parkes	Australia	34	France	2	12 384
1990	Avignon	Australia	60	France	4	2200
1990	Perpignan	Australia	34	France	10	3428

Australia v Papua New Guinea

Year	Venue	Results				Attendance
1982	Port Moresby	Australia	38	Papua New Guinea	2	15 000
1986	Port Moresby	Australia	62	Papua New Guinea	12	17 000
1988	Wagga Wagga	Australia	70	Papua New Guinea	8	11 685
1991	Goroka	Australia	58	Papua New Guinea	2	13 000
1991	Port Moresby	Australia	40	Papua New Guinea	6	14 500

Australia v South Africa

Year	Venue	Results				Attendance
1963	Brisbane	Australia	34	South Africa	6	10 210
1963	Sydney	Australia	54	South Africa	21	16 995

Great Britain v France

Year	Venue	Results				Attendance
1956	Bradford	Great Britain	18	France	10	
1957	Leeds	Great Britain	45	France	12	20 221
1957	Toulouse	France	19	Great Britain	19	16 000
1957	St Helens	Great Britain	29	France	14	23 250
1957	Toulouse	Great Britain	25	France	14	15 000
1957	Wigan	Great Britain	44	France	15	19 152
1958	Grenoble	Great Britain	23	France	9	20 000
1959	Leeds	Great Britain	50	France	15	22 000
1959	Grenoble	France	24	Great Britain	15	8500
1960	Toulouse	France	20	Great Britain	18	
1960	St Helens	Great Britain	17	France	17	14 000
1960	Bordeaux	Great Britain	21	France	10	8000
1961	St Helens	Great Britain	27	France	8	18 000
1962	Wigan	France	20	Great Britain	15	17 277
1962	Perpignan	France	23	Great Britain	13	14 000
1962	Perpignan	France	17	Great Britain	12	5000
1963	Wigan	Great Britain	20	France	15	17 277
1964	Perpignan	Great Britain	11	France	5	
1964	Leigh	Great Britain	39	France	0	4750
1964	Perpignan	France	18	Great Britain	8	15 000
1965	Swinton	Great Britain	17	France	7	9959
1966	Perpignan	France	18	Great Britain	13	6000
1966	Wigan	France	8	Great Britain	4	14 004
1967	Carcassonne	Great Britain	16	France	13	
1967	Wigan	France	23	Great Britain	13	7448
1968	Paris	Great Britain	22	France	13	8000
1968	Bradford	Great Britain	19	France	8	14 196
1968	St Helens	Great Britain	34	France	10	6080
1969	Toulouse	France	13	Great Britain	9	10 000
1971	Toulouse	France	18	Great Britain	8	14 960
1971	St Helens	Great Britain	24	France	2	7783
1972	Toulouse	Great Britain	10	France	0	11 508
1972	Bradford	Great Britain	45	France	10	7313
1974	Grenoble	Great Britain	24	France	5	5500
1974	Wigan	Great Britain	29	France	0	10 105
1981	Hull	Great Britain	37	France	0	13 173
1981	Marseille	France	19	Great Britain	2	6500
1983	Carcassonne	Great Britain	20	France	5	3826
1983	Hull	Great Britain	37	France	0	6055
1984	Avignon	Great Britain	12	France	0	4000
1984	Leeds	Great Britain	10	France	0	7596
1985	Avignon	France	10	Great Britain	10	6000
1985	Wigan	Great Britain	24	France	10	8112
1987	Leeds	Great Britain	52	France	4	6567
1987	Carcassonne	Great Britain	20	France	10	3000
1988	Avignon	Great Britain	28	France	14	6000
1988	Leeds	Great Britain	30	France	12	7007
1989	Wigan	Great Britain	26	France	10	8012
1989	Avignon	Great Britain	30	France	8	6000
1990	Perpignan	Great Britain	8	France	4	6000
1990	Leeds	France	25	Great Britain	18	6554
1991	Perpignan	Great Britain	45	France	10	5500
1991	Wigan	Great Britain	60	France	4	5284

Great Britain v New Zealand

Year	Venue	Results				Attendance
1908	Leeds	Great Britain	14	New Zealand	6	
1908	Leeds	Great Britain	14	New Zealand	6	
1908	Chelsea	New Zealand	18	Great Britain	6	
1908	Cheltenham	New Zealand	8	Great Britain	5	
1910	Wellington	Great Britain	52	New Zealand	20	20 000
1914	Auckland	Great Britain	16	New Zealand	13	24 600
1920	Auckland	Great Britain	31	New Zealand	73	4000
1920	Christchurch	Great Britain	19	New Zealand	3	10 000
1920	Wellington	Great Britain	11	New Zealand	10	5000
1924	Auckland	New Zealand	16	Great Britain	8	22 000
1924	Wellington	New Zealand	13	Great Britain	11	6000
1924	Dunedin	Great Britain	31	New Zealand	18	14 000
1926	Wigan	Great Britain	28	New Zealand	20	
1926	Hull	Great Britain	21	New Zealand	11	
1927	Leeds	Great Britain	32	New Zealand	17	
1928	Auckland	New Zealand	17	Great Britain	13	20 000
1928	Dunedin	Great Britain	13	New Zealand	5	12 000
1928	Christchurch	Great Britain	6	New Zealand	5	21 000
1932	Auckland	Great Britain	24	New Zealand	9	25 000
1932	Christchurch	Great Britain	25	New Zealand	14	8000
1932	Auckland	Great Britain	20	New Zealand	18	20 000
1936	Auckland	Great Britain	10	New Zealand	8	25 000
1936	Auckland	Great Britain	23	New Zealand	11	16 000
1946	Auckland	New Zealand	13	Great Britain	8	11 000
1947	Leeds	Great Britain	11	New Zealand	10	28 445
1947	Swinton	New Zealand	10	Great Britain	7	28 531
1947	Bradford	Great Britain	25	New Zealand	9	45 680
1950	Christchurch	New Zealand	16	Great Britain	10	
1950	Auckland	New Zealand	20	Great Britain	13	
1951	Bradford	Great Britain	21	New Zealand	15	37 475
1951	Swinton	Great Britain	20	New Zealand	19	27 065
1951	Leeds	Great Britain	16	New Zealand	12	18 649
1954	Auckland	Great Britain	27	New Zealand	7	22 097
1954	Greymouth	New Zealand	20	Great Britain	14	4240
1954	Auckland	Great Britain	12	New Zealand	6	6186
1955	Swinton	Great Britain	25	New Zealand	6	21 613
1955	Bradford	Great Britain	27	New Zealand	12	24 443
1955	Leeds	New Zealand	28	Great Britain	13	10 438
1958	Auckland	New Zealand	15	Great Britain	10	18 000
1958	Auckland	Great Britain	32	New Zealand	15	20 000
1961	Leeds	New Zealand	29	Great Britain	11	16 479
1961	Bradford	Great Britain	23	New Zealand	10	20 049
1961	Swinton	Great Britain	35	New Zealand	19	22 558
1962	Auckland	New Zealand	19	Great Britain	0	14 976
1962	Auckland	New Zealand	27	Great Britain	8	6411
1965	Swinton	Great Britain	7	New Zealand	2	8497
1965	Bradford	Great Britain	15	New Zealand	9	15 849
1965	Wigan	Great Britain	9	New Zealand	9	7919
1966	Auckland	Great Britain	25	New Zealand	8	14 494
1966	Auckland	Great Britain	22	New Zealand	14	10 657
1970	Auckland	Great Britain	19	New Zealand	15	15 948
1970	Christchurch	Great Britain	23	New Zealand	9	8600
1970	Auckland	Great Britain	33	New Zealand	16	13 137
1971	Salford	New Zealand	18	Great Britain	13	3764
1971	Castleford	New Zealand	17	Great Britain	14	4105
1971	Leeds	Great Britain	12	New Zealand	3	5479
1974	Auckland	New Zealand	13	Great Britain	8	15 000
1974	Christchurch	Great Britain	17	New Zealand	8	
1974	Auckland	Great Britain	20	New Zealand	0	
1979	Auckland	Great Britain	16	New Zealand	8	12 000
1979	Christchurch	Great Britain	22	New Zealand	7	7000
1979	Auckland	New Zealand	18	Great Britain	11	10 000
1980	Wigan	Great Britain	14	New Zealand	14	7000
1980	Bradford	New Zealand	12	Great Britain	8	10 946
1980	Leeds	Great Britain	10	New Zealand	2	8089
1984	Auckland	New Zealand	12	Great Britain	0	8500
1984	Christchurch	Great Britain	28	New Zealand	12	3824
1984	Auckland	New Zealand	32	Great Britain	16	7800
1985	Leeds	New Zealand	24	Great Britain	22	12 591
1985	Wigan	Great Britain	25	New Zealand	8	15 506
1985	Leeds	New Zealand	6	Great Britain	6	14 000
1988	Auckland	New Zealand	12	Great Britain	10	8525
1989	Manchester	New Zealand	24	Great Britain	16	18 723

Continued

553

Great Britain v New Zealand *continued*

Year	Venue	Results			Attendance
1989	Leeds	Great Britain	26	New Zealand	6	13 073
1989	Wigan	Great Britain	10	New Zealand	6	20 346
1990	Palmerston North	Great Britain	11	New Zealand	10	10 000
1990	Auckland	Great Britain	16	New Zealand	14	7500
1990	Christchurch	New Zealand	21	Great Britain	18	5000

New Zealand v France

Year	Venue	Results			Attendance
1948	Paris	New Zealand	11	France	7	12 000
1948	Bordeaux	France	25	New Zealand	7	22 000
1951	Auckland	New Zealand	16	France	15	19 229
1951	Paris	France	17	New Zealand	7	23 459
1952	Bordeaux	France	8	New Zealand	3	8954
1955	Auckland	France	19	New Zealand	9	
1955	Auckland	New Zealand	11	France	6	
1955	Toulouse	France	24	New Zealand	7	10 184
1956	Lyon	New Zealand	31	France	22	7051
1956	Paris	France	24	New Zealand	3	14 752
1960	Auckland	New Zealand	9	France	2	17 914
1960	Auckland	New Zealand	9	France	3	14 007
1961	Bordeaux	New Zealand	16	France	6	2375
1961	Perpignan	New Zealand	23	France	2	9000
1962	Paris	New Zealand	5	France	5	3307
1964	Auckland	New Zealand	24	France	16	10 148
1964	Christchurch	New Zealand	18	France	8	4935
1964	Auckland	New Zealand	10	France	2	7279
1965	Marseille	France	14	New Zealand	3	31 431
1965	Perpignan	France	6	New Zealand	2	9000
1966	Toulouse	France	28	New Zealand	5	7000
1971	Perpignan	New Zealand	27	France	11	
1971	Carcassonne	New Zealand	24	France	2	
1971	Toulouse	France	3	New Zealand	3	
1980	Perpignan	France	6	New Zealand	5	6000
1980	Toulouse	New Zealand	11	France	3	1956
1981	Auckland	New Zealand	26	France	3	12 200
1981	Auckland	New Zealand	25	France	2	8100
1985	Marseille	New Zealand	22	France	0	1500
1985	Perpignan	New Zealand	22	France	0	5000
1989	Carcassonne	New Zealand	16	France	14	3500
1989	Narbonne	New Zealand	34	France	0	6000
1991	Auckland	New Zealand	60	France	6	7000
1991	Christchurch	New Zealand	32	France	10	2000

New Zealand v South Africa

Year	Venue	Results		
1963	Auckland	South Africa	4	New Zealand	3

Great Britain v Papua New Guinea

Year	Venue	Results			Attendance
1984	Mount Hagen	Great Britain	38	Papua New Guinea	20	7510
1987	Wigam	Great Britain	42	Papua New Guinea	0	9120
1988	Port Moresby	Great Britain	42	Papua New Guinea	22	12 107
1990	Goroka	Papua New Guinea	20	Great Britain	18	11 598
1990	Port Moresby	Great Britain	40	Papua New Guinea	8	7837
1991	Wigan	Great Britain	56	Papua New Guinea	4	4193

New Zealand v Papua New Guinea

Year	Venue	Results			Attendance
1978	Port Moresby	New Zealand	30	Papua New Guinea	21	12 000
1982	Port Moresby	New Zealand	56	Papua New Guinea	5	13 000
1983	Auckland	New Zealand	60	Papua New Guinea	20	7000
1986	Goroka	New Zealand	36	Papua New Guinea	26	11 000
1986	Port Moresby	Papua New Guinea	24	New Zealand	22	15 000
1987	Port Moresby	New Zealand	36	Papua New Guinea	22	15 000
1988	Auckland	New Zealand	66	Papua New Guinea	14	14 000
1990	Goroka	New Zealand	36	Papua New Guinea	6	8475
1990	Port Moresby	New Zealand	18	Papua New Guinea	10	4478

France v Papua New Guinea

Year	Venue	Results				Attendance
1979 _____	Albi	France _____	16	Papua New Guinea _____	9	4500
1979 _____	Carcassonne	France _____	15	Papua New Guinea _____	2	3500
1981 _____	Port Moresby	France _____	15	Papua New Guinea _____	15	16 000
1987 _____	Carcassonne	France _____	21	Papua New Guinea _____	4	3500
1991 _____	Goroka	France _____	20	Papua New Guinea _____	18	11 485
1991 _____	Carcassonne	France _____	28	Papua New Guinea _____	14	2000

TOP AUSTRALIAN POINT-SCORERS IN ALL TESTS

	Tries	Goals	Field goals	Points
Mal Meninga	15	85	—	220
Mick Cronin	5	93	—	201
Michael O'Connor	17	61	—	190
Graeme Langlands	17	69	—	189
Noel Pidding	6	53	—	124
Ken Irvine	33	11	—	121
Keith Barnes	—	54	—	108
Reg Gasnier	26	—	—	78
Dave Brown	7	26	—	73
Les Johns	2	30	—	66
Keith Holman	14	6	—	54
Harold Horder	11	10	—	53
Kerry Boustead	15	—	—	46
Wally Lewis	11	—	2	45
Dally Messenger	4	16	—	—
Garry Jack	11	—	—	44
Johnny Graves	5	14	—	43
Brian Carlson	10	5	—	40
Bob Fulton	12	—	4	40

VIV THICKNESSE

Seven Tests for Australia (1933-36). Also played 16 minor games on one Kangaroo tour (1933-34).

When Viv Thicknesse joined Sydney's Eastern Suburbs club in 1931 there was no doubt that a great Rugby League career lay ahead of him. Thicknesse, a brilliant halfback, had already played for New South Wales in Rugby Union and was shaping as a future international in the amateur code. Easts took him on a tour of New Zealand at the end of 1931 and from then on his status was never in doubt.

Viv Thicknesse

Thicknesse played in his first major Rugby League representative match (City v Country) in 1932 and a year later was selected in the Kangaroo side to tour Great Britain. He was one of the Kangaroo stars, with a sensational match in the Second Test at Headingley, Leeds. During the match he was a vital link in Australia's only try, a spectacular length-of-the-field effort. Sadly he missed the Third Test through injury. In the next three years he was to play five more Tests, against New Zealand and the touring 1936 British Lions. In the green and gold, Thicknesse formed formidable combinations with his Easts' team-mate Ernie Norman and Vic Hey, the all-time great from Western Suburbs.

Thicknesse was a vital cog in the Eastern Suburbs machine which swept to three straight Premierships in 1935, 1936 and 1937. Such was the superiority of Easts that in 1936 they were unbeaten, and provided no less than six of the 13 players in Australia's First Test side.

THIESS-TOYOTA TROPHY see *Extinct Competitions*

ALAN THOMPSON

Seven Tests for Australia (1978-80). Also played 14 minor games on one Kangaroo tour (1978) and one New Zealand tour (1980).

Manly-Warringah five-eighth Alan Thompson had the distinction of being selected in a Kangaroo touring squad before he had played for either City (Sydney) or New South Wales. His 26 first-grade games for the Sea Eagles in 1978 were enough to impress the selectors. He was a vital link in the Manly backline that year during which the Sea Eagles notched a Premiership success.

On the Kangaroo tour, Thompson made his Test debut, not as a five-eighth (captain Bob Fulton had that position well and truly wrapped up), but as a centre replacement for Mick Cronin in the second encounter with Great Britain, at Odsal Stadium, Bradford. His next Test was also as a replacement, this time for Cronin's centre partner, Steve Rogers, in the series decider at Headingley, Leeds. Thompson appeared against the visiting British in 1979 and New Zealand the following year. But injury cost him his Test spot against the touring Frenchmen in 1981—and his replacement, the great Wally Lewis, never gave him a chance to regain his Test place.

Thompson's club relied heavily upon him. When he was out, the Manly attack was stifled. When he was on the field, the Sea Eagles fired. He played 263 first grade games for Manly. Although other players, who changed teams, have appeared in more matches in the senior grade, Thompson's figure, at the time, was a record for a single club in the Sydney Premiership. It has since been topped by Steve Mortimer's 267 for Canterbury.

After he retired, Thompson turned to coaching. He was Manly's mentor in 1989, but, after a poor season by the first-grade side, he was unceremoniously sacked.

DUNCAN THOMPSON

Nine Tests for Australia (1920-24). Also played minor games on one Kangaroo tour (1921-22).

A bullet fired by a German soldier during World War I almost spelled an end to the footballing career of one of Australia's most promising halfbacks, Duncan Thompson. Thompson was hit in the lung while fighting at Dernancourt, France, in 1918. Doctors warned him against playing again, but their advice fell on deaf ears and Thompson went on to make a name for himself as one of Australia's finest halfbacks of all time.

The Ipswich-based Thompson was already a Queensland State representative when he was wounded. After the War, he joined North Sydney and gained Test honours. He toured New Zealand (with the 1919 NSW side) and Britain (with the 1921-22 Kangaroos). He was one of four players to top the century on the British tour, scoring 107 points (three tries and 49 goals). The 1921-22 Kangaroos had a distinctive North Sydney look about their line-up. As well as Thompson, four other Norths' players made the tour: wingers Harold Horder and Cec Blinkhorn (both of whom topped the century of points), centre Herman Peters and forward Clarrie Ives. Another Norths' star, centre Frank Rule, was selected but could not make the visit.

Thompson played a major role in the 1921 and 1922 Premiership successes by Norths (which, by the 1990s, were still the club's only Premierships). He captained the side in 1922. He returned to his native Queensland to succeed as coach of several fine Toowoomba sides, both before and after his retirement as a player in 1925.

THORNETT BROTHERS
DICK THORNETT

Eleven Tests for Australia (1963-66). Also played two matches one World Cup (1968) and 18 minor games on one Kangaroo tour (1963-64).

KEN THORNETT

Twelve Tests for Australia (1963-64). Also played 10 minor games on one Kangaroo tour (1963-64).

It is doubtful whether any brothers made a greater impact on the two codes of Rugby than did the Thornetts - John, Ken and Dick. The talented trio played Tests for Australia in Rugby Union or Rugby League and, in the case, of Dick, both. Between them they played 70 Test matches.

John, the eldest, stayed in the amateur ranks where he played 37 internationals and was captain of Australia in the last 17 of them. A well-stocked cheque-book wielded by Leeds Rugby League officials meant that Ken, unlike his brothers, never played Rugby Union for Australia. A robust fullback, he changed codes before catching the eye of the Union selectors, and went on to become one of the professional code's great players.

Ken Thornett, the man the fans dubbed 'The Mayor of Parramatta', played in 12 Tests, against every major Rugby League nation (three each against Great Britain and New Zealand, five versus France and one against South

Africa). He might have played many more but for sharing an era of great fullbacks (including Graeme Langlands, Les Johns and Keith Barnes) and having his career cut short by injury problems. Ken's best performances came in 1965. Although he had no international appearances to his credit that year, he helped Parramatta to the Sydney Premiership semi-finals and was named NSW Player-of-the-Year.

Dick Thornett was the last of the brothers to win fame on the football field, but he went further than the other two. A second-rower, Dick represented his country in major internationals 11 times as a Rugby Union player and 13 times in the professional code. To cap a fine sporting career, he also represented Australia at water polo.

Dick joined Ken in the Parramatta team upon turning professional in 1963, after a furious bidding war between the Eels and several other Sydney clubs. Dick was an immediate success and before the season had ended had made his first Test appearance, against the ill-fated South African touring side. He followed that up with a good tour of Britain and France with the 1963-64 Kangaroos. When he and Ken appeared in a Test together on that tour, it was the first time since 1911 that brothers had played in the same international. Dick Thornett virtually faded from the international scene after that tour, although he made brief re-appearances in the green and gold as a second-half replacement in a 1966 Test against Britain and in two matches in the 1968 World Cup, held in Australia.

Dick Thornett

Ken Thornett

BRENT TODD

22 Tests for New Zealand (1985–91). Also played 13 minor games on one tour of Australia and Papua New Guinea (1986) and two tours of Britain and France (1985 and 1989)

Brent Todd had already represented New Zealand in water polo when, as a rugged 20-year-old, he was flown to Britain as a replacement for injured prop Ross Taylor on the Kiwis' 1985 tour. A few weeks later, after just four appearances in minor tour matches, he made his Test debut, in New Zealand's 22–0 victory over France at Perpignan. It was the start of a distinguished career in which he was to stamp himself as one of the finest Kiwi forwards of the modern era.

Canberra scouts were impressed by the potential Todd showed on the 1986 tour of Australia and Papua New Guinea (in which he played his second Test, against the Kumuls). They signed him up to form an imposing front-row combination with future internationals, prop Sam Backo and hooker Steve Walters. In his first season with the Raiders, Todd played in all 26 first grade games and was on hand for Canberra's first ever grand final (the Raiders going down to Manly 18–8).

Sadly, the following season was not as happy. Todd broke an arm in the first pre-season trial match and missed the rest of the football year. But a nine-match, off-season stint in England with Wakefield Trinity gave him the enthusiasm for a big year in 1989. He was a cornerstone of the Kiwi Test side which played three Tests against the touring Australian side. And he was an important cog in the Canberra machine which won its first NSWRL Premiership. At the end of the season Todd made his second tour of Britain and France, playing in all five Tests.

Todd collected his second Premiership-winners' medal in 1990, a season in which he played six Tests (one versus Australia, three against the touring British and two against Papua New Guinea). In 1991, he appeared in both Tests against the touring Frenchmen and then was one of his country's best players in the three-match series against Australia, including New Zealand's shock 24–8 victory at Olympic Park, Melbourne. On the club scene, Canberra won a series of sudden-death matches to reach the grand final for the third straight year, only to go down 19–12 to Penrith.

But Canberra's financial problems meant that, after 87 first-grade games for the Raiders, Todd had to look elsewhere to secure his footballing future and signed with the Gold Coast for the 1992 season.

TOOHEYS CHALLENGE see *Challenge Cup*

TOOTH CUP see *Midweek Cup*

GEOFF TOOVEY

Two Tests for Australia (1991). Also played three minor matches on one Papua New Guinea tour (1991).

Blonde-haired Geoff Toovey had the size and looks of a schoolboy. But that image was deceiving. Pound for pound the brilliant halfback was one of the toughest footballers of the modern era.

Test coach Bob Fulton was quick to spot his ability when Toovey was playing for Manly-Warringah in the Jersey Flegg competition for under-18s, in 1987. Fulton, then coach of the Sea Eagles, included the youngster in the first-grade squad training for the grand final (which Manly ultimately won) to give him a taste of what it took to reach the top. It was a good education. Toovey made his first-grade debut the following year. And from 1989 on, he made the halfback spot his own, forcing Test man Des Hasler to play five-eighth or lock despite playing almost every week with his left shoulder heavily strapped to ease the pain of a chronic injury.

In 1990, Toovey was included in the Kangaroo train-on squad but with a host of fine experienced halves, including Ricky Stuart (Canberra), Allan

Langer (Brisbane) and Greg Alexander (Penrith) in great form, he missed out on the tour of Britain and France. Toovey had another great year in 1991 helping Manly to the semi-finals. At the end of the season he had planned to have an operation to tie the ligaments in his shoulder to the bone. But the operation was postponed when, after Stuart, Langer and Alexander were all ruled out of the Papua New Guinea tour, Toovey was called into the Australian side. On tour, he played his first two Tests, against the Kumuls.

TRANS-TASMAN TROPHY

The Trans-Tasman Trophy was, for decades, up for grabs every time Australia and New Zealand played each other in Test series. However, in 1991, in deference to the sponsors, the XXXX Trophy was substituted. Australia has had a virtual mortgage on the series played at home. However, the Australians have often met their downfall in New Zealand where most of the Tests have been played on Auckland's Carlaw Park, where heavy conditions often favoured the home sides.

Results of the Trans-Tasman Series

Year	Venue	Result	Tests to Australia	Tests to New Zealand
1908	Australia	New Zealand	1	2
1909	Australia	Australia	2	1
1919	New Zealand	Australia	3	1
1935	New Zealand	Australia	2	1
1948	Australia	Australia	2	1
1949	New Zealand	Drawn	1	1
1952	Australia	New Zealand	1	2
1953	New Zealand	New Zealand	1	2
1956	Australia	Australia	3	—
1959	Australia	Australia	2	1
1961	New Zealand	Drawn	1	1
1963	Australia	Australia	2	1
1965	New Zealand	Drawn	1	1
1967	Australia	Australia	3	—
1969	New Zealand	Drawn	1	1
1971	New Zealand	New Zealand	—	1
1972	Australia	Australia	2	—
1978	Australia	Australia	3	—
1980	New Zealand	Australia	2	—
1982	Australia	Australia	2	1
1983	Australia & New Zealand	Drawn	1	1
1985	Australia & New Zealand	Australia	2	1
1986	Australia & New Zealand	Australia	3	—
1987	Australia	New Zealand	—	1
1989	New Zealand	Australia	3	—
1990	New Zealand	Australia	1	—
1991	Australia	Australia	2	1

GEORGE TREWEEK

Seven Tests for Australia (1928-30). Also played 18 minor games on one Kangaroo tour (1929-30).

George Treweek was one of the best forwards of all time. Some critics, such as noted Australian sporting journalist Tom Goodman, rated him the finest second-rower ever to pull on a green and gold jumper for Australia. Treweek was a tall, gangling footballer, weighing just 99kg (14 st) and nicknamed 'Arms and Legs' because of his high-stepping run and flailing arms. He was noted for his speed in attack, tough scrummaging and ferocious cover defence. Such was his tackling ability that his club, South Sydney, was able to play a five-forward pack, with the lock playing as an extra five-eighth.

Treweek made his Test debut against the touring British side in 1928, and played a second series against the British while touring with the 1929-30 Kangaroos. This visit was perhaps the highlight of his career. He played in 22 games (including all four Tests) and was one of the Kangaroos' top players.

On the club scene, Treweek played in the Riverina in 1921 and 1922, then spent three seasons with Mascot in the Sydney competition before joining Souths. He was one of the mainstays of the fine Rabbitohs' combination which won six of the next seven Premierships. He skippered Souths in the last two of those successes (1931 and 1932). All told, when he retired after the 1934 season, Treweek had played 119 first-grade games with the Rabbitohs.

TRUTH AND SPORTSMAN CUP

The Truth and Sportsman Gold Cup was awarded to the winner of the Sydney Premiership during the early days of Rugby League. It replaced the Hugh McIntosh Shield, which was won outright by Balmain when it scored its third successive Premiership in 1915. South Sydney won the Gold Cup outright after its third win (in 1927), and then won a second Gold Cup outright by winning three more Premierships.

Winners of the Truth and Sportsman Gold Cup

Year	Winner
1918	South Sydney
1919	Balmain
1920	Balmain
1921	North Sydney
1922	North Sydney
1923	Eastern Suburbs
1924	Balmain
1925	South Sydney
1926	South Sydney
1927	South Sydney
1928	South Sydney
1929	South Sydney
1930	Western Suburbs
1931	South Sydney

DENNIS TUTTY

One Test for Australia (1967)

Dennis Tutty was a most accomplished sportsman. He rowed for Australia and as a footballer he played more than 100 first-grade games in the Sydney Premiership and one Test match for Australia (against New Zealand, in 1967)—but he will best be remembered as the man who forced the transfer system to be scrapped in Australia.

When his club, Balmain, refused to put him on the transfer list in 1968, Tutty took the matter to the Equity Court. From there it went to the High Court and, after three years of litigation, a decision was handed down indicating that the system of clubs having the power over whether a player should be allowed to swap to another side was illegal. For Tutty it was a Pyhrric victory. He got his transfer - to Penrith - but he had already lost many thousands of dollars in football earnings waiting for the court decision to be handed down. Ironically, Balmain and Tutty eventually made their peace. In 1980, he took over as non-playing coach of the Tigers' top team.

TYQUIN BROTHERS

BILL TYQUIN

Six Tests for Australia (1948-49). Also played 10 minor games on one Kangaroo tour (1948-49).

TOM TYQUIN

Six Tests for Australia (1956). Also played 13 minor games on one Kangaroo tour (1956-57) and was a member of the 1957 World Cup squad.

Bill and Tom Tyquin each had just a brief 12-month spell of glory on the international scene—but they go into the record books as one of a select few brothers to have represented Australia.

Bill's success was more notable. A strong-running lock-forward with excellent cover-defence, he captained Queensland in 1948 and 1949, and was vice-captain (to Col Maxwell) of the 1948-49 Kangaroos on their tour of Britain and France. He missed only the first Test of that tour, through injury. He had earlier played two Tests against New Zealand, at home. On the club scene, Bill Tyquin was captain-coach of Brisbane's Southern Suburbs side which took out the Brisbane Premiership in 1949, and he was later the club's president.

Tom made his Test debut against the touring 1956 New Zealand Kiwis. He was also a lock, but the selectors switched him to the second-row after only two games of the Kangaroo tour later that year. In 1957 Tom Tyquin was chosen in the Australian squad for the World Cup—but he did not play in any of the four games.

U

UNITED STATES

Australian Harry Sunderland played a major role in the lead-up to the successful introduction of Rugby League into France in the 1930s. Twenty years later he tried in vain to get the sport started in another country—the United States. It was largely through his efforts that American footballer-cum-promoter Mike Dimitro decided to gather a team of gridiron players to tour Australia and New Zealand in 1953. The tour was a failure. The American Allstars (as the team was known) had intensive coaching in the finer points of Rugby League but the tourists managed to win only seven of their 26 matches. A few did continue in Rugby League and one, Al E Kirkland, turned out on the wing for Parramatta in the Sydney Premiership competition.

Officials were not entirely disheartened by the experiment and, the following year, tried to promote the code in the United States itself. The Australian and New Zealand sides played two exhibition games in California on their way home from the inaugural World Cup series in France. The ballyhoo before the games at Long Beach Memorial Stadium and the Los Angeles Coliseum was typically American. Australian captain, Clive Churchill, was given the Key to the City and escorted to the arena by police with their car sirens blaring. Australia won both matches—30–13 (before 1000 spectators) and 28–18 (4554 attendance). The Los Angeles promoters lost about $4000, the English Rugby League Council (which had offered to help) incurred expenses of about $1500 and the Australian and New Zealand authorities each spent $1000. This was a sizable amount in those days.

In the late 1960s, Dimitro expressed interest in staging the World Cup in the United States, but none of the major Rugby League countries showed any interest in his proposals. Then, in the late 1970s, another ex-gridiron player, Mike Mayer, made a vain attempt to get the game underway. In 1987, the Australian Rugby League staged a State-of-Origin match between New South Wales and Queensland at Long Beach. The match drew 12 349 spectators, who saw New South Wales win 30–18, but created little interest among the local media. In 1989, English clubs Wigan and Warrington played an exhibition game in Milwaukee.

UNIVERSITY

University was one of the Sydney Premiership clubs during the period between the two World Wars. It joined the competition in 1920 and pulled out after the end of the 1937 season. It's players were all amateurs and, as such, did not have the experience to match the top sides. They lost almost three-quarters of their games—notching just 44 wins in 226 matches—and they ended up with the wooden spoon on 11 occasions during their 18 seasons in the Premiership. However University did manage to be runner-up in 1926, going down 11–0 to a very good South Sydney combination in the final, after winning seven of its nine games in the competition proper.

Only one player managed to make an Australian side while playing for the club—Ray Morris—but there was a sad finale to his selection. He was chosen for the 1933–34 Kangaroos, but died of an ear infection in Malta en route to Britain without ever playing a game in the green and gold. Another University player, who later made his name after joining Eastern Suburbs, was Ross McKinnon. He is regarded as one of the finest coaches Australia has known.

V

PAUL VAUTIN

Thirteen Tests for Australia (1982–89). Also played three minor games on two New Zealand tours (1985 and 1989).

One of the great disappointments of Paul Vautin's football career was that he never made a Kangaroo tour. In 1982, the year he made his Test debut, he missed out on a lock spot to the great Ray Price and a rising young star who was destined for greatness, Wayne Pearce. Four years later a broken arm put him out for most of the season and he did not have enough time to impress the selectors—and in 1990, he was dropped from the Queensland State-of-Origin side just four months before the Kangaroo selections were made. However 'Fatty' Vautin is worthy of inclusion in the Rugby League history books. A courageous and inspiring forward he turned many a game for Australia, his native Queensland and the club for which he played 11 seasons, Manly-Warringah.

Vautin came to Sydney in 1979 as a raw 20-year-old, but he was so talented that for a while he was the only non-international in the powerful Manly pack. That changed in 1982. He came on as a replacement in the second State-of-Origin match and scored a try which swung the game for Queensland. Soon after he was a last minute inclusion in the Test side against New Zealand, after Price was forced out through injury.

The Manly star was back in the Test side when the British Lions toured in 1984, but during the Second Test at Lang Park, he suffered a depressed fracture of the cheekbone after being hit by an elbow in a highly suspect tackle. He was ruled out of the First Test, against New Zealand, the following year with an injured shoulder, but made the subsequent tour of the Shaky Isles. Vautin played all Tests in 1988 (against Britain and Papua New Guinea) before ending his international career as Australia's vice-captain on the 1989 tour of New Zealand.

The highlight of Vautin's footballing days came in 1987 when he captained Manly to Premiership success. All told, he played 201 first-grade games for the Sea Eagles, but their relationship soured in 1989, soon after he returned from New Zealand. Manly made it clear that they no longer required his services and a disappointed Vautin moved to Easts. Then, after captaining Queensland in the first 1990 State-of-Origin match, he was dropped from the Maroons squad. His 1990 Kangaroo dreams shattered. However under manager Jack Gibson and coach Mark Murray at Easts, Vautin gained a new lease of life in 1991, rekindling his hopes of more Test football, but when the representative selectors overlooked him he decided to call it a day and retire at the end of the season.

MICK VEIVERS

Six Tests for Australia (1962–66). Also played three minor games on a New Zealand tour (1965).

An HD Holden station wagon was one of the fringe benefits which helped lure giant Queensland forward Mick Veivers to Sydney in the mid-1960s. Veivers had not been able to afford a car in his native Brisbane, but the huge Manly-Warringah offer of cash and other comforts persuaded him to migrate south.

Veivers, a second-rower from Brisbane Souths, had made his interstate debut for Queensland in 1961 and a year later played two Tests against the great British Lions touring combination. Although still playing interstate football, he was then continually overlooked by the Test selectors until making the move to Manly in 1965.

His international career was resurrected, with Veivers one of the first chosen to tour New Zealand that year. He starred in both Tests and in the three minor games in which he played. Veivers had a second sortie against curtain on his Test match playing career, although he was a reserve against New Zealand the following year.

After he retired, Veivers turned his talents to politics and served as a National Party MP in the Queensland Parliament.

WALES

Wales has provided some of the greatest players in the history of Rugby League. They include the immortals, Jim Sullivan and Gus Risman as well as the more recent goal-kicking wizard David Watkins. In the early 1990s, the Welsh Rugby Union officials were bewailing the fact that more than a dozen international players, headed by another pointscoring freak, Jonathan Davies, had switched to the professional code in the space of a couple of years.

The Australian Kangaroos began their first-ever tour of Britain with a match at Tonypandy in Wales, in which they beat Mid Rhondda 20–6. Since then, with a few notable exceptions, most Kangaroo sides have played at least one game in Wales. Wales' only venture overseas was for the 1975 World Championships, in which it finished a disappointing third behind Australia and England.

WALES V AUSTRALIA
WORLD CHAMPIONSHIP MATCHES

At Sydney Cricket Ground, Saturday, 14 June 1975
Crowd: 25 386
AUSTRALIA 30 (Harris, Langlands, Raudonikis, Fulton tries, Cronin 9 goals) d WALES 13 (Fisher try, Watkins 5 goals)
Australia: G Langlands (c), M Harris, R Fulton, M Cronin, J Rhodes, T Pickup, T Raudonikis, P Sait, L Platz, G Stevens, T Randall, J Lang, J O'Neill. Replacement: J Donnelly (for Stevens)
Wales: W Francis, C Sullivan, D Watkins (c), D Willicombe, R Mathias, G Turner, D Treasure, K Coslett, E Cunningham, J Mantle, R Wanbon, T Fisher, J Mills Replacements: F Wilson (for Sullivan) and P Rowe (for Treasure)
Referee: F Escande (France)

At St Helen's Ground, Swansea, Sunday, 19 October 1975'
Crowd: 11 112
AUSTRALIA 18 (Schubert 3, Peard tries, Cronin 3 goals) d WALES 6 (Watkins 3 goals)
Australia: G Eadie, A McMahon, M Cronin, S Rogers, I Schubert, J Peard, J Mayes, J Quayle, R Higgs, T Randall, G Veivers, G Piggins, A Beetson (c). Replacements: I Mackay (for Quayle) and J Porter (for Mayes)
Wales: D Watkins (c), R Mathias, W Francis, F Wilson, J Bevan, G Turner, P Banner, K Coslett, C Dixon, E Cunningham, J Mantle, T Fisher, J Mills. Replacement: P Rowe (for Dixon).
Referee: J Percival (New Zealand)

WALES V AUSTRALIA
INTERNATIONAL MATCHES

1909

At Ebbw Vale, Saturday, 6 March 1909
(Match abandoned because of snow)

1911

At Ebbw Vale, Saturday, 7 October 1911
Crowd: 7000
AUSTRALIA 28 d WALES 20

1921

At Pontypridd, Saturday, 10 December 1921
Crowd: 13 000
AUSTRALIA 21 d WALES 16

1930

At Wembley Stadium, London, Saturday, 18 January 1930
Crowd: 16 000
AUSTRALIA 26 d WALES 10

1933

At Wembley Stadium, London, Saturday, 30 December 1933
Crowd: 10 000
AUSTRALIA 51 d WALES 19

1948

At St Helen's Ground, Swansea, Saturday, 20 November 1948
Crowd: 9161
AUSTRALIA 12 d WALES 5

1978

At St Helen's Ground, Swansea, Sunday, 15 October 1978
Crowd: 4250
AUSTRALIA 8 (Fulton, Raudonikis tries, Cronin goal) d WALES 3 (Watkins try)
Australia: G Eadie, I Schubert, M Cronin, S Rogers, K Boustead, R Fulton (c), T Raudonikis, R Price, R Reddy, G Pierce, I Thomson, G Peponis, G Olling. Replacements: A Thompson and C Young
Wales: D Watkins (c), C Sullivan, E Cunningham, D Willicombe, J Bevan, W Francis, P Woods, R Mathias, G Shaw, T Skerrett, J Mills, A Fisher, M James. Replacements: G Johns and B Juliff
Referee: R Campbell (Great Britain)

1982

At Ninian Park, Cardiff, Sunday, 24 October 1982
Crowd: 5 617
AUSTRALIA 37 (Ella 4, Ribot 2, Murray, Lewis, McKinnon tries, Lewis 4, McKinnon goals) d WALES 7 (Williams try, Hopkins, Fenwick goals)
Australia: S Ella, C Anderson, W Lewis (c), G Miles, J Ribot, M Murray, S Mortimer, I Schubert, R Reddy, P McCabe, R Morris, R Brown, D McKinnon. Replacements: K Boustead (for Ella) and G Conescu (for Morris)
Wales: L Hopkins, C Camilleri, S Fenwick, J Bevan (c), P Prendiville, L Hallett, B Williams, P Ringer, B Juliff, M Herdman, T David, D Parry, G Shaw. Replacements: M McJennett (for David). D Wilson not used
Referee: G Kershaw (Great Britain)

IAN WALSH

Twenty-five Tests for Australia (1959-66). Also played 39 minor games on two Kangaroo tours (1959-60 and 1963-64) and two New Zealand tours (1961 and 1965).

Ian Walsh was one of Australia's finest hookers. He was also a great captain and coach, both at a club and international level. Indeed, there were few more astute football brains in his era.

Walsh began his football in the country districts of western New South Wales. At the age of 17, he had his first taste of big-time Rugby League, when chosen to play for Western Division against the great 1951 touring French side. He was to go on to play against every national team which came to Australia until he retired in 1966. In 1958 he captained Western Division against the British Lions. They lost only one match in Australia— a Test. But Walsh's Westerners managed a 24–all draw. 'That performance was one of the highlights of my career,' he explained.

Walsh first represented Australia in 1959, while touring Britain and France with the Kangaroos. He had been chosen only as a second-string to hooker Noel Kelly—but Kelly was injured early in the tour and Walsh played all three Tests against the traditional foe, Britain. He made another tour north four years later. Captain-coach Arthur Summons suffered a recurring injury and Walsh, his deputy, led the Australians in the Tests to an historic Ashes victory (the first by an entirely-Australian Kangaroo side).

Walsh moved into the Sydney Premiership scene in 1962 and figured in five of St George's record 11 successive titles. In 1966 he was captain-coach of the Dragons for the last of their long string of triumphs and, during that same season, led Australia in its successful defence of the Ashes, against the touring British line–up. He bowed out of representative football but continued as captain-coach of St George for one last season. It was a disappointing finale to his career, for the Dragons' reign finally came to an end. Walsh had a stint as non-playing coach of Parramatta and branched out as a long-serving columnist for the Sydney *Daily Telegraph*.

ELWYN WALTERS

Twelve Tests for Australia (1969-74). Also played seven matches in two World Cups (1970 and 1972), one minor international (1970) and 18 minor games on two Kangaroo tours (1967-68 and 1973) and one New Zealand tour (1969).

Elwyn Walters was one of the finest hooker-forwards produced by Australia in the post-World War II era. As well being a top rake, he was superb in the open and a tough defender. In the later 1960s and early 1970s he played a major role in the success of Australia and his Sydney clubs, Souths and Easts.

Walters first wore the green and gold on the 1967 Kangaroo tour, but played second-fiddle to hooker-cum-prop Noel Kelly. Walters made a second Kangaroo tour six years later, appeared in two World Cup tournaments and played in Tests against all major Rugby League nations before his international career came to an end in 1974.

He was a member of Souths' Premiership-winning sides in 1967, 1968 and 1970. Injury forced him to miss the 1971 grand final, also won by the Rabbitohs. Walters finished his career with Eastern Suburbs, figuring in the Roosters' 1974 and 1975 grand final successes.

WALTERS BROTHERS

KERROD WALTERS

Eight Tests for Australia (1989–91). Also played 11 minor games on one Kangaroo tour (1990) one New Zealand tour (1989) and one Papua New Guinea tour (1991).

KEVIN WALTERS

Two Tests for Australia (1991). Also played 11 minor games on one Kangaroo tour (1990) and one Papua New Guinea tour (1991).

STEVE WALTERS

Three Tests for Australia (1991). Also toured Papua New Guinea (1991) without playing a game.

The Walters brothers, from the Queensland city of Ipswich, played their way into the record books in 1990. All three turned out for Queensland in the State-of-Origin series against New South Wales. Kerrod, the incumbent Test hooker, played in two of the three clashes, missing the first match, at the Sydney Football Stadium, when he was replaced by his older brother Steve. And Kerrod's twin, Kevin, came on as a replacement in both the first and third encounters. It was the first time in history that three brothers had played in the one interstate series.

To add to the record, Kerrod and Kevin were chosen in the Kangaroo squad for the tour of Britain and France at the end of the season. It was the first time that twins had worn the green and gold for Australia. Steve, after a sensational display for Canberra's Premiership-winning side in the play-offs, was considered unlucky not to have made the Kangaroo side, too. But the following year he finally was rewarded with a Test spot. Never before had three brothers played for any one country in Rugby League.

Kerrod Walters was the first to make a name for himself. At the start of the 1989 season, Brisbane Broncos' coach Wayne Bennett shocked the football world when he dropped Test hooker Greg Conescu and promoted Kerrod to his first grade side. Bennett knew what he was doing. Within a couple of months Walters was in the Queensland State-of-Origin side and, soon after, was chosen as number-one hooker for the Australian tour of New Zealand. He played in all five matches, including the three Tests.

Despite a strong challenge from NSW skipper Ben Elias, Walters held his spot in the Test lineup for the 1990 clashes with France and New Zealand. But, after Australia's shock loss to Britain in the First Test on the Kangaroo tour, he was replaced by Elias.

Kerrod's form was so good in 1991, that he looked certain to regain his Test spot. But he was sent off in a club game and suspended just before the First Test against New Zealand. The selectors turned to brother Steve and he turned in such a sensational display that even when Kerrod returned from suspension he had to watch from the stands for the final two Tests. Kerrod was back in the Test XIII, however, when rushed to Papua New Guinea after Steve injured an ankle before the first match of the end-of-season tour.

Bennett dropped another bombshell, at the start of 1990, when he switched Test captain Wally Lewis from five-eighth to lock to make way for Kevin Walters, who had joined the Broncos from Canberra. Once again, it was a master-stroke. Kevin Walters finished the season with a host of awards, including that of the Broncos' top player and the Daily M Players' Player (voted by his contemporaries in all 16 Premiership clubs). Kevin Walters showed his versatility on the Kangaroo tour by playing centre as well as five-eighth. And when brother Kerrod was ruled out of the last minor match on the French leg of the tour, Kevin filled in for him at hooker.

While 1990 Kangaroo selection eluded Steve, he gained some consolation with a second Premiership-winners' medal with Canberra. Ironically, when Steve was injured at the start of Australia's 1991 tour of Papua New Guinea, brother Kevin deputised for him as hooker, just as he had done for Kerrod in France. In Papua New Guinea, Kevin finally made his Test debut, coming on as a replacement in the first encounter, at Goroka.

KEVIN WARD

Sixteen Tests for Great Britain (1984–90). Also played for the Rest-of-the-World against Australia (1988) and for Britain against the Rest-of-the-World (1988) and five minor games on one tour of Papua New Guinea, Australia and New Zealand (1988).

When Manly-Warringah won the 1987 Sydney Premiership grand final, many keen judges reckoned the Sea Eagles owed their success to the powerhouse display in the front-row by Kevin Ward. The Castleford prop had joined

St Helen's prop Kevin Ward looks for support as he's tackled by Bob Lindner in the opening match of the 1990 Kangaroo tour

the club for 12 matches—and like other British players before him at Manly had been an outstanding success. However the Clive Churchill Medal, as Man-of-the-Match, went to one of Ward's team-mates. Australians were to see Ward at his best again, 12 months later, when Great Britain gave Australia its first real taste of competition for the Ashes in years.

Ward had made his Test debut against France in 1984, but it was not until the Kangaroos toured in 1986 that he really showed his worth. It was his showing in the three Tests that year that caught the eye of the Manly officials. After being dropped from the British squad for the final Test of the 1990 series against Australia, Ward, who had by then transferred to St Helens, announced his retirement from representative football. He had played in 16 Tests (eight against Australia, five against France and three versus New Zealand). Injury cost him several more caps.

LAURIE WARD

Ten Tests for Australia (1935–38). Also played 24 minor games on one Kangaroo tour (1937–38) and one New Zealand tour (1935).

Laurie Ward was a great fullback of the 1930s who had the uncanny knack of turning defence into attack. He would regularly gather the ball near his own line and run it half the length of the field. The Eastern Suburbs scoring freak Jack Beaton recalled how Ward was one of the great successes of the 1937–38 Kangaroo tour, with only one fault—'he'd make a run and beat 10 players, then he'd want to beat the eleventh'.

Ward, from Newcastle, made his Test debut on the 1935 tour of New Zealand. He missed the Tests against the touring British side the following year (Beaton, normally a centre, played fullback in the 1936 Ashes series). Switching to North Sydney, Ward returned for the five Tests on the Kangaroo tour of Britain and France and the two internationals in New Zealand en route to the northern hemisphere. Ward's last Test was the most memorable. It was the third encounter with Britain, at Huddersfield. The Kangaroos were underdogs, but won the match 13–3. Ward had a blinder. He looked certain to hold down the Test fullback spot for many years to come— but the outbreak of World War II brought a halt to international football.

JACK WATKINS

Seven Tests for Australia (1914–21). Also played 13 minor games on one Kangaroo tour (1921–22) and one New Zealand tour (1919).

Jack 'Bluey' Watkins was one of the real personalities of the early days of Australian Rugby League. He was a fiery forward noted for his footballing knowledge and outstanding cover defence. Watkins played mainly as a lock, but was equally at home anywhere in the pack. Indeed, he began his 14–year stint with Eastern Suburbs in the front-row, even though he weighed only 63.5 kg (10 stone) at the time.

He made his Test debut against the touring British Lions in 1914, but then had his international career interrupted by World War I He was back in the limelight soon after the Armistice. Watkins toured New Zealand in 1919, playing in all four Tests. Despite being sidelined for some time on the 1921–22 Kangaroo tour because of a cartilage injury, he managed to make two more Test appearances.

He last played for New South Wales against Queensland in 1924, but he remained a force in club football even after that, captaining Sydney's Eastern Suburbs club in 1926, at the age of 35. He played 137 first-grade games for Easts and was a member of two of their Premiership-winning combinations (in 1913 and 1923).

His status was ably summed up in a 1935 Rugby League Annual: 'A demon tackler, it is said of him that he grassed more wing-threequarters than any other lock man'. And the British newspaper, *The Sporting Chronicle*, not known for its hyperbole, commented after the Kangaroo tour: 'The best loose forward we have seen for some time'.

ALEX WATSON

Fourteen Tests for Australia (1954–56). Also played five matches in two World Cups (1954 and 1957) and 18 minor games on one Kangaroo tour (1956–57) and one New Zealand tour (1953).

Brisbane centre Alex Watson was one of Australia's most consistent players during the mid-1950s. Big and fast, he had the ability to leave opposing three-quarters groping for thin air. He first played for Queensland as an 18–year-old in 1951, and two years later was the baby of the Australian team which toured New Zealand. He did not play in any of the Tests, but managed to bag six tries in five minor games.

Watson made his Test debut in 1954, playing in all three Tests against Great Britain. Later in the year, he turned out in each of Australia's three World Cup games in France, in the first ever competition for world supremacy. The big Queenslander made his third overseas trip with the 1956–57 Kangaroos. On this tour he played 18 games (only Ken Kearney and Roy Bull appeared in more), including five Tests. Watson would have played in the sixth but was dropped at the last moment as a disciplinary measure for having skipped a training session. Watson bowed out of international and representative football as a member of the triumphant Australian side in the 1957 World Cup.

On the club scene, he was with Western Suburbs when it carried off the Brisbane Premiership in 1952 and 1954.

CLIFF WATSON

Twenty-three Tests for Great Britain (1963–1971). Also played seven matches in two World Cups (1968 and 1970).

Cliff Watson's Rugby League career is unique. It only began as the result of a newspaper advertisement. Watson had played some Rugby Union, but had never even seen a game of League until he answered the call for 'big, fast, tough forwards'. Londoner Watson was an instant success and became the backbone of the St Helens' club pack and the British international six.

His first Test was against Australia, in 1963. He went on to play 23 (11 against Australia, seven against France and five versus New Zealand) and appear in two World Cups. He captained Britain several times.

In 11 years with St Helens, Watson figured in the sides which won two Challenge Cups (1966 and 1970) and two English Championships (1965 and 1967). In 1973, he headed south to an old battleground, Australia, to join former clubmate Tommy Bishop, who was captain-coach of Cronulla-Sutherland. The pair were instrumental in lifting the side from near the bottom of the Sydney Premiership table to that year's grand final. However, because of a ceiling on player payments, Watson then headed off, finishing his career as a player-coach in Wollongong.

GEORGE WATT
Three Tests for Australia (1946).

Although he played in only three Tests for Australia, George Watt is universally acknowledged as being one of the finest hookers his country has known. He was only lightly-framed but had an amazing turn of speed over a short distance, which helped him net many tries—and there were few who could match his ball-winning ability in the scrums.

Watt's three Tests were against the 1946 British touring side, dubbed The Indomitables, after the aircraft carrier which brought them to Australia. He lost nothing in comparison to his opposite number, Joe Egan, regarded by many as the greatest ever British hooker.

On the club scene, Watt is one of only a handful of players to have won Sydney Premierships with different clubs. He was a member of the Balmain side which thrashed South Sydney 33–4 in the 1939 decider and was on the winning side again in 1944, when Balmain downed Newtown 12–8. The following year he switched clubs and was with Easts when they downed his old side, Balmain, 22–18 in the Premiership finale.

BENNY WEARING
One Test for Australia (1928).

It seems incredible that Benny Wearing played only one Test match for Australia, for he was one of the best wingers ever to step onto a football field.

Wearing's lone Test appearance was in the third encounter with the 1928 touring British Lions side. He scored two brilliant tries and kicked three goals to help Australia to a face-saving 21–14 victory over the British side (the British side had won the first two Tests, 15–12 and 8–0). After that final encounter, Britain's captain, Jonty Parkin, exclaimed: 'Where art thou been hiding yon winger?'. Despite this great Test performance and good club form the following year, Wearing was overlooked by the selectors when they sat down to choose the 1929–30 Kangaroo squad. Prominent journalist J C Davis, writing in *The Referee* newspaper under the nom-de-plume of The Cynic attacked the selectors, noting '(Wearing is) the finest wing three-quarter of this century'.

On the club scene, Wearing played a major role in South Sydney's seven Premiership successes in eight years from 1925 to 1932. His 196 first-grade games for the Rabbitohs remained a club record for almost half a century. Wearing scored 903 points (163 tries and 207 goals) during his club career.

ERIC WEISSEL

Eight tests for Australia (1928–32). Also played 17 minor games on one Kangaroo tour (1929–30).

Eric Weissel, the country star who refused to play club football anywhere but in his home area of the Riverina, in southern New South Wales, is regarded as one of Australia's greatest five-eighths. His play was characterised by a brilliant turn of speed and robust tackling.

Weissel rose to the top in 1928 when, after playing for his State, he was selected in the last two Tests against the touring British side. He went to Britain the following year with the Kangaroos, appearing in all three Tests and topping the tour scoring with 127 points (five tries and 56 goals). He had a particularly successful opening to the tour with six goals in his first game, against Rochdale Hornets, followed by seven against Hull and then two tries and 11 goals against Halifax. In the First Test, at Hull, Weissel spearheaded a fine 31–8 Australian victory with a try and five goals. The country five-eighth finished his international career with three Tests against Britain in 1932, including the infamous 'Battle of Brisbane', in which he just missed a try after a 75–metre run on a badly injured ankle which would have sidelined any lesser player.

Weissel turned out with five different clubs in the Riverina—Cootamundra, Temora, Bardmedman, Narrandera and Wagga. With Cootamundra, he was skipper during two years when they retained the famous Maher Cup with an unbeaten record.

HARRY WELLS

Twenty-one Tests for Australia (1952–1960). Also played eight matches in three World Cups (1954, 1957 and 1960), one minor international (1960) and 34 minor games on two Kangaroo tours (1952–53 and 1959–60), one New Zealand tour (1953) and one World Cup tour (1960).

A robust centre, Harry Wells played a vital role in Australian successes throughout the 1950s. Although much of his club form was only average, 'Dealer' Wells was a true big-match player, especially against British sides.

Wells first strode into the limelight in 1952 and gained selection for the Kangaroo tour of Britain and France. He played a Test against each country and on his return home was one of the first chosen for the 1953 tour of New Zealand. After a good performance in the inaugural World Cup in 1954, and against France the following year, Wells slipped from the international scene, with only a brief return for the 1957 World Cup.

He was back with a vengeance in 1959. Teaming up with the new sensation, Reg Gasnier, Wells set about proving just what a great player he was. Many experts suggest it was having Wells as a foil which saw Gasnier through his international baptism unscathed. At the very least, they were the ideal centre pairing. They played eight Tests together in the next 12 months and starred in the unsuccessful 1960 bid by Australia to retain the World Cup. Wells showed his versatility in an international against France, at Toulouse, after that series. He turned out as lock-forward and played a sensational game.

Harry Wells, star Western Suburbs Rugby League centre of the 1950s, crashes into Manly fullback Bob Batty

Wells, who had won a Premiership with South Sydney in 1951 and had captained Western Suburbs in the 1958 grand final, (a year after he won the *Sun Herald* award for the best-of-fairest player in the Sydney competition), eventually faded into NSW country football. He made a brief return to international play when chosen for the Monaro side which took on the 1966 touring British team. By then however, he was but a shell of his former self and no match for his younger and faster opponents. He continued playing around the country until a knee reconstruction brought an end to his career, at Port Macquarie on the NSW north coast, in 1972.

Harry Wells' real name was Harry Wills. Early in his career, an errant sporting scribe spelled it incorrectly—and the mistake was perpetuated by writer after writer for the rest of Wells' playing career. Only once, on the official listing of the 1952–53 Kangaroos, was his correct name used.

WESTERN SUBURBS

Western Suburbs players have, over the years, built up a reputation as the giant killers of the Sydney Premiership competition. Many times the Magpies have halted the winning streak of another club, or put paid to the chances of Premiership favourites.

Wests' success in the 1930 competition interrupted South Sydney's succession of Premierships which stretched from 1925 to 1932. The Magpies also split a winning streak by Souths in the 1950s, their 1952 Premiership victory coming in the middle of South Sydney's reign at the top between 1950 and 1955. Western Suburbs nearly did the same thing to the mighty St George combination which won a world record 11 straight competitions in the late 1950s and 1960s. In 1963, Wests beat St George in three of their four clashes, including the major semi-final—but the Magpies went down 8–3 in a controversial grand final, in which a seemingly good try by Wests was disallowed.

One of the original eight clubs in the Sydney Premiership, Wests holds an important place in the history of the game down-under for the number of fine Test captains who have worn the black and white. Wests have supplied the captains of three Kangaroo touring sides—Frank 'Skinny' McMillan (1933–34), Col Maxwell (1948–49) and Arthur Summons (1963–64). Only St George can boast a similar record. Other Test skippers from the Magpies include Jimmy Craig, the great utility back of the 1930s, and halfback Tom Raudonikis, who led the Australians in 1973 Tests.

Wests have always been great around the scrum-base. In the 1930s, the club had the services of Jimmy Craig, Vic Hey and Les Mead. Hey is considered by many experts to have been the greatest Australian five-eighth of all time. In the 1950s, Wests could boast the services of the Test combination of Keith Holman and Frank Stanmore. Holman was one of the greatest halfbacks to represent Australia, appearing in 32 Tests (in 12 series), including a record tally of Anglo-Australian internationals of 14. Three times he was named NSW Player-of-the-Year (in 1951, 1956 and 1958). In the following decade, it was the turn of Arthur Summons, who was equally at home at either half or five-eighth, representing Australia in both positions. In the 1970s, came Raudonikis, recommended to Wests by Summons, who had followed Raudonikis' early career in the Riverina area of southern New South Wales.

All Rugby League players, no matter what their club, owe a debt to Western Suburbs, for it was Wests, in the 1950s, which set the pace in paying players big money—a trend which has been continued by all clubs ever since. The Wests move was prompted by a slump in form which saw them drop from Premiers in 1952 to wooden-spooners the following season. The Magpies were near the bottom in 1954 and once again last in 1955. Before the start of the 1956 season, the club signed Test centre Harry Wells, international second-rower Kel O'Shea, Test five-eighth Darcy Henry and representative back Ian Johnston. The move paid off handsomely. Wests just missed out on the Premiership after scraping into the semi-finals following a dream second round run and a play-off for fourth spot with Newtown, a grand finallist the previous year. The Magpies were the only real threat to the great St George side in the next few seasons.

It was perhaps ironic that, in the mid-1970s, Wests could not match the big spending of some of the other clubs and had to sit back and watch as stars 'defected'. The biggest loss came at the end of the 1979 season, during which Wests had managed to make the semi-finals. Four of the club's five Test stars left—centre John Dorahy and forwards Ray Brown and Les Boyd to Manly-Warringah and skipper Tom Raudonikis to Newtown.

Wests again managed to make the semi-finals in 1980. The plunder of Wests players by other clubs continued, including Test winger John Ribot, another to switch to Manly. Bled of its stars, Wests once more languished at the bottom of the table. In 1983, the NSW Rugby League axed the Magpies from the competition, but a court appeal forced them to be reinstated.

To try to establish a strong base for the future, Wests moved, in 1987, from the inner city to the fringe metropolis of Campbelltown, south-west of Sydney. In 1989, they shocked everyone by signing the Great Britain captain Ellery Hanley for a reputed $6000 per match. Another British Test player, Garry Schofield, also joined the Magpies for the season. It provided a boost for the young Wests players.

An even bigger boost came at the end of the 1990 season. Wests signed the fine coach Warren Ryan, who had won two Premierships at Canterbury-Bankstown and had guided Balmain to two grand finals. His influence helped persuade Test forward David Gillespie and former internationals Andrew Farrar and Paul Langmack to link up with the Magpies for 1991. Already in the black and white were Test forward Bob Lindner, the Man-of-the-Tour with the 1990 Kangaroos and 1989 Rookie-of-the-Year, second-rower Cameron Blair.

Under Ryan, Wests made the semi-finals for the first time since 1982, beating off a challenge from Canterbury in the play-off for fifth place. In doing so, the club drew down the curtain on one of the most frustrating periods in its long history (with the wooden spoon in 1983, 1984, 1987 and 1988, second last in 1985 and 1986 and with only two sides below it in the other two seasons). Injuries didn't help the Magpies effort. Langmack was badly hurt in a trial match and forced to have a knee reconstruction which kept him out of the side until the last handful of games. And Lindner broke his leg in a match against Cronulla in April, made a dramatic comeback two months later and then, in the First Test against New Zealand, broke it again. During the season Gillespie and Lindner both made the Test side and second-rower Steve Jackson joined them in the State-of-Origin series. Halfback Jason Taylor, a former schoolboy star, who won the 1989 Commonwealth Bank Cup Superstar award, topped the Premiership goalkicking lists with 80 goals.

WESTERN SUBURBS

Founded: 1908
Entered Sydney Premiership competition: 1908
Home ground: Campbelltown Sports Ground (formerly called Orana Park) (Record crowd—17 286)
Colours: Black and white
Nickname: The Magpies
Honours:
    Sydney Premiership—Winners, 1930, 1934, 1948, 1952; Runners-up, 1918, 1925, 1932, 1950, 1958, 1961, 1962, 1963
      Midweek Cup—1977
      City Cup—1918
      State Cup—1965
      Ampol Cup—1963
      Flowers Memorial Pennant (Club Championship)—1948, 1960, 1961
      Reserve-grade Premiership—1936, 1961, 1981
      League Cup—1926
      President's Cup—1925, 1947, 1958
      Third-grade Premiership—1936, 1938, 1939, 1944, 1958, 1961, 1967
      Under-23 Premiership—1977
      Flegg Memorial Trophy—1965
      S G Ball Cup—1971
Most first grade games: 201 by Tom Raudonikis
Most points in a career: 767 by Bill Keato
Most tries in a career: 84 by Trevor Cogger
Most points in a season: 215 by Peter Rowles, 1978
Most tries in a season: 18 by Alan Ridley, 1932
Rothmans Medal winner: Tom Raudonikis (1972)
NSW Player-of-the-Year: Keith Holman (1951, 1956 and 1958), Arthur Summons (1962)
Sun Herald Best-and-Fairest Player: Keith Holman (1950, 1951, 1956 and 1958), Harry Wells (1957), Tom Raudonikis (1974)
Coach-of-the-Year: Don Parish (1974), Roy Masters (1978)

RON WILLEY

Played in 17 minor games for Australia on one Kangaroo tour (1952–53).

Ron Willey was an efficient goal-kicking fullback, who had the misfortune to be playing at the same time as the legendary Clive Churchill, the man they called 'The Little Master'. Churchill kept Willey out of the Test sides. Willey also suffered from cartilage trouble which forced him out of football for 12 months at the height of his career. However he still managed a Kangaroo tour of Britain in 1952–53 as Churchill's understudy and was the squad's second top-scorer, with 141 points (five tries and 63 goals) in his 17 games.

On the club scene, Willey was a member of the Manly-Warringah sides which reached the grand finals in 1957 and 1959, only to be beaten by the incredible St George combination. His 968 points in 124 games for Manly broke the club record of 847 set by Ron Rowles. He was captain-coach of Manly in 1962, and he continued coaching after he retired as a player, in 1964. The highlight of his career was in 1972 when he steered Manly to its first Premiership. He was at the helm again when the Sea Eagles made it two straight titles 12 months later.

Willey later coached Balmain (getting the Tigers to the semi-finals for the first time in almost a decade, in 1977), North Sydney (which reached the Semis for the first time in 17 years in 1982) and Penrith (steering the Panthers to the semi-finals for the first time in the club's history, in 1989), as well as Bradford Northern in the English Championship competition.

LIONEL WILLIAMSON

Five Tests for Australia (1971–74). Also played six matches in two World Cups (1968 and 1970), one minor international (1970) and 10 minor games on one Kangaroo tour (1973), one New Zealand tour (1971) and one World Cup tour (1970).

Many record books refer to the burly winger Lionel Williamson as being a champion Aborigine. Indeed, his story appeared in a book on Aboriginal sporting stars. However while Williamson was unfazed by the description, he was in fact, of Anglo-Saxon descent. Nevertheless his dark features will be remembered by many an opposition winger left groping, as Williamson ducked and bumped his way past en route to the tryline.

Williamson was from the North Queensland town of Innisfail, the home of another great winger, Kerry Boustead. He had a couple of seasons with Halifax in the English competition, but first hit the headlines in Australia with some great form in the interstate series in 1967. He was surprisingly overlooked when the Kangaroo side was chosen at the end of the year. Disappointed, Williamson briefly considered retirement, but a year later he made the 1968 Australian World Cup squad. He was on the bench for the first two games (against Great Britain and New Zealand) but came on for the last preliminary match and the final (both against France)— and he made his mark with two tries in each game.

He moved to Sydney to join the Newtown club in 1969. After missing the series against the touring 1970 British Lions, he was back at the end of that season for another World Cup, as the only specialist winger in the squad. His displays in the Cup were such that the great Graeme Langlands chose him in his form side of the series. Williamson eventually earned himself a Kangaroo tour, in 1973, before bowing out of international football, at the age of 30, in the 1974 Ashes series against Britain.

WILLS CUP see *Pre-Season Competition*

BILLY WILSON

Ten Tests for Australia (1959–63). Also played 14 minor games on one Kangaroo tour (1959–60).

When St George selectors decided, in 1958, to switch backrower Billy Wilson to prop, in a sporting gesture he offered to quit football rather than keep a specialist front-rower out of the side. Luckily he was talked out of this idea, for Wilson went on to became one of the best props in the game—and five years later he achieved the ultimate of captaining his country in a Test series.

The versatile Wilson first attracted attention in the mid-1950s. As lock forward he had played a major role in the first of St George's record 11 straight Sydney Premierships. He played most of that match in 1956, at outside centre, after the regular centre Merv Lees was carried off with a badly-damaged shoulder. Wilson moved to Wagga for a season in 1957 (from where he represented Country Firsts) before coming back to the Dragons a year later. He made his Test debut, in the front-row, against the touring New Zealand Kiwis, in 1959, and, later that year, toured Britain and France with the Kangaroos.

After six Premierships with the Dragons, the tough forward quit the club at the end of the 1962 season, linking up with North Sydney. He had a new lease of life and was chosen to skipper the Test sides in the first two clashes against the 1963 New Zealand tourists, his last appearances in the international arena.

GRAHAM WILSON

Three Tests for Australia (1963–64). Also played 16 minor games on one Kangaroo tour (1963–64).

Graham Wilson is the only Rugby League player of the modern era to have played for more than one country at an international level. The Newtown second-rower was one of two Sydney players seconded to the South African side to bolster its strength for the New Zealand leg of its 1963 Australasian tour (the other was Canterbury-Bankstown hooker Fred Anderson). Later that year Wilson was chosen in the Kangaroo squad for the tour of Britain and France. He had shown great potential a few years earlier, playing in the Metropolitan side against NSW Country in 1960 and making his interstate debut in Brisbane the following season. However the tough tackler had been inconsistent and it was only in 1963 that he had started to live up to his potential, turning out for Sydney against South

Africa before touring the Shaky Isles with the South Africans. Wilson played in two Tests against France on the Kangaroo tour and was a member of the Third Test side when France visited Australia in 1964. His last representative football was for New South Wales, in 1966.

WINFIELD CUP see *Sydney Premiership and Brisbane Premiership*

WINFIELD STATE LEAGUE see *Queensland State League*

ROD WISHART

Four Tests for Australia (1991). Also played two minor games on one Papua New Guinea tour (1991).

Winger Rod Wishart earned a spot in the record books when chosen to wear the green and gold against New Zealand in 1991. He became the first Illawarra player to represent Australia in the Test arena.

The 22-year-old had almost given up hope after being overlooked for the previous year's Kangaroo tour and the First Test against the touring Kiwis. But when Australia suffered a humiliating loss in that Test, there were wholesale changes for the second encounter and Wishart got his chance.

Wishart scored a try in his debut Test, won 44–0 by Australia. But his effort was soured when he was hit by a heavy tackle from second-rower Dean Lonergan after grounding the ball. His face blew up and a fractured cheekbone was suspected. But Wishart surprised everyone by proving his fitness for the Third Test. He scored again, in Australia's 40–12 victory, making his selection for the end-of-season tour of Papua New Guinea a mere formality. On tour he continued his try-scoring endeavours, notching a hat-trick in the First Test, at Goroka, and another try in the second encounter, at Port Moresby.

Wishart, joined Illawarra from Gerringong, where he was coached by the great Mick Cronin. He represented both Southern Division and Country Firsts in 1988. In each of his first three seasons with Illawarra, he topped the Steelers' pointscoring (82 in 1989, 112 in 1990 and 124 in 1991). In Illawarra's 44–4 victory over Canterbury in March 1991, Wishart's eight goals set a new club record and his 20 points equalled another.

JOHN WITTENBERG

Six Tests for Australia (1966–70). Also played four matches in one World Cup (1968) and three minor matches on one New Zealand tour (1969).

Big Queensland forward John Wittenberg showed just what a tough man he was with his first taste of international football. Playing for Central Queensland against the 1966 British Lions he was regularly splitting the tourists' defence with crashing runs up the middle. Soon after half-time he was laid out by a suspect tackle and carried in agony from the field. However, within minutes he was back in the fray—and his inspiration helped the local side to a shock 10–5 victory over the British. That display and some fine performances for Queensland by the tough prop from Theodore, 200 km south of Rockhampton, caught the eye of the selectors. When Britain clearly won the First Test 17–13 he became an automatic selection for the remaining two Ashes encounters.

The lure of the St George dollars brought Wittenberg to Sydney. He was prevented from joining the Dragons straight after the 1966 clashes with Britain because of rules designed to curb the flow of talent from Queensland to the Sydney competition—but he was willing to sit out a season on the sidelines to ensure his move south. With St George, Wittenberg won a spot in the 1968 World Cup side, which carried all before it. The following year he toured New Zealand, but the tour ended badly for Wittenberg, who suffered a depressed fracture of the cheekbone in the final match, against Auckland. He was back on deck 12 months later to ring down the curtain on his international career, against the 1970 British tourists.

WOODEN SPOON

The one award no club wants is the wooden spoon. In the Sydney Premiership competition only two clubs (Manly-Warringah and Brisbane) had, by 1992, managed to avoid the humiliation of finishing last. And Brisbane had only been in the Premiership race for four seasons. The worst record is by Western Suburbs with 14 wooden spoons since the club began in 1908. But considering when each club first appeared, of the current sides the most disappointing is Illawarra, with three in just nine seasons, followed by Parramatta, with 11 in 44 years. Twice the Eels picked up the wooden spoon in all three grades.

There were some great comebacks, though. Wests, wooden spooners in 1955, winning only three games, were semi-finalists in the next eight seasons. In 1966, Eastern Suburbs failed to win a match (and took out its third wooden spoon in four years). But a year later the Roosters were in the semi-finals.

By 1992, the tally of wooden spoons was: Western Suburbs (14), Parramatta (11), University (11), North Sydney (10), Newtown (6), Annandale (4), Eastern Suburbs (4), South Sydney (4), Balmain (3), St George (3), Canterbury-Bankstown (3), Illawarra (3), Penrith (2), Cronulla-Sutherland (2), Canberra (1), Gold Coast (1).

WORLD CHAMPIONSHIP see *World Cup*

WORLD CLUB CHAMPIONSHIP

For years, Rugby League critics had called for a World Club Championship in which the top sides from Britain and Australia could meet to decide the relative merits of their competitions. In the 1950s and 1960s several tentative plans for leading clubs to make tours were vetoed by the League hierarchy. However, in 1976, St Helens, who had just won the Challenge Cup and the Premiership in Britain, made a quick visit to play Eastern Suburbs, reigning Sydney Premiers. St Helens was no match for the home side which ran out easy winners 25–2. The slipshod performance by the visitors put paid to any further clashes in the immediate future.

The idea was revived a decade later. Wigan, the English champions, invited Manly-Warringah, the Sydney Premiers, to fight for the world crown at Wigan's home ground of Central Park. Wigan's side contained only one player who was not an international, winger Richard Russell. The team was Steve Hampson, Russell, Joe Lydon, David Stephenson, Henderson Gill, Shaun Edwards, Andy Gregory, Ellery Hanley, Andy Goodway, Ian Potter, Shaun Wane, Nicky Kiss and Brian Case. Manly had a star-studded line-up, too, including seven current or future Test players. The line-up was Dale Shearer, David Ronson, Darrell Williams, Michael O'Connor, Stuart Davis, Cliff Lyons, Des Hasler, Paul Vautin, Owen Cunningham, Ron Gibbs, Ian Gately, Mal Cochrane and Phil Daley.

The match was a titanic struggle from the opening whistle. Despite some glorious attacking moves, the rock-like defence of both sides prevented even one try from being scored. Manly put up a great effort after being reduced to 12-men for most of the second half, following the dismissal of second-rower Ron Gibbs. Wigan finally won 8-2. The success of the match was such that another world club confrontation was arranged in 1989 at Old Trafford, the home of the famous Manchester United Soccer Club, between English Champions Widnes and Sydney Premiers Canberra. Widnes had nine internationals in its side, Canberra had five and two who were to make their Test debuts on the Kangaroo tour of Britain a year later.

The Widnes side was Alan Tait, Andy Currier, Jonathan Davies, Darren Wright, Martin Offiah, Tony Myler, David Hulme, Richard Eyres, Paul Hulme, Kurt Sorensen (c), Joe Grima, Phil McKenzie and Derrick Pyke. Playing for Canberra were Gary Belcher, Matthew Wood, Mal Meninga (c), Laurie Daley, John Ferguson, Chris O'Sullivan, Ricky Stuart, Bradley Clyde, Gary Coyne, Dean Lance, Steve Jackson, Steve Walters, Glenn Lazarus.

Canberra rushed to a 12-0 lead after only 11 minutes of play and looked like running away easy winners, but the English club fought back. Then Canberra were badly hit. Meninga, the inspiration behind the Raiders could not resume after half-time, and centre Laurie Daley was sin-binned for a head-high tackle on former Rugby Union international Davies as the Welshman was crossing the line for a try. While Daley was off the field, Widnes ran in two more tries to take an unbeatable 12 point lead. The locals finally ran out winners 30-18.

Penrith won its first ever Sydney Premiership in 1991, the 25th anniversary of the Panthers' entering the competition. And it was hard to come down off 'Cloud Nine' to play Wigan in the World Club Challenge on the latter club's home territory. And the Panthers were without star centre Brad Fittler (who was on Test duty in Papua New Guinea), tough second-rower Mark Geyer (thanks to a passport mixup) and several other young grand final heroes (who for personal reasons declined the trip to England). Captain Greg Alexander and international second-rower John Cartwright were also under a fitness cloud. But Penrith still could field a strong lineup which included international forwards Royce Simmons and Paul Dunn as well as Graham Mackay, the man who that year had broken Alexander's Penrith tryscoring record with 16 touchdowns.

Wigan had a side chock full of talent: Steve Hampson, Frano Botica, Sam Panapa, Joe Lydon, David Myers, Shaun Edwards, Andy Gregory (c),

Paul Clarke, Billy McGinty, Denis Betts, Andy Platt, Martin Dermott and Kelvin Skerrett. Botica and Panapa were Kiwi internationals and, of the rest, only Myers, Clarke and McGinty had not played Tests for Britain (Myers had represented for the Under-21s).

The Panthers could not come to grips with French referee Alain Sablayrolles, who caned them in the penalties. After 13 minutes the penalty count was 6–1 and Botica had kicked goals from four of them to put Wigan ahead 8–0. Penrith fought back to be 8–4. But the Panthers never seemed to be able to finish off promising movements. They were still in it, down 4–14, until 10 minutes from fulltime, when a Botica penalty and a try by Myers put the game out of reach. Lydon kicked a cheeky field goal a minute from the end to rub salt in the wound. Botica was named Man-of-the-Match.

RESULTS OF WORLD CLUB CHAMPIONSHIP MATCHES

1976

At Sydney Cricket Ground, Tuesday, 29 June 1976
Crowd: 26 856
EASTERN SUBURBS 25 (R Fairfax, K Stevens, R Ayliffe, I Schubert, G Townsend tries, J Brass 5 goals) d ST HELENS 2 (G Pimblett goal)

1987

At Central Park, Wigan, Wednesday, 7 October 1987
Crowd: 36 895
WIGAN 8 (D Stephenson 4 goals) d MANLY-WARRINGAH 2 (M O'Connor goal)

1989

At Old Trafford, Manchester, Wednesday, 10 October 1989
Crowd: 30 786
WIDNES 30 (M Offiah 2, P Hulme, J Davies, R Eyres, D Wright tries, J Davies 3 goals) d CANBERRA 18 (M Meninga, C O'Sullivan, S Walters tries, M Wood 2, C O'Sullivan goals)

1991

At Anfield Stadium, Liverpool, Wednesday, October 2,
Crowd: 15 000
WIGAN 21 (S Panapa, D Myers tries, F Botica 6 goals, J Lydon field goal) d PENRITH 4 (D Willis try)

WORLD CUP

The possibility of staging a world Rugby League championship was first mooted as far back as 1933. France, which had just entered the international sphere, suggested that a tournament between England, Wales, France, Australia and New Zealand could be held in May 1935. Britain agreed to consider the proposal—but it was soon pigeon-holed.

The idea was revived when the International Board of Rugby League was formed in Bordeaux in 1948. France called for a World Cup to be held three years later. Again the idea gathered dust. France tried again in 1952, with a firm offer to stage the tournament in May 1954. Australia complained that this would mean the cancellation of Britain's tour 'Down Under'. A compromise saw the tour go ahead with the Cup taking place after the tourists returned home. Even at the last minute the tournament was nearly cancelled. A vicious end to the British visit prompted their Australian hosts to call for the Cup's abandonment until, as they put it, 'sanity returns'. The four major Rugby League nations—Australia, France, Great Britain and New Zealand—eventually took the field in France.

Subsequent World Cup tournaments have been held in both the Northern and Southern Hemispheres—although at one stage, in the mid-1960s, it looked likely that the Cup would be scrapped. Australia was due to host the 1965 series but, because of France's poor international form, feared it would be a financial flop and cancelled. Three years later, the Australians had second thoughts and a tournament took place in Sydney, Brisbane and Auckland (New Zealand). An improved France finished as runner-up to Australia.

There was a change of format for the series, re-named the World Championship, in 1975. Britain was split into two sides, England and Wales, for a five-sided contest, with each side playing the others at home and away. The experiment was not a financial success and the old system was resumed in 1977. After yet another financially disastrous series, the Rugby League chiefs decided to scrap the whole idea.

It was again revived in 1985. This time there were a series of home-and-away qualifying games for a 1988 final. The last Test of each series was deemed to be a qualifying match—thus breathing some life into several series which had already been decided in the first two Tests. Australia was the first to make the final. It's opponent was only decided in a Test between Great Britain and New Zealand, at Christchurch—the penultimate qualifying match. However despite enormous hype, New Zealand found the Australians too strong in the final.

The final in the next World Cup under this format is set for late 1992.

1954 Tournament

Paul Barriere, president of the French Rugby League, donated a silver trophy costing three million francs (about $8000) for the winning side in the inaugural World Cup competition held in France in 1954. An extraordinary number of players made themselves unavailable or withdrew from the British side. This lack of player enthusiasm—especially among Oldham and St Helens stars—was because of what they described as paltry financial terms for members of the British team. The eventual 18–man British squad contained only three players who had appeared in the Tests against Australia earlier that year—captain and lock-forward Dave Valentine, halfback Gerry Helme and centre Phil Jackson. The scratch British side surprised all the critics (no to mention themselves) by carrying off the trophy.

The British downed Australia, drew with France and then beat New Zealand. France also beat Australia and New Zealand—although the Australians claimed they had two legitimate tries and a goal disallowed in their 15–5 loss. In the final, at the Parc de Princes in Paris, the tough match against Australia two days earlier told on France. Britain led 8–2, but France hit the front 9–8 when captain Puig Aubert converted a try by winger Vincent Cantoni. Inspired play by Valentine helped lift the British performance in the latter stages and his team ran out winners 16–12. France showed a small profit on the series, but the other three countries lost money.

1st World Cup, France, 1954

Venue	Result					Attendance
Paris	France	22	New Zealand	13		13 240
Lyon	Great Britain	28	Australia	13		10 250
Marseille	Australia	34	New Zealand	15		20 000
Toulouse	France	13	Great Britain	13		37 471*
Nantes	France	15	Australia	3		13 000
Bordeaux	Great Britain	26	New Zealand	6		14 000

* Record for a Rugby League game in France

Final table

	W	D	L	F	A	Pts
Great Britain	2	1	—	67	32	5
France	2	1	—	50	31	5
Australia	1	—	2	52	58	2
New Zealand	—	—	3	34	82	—

Final

At Parc de Princes, Paris, Saturday, 13 November 1954
Crowd: 30 368
GREAT BRITAIN 16 (Brown 2, Rose, Helme tries, Ledgard 2 goals) d FRANCE 12 (Cantoni, Contrastin tries, Puig Aubert 3 goals)
Great Britain: J Ledgard, D Rose, P Jackson, A Naughton, M Sullivan, G Brown, G Helme, D Valentine (c), D Robinson, B Watts, R Coverdale, S Smith, J Thorley
France: Puig Aubert (c), V Cantoni, C Teisseire, J Merquey, R Contrastin, A Jiminez, J Crespo, G Verdier, J Pambrun, A Save, F Rinaldi, J Audobert, J Krawzyck
Referee: C Appleton (Great Britain)

The squads

Australia: C Churchill (c), I Moir, N Pidding, D Flannery, A Watson, H Wells, K McCaffery, R Banks, K Holman, G Hawick, H Crocker, P Diversi, N Provan, K O'Shea, R Bull, B Davies, D Hall, K Kearney
France: Puig Aubert (c), C Teissiere, J Merquey, A Jiminez, R Contrastin, V Cantoni, M Voron, J Crespo, G Benausse, R Guilhem, G Verdier, J Pambrun, A Save, A Carrere, J Audobert, F Rinaldi, G Delaye, J Krawzyck
Great Britain: J Ledgard, D Rose, P Jackson, M Sullivan, F Kitchen, A Naughton, G Brown, G Helme, W Banks, R Rylance, J Whiteley, H Bradshaw, D Valentine (c), B Watts, D Robinson, R Coverdale, S Smith, J Thorley
New Zealand: H Anderson, J Edwards, N Denton, J Austin, R McKay, C Eastlake (c), W Sorensen, G Menzies, L Erikson, A Atkinson, I Grey, J Bond, J Yates, G McDonald, J Butterfield, W mcLennan, D Blanchard, C Johnson
Referees: C Appleton (Great Britain) and M Guidicelli (France)

1957 Tournament

The 1957 World Cup in Australia coincided with the country's Golden Jubilee of Rugby League. And what a celebration it turned out to be! The Australian combination swept all before it—despite injuries to three key players in the first match.

This game, against New Zealand, was won easily 25–5, but star halfback Keith Holman, goal-kicking fullback Keith Barnes and classy five-eighth Greg Hawick were lost for the subsequent encounters. In the reshuffle, winger Brian Carlson moved to fullback, lock Brian Clay to stand-off and reserve five-eighth Ken McCaffery came into the side as half.

All proved outstanding successes in Australia's 31–6 drubbing of Britain and 26–9 win over France. Carlson scored 17 points (one try and seven goals) against France, in wet and windy conditions. No final was required to confirm Australia's win. Instead, the home team went out against a team chosen from the other three countries (four Frenchmen, four Britons and five New Zealanders). The Rest-of-the-World, captained by French centre Jacques Merquey, were no match for the Cup champions who, after leading 5–3 at half-time, went on to win 20–11.

Front row—BJ Clay, K Kearney, R Poole (Capt. & Coach),
NC Robinson (Manager), K McCaffery, KV Holan, K Barnes
*Second row—***G Hawick, R Ritchie, N Provan, KJ O'Shea, B Carlson,**
H Wells
*Back row—***A Watson, WL Marsh, B Davies (V. Capt.), T Tyquin,**
DF Schofield, I Moir

2nd World Cup, Australia, 1957

Venue	Result			Attendance
Sydney	Great Britain	23	France	5	50 077
Brisbane	Australia	25	New Zealand	5	29 636
Sydney	Australia	31	Great Britain	6	57 955
Brisbane	France	14	New Zealand	10	22 142
Sydney	Australia	26	France	9	35 158
Sydney	New Zealand	29	Great Britain	21	14 263

Final table

	W	D	L	F	A	Pts
Australia	3	—	—	82	20	6
Great Britain	1	—	2	50	65	2
New Zealand	1	—	2	44	60	2
France	1	—	2	28	59	2

No Final required.

Non-Cup match
At Sydney Cricket Ground, Saturday, 29 June 1957
Crowd: 30 675
AUSTRALIA 20 (Provan, Moir, Poole, Ritchie tries, Carlson 3 goals & field goal) d REST-OF-THE-WORLD
11 (Benausse, Ashton, Merquey tries, Soremsen goal)
Australia: B Carlson, R Ritchie, R Poole (c), H Wells, I Moir, G Hawick, K McCaffery, B Clay, N Provan,
K O'Shea, B Davies, K Kearney, W Marsh

587

Rest-of-the-World: L Jones (GB), M Voron (F), J Merquey (F) (c), W Sorensen (NZ), E Ashton (GB), G Benausse (F), S Belsham (NZ), J Whiteley (GB), J Riddell (NZ), G Gunney (GB), H Maxwell (NZ), N Appelian (F), C Johnson (NZ)
Referee: V Belsham (New Zealand)

The squads:
Australia: K Barnes, B Carlson, R Ritchie, I Moir, R Poole (c), H Wells, A Watson, K McCaffery, G Hawick, K Holman, B Clay, D Schofield, N Provan, K O'Shea, T Tyquin, B Davies, K Kearney, W Marsh
France: A Rives, G Husson, J Foussat, J Merquey (c), M Voron, G Benausse, R Jean, R Medus, F Levy, A Save, G Verdier, R Ferrero, A Jiminez, J Rouqueriol, A Parent, G Berthomieu, H Delhoste, A Appellian
Great Britain: G Moses, W Boston, P Jackson, A Davies, L Jones, E Ashton, M Sullivan, R Price, A Rhodes, J Stevenson, D Turner, J Grundy, J Whiteley, G Gunney, S Little, A Prescott (c), T McKinney, T Harris
New Zealand: P Creedy, V Bakalich, K Bell, R Griffiths, T Hadfield, W Sorensen, G Turner, R Ackland, S Belsham, G Menzies, J Yates, J Riddell, R Percy, K Pearce, H Maxwell, W mcLennan, C Johnson (c), J Butterfield
Referees: V Belsham (New Zealand), D Lawler (Australia)

1960 Tournament

Britain, the host country, was a decisive winner of the 1960 World Cup. Like Australia three years earlier, the British succeeded with an unbeaten sequence in the preliminary matches—beating New Zealand 23–8, France 22–7 and Australia 10–3. It was the last match, on a muddy Odsal Stadium field, that decided the series. The British won through a concerted forward display—and their ability to bottle up the legendary Australian centre combination of Reg Gasnier and Harry Wells. The match was ruined as a spectacle by French referee Edouard Martung, who allowed both sides to encroach offside.

Five Australians were selected in the Rest-of-the-World side which was beaten 33–27 by the Cup-winning British combination.

3rd World Cup, Britain, 1960

Venue	Result				Attendance
Bradford	Great Britain	23	New Zealand	8	20 577
Wigan	Australia	13	France	12	20 278
Leeds	Australia	21	New Zealand	15	10 773
Swinton	Great Britain	33	France	7	22 923
Wigan	New Zealand	9	France	0	6500
Bradford	Great Britain	10	Australia	3	32 773

Final table

	W	D	L	F	A	Pts
Great Britain	3	—	—	66	18	6
Australia	2	—	1	37	37	4
New Zealand	1	—	2	32	44	2
France	—	—	3	19	55	—

No Final required

Non-Cup match
At Odsal Stadium, Bradford, Monday, 10 October 1960
Crowd: 3908
GREAT BRITAIN 33 (Ashton 2, Murphy 2, Myler 2, Davies, Shaw, Sullivan tries, Rhodes 3 goals) d REST-OF-THE-WORLD 27 (Menzies 3, Gruppi 2, Gourbal, Hadfield tries, Mantoulan 2, Eastlake goals)
Great Britain: A Rhodes, J Challinor, E Ashton (c), A Davies, M Sullivan, F Myler, A Murphy, V Karalius, B Shaw, D Turner, J Wilkinson, J Shaw, B McTigue.
Rest-of-the-World: C Eastlake (NZ), T Hadfield (NZ), R Boden (A), C Mantoulan (F), R Gruppi (F), G Menzies (NZ), B Muir (A), Y Gourbal (F), B Hambly (A), R Eramouspe (F), D Beattie (A), W Rayner (A), C Johnson (NZ) (c)
Referee: M Martung (France)

The squads:
Australia: K Barnes (c), K Irvine, B Carlson, L Morgan, R Gasnier, H Wells, R Boden, A Brown, B Muir, R Bugden, J Raper, R Mossop, E Rasmussen, G Parcell, D Beattie, B Hambly, N Kelly, W Rayner
France: J Barthe (c), L Poletti, J Dubon, R Gruppi, J Merquey, C Mantoulan, R Rey, G Fages, J Guiraud, A Lacaze, R Eramouspe, A Quaglio, A Vaden, A Boldini, Y Gourbal, A Marty, A Casas, V Mezzard

Great Britain: E Ashton (c), W Boston, J Challinor, A Davies, E Fraser, R Greenough, T Harris, V Karalius, B McTigue, A Murphy, F Myler, A Rhodes, B Shaw, J Shaw, M Sullivan, D Turner, J Whiteley, J Wilkinson
New Zealand: C Johnson (c), C Eastlake, T Hadfield, G Turner, W Sorensen, N Denton, G Menzies, K Roberts, G Phillips, R Griffiths, R Cooke, H Maxwell, J Butterfield, R Ackland, T Kilkelly, M Cooke, L Olliff, T Reid
Referees: E Clay (Great Britain) and M Martung (France)

1968 Tournament

The 1968 World Cup—the first in eight years—was co-hosted by Australia and New Zealand. For the first time it was decided to award the Cup to the winner of a play-off between the top two sides after the preliminary rounds, to ensure crowd interest right up until the last game.

Australia went through the early games undefeated. Britain had been expected to be Australia's biggest threat, but it suffered a 7–2 defeat by France in appalling conditions at Auckland's Carlaw Park and could finish only third. In the final, at the Sydney Cricket Ground, Australia easily accounted for France 20–2. Star of the series was Australia's Aboriginal fullback Eric Simms. In four matches, he kicked a fantastic 25 goals. His 50 points were 21 more than the previous World Cup individual record set by Britain's Jack Ledgard in the inaugural contest in 1954.

Johnny Raper with the World Cup won by Australia in 1968

4th World Cup, Australasia, 1968

Venue	Result				Attendance
Sydney	Australia	25	Great Britain	10	62 256
Auckland	France	15	New Zealand	10	18 000
Brisbane	Australia	31	New Zealand	12	23 608
Auckland	France	7	Great Britain	2	15 760
Brisbane	Australia	37	France	4	32 600
Sydney	Great Britain	38	New Zealand	14	14 105

Final table

	W	D	L	F	A	Pts
Australia	3	—	—	93	26	6
France	2	—	1	26	49	4
Great Britain	1	—	2	50	46	2
New Zealand	—	—	3	36	84	—

Final
At Sydney Cricket Ground, Monday, 10 June 1968
Crowd: 54 290
AUSTRALIA 20 (Williamson 2, Greaves, Coote tries, Simms 4 goals) d FRANCE 2 (Capdouze goal)
Australia: E Simms, J Rhodes, J Greaves, L Williamson, R Fulton, W Smith, J Raper (c),
R Coote, R Thornett, A Beetson, F Jones, J Wittenberg
France: J Cros, D Pellerin, J Lecompte, J Gruppi, J Ledru, J Capdouze, R Garrigues, J Clar, H Marracq,
F de Nadai, G Ailleres (c), Y Begon, C Sabatie
Referee: J Percival (New Zealand)

The squads
Australia: E Simms, G Langlands, J King, B James, J Greaves, J Rhodes, L Williamson, A Branson, R Fulton,
W Smith, J Raper (c), R Coote, R Thornett, A Beetson, E Rasmussen, J Wittenberg, D Manteit, F Jones,
B Fitzsimmons
France: J Cros, D Pellerin, A Ferren, J Ledru, M Molinier, J Lecompte, J Gruppi, J Capdouze, R Garrigues,
M Frattini, J Clar, F de Nadai, H Marracq, H Mazard, A Alesina, G Ailleres (c), C Sabatie, V Serrano,
Y Begon
Great Britain: B Risman (c), D Edwards, C Young, C Sullivan, J atkinson, I Brooke, A Burwell, R Millward,
M Shoebottom, T Bishop, C Renilson, R Haigh, R Warlow, A Morgan, R French, C Watson, M Clark,
P Flanagan, K Ashcroft
New Zealand: R Tait, D Ellwood, R Mincham, E Wiggs, R Sinel, P Schultz, S Dunn, J Bond (c), G Clarke,
E Carson, A Kriletich, K Dixon, B Lee, D Parkinson, G Smith, O Danielson, H Tatana, C O'Neil, C McMaster
Referees: C Pearce (Australia), J Percival (New Zealand)

1970 Tournament

Australia was lucky to reach the final of the 1970 World Cup, in England—
but having done so, it scored a great 12–7 win over the previously unbeaten
British side, to retain the trophy it had won two years earlier. Ironically,
the Cup went missing soon after the final and was not seen again until
a fan found it on a rubbish dump 20 years later.

Australia thrashed New Zealand 47–11 in the opening match of the
tournament but had its colours lowered first by Britain (11–4) and then,
surprisingly, by France (17–15). It sneaked into the final on points average
from France and New Zealand, who also scored one win each.

The final was a vicious match! Australian halfback Billy Smith and British
centre Syd Hynes became the first players ever sent off in a World Cup
match, when they received their marching orders two minutes from the
end. *The Daily Mail* noted that had the fighting which characterised the
final taken place on a public street, 'the parties would have been
arrested' . . . 'This was pure, bloody mayhem paraded as sport,' *the Mail*
said.

Eric Simms, a last-minute replacement for injured captain Graeme
Langlands in the Australian squad, topped the Cup pointscoring for the
second time. He notched 37 points (one try, 15 goals and two field goals,
then worth two points). In the match against New Zealand, he scored
a Cup record 23 points (one try, nine goals and a field goal).

Captain Ron Coote holds up the World Cup after the Australians had beaten Great Britain in the final of the 1970 series

5th World Cup, England, 1970

Venue	Result					Attendance
Wigan	Australia	47	New Zealand	11		9586
Leeds	Great Britain	11	Australia	4		15 084
Hull	New Zealand	16	France	15		3900
Castleford	Great Britain	6	France	0		9150
Swinton	Great Britain	27	New Zealand	17		5609
Bradford	France	17	Australia	15		6215

Final table

	W	D	L	F	A	Pts
Great Britain	3	—	—	44	21	6
Australia	1	—	2	66	38	2
France	1	—	2	32	37	2
New Zealand	1	—	2	44	89	2

Final

At Headingley, Leeds, Saturday, 7 November 1970
Crowd: 18 776
AUSTRALIA 12 (Cootes, Williamson tries, Simms 2 goals & field goal) d GREAT BRITAIN 7 (Atkinson try, Dutton goal, Hynes field goal)
Australia: E Simms, M Harris, J Cootes, P Sait, L Williamson, R Fulton, W Smith, R Coote (c), R McCarthy, R Costello, J O'Neill, R Turner, R O'Reilly. Replacements: R Branighan (for Sait) and E Walters (for Turner)
Great Britain: R Dutton, A Smith, F Myler (c), S Hynes, J Atkinson, M Shoebottom, K Hepworth, M Reilly, D Laughton, J Thompson, C Watson, A Fisher, D Hartley. Replacement: C Hesketh
Referee: F Lindop (Great Britain)

The squads

Australia: E Simms, L Williamson, R Branighan, M Harris, J Cootes, R Fulton, P Sait, D Pittard, W Smith, J Brown, R Coote (c), G Sullivan, B McTaggart, R McCarthy, R Costello, R O'Reilly, J O'Neill, R Turner, E Walters
France: J Cros, S Marsolan, E Bonal, D Pellerin, M Molinier, A Ruiz, J Gruppi, J Capdouze, R Garrigues, G Guiraud, J Clar (c), H Mazard, R Biffi, G Cremoux, C Sabatie, F Bonet, F de Nadai, J Cabere
Great Britain: R Dutton, P Charlton, A Smith, K Jones, J Atkinson, F Myler (c), S Hynes, C Hesketh, M Shoebottom, K Hepworth, R Haigh, M Reilly, D, Laughton, J Thompson, D Chisnall, C Watson, D Hartley, A Fisher, K Ashcroft
New Zealand: D Ladner, J Whittaker, B McGuinn, M Brereton, B Lowther, R Christian (c), L Graham, G Woolard, G Cooksley, E Carson, A Kriletich, B Deacon, E Heatley, E Kereopa, G Smith, D Gailey, J Greengrass, C O'Neill, W Burgoyne
Referees: F Lindop (great Britain), W Thompson (Great Britain)

1972 Tournament

Britain won the 1972 World Cup series, held in France, after the only drawn final in the history of the championships. Britain and Australia finished 10–all in the final at Lyon's Gerland Stadium, and neither side scored in the 20 minutes extra time. The British were awarded the Cup for their better showings in the preliminary matches, in which they had beaten each of their three opponents. Australia claimed a try by captain Graeme Langlands, disallowed by French referee Georges Jameau, was legitimate— and this would have changed the result of the whole series.

As in 1970, the crowds were very small by international standards. Only twice did more than 10 000 attend. On one of these occasions, the match (France against New Zealand) was a curtain-raiser for a Soccer game and most of the crowd had come to watch the 11–a-side clash.

6th World Cup, France, 1972

Venue	Result				Attendance
Marseille	France	20	New Zealand	9	20 748
Perpignan	Great Britain	27	Australia	21	6300
Grenoble	Great Britain	13	France	4	5321
Paris	Australia	9	New Zealand	5	8000
Pau	Great Britain	53	New Zealand	19	7500
Toulouse	Australia	31	France	9	10 332

Final table

	W	D	L	F	A	Pts
Great Britain	3	—	—	93	44	6
Australia	2	—	1	61	41	4
France	1	—	2	33	53	2
New Zealand	—	—	3	33	83	—

Final

At Stade de Gerland, Lyon, Saturday, 11 November 1972
Crowd: 4500
GREAT BRITAIN 10 (Sullivan, Stephenson tries, Clawson 2 goals) drew with AUSTRALIA 10 (O'Neill, Beetson tries, Branighan 2 goals)
Great Britain: P Charlton, J Atkinson, J Walsh, C Hesketh, C Sullivan (c), J Holmes, S Nash, G Nicholls, P Lowe, B Lockwood, T Clawson, M Stephenson, D Jeanes
Australia: G Langlands (c), R Branighan, G Starling, M Harris, J Grant, R Fulton, D Ward, G Sullivan, A Beetson, G Stevens, J O'Neill, E Walters, R O'Reilly
Referee: G Jameau (France)

The squads

Australia: G Langlands (c), J Grant, R Branighan, M Harris, G Starling, S Knight, P Sait, R Fulton, T Raudonikis, D Ward, G Sullivan, G Stevens, R McCarthy, J Elford, J O'Neill, R O'Reilly, A Beetson, E Walters, F Jones
France: F Toujas, S Marsolan, E Bonal, M Molinier, A Ruiz, M Mazare, G Guilham, J Imbert, M Frattini, M Anglade, A Rodrigues, S Gleyzes, V Serrano, J Sauret, F de Nadai (c), J Garzino, C Zaluendo, J Franc, J Bonal
Great Britain: P Charlton, J Holmes, D Redfearn, J Atkinson, C Sullivan (c), C Hesketh, J Walsh, D O'Neill, D Topliss, S Nash, G Nicholls, R Irving, C Dixon, P Lowe, B Lockwood, T Clawson, D Jeanes, A Karalius, M Stephenson
New Zealand: W Collicoat, J Wilson, J Whittaker, P Orchard, M Brereton, J O'Sullivan, R Christian (c), D Williams, B Tracey, G Cooksley, P Gurnick, M Eade, R Walker, A Coll, R Paul, D Gailey, D Mann, M Mohi, W Burgoyne
Referees: G Jameau (France), F Gril (France), M Naughton (Great Britain)

In the first six World Cups, each country had to nominate 19 players. Even if a side was plagued with injuries, no other players could be added to the squad during the series. However some players never even had the chance to show their wares. Four Australians were chosen in World Cup squads but never played a game in the green and gold—Brisbane forward Tom Tyquin (1957), St George halfback Bob Bugden (1960), Parramatta hooker Bill Rayner (1960) and Brisbane half Johnny Brown (1970). Rayner however did however play for the Rest-of-the-World against Britain.

1975 Tournament

Britain was split into two sides—England and Wales—for the 1975 World Championships. In another change of format, each of the sides played the other four at home and away. England and Wales played their 'away' games on neutral territory—in Brisbane, Australia. The series was played in three stages. France met England and Wales at the end of their 1974–75 domestic season. The three sides then travelled south for their away matches in Australia and New Zealand. Finally, at the end of the southern season, the Australasian teams visited Britain and France.

There was no final scheduled and, as a result, Australia virtually had the series sewn up before it went on tour. The Australians did not lose a match in the early stages but their main rivals, England, managed a draw on the Sydney Cricket Ground. At home, England became the only side to beat Australia during the series, but had left its run too late and failed by one point to catch the Aussies on the final table.

Wales was involved in a couple of vicious matches. There were all-in brawls at Swansea in the match against Australia. New Zealand swore it would never again take the field against a team in which Welsh prop Jim Mills was chosen, following an incident in its Swansea game.

1st World Championships

Venue	Result				Attendance
Toulouse	France	14	Wales	7	7563
Leeds	England	20	France	2	10 842
Brisbane	Australia	36	New Zealand	8	10 000
Brisbane	Wales	12	England	7	6000
Sydney	Australia	30	Wales	13	25 386
Christchurch	New Zealand	27	France	0	2500
Auckland	New Zealand	17	England	17	12 000
Brisbane	Australia	26	France	6	9000
Sydney	Australia	10	England	10	33 858
Auckland	New Zealand	13	Wales	8	18 000
Warrington	England	22	Wales	16	5034
Auckland	Australia	24	New Zealand	8	18 000
Bordeaux	England	48	France	2	2000
Marseille	France	12	New Zealand	12	8000
Swansea	Australia	18	Wales	6	11 112
Bradford	England	27	New Zealand	12	5937
Perpignan	Australia	41	France	2	10 440
Wigan	England	16	Australia	13	9393
Swansea	Wales	25	New Zealand	24	2645
Salford	Wales	23	France	2	2247

593

Final table

	W	D	L	F	A	Pts
Australia	6	1	1	198	69	13
England	5	2	1	167	84	12
Wales	3	—	5	110	130	6
New Zealand	2	2	4	121	149	6
France	1	1	6	40	204	3

The squads

Australia: G Langlands, G Eadie, C Anderson, A McMahon, J Rhodes, T Fahey, R Branighan, I Schubert, J Porter, J Brass, R Fulton, M Cronin, S Rogers, T Pickup, J Peard, J Mayes, T Raudonikis, R Strudwick, R Coote, J Quayle, G Pierce, R Higgs, P Sait, L Platz, D Fitzgerald, G Stevens, D Wright, T Randall, J Donnelly, J O'Neill, A Beetson, G Veivers, I Mackay, G Piggins, J Lang

England: G Fairbairn, P Charlton, K Fielding, J Atkinson, G Dunn, D Noonan, E Hughes, J Holmes, L Dyl, J Walsh, D Eckersley, K Gill, R Millward, S Nash, S Norton, M Philbin, M Morgan, E Chisnall, P Cookson, M Couleman, M Adams, G Nicholls, T Martyn, R Irving, P Jackson, C Forsyth, B Hogan, D Chisnall, J Thompson, J Grayshon, J Gray, J Bridges

France: F Tranier, M De Matos, M Pillon, J F Grechi, M Laffargue, A Dumas, B Curt, E Bonal, A Ruiz, M Molinier, B Guilhem, P Clergeau, P Chauvet, R Terrats, J Calle, J P Lacoste, J M Imbert, C Zaluendo, Y Alvernhe, G Garcia, F Duthil, J M Bosc, G Bucchi, G Vigouroux, C Thenegal, M Gonzales, M Moussard, F De Nadia, F Kaminski, V Serrano, M Cassin, J P Tremouille, J C Mayorgas, M Maique, J P Sauret, S Gleyzes, D Hermet, M Anglade

New Zealand: W Collicoat, M Brereton, P Orchard, J O'Sullivan, J Whittaker, P Matete, B Dickison, A Gordon, F Ah Kuoi, D Munro, D Williams, R Jarvis, J Smith, K Stirling, M Eade, P Gurnick, R Baxendale, A Coll, K Sorensen, D Sorensen, J Greengrass, L Proctor, G West, J Hibbs, T Conroy

Wales: W Francis, C Sullivan, M Richards, F Wilson, D Willicombe, D Watkins, R Wallace, G Turner, P Rowe, D Treasure, P Banner, J Mantle, K Coslett, C Dixon, B Butler, B Gregory, S Gallagher, C Jones, M Murphy, E Cunningham, R Wanbon, J Mills, M James, R Evans, A Fisher

Referees: L Bruyeres (Australia), M Caillot (France), F Escande (France), G Jameau (France), A Lacaze (France), D Lancashire (Australia), F Lindop (Great Britain), K Page (Australia), J Percival (New Zealand), W Thompson (Great Britain)

1977 Tournament

From the opening game of the 1977 series, it was obvious that the final would be an Anglo-Australian affair. Neither France nor New Zealand could offer any real opposition. Australia won the preliminary clash with Britain 19–5, thanks largely to a brilliant effort by fullback Graham Eadie. He became the first Australian fullback to score two tries in an international, in that Brisbane clash.

The final was a tougher affair. Only great defence and a couple of lucky breaks allowed Australia to hold on to win 13–12. The most significant piece of luck occurred when British referee Billy Thompson blew his whistle to award a penalty to Britain for shepherding. At that very moment, British winger Stuart Wright took an intercept and headed off for what would have been a certain try under the post. Later in the match, British fullback George Fairbairn missed a simple kick for goal from in front of the posts.

2nd World Championships, Australasia, 1977

Venue	Result				Attendance
Auckland	Australia	27	New Zealand	12	18 000
Auckland	Great Britain	23	France	4	10 000
Sydney	Australia	21	France	9	13 231
Christchurch	Great Britain	30	New Zealand	12	9000
Brisbane	Australia	19	Great Britain	5	25 200
Auckland	New Zealand	28	France	20	8000

Final table

	W	D	L	F	A	Pts
Australia	3	—	—	60	26	6
Great Britain	2	—	1	63	35	4
New Zealand	1	—	2	52	77	2
France	—	—	3	33	72	—

Final

At Sydney Cricket Ground, Saturday, 25 June 1977

Crowd: 24 457

AUSTRALIA 13 (Gartner, McMahon, Kolc tries, Cronin 2 goals) d GREAT BRITAIN 12 (Pitchford, Gill tries, Fairbairn 3 goals)

Australia: G Eadie, A McMahon, M Cronin, R Gartner, M Harris, J Peard, J Kolc, G Pierce, R Higgs, A Beetson (c),T Randall, N Geiger, G Veivers. Replacement: D Fitzgerald

Great Britain: G Fairbairn, S Wright, J Holmes, L Dyl, W Francis, R Millward (c), S Nash, P Hogan, E Bowman, G Nicholls, S Pitchford, K Elwell, J Thompson. Replacements: K Gill and L Casey

Referee: W Thompson (Great Britain)

The Squads

Australia: G Eadie, A McMahon, M Harris, T Fahey, M Cronin, M Thomas, R Gartner, J Peard, S Crear, T Raudonikis, J Kolc, G Pierce, R Reddy, R Higgs, A Beetson (c), T Randall, D Fitzgerald, G Veivers, N Geiger

France: P Saboureau, J Guigue, J Moya, P Chauvet, C Baile, G Lepine, J M Bourret, R Terrats, A Ruiz, J Calle (c), J Imbert, G Alard, J M Imbert, M Caraca, J Roosebrouck, J J Cologni, J P Sauret, G Rodriguez, J C Mayorgas, J Brial, H Daniel, M Cassin, M Chantal, M Moussard, H Bonnet, G Garcia

Great Britain: G Fairbairn, K Fielding, S Wright, L Dyl, W Francis, J Holmes, K Gill, R Millward (c), S Nash, L Casey, P Hogan, S Lloyd, G Nicholls, S Pitchford, E Bowman, A Hodginson, J Thompson, P Smith, D Ward, K Elwell

New Zealand: W Collicoat, M Collicoat, M O'Donnell, K Fisher, D O'Hara, J Whittaker, C Jordan, F Ah Kuoi, O Filipaina, L Proctor, D Williams, J Smith, Whetu henry, Whare Henry, A Rushton, D Sorensen, K Sorensen, T Coll (c), R Baxendale, M Graham

Referees: M Caillol (France), R Cooper (New Zealand), D Lancashire (Australia) and W Thompson (Great Britain)

1985-1988 Tournament

The four-year home-and-away format for the World Cup received a jolt when France cancelled its visit to the southern hemisphere, forfeiting its away games to Australia, New Zealand and Papua New Guinea. Great Britain's shock win over Australia in the Third Test of the 1988 series meant that the penultimate game (between the Lions and New Zealand) decided which side met the Australians in the final. After a narrow win at Christchurch, New Zealand qualified. Such was the interest in the game that the Rugby Union ground Eden Park was needed to hold the 46 000 fans. However the match hardly lived up to the pre-match hype, with Australia winning easily 25-12.

7th World Cup, 1985-1988

Venue	Result				Attendance
Auckland	New Zealand	18	Australia	0	22 000
Leeds	Great Britain	6	New Zealand	6	22 209
Perpignan	New Zealand	22	France	0	5000
Avignon	Great Britain	10	France	10	6000
Brisbane	Australia	32	New Zealand	12	22 811
Port Moresby	Papua New Guinea	24	New Zealand	22	15 000
Port Moresby	Australia	62	Papua New Guinea	12	17 000
Wigan	Australia	24	Great Britain	15	20 169
Carcassonne	Australia	52	France	0	5000
Leeds	Great Britain	52	France	4	6567
Wigan	Great Britain	42	Papua New Guinea	0	9121
Carcassonne	France	21	Papua New Guinea	4	3500
Port Moresby	Great Britain	42	Papa New Guinea	22	12 107
Sydney	Great Britain	26	Australia	12	15 944
Auckland	New Zealand	66	Papua New Guinea	14	14 000
Wagga Wagga	Australia	70	Papua New Guinea	8	11 685
Christchurch	New Zealand	12	Great Britain	10	8525

(France forfeited away matches against Australia, New Zealand and Papua New Guinea)

Final table

	W	D	L	F	A	Pts
Australia	6	—	2	252	91	12
New Zealand	5	1	2	158	85	11
Great Britain	4	2	2	203	90	10
Papua New Guinea	2	—	6	84	325	4
France	1	1	6	35	140	3

Final

At Eden Park, Auckland, Sunday, 9 October 1988
Crowd: 46 000
AUSTRALIA 25 (Langer 2, Miller, Shearer tries, O'Connor 4 goals, Elias field goal) d NEW ZEALAND 12
(T Iro, K Iro tries, Brown 2 goals)
Australia: G Jack, D Shearer, A Farrar, M McGaw, M O'Connor, W Lewis (c), A Langer, W Pearce, G Miller, P Sironen, S Roach, B Elias, P Dunn. Replacements: T Lamb (for Lewis) and D Gillespie (for Roach)
New Zealand: G Mercer, T Iro, K Iro, D Bell (c), M Elia, G Freeman, C Friend, M Horo, M Graham, K Sorensen, P Brown, W Wallace, A Shelford. Replacements: S Cooper (for Mercer) and S Stewart (for Shelford)
Referee: G Ainui (Papua New Guinea)

1989–1992 Tournament

The Rugby League authorities decided to continue with the new four-year home-and-away format in 1989. New Zealand, finalist the previous year, got off to a disastrous start losing to both Australia and Great Britain in the first two games, but managed to salvage some hope with success over Britain in the return game in Christchurch and against Papua New Guinea in Port Moresby. France had an even more catastrophic beginning to its campaign, losing by cricket scores to New Zealand, Australia (twice) and Great Britain.

By the end of 1991, Australia had secured one spot in the final. And Britain's 65–4 thrashing of Papua New Guinea gave it the edge over New Zealand for the other place.

8th World Cup, 1989–1992

Venue	Result				Attendance
Auckland	Australia	22	New Zealand	14	20 000
Wigan	Great Britain	10	New Zealand	6	20 346
Carcassonne	New Zealand	34	France	0	6000
Port Moresby	Great Britain	40	Papua New Guinea	8	7837
Parkes	Australia	34	France	2	12 384
Christchurch	New Zealand	21	Great Britain	18	5000
Port Moresby	New Zealand	18	Papua New Guinea	10	7837
Leeds	Australia	14	Great Britain	0	32 500
Perpignan	Australia	34	France	10	3428
Perpignan	Great Britain	45	France	10	5500
Christchurch	New Zealand	32	France	10	2000
Goroka	France	20	Papua New Guinea	18	11 485
Brisbane	Australia	40	New Zealand	12	29 139
Port Moresby	Australia	40	Papua New Guinea	6	14 500
Wigan	Great Britain	56	Papua New Guinea	4	4193
Carcassonne	France	28	Papua New Guinea	14	2000

Progress Points

	P	W	D	L	F	A	Pt
Australia	6	6	—	—	184	44	12
Great Britain	6	4	2	—	169	63	8
New Zealand	7	4	3	—	137	110	8
France	7	2	5	—	52	213	4
Papua New Guinea	6	—	6	—	46	202	—

Matches still to be played:
(Home side first)

1992

Great Britain v France
Australia v Great Britain
Australia v Papua New Guinea
New Zealand v Papua New Guinea
Final (October)

OTHER MATCHES PLAYED BY AUSTRALIA ON WORLD CUP OR CHAMPIONSHIP TOURS

Year	Opponents	Venue (Attendance)	For	Against
1954	New Zealand	Leigh (3000)	18	5
	New Zealand	Long Beach (1000)	30	13
	New Zealand	Los Angeles (4554)	28	18
1960	St Helens	St Helens (12 250)	12	15
	France	Toulouse (5304)	37	12
1970	St Helens	St Helens (15 570)	10	37
	France	Perpignan (14 700)	7	4
	France B	Paris (1570)	36	8
1975	Auckland	Auckland (14 000)	17	6
	Salford	Salford (5357)	44	6
	St Helens	St Helens (10 170)	32	7
	Oldham	Oldham (3575)	20	10
	York	York (4082)	45	4
	England	Leeds (7727)	25	0
	Rouergue	Albi (2000)	35	4
1977	South Island	Christchurch (2500)	68	5
1988	Invitational XIII	Wellington (2000)	24	12

MATCH PLAYED BY AUSTRALASIA ON WORLD CUP TOUR

Year	Opponents	Venue (Attendance)	For	Against
1954	England XIII	Bradford (6000)	25	13

WORLD RECORDS

Because British football involves many more matches than in other countries, most of the individual world records are held by players who turned out in the English competitions. Two involve Australians who played for many years in Britain—the most tries in a career (834 by Brian Bevan) and the most in a season (80 by Albert Rosenfeld). When it comes to Test football however, Australia and Australians lay claim to most of the records.

INDIVIDUAL

MOST POINTS DURING A CAREER
6220 by Neil Fox (in 828 appearances for Great Britain, Yorkshire, Wakefield Trinity, Bradford Northern, Hull Kingston Rovers, York, Bramley, Huddersfield). Total comprises 358 tries and 2575 goals, including four one-point field goals.

MOST TRIES DURING A CAREER
834* by Brian Bevan (for Other Nationalities, Warrington, Blackpool Borough and various representative teams).
* Total includes 38 tries scored in so-called friendly matches.

MOST GOALS DURING A CAREER
2867 by Jim Sullivan (for Great Britain, Wales, Other Nationalities, Wigan, Bradford Northern, Dewsbury, Keighley and various representative teams).

MOST POINTS IN SINGLE CALENDAR YEAR
547 by Mick Cronin (in 52 games for Australia, New South Wales, City and Parramatta during 1978).

MOST POINTS IN ONE SEASON
496 by Lewis Jones (in 48 games for Great Britain, Leeds and various representative teams in 1956–57).

MOST TRIES IN ONE SEASON
80 by Albert Rosenfeld (in 42 games for Huddersfield in 1913–14).

MOST GOALS IN ONE SEASON
221 by David Watkins (in 47 games for Salford in 1972–73).

MOST POINTS IN A MATCH
65 by Alf Fairhall (for North Newcastle against Morpeth-East Maitland, in 1940). Total comprised 11 tries and 14 goals.

MOST TRIES IN A MATCH
11 by George West (for Hull Kingston Rovers against Brookland Rovers, in 1905); and by Alf Fairhall (for North Newcastle against Morpeth-East Maitland).

MOST GOALS IN A MATCH
22 by Jim Sullivan (for Wigan against Flimby and Fothergill, in 1925).

MOST CONSECUTIVE GOALS
26 by Mick Cronin (for Australia and Parramatta, in 1978).

MOST POINTS IN A TEST
30 by Michael O'Connor (for Australia against Papua New Guinea, at Parkes, in 1988). Total comprised four tries and seven goals.

MOST TRIES IN A TEST
6 by Hugh McGahan (for New Zealand against Papua New Guinea, at Auckland, in 1983).

MOST GOALS IN A TEST
11 by Des White (for New Zealand against Australia, at Brisbane, in 1952).

MOST POINTS IN A TEST SERIES
54 by Mick Cronin (for Australia against Great Britain, in 1979). Total comprised two tries and 24 goals.

MOST GOALS IN A TEST SERIES
24 by Mick Cronin (for Australia against Great Britain, in 1979).

MOST TEST APPEARANCES
37 by Gilbert Benausse (France).

MOST WORLD CUP AND CHAMPIONSHIP APPEARANCES
15 by Bob Fulton (Australia).

MOST INTERNATIONAL APPEARANCES
56 by Jim Sullivan (Great Britain, Wales and Other Nationalities).

The biggest crowd at Odsal Stadium, 1954

TEAMS

MOST POINTS IN A MATCH
136 by Glen Innes (against Narwan, 0, in 1988).

BIGGEST WINNING MARGIN
136 by Glen Innes (against Narwan, 0, in 1988).

MOST POINTS IN A TEST
70 by Australia (against Papua New Guinea, 8, at Wagga Wagga, in 1988).

BIGGEST WINNING MARGIN IN A TEST
62 by Australia (which beat Papua New Guinea 70–8, at Wagga Wagga, in 1988).

BIGGEST CROWD
104 569 at Odsal Stadium, Bradford, for Warrington v Halifax, 1954.

BIGGEST TEST CROWD
70 204 for First Test, Australia v Great Britain, Sydney Cricket Ground, 1932.

BIGGEST TEST CROWD see *Nissan Sevens*

WORLD SEVENS see *Nissan Sevens*

DAVID WRIGHT

One match for Australia in one World Championship (1975).

Two crucial injuries cost big Queensland front-rower David Wright the chance to establish himself as a regular in the Australian international sides. In 1975 he beat a star-studded line–up to gain one of the two prop positions in the Australian side for the first match of the World Championship, over all–time greats Arthur Beetson, John O'Neill and Bob O'Reilly. However, in the match against New Zealand at Brisbane's Lang Park, he tore a hamstring and missed the rest of the Championship matches. There were no international games the following season and just before the 1977 games, Wright broke an arm. His international career was well and truly over.

Despite this, Wright is in the record books as one of only a handful of Australians to have won a Challenge Cup-winners medal in England. In 1973 he was named Brisbane's Player-of-the-Year, and received a trip to Britain where he played for Warrington, coached by the great Alex Murphy. That year Warrington swept all before it, winning the English Championship, the John Player Trophy, the Captain Morgan Trophy and the Cup.

After his retirement in 1978, Wright turned his talents to television, and for several years was the expert commentator for the Ten Network's Queensland stations.

X

XXXX TROPHY see *Trans-Tasman Trophy*

Y

CRAIG YOUNG

Twenty Tests for Australia (1978–84). Also played 21 minor games on two Kangaroo tours (1978 and 1982) and one New Zealand tour (1980).

One of the stars unearthed on the 1972 schoolboys' tour of Britain, prop-forward Craig Young, achieved greater success than did most of his colleagues on that trail-blazing tour. He was one of three team members to go on to represent Australia in Tests or World Series matches. He capped a fine career by leading St George to victory in the 1979 Sydney Premiership.

Young was one of the inexperienced St George side which had shocked the critics by winning the title two years earlier. He had his chance in the international arena a year later, in 1978, in the Third Test against the touring New Zealand Kiwis. Young was, from then on, a Test regular. He visited Britain and France with the 1978 Kangaroos and was in the Australian side which humiliated the touring British Lions the following year.

His Test career seemed in jeopardy after he was dropped to reserve–grade for St George in 1982—but he bounced back to play against the touring Kiwis. He was then one of the first chosen for the triumphant Kangaroo side which white-washed its opponents in Papua New Guinea, Britain and France. He wound up his Test career against the British in 1984, although he continued in club football for another four seasons, quitting at the end of 1988 to take over as his club's coach. His 234 first-grade games was the second highest tally for St George behind Norm Provan's 256.

Unfortunately, Young's coaching career never really got off the ground. After less than two years at the helm of his beloved Dragons, Young was unceremoniously dumped by officials demanding better results on the field.

Craig Young

YOUNG FOOTBALLERS

Many young footballers have played in major competitions and Test matches while still in their teens.

Balmain centre Geoff Starling was only 18 years and 178 days old when he played in the first of his two matches for Australia on the short tour of New Zealand in 1971. This made him the youngest player ever to wear the green and gold for his country. However, Starling is not the youngest to play Test football. That honour belongs to Queensland winger Kerry Boustead, who was 18 years and 310 days old when he turned out in the First Test of the 1978 series against New Zealand. Four other Australians have toured with Kangaroo sides while still 18—Chook Fraser (1911–12), Bobby Dimond (1948–49), Steve Rogers (1973) and Brad Fittler (1990).

On the club scene, Ray Stehr was only 15 when he played in a 'friendly' match against Newcastle, in 1928. Frank Burge, the great try-scoring forward, played first grade Rugby Union when 14 and, in 1911, at the age of 16 switched to League where he immediately became a first-grader with Glebe.

He pressed for selection with that year's Kangaroos, but the selectors thought that he was too young to mix it with the tough British forwards. However he did tour before he was 17—with the NSW side which visited New Zealand in 1912.

YUGOSLAVIA

For a brief period in the 1950s and early 1960s Rugby League was played in Yugoslavia. Thanks to the efforts of a Serbian sports administrator, Dragan Marsicevic, two French university teams were brought to Belgrade in September 1953 to launch the game.

In the next few years isolated club games were held and, in 1957, the first full-scale competition kicked off. The most successful teams were Jedinstvo (United) based in the industrial city of Pancevo, Partizan in the capital Belgrade, Mladost (Youth) in Zagreb and Nada (Hope) in the holiday playground of Split. In 1964, most of the clubs switched to Rugby Union and the 13–a-side code died out. The champions of the final two seasons, Nada, went on to take out the Rugby Union Championship 10 times.

Yugoslavia's Winning Clubs

Year	Championship	Cup
1957	Pancevo Jedinstvo	
1958	Zagreb Mladost	Pancevo Jedinstvo
1959	Belgrade Partizan	Zagreb Mladost
1960	Belgrade Partizan	Belgrade Partizan
1961	Belgrade Partizan	Zagreb Mladost
1962	Split Nada	Zagreb Mladost
1963	Split Nada	